OUR *Healing* COVENANT

GOD'S PROMISES
FOR DIVINE HEALTH

DR. CHIP BEAULIEU

Unless otherwise indicated, all Scripture quotations are taken from the *King James Version* of the Bible.

Additional scripture copyright information is found in the bibliography.

Our Healing Covenant
ISBN-13: 978-0-9847542-8-1
ISBN-10: 0-9847542-8-1

PREFACE

In the original edition of the King James Bible printed in 1611, the preface from the translators included a quote from Saint Augustine, *"a variety of Translations is profitable for the finding out the sense of the Scriptures."*[1] Saint Augustine lived a thousand years before the King James Bible was printed.

One of the best methods for studying a biblical doctrine is to read relevant verses in multiple translations. Bible language scholars have a way of pulling out nuance meanings of verses that may not be possible by using a dictionary or through other methods. Dr. Robert Young, for example, wrote both the Young's Analytical Concordance and Young's Literal Translation of the Bible. An area he focuses on in the translation is the tense of verbs. Many times, the English language would seem to prefer a verb to be in the past tense while the original language often is written either in a present tense or even a continuous tense. In Exodus 15:26, the King James version ends with, "…for I am the Lord that healeth thee." In Young's translation he writes, "for I, Jehovah, am healing thee." He brings out the thought of present, continuous action of the healing power of the Lord.

Of all the doctrines and promises in the Bible, the healing of our bodies is one of the most documented parts of the covenant that the Lord made with mankind. There are many good books about healing. *Christ the Healer* by F. F. Bosworth is almost required reading in the Word of Faith movement. In this book, I wanted the central focus to be on scripture. I wanted to put together a reference book that overwhelms the reader with scripture after scripture regarding healing. Although there are sections of teaching and instruction, the primary intent is to develop a reference book focused on divine healing.

When I started this project many years ago, my plan was to first search the Bible for verses related to the topic of healing. I wanted the list of verses to be as exhaustive as possible and to include verses from every book of the Bible. I ended up with a list of 454 verses from the King James Version.

The next step was to review these verses in as many translations as I could. I never expected this part of the project to consume several years of research. I scoured reference books of lists of translations and many sources on the internet. I ended up reviewing 618 unique translations of the Bible (and sometimes dozens of revisions of each of those). To aid the process, I collected as many translations in a database computer program as possible. The result was a system with 238 translations totaling 4.5 million verses. Between my wife and I, we have read more than 100,000 verses from those hundreds of translations. A dear friend, Sue Ziegenhorn, helped in the final selection by reading thousands of verses as well. We have enjoyed the journey of reading all those verses as much as we will enjoy the final product. There have been so many translations of the Bible that have been essentially lost to time.

One example is a translation called *"The Life and Epistles of St. Paul"* by William John Conybeare and John Saul Howson. First published in 1852, it went through more that 30 revisions and was printed at

---

[1] S. Aug. 2. de doctr. Christian. cap 14

multiple locations in the United States, Canada, and London over a period of about 60 years. Yet, most Christians today have never heard of this great work. A secondary hope for this project is to bring to light many wonderful translations of the Bible and spark an interest in further reading these translations.

The result contained in this work is the 454 verses from 430 translations totaling 6,549 total references. To put this in perspective, the King James New Testament contains 7,957 verses.

There is no substitute for reading the Word to develop one's faith. It is my great desire to strengthen every reader's faith in the doctrine of divine healing by reading the verses found in this book.

TABLE OF

INTRODUCTION

After a short chapter discussing the will of God related to healing, you will find verses from each book of the Bible that will build up your faith in divine healing. The first version of each verse is the King James version followed by carefully selected translations that clarify or enhance the thought of the primary verse.

After the section of divine healing scriptures, there is a section of scriptures related to long life. The conclusion that the reader should arrive at after completing this section is that the length of our natural life on this earth is not an unknown, is not "in the hands of God", is surely not "you just never know when your time is up", but is rather a process and a walk of faith. Our natural life should conclude after a long, satisfying time on this earth according to Psalms 91:16.

A few comments are sprinkled among the verses to give insight to the purpose of the inclusion of that verse in this work or to perhaps clarify its general meaning. Most scriptures are sufficiently clear as to not need any additional discussion.

In the topic of divine healing, there are a few key words from the original languages of the Bible that will be helpful to be aware of. In the Old Testament, the Hebrew word for healer is *raphah*. This is most famously found at the end of Exodus 15:26, "…for I am the Lord[Jehovah] that healeth[raphah] thee. The Lord called Himself Jehovah Raphah – the Lord that heals. This is one of the seven covenant names of God. Wherever *raphah* is used in one of the Old Testament verses, it is marked as shown here.

In the New Testament, there are many Greek words that are translated into the English word *life*. One of those Greek words is *zoé*. This Greek word means the God kind and the God quality of life. It is the eternal, everlasting life of God that comes into every believer who receives the Lord Jesus as their Savior. This eternal life can affect our physical lives if we will trust in it. Paul said in 2 Corinthians 4:11, "…the life[zoé] also of Jesus might be made manifest in our mortal flesh." The *zoé* life of Jesus manifested in our natural, death-doomed bodies can replace the death of sickness with the life of God. This Greek word is also marked where used. The last Greek word of interest is *sozo* and is the subject of the next chapter. It is marked in the same manner as the other key words.

The final section of the book is an extensive bibliography so the reader can find the exact reference source of any used translation. Note that translations often went through many editions. In most cases, the most recent edition of a translation was used. The bibliography not only names the translation, but also gives the publication date, the publisher, and location as applicable. The names in brackets prior to a verse, e.g. [Anchor] is the name found in the bibliography. If the same name is found more than once in the bibliography, it is either from multiple books by the same author, or multiple volumes of a complete work.

THE WILL OF GOD IN

In discussing the topic of divine healing, the most common issue Christians deal with is the question, "Is it God's will to heal me?". To answer this question, it is helpful to answer another question, "Is it God's will to save everyone?" A few key verses can answer the second question.

> For God so loved the world, that he gave his only begotten Son, that whosoever believeth in him should not perish, but have everlasting life.
> — John 3:16

> Who will have all men to be saved, and to come unto the knowledge of the truth.
> — 1 Timothy 2:4

> The Lord is not slack concerning his promise, as some men count slackness; but is longsuffering to us-ward, not willing that any should perish, but that all should come to repentance.
> — 2 Peter 3:9

From these few verses, the will of God the Father is that every person in the earth receive Jesus as their Lord and Savior. Yet from a practical standpoint, we know everyone will not accept Jesus and many will die in their sins and spend eternity in the region of the damned. That is not a reflection on God's desire at all, but is the reality that mankind has the God breathed sovereignty of their own will. God has completed all the work necessary for every person to become a Christian up to the edge of their will. He leaves the final choice with each person.

The same understanding holds true for the topic of divine healing in that it is God's will, every single time, without exception to heal every person of every disease.

> Who his own self bare our sins in his own body on the tree, that we, being dead to sins, should live unto righteousness: by whose stripes ye were healed.
> — 1 Peter 2:24

The payment for our healing occurred on the same cross where the payment for our sins occurred. It is God's perfect will that every Christian live a life free from sickness and disease so we can complete the great commission to preach salvation to the whole earth. At the end of our stay on the earth, we should die in the same fashion as the great Moses did.

> And Moses was an hundred and twenty years old when he died: his eye was not dim, nor his natural force abated.
> — Deuteronomy 34:7

OUR HEALING COVENANT

Moses just gave up the ghost. He had no sickness, no chronic illness, no disease. He just died when it was his time. This is God's best for His people. But just as with salvation, every person may not walk in God's best. Since I am not any one's judge, I cannot make sweeping statements as to why someone is not healed. In the Word of God, we see many reasons why people are sick including sin, not being part of the covenant of God, being born that way etc. It is unkind and improper to stand in judgment and state that if someone just had enough faith, they could be healed. I cannot tell you why everyone is not healed, but I can tell you it is always God's will to heal. If everyone would start with understanding of God's will, He will reveal any hinderances in our lives that may stand in the way of healing. If we start with accusing God of desiring, or even "allowing" sickness, there is no room for God to work.

Picking up the topic of salvation again, the Greek word for saved is *sozo*. This Greek word is used 118 times in the New Testament and has three primary meanings. The first meaning is salvation in the sense of accepting Jesus as our Savior.

> For by grace are ye saved[sozo] through faith; and that not of yourselves: it is the gift of God:
> — Ephesians 2:8

> [9]That if thou shalt confess with thy mouth the Lord Jesus, and shalt believe in thine heart that God hath raised him from the dead, thou shalt be saved[sozo]. [13]For whosoever shall call upon the name of the Lord shall be saved[sozo].
> — Romans 10:9,13

The most important use of the Greek word *sozo* is for our salvation. Becoming born again. Accepting Jesus. Becoming a child of God. All of these are the result of "getting saved". The foundation of the Christian life is salvation by faith–*sozo*.

The second use of this same word is for deliverance. The Lord will deliver us in time of trouble.

> And his disciples came to him, and awoke him, saying, Lord, save[sozo] us: we perish.
> — Matthew 8:25

> [30]But when he saw the wind boisterous, he was afraid; and beginning to sink, he cried, saying, Lord, save[sozo] me. [31]And immediately Jesus stretched forth his hand, and caught him, and said unto him, O thou of little faith, wherefore didst thou doubt?
> — Matthew 14:30-31

In these verses, the disciples were not asking for eternal salvation, but rather natural deliverance from the threatening storms and waves. The Lord is always prepared to deliver His children from the dangers of this earth.

> Many are the afflictions of the righteous: but the LORD delivereth him out of them all.
> — Psalms 34:19

The final use of the Greek word *sozo* is for the divine healing of our bodies.

THE WILL OF GOD IN HEALING

But Jesus turned him about, and when he saw her, he said, Daughter, be of good comfort; thy faith hath made thee whole[sozo]. And the woman was made whole[sozo] from that hour.
— Matthew 9:22

And besought him greatly, saying, My little daughter lieth at the point of death: I pray thee, come and lay thy hands on her, that she may be healed[sozo]; and she shall live.
— Mark 5:23

And Jesus said unto him, Receive thy sight: thy faith hath saved[sozo] thee.
— Luke 18:42

[9]The same heard Paul speak: who stedfastly beholding him, and perceiving that he had faith to be healed[sozo], [10]Said with a loud voice, Stand upright on thy feet. And he leaped and walked.
— Acts 14:9-10

The translators of the King James version chose to use several English words to denote restoration of physical bodies – *make whole, healed, saved.* They all refer to physical healing from sickness and disease.

If the Lord Jesus is still saving people by becoming their Lord today, and if He is still delivering His people from natural calamities today, then the only conclusion we can come to is that He is still healing people today. Understanding the will of God separate from our natural observations is the first step towards faith. F. F. Bosworth coined the phrase, "*Faith begins where the will of God is known.*"[1] Know with a surety that the Saving God is still the Healing God.

---

[1]*Christ the Healer* by F. F. Bosworth © 1924, 1948, chapter 3.

A SURVEY OF *Healing* SCRIPTURES

Each section in this chapter covers healing scriptures from a book in the Bible in order of appearance. This is a good place to go to when you want to build your faith up in healing.

Key portions of scriptures are in bold text. Important Hebrew or Greek words are identified following the English word. Definitions of these key words can be found in the Introduction.

The Kings James version of the scripture is always listed first. Alternate versions of the same verse from different translations may follow and will be indented from the King James Version to recognize verses with the same reference.

GENESIS

Genesis 20:17 So Abraham prayed unto God: and **God healed**[raphah] **Abimelech**, and his wife, and his maidservants; and they bare children.

> **[Anchor] Genesis 20:17** Abraham then interceded with God, and **God restored full health to Abimelech**, namely, his wife and his maidservants, so that they could bear again.

> **[CCB] Genesis 20:17** Then Abraham prayed to God and **God healed Abimelech**, his wife and his servants, so that they were able to have children again.

> **[EEBT] Genesis 20:17** Then Abraham prayed to God. And **God made Abimelech well again**. He also made his wife and his female slaves well again. So, they could have children again.

> **[Macrae] Genesis 20:17** So Abraham prayed to God, and **he healed Abimelech**, and his wife, and all the females of his house, and they became prolific;

> **[NABRE] Genesis 20:17** Abraham then interceded with God, and **God restored health to Abimelech**, to his wife, and his maidservants, so that they bore children;

> **[NIRV] Genesis 20:17** Then Abraham prayed to God, and **God healed Abimelek**. He also healed his wife and his female slaves so they could have children again.

> **[T4T] Genesis 20:17** Then Abraham prayed to God, and **God healed Abimelech's wife** and his slave girls so that they could become pregnant.

> **[TVB] Genesis 20:17** Abraham prayed to God on Abimelech's behalf, and **God healed Abimelech**. He also healed the infertility that plagued Abimelech's wife and female slaves enabling them to again bear children

Genesis 21:2 For Sarah conceived, and bare Abraham a son in his old age, at the set time of which God had spoken to him.

> **[CBC]** <u>Genesis 21:2</u> For Sarah conceived, and bare Abraham a son in his old age, at the exact time of which God [the Creator] had spoken to him.

> **[CEV]** <u>Genesis 21:2</u> Although Abraham was very old, Sarah had a son exactly at the time God had said.

> **[Cohn-OT]** <u>Genesis 21:2</u> And Sarah conceived, and bore Abraham a son in his old age, at the set time which God had told him.

> **[CWB]** <u>Genesis 21:2</u> She became pregnant and gave Abraham a son in his old age. The baby was born when the Lord had said he would be.

> **[GW]** <u>Genesis 21:2</u> So she became pregnant, and at the exact time God had promised, she gave birth to a son for Abraham in his old age.

> **[ICB]** <u>Genesis 21:2</u> Sarah became pregnant. And she gave birth to a son for Abraham in his old age. Everything happened at the time God had said it would.

> **[MOTB]** <u>Genesis 21:2</u> At last faith had its miraculous reward. Through Sarah, Abraham had a son in his old age.

> **[NIVUK]** <u>Genesis 21:2</u> Sarah became pregnant and bore a son to Abraham in his old age, at the very time God had promised him.

> **[T4T]** <u>Genesis 21:2</u> She became pregnant and gave birth to a son for Abraham when he was very old, at the time God promised it would happen.

Genesis 25:21 And Isaac intreated the LORD for his wife, because she was barren: and the LORD was intreated of him, and Rebekah his wife conceived.

> **[AMP]** <u>Genesis 25:21</u> Isaac prayed to the LORD for his wife, because she was unable to conceive children; and the LORD granted his prayer and Rebekah his wife conceived [twins].

> **[AMPC]** <u>Genesis 25:21</u> And Isaac prayed much to the Lord for his wife because she was unable to bear children; and the Lord granted his prayer, and Rebekah his wife became pregnant.

> **[BLE]** <u>Genesis 25:21</u> And Isaac invoked Jehovah with regard to his wife, because she was barren; and Jehovah let himself be invoked, and his wife Rebekah became pregnant.

> **[CEB]** <u>Genesis 25:21</u> Isaac prayed to the Lord for his wife, since she was unable to have children. The Lord was moved by his prayer, and his wife Rebekah became pregnant.

> **[CEV]** <u>Genesis 25:21</u> Rebekah still had no children. So Isaac asked the Lord to let her have a child, and the Lord answered his prayer.

> **[CWB]** <u>Genesis 25:21</u> Rebecca was not able to have children, so Isaac prayed to the Lord, and the Lord answered his prayer. Soon afterward Rebecca became pregnant.

> **[Macrae]** <u>Genesis 25:21</u> Isaac intreated the Eternal for his wife, because she was barren, and obtained his desire;

> **[NIVUK]** <u>Genesis 25:21</u> Isaac prayed to the LORD on behalf of his wife, because she was childless. The LORD answered his prayer, and his wife Rebekah became pregnant.

> **[T4T]** <u>Genesis 25:21</u> Almost twenty years after they were married, Rebekah still had no children. So Isaac prayed to Yahweh concerning his wife, and Yahweh answered his prayer. His wife Rebekah became pregnant.

EXODUS

Exodus 15:26 And said, If thou wilt diligently hearken to the voice of the Lord thy God, and wilt do that which is right in his sight, and wilt give ear to his commandments, and keep all his statutes, I will put none of these diseases upon thee, which I have brought upon the Egyptians: **for I am the Lord that healeth**[raphah] **thee.**

[AMP] **Exodus 15:26** saying, "If you will diligently listen and pay attention to the voice of the Lord your God, and do what is right in His sight, and listen to His commandments, and keep [foremost in your thoughts and actively obey] all His precepts and statutes, then I will not put on you any of the diseases which I have put on the Egyptians; **for I am the Lord who heals you.**"

[BBE] **Exodus 15:26** And he said, If with all your heart you will give attention to the voice of the Lord your God, and do what is right in his eyes, giving ear to his orders and keeping his laws, I will not put on you any of the diseases which I put on the Egyptians: **for I am the Lord your life-giver.**

[BLE] **Exodus 15:26** and he said "If you obey your God Jehovah and give ear to his commandments and keep his rules, I will never lay on you any of the maladies I laid on Egypt; **for I am Jehovah your Healer.**"

[CCB] **Exodus 15:26** and said, "If you listen carefully to the voice of Yahweh, your God, and if you do what is right in his eyes, if you obey his commands and statutes, I will not inflict on you any of the diseases I brought on the Egyptians, **for I am Yahweh, the One who heals you.**"

[CWB] **Exodus 15:26** The Lord said to Moses, "If you will listen to me and do what is right, if you will keep my commandments and laws, I will not let any of you come down with the diseases of the Egyptians. **I will heal you, for I am the Lord.**"

[FAA] **Exodus 15:26** and he said, "If you carefully obey the Lord your God, and do what is right in his sight, and hearken to his commandments and keep all his statutes, then I will not lay on you any of the diseases which I laid on Egypt, for **I am the Lord your healer.**"

[Fenton] **Exodus 15:26** But he said; "If you will listen to the voice of your Ever-living God, and do what is right in His eyes, and give your ears to His commands, and keep all His institutions, all the plagues which I laid upon the Mitzerites I will not lay upon you, **for I am your Ever-living Restorer.**"

[Haak] **Exodus 15:26** And said; if so be, that thou wilt earnestly hearken to the voice of the Lord thy God, and do what is right in his eyes, and incline thine ears to his Commandments, and keep all his Institutions; then shall I lay none of the diseases upon thee, which I laid upon the land of Egypt, **for I am the Lord thy healer, (or, Physician) [i.e. I am he that is able to heal and help thee in body and soul, and to keep and preserve thee from all hurt and misery present and to come.]**

[ICB] **Exodus 15:26** He said, "You must obey the Lord, your God. You must do what the Lord said is right. You must obey all his laws and keep his rules. If you do these things, I will not give you any of the sicknesses I gave the Egyptians. **I am the Lord. I am the Lord who heals you.**"

[Knox] **Exodus 15:26** If thou wilt listen to the voice of the Lord thy God, his will doing, his word obeying, and all he bids thee observe, observing faithfully, never shall they fall on thee, the many woes brought on Egypt; **I am the Lord, and it is health I bring thee.**

[Lesser-OT] **Exodus 15:26** And he said, If thou wilt diligently hearken to the voice of the Lord thy God, and wilt do that which is right in his eyes, and wilt give ear to his commandments, and wilt keep all his statutes: I will put none of those diseases upon thee, which I have brought upon the Egyptians; **for I the Lord am thy physician.**

[MSTC] <u>Exodus 15:26</u> and said, "If ye will hearken unto the voice of the Lᴏʀᴅ your God, and will do that which is right in his sight and will give an ear unto his commandments, and keep all his ordinances: then will I put none of these diseases upon thee which I brought upon the Egyptians, **for I am the Lᴏʀᴅ thy surgeon.**"

[NEB] <u>Exodus 15:26</u> He said, 'If only you will obey the Lord your God, if you will do what is right in his eyes, if you will listen to his commands and keep all his statutes, then I will never bring upon you any of the sufferings which I brought on the Egyptians; **for I the Lord am your healer.**'

[NIRV] <u>Exodus 15:26</u> He said, "I am the Lord your God. Listen carefully to me. Do what is right in my eyes. Pay attention to my commands. Obey all my rules. If you do, I will not send on you any of the sicknesses I sent on the Egyptians. **I am the Lord who heals you.**"

[Rotherham] <u>Exodus 15:26</u> And he said: If thou, wilt indeed hearken, to the voice of Yahweh thy God, And, the thing that is right in his eyes, thou wilt do, And so give ear to his commandments, And keep all his statutes, None of the sicknesses which I laid on the Egyptians, will I lay upon thee, **For, I, am Yahweh, thy physician.**

[SG] <u>Exodus 15:26</u> "If you will but heed the injunction of the Lᴏʀᴅ your God," he said, "and do what is right in his eyes, and pay attention to his commands, and observe all his statutes, I will inflict none of the diseases on you which I inflicted on the Egyptians; **for I, the Lᴏʀᴅ, make you immune to them.**"

[Tyndale] <u>Exodus 15:26</u> and said: If ye will harken unto the voice of the Lord your God, and will do that which is right in his sight and will give and ear unto his commandments, and keep all his ordinances: then will I put none of these diseases upon the which I brought upon the Egyptians: **for I am the Lord thy surgeon.**

[YLT] <u>Exodus 15:26</u> and He saith, 'If thou dost really hearken to the voice of Jehovah thy God, and dost that which is right in His eyes, and hast hearkened to His commands, and kept all His statutes: none of the sickness which I laid on the Egyptians do I lay on thee, **for I, Jehovah, am healing thee.**

Note the present and continuous tense in Young's translation of how the Lord is healing us.

<u>Exodus 23:25</u> And ye shall serve the Lᴏʀᴅ your God, and he shall bless thy bread, and thy water; and **I will take sickness away from the midst of thee.**

[ABP] <u>Exodus 23:25</u> And you shall serve to the Lord your God; and I will bless your bread, and your wine, and your water; and **I will turn infirmity from you.**

[AMP] <u>Exodus 23:25</u> You shall serve [only] the Lᴏʀᴅ your God, and He shall bless your bread and water. **I will also remove sickness from among you.**

[BBE] <u>Exodus 23:25</u> And give worship to the Lord your God, who will send his blessing on your bread and on your water; and **I will take all disease away from among you.**

[BrownKrueger] <u>Exodus 23:25</u> For ye shall serve the Lord your God, and he shall bless thy bread and thy water, and **I will take all sickness away from the midst of thee.**

[CEV] <u>Exodus 23:25</u> Worship only me, the Lord your God! **I will** bless you with plenty of food and water and **keep you strong.**

[CPDV] <u>Exodus 23:25</u> And you shall serve the Lord your God, so that I may bless your bread and your waters, and so that **I may take away sickness from your midst.**

[CT-OT] <u>Exodus 23:25</u> And you shall worship the Lord, your God, and He will bless your food and your drink, and **I will remove illness from your midst.**

[EEBT] <u>Exodus 23:25</u> Worship me, the Lord your God, and then I will make your bread and water very good. **I will remove illness from among you.**

[Knox] <u>Exodus 23:25</u> All your loyalty must be for the Lord your God. So I will enrich thee with the bread and the water thou needest, and **keep sickness far away from thy company;**

[LTN-OT] <u>Exodus 23:25</u> You will then serve God your Lord, and He will bless your bread and your water. **I will banish sickness from among you.**

[Moffatt] <u>Exodus 23:25</u> You shall worship the Eternal you God, and then I will bless your food and water, and **I will free you from disease;**

[NIRV] <u>Exodus 23:25</u> Worship the Lord your God. Then he will bless your food and water. **I, the Lord, will take away any sickness you may have.**

[NJB] <u>Exodus 23:25</u> You will worship Yahweh your God, and then **I shall** bless your food and water, and **keep you free of sickness.**

[Purver] <u>Exodus 23:25</u> And you shall serve the Lord your God, who will bless thy Victuals and Drink; and **I will put away Sickness from within thee.**

[Thomson] <u>Exodus 23:25</u> and worship the Lord thy God. And I will bless thy bread and thy wine and thy water, and **turn away sickness from you.**

[Wycliffe-Noble] <u>Exodus 23:25</u> And ye shall serve to your Lord God, (so) that I (can) bless thy loaves, and thy waters, and **do away sickness from the midst of thee;**

[YLT] <u>Exodus 23:25</u> 'And ye have served Jehovah your God, and He hath blessed thy bread and thy water, and **I have turned aside sickness from thine heart;'**

LEVITICUS

<u>Leviticus 14:2</u> This shall be the law of the leper **in the day of his cleansing**: He shall be brought unto the priest:

The only time anyone was cleansed of leprosy in the Old or New Testament was by a supernatural miracle.

[BLE] <u>Leviticus 14:2</u> These shall be the instructions for the man who has had leprosy, **on the day that he is declared clean**: he shall be brought to the priest,

[EEBT] <u>Leviticus 14:2</u> 'These rules are for a person who has had an illness on his skin. They are rules about how to make him clean. **When the illness leaves the person**, you must bring him to the priest.

[ICB] <u>Leviticus 14:2</u> "These are the teachings for people who had a harmful skin disease and have become well. **These teachings are for making that person clean.**

[JPS-OT 1985] <u>Leviticus 14:2</u> This shall be the ritual for a leper **at the time that he is to be cleansed.** When it has been reported to the priest,

[T4T] <u>Leviticus 14:2</u> "These are the regulations for **anyone who has been healed of a contagious skin disease.**

<u>Leviticus 18:5</u> Ye shall therefore keep my statutes, and my judgments: which if a man do, **he shall live in them**: I am the Lord.

[BBE] <u>Leviticus 18:5</u> So keep my rules and my decisions, which, if a man does them, **will be life to him**: I am the Lord.

[CWB] <u>Leviticus 18:5</u> Do what I ask you to do; the one who listens to me and keeps my laws **will save his life** by doing so. I am the Lord.

[GNT] <u>Leviticus 18:5</u> Follow the practices and the laws that I give you; **you will save your life by doing so**. I am the Lord."

[ICB] <u>Leviticus 18:5</u> Obey my laws and rules. A person who obeys my laws and rules **will live because of them**. I am the Lord.

[Moffatt] <u>Leviticus 18:5</u> So keep my rules and regulations; if a man obeys them, **it means life for him**. I am the Eternal.

[NAB] <u>Leviticus 18:5</u> Keep, then, my statutes and decrees, for **the man who carries them out will find life through them**. I am the Lord.

[NOG] <u>Leviticus 18:5</u> Live by my standards, and obey my rules. **You will have life through them**. I am Yahweh.

[T4T] <u>Leviticus 18:5</u> If you obey all my laws and decrees, **you will continue to remain alive for a long time**. I, Yahweh, am the one who is promising that to you. These are some of my laws:

<u>Leviticus 26:3,9</u> If ye walk in my statutes, and keep my commandments, and do them; ⁹For I will have respect unto you, and **make you fruitful, and multiply you**, and establish my covenant with you.

[BBE] <u>Leviticus 26:3,9</u> If you are guided by my rules, and keep my laws and do them, ⁹And I will have pleasure in you and **make you fertile and greater in number**; and I will keep my agreement with you.

[Besorah] <u>Leviticus 26:3,9</u> 'If you walk in My laws and guard My commands and shall do them, ⁹'And I shall turn to you and **make you bear fruit and shall increase you** and shall establish My covenant with you.

[CEV] <u>Leviticus 26:3,9</u> Faithfully obey my laws, ⁹I will treat you with such kindness that **your nation will grow strong**, and I will also keep my promises to you.

[CPDV] <u>Leviticus 26:3,9</u> If you will walk in my precepts, and observe my commandments, and accomplish them, I will give to you rain in its time, ⁹I will look with favor upon you, and **I will cause you to increase; you will be multiplied**, and I will confirm my covenant with you.

[Darby] <u>Leviticus 26:3,9</u> If ye walk in my statutes, and observe my commandments and do them, ⁹And I will turn my face towards you and **make you fruitful, and multiply you**, and establish my covenant with you.

[Douay-Rheims] <u>Leviticus 26:3,9</u> If you walk in my precepts, and keep my commandments, and do them, I will give you rain in due seasons. ⁹I will look on you, and **make you increase: you shall be multiplied**, and I will establish my covenant with you.

[Douay-Rheims-Peters] <u>Leviticus 26:3,9</u> If you walk in my precepts, and keep my commandments, and do them, I will give you rain in their seasons, ⁹I will respect you, and **make you increase: you shall be multiplied**, and I will establish my covenant with you.

[EEBT] <u>Leviticus 26:3,9</u> The people must carefully obey the rules. ⁹I will do good things for your people and **I will give many children to them. Their number will grow**. I will do everything that I have promised to do for them.

[HRB] <u>Leviticus 26:3,9</u> If you walk in My statutes, and keep My commandments, and do them, ⁹And I shall turn My face toward you and **make you fruitful, and multiply you**, and shall establish My covenant with you.

[ICB] <u>Leviticus 26:3,9</u> "'Remember my laws and commands, and obey them. ⁹"'Then I will show kindness to you. **I will let you have many children**. I will keep my agreement with you.

[Jerusalem] <u>Leviticus 26:3,9</u> If you live according to my laws, if you keep my commandments and put them into practice, ⁹"I will turn towards you, **I will make you be fruitful and multiply**, and I will uphold my Covenant with you.

[MEV] <u>Leviticus 26:3,9</u> If you walk in My statutes and keep My commandments and do them, ⁹I will turn toward you and **make you fruitful and multiply you**, and I will confirm My covenant with you.

[NAB] <u>Leviticus 26:3,9</u> If you live in accordance with my precepts and are careful to observe my commandments, ⁹I will look with favor upon you, and **make you fruitful and numerous**, as I carry out my covenant with you.

[NEB] <u>Leviticus 26:3,9</u> If you conform to my statutes, if you observe my commandments and carry them out, ⁹I will look upon you with favour, **I will make you fruitful and increase your numbers**: I will give my covenant with you its full effect.

[REAL] <u>Leviticus 26:3,9</u> If you walk in my rules, and you guard my commands, and you do them, ⁹because I shall respect you, and **I shall make you fruitful, and I shall multiply you**, and I shall raise up my Binding Contract with you,

[T4T] <u>Leviticus 26:3,9</u> If you carefully obey all my commands, ⁹If you obey all my laws, I will bless you and **cause you to have many children**. And I will do what I said that I would do in the agreement that I made with you.

[Thomson] <u>Leviticus 26:3,9</u> if you walk in my statutes, and keep my commandments, and do them, ⁹And I will watch over you, and **increase you, and multiply you**, and establish my covenant with you.

NUMBERS

<u>Numbers 12:13</u> And Moses cried unto the Lᴏʀᴅ, saying, **Heal**[ʳᵃᵖʰᵃʰ] **her now**, O God, I beseech thee.

[CJB] <u>Numbers 12:13</u> Moshe cried to Adonai, "Oh God, I beg you, **please, heal her!**"

[MEV] <u>Numbers 12:13</u> And Moses cried out to the Lᴏʀᴅ, saying, "O God, **heal her, I pray!**"

[NHEB] <u>Numbers 12:13</u> Moses cried to the Lᴏʀᴅ, saying, "**Heal her, God**, I beg you."

[Rotherham] <u>Numbers 12:13</u> Then Moses made outcry unto Yahweh, saying, —O Gᴏᴅ, I beseech thee, **grant healing, I beseech thee, unto her**.

[UDB] <u>Numbers 12:13</u> So Moses cried out to Yahweh, saying, "Almighty, **I plead with you to heal her!**"

<u>Numbers 16:48</u> And he stood between the dead and the living; and the plague was stayed.

[AMP] <u>Numbers 16:48</u> He stood between the dead and the living, so that the plague was brought to an end.

[BLE] <u>Numbers 16:48</u> and stood between the dead and the living, and the deaths were shut off.

[CLV] <u>Numbers 16:48</u> He stood between the dead and the living, and the stroke was restrained.

[CPDV] <u>Numbers 16:48</u> And standing between the dead and the living, he prayed for the people, and the scourge ceased.

[Douay-Rheims-Peters] <u>Numbers 16:48</u> and standing between the dead and the living, he prayed for the people, and the plague ceased.

[ECB] <u>Numbers 16:48</u> and he stands between the dying and the living; and the plague restrains.

[Fox-OT] <u>Numbers 16:48</u> now he stood between the dead and the living, and the plague was held-back.

[LTPB] <u>Numbers 16:48</u> Standing between the dead and the living, he pleaded for the people and the plague ceased.

[T4T] <u>Numbers 16:48</u> He stood between the people who had already died and those who were still alive, and then the plague stopped.

[TVB] <u>Numbers 16:48</u> and where he stood, the plague stopped—dead people on one side, the living on the other.

[ULB] <u>Numbers 16:48</u> Aaron stood between the dead and the living; in this way the plague was stopped.

<u>Numbers 21:9</u> And Moses made a serpent of brass, and put it upon a pole, and it came to pass, that if a serpent had bitten any man, **when he beheld the serpent of brass, he lived**.

The serpent on the pole represents the Lord Jesus. See John 3:14-15 where Jesus references this story. If we look upon Jesus now, we get the same results that the children of Israel received—we will be healed.

[AMPC] <u>Numbers 21:9</u> And Moses made a serpent of bronze and put it on a pole, and if a serpent had bitten any man, **when he looked to the serpent of bronze [attentively, expectantly, with a steady and absorbing gaze], he lived.**

[BBE] <u>Numbers 21:9</u> So Moses made a snake of brass and put it on a rod; and **anyone who had a snakebite, after looking on the snake of brass, was made well**.

[CPDV] <u>Numbers 21:9</u> Therefore, Moses made a bronze serpent, and he placed it as a sign. **When those who had been struck gazed upon it, they were healed.**

[Kenrick] <u>Numbers 21:9</u> Moses therefore made a brazen serpent, and set it up for a sign, on which **when they who were bitten looked, they were healed.**

[MSTC] <u>Numbers 21:9</u> And Moses made a serpent of brass and set it up for a sign. And when the serpents had bitten any man, **he went and beheld the serpent of brass and recovered**.

[NET] <u>Numbers 21:9</u> So Moses made a bronze snake and put it on a pole, so that **if a snake had bitten someone, when he looked at the bronze snake he lived.**

[YLT] <u>Numbers 21:9</u> And Moses maketh a serpent of brass, and setteth it on the ensign, and it hath been, **if the serpent hath bitten any man, and he hath looked expectingly unto the serpent of brass—he hath lived.**

<u>Numbers 23:19</u> God is not a man, that he should lie; neither the son of man, that he should repent: hath he said, and shall he not do it? or hath he spoken, and shall he not make it good?

[Anchor] <u>Numbers 23:19</u> El is no human that he would fail, nor a mortal man that he would renege. Would he promise and not perform? Ordain, and not fulfill it?

[Benisch-OT] <u>Numbers 23:19</u> God is not a man, that he should be false; neither the son of man, that he should repent: hath he said, and shall he not do it? or hath he spoken, and shall he not establish it?

[Berkeley] <u>Numbers 23:19</u> For God is not man that He should lie, neither human that He should change his mind. When He gives His word, does He not perform it? Or does He promise and not fulfill it?

[CE] <u>Numbers 23:19</u> God is not man that he should speak falsely, nor human, that he should change his mind. Is he one to speak and not act, to decree and not fulfill?

[CEV] <u>Numbers 23:19</u> God is no mere human! He doesn't tell lies or change his mind. God always keeps his promises.

[CJB] <u>Numbers 23:19</u> God is not a human who lies or a mortal who changes his mind. When he says something, he will do it; when he makes a promise, he will fulfill it.

[CLV] <u>Numbers 23:19</u> El is not a man that He should lie. Or a son of humanity that He should feel regret. Does He say it and then not do it? Or speak and then not carry it out?

[EEBT] <u>Numbers 23:19</u> The Lord is not a man. He does not speak words that are not true. If he promises something, it happens.

[ERV] <u>Numbers 23:19</u> God is not a man; he will not lie. God is not a human being; his decisions will not change. If he says he will do something, then he will do it. If he makes a promise, then he will do what he promised.

[Haak] <u>Numbers 23:19</u> God is no man that he should lie, not a child of man, that it should repent him; should he say, and not do it? or speak, and not make it stedfast?

[Hall] <u>Numbers 23:19</u> God hath already spoken a word of blessing, and hath accordingly decreed a large benediction for Israel; do not therefore hope vainly, that he will, upon any entreaty, reverse his word, and do contrary to what he hath determined and revealed.

[ICB] <u>Numbers 23:19</u> God is not a man. He will not lie. God is not a human being. He does not change his mind. What he says he will do, he does. What he promises, he keeps.

[Kenrick] <u>Numbers 23:19</u> God is not a man, that He should lie, nor as the son of man, that He should be changed. Hath He said then, and will He not do? hath He spoken, and will He not fulfil?

[Moffatt] <u>Numbers 23:19</u> God is no man to break his word, no mortal to change his mind; he promises, and does he not perform? Does he not carry out his word?

[NEB] <u>Numbers 23:19</u> God is not a mortal that he should lie, not a man that he should change his mind. Has he not spoken, and will he not make it good? What he has proclaimed, he will surely fulfil.

[NIRV] <u>Numbers 23:19</u> God isn't a mere human. He can't lie. He isn't a human being. He doesn't change his mind. He speaks, and then he acts. He makes a promise, and then he keeps it.

[Orton-OT] <u>Numbers 23:19</u> God is not a man, that he should lie, or fail in the performance of what he hath spoken; neither the son of man, that he should repent, so as to change his purpose; hath he said, and shall he not do it? or hath he spoken, and shall he not make it good? It is in vain for thee ever to expect he will alter his purpose.

[SG] <u>Numbers 23:19</u> God is not a man that he should break his word, Nor a human being that he should change his mind. When he has said something, will he not do it? What he has asserted something, will he not make it good?

[Sharpe] <u>Numbers 23:19</u> God is not a man, that he should lie; Neither a son of Adam, that he should repent. Hath he said, and will he not do it? Or hath he spoken, and will he not perform it?

[Spurrell-OT] <u>Numbers 23:19</u> God is not a man, that He should deceive; Neither the son of man, that He should change. Hath He spoken, and will He not perform? Or hath He said, and will He not establish it?

[T4T] <u>Numbers 23:19</u> God is not a human being. Humans lie, but God never lies. He never changes his mind/thoughts, as humans do. Whatever he has said that he will do, he does. Whatever he has promised to do, he has done it.

DEUTERONOMY

<u>Deuteronomy 4:1</u> Now therefore hearken, O Israel, unto the statutes and unto the judgments, which I teach you, for to do them, that ye may live, and go in and possess the land which the LORD God of your fathers giveth you.

[CSB] <u>Deuteronomy 4:1</u> "Now, Israel, listen to the statutes and ordinances I am teaching you to follow, so that you may live, enter, and take possession of the land the LORD, the God of your fathers, is giving you.

[CWB] <u>Deuteronomy 4:1</u> Then Moses said to the people, "Now listen to me before you cross over Jordan. Obey the Lord your God and make Him first in your lives. Follow His instructions so that you may live and occupy the land which He promised to our ancestors, which He's now ready to give you.

[ICB] <u>Deuteronomy 4:1</u> Now, Israel, listen to the laws and commands I will teach you. Obey them so you will live. Then you will go over and take the land. The Lord, the God of your ancestors, is giving it to you.

[NIRV] <u>Deuteronomy 4:1</u> Now, Israel, listen to the rules and laws I'm going to teach you. Obey them and you will live. You will go in and take over the land. The Lord was the God of your people of long ago. He's giving you the land.

[NRSV] <u>Deuteronomy 4:1</u> So now, Israel, give heed to the statutes and ordinances that I am teaching you to observe, so that you may live to enter and occupy the land that the Lord, the God of your ancestors, is giving you.

<u>Deuteronomy 6:24</u> And the LORD commanded us to do all these statutes, to fear the LORD our God, for our good always, **that he might preserve us alive**, as it is at this day.

[Beck] <u>Deuteronomy 6:24</u> The LORD ordered us to keep all these laws and to fear the LORD our God, so that we might always prosper and **be kept alive** as we are today.

[Berkeley] <u>Deuteronomy 6:24</u> So it was that the Lord commanded us to keep all these laws and to show reverence for the Lord our God, for our welfare **so He might keep us alive**, as we are kept alive today.

[CPDV] <u>Deuteronomy 6:24</u> And the Lord instructed us that we should do all these ordinances, and that we should fear the Lord our God, **so that it may be well with us all the days of our life**, just as it is today.

[CWB] <u>Deuteronomy 6:24</u> He also gave us these commandments and laws and asked us to keep them and reverence Him **because He doesn't want us to lose His protection. When you look around you can see how He has prospered us**. He has kept His word.

[JPS-OT 1985] <u>Deuteronomy 6:24</u> Then the LORD commanded us to observe all these laws, to revere the LORD our God, **for our lasting good and for our survival**, as is now the case.

[LTPB] <u>Deuteronomy 6:24</u> The Lord commanded us that we do all these laws, and we fear the Lord our God, and **it may be well with us all our life's days**, as it is today.

[MSG] <u>Deuteronomy 6:24</u> That's why God commanded us to follow all these rules, so that we would live reverently before God, our God, as he gives us this good life, **keeping us alive** for a long time to come.

[NIVUK] <u>Deuteronomy 6:24</u> The Lord commanded us to obey all these decrees and to fear the Lord our God, **so that we might always prosper and be kept alive**, as is the case today.

[UDB] <u>Deuteronomy 6:24</u> And he commanded us to obey all these laws and to honor him, so that things would go well with us, and so **that he would protect our nation and enable us to prosper**, as he is doing now.

<u>Deuteronomy 7:15</u> **And the Lord will take away from thee all sickness**, and will put none of the evil diseases of Egypt, which thou knowest, upon thee; but will lay them upon all them that hate thee.

[Abegg-OT] <u>Deuteronomy 7:15</u> **And the Lord will take away from you all [sickness]**; none of the evil diseases of Egypt, which you have seen and which you know, will he inflict on you, but will lay them on all of those that hate you.

[BBE] <u>Deuteronomy 7:15</u> **And the Lord will take away from you all disease**, and will not put on you any of the evil diseases of Egypt which you have seen, but will put them on your haters.

[Berkeley] <u>Deuteronomy 7:15</u> **The Lord will preserve you from every sickness**, and He will not inflict upon you any of those hurtful diseases of Egypt, with which you are familiar; but He will lay them upon all who hate you.

[BLE] <u>Deuteronomy 7:15</u> **and Jehovah will keep every disease away from you**, and not give you any of the malignant distempers of Egypt that you knew about, but will put them on all your haters.

[CAB] <u>Deuteronomy 7:15</u> **And the Lord your God shall remove all sickness from you**; and none of the evil diseases of Egypt, which you have seen, and all that you have known, will He lay upon you; but He will lay them upon all those that hate you.

[CE] <u>Deuteronomy 7:15</u> **The Lord will remove all sickness from you**; he will not afflict you with any of the malignant diseases that you know from Egypt, but will leave them with all your enemies.

[CEB] <u>Deuteronomy 7:15</u> **The Lord will remove all sickness from you**. As for all those dreadful Egyptian diseases you experienced, the Lord won't put them on you but will inflict them on all who hate you.

[CLV] <u>Deuteronomy 7:15</u> **Yahweh will take away from you every illness**; and all the bad diseases of Egypt about which you know, He shall not place them among you, but He will give them to all those hating you.

[CWB] <u>Deuteronomy 7:15</u> **You will be healthy because the Lord will protect you from those dreadful diseases** that you had when you were in Egypt, but He will not take them away from those who hate you.

[GNV] <u>Deuteronomy 7:15</u> **Moreover, the Lord will take away from thee all infirmities**, and will put none of the evil diseases of Egypt (which thou knowest) upon thee, but will send them upon all that hate thee.

[GW] <u>Deuteronomy 7:15</u> **The Lord will keep you from having any kind of illness**. He will not strike you with any of the terrible diseases you experienced in Egypt. Instead, he will strike all those who hate you.

[ICB] <u>Deuteronomy 7:15</u> **The Lord will take away all disease from you**. You will not have the terrible diseases that were in Egypt. But he will give them to your enemies.

[Jerusalem] <u>Deuteronomy 7:15</u> **Yahweh will keep all sickness far from you**; he will not afflict you with those evil plagues of Egypt which you have known, but will save them for all those who hate you.

[MSG] <u>Deuteronomy 7:15</u> **God will get rid of all sickness**. And all the evil afflictions you experienced in Egypt he'll put not on you but on those who hate you.

[NET] <u>Deuteronomy 7:15</u> **The Lord will protect you from all sickness**, and you will not experience any of the terrible diseases that you knew in Egypt; instead he will inflict them on all those who hate you.

[NIRV] <u>Deuteronomy 7:15</u> **The Lord will keep you from getting sick**. He won't send on you any of the horrible sicknesses you saw all around you in Egypt. But he'll send them on everyone who hates you.

[NIV] <u>Deuteronomy 7:15</u> **The Lord will keep you free from every disease**. He will not inflict on you the horrible diseases you knew in Egypt, but he will inflict them on all who hate you.

[NOG] <u>Deuteronomy 7:15</u> **Yahweh will keep you from having any kind of illness**. He will not strike you with any of the terrible diseases you experienced in Egypt. Instead, he will strike all those who hate you.

[SG] <u>Deuteronomy 7:15</u> **The Lord will also free you from all sickness**, and none of the malignant diseases of Egypt, with which you are acquainted, will he inflict on you; but he will inflict them on all who hate you.

[T4T] <u>Deuteronomy 7:15</u> And **Yahweh will protect you from all illnesses**. You will not be afflicted with any of the dreadful diseases that our ancestors knew about in Egypt, but all your enemies will be inflicted with those diseases.

[Wycliffe-Noble] <u>Deuteronomy 7:15</u> **The Lord shall do away from thee all ache (The Lord shall take away all thy aches and pains)**; and he shall not bring to thee the full evil sicknesses of Egypt, that thou hast known, but to all thine enemies these sicknesses shall come.

<u>Deuteronomy 8:1</u> All the commandments which I command thee this day **shall ye observe to do, that ye may live, and multiply**, and go in and possess the land which the LORD sware unto your fathers.

[CEV] <u>Deuteronomy 8:1</u> Israel, do you want to go into the land the Lord promised your ancestors? **Do you want to capture it, live there, and become a powerful nation?** Then be sure to obey every command I am giving you.

[CSB] <u>Deuteronomy 8:1</u> "**Carefully follow every command I am giving you today, so that you may live and increase**, and may enter and take possession of the land the LORD swore to your fathers.

[ERV] <u>Deuteronomy 8:1</u> **You must obey all the commands that I give you today, because then you will live and grow to become a great nation.** You will get the land that the Lord promised to your ancestors.

[Knox] <u>Deuteronomy 8:1</u> Life, increase, entrance into the land the Lord promised to thy fathers, **secure possession of it, all shall be thine if thou wilt take good heed to follow the commandments I am giving thee this day.**

[LTN-OT] <u>Deuteronomy 8:1</u> You must safeguard and **keep the entire mandate that I am prescribing to you today. You will then survive, flourish**, and come to occupy the land that God swore to your fathers.

[NLV] <u>Deuteronomy 8:1</u> **Be careful to do all that I am telling you today. Then you will live and have many children**, and go in to own the land the Lord promised to give to your fathers.

[T4T] <u>Deuteronomy 8:1</u> "**You must faithfully obey all the commandments that I am giving you today. If you do that, you will live a long time, you will become very numerous**, and you will occupy the land that Yahweh solemnly promised your ancestors that he would give to you.

[TNIV] <u>Deuteronomy 8:1</u> Be careful to **follow every command I am giving you today, so that you may live and increase** and may enter and possess the land that the LORD promised on oath to your ancestors.

<u>Deuteronomy 8:4</u> Thy raiment waxed not old upon thee, **neither did thy foot swell, these forty years**.

[AMP] <u>Deuteronomy 8:4</u> Your clothing did not wear out on you, **nor did your feet swell these forty years**.

[CAB] <u>Deuteronomy 8:4</u> Your garments grew not old from off you, your shoes were not worn from off you, **your feet were not painfully hardened, behold, for these forty years**!

[CE] <u>Deuteronomy 8:4</u> The clothing did not fall from you in tatters, **nor did your feet swell these forty years**.

[CWB] <u>Deuteronomy 8:4</u> He also blessed you in other ways. During all those years your clothes didn't wear out, and **your feet didn't swell from all the walking you had to do**.

[EEBT] <u>Deuteronomy 8:4</u> Your clothes did not become too old to wear. Your feet did not become too painful to walk on during all those 40 years.

[LTPB] <u>Deuteronomy 8:4</u> Your clothes with which you covered yourself did not fall apart from age. **Your foot was not blistered—look, this is the fortieth year**! —

[REB] <u>Deuteronomy 8:4</u> The clothes on your backs did not wear out, **nor did your feet blister, all these forty years**.

[Spurrell-OT] <u>Deuteronomy 8:4</u> Thy raiment waxed not old upon thee, **neither did thy feet become tender, these forty years**.

[T4T] <u>Deuteronomy 8:4</u> During those forty years of walking through the desert, our clothes did not wear out and **our feet did not swell from walking very much through the desert**.

[TVB] <u>Deuteronomy 8:4</u> Your clothes didn't wear out, and **your feet didn't swell throughout your 40 years of wandering**.

<u>Deuteronomy 11:8</u> Therefore **shall ye keep all the commandments which I command you this day, that ye may be strong**, and go in and possess the land, whither ye go to possess it;

[CCB] <u>Deuteronomy 11:8</u> Therefore, **observe all these commandments that I give you, that you may gather strength** and occupy the land which you are going over to possess.

[CE] <u>Deuteronomy 11:8</u> **Keep all the commandments, then, which I enjoin on you today, that you may be strong** enough to enter in and take possession of the land into which you are crossing.

[Fenton] <u>Deuteronomy 11:8</u> therefore **attend to all the commands that I command you to-day, so that you may be hearty**, and go and seize the country that you are advancing to possess;

[LTN-OT] <u>Deuteronomy 11:8</u> **Safeguard the entire mandate that I am prescribing to you today, so that you will be strong** and come to occupy the land which you are crossing to occupy.

[NASB] <u>Deuteronomy 11:8</u> **You shall therefore keep every commandment which I am commanding you today, so that you may be strong** and go in and possess the land into which you are about to cross to possess it;

[NIRV] <u>Deuteronomy 11:8</u> **So obey all the commands I'm giving you today. Then you will be strong enough** to go in and take over the land. You will go across the Jordan River and take the land as your own.

[NOG] <u>Deuteronomy 11:8</u> **Obey all the commands I'm giving you today. Then you will have the strength** to enter and take possession of the land once you've crossed the Jordan River.

[Smith] <u>Deuteronomy 11:8</u> **And watch ye every command which I command thee this day, so that ye shall be strengthened** and go in and possess the land where ye are passing over there to possess it;

<u>Deuteronomy 16:20</u> **That which is altogether just shalt thou follow, that thou mayest live**, and inherit the land which the LORD thy God giveth thee.

[AMP] <u>Deuteronomy 16:20</u> **You shall pursue justice, and only justice [that which is uncompromisingly righteous], so that you may live** and take possession of the land which the LORD your God is giving you.

[AMPC] <u>Deuteronomy 16:20</u> **Follow what is altogether just (uncompromisingly righteous), that you may live** and inherit the land which your God gives you.

[BBE] <u>Deuteronomy 16:20</u> **Let righteousness be your guide, so that you may have life**, and take for your heritage the land which the Lord your God is giving you.

[Beck] <u>Deuteronomy 16:20</u> **Strive for total justice, so that you will live** and take the land the LORD your God is giving you.

[BrownKrueger] <u>Deuteronomy 16:20</u> **That which is just and right shalt thou follow, that thou mayest live**, and possess the land which the Lord thy God giveth thee.

[FAA] <u>Deuteronomy 16:20</u> **You shall pursue justice and nothing but justice, so that you may live** and possess the land which the Lord your God is giving you.

[ICB] <u>Deuteronomy 16:20</u> **Always do what is right. Then you will live** and own the land the Lord your God is giving you.

[Kent-OT] <u>Deuteronomy 16:20</u> **Justice and only justice shalt thou follow, that thou mayst live** and inherit the land which the Lord thy God giveth thee.

[NLV] <u>Deuteronomy 16:20</u> **Follow what is right, and only what is right. Then you will live** and receive the land the Lord your God is giving you.

<u>Deuteronomy 23:5</u> Nevertheless the LORD thy God would not hearken unto Balaam; but the LORD **thy God turned the curse into a blessing** unto thee, because the LORD thy God loved thee.

Recall from Galatians 3:13, that sickness and disease are part of the curse from which we've been redeemed.

[CAB] <u>Deuteronomy 23:5</u> But the Lord your God would not hearken to Balaam; and the **Lord your God changed the curses into blessings**, because the Lord your God loved you.

[CEB] <u>Deuteronomy 23:5</u> But the Lord your God wasn't interested in listening to Balaam. The Lord **your God turned that curse into a blessing** because the Lord your God loves you.

[FAA] <u>Deuteronomy 23:5</u> But the Lord your God was not willing to listen to Balaam, and **the Lord your God changed the curse into a blessing** for you, for the Lord your God loves you.

[JPS-OT 1985] <u>Deuteronomy 23:5</u> But the LORD your God refused to heed Balaam; instead, **the LORD your God turned the curse into a blessing for you**, for the LORD your God loves you.

[LTPB] <u>Deuteronomy 23:5</u> The Lord your God did not want to hear Balaam, and **He turned his curse into your blessing** because He loved you.

[MLV] <u>Deuteronomy 23:5</u> Nevertheless Jehovah your God would not listen to Balaam, but **Jehovah your God turned the curse into a blessing to you**, because Jehovah your God loved you.

[NIRV] <u>Deuteronomy 23:5</u> The Lord your God wouldn't listen to Balaam. Instead, **he turned the curse into a blessing for you**. He did it because he loves you.

[TLB] <u>Deuteronomy 23:5</u> But the Lord wouldn't listen to Balaam; instead, **he turned the intended curse into a blessing for you** because the Lord loves you.

<u>Deuteronomy 28:4</u> **Blessed shall be the fruit of thy body**, and the fruit of thy ground, and the fruit of thy cattle, the increase of thy kine, and the flocks of thy sheep.

[Beck] <u>Deuteronomy 28:4</u> **Your children will be blessed**, and what your ground produces, the young of your animals, the calves of your cattle, and the lambs of your flocks.

[CEB] <u>Deuteronomy 28:4</u> **Your own fertility**, your soil's produce, and your livestock's offspring—the young of both cattle and flocks—**will be blessed**.

[CSB] <u>Deuteronomy 28:4</u> **Your offspring will be blessed**, and your land's produce, and the offspring of your livestock, including the young of your herds and the newborn of your flocks.

[CWB] <u>Deuteronomy 28:4</u> **The Lord will bless you with healthy children and many descendants**, and your herds and flocks will overflow with calves and lambs.

[EEBT] <u>Deuteronomy 28:4</u> **The LORD will give you many children**, many cows and many sheep. He will make much food grow in your fields.

[ESV] <u>Deuteronomy 28:4</u> **Blessed shall be the fruit of your womb** and the fruit of your ground and the fruit of your cattle, the increase of your herds and the young of your flock.

[ICB] <u>Deuteronomy 28:4</u> **Your children will be blessed**. Your crops will be blessed. Your cattle will be blessed with calves and your sheep with lambs.

[NIRV] <u>Deuteronomy 28:4</u> **Your children will be blessed.** Your crops will be blessed. The young animals among your livestock will be blessed. That includes your calves and lambs.

[NLT] <u>Deuteronomy 28:4</u> **Your children and your crops will be blessed**. The offspring of your herds and flocks will be blessed.

[T4T] <u>Deuteronomy 28:4</u> **He will bless you by giving you many children** and by giving you abundant crops, and plenty of cattle and sheep.

[Thomson] <u>Deuteronomy 28:4</u> **blessed shall be the fruit of thy body, and the products of thy land**, and thy herds, and thy flocks.

[TVB] <u>Deuteronomy 28:4</u> **You'll be blessed with children** and crops and cattle. Your herds will multiply, and your flocks will increase.

<u>Deuteronomy 30:16</u> In that I command thee this day to love the LORD thy God, to walk in his ways, and to keep his commandments and his statutes and his judgments, that thou mayest live and multiply: and the LORD thy God shall bless thee in the land whither thou goest to possess it.

[BBE] <u>Deuteronomy 30:16</u> In giving you orders today to have love for the Lord your God, to go in his ways and keep his laws and his orders and his decisions, so that you may have life and be increased, and that the blessing of the Lord your God may be with you in the land where you are going, the land of your heritage.

[CEV] <u>Deuteronomy 30:16</u> I am commanding you to be loyal to the Lord, to live the way he has told you, and to obey his laws and teachings. You are about to cross the Jordan River and take the land that he is giving you. If you obey him, you will live and become successful and powerful.

[Fenton] <u>Deuteronomy 30:16</u> What I propose to you is Life, —to love the Ever-Living, your God, —to walk in His ways, to preserve His Legislation, and Institutions, and Decrees, when your Ever-Living God will increase you, and bless you in the land which you are going to process!

[LTN-OT] <u>Deuteronomy 30:16</u> I have commanded you today to love God your Lord, to walk in His paths, and to keep His commandments, decrees and laws. You will then survive and flourish, and God your Lord will bless you in the land that you are about to occupy.

[NCV] <u>Deuteronomy 30:16</u> I command you today to love the Lord your God, to do what he wants you to do, and to keep his commands, his rules, and his laws. Then you will live and grow in number, and the Lord your God will bless you in the land you are entering to take as your own.

[NIVUK] <u>Deuteronomy 30:16</u> For I command you today to love the Lord your God, to walk in obedience to him, and to keep his commands, decrees and laws; then you will live and increase, and the Lord your God will bless you in the land you are entering to possess.

[TLB] <u>Deuteronomy 30:16</u> I have commanded you today to love the Lord your God and to follow his paths and to keep his laws, so that you will live and become a great nation, and so that the Lord your God will bless you and the land you are about to possess.

<u>Deuteronomy 30:19</u> I call heaven and earth to record this day against you, that I have set before you life and death, blessing and cursing: therefore choose life, that both thou and thy seed may live:

[Fox-OT] <u>Deuteronomy 30:19</u> I call-as-Witness against you today the heavens and the earth: life and death I place before you, blessing and curse; now choose life, in order that you may stay-alive, you and your seed,

[ICB] <u>Deuteronomy 30:19</u> Today I ask heaven and earth to be witnesses. I am offering you life or death, blessings or curses. Now, choose life! Then you and your children may live.

[Knox] <u>Deuteronomy 30:19</u> I call heaven and earth to witness this day that I have set such a choice before thee, life or death, a blessing or a curse. Wilt thou not choose life, long life for thyself and for those that come after thee?

[LTN-OT] <u>Deuteronomy 30:19</u> I call heaven and earth as witnesses! Before you I have placed life and death, the blessing and the curse. You must choose life, so that you and your descendants will survive.

[NLT] <u>Deuteronomy 30:19</u> Today I have given you the choice between life and death, between blessings and curses. Now I call on heaven and earth to witness the choice you make. Oh, that you would choose life, so that you and your descendants might live!

[REAL] <u>Deuteronomy 30:19</u> "I call the heavens and the Earth to record today against you, I have put in front of you life and death, blessing and cursing. So choose life, so you and your seed can live,

[TLV] <u>Deuteronomy 30:19</u> "I call the heavens and the earth to witness about you today, that I have set before you life and death, the blessing and the curse. Therefore choose life so that you and your descendants may live,

[TVB] <u>Deuteronomy 30:19</u> Moses: I'm calling on the heavens and the earth to be the witnesses against you. I gave you the choice today between life and death, between being blessed or being cursed. Choose life, so that you and your descendants may live!

[UDB] <u>Deuteronomy 30:19</u> I am requesting everyone in heaven and on the earth to testify to you, that today I am allowing you to choose whether you want to live for a long time or to soon die, whether you want Yahweh to bless you or to curse you. So choose to live.

<u>Deuteronomy 33:25</u> Thy shoes shall be iron and brass; and **as thy days, so shall thy strength be.**

[Beck] <u>Deuteronomy 33:25</u> May your doorbolts be iron and copper. **May your strength last as long as your days.**

[CEB] <u>Deuteronomy 33:25</u> I pray that your dead bolts are iron and copper, and **that your strength lasts all your days.**

[CEV] <u>Deuteronomy 33:25</u> and have strong town gates with bronze and iron bolts. **Your people will be powerful for as long as they live.**

[CJB] <u>Deuteronomy 33:25</u> May your bolts be of iron and bronze and **your strength last as long as you live.**

[CPDV] <u>Deuteronomy 33:25</u> His shoe shall be of iron and of brass. **As were the days of your youth, so also shall be your old age.**

[Douay-Rheims] <u>Deuteronomy 33:25</u> His shoe shall be iron and brass. **As the days of thy youth, so also shall thy old age be.**

[ERV] <u>Deuteronomy 33:25</u> Your gates will have locks made from iron and bronze. **You will be strong all your life.**

[GNV-Zychal] <u>Deuteronomy 33:25</u> Thy shoes shall be iron and brass, and **thy strength shall continue as long as thou livest.**

[ICB] <u>Deuteronomy 33:25</u> Your gates will have locks of iron and bronze. **You will be strong as long as you live.**

[NEB] <u>Deuteronomy 33:25</u> May your bolts be of iron and bronze, and **your strength last as long as you live.**

[NIRV] <u>Deuteronomy 33:25</u> The bars of his gates will be made out of iron and bronze. **His strength will last as long as he lives.**

JOSHUA

<u>Joshua 14:10-11</u> And now, behold, the L<small>ORD</small> hath kept me alive, as he said, these forty and five years, even since the L<small>ORD</small> spake this word unto Moses, while the children of Israel wandered in the wilderness: and now, lo, **I am this day fourscore and five years old. ¹¹As yet I am as strong this day as I was in the day that Moses sent me: as my strength was then, even so is my strength now,** for war, both to go out, and to come in.

[BBE] <u>Joshua 14:10-11</u> And now, as you see, the Lord has kept me safe these forty-five years, from the time when the Lord said this to Moses, while Israel was wandering in the waste land: and **now I am eighty-five years old. ¹¹And still, I am as strong today as I was when Moses sent me out: as my strength was then, so is it now,** for war and for all the business of life.

[CCB] <u>Joshua 14:10-11</u> From then till now, Yahweh has kept me alive in accordance with his promise. It is forty-five years since Yahweh made this promise to Moses (Israel was then journeying through the wilderness), and **now I am eighty-five years old. ¹¹Today I am still as strong as the day when Moses sent me out on the raid; for fighting, for going and coming, I am as strong now as then**.

[CEV] <u>Joshua 14:10-11</u> Joshua, it was 45 years ago that the Lord told Moses to make that promise, and **now I am 85**. Even though Israel has moved from place to place in the desert, the Lord has kept me alive all this time as he said he would. **¹¹I'm just as strong today as I was then, and I can still fight as well in battle.**

[CEVUK2012] <u>Joshua 14:10-11</u> Joshua, it was forty-five years ago that the Lᴏʀᴅ told Moses to make that promise, and **now I am eighty-five. Even though Israel has moved from place to place in the desert, the Lᴏʀᴅ has kept me alive all this time as he said he would. ¹¹I'm just as strong today as I was then**, and I can still fight as well in battle.

[CPDV] <u>Joshua 14:10-11</u> Therefore, the Lord has granted life to me, just as he promised, even to the present day. It has been forty-five years since the Lord spoke this word to Moses, when Israel was wandering through the wilderness. **Today, I am eighty-five years old, ¹¹being just as strong as I was at that time, when I was sent to explore the land. The fortitude in me at that time continues even until today**, as much to fight as to march.

[CSB] <u>Joshua 14:10-11</u> "As you see, the Lᴏʀᴅ has kept me alive these forty-five years as he promised, since the Lᴏʀᴅ spoke this word to Moses while Israel was journeying in the wilderness. **Here I am today, eighty-five years old. ¹¹I am still as strong today as I was the day Moses sent me out. My strength for battle and for daily tasks is now as it was then**.

[CWB] <u>Joshua 14:10-11</u> That was forty-five years ago when we were making our way through the wilderness. All these years the Lord has kept me alive and blessed me with good health. **I'm now eighty-five years old and as strong as ever. ¹¹I'm just as full of energy as I was when Moses sent me to spy out the land**. I can still go to war and fight side by side with those half my age.

[JPS-OT 1985] <u>Joshua 14:10-11</u> Now the Lᴏʀᴅ has preserved me, as He promised. It is forty-five years since the Lᴏʀᴅ made this promise to Moses, when Israel was journeying through the wilderness; and **here I am today, eighty-five years old. ¹¹I am still as strong today as on the day that Moses sent me; my strength is the same now as it was then**, for battle and for activity.

[NCV] <u>Joshua 14:10-11</u> "Now then, the Lord has kept his promise. He has kept me alive for forty-five years from the time he said this to Moses during the time we all wandered in the desert. Now **here I am, eighty-five years old. ¹¹I am still as strong today as I was the day Moses sent me out**, and I am just as ready to fight now as I was then.

[NETS-OT] <u>Joshua 14:10-11</u> And now the Lord has sustained me, as he said; this is the forty-fifth year from when the Lord spoke this word to Moyses, and Israel journeyed in the wilderness, and now, look, **I am today eighty-five years old. ¹¹I am still strong today, as when Moyses sent me**; I am now just as strong to go out and to go into war.

[NJB] <u>Joshua 14:10-11</u> From then till now, Yahweh has kept me alive in observance of his promise. It is forty-five years since Yahweh said this to Moses—Israel was then going through the desert—and **now I am eighty-five years old. ¹¹Today I am still as strong as the day when Moses sent me out on that errand**; for fighting, for going and coming, I am as strong now as then.

[RNV] <u>Joshua 14:10-11</u> And now, behold, Yahuwah has kept me alive, as He said, these forty-five years, ever since Yahuwah spoke this word to Mosheh while Yisra'el wandered in the wilderness, and **now here I am this day, a son of eighty-five years. ¹¹As yet I am as strong this day as on the day that Mosheh sent me. Just as my strength was then, so now is my strength** for battle, both for going out and for coming in.

[T4T] Joshua 14:10-11 Now Yahweh has done for me what he promised. Forty-five years have passed since Moses said that to me during the time that we were wandering around in the desert. And just like Yahweh promised, he has kept me alive and well all during that time. **Now I am eighty-five years old.** **[11]I am as strong today as I was on the day that Moses sent me to explore this land. I am as ready to fight now as I was then.**

[Thomson] Joshua 14:10-11 Now **the Lord hath kept me alive as he said. This is the forty fifth year since the Lord spoke this word to Moses,** and Israel commenced their wanderings in the wilderness. And behold I am now eighty five years of age; **[11]yet I am now as strong as when Moses sent me; as able now as then to go out and come in to battle;**

[TNIV] Joshua 14:10-11 "Now then, just as the LORD promised, he has kept me alive for forty-five years since the time he said this to Moses, while Israel moved about in the wilderness. So here **I am today, eighty-five years old! [11]I am still as strong today as the day Moses sent me out;** I'm just as vigorous to go out to battle now as I was then.

[UDB] Joshua 14:10-11 Now Yahweh has done for me as he promised he would. Forty-five years have passed since Moses said that to me during the time that we were still in the wilderness. And just as Yahweh promised, he has kept me alive and well all during that time. Look at me! **I am eighty-five years old. [11]I am as strong today as I was on the day that Moses sent me to explore this land.** My strength is now as my strength was when I was young. I can wage war or I can travel far away and still have the strength to come home.

Joshua 21:45 There failed not ought of any good thing which the LORD had spoken unto the house of Israel; all came to pass.

[Anchor] Joshua 21:45 Not a word of all the Good Word which Yahweh had spoken to the house of Israel proved untrue. It all happened.

[Beck] Joshua 21:45 Of all the good the LORD promised the people of Israel not one thing failed to be carried out; all of it came true.

[CEB] Joshua 21:45 Not one of all the good things that the Lord had promised to the house of Israel failed. Every promise was fulfilled.

[CEV] Joshua 21:45 The Lord promised to do many good things for Israel, and he kept his promise every time.

[CPDV] Joshua 21:45 Indeed, not so much as one word that he had promised to provide for them was left empty; instead, everything was fulfilled.

[CSB] Joshua 21:45 None of the good promises the LORD had made to the house of Israel failed. Everything was fulfilled.

[CWB] Joshua 21:45 The Lord kept every one of His promises that He had made. Not one of them failed.

[Douay-Rheims] Joshua 21:45 Not so much as one word, which he had promised to perform unto them, was made void, but all came to pass.

[EXB] Joshua 21:45 He kept every promise he had made to the Israelites; each one came true.

[FAA] Joshua 21:45 And not a word failed of all the good words which the Lord had spoken to the house of Israel—it all came about.

[FV] Joshua 21:45 Not a word failed from any good thing which the LORD had spoken to the house of Israel. All came to pass.

[GNV] <u>Joshua 21:45</u> There failed nothing of all the good things, which the Lord had said unto the house of Israel, but all came to pass.

[ICB] <u>Joshua 21:45</u> He kept every promise he had made to the Israelites. No promises failed. Each one came true.

[MEV] <u>Joshua 21:45</u> Not a single word of all the good things that the LORD had spoken to the children of Israel failed. They all came to pass.

[NJB] <u>Joshua 21:45</u> Of all the promises that Yahweh had made to the House of Israel, not one failed; all were fulfilled.

[TLB] <u>Joshua 21:45</u> Every good thing the Lord had promised them came true.

[ULB] <u>Joshua 21:45</u> Not one thing among all the good promises that Yahweh had spoken to the house of Israel failed to come true. All of them came to be.

JUDGES

<u>Judges 13:2-3</u> And there was a certain man of Zorah, of the family of the Danites, whose name was Manoah; and his wife was barren, and bare not. ³And the angel of the LORD appeared unto the woman, and said unto her, Behold **now, thou art barren, and bearest not: but thou shalt conceive, and bear a son**.

[CWB] <u>Judges 13:2-3</u> During this time there was a man living in Zorah in the territory of Dan named Manoah. His wife was not able to have children. ³One day the Angel of the Lord who had led the children of Israel out of Egypt appeared to her and said, "**I know you haven't been able to have children, but soon you'll become pregnant and have a son.**"

[ICB] <u>Judges 13:2-3</u> There was a man named Manoah from the city of Zorah. Manoah was from the tribe of Dan. He had a wife, but she could not have children. ³The angel of the Lord appeared to Manoah's wife. He said, "**You have not been able to have children. But you will become pregnant and have a son**!"

[NIVUK] <u>Judges 13:2-3</u> A certain man of Zorah, named Manoah, from the clan of the Danites, had a wife who was childless, unable to give birth. ³The angel of the LORD appeared to her and said, '**You are barren and childless, but you are going to become pregnant and give birth to a son**.'

RUTH

<u>Ruth 4:13</u> So Boaz took Ruth, and she was his wife: and when he went in unto her, the LORD gave her conception, and she bare a son.

[AMP] <u>Ruth 4:13</u> So Boaz took Ruth, and she became his wife. And he went in to her, and the LORD enabled her to conceive, and she gave birth to a son.

[CEV] <u>Ruth 4:13</u> Boaz married Ruth, and the Lord blessed her with a son.

[CJB] <u>Ruth 4:13</u> So Bo'az took Rut, and she became his wife. He had sexual relations with her, Adonai enabled her to conceive, and she gave birth to a son.

[CWB] <u>Ruth 4:13</u> So Boaz bought the property and married Ruth, and she was accepted by the townspeople as one of their own. The Lord blessed her and she became pregnant and gave birth to a son.

[FV] <u>Ruth 4:13</u> And Boaz took Ruth, and she became his wife. And when he went in to her, the LORD enabled her to conceive. And she bore a son.

[GW] <u>Ruth 4:13</u> Then Boaz took Ruth home, and she became his wife. He slept with her, and the Lord gave her the ability to become pregnant. So she gave birth to a son.

FIRST SAMUEL

<u>1 Samuel 1:11,20</u> And she vowed a vow, and said, O LORD of hosts, if thou wilt indeed look on the affliction of thine handmaid, and remember me, and not forget thine handmaid, but wilt **give unto thine handmaid a man child**, then I will give him unto the LORD all the days of his life, and there shall no razor come upon his head. [20]Wherefore it came to pass, when the time was come about after Hannah had conceived, that she bare a son, and called his name Samuel, saying, Because I have asked him of the LORD. Hannah received her request to be healed of a barren womb.

[AMP] **1 Samuel 1:11,20** She made a vow, saying, "O LORD of hosts, if You will indeed look on the affliction (suffering) of Your maidservant and remember, and not forget Your maidservant, but will **give Your maidservant a son**, then I will give him to the LORD all the days of his life; a razor shall never touch his head." [20]It came about in due time, after Hannah had conceived, that she gave birth to a son; she named him Samuel, saying, "Because I have asked for him from the LORD."

[ICB] **1 Samuel 1:11,20** She made a promise. She said, "Lord of heaven's armies, see how bad I feel. Remember me! Don't forget me. If **you will give me a son**, I will give him back to you all his life. And no one will ever use a razor to cut his hair." [20]So Hannah became pregnant, and in time she gave birth to a son. She named him Samuel. She said, "His name is Samuel because I asked the Lord for him."

[LEB] **1 Samuel 1:11,20** She made a vow and said: "O Yahweh of hosts, if you will look with compassion on the misery of your female servant, and will remember me, and not forget your female servant, and will **give to your female servant a male child** then I will give him to Yahweh all the days of his life, and a razor will never pass over his head." [20]In due time, Hannah conceived and gave birth to a son. She called his name Samuel, for she said, "I requested him from Yahweh."

[TNIV] **1 Samuel 1:11,20** And she made a vow, saying, "LORD Almighty, if you will only look on your servant's misery and remember me, and not forget your servant but **give her a son**, then I will give him to the LORD for all the days of his life, and no razor will ever be used on his head." [20]So in the course of time Hannah became pregnant and gave birth to a son. She named him Samuel, saying, "Because I asked the LORD for him."

[UDB] **1 Samuel 1:11,20** She made a solemn promise, saying, "O Yahweh, Commander of the angel armies, if you will look at me and see how miserable I am, and think kindly about me and **allow me to give birth to a son**, then I will dedicate him to you for the rest of his life. And to show that he is dedicated to you, no one will ever be allowed to cut his hair." [20]She became pregnant and gave birth to a son. She named him Samuel, which sounds like the words in the Hebrew language that mean "heard by God," because she said, "Yahweh heard me when I requested a son from him."

<u>1 Samuel 2:4</u> The bows of the mighty men are broken, and **they that stumbled are girded with strength**.

[AMP] <u>1 Samuel 2:4</u> "The bows of the mighty are broken, But **those who have stumbled equip themselves with strength**.

[CJB] <u>1 Samuel 2:4</u> The bows of the mighty are broken, while **the feeble are armed with strength**.

[CWB] <u>1 Samuel 2:4</u> The bows of proud warriors break, but **the Lord gives strength to those who stumble in their weakness**.

[ERV] <u>1 Samuel 2:4</u> The bows of strong soldiers break, and **weak people become strong**.

[ICB] <u>1 Samuel 2:4</u> "The bows of warriors break, but **weak people become strong**.

[MSG] <u>1 Samuel 2:4</u> The weapons of the strong are smashed to pieces, while **the weak are infused with fresh strength**.

[NIVUK] <u>1 Samuel 2:4</u> 'The bows of the warriors are broken, but **those who stumbled are armed with strength**.

[NLT] <u>1 Samuel 2:4</u> The bow of the mighty is now broken, and **those who stumbled are now strong**.

[TVB] <u>1 Samuel 2:4</u> The bows of the mighty crack in two, but **the feeble are given new strength**.

<u>1 Samuel 6:1-3</u> And the ark of the Lord was in the country of the Philistines seven months. ²And the Philistines called for the priests and the diviners, saying, What shall we do to the ark of the Lord? tell us wherewith we shall send it to his place. ³And they said, If ye send away the ark of the God of Israel, send it not empty; but in any wise return him a trespass offering: then **ye shall be healed**[raphah], and it shall be known to you why his hand is not removed from you.

The Philistines had the ark for seven months and suffered in sickness. Using the glory of the Lord incorrectly will open the door to sickness and disease. The solution is simple—repentance.

[ICB] <u>1 Samuel 6:1-3</u> The Philistines kept the Ark of the Covenant of God in their land seven months. ²Then they called for their priests and magicians. They said, "What should we do with the Ark of the Covenant of the Lord? Tell us how to send it back home!" ³The priests and magicians answered them. They said, "If you send back the Ark of the Covenant of the God of Israel, don't send it away empty. You must offer a penalty offering so the God of Israel will forgive your sins. **Then you will be healed**. When God has forgiven you, he will stop punishing you."

[JPS-OT 1963] <u>1 Samuel 6:1-3</u> The Ark of the Lord remained in the territory of the Philistines seven months. ²Then the Philistines summoned the priests and the diviners and asked, "What shall we do about the Ark of the Lord? Tell us with what we shall send it off to its own place." ³They answers, "If you are going to send the Ark of the God of Israel away, do not send it away without anything; you must also pay an indemnity to Him. **Then you will be healed, and He will make Himself known** to you; otherwise His hand will not turn away from you."

[LEB] <u>1 Samuel 6:1-3</u> Now the ark of Yahweh had been in the territory of the Philistines for seven months, ²and the Philistines called to the priests and to those who practiced divination, saying, "What should we do with the ark of Yahweh? Inform us how we should send it to its place." ³They said, "If you are sending the ark of the God of Israel away, you must not send it away empty, but by all means return it with a guilt offering. **Then you will be healed** and it will become known to you why his hand is not turned aside from you."

[NIRV] <u>1 Samuel 6:1-3</u> The ark of the Lord had been in Philistine territory for seven months. ²The Philistines called for the priests and for those who practice evil magic. They wanted their advice. They said to them, "What should we do with the ark of the Lord? Tell us how we should send it back to its place." ³They answered, "If you return the ark of the god of Israel, don't send it back to him without a gift. Be sure you send a guilt offering to their god along with it. **Then you will be healed**[raphah]. You will find out why his power has continued to be against you."

[ULB] 1 Samuel 6:1-3 Now the ark of Yahweh was in the country of the Philistines for seven months. ²Then the Philistine people called for the priests and the diviners; they said to them, "What should we do with the ark of Yahweh? Tell us how we should send it back to its own country." ³The priests and diviners said, "If you send back the ark of the God of Israel, do not send it without a gift; by all means send him a guilt offering. **Then you will be healed**, and you will know why his hand has not been lifted off of you until now."

SECOND SAMUEL

2 Samuel 24:25 And David built there an altar unto the LORD, and offered burnt offerings and peace offerings. So the LORD was intreated for the land, and **the plague was stayed from Israel**.

[BBE] **2 Samuel 24:25** And there David put up an altar to the Lord, making burned offerings and peace-offerings. So the Lord gave ear to his prayer for the land, and **the disease came to an end in Israel**.

[CCB] **2 Samuel 24:25** David built there an altar to Yahweh and offered burnt offerings and peace offerings. So Yahweh had mercy on the land and **the plague ended in Israel**.

[CEVUK2012] **2 Samuel 24:25** Then he built an altar for the LORD. He sacrificed animals and burnt them on the altar. The LORD answered the prayers of the people, and **no one else died from the terrible disease**.

[CSB] **2 Samuel 24:25** He built an altar to the LORD there and offered burnt offerings and fellowship offerings. Then the LORD was receptive to prayer for the land, and **the plague on Israel ended**.

[EEBT] **2 Samuel 24:25** Then he built an altar and he sacrificed burnt offerings and peace offerings there. Then the LORD answered David's prayer and **the illness stopped.**

[ERV] **2 Samuel 24:25** Then David built an altar to the Lord there and offered burnt offerings and peace offerings. The Lord answered his prayer for the country. **He stopped the disease in Israel**.

[Fenton] **2 Samuel 24:25** and David built there an altar to the Ever-Living, and offered a burnt-offering, and thank-offering, when the Ever-Living was entreated for the land, and **removed the plague from the country**.

[ICB] **2 Samuel 24:25** Then he built an altar to the Lord there. And he offered whole burnt offerings and fellowship offerings. Then the Lord answered his prayer for the country. And **the disease in Israel stopped**.

[JPS-OT 1963] **2 Samuel 24:25** And David built there an altar to the LORD and sacrificed burnt offerings and offerings of well-being. The LORD responded to the plea for the land, and **the plague against Israel was checked**.

[T4T] **2 Samuel 24:25** Then David built an altar to Yahweh, and he offered the oxen to be completely burned on the altar, and he also offered sacrifices to maintain fellowship with Yahweh. Then, Yahweh answered David's prayers, and **he caused the plague in Israel to end**.

[TNIV] <u>2 Samuel 24:25</u> David built an altar to the Lord there and sacrificed burnt offerings and fellowship offerings. Then the Lord answered his prayer in behalf of the land, and **the plague on Israel was stopped**.

FIRST KINGS

<u>1 Kings 8:37-39</u> If there be in the land famine, if there be pestilence, blasting, mildew, locust, or if there be caterpiller; if their enemy besiege them in the land of their cities; whatsoever plague, whatsoever sickness there be; [38]What prayer and supplication soever be made by any man, or by all thy people Israel, which shall know every man the plague of his own heart, and spread forth his hands toward this house: [39]Then hear thou in heaven thy dwelling place, and forgive, and do, and give to every man according to his ways, whose heart thou knowest; (for thou, even thou only, knowest the hearts of all the children of men;)

[CPDV] <u>1 Kings 8:37-39</u> Then, if famine rises over the land, or pestilence, or corrupt air, or blight, or locust, or mildew, or if their enemy afflicts them, besieging the gates, or any harm or infirmity, 38or whatever curse or divine intervention may happen to any man among your people Israel, if anyone understands, having been wounded in his heart, and if he will have extended his hands in this house, 39you will hear in heaven, in your dwelling place, and you will forgive. And you will act so that you give to each one in accord with his own ways, just as you see in his heart, for you alone know the heart of all the sons of men.

[Douay-Rheims-Peters] <u>1 Kings 8:37-39</u> If famine Arise in the land, or pestilence, or corrupt air, or blasting, or locust, or rust, and their enemy afflict them besieging the gates, all plague, all infirmity, [38]all cursing, and banning, that shall chance to any man of thy people Israel: if any man shall know the wound of his heart, and shall spread forth his hands in this house, [39]thou shalt hear in heaven, in the place of thy habitation, and shalt be merciful again, and shalt so do that thou give to every one according to his ways, as thou shalt see his heart (for thou only knowest the heart of all the children of men)

[EXB] <u>1 Kings 8:37-39</u> ·At times the land will become so dry that no food will grow [If there is a famine in the land], or ·a great sickness will spread among the people [pestilence]. ·Sometimes all the crops will be destroyed by […or blight or mildew or] locusts or grasshoppers. ·Your people will be attacked in […or the people are besieged in the land of] their cities by their enemy or ·will become sick [struck by plague or sickness…]. [38]When any of these things happen, ·the people will become truly sorry [each will know the affliction of his own heart]. ·If your people spread their hands in prayer […and spread his hands] toward this ·Temple [house], [39]then hear their prayers from your ·home [dwelling place] in heaven. Forgive and ·treat [act and give to] each person ·as he should be treated [according to his ways/conduct] because you know what is in a person's heart. Only you know what is in everyone's heart.

[GW] <u>1 Kings 8:37-39</u> There may be famine in the land. Plant diseases, heat waves, funguses, locusts, or grasshoppers may destroy crops. Enemies may blockade Israel's city gates. During every plague or sickness [38]hear every prayer for mercy, made by one person or by all the people in Israel, whose consciences bother them, who stretch out their hands toward this temple. [39]Hear them in heaven, where you live. Forgive them, and take action. Give each person the proper reply. (You know what is in their hearts, because you alone know what is in the hearts of all people.)

[ICB] <u>1 Kings 8:37-39</u> "At times the land will become so dry that no food will grow. Or, a great sickness will spread among the people. Sometimes all the crops will be destroyed by locusts or grasshoppers. Your people will be attacked in their cities by their enemies. Your people will become sick. 38When any of these things happen, the people will become truly sorry. If anyone of your people Israel spreads his hands in prayer toward this Temple, 39please hear his prayer. Hear it from your home in heaven. Then forgive the people and help them. Only you know what people are really thinking. So judge each person, and do to him what is right.

[NETS-OT] <u>1 Kings 8:37-39</u> "If there is famine, if there is death—for there will be burning, locust larva—if there is mildew and if their enemy afflicts them in one of their cities, any plague, any pain, 38any prayer, any petition, if it be to any person, when each knows the grip of his own heart and spreads out his hands toward this house, 39then you shall listen from heaven from your established dwelling place, and will be merciful and act and give to a man according to his ways, just as you know his heart, for you alone know the heart of all the sons of people,

[NHEB] <u>1 Kings 8:37-39</u> "If there is famine in the land, if there is pestilence, if there is blight, mildew, locust or caterpillar; if their enemy besieges them in the land of their cities; whatever plague, whatever sickness there is; 38whatever prayer and supplication is made by any man, or by all your people Israel, who shall each know the plague of his own heart, and spread forth his hands toward this house: 39then hear in heaven, your dwelling place, and forgive, and do, and render to every man according to all his ways, whose heart you know; (for you, even you only, know the hearts of all the children of men;)

[NOG] <u>1 Kings 8:37-39</u> "There may be famine in the land. Plant diseases, heat waves, funguses, locusts, or grasshoppers may destroy crops. Enemies may blockade Israel's city gates. During every plague or sickness 38hear every prayer for mercy, made by one person or by all the people in Israel, whose consciences bother them, who stretch out their hands toward this temple. 39Hear them in heaven, where you live. Forgive them, and take action. Give each person the proper reply. (You know what is in their hearts, because you alone know what is in the hearts of all people.)

[Thomson] <u>1 Kings 8:37-39</u> If there be famine, if there be pestilence [for such things will be] if there be blasting, locust, mildew; or if their enemy afflict them in any of their cities, in every occurrence, in every distress, 38whatever prayer, whatever supplication any man shall make, when they know every one the plague of his own heart, and shall spread forth his hands toward this house; 39thou indeed wilt hearken from heaven—from thy settled habitation and be merciful, and do and give to every man as thou knowest his heart [for thou alone knowest the hearts of all the children of men]

<u>1 Kings 13:6</u> And the king answered and said unto the man of God, Intreat now the face of the Lord thy God, and pray for me, that my hand may be restored me again. And the man of God besought the Lord, and **the king's hand was restored him again, and became as it was before**.

[Berkeley] <u>1 Kings 13:6</u> The king begged the man of God, "Plead with the Lord your God and pray on my behalf, that my hand may be restored." So the man of God interceded with the Lord, and **the hand of the king was restored to its former condition**.

[CWB] <u>1 Kings 13:6</u> Jeroboam said to the man of God, "Please pray to the Lord for me and ask Him to restore my arm." So the prophet prayed and **the king's arm was restored to normal**.

[EEBT] <u>1 Kings 13:6</u> Then the king said to God's servant, 'Pray for me. (Pray) to the Lord (who is) your God. Pray that my hand will become well again.' So God's servant prayed to the Lord. And **the king's hand became well again, as it was before**.

[ERV] <u>1 Kings 13:6</u> Then King Jeroboam said to the man of God, "Please pray to the Lord your God for me. Ask him to heal my arm." So the man of God prayed to the Lord, and **the king's arm was healed, as it was before**.

[GNV-Zychal] <u>1 Kings 13:6</u> Then the King answered, and said unto the man of God, I beseech thee, pray unto ye Lord thy God, and make intercession for me, that mine hand may be restored unto me. And the man of God besought the Lord, and **the King's hand was restored, and became as it was afore**.

[ICB] <u>1 Kings 13:6</u> Then the king said to the man of God, "Please pray to the Lord your God for me. Ask him to heal my arm." So the man of God prayed to the Lord. And **the king's arm was healed. It became as it was before.**

[ISV] <u>1 Kings 13:6</u> "Please!" the king begged the man of God, "Ask the Lord your God and pray for me that my hand may be restored for me!" So the man of God asked the Lord, and the **king's hand was immediately and fully restored, just like it had been before.**

[Knox] <u>1 Kings 13:6</u> Plead with the Lord thy God, the king said to him, and pray for me, that I may have the use of my hand again. So the prophet entreated God's mercy for him, and **his hand was restored to him, as sound as before.**

[Koren-OT] <u>1 Kings 13:6</u> And the king answered and said to the man of God, Entreat now the face of the Lord thy God, and pray for me, that my hand may be restored me again. And the man of God entreated the Lord, and **the king's hand was restored him again, and became as it was before.**

[MSG] <u>1 Kings 13:6</u> The king pleaded with the holy man, "Help me! Pray to your God for the healing of my arm." The holy man prayed for him and **the king's arm was healed—as good as new!**

[NIRV] <u>1 Kings 13:6</u> King Jeroboam spoke to the man of God. He said, "Pray to the Lord your God for me. Pray that my hand will be as good as new again." So the man of God prayed to the Lord for the king. And **the king's hand became as good as new. It was just as healthy as it had been before.**

[NIVUK] <u>1 Kings 13:6</u> Then the king said to the man of God, 'Intercede with the LORD your God and pray for me that my hand may be restored.' So the man of God interceded with the LORD, and **the king's hand was restored and became as it was before.**

[T4T] <u>1 Kings 13:6</u> Then the king said to the prophet, "Please pray that Yahweh will be merciful to me and heal my arm!" So the prophet prayed, and **Yahweh completely healed the king's arm.**

[ULB] <u>1 Kings 13:6</u> King Jeroboam answered and said to the man of God, "Plead for the favor of Yahweh your God and pray for me, so that my hand may be restored to me again." So the man of God prayed to Yahweh, and **the king's hand was restored to him again, and it became as it was before.**

<u>1 Kings 17:22</u> And the LORD heard the voice of Elijah; and the **soul of the child came into him again, and he revived.**

[Bate-OT] <u>1 Kings 17:22</u> And Jehovah hearkened to the voice of Alijeh; and the **soul of the child came into him again, and he revived.**

[Berkeley] <u>1 Kings 17:22</u> The Lord heard the prayer of Elijah; **the life of the child returned to him, and he lived again.**

[CEV] <u>1 Kings 17:22</u> The Lord answered Elijah's prayer, and **the boy started breathing again.**

[CSB] <u>1 Kings 17:22</u> So the LORD listened to Elijah, and **the boy's life came into him again, and he lived.**

[ICB] <u>1 Kings 17:22</u> The Lord answered Elijah's prayer. **The boy began breathing again, and he was alive.**

[NABRE] <u>1 Kings 17:22</u> The Lord heard the prayer of Elijah; **the life breath returned to the child's body and he lived.**

[T4T] <u>1 Kings 17:22</u> Yahweh heard what Elijah prayed, and **he caused the boy to become alive again.**

[TLB] <u>1 Kings 17:22</u> And the Lord heard Elijah's prayer; and **the spirit of the child returned, and he became alive again!**

[TNIV] <u>1 Kings 17:22</u> The LORD heard Elijah's cry, and **the boy's life returned to him, and he lived**.

SECOND KINGS

<u>2 Kings 2:21-22</u> And he went forth unto the spring of the waters, and cast the salt in there, and said, Thus saith the LORD, **I have healed**[raphah] **these waters; there shall not be from thence any more death or barren land.** ²²**So the waters were healed**[raphah] **unto this day**, according to the saying of Elisha which he spake.

[AMP] <u>2 Kings 2:21-22</u> Then Elisha went to the spring of water and threw the salt in it and said, "Thus says the LORD: '**I [not the salt] have purified and healed these waters; there shall no longer be death or barrenness because of it.'**" ²²**So the waters have been purified to this day**, in accordance with the word spoken by Elisha.

[BSV] <u>2 Kings 2:21-22</u> And he went forth to the spring of the waters, and cast the salt in there, and said, Thus says the LORD, **I have healed these waters; there will not be from thence any more death or barren land.** ²²**So the waters were healed to this day**, according to the saying of Elisha which he spoke.

[CCB] <u>2 Kings 2:21-22</u> Elisha went to the fountain and threw salt in it saying, "This is what Yahweh says: **I have healed this water, never more will it cause death or sickness.**" ²²**And the water has remained wholesome to this day**, just as Elisha said.

[CEB] <u>2 Kings 2:21-22</u> Elisha then went out and threw salt into the spring. He said, "This is what the Lord has said: **I have purified this water. It will no longer cause death and miscarriage.**" ²²**The water has stayed pure right up to this very day**, in agreement with the word that Elisha spoke.

[CSB] <u>2 Kings 2:21-22</u> Elisha went out to the spring, threw salt in it, and said, "This is what the LORD says: '**I have healed this water. No longer will death or unfruitfulness result from it.'**" ²²**Therefore, the water still remains healthy today** according to the word that Elisha spoke.

[CWB] <u>2 Kings 2:21-22</u> He took it and went out to the city spring and dumped the salt in it. He said, "This is what the Lord says: '**The water in this spring is now healed and never again will it cause death or keep the land from producing good crops.'**" ²²**From that moment, the water of the city was pure**, just as Elisha had said.

[Moffatt] <u>2 Kings 2:21-22</u> Then he went to the source of their water-supply and, throwing salt in, he uttered this word from the Eternal, **"I herby heal these waters; never again shall they cause death or miscarriages."** ²²**To this day the waters remain healed**, exactly as Elisha said.

[NCV] <u>2 Kings 2:21-22</u> Then he went out to the spring and threw the salt in it. He said, "This is what the Lord says: '**I have healed this water. From now on it won't cause death, and it won't keep the land from growing crops.'**" ²²**So the water has been healed to this day** just as Elisha had said.

[NET] <u>2 Kings 2:21-22</u> He went out to the spring and threw the salt in. Then he said, "This is what the Lord says, '**I have purified this water. It will no longer cause death or fail to produce crops.**'" ²²**The water has been pure to this very day**, just as Elisha prophesied.

[NIVUK] <u>2 Kings 2:21-22</u> Then he went out to the spring and threw the salt into it, saying, 'This is what the LORD says: "**I have healed this water. Never again will it cause death or make the land** unproductive.'" ²²**And the water has remained pure to this day**, according to the word Elisha had spoken.

[RSV] 2 Kings 2:21-22 Then he went to the spring of water and threw salt in it, and said, "Thus says the Lord, **I have made this water wholesome; henceforth neither death nor miscarriage shall come from it.**" ²²**So the water has been wholesome to this day**, according to the word which Elisha spoke.

[Thomson] 2 Kings 2:21-22 Elisha went to the spring of the waters, and threw the salt in there and said, Thus saith the Lord, **I cure the waters. There shall no more be thence death or barren ground.** ²²**So the waters were healed, and continue so to this day**, according to the word which Elisha spoke.

[TLB] 2 Kings 2:21-22 Then he went out to the city well and threw the salt in and declared, "**The Lord has healed these waters. They shall no longer cause death or miscarriage.**" ²²**And sure enough! The water was purified**, just as Elisha had said.

[WEB] 2 Kings 2:21-22 He went out to the spring of the waters, and threw salt into it, and said, "Yahweh says, '**I have healed these waters. There shall not be from there any more death or barren wasteland.**'" ²²**So the waters were healed to this day**, according to Elisha's word which he spoke.

2 Kings 4:16-17 And he said, **About this season, according to the time of life, thou shalt embrace a son**. And she said, Nay, my lord, thou man of God, do not lie unto thine handmaid. ¹⁷And the woman conceived, and bare a son at that season that Elisha had said unto her, according to the time of life.

[AMP] 2 Kings 4:16-17 Elisha said, "**At this season next year, you will embrace a son.**" She said, "No, my lord. O man of God, do not lie to your maidservant." ¹⁷But the woman conceived and gave birth to a son at that season the next year, just as Elisha had said to her.

[BBE] 2 Kings 4:16-17 And Elisha said, **At this time in the coming year you will have a son in your arms**. And she said, No, my lord, O man of God, do not say what is false to your servant. ¹⁷Then the woman became with child and gave birth to a son at the time named, in the year after, as Elisha had said to her.

[Darby] 2 Kings 4:16-17 And he said, **At this appointed time, when thy term is come, thou shalt embrace a son**. And she said, No, my lord, man of God, do not lie to thy handmaid. ¹⁷And the woman conceived, and bore a son at that appointed time in the next year as Elisha had said to her.

[ICB] 2 Kings 4:16-17 Then Elisha said, "**About this time next year, you will hold a son in your arms.**" The woman said, "No, master, man of God. Don't lie to me!" ¹⁷But the woman became pregnant. And she gave birth to a son at that time the next year as Elisha had told her.

[NJB] 2 Kings 4:16-17 '**This time next year**', he said, '**you will hold a son in your arms.**' But she said, 'No, my lord, do not deceive your servant.' ¹⁷But the woman did conceive, and she gave birth to a son at the time that Elisha had said she would.

[NLT] 2 Kings 4:16-17 "**Next year at this time you will be holding a son in your arms!**" "No, my lord!" she cried. "O man of God, don't deceive me and get my hopes up like that." ¹⁷But sure enough, the woman soon became pregnant. And at that time the following year she had a son, just as Elisha had said.

2 Kings 4:32-35 And when Elisha was come into the house, behold, the child was dead, and laid upon his bed. ³³He went in therefore, and shut the door upon them twain, and prayed unto the LORD. ³⁴And he went up, and lay upon the child, and put his mouth upon his mouth, and his eyes upon his eyes, and his hands upon his hands: and **he stretched himself upon the child; and the flesh of the child waxed warm**.

[35]Then he returned, and walked in the house to and fro; and went up, and stretched himself upon him: and the child sneezed seven times, and the child opened his eyes.

[AMP] 2 Kings 4:32-35 When Elisha came into the house, the child was dead and lying on his bed. [33]So he went in, shut the door behind the two of them, and prayed to the LORD. [34]Then he went up and lay on the child and put his mouth on his mouth, his eyes on his eyes, and his hands on his hands. And **as he stretched himself out on him and held him, the boy's skin became warm**. [35]Then he returned and walked in the house once back and forth, and went up [again] and stretched himself out on him; and the boy sneezed seven times and he opened his eyes.

[CWB] 2 Kings 4:32-35 When Elisha got there, he went up to his room and found the dead child lying on his bed. [33]He closed the door, fell on his knees and prayed earnestly to the Lord, asking Him to return life to the boy. [34]Then he got up, laid on top of the boy, face to face, eye to eye, mouth to mouth and hands to hands. **As he stretched himself out on the boy's body it began to grow warm**. [35]Elisha got up, paced the floor and continued praying to the Lord. Then he stretched himself out on the boy's body a second time. This time the boy sneezed seven times and opened his eyes.

[HCSB] 2 Kings 4:32-35 When Elisha got to the house, he discovered the boy lying dead on his bed. [33]So he went in, closed the door behind the two of them, and prayed to the Lord. [34]Then he went up and lay on the boy: he put mouth to mouth, eye to eye, hand to hand. **While he bent down over him, the boy's flesh became warm**. [35]Elisha got up, went into the house, and paced back and forth. Then he went up and bent down over him again. The boy sneezed seven times and opened his eyes.

[ICB] 2 Kings 4:32-35 Elisha came into the house. There was the child, lying dead on his bed. [33]When Elisha entered the room, he shut the door. Only he and the child were in the room. Then Elisha prayed to the Lord. [34]He went to the bed and lay on the child. He put his mouth on the child's mouth. He put his eyes on the child's eyes and his hands on the child's hands. **He stretched himself out on top of the child. Then the child's skin became warm**. [35]Elisha turned away and walked around the room. Then he went back and put himself on the child again. Then the child sneezed seven times and opened his eyes.

[NLT] 2 Kings 4:32-35 When Elisha arrived, the child was indeed dead, lying there on the prophet's bed. [33]He went in alone and shut the door behind him and prayed to the Lord. [34]Then he lay down on the child's body, placing his mouth on the child's mouth, his eyes on the child's eyes, and his hands on the child's hands. **And as he stretched out on him, the child's body began to grow warm again!** [35]Elisha got up, walked back and forth across the room once, and then stretched himself out again on the child. This time the boy sneezed seven times and opened his eyes!

2 Kings 4:40-41 So they poured out for the men to eat. And it came to pass, as they were eating of the pottage, that they cried out, and said, O thou man of God, there is death in the pot. And they could not eat thereof. [41]But he said, Then bring meal. And he cast it into the pot; and he said, Pour out for the people, that they may eat. **And there was no harm in the pot**.

[CAB] 2 Kings 4:40-41 And he poured it out for the men to eat. And it came to pass, when they were eating of the stew, that behold, they cried out, and said, There is death in the pot, O man of God! And they could not eat. [41]And he said, Take meal, and cast it into the pot. And Elisha said to his servant Gehazi, Pour out for the people, and let them eat. **And there was no longer there any hurtful thing in the pot**.

[CCB] 2 Kings 4:40-41 Then the broth was served to the men to eat. But as soon as they tasted the soup, they cried out, "Man of God, this is pure poison!" So they did not eat any more. [41]Then Elisha said,

"Bring me flour." And he put it into the pot. Then he said, "Serve these men and let them eat." **And there was no longer anything harmful in the pot**.

[ISV] <u>2 Kings 4:40-41</u> When they served the men, they began to eat the stew. But they cried out, "That pot of stew is deadly, you man of God!" So they couldn't eat the stew. [41]But he replied, "Bring me some flour." He tossed it into the pot and said, "Serve the people so they can eat." **Then there was nothing harmful in the pot**.

[NABRE] <u>2 Kings 4:40-41</u> The stew was served, but when they began to eat it, they cried, "Man of God, there is death in the pot!" And they could not eat it. [41]He said, "Bring some meal." He threw it into the pot and said, "Serve it to the people to eat." **And there was no longer anything harmful in the pot**.

[T4T] <u>2 Kings 4:40-41</u> He served the stew to the prophets, but after the men had eaten only a couple bites, they cried out, "Elisha, there is something in the pot that will kill us!" So they would not eat it. [41]Elisha said, "Bring me some flour." They brought him some, and he threw it in the pot and he said, "It is all right now. You can eat it." **And they ate it, and it did not harm them**.

[ULB] <u>2 Kings 4:40-41</u> So they poured out the stew for the men to eat. Later, as they were eating, they cried out and said, "Man of God, there is death in the pot!" So they could not eat it anymore. [41]But Elisha said, "Bring some flour." He threw it into the pot and said, "Pour it out for the people, so that they may eat." **Then there was no longer anything hurtful in the pot**.

<u>2 Kings 5:14</u> Then went he down, and dipped himself seven times in Jordan, according to the saying of the man of God: and **his flesh came again like unto the flesh of a little child, and he was clean**.

[CT-OT] <u>2 Kings 5:14</u> And he went down and immersed himself in the Jordan seven times according to the word of the man of God: and **his flesh was restored like the flesh of a young lad, and he became clean**.

[CWB] <u>2 Kings 5:14</u> Naaman listened and decided to do as Elisha had told him. He went to the Jordan River and dipped his whole body in the water seven times. As he came up the seventh time, suddenly, **his body was firm and healthy again like that of a young man. His leprosy was gone!**

[ERV] <u>2 Kings 5:14</u> So Naaman did what the man of God said. He went down and dipped himself in the Jordan River seven times, and **he became pure and clean. His skin became soft like the skin of a baby**.

[ICB] <u>2 Kings 5:14</u> So Naaman went down and dipped in the Jordan seven times. He did just as Elisha had said. **Then Naaman's skin became new again. It was like the skin of a little boy. And Naaman was clean!**

[NIRV] <u>2 Kings 5:14</u> So Naaman went down to the Jordan River. He dipped himself in it seven times. He did exactly what the man of God had told him to do. **Then his skin was made pure again. It became "clean" like the skin of a young boy**.

[Thomson] <u>2 Kings 5:14</u> Then Naiman went down, and when he had dipped himself seven times in the Jordan, according to the word of the prophet, **his flesh became again like the flesh of a little child, and he was cleansed**.

[TLB] <u>2 Kings 5:14</u> So Naaman went down to the Jordan River and dipped himself seven times, as the prophet had told him to. **And his flesh became as healthy as a little child's, and he was healed!**

[TVB] <u>2 Kings 5:14</u> So Naaman swallowed his pride, walked down to the Jordan River, and washed himself seven times, just as the man of God had instructed him to do. **There, the miracle occurred.**

Naaman's disease was healed: his skin was as new as an infant's, and he was clean from the disease.

[ULB] <u>2 Kings 5:14</u> Then he went down and dipped himself seven times in the Jordan, obeying the instructions of the man of God. **His flesh was restored again like the flesh of a little child, and he was healed.**

<u>2 Kings 13:21</u> And it came to pass, as they were burying a man, that, behold, they spied a band of men; and they cast the man into the sepulchre of Elisha: and **when the man was let down, and touched the bones of Elisha, he revived, and stood up on his feet.**

[CCB] <u>2 Kings 13:21</u> It happened that at that time some people were burying a dead man, when they saw the Moabites. So they quickly threw the body into the grave of Elisha, and then fled to safety. But **as soon as the man's body touched the bones of Elisha, the man revived and stood on his feet.**

[CJB] <u>2 Kings 13:21</u> Once it happened that just as they were burying a man, they spotted a raiding party; so they threw the man's body into Elisha's burial cave; and **the moment the man touched the bones of Elisha, he revived and stood on his feet.**

[CSB] <u>2 Kings 13:21</u> Once, as the Israelites were burying a man, suddenly they saw a raiding party, so they threw the man into Elisha's tomb. **When he touched Elisha's bones, the man revived and stood up!**

[EEBT] <u>2 Kings 13:21</u> Once, while they were burying a man, some people saw a group of those men from Moab. So they threw the man's dead body into Elisha's grave. **When the dead body touched Elisha's bones, the man became alive again! He stood on his feet.**

[GNT] <u>2 Kings 13:21</u> One time during a funeral, one of those bands was seen, and the people threw the corpse into Elisha's tomb and ran off. **As soon as the body came into contact with Elisha's bones, the man came back to life and stood up.**

[NIRV] <u>2 Kings 13:21</u> One day some Israelites were burying a man. Suddenly they saw a group of robbers. So they threw the man's body into Elisha's tomb. **The body touched Elisha's bones. When it did, the man came back to life again. He stood up on his feet.**

[T4T] <u>2 Kings 13:21</u> One year, when some Israeli people were burying a man's body, they saw a group of those raiders. They were afraid; so quickly they threw that man's body into the tomb where Elisha had been buried, and they ran away. But **as soon as the man's body touched Elisha's bones, the dead man became alive again and jumped up**!

[TLB] <u>2 Kings 13:21</u> Once some men who were burying a friend spied these marauders so they hastily threw his body into the tomb of Elisha. **And as soon as the body touched Elisha's bones, the dead man revived and jumped to his feet!**

[TVB] <u>2 Kings 13:21</u> During the springtime, while a group of men were out burying a man, they spied a gang of bandits approaching them. They became afraid, so they threw the dead man's body into Elisha's grave. **As soon as the dead man's body touched the bones of Elisha, the dead man miraculously came back to life and stood up.**

[UDB] <u>2 Kings 13:21</u> One year, when some Israelite people were burying a man's body, they saw a group of those raiders. They were afraid, so quickly they threw that man's body into the grave where Elisha had been buried, and they ran away. But **as soon as the man's body touched Elisha's bones, the dead man became alive again and jumped up!**

2 Kings 20:5-6 Turn again, and tell Hezekiah the captain of my people, Thus saith the Lord, the God of David thy father, I have heard thy prayer, I have seen thy tears: behold, **I will heal**[raphah] **thee**: on the third day thou shalt go up unto the house of the Lord. ⁶And I will add unto thy days fifteen years; and I will deliver thee and this city out of the hand of the king of Assyria; and I will defend this city for mine own sake, and for my servant David's sake.

[AMP] 2 Kings 20:5-6 "Go back and tell Hezekiah the leader of My people, 'Thus says the Lord, the God of David your father (ancestor): "I have heard your prayer, I have seen your tears. Behold, **I am healing you**; on the third day you shall go up to the house of the Lord. ⁶I will add fifteen years to your life and save you and this city [Jerusalem] from the hand of the king of Assyria; and I will protect this city for My own sake and for My servant David's sake."'"

[CT-OT] 2 Kings 20:5-6 "Return and say to Hezekiah the ruler of My people, 'So has the Lord God of your father David said, "I have heard your prayer; I have seen your tears. Behold **I shall heal you**. On the third day you shall go up to the house of the Lord. ⁶And I will add fifteen years to your life and I will save you from the hand of the king of Assyria, I will save you and this city, and I will protect this city for My sake and for the sake of My servant David."'"

[CWB] 2 Kings 20:5-6 "Go back to Hezekiah and say to him, 'This is what the Lord, the God of your ancestor David says: I have heard your prayer and seen your tears. **I will heal you**. The day after tomorrow you'll be up, strong enough to go to the Temple to worship me. ⁶I will add fifteen years to your life and will deliver Jerusalem from the hand of the Assyrians. I will defend this city for the sake of my name and for the sake of my servant David.'"

[ICB] 2 Kings 20:5-6 "Go back and tell Hezekiah, the leader of my people: 'This is what the Lord, the God of your ancestor David, says: I have heard your prayer. And I have seen your tears. So **I will heal you**. Three days from now you will go up to the Temple of the Lord. ⁶I will add 15 years to your life. I will save you and this city from the king of Assyria. And I will protect the city for myself and for my servant David.'"

[NOG] 2 Kings 20:5-6 "Go back and say to Hezekiah, leader of my people, 'This is what Yahweh Elohim of your ancestor David says: I've heard your prayer. I've seen your tears. Now **I'm going to heal you**. The day after tomorrow you will go to Yahweh's temple. ⁶I'll give you 15 more years to live. I'll rescue you and defend this city from the control of the king of Assyria for my sake and for the sake of my servant David.'"

[Palmer] 2 Kings 20:5-6 Turn back, and say to Hezekiah the prince of my people, Thus says Yahweh, the God of David your father, I have heard your prayer, I have seen your tears: behold, **I will heal you**; on the third day you shall go up to the house of Yahweh. ⁶And I will add to your days fifteen years; and I will deliver you and this city out of the hand of the king of Assyria; and I will defend this city for my own sake, and for my servant David's sake.

[TLB] 2 Kings 20:5-6 "Go back to Hezekiah, the leader of my people, and tell him that the Lord God of his ancestor David has heard his prayer and seen his tears. **I will heal him**, and three days from now he will be out of bed and at the Temple! ⁶I will add fifteen years to his life and save him and this city from the king of Assyria. And it will all be done for the glory of my own name and for the sake of my servant David."

2 Kings 20:7 And Isaiah said, Take a lump of figs. **And they took and laid it on the boil, and he recovered**.

Although Hezekiah was healed with a natural remedy, how did they know what to administer? If the Lord reveals a natural remedy to us, it is still supernatural.

[CWB] <u>2 Kings 20:7</u> So Isaiah turned around and told Hezekiah what the Lord had said. He also told the king's servants to make a poultice of figs and put it on the infection and their master would get well. **They did what Isaiah said and the king began to recover.**

[Douay-Rheims] <u>2 Kings 20:7</u> And Isaias said: Bring me a lump of figs. **And when they had brought it, and laid it upon his boil, he was healed.**

[ERV] <u>2 Kings 20:7</u> Then Isaiah said, "Crush figs together and put them on your sore; you will get well." **So they took the mixture of figs and put it on Hezekiah's sore place, and he got well.**

[ICB] <u>2 Kings 20:7</u> Then Isaiah said, "Make a paste from figs." So **they made it and put it on Hezekiah's boil. And he got well.**

[NOG] <u>2 Kings 20:7</u> Then Isaiah said, "Get a fig cake, and **put it on the boil so that the king will get well."**

[TVB] <u>2 Kings 20:7</u> Isaiah: Fetch a lump of figs. **They placed the figs on the king's open sore, and he was healed.**

[UDB] <u>2 Kings 20:7</u> Isaiah returned to the palace and told Hezekiah what Yahweh had said. Then he said to Hezekiah's servants, "Bring a paste made of boiled figs. Put some of it on his boils, and he will get well." **The servants did that, and the king recovered.**

FIRST CHRONICLES

<u>1 Chronicles 21:22</u> Then David said to Ornan, Grant me the place of this threshingfloor, that I may build an altar therein unto the Lord: thou shalt grant it me for the full price: that the plague may be stayed from the people.

[AMPC] **1 Chronicles 21:22** Then David said to Ornan, Grant me the site of this threshing floor, that I may build an altar on it to the Lord. You shall charge me the full price for it, that the plague may be averted from the people.

[BBE] **1 Chronicles 21:22** Then David said to Ornan, Give me the place where this grain-floor is, so that I may put up an altar here to the Lord: let me have it for its full price; so that this disease may be stopped among the people.

[BLE] **1 Chronicles 21:22** And David said to Ornan "Give me the site of the threshing-floor to build an altar to Jehovah on—give it to me for full money—to have the deaths among the people shut off."

[EEBT] **1 Chronicles 21:22** David said to Ornan, 'Let me buy this ground so that I can build an altar to the Lord here. Then God will stop the illness that is killing people. I will pay the whole price for the land.'

[ERV] **1 Chronicles 21:22** David said to Araunah, "Sell me your threshing floor. I will pay you the full price. Then I can use the area to build an altar to worship the Lord. Then the terrible sicknesses will be stopped."

[GNT] **1 Chronicles 21:22** David said to him, "Sell me your threshing place, so that I can build an altar to the Lord, to stop the epidemic. I'll give you the full price."

[LTPB] **1 Chronicles 21:22** David said to him, "Give me the site of your threshing floor so I can build the Lord's altar in it, so that you receive however much it is worth in silver, and the plague may cease from the people!"

[MSG] **1 Chronicles 21:22** David said to Araunah, "Give me the site of the threshing floor so I can build an altar to God. Charge me the market price; we're going to put an end to this disaster."

[NHEB] **1 Chronicles 21:22** Then David said to Ornan, "Give me the place of this threshing floor, that I may build thereon an altar to the Lord. You shall sell it to me for the full price, that the plague may be stopped from afflicting the people."

[NLV] **1 Chronicles 21:22** David said to him, "Give me this part of the grain-floor, that I may build an altar on it to the Lord. Give it to me for the full price. Then the disease will be turned away from the people."

[NWT] **1 Chronicles 21:22** David said to Or nan: "Sell me the site of the threshing floor, so that I may build an altar to Jehovah on it. Sell it to me for the full price, so that the scourge against the people may be halted."

[REAL] **1 Chronicles 21:22** Then David told Ornan, "Give me the position of this threshing floor, so I can build an Altar on it to Ya-HoVaH. Give it to me for the full price, so the outbreak can be held back from the people,"

[TVB] **1 Chronicles 21:22** David: Sell me this threshing floor so I may build on it an altar to the Eternal. I will pay you the full price so the plague against the people may end.

[YLT] **1 Chronicles 21:22** And David saith unto Ornan, 'Give to me the place of the threshing-floor, and I build in it an altar to Jehovah; for full silver give it to me, and the plague is restrained from the people.'

1 Chronicles 29:11-12 Thine, O Lord, is the greatness, and the power, and the glory, and the victory, and the majesty: for all that is in the heaven and in the earth is thine; thine is the kingdom, O Lord, and thou art exalted as head above all. ¹²Both riches and honour come of thee, and thou reignest over all; and **in thine hand is power and might; and in thine hand it is to make great, and to give strength unto all**.

[AMP] **1 Chronicles 29:11-12** Yours, O Lord, is the greatness and the power and the glory and the victory and the majesty, indeed everything that is in the heavens and on the earth; Yours is the dominion and kingdom, O Lord, and You exalt Yourself as head over all. ¹²Both riches and honor come from You, and You rule over all. **In Your hand is power and might; and it is in Your hands to make great and to give strength to everyone**.

[AMPC] **1 Chronicles 29:11-12** Yours, O Lord, is the greatness and the power and the glory and the victory and the majesty, for all that is in the heavens and the earth is Yours; Yours is the kingdom, O Lord, and Yours it is to be exalted as Head over all. ¹²Both riches and honor come from You, and You reign over all. **In Your hands are power and might; in Your hands it is to make great and to give strength to all.**

[ASV-2014] **1 Chronicles 29:11-12** Thine, O Yahweh, is the greatness, and the power, and the glory, and the victory, and the majesty: for all that is in the heavens and in the earth [is thine]; thine is the kingdom, O Yahweh, and thou art exalted as head above all. ¹²Both riches and honor come of thee, and thou rulest over all; and **in thy hand is power and might; and in thy hand it is to make great, and to give strength unto all.**

[CCB] **1 Chronicles 29:11-12** Yours, Yahweh, is the greatness, the power, splendor, length of days, glory, for all that is in the heavens and on the earth is yours. Yours is the sovereignty forever, O Yahweh; you are supreme ruler over all. ¹²Riches and honor go before you, you are ruler of all, **in your hand lie strength and power; You are the one who gives greatness and strength to all**.

[CEB] <u>1 Chronicles 29:11-12</u> To you, Lord, belong greatness and power, honor, splendor, and majesty, because everything in heaven and on earth belongs to you. Yours, Lord, is the kingship, and you are honored as head of all. [12]You are the source of wealth and honor, and you rule over all. **In your hand are strength and might, and it is in your power to magnify and strengthen all.**

[CJB] <u>1 Chronicles 29:11-12</u> Yours, Adonai, is the greatness, the power, the glory, the victory and the majesty; for everything in heaven and on earth is yours. The kingdom is yours, Adonai; and you are exalted as head over all. [12]Riches and honor come from you, you rule everything, **in your hand is power and strength, you have the capacity to make great and to give strength to all.**

[CWB] <u>1 Chronicles 29:11-12</u> Lord, you are great and powerful, surrounded by glory, splendor and majesty. Everything in heaven and earth is yours. The kingdom is yours and you are its rightful Ruler. [12]Wealth and honor come from you. **You rule over everything by your own strength and power. No one has given you what you have. You are the One who makes others great and gives them strength and power.**

[ICB] <u>1 Chronicles 29:11-12</u> Lord, you are great and powerful. You have glory, victory and honor. Everything in heaven and on earth belongs to you. The kingdom belongs to you, Lord. You are the ruler over everything. [12]Riches and honor come from you. You rule everything. **You have the power and strength to make anyone great and strong.**

[Jerusalem] <u>1 Chronicles 29:11-12</u> Yours, Yahweh, is the greatness, the power, splendour, length of days, glory, for all that is in the heavens and on the earth is yours. Yours is the sovereignty, Yahweh; you are exalted over all, supreme. [12]Riches and honour go before you, you are ruler of all, **in your hand lie strength and power; in your hand it is to give greatness and strength to all.**

[Kent-OT] <u>1 Chronicles 29:11-12</u> Thine, O Jehovah, is the greatness, and the might, and the glory, and the eminence, and the majesty, for all that is in the heavens and in the earth is thine. Thine is the kingdom, O Jehovah, and thou art exalted as head above all. [12]Riches and honor come from thee, and thou rulest over all, and **in thy hand is might and strength, and in thy hand it is the power to make every one great and strong.**

[Knox] <u>1 Chronicles 29:11-12</u> Thine, Lord, the magnificence, thine the power, splendour and glory and majesty are thine; to thee all that is in heaven, all that is on earth, belongs, to thee the kingdom, of all princes thou art overlord. [12]Riches and honour come from thee; all things obey thy will; **from thee power comes and dominion; only thy hand exalts, only thy hand makes strong.**

[LTPB] <u>1 Chronicles 29:11-12</u> Magnificence is Yours, Lord, and power and glory and victory! Praise be to You—for all that are in sky and on earth are Yours. The kingdom is Yours, and You are above all princes. [12]**Riches are Yours, and glory is Yours. You rule in all things by Your hand. Strength and power are in Your hand, greatness and dominion over all!**

[MEV] <u>1 Chronicles 29:11-12</u> Yours, O Lord, is the greatness, and the power, and the glory, and the victory, and the majesty, for everything in the heavens and the earth is Yours. Yours is the kingdom, O Lord, and You exalt Yourself as head above all. [12]Riches and honor flow from You, and You rule over all. **In Your hand are power and might, and in Your hand it is to make great and to strengthen all.**

[SAAS-OT] <u>1 Chronicles 29:11-12</u> Yours, O Lord, is the greatness and the power and the glory and the victory and the might. You are master over all that is in heaven and on the earth. Every king and nation is thrown into confusion before You. [12]From the first, You are the wealth and the glory who reigns over all, as the Lord and dominion of all. **In Your hand is power and authority, and you are almighty with Your hand to increase and establish all things.**

[TVB] <u>1 Chronicles 29:11-12</u> All that is great and powerful and glorious and victorious and majestic is Yours, O Eternal One. Indeed everything that is in the heavens and the earth belongs to You. The kingdom belongs to You, O Eternal One, and You are the head of it all. [12]Wealth and glory come from You, and You rule over them all. **In Your hand is power and strength, and You use them to make great and strengthen everyone.**

SECOND CHRONICLES

<u>2 Chronicles 6:28-30</u> If there be dearth in the land, if there be pestilence, if there be blasting, or mildew, locusts, or caterpillers; if their enemies besiege them in the cities of their land; whatsoever sore or whatsoever sickness there be: [29]Then what prayer or what supplication soever shall be made of any man, or of all thy people Israel, when every one shall know his own sore and his own grief, and shall spread forth his hands in this house: [30]Then hear thou from heaven thy dwelling place, and forgive, and render unto every man according unto all his ways, whose heart thou knowest; (for thou only knowest the hearts of the children of men:)

[CAB] <u>2 Chronicles 6:28-30</u> If there should be famine upon the land, if there should be death, a pestilent wind and blight; if there should be locusts and caterpillars, and if the enemy should harass them before their cities; in whatever plague and whatever distress they may be; [29]then whatever prayer and whatever supplication shall be made by any man and all Your people Israel, if a man should know his own plague and his own sickness, and should spread forth his hands toward this house; [30]then shall You hear from heaven, out of Your prepared dwelling place, and shall be merciful, and shall recompense to the man according to his ways, as You shall know his heart; for You alone know the heart of the children of men;

[CPDV] <u>2 Chronicles 6:28-30</u> If a famine will have risen up in the land, or pestilence, or fungus, or mildew, or locusts, or beetles, or if enemies will have laid waste to the countryside and will have besieged the gates of the cities, or whatever scourge or infirmity will have pressed upon them, [29]if anyone from your people Israel, knowing his own scourge and infirmity, will have made supplication and will have extended his hands in this house, [30]you will heed him from heaven, indeed from your sublime habitation, and you will forgive, and you will repay each one according to his ways, which you know him to hold in his heart. For you alone know the hearts of the sons of men.

[MSG] <u>2 Chronicles 6:28-30</u> When disasters strike, famine or catastrophe, crop failure or disease, locust or beetle, or when an enemy attacks their defenses—calamity of any sort— [29]any prayer that's prayed from anyone at all among your people Israel, their hearts penetrated by disaster, hands and arms thrown out for help to this Temple, [30]Listen from your home in heaven, forgive and reward us: reward each life and circumstance, For you know each life from the inside, (you're the only one with such inside knowledge!),

[NIRV] <u>2 Chronicles 6:28-30</u> "Suppose there isn't enough food in the land. And a plague strikes the land. The hot winds completely dry up our crops. Or locusts or grasshoppers come and eat them up. Or enemies surround one of our cities and get ready to attack it. Or trouble or sickness comes. [29]But suppose one of your people prays to you. They ask you to help them. They are aware of how much they are suffering. And they spread out their hands toward this temple to pray. [30]Then listen to them from heaven. It's the place where you live. Forgive them. Deal with everyone in keeping with everything they do. You know their hearts. In fact, you are the only one who knows every human heart."

[NOG] <u>2 Chronicles 6:28-30</u> "There may be famine in the land. Plant diseases, heat waves, funguses, locusts, or grasshoppers may destroy crops. Enemies may blockade Israel's city gates. During every plague or sickness [29]hear every prayer for mercy made by one person or by all the people in Israel, all who know suffering or pain, who stretch out their hands toward this temple. [30]Hear them in heaven, where you live. Forgive them, and give each person the proper reply. (You know what is in their hearts, because you alone know what is in people's hearts.)"

[SAAS-OT] 2 Chronicles 6:28-30 When there is famine in the land, death and blight and mildew and locusts and grasshoppers, when their enemies besiege their cities, whatever plague or whatever sickness there may be; [29]whatever prayer, whatever supplication anyone makes, or all Your people Israel make, when each one knows his own burden and his own grief and spreads out his hands in this house; [30]then hear from heaven, Your dwelling place, and forgive them. And give to everyone according to his ways, for You know his heart, since You alone know the hearts of the sons of men;

[TLB] 2 Chronicles 6:28-30 "If there is a famine in the land, or plagues, or crop disease, or attacks of locusts or caterpillars, or if your people's enemies are in the land besieging our cities—whatever the trouble is— [29]listen to every individual's prayer concerning his private sorrow, as well as all the public prayers. [30]Hear from heaven where you live and forgive, and give each one whatever he deserves, for you know the hearts of all mankind."

2 Chronicles 30:18-20 For a multitude of the people, even many of Ephraim, and Manasseh, Issachar, and Zebulun, had not cleansed themselves, yet did they eat the passover otherwise than it was written. But Hezekiah prayed for them, saying, The good LORD pardon every one [19]That prepareth his heart to seek God, the LORD God of his fathers, though he be not cleansed according to the purification of the sanctuary. [20]**And the LORD hearkened to Hezekiah, and healed**[raphah] **the people.**

[CPDV] 2 Chronicles 30:18-20 And now a great portion of the people from Ephraim, and Manasseh, and Issachar, and Zebulun, who had not been sanctified, ate the Passover, which is not in accord with what was written. And Hezekiah prayed for them, saying: "The good Lord will be forgiving 19 to all who, with their whole heart, seek the Lord, the God of their fathers. And he will not impute it to them, though they have not been sanctified." [20]**And the Lord heeded him, and was reconciled to the people.**

[CWB] 2 Chronicles 30:18-20 But others, particularly those from the northern tribes of Ephraim, Manasseh, Issachar and Zebulun who were ritually unclean, had killed their Passover lamb and eaten its meat before consecrating themselves to the Lord. The king prayed for them, saying, "O Lord, forgive them. You are a compassionate God, a God who pardons. [19]I know you forgive those who worship you with their whole hearts, even if they are not ritually clean according to the rules of the Sanctuary." [20]**The Lord heard Hezekiah's prayer and showed His compassion and forgiveness to those people.**

[FAA] 2 Chronicles 30:18-20 For a large number of the people, many from Ephraim and Manasseh and Issachar and Zebulun, had not purified themselves, for they had eaten the Passover lamb in a way not as written, but Hezekiah prayed for them and said, "May the good Lord forgive this for [19]everyone who has prepared his heart to seek God—the Lord God of his fathers—but is not clean according to the standards of holy cleanness." [20]And **the Lord heard Hezekiah and he healed the people.**

[ICB] 2 Chronicles 30:18-20 Many people from Ephraim, Manasseh, Issachar and Zebulun had not purified themselves for the feast. But they ate the Passover even though it was against the law. So Hezekiah prayed for them. He said, "Lord, you are good. You are the Lord, the God our ancestors obeyed. Please forgive everyone who tries to obey you. Forgive them even if they did not make themselves clean as the rules of the Temple command." [20]**The Lord listened to Hezekiah's prayer, and he healed the people.**

[KJV-Miller] 2 Chronicles 30:18-20 For a multitude of the people, even many of Ephraim and Manasseh, Issachar and Zebulun, had not cleansed themselves, yet they ate the Passover other than it was written. But Hezekiah prayed for them, saying, The good LORD pardon every one [19]Who prepares his heart to seek God, the Lord God of his fathers, though he is not cleansed according to the purification of the sanctuary. **[20]And the Lord listened to Hezekiah and healed the people**.

[MSG] <u>2 Chronicles 30:18-20</u> There were a lot of people, especially those from Ephraim, Manasseh, Issachar, and Zebulun, who did not eat the Passover meal because they had not prepared themselves adequately. Hezekiah prayed for these as follows: "May God who is all good, pardon and forgive [19]everyone who sincerely desires God, the God of our ancestors. Even—especially! —these who do not meet the literal conditions stated for access to The Temple." **[20]God responded to Hezekiah's prayer and healed the people**.

[MSTC] <u>2 Chronicles 30:18-20</u> There was very much people out of Ephraim, Manasseh, Issachar and Zebulun that were not clean, and therefore did eat Passover otherwise than writing specifieth. But Hezekiah prayed for them, and said, [19]"The good Lord be merciful to all that set their hearts to seek the God that is the Lord God of their fathers, though they do it not according to the cleanness of the holy place." **[20]And the Lord heard Hezekiah and healed the people**.

[NCV] <u>2 Chronicles 30:18-20</u> Although many people from Ephraim, Manasseh, Issachar, and Zebulun had not purified themselves for the feast, they ate the Passover even though it was against the law. So Hezekiah prayed for them, saying, "Lord, you are good. You are the Lord, the God of our ancestors. Please forgive all those [19]who try to obey you even if they did not make themselves clean as the rules of the Temple command." **[20]The Lord listened to Hezekiah's prayer, and he healed the people**.

[TVB] <u>2 Chronicles 30:18-20</u> Many of the people from the tribes of Ephraim, Manasseh, Issachar, and Zebulun, had not cleansed themselves as prescribed, but they were able to eat the Passover feast because Hezekiah prayed on their behalf. Hezekiah: Eternal One, because You are good, cover their sins for [19]everyone here who has neglected to ritually cleanse himself in order to properly enter the temple of the True God, the Eternal God of our ancestors. Everyone here wants to follow You. **[20]The Eternal One heard Hezekiah's prayer and healed them from the threat of disease for not approaching God as instructed**.

EZRA

<u>Ezra 7:28</u> And hath extended mercy unto me before the king, and his counsellors, and before all the king's mighty princes. **And I was strengthened as the hand of the Lord my God was upon me**, and I gathered together out of Israel chief men to go up with me.

[ABP] <u>Ezra 7:28</u> And upon me [leaned mercy] in the eyes of the king, and his counselors, and all the rulers of the king of the mighty ones. And **I was strengthened by the [hand of the Lord my God good] upon me,** and I gathered from Israel rulers to ascend with me.

[BBE] <u>Ezra 7:28</u> And has given mercy to me before the king and his government and before all the king's great captains. **And I was made strong by the hand of the Lord my God which was on me**, and I got together out of Israel chief men to go up with me.

[LXX-1844] <u>Ezra 7:28</u> and has given me favour in the eyes of the king, and of his councillors, and all the rulers of the king, the exalted ones. **And I was strengthened according to the good hand of God upon me**, and I gathered chief men of Israel to go up with me.

[Macrae] <u>Ezra 7:28</u> And extended mercy to me before the king his counsellors, and all his mighty princes; **for I was strengthened by the Eternal, my God's power**, with me; and gathered the chief of Israel to go up with me.

[NIRV] <u>Ezra 7:28</u> The Lord has been kind to me. He has caused the king and his advisers to be kind to me. In fact, all the king's powerful officials have been kind to me. **The strong hand of the Lord my God helped me. That gave me new strength.** So I gathered together leaders from Israel to go up to Jerusalem with me."

[TLV] <u>Ezra 7:28</u> and who has extended lovingkindness to me before the king and his counselors and all the king's mighty princes. **I gained strength, as the hand of Adonai my God was upon me,** and I gathered leading men from Israel to go up with me.

<u>Ezra 9:8</u> And now for a little space grace hath been shewed from the Lᴏʀᴅ our God, to leave us a remnant to escape, and to give us a nail in his holy place, that **our God may lighten our eyes, and give us a little reviving in our bondage.**

[CAB] <u>Ezra 9:8</u> And now our God has dealt mercifully with us, so as to leave us a remnant to escape, and to give us an establishment in the place of His sanctuary, **to enlighten our eyes, and give us a measure of revival in our bondage.**

[CEV] <u>Ezra 9:8</u> But for now, Lord God, you have shown great kindness to us. You made us truly happy by letting some of us settle in this sacred place and **by helping us in our time of slavery.**

[CWB] <u>Ezra 9:8</u> Now for a little while, you, the Lord our God, have been gracious to us by letting some of us return in safety to your city to worship again in your Temple. You have given us a new outlook on life **by taking us out of bondage and setting us free.**

[EXB] <u>Ezra 9:8</u> "But now, for a short time, the Lord our God has been ·kind [gracious; merciful] to us. He has let ·some of us [a remnant] ·come back from [escape; or survive] ·captivity [exile] and has ·let us live in safety [given us a peg; a tent peg symbolizing pitching a tent after travel] in his holy place. And **so our God ·gives us hope [causes our eyes to shine; that is, revives] and a little relief ·from [in] our ·slavery [bondage].**

[GNT] <u>Ezra 9:8</u> Now for a short time, O Lord our God, you have been gracious to us and have let some of us escape from slavery and live in safety in this holy place. **You have let us escape from slavery and have given us new life.**

[NABRE] <u>Ezra 9:8</u> "And now, only a short time ago, mercy came to us from the Lord, our God, who left us a remnant and gave us a stake in his holy place; **thus our God has brightened our eyes and given us relief in our slavery.**

[T4T] <u>Ezra 9:8</u> But now, Yahweh God, you have acted very kindly toward us. You have allowed some of us to survive/continue to live. **You have revived our spirits** and allowed us to escape from being slaves in Babylonia and to return safely to live in this sacred place.

[TNIV] <u>Ezra 9:8</u> "But now, for a brief moment, the Lᴏʀᴅ our God has been gracious in leaving us a remnant and giving us a firm place in his sanctuary, and **so our God gives light to our eyes and a little relief in our bondage.**

NEHEMIAH

<u>Nehemiah 6:9</u> For they all made us afraid, saying, Their hands shall be weakened from the work, that it be not done. Now therefore, O God, strengthen my hands.

[BBE] <u>Nehemiah 6:9</u> For they were hoping to put fear in us, saying, Their hands will become feeble and give up the work so that it may not get done. But now, O God, make my hands strong.

[EXB] <u>Nehemiah 6:9</u> Our enemies were trying to ·scare [intimidate; terrorize] us, thinking, "They will get too ·weak [discouraged; their hands will grow slack] to work. Then the wall will not be finished." ·But I prayed [So now], "God, ·make me strong [strengthen my hands]."

[GW] <u>Nehemiah 6:9</u> They were all trying to intimidate us. They thought we would give up and not finish the work. But God made me strong.

[ICB] <u>Nehemiah 6:9</u> Our enemies were trying to scare us. They were thinking, "They will get too weak to work. Then the wall will not be finished." But I prayed, "God, make me strong."

[MSG] <u>Nehemiah 6:9</u> They were trying to intimidate us into quitting. They thought, "They'll give up; they'll never finish it." I prayed, "Give me strength."

[TNIV] <u>Nehemiah 6:9</u> They were all trying to frighten us, thinking, "Their hands will get too weak for the work, and it will not be completed." But I prayed, "Now strengthen my hands."

[VW] <u>Nehemiah 6:9</u> For they all were trying to make us afraid, saying, Their hands will be weakened in the work, and it will not be done. Now therefore, O God, strengthen my hands.

<u>Nehemiah 8:10</u> Then he said unto them, Go your way, eat the fat, and drink the sweet, and send portions unto them for whom nothing is prepared: for this day is holy unto our Lord: neither be ye sorry; for **the joy of the Lᴏʀᴅ is your strength**.

[AMPC] <u>Nehemiah 8:10</u> Then [Ezra] told them, Go your way, eat the fat, drink the sweet drink, and send portions to him for whom nothing is prepared; for this day is holy to our Lord. And be not grieved and depressed, for the **joy of the Lord is your strength and stronghold**.

[BBE] <u>Nehemiah 8:10</u> Then he said to them, Go away now, and take the fat for your food and the sweet for your drink, and send some to him for whom nothing is made ready: for this day is holy to our Lord: and let there be no grief in your hearts; for **the joy of the Lord is your strong place**.

[Beck] <u>Nehemiah 8:10</u> Then he told them, "Go, eat fat meat, drink sweat drinks, and send portions of food to those for whom none is prepared, because this is the Lord's holy day; don't feel sad. **The joy you have in the Lᴏʀᴅ is your fortress**."

[CBC] <u>Nehemiah 8:10</u> Then he said unto them, "Go your way, eat the fat, and drink the sweet, and send portions unto them for whom nothing is prepared: for this day it is holy unto our Lord: neither be ye sorry; for **the joy of the Lᴏʀᴅ that is your defence and refuge**."

[ERV] <u>Nehemiah 8:10</u> Nehemiah said, "Go and enjoy the good food and sweet drinks. Give some food and drinks to those who didn't prepare any food. Today is a special day to our Lord. Don't be sad, because **the joy of the Lord will make you strong**."

[FAA] <u>Nehemiah 8:10</u> And he said to them, "Go and eat rich food, and drink sweet drinks, and send portions to him who has nothing prepared for him, for the day is holy to our Lord. And do not be grieved, **for the joy of the Lord is your stronghold**."

[ICB] <u>Nehemiah 8:10</u> Nehemiah said, "Go and enjoy good food and sweet drinks. Send some to people who have none. Today is a holy day to the Lord. Don't be sad. **The joy of the Lord will make you strong**."

[JPS-OT 1985] <u>Nehemiah 8:10</u> He further said to them, "Go, eat choice foods and drink sweet drinks and send portions to whoever has nothing prepared, for the day is holy to our Lord. Do not be sad, **for your rejoicing in the Lᴏʀᴅ is the source of your strength**."

[Lamsa] <u>Nehemiah 8:10</u> Then he said to them, Go your way, eat and drink and send portions to them for whom nothing is prepared; for this day is holy to the Lord; and do not be sad, **for this is a day of joy of the Lord, and he will be your strength.**

[LEB] <u>Nehemiah 8:10</u> Then he said to them, "Go, eat festive food and drink sweet drinks, and send a share to those for whom nothing is prepared; for this day is holy to our lord. Do not be grieved because **the joy of Yahweh is your refuge.**"

[SG] <u>Nehemiah 8:10</u> Then he said to them, "Go your way, eat the fat and drink the sweet, and send portions to him for whom nothing is prepared, for this day is holy to the Lord; and do not be depressed, for **the joy of the Lord is your refuge.**"

[SPV] <u>Nehemiah 8:10</u> Then he said to them, "Go, eat fat [things] and drink sweet [things] and send portions to [him who] has nothing prepared, for this day [is] holy to our Lord; and do not grieve, **for the joy of the Lord is your fortress.**"

[TLB] <u>Nehemiah 8:10</u> it is a time to celebrate with a hearty meal and to send presents to those in need, **for the joy of the Lord is your strength**. You must not be dejected and sad!

[UDB] <u>Nehemiah 8:10</u> Then Nehemiah said to them, "Now go home and enjoy some good food and have something sweet to drink. And send some of it to people who do not have anything to eat or drink. This is a day set apart to worship our Lord. Do not be filled with sadness! **The joy that Yahweh gives will make you strong.**"

Nehemiah 9:6 Thou, even thou, art Lord alone; thou hast made heaven, the heaven of heavens, with all their host, the earth, and all things that are therein, the seas, and all that is therein, and thou preservest them all; and the host of heaven worshippeth thee.

[BBE] <u>Nehemiah 9:6</u> You are the Lord, even you only; you have made heaven, the heaven of heavens with all their armies, the earth and all things in it, the seas and everything in them; and you keep them from destruction: and the armies of heaven are your worshippers.

[CCB] <u>Nehemiah 9:6</u> Then Ezra said, "You, Yahweh, you alone made the heavens, the heaven of heavens, and all their army, the earth and all that is on it, the seas and all that is in them. You give life to all, and all the angels of heaven adore you.

[CEV] <u>Nehemiah 9:6</u> You alone are the Lord, Creator of the heavens and all the stars, Creator of the earth and those who live on it, Creator of the ocean and all its creatures. You are the source of life, praised by the stars that fill the heavens.

[CLV] <u>Nehemiah 9:6</u> You are He, Yahweh You alone. You Yourself have made the heavens, the heavens of the heavens and all their host, the earth and all that is on it, the seas and all that is in them. You are keeping all of them alive, and the host of the heavens are prostrating themselves before You.

[CPDV] <u>Nehemiah 9:6</u> You yourself alone, O Lord, made heaven, and the heaven of the heavens, and all their host, the earth and all things that are in it, the seas and all things that are in them. And you gave life to all these things. And the host of heaven adores you.

[CWB] <u>Nehemiah 9:6</u> With all the people standing, the Levites led them in a joint prayer of praise, saying, "You alone, O Lord, are the Lord of heaven and earth. You made the heavens and the heaven of heavens, together with all the planets and stars. You made the earth and everything that's in it. You made the seas and everything in them. You gave life and breath to everything. All creation respects you and worships you.

[ECB] <u>Nehemiah 9:6</u> You are he, Yah Veh alone; you worked the heavens—the heavens of the heavens and all their host; the earth and all thereon; the seas and all therein; and you enliven them all; and the host of the heavens prostrates to you.

[ERV] <u>Nehemiah 9:6</u> You are God. Lord, only you are God. You made the sky and the highest heavens and everything in them. You made the earth and everything on it. You made the seas and everything in them. You give life to everything. All the heavenly angels bow down and worship you.

[ISV] <u>Nehemiah 9:6</u> You are the Lord; you alone crafted the heavens, the highest heavens with all of their armies; the earth, and everything in it; the seas, and everything in them; you keep giving all of them life, and the army of heaven continuously worships you.

[KJ3] <u>Nehemiah 9:6</u> You alone are He, O Jehovah; You have made the heavens, and heaven of the heavens, and all their host; the earth and all which is on it; the seas, and all that is in them; and You shall preserve them all alive. And the host of the heavens bows down to You.

[REAL] <u>Nehemiah 9:6</u> You, you alone are Ya-HoVaH. You have made the heavens, the heavens of heavens, with all their mobilized army, the Earth and everything are in it, the seas and everything in it, and you rescue them all, and the mobilized army of the heavens worships you.

[T4T] <u>Nehemiah 9:6</u> You only are God. You made the sky and the heavens and all the stars. You made the earth and everything that is on it, and you made the seas/oceans and everything that is in them. You are the one who gives life to everything and helps them remain alive. All the angels who are in heaven worship you.

[TVB] <u>Nehemiah 9:6</u> You are the Eternal, the only One. The skies are Your work alone—You made the heavens above those skies and the stars that fill them. You made the earth and everything upon it, the seas and all that lives within their depths. Your creation lives and is sustained by You, and those who dwell in the heavens Fall down before You and worship.

<u>Nehemiah 9:21</u> Yea, forty years didst thou sustain them in the wilderness, so that they lacked nothing; their clothes waxed not old, and **their feet swelled not**.

[BBE] <u>Nehemiah 9:21</u> Truly, for forty years you were their support in the waste land, and they were in need of nothing; **their clothing did not get old or their feet become tired.**

[Beck] <u>Nehemiah 9:21</u> For 40 years You fed them in the wilderness, and they had everything they needed. Their clothes didn't wear out, **and their feet didn't blister**.

[CE] <u>Nehemiah 9:21</u> Forty years didst thou feed them in the desert, and nothing was wanting to them; their garments did not grow old, and **their feet were not worn**.

[CWB] <u>Nehemiah 9:21</u> "For forty years you kept them in the desert and gave them all they needed. Their clothes didn't wear out. **They never had swollen feet from all that walking. And they were never sick.**

[ERV] <u>Nehemiah 9:21</u> You took care of them for 40 years. They had all they needed in the desert. Their clothes didn't wear out, and **their feet didn't swell and hurt**.

[LTPB] <u>Nehemiah 9:21</u> You fed them forty years in the desert, and nothing was lacking to them. Their clothing did not get old, and their feet were not bruised.

[Moffatt] <u>Nehemiah 9:21</u> For forty years thou didst support them in the desert, and they lacked for nothing; their clothes never grew old, and **their feet never blistered**.

[NOG] <u>Nehemiah 9:21</u> You provided for them in the desert for 40 years, and they had everything they needed. Their clothes didn't wear out, and **their feet didn't swell**.

[T4T] <u>Nehemiah 9:21</u> For forty years you took care of them in the desert. During all that time, they did not lack anything that they needed. Their clothes did not wear out, and **their feet did not swell up even though they were continually walking**.

[TVB] <u>Nehemiah 9:21</u> In 40 years of living in the wilderness, You provided for every need they had: Their clothing did not wear out, **nor did their feet swell from endless walking**.

<u>Nehemiah 13:2</u> Because they met not the children of Israel with bread and with water, but hired Balaam against them, that he should curse them: howbeit **our God turned the curse into a blessing.**

[ERV] <u>Nehemiah 13:2</u> That law was written because those people didn't give the Israelites food and water. And they had paid Balaam to say a curse against the Israelites. But **our God changed that curse and made it a blessing for us.**

[Knox] <u>Nehemiah 13:2</u> by refusing to provide food and drink, when Israel came by; it was they, too, that hired Balaam to curse Israel, only **our God transformed that curse into a blessing.**

[Lamsa] <u>Nehemiah 13:2</u> Because they did not meet the children of Israel with bread and water, but hired Baalam to curse them; but our **God turned his curses into blessings.**

[LEB] <u>Nehemiah 13:2</u> because they did not come to meet the Israelites with bread and water, but hired Balaam against them in order to curse them—but **our God changed the curse into a blessing.**

[UDB] <u>Nehemiah 13:2</u> The reason for that was that the people of Ammon and the people of Moab did not give any food or water to the Israelites while the Israelites were going through their areas after they left Egypt. Instead, the people of Ammon and Moab paid money to Balaam to influence him to curse the Israelites. But **God turned that attempt to curse Israel into a blessing.**

[YLT] <u>Nehemiah 13:2</u> because they have not come before the sons of Israel with bread and with water, and hire against them Balaam to revile them, and **our God turneth the reviling into a blessing.**

ESTHER

<u>Esther 9:22</u> As the days wherein the Jews rested from their enemies, and the month which was **turned unto them from sorrow to joy, and from mourning into a good day**: that they should make them days of feasting and joy, and of sending portions one to another, and gifts to the poor.

[CAB] <u>Esther 9:22</u> for on these days the Jews obtained rest from their enemies. And as to the month, which was Adar, in which **a change was made for them, from mourning to joy, and from sorrow to a good day**, to spend the whole of it in good days of feasting and gladness, sending portions to their friends, and to the poor.

[CEB] <u>Esther 9:22</u> They are the days on which the Jews finally put to rest the troubles with their enemies. The month is **the one when everything turned around for them from sadness to joy, and from sad, loud crying to a holiday.** They are to make them days of feasts and joyous events, days to send food gifts to each other and money gifts to the poor.

[CWB] <u>Esther 9:22</u> He urged them to remember both of these days as the time when God delivered them from their enemies and **turned their sorrow into joy and their mourning into gladness.** He told them to always keep these days as days of joy, not only to give presents to each other but to give presents to those in need.

[MSTC] <u>Esther 9:22</u> as the days wherein the Jews came to rest from their enemies, and as a month wherein **their pain was turned to joy, and their sorrow to prosperity**: that they should observe the same days of wealth and gladness, and one to send gifts to another, and to distribute unto the poor.

[NOG] <u>Esther 9:22</u> They were to observe them just like the days when the Jews freed themselves from their enemies. In that month **their grief turned to joy and their mourning into a holiday**. He declared that these days are to be days for feasting and celebrating and for sending gifts of food to one another, especially gifts to the poor.

[Rotherham] <u>Esther 9:22</u> according to the days wherein the Jews found rest from their enemies, and the month which was **turned for them, from sorrow to joy, and from mourning to a happy day**, — that they should make them days of banqueting and rejoicing, and of sending portions, every one to his neighbour, and gifts, unto the needy.

JOB

<u>Job 2:7</u> So went **Satan** forth from the presence of the LORD, and **smote Job with sore boils** from the sole of his foot unto his crown.

It is clear from this verse that Satan was the source of all of Job's sicknesses.

[Benisch-OT] <u>Job 2:7</u> So the **obstructor** went forth from the presence of the Eternal, and **smote Job with sore boils** from the sole of his foot unto his crown.

[CSB] <u>Job 2:7</u> So **Satan** left the Lord's presence and **infected Job with terrible boils** from the soles of his feet to the top of his head.

[EEBT] <u>Job 2:7</u> So **Satan** left. And he **caused Job to have very painful skin all over his body**, from his head to his feet.

[Fenton] <u>Job 2:7</u> The **Accuser** consequently went out from the presence of the Lord, and **struck Job with a painful ulcerous inflammation**, from the sole of his foot to the crown of his head.

[GHBWright-OT] <u>Job 2:7</u> And **Satan** went forth from the presence of Jahveh. And he **smote Job with grievous boils** from the sole of his foot to the crown of his head.

[Kent-OT] <u>Job 2:7</u> So **the Adversary** left the presence of Jehovah, and **afflicted Job from the sole of his foot to the crown of his head with leprosy** so terrible

[SAAS-OT] <u>Job 2:7</u> Thus **the devil** went out from the Lord and **struck Job with malignant sores** from head to foot.

[T4T] <u>Job 2:7</u> So **Satan** left, and he caused Job to be **afflicted with very painful boils, from the top of his head to the soles of his feet**.

[Thomson] <u>Job 2:7</u> Thereupon **Satan** withdrew from the presence of the Lord, and **smote Job with foul ulcers from head to foot**,

[TVB] <u>Job 2:7</u> With that, the **Accuser** left the court and the Eternal's presence, and he **infected Job with a painful skin disease. From the soles of his feet to the crown of his head, his body was covered with boils.**

<u>Job 33:4</u> The Spirit of God hath made me, and **the breath of the Almighty hath given me life**.

[CCB] <u>Job 33:4</u> The Spirit of God has made me; **the breath of the Almighty keeps me alive**.

[CLV] Job 33:4 The spirit of El, it has made me, And **the breath of Him Who-Suffices, it preserves me alive.**

[EEBT] Job 33:4 The Spirit of God has made me. **I am alive because of him.**

[GNT] Job 33:4 God's spirit made me and **gave me life.**

[ICB] Job 33:4 The Spirit of God created me. **The breath of God All-Powerful gave me life.**

[NAB] Job 33:4 For the spirit of God has made me, **the breath of the Almighty keeps me alive.**

[NIRV] Job 33:4 The Spirit of God has made me. **The breath of the Mighty One gives me life.**

[Smith] Job 33:4 The spirit of God made me, and **the breath of the Almighty will cause me to live.**

[T4T] Job 33:4 Almighty God has created me as well as you, and with **his breath he has caused me to live.**

[TVB] Job 33:4 God's Spirit has fashioned me and the breath of **the Highest One imparts life to me.**

Job 33:24-25 Then he is gracious unto him, and saith, Deliver him from going down to the pit: I have found a ransom. ²⁵**His flesh shall be fresher than a child's: he shall return to the days of his youth:**

[AMP] Job 33:24-25 Then the angel is gracious to him, and says, 'Spare him from going down to the pit [of destruction]; I have found a ransom [a consideration, or reason for redemption, an atonement]!' ²⁵**"Let his flesh be restored and become fresher than in youth; Let him return to the days of his youthful strength.**

[BBE] Job 33:24-25 And if he has mercy on him, and says, Let him not go down to the underworld, I have given the price for his life: ²⁵**Then his flesh becomes young again, and he comes back to the days of his early strength;**

[Berkeley] Job 33:24-25 then He is gracious and says, 'Release him from going down to the pit; I have found a ransom; ²⁵having repented, **his flesh shall return fresh as in youth, let him return to the days of youthful vigor.'**

[CPDV] Job 33:24-25 he will have mercy on him, and he will say, "Free him, so that he will not descend to destruction. I have found a reason to be favorable to him. ²⁵His body is consumed by suffering. **Let him return to the days of his youth."**

[EEBT] Job 33:24-25 Then God will be kind to that sick person. And God will say, "I have found someone to pay on behalf of this person. So keep him alive." ²⁵**He will become well again. And he will be strong, like a young man.**

[ERV] Job 33:24-25 Maybe the angel will be kind and say to God, 'Save this one from the place of death! I have found a way to pay for his life.' ²⁵**Then that person's body will become young and strong again. He will be as he was when he was young.**

[HCSB] Job 33:24-25 and to be gracious to him and say, "Spare him from going down to the Pit; I have found a ransom," ²⁵**then his flesh will be healthier than in his youth, and he will return to the days of his youthful vigor.**

[ICB] Job 33:24-25 The angel will beg for mercy and say: 'Save this man from the place of death. I have found a way to pay for his life.' ²⁵**Then his body is made new like a child's body. It will be returned to the way it was when he was young.**

[ISV] Job 33:24-25 to show favor to him and to plead, 'Deliver him from having to go down to the Pit— I know where his ransom is!' ²⁵**Let his flesh be rejuvenated as he was in his youth! Let him recover the strength of his youth.**

[NIRV] Job 33:24-25 That angel will be gracious to them. He'll say to God, 'Spare them from going down into the grave. I know a way that can set them free.' **²⁵Then their body is made like new again. They become as strong and healthy as when they were young**.

[NLT] Job 33:24-25 he will be gracious and say, 'Rescue him from the grave, for I have found a ransom for his life.' **²⁵Then his body will become as healthy as a child's, firm and youthful again.**

[Palmer] Job 33:24-25 Then God is gracious to him, and says, Deliver him from going down to the pit, I have found a ransom. **²⁵His flesh shall be fresher than a child's; He returns to the days of his youth.**

[RVIC] Job 33:24-25 Then God is gracious unto him, and saith, Deliver him from going down to the pit, I have found an atoning payment. **²⁵His flesh shall be fresher than a child's; He returneth to the days of his youth.**

[TNIV] Job 33:24-25 and he is gracious to them and says to God, 'Spare them from going down to the pit; I have found a ransom for them— **²⁵let their flesh be renewed like a child's; let them be restored as in the days of their youth'—**

[ULB] Job 33:24-25 and if the angel is kind to him and says to God, 'Save this person from going down to the pit; I have found a ransom for him,' **²⁵then his flesh will become fresher than a child's; he will return to the days of his youthful strength.**

Job 42:10 And the Lord turned the captivity of Job, when he prayed for his friends: also the Lord gave Job twice as much as he had before.

Job's captivity was not just financial, but also physical with all the sickness he endured. Job had opened the door to the devil through fear (Job 3:25) and once he repented (Job 42:6), everything was restored to him including his health.

[BBE] Job 42:10 And the Lord made up to Job for all his losses, after he had made prayer for his friends: and all Job had before was increased by the Lord twice as much.

[CWB] Job 42:10 After Job had prayed for his three friends, **the Lord healed Job** and prospered him and gave him twice as much as he had had before.

[KJ21] Job 42:10 And the Lord released Job from captivity when he prayed for his friends. Also the Lord gave Job twice as much as he had before.

[Lamsa] Job 42:10 And **the Lord restored to Job all that he had lost**, when he prayed for his friends; also the Lord gave Job twice as much as he had before.

[NET] Job 42:10 So the Lord restored what Job had lost after he prayed for his friends, and the Lord doubled all that had belonged to Job.

[NJB] Job 42:10 And **Yahweh restored Job's condition**, while Job was interceding for his friends. More than that, Yahweh gave him double what he had before.

[Orton-OT] Job 42:10 And the Lord turned the captivity of Job, when he prayed for his friends: also the Lord gave Job twice as much as he had before; he restored the cattle of which he had been before plundered, **healed his bodily disorders** and restored the peace of his mind.

[Spurrell-OT] Job 42:10 And Jehovah reversed Job's afflicted dispensation when he made intercession on behalf of his friends; and Jehovah increased all that Job had possessed twofold.

[VW] Job 42:10 And **Jehovah returned what had been taken captive from Job** when he prayed for his friends. Indeed Jehovah gave Job twice as much as he had before.

[WSP-OT] <u>Job 42:10</u> And **Jehovah repaired the calamities of Job**, when he prayed for his friends: also Jehovah gave to Job twice as much as he had before.

PSALMS

<u>Psalms 6:2</u> Have mercy upon me, O LORD; for I am weak: O LORD, heal^[raphah] **me; for my bones are vexed.**

[Alexander-OT] <u>Psalms 6:2</u> Have mercy upon me, or be gracious unto me, oh Lord, Jehovah, for drooping, languishing, am I. **Heal me oh Lord, Jehovah, for shaken, agitated with distress and terror, are my bones.**

[AMP] <u>Psalms 6:2</u> Have mercy on me and be gracious to me, O Lord, for I am weak (faint, frail); **Heal me, O Lord, for my bones are dismayed and anguished.**

[Anchor] <u>Psalms 6:2</u> Have pity on me, O Yahweh, for I am spent, **heal me, O Yahweh, for my bones are racked.**

[Boothroyd] <u>Psalms 6:2</u> Have mercy on me, Jehovah, for I am weak; **Heal me, O Jehovah, for my bones are troubled;**

[Buttenwieser-OT] <u>Psalms 6:2</u> Have mercy on me, O Lord, for I wither away. **O Lord, heal me, for my body is shattered.**

[CLV] <u>Psalms 6:2</u> Be gracious to me, O Yahweh, for I am feeble; **Heal me, O Yahweh, for my bones are flustered,**

[Coles-Ps] <u>Psalms 6:2</u> Have mercy, Lord! for I am weak; **O heal me and restore! With anguish all my bones are vexed**, My soul is troubled sore.

[Didham-Ps] <u>Psalms 6:2</u> Have mercy upon me, O Jehovah, for I am weak, **heal me, O Jehovah, for my bones tremble.**

[EHV] <u>Psalms 6:2</u> Be merciful to me, Lord, for I am fading away. **Heal me, Lord, for my bones are trembling,**

[Ewald-OT] <u>Psalms 6:2</u> Be gracious to me, Jahvé! for I wither—**heal me, Jahvé! for my bones are deeply shaken;**

[EXB] <u>Psalms 6:2</u> Lord, ·have mercy on [be gracious to] me because I ·am weak [languish; faint]. **Heal me, Lord, because my bones ·ache [are in agony].**

[Fysh-Ps] <u>Psalms 6:2</u> Be gracious to me, Jehovah: For I am faint. **Heal me, Jehovah: For my bones are agitated:**

[GAC-Ps-Third] <u>Psalms 6:2</u> Have mercy, Lord, for I am weak; Regard my heavy groans: O let thy voice of comfort speak, And **heal my broken bones.**

[Grail-Ps] <u>Psalms 6:2</u> Have mercy on me, LORD, for I languish. LORD, **heal me; my bones are shaking,**

[ICB] <u>Psalms 6:2</u> Lord, be kind to me because I am weak. **Heal me, Lord, because my bones ache.**

[Jones-Ps] <u>Psalms 6:2</u> Oh Jehovah, I'm drooping, most graciously look, **And heal, for with terrors I shake.**

[JPS-Ps 1972] <u>Psalms 6:2</u> Have mercy on me, O LORD, for I languish; **heal me, O LORD, for my bones shake with terror.**

OUR HEALING COVENANT

[Lamsa] <u>Psalms 6:2</u> Have mercy upon me, O Lᴏʀᴅ; for I am weak; O Lᴏʀᴅ, **heal me; for my bones are troubled.**

[Purver] <u>Psalms 6:2</u> Be gracious to me, O Lord; for I am languishing: **heal me, O Lord, for my Bones are disturbed.**

[Spurrell-OT] <u>Psalms 6:2</u> Compassionate me, O Jᴇʜᴏᴠᴀʜ, for I am faint; **Assuage my pain, O Jᴇʜᴏᴠᴀʜ, for my bones ache.**

[T4T] <u>Psalms 6:2</u> Yahweh, act kindly toward me and **heal me because I have become weak. My body shakes because I am experiencing much pain.**

[TPT] <u>Psalms 6:2</u> Please deal gently with me; show me mercy, for I'm sick and frail. I'm fading away with weakness. **Heal me, for I'm falling apart.**

<u>Psalms 22:26</u> The meek shall eat and be satisfied: they shall praise the Lᴏʀᴅ that seek him: **your heart shall live for ever.**

[Burgess-Ps] <u>Psalms 22:26</u> There, the meek suff'rer shall rejoice, Feast in thy love, and lift his voice: **The heart that pray'd, in praise shall soar, And beat with life that dies no more.**

[CSB] <u>Psalms 22:26</u> The humble will eat and be satisfied; those who seek the Lord will praise him. **May your hearts live forever!**

[De Witt-Ps] <u>Psalms 22:26</u> The lowly shall eat and be filled, They that seek for Jehovah shall praise Him; **May your heart get new life evermore.**

[EXB] <u>Psalms 22:26</u> ·Poor [or Afflicted] people will eat ·until they are full [and be satisfied]; those who ·look to the Lord [seek him] will praise him. **May your hearts live forever!**

[Haupt] <u>Psalms 22:26</u> The godly eat, and are satisfied. The followers of Jʜᴠʜ praise Him. **May your hearts revive for ever!**

[JPS-OT 1917] <u>Psalms 22:26</u> Let the humble eat and be satisfied; let them praise the Lᴏʀᴅ that seek after Him; **may your heart be quickened for ever!**

[MP1650] <u>Psalms 22:26</u> The meek shall eat, and shall be filled; they also praise shall give Unto the Lord that do him seek: **your heart shall ever live.**

[NLT] <u>Psalms 22:26</u> The poor will eat and be satisfied. All who seek the Lord will praise him. **Their hearts will rejoice with everlasting joy.**

[UDB] <u>Psalms 22:26</u> The poor people whom I have invited to the meal will eat as much as they want. All who come to worship Yahweh will praise him. I pray that **God will enable you all to live a long and happy life!**

[Wycliffe-Noble] <u>Psalms 22:26</u> Poor men shall eat, and shall be [ful]filled, and they shall praise the Lord, that seek him; **the hearts of them shall live into the world of world.** (The poor shall eat, and shall be satisfied; and they who seek the Lord shall praise him, and **their hearts shall live forever and ever.**)

<u>Psalms 23:1</u> The Lᴏʀᴅ is my shepherd; **I shall not want.**

[Allen-Ps-First] <u>Psalms 23:1</u> My Shepherd is the living Lord; **Now shall my wants be well supplied:**

[Allen-Ps-Third] <u>Psalms 23:1</u> The Lord, my Shepherd, is on high, **To every want He brings supply,**

[AMP] <u>Psalms 23:1</u> The Lord is my Shepherd [to feed, to guide and to shield me], **I shall not want.**

[Aston-Ps] <u>Psalms 23:1</u> The Lord my pasture shall prepare, And **feed me with a shepherd's care;**

[Barton-Ps] <u>Psalms 23:1</u> The Lord my shepherd is, and **he that doth me feed: since he is mine and I am his, what comfort can I need?**

[BBE] <u>Psalms 23:1</u> The Lord takes care of me as his sheep; **I will not be without any good thing.**

[Beck] <u>Psalms 23:1</u> The LORD is my Shepherd—**I have everything I need.**

[Belknap-Ps] <u>Psalms 23:1</u> The Lord himself, the mighty Lord, is pleased to be my guide; **The shepherd by whose constant care My wants are all supplied.**

[Berkeley] <u>Psalms 23:1</u> The Lord is my Shepherd; **I shall not lack;**

[Birks-OT] <u>Psalms 23:1</u> The Lord my Shepherd is and He my soul will keep; He knoweth who are his, and watches o'er his sheep; Away with every anxious fear! **I cannot want, while He is near.**

[BWilliams-Ps] <u>Psalms 23:1</u> While my Creator's near, My Shepherd and my Guide, I bid farewell to anxious Fear, **My wants are all supply'd.**

[CEV] <u>Psalms 23:1</u> You, Lord, are my shepherd. **I will never be in need.**

[Cheyne-OT] <u>Psalms 23:1</u> Jehovah is my shepherd; **I want for nothing.**

[Churton-Ps] <u>Psalms 23:1</u> My shepherd is the gracious Lord, Amidst His flock I feed: **While I am His, and He is mine, I cannot suffer need.**

[Cottle-Ps] <u>Psalms 23:1</u> God is my Shepherd ever near, I live beneath his watchful eye, Nor shall I any evil fear, **For he will all my wants supply.**

[CPDV] <u>Psalms 23:1</u> The Lord directs me, and **nothing will be lacking to me.**

[CWB] <u>Psalms 23:1</u> The Lord is my shepherd; **I have everything I need.**

[Davis-Ps] <u>Psalms 23:1</u> The Lord, my Shepherd, knows his sheep, And **will for all their wants provide**; He doth my soul in safety keep, And is mine everlasting guide.

[De Witt-Ps] <u>Psalms 23:1</u> Jehovah is my Shepherd, **I suffer no want;**

[Didham-Ps] <u>Psalms 23:1</u> Jehovah is my Shepherd: **I can want nothing.**

[EXB] <u>Psalms 23:1</u> The Lord is my shepherd; **I ·have everything I need [will lack nothing].**

[Fenton] <u>Psalms 23:1</u> The Lord attends; —**I shall not want;**

[Goode-Ps] <u>Psalms 23:1</u> I hear my shepherd's voice, and in His care confide: **In Thee, Jehovah, I rejoice, My wants are all supplied.**

[Haupt] <u>Psalms 23:1</u> JHVH is my shepherd; **Therefore I can lack nothing.**

[HCSB] <u>Psalms 23:1</u> The Lord is my shepherd; **there is nothing I lack.**

[ICB] <u>Psalms 23:1</u> The Lord is my shepherd. **I have everything I need.**

[JPS-OT 1985] <u>Psalms 23:1</u> The LORD is my shepherd; **I lack nothing.**

[Keble-Ps] <u>Psalms 23:1</u> My Shepherd is the Lord; **I know No care, or craving need:**

[Kennedy-Ps] <u>Psalms 23:1</u> My shepherd is the Lord: **no care or craving want I know:**

[Kenrick] <u>Psalms 23:1</u> The Lord ruleth me: and **I shall want nothing.**

[Knox] <u>Psalms 23:1</u> The Lord is my shepherd; **how can I lack anything?**

[LTPB] <u>Psalms 23:1</u> The Lord will guide me. **Nothing will be lacking to me.**

[Lyte-Ps] <u>Psalms 23:1</u> The living Lord my Shepherd is; **What can I want while I am His?**

[Merrick-Ps] <u>Psalms 23:1</u> Lo, my Shepherd's hand divine! **Want shall never more be mine.**

[Moffat] <u>Psalms 23:1</u> The Eternal shepherds me, **I lack for nothing;**

[NIRV] <u>Psalms 23:1</u> The Lord is my shepherd. **He gives me everything I need.**

[Norlie-NT] <u>Psalms 23:1</u> The Lord shepherds me, **I shall never be in need.**

[OEB-NT] <u>Psalms 23:1</u> The Lord is my shepherd: **I am never in need.**

[Oliver-Ps] <u>Psalms 23:1</u> The Lord shall feed me, **nor shall he suffer anything to be lacking to me.**

[Spurrell-OT] <u>Psalms 23:1</u> JEHOVAH is my shepherd, **I cannot want**:

[Sternhold-Ps] <u>Psalms 23:1</u> The Lord is only my support, and he that doth me feed; **How can I then lack any thing; whereof I stand in need?**

[Street-Ps] <u>Psalms 23:1</u> JEHOVAH is my shepherd, **I shall never want;**

[T4T] <u>Psalms 23:1</u> Yahweh, you care for me like a shepherd cares for his sheep. So **I have everything that I need.**

[Tate-Ps] <u>Psalms 23:1</u> The Lord himself, the mighty Lord, Vouchsafes to be my guide; **The shepherd by whose constant care My wants are all supplied.**

[TPT] <u>Psalms 23:1</u> The Lord is my best friend and my shepherd. **I always have more than enough.**

<u>Psalms 27:14</u> Wait on the LORD: be of good courage, and **he shall strengthen thine heart**: wait, I say, on the LORD.

[AMPC] <u>Psalms 27:14</u> Wait and hope for and expect the Lord; be brave and of good courage and **let your heart be stout and enduring**. Yes, wait for and hope for and expect the Lord.

[Cheyne-OT] <u>Psalms 27:14</u> Wait for Jehovah: be courageous, and **let thine heart gather strength**, wait, I say, for Jehovah.

[CWB] <u>Psalms 27:14</u> Trust in the Lord and take courage. Wait for Him and **He will strengthen your heart**. Wait, I say, on the Lord!

[Delitzsch-Ps] <u>Psalms 27:14</u> Hope in Jahve, Be of good courage, and **let thine heart be strong**, And hope in Jahve.

[Haak] <u>Psalms 27:14</u> Wait on the LORD, be strong, and **he shall fortify thy heart**: yea, wait on the LORD.

[Hawley-Ps] <u>Psalms 27:14</u> **But make thou my heart strong**, And more joyful my song, While still hoping, I wait upon thee.

[MKJV] <u>Psalms 27:14</u> Hope in the LORD; be of good courage, and **He shall make your heart strong**; yea, hope in the LORD.

[Spurrell-OT] <u>Psalms 27:14</u> Wait on JEHOVAH: Be assured that **He will strengthen thine heart**; Yea, eagerly expect from JEHOVAH.

[TPT] <u>Psalms 27:14</u> Here's what I've learned through it all: Don't give up; don't be impatient; be entwined as one with the Lord. Be brave and courageous, and **never lose hope**. Yes, keep on waiting—for he will never disappoint you!

[UKJV] <u>Psalms 27:14</u> Wait on the LORD: be of good courage, and **he shall strengthen your heart**: wait, I say, on the LORD.

[YLT] <u>Psalms 27:14</u> Look unto Jehovah—be strong, And **He doth strengthen thy heart**, Yea, look unto Jehovah!

<u>Psalms 29:11</u> **The LORD will give strength unto his people;** the LORD will bless his people with peace.

[AMPC] <u>Psalms 29:11</u> **The Lord will give [unyielding and impenetrable] strength to His people**; the Lord will bless His people with peace.

[Barton-Ps] <u>Psalms 29:11</u> **The Lord that is our strength and tower, will give his people ample power**, the Lord will bless his Church with peace.

[BLE] <u>Psalms 29:11</u> **Jehovah will give might to his people**, Jehovah will bless his people with peace.

[EEBT] <u>Psalms 29:11</u> **The LORD will make his people strong**. The LORD will give his people peace.

[GAC-Ps-Second] <u>Psalms 29:11</u> **The Lord is the strength of his people;** the Lord Gives health to his chosen, and peace.

[GW] <u>Psalms 29:11</u> **The Lord will give power to his people**. The Lord will bless his people with peace.

[JMontgomery-Ps] <u>Psalms 29:11</u> **The Lord is the strength of his people; the Lord Gives health to his people**, and peace evermore;

[JPS-OT 1985] <u>Psalms 29:11</u> **May the LORD grant strength to His people**; may the LORD bestow on His people wellbeing.

[Lang-Ps] <u>Psalms 29:11</u> **Jehovah will strengthen his people,** and bless The seed of his saints with unchangeable peace.

[MOTB] <u>Psalms 29:11</u> **This glorious God is Israel' God; and the strength he has shown in the storm he will impart to his people**, and give them the blessing of peace.

[MSG] <u>Psalms 29:11</u> **God makes his people strong**. God gives his people peace.

[Street-Ps] <u>Psalms 29:11</u> **Jehovah giveth might to his people**, Jehovah blesseth his people with peace.

[TPT] <u>Psalms 29:11</u> **This is the one who gives his strength and might to his people**. This is the Lord giving us his kiss of peace.

[Wheatland-Ps] <u>Psalms 29:11</u> **JEHOVAH will his people's strength increase**, JEHOVAH will his people bless with peace.

<u>Psalms 30:2</u> O LORD my God, I cried unto thee, and thou hast healed[raphah] me.

[AMP] <u>Psalms 30:2</u> O Lord my God, I cried to You for help, and You have healed me.

[BBE] <u>Psalms 30:2</u> O Lord my God, I sent up my cry to you, and you have made me well.

[CJB] <u>Psalms 30:2</u> Adonai my God, I cried out to you, and you provided healing for me.

[EEBT] <u>Psalms 30:2</u> LORD, my God, I prayed to you for help, and you gave me health.

[Haak] <u>Psalms 30:2</u> LORD, my God; I have called unto thee, and thou hast healed me, (or, made me whole;)

[Hielscher-Ps] <u>Psalms 30:2</u> And when I raised my voice to Him, In mercy He hath heard and healed me.

[ICB] <u>Psalms 30:2</u> Lord, my God, I prayed to you. And you healed me.

[Knox] <u>Psalms 30:2</u> I cried out to the Lord my God, and thou didst grant me recovery.

[Lamsa] <u>Psalms 30:2</u> O LORD, my God, I have sought thee, and thou hast healed me.

[Milborne-Ps] <u>Psalms 30:2</u> I cry'd, my Lord, my God, to Thee, And Health thy Mercy gave.

[NCV] <u>Psalms 30:2</u> Lord, my God, I prayed to you, and you healed me.

[NIRV] <u>Psalms 30:2</u> Lord my God, I called out to you for help. And you healed me.

[NLT] <u>Psalms 30:2</u> O Lord my God, I cried to you for help, and you restored my health.

[REM-NT] <u>Psalms 30:2</u> My Lord and my God, I called to you for help and you healed me.

[Rosenburg-Ps] <u>Psalms 30:2</u> Lord Most High I called you and I was made new

[T4T] <u>Psalms 30:2</u> Yahweh, my God, I called out for you to help me when I was ill, and you healed me.

[Tate-Ps] <u>Psalms 30:2</u> In my distress I cried to thee, Who kindly didst relieve

[TLB] <u>Psalms 30:2</u> O Lord my God, I pleaded with you, and you gave me my health again.

[TPT] <u>Psalms 30:2</u> O Lord, my healing God, I cried out for a miracle and you healed me!

[Wheatland-Ps] <u>Psalms 30:2</u> My God, Jehovah, did my cries implore, Soon his all-healing hand relieved my sore:

[YLT] <u>Psalms 30:2</u> Jehovah my God, I have cried to Thee, And Thou dost heal me.

[York-Ps] <u>Psalms 30:2</u> To Thee, my God Jehovah, I appealed, On Thee I called, and by Thy power am healed:

<u>Psalms 30:3</u> O Lord, thou hast brought up my soul from the grave: **thou hast kept me alive**, that I should not go down to the pit.

[EHV] <u>Psalms 30:3</u> Lord, you snatched my life from the grave. **You kept me alive** so I did not go down into the pit.

[GAC-Ps-Second] <u>Psalms 30:3</u> **Thy mercy chased the shades of death**. And snatched me from the grave; O may thy praise employ that breath Which mercy deigns to save.

[ISV] <u>Psalms 30:3</u> Lord, you brought me from death; **you kept me alive** so that I did not descend into the Pit.

[NKJV] <u>Psalms 30:3</u> O Lord, You brought my soul up from the grave; **You have kept me alive**, that I should not go down to the pit.

[Norlie-NT] <u>Psalms 30:3</u> You, Lord, have snatched me from death; **You have revived me**, and have not allowed me to die.

[REAL] <u>Psalms 30:3</u> Ya-HoVaH, you have brought up my soul from the tomb. **You have guarded me alive**, so I would not go down to the pit.

[REM-NT] <u>Psalms 30:3</u> O Lord, you pulled me from the grave—I was dying and **you restored my life**.

[T4T] <u>Psalms 30:3</u> You saved/restored me when I was dying. I was nearly dead, but **you caused me to become healthy again**.

[Tate-Ps] <u>Psalms 30:3</u> And from the grave's expecting jaws **My hopeless life retrieve**.

[TLB] <u>Psalms 30:3</u> You brought me back from the brink of the grave, from death itself, **and here I am alive!**

[TPT] <u>Psalms 30:3</u> You brought me back from the brink of death, from the depths below. Now here I am, **alive and well, fully restored!**

[UDB] <u>Psalms 30:3</u> You saved me from death. I was nearly dead, but **you caused me to become healthy again**.

<u>Psalms 31:24</u> Be of good courage, and **he shall strengthen your heart**, all ye that hope in the Lord.

[MEV] <u>Psalms 31:24</u> Be strong, and **He will strengthen your heart**, all you who wait for the Lord.

[MP1650] <u>Psalms 31:24</u> Be of good courage, and **he strength unto your heart shall send**, All ye whose hope and confidence doth on the Lord depend.

[PCB-Ps] <u>Psalms 31:24</u> Ye that on God rely, courageously proceed; for **He will still your hearts supply with strength in time of need.**

[REB] <u>Psalms 31:24</u> **Be strong and stout-hearted**, all you whose hope is in the Lord.

[Turner-Ps] <u>Psalms 31:24</u> Have courage then, **For He shall steel your hearts with strength**, All ye that trust upon the Lord.

[Woodd-Ps] <u>Psalms 31:24</u> **Be of good courage then, establish'd on His word; Your heart He strengthens**; trust His name, And triumph in the Lord.

<u>Psalms 33:19</u> To deliver their soul from death, and to keep them alive in famine.

[Anchor] <u>Psalms 33:19</u> To rescue them from Death, to preserve their lives from the Hungry One.

[BBE] <u>Psalms 33:19</u> To keep their souls from death; and to keep them living in time of need.

[CE] <u>Psalms 33:19</u> to deliver them from death and preserve them in spite of famine.

[CEV] <u>Psalms 33:19</u> He protects them from death and starvation.

[CLV] <u>Psalms 33:19</u> To rescue their soul from death And to preserve them alive in famine.

[CWB] <u>Psalms 33:19</u> He delivers us from death and keeps us alive in times of hunger.

[ERV] <u>Psalms 33:19</u> He saves them from death. He gives them strength when they are hungry.

[Hawley-Ps] <u>Psalms 33:19</u> He forbids death should them kill, And in famine feeds them still.

[ICB] <u>Psalms 33:19</u> He saves them from death. He spares their lives in times of hunger.

[JPS-OT 1985] <u>Psalms 33:19</u> to save them from death, to sustain them in famine.

[NCV] <u>Psalms 33:19</u> He saves them from death and spares their lives in times of hunger.

[REAL] <u>Psalms 33:19</u> to snatch their soul from death, and keep them alive in hunger.

[TPT] <u>Psalms 33:19</u> God will deliver them from death, even the certain death of famine, with no one to help.

<u>Psalms 34:19-20</u> Many are the afflictions of the righteous: but the Lord delivereth him out of them all. [20]He keepeth all his bones: not one of them is broken.

[ABP] <u>Psalms 34:19-20</u> Many are the afflictions of the just; and from out of all of them [shall rescue them the Lord]. [20]The Lord guards all their bones; [one of them not] shall be broken.

[AMP] <u>Psalms 34:19-20</u> Many hardships and perplexing circumstances confront the righteous, But the Lord rescues him from them all. [20]He keeps all his bones; Not one of them is broken.

[BBE] <u>Psalms 34:19-20</u> Great are the troubles of the upright: but the Lord takes him safely out of them all. [20]He keeps all his bones: not one of them is broken.

[Beck] <u>Psalms 34:19-20</u> If you're righteous, you have many griefs, but the Lord rescues you from all of them, [20]and protects every bone in you so that not one of them is broken.

[CEV] <u>Psalms 34:19-20</u> The Lord's people may suffer a lot, but he will always bring them safely through. [20]Not one of their bones will ever be broken.

[CJB] <u>Psalms 34:19-20</u> The righteous person suffers many evils, but Adonai rescues him out of them all. [20]He protects all his bones; not one of them gets broken.

[Ewald-OT] <u>Psalms 34:19-20</u> Unnumbered are the good man's ills: but out of all Jahvé frees him, [20]Upholds all his bones, not one of them is crushed,

[Goode-Ps] <u>Psalms 34:19-20</u> What num'rous scenes of varied grief His saints and servants share? [20]But mercy quickly sends relief, and makes their bones its care.

[Haupt] <u>Psalms 34:19-20</u> Many the sorrows of the righteous, But out of them all J<small>HVH</small> delivers him. [20]His every bone J<small>HVH</small> guards, Not one of them is broken.

[ICB] <u>Psalms 34:19-20</u> People who do what is right may have many problems. But the Lord will solve them all. [20]He will protect their very bones. Not one of them will be broken.

[JPS-Ps 1972] <u>Psalms 34:19-20</u> Though the misfortunes of the righteous be many, the L<small>ORD</small> will save him from them all, [20]Keeping all his bones intact, not one of them being broken.

[NIRV] <u>Psalms 34:19-20</u> The person who does what is right may have many troubles. But the Lord saves him from all of them. [20]The Lord watches over all his bones. Not one of them will be broken.

[T4T] <u>Psalms 34:19-20</u> Righteous people may have many troubles, but Yahweh rescues them from all those troubles. [20]Yahweh protects them from being harmed; when their enemies attack them, they will not break any bones of those righteous people.

[Tehillim-Ps] <u>Psalms 34:19-20</u> Though many evils reach a righteous man, From all these will Jehovah rescue him; [20]He keeping watchfully his every bone, Not even one of them shall have been broke.

[TLB] <u>Psalms 34:19-20</u> The good man does not escape all troubles—he has them too. But the Lord helps him in each and every one. [20]Not one of his bones is broken.

[TNIV] <u>Psalms 34:19-20</u> The righteous may have many troubles, but the L<small>ORD</small> delivers them from them all; [20]he protects all their bones, not one of them will be broken.

[TPT] <u>Psalms 34:19-20</u> Even when bad things happen to the good and godly ones, the Lord will save them and not let them be defeated by what they face. [20]God will be your bodyguard to protect you when trouble is near. Not one bone will be broken.

[York-Ps] <u>Psalms 34:19-20</u> Though countless ills the Just befall, The Lord redeems Him from them all: [20]His bones He keeps, and therefore none Of them is broken—no, not one!

<u>Psalms 40:6</u> Sacrifice and offering thou didst not desire; **mine ears hast thou opened**: burnt offering and sin offering hast thou not required.

[AMP] <u>Psalms 40:6</u> Sacrifice and meal offering You do not desire, nor do You delight in them; **You have opened my ears and given me the capacity to hear [and obey Your word];** Burnt offerings and sin offerings You do not require.

[FHV-NT] <u>Psalms 40:6</u> Neither sacrifice nor offering do you desire. **You have opened my ears**. Neither burnt sacrifice nor a sin offering have you requested.

[GNT] <u>Psalms 40:6</u> You do not want sacrifices and offerings; you do not ask for animals burned whole on the altar or for sacrifices to take away sins. Instead, **you have given me ears to hear you,**

[MEV] <u>Psalms 40:6</u> Sacrifice and offering You did not desire; **You have opened up my ears to listen**. Burnt offering and sin offering You have not required.

[NIRV] <u>Psalms 40:6</u> You didn't want sacrifices and offerings. You didn't require burnt offerings and sin offerings. **You opened my ears so that I could hear you and obey you.**

<u>Psalms 41:2-3</u> **The L**ORD **will preserve him, and keep him alive**; and he shall be blessed upon the earth: and thou wilt not deliver him unto the will of his enemies. ³**The L**ORD **will strengthen him upon the bed of languishing**: thou wilt make all his bed in his sickness.

[Anchor] <u>Psalms 41:2-3</u> **May Yahweh protect him, give him long life**, bless him upon the earth, Do not put him into the maw of his Foe! ³**May Yahweh support him on his bed of illness; Sustain his confinement, overthrow the sickness itself!**

[BBE] <u>Psalms 41:2-3</u> **The Lord will keep him safe, and give him life**; the Lord will let him be a blessing on the earth, and will not give him into the hand of his haters. ³**The Lord will be his support on his bed of pain**: by you will all his grief be turned to strength.

[Beck] <u>Psalms 41:2-3</u> May the L**ORD** **protect him and keep him alive**. May he enjoy happiness in the land, and not be surrendered to the greed of his enemies. ³**May the L**ORD **strengthen him on his sickbed—sustain him on his bed and overthrow his sickness!**

[Berkeley] <u>Psalms 41:2-3</u> **The Lord will preserve him and keep him alive**; he shall be counted blessed in the land; Thou shalt not hand him over to the desires of his enemies. ³**The Lord will uphold him on his bed of sickness.**

[CCB] <u>Psalms 41:2-3</u> **The Lord protects him, preserves his life**, and gives him happiness in the land; he yields him not to the will of his foes. ³**The Lord helps him when he gets sick, and heals him of all his ailments.**

[CE] <u>Psalms 41:2-3</u> **The Lord will keep and preserve him**; he will make him happy on the earth, and not give him over to the will of his enemies. ³**The Lord will help him on his sickbed, he will take away all his ailment when he is ill.**

[CEB] <u>Psalms 41:2-3</u> **The Lord protects them and keeps them alive**; they are widely regarded throughout the land as happy people. You won't hand them over to the will of their enemies. ³**The Lord will strengthen them when they are lying in bed, sick.** You will completely transform the place where they lie ill.

[Cheyne-OT] <u>Psalms 41:2-3</u> **Jehovah will preserve him and keep him alive**, and he shall be called happy in the land; and do not thou deliver him unto the greed of his enemies. ³**Jehovah will support him upon the bed of languishing:** as oft as he lies low, **thou recoverest him in his sickness.**

[Collier-Ps] <u>Psalms 41:2-3</u> **The L**ORD **will guard and let him live**, will bless him in the land; and never to his foes will give his life within their hand. ³**Upon the couch of languishing the L**ORD **will still sustain**; and by the comforts He will bring. **Transform his bed of pain.**

[EEBT] <u>Psalms 41:2-3</u> **The L**ORD **will make him safe and keep him alive.** He will be happy where he lives. (The L**ORD**) will not give him to his enemies (for them) to do what they want to do (with him). ³The L**ORD** will be like a nurse to him when he is ill in bed. Every time that he is ill you will make him well again.

[EHV] <u>Psalms 41:2-3</u> May **the Lord guard him and keep him alive.** May he be blessed in the land. May you not surrender him to the desire of his enemies. ³**May the Lord sustain him on his sickbed. You raise him up from his bed.**

[FHV-NT] <u>Psalms 41:2-3</u> **Yahweh will guard him and keep him alive.** He will be blessed in the land and you will not deliver him to the desire of his enemies. ³**Yahweh will support him on his sickbed and turn his illness into good health,**

[JPS-Ps 1972] <u>Psalms 41:2-3</u> **May the L**ORD **guard him and preserve him**; and may he be thought happy in the land. Do not subject him to the will of his enemies. ³**The L**ORD **will sustain him on his sickbed; You shall wholly transform his bed of suffering.**

[Knox] <u>Psalms 41:2-3</u> **The Lord will watch over him, and give him long life** and happiness on earth, and baulk his enemies of their will. ³**The Lord will sustain him when he lies bed-ridden, turn all to health in his sickness.**

[Leeser-OT] <u>Psalms 41:2-3</u> **The Lord will preserve him, and keep him alive;** he shall be made happy on the earth: and thou wilt not deliver him unto the revengeful desire of his enemies. ³**The Lord will sustain him upon the bed of painful disease:** thou changest all his couch in his sickness.

[Moffatt] <u>Psalms 41:2-3</u> **the Eternal will preserve his life,** nor hand him over to his eager foes; ³**the Eternal sustains him on a sick bed, and brings him back to health.**

[MSG] <u>Psalms 41:2-3</u> **God looks after us all, makes us robust with life**—Lucky to be in the land, we're free from enemy worries. ³**Whenever we're sick and in bed, God becomes our nurse, nurses us back to health.**

[NIRV] <u>Psalms 41:2-3</u> **The Lord guards them and keeps them alive.** They are counted among those who are blessed in the land. The Lord won't hand them over to the wishes of their enemies. ³**The Lord will take care of them when they are lying sick in bed. He will make them well again.**

[NIVUK] <u>Psalms 41:2-3</u> **The Lord protects and preserves them**—they are counted among the blessed in the land—he does not give them over to the desire of their foes. ³**The Lord sustains them on their sick-bed and restores them from their bed of illness.**

[NLT] <u>Psalms 41:2-3</u> **The Lord protects them and keeps them alive.** He gives them prosperity in the land and rescues them from their enemies. ³**The Lord nurses them when they are sick and restores them to health.**

[NLV] <u>Psalms 41:2-3</u> **The Lord will keep him alive and safe.** And he will be happy upon the earth. You will not give him over to the desire of those who hate him. ³**The Lord will give him strength on his bed of sickness. When he is sick, You will make him well again.**

[REB] <u>Psalms 41:2-3</u> **the Lord protects him and gives him life,** making him secure in the land; the Lord never leaves him to the will of his enemies. ³**On his sick-bed he nurses him, transforming his every illness to health.**

[Sullivan-OT] <u>Psalms 41:2-3</u> **God keep them from danger, protect, prolong their lives,** enrich their days on earth, save them from hungry death. ³**If sickness lays them low, may God look after them and nurse them back to health, and stand them on their own.**

[UPBOP-Ps] <u>Psalms 41:2-3</u> **The Lord will keep him, guard his life,** On earth he shall be blest, The Lord will not surrender him By foes to be distressed. ³**Upon the suffering Jehovah will sustain, And in his sickness God will soothe The weariness and pain.**

[YLT] <u>Psalms 41:2-3</u> **Jehovah doth preserve him and revive him,** He is happy in the land, And Thou givest him not into the will of his enemies. ³**Jehovah supporteth on a couch of sickness, All his bed Thou hast turned in his weakness.**

<u>Psalms 41:4</u> I said, Lord, be merciful unto me: heal[raphah] my soul; for I have sinned against thee.

[CWB] <u>Psalms 41:4</u> I know I have sinned against you, Lord. But please be merciful to me. Forgive and heal me.

[ERV] <u>Psalms 41:4</u> I say, "Lord, be kind to me. I sinned against you, but forgive me and make me well."

[EXB] <u>Psalms 41:4</u> I said, "Lord, have ·mercy [compassion] on me. Heal me, because I have sinned against you."

[Horsley-OT] <u>Psalms 41:4</u> For me, I have said, O Jehovah, have pity upon me, O heal my soul. Surely I bear blame before thee.

[ICB] <u>Psalms 41:4</u> I said, "Lord, be kind to me. Heal me because I have sinned against you."

[Knox] <u>Psalms 41:4</u> Lord have mercy on me, is my prayer; bring healing to a soul that has sinned against thee.

[MSG] <u>Psalms 41:4</u> I said, "God, be gracious! Put me together again—my sins have torn me to pieces."

[NEB] <u>Psalms 41:4</u> But I said, 'Lord, be gracious to me; heal me, for I have sinned against thee.'

[TPT] <u>Psalms 41:4</u> So in my sickness I say to you, "Lord, be my kind healer. Heal my body and soul; heal me, God! For I have confessed my sins to you."

[UDB] <u>Psalms 41:4</u> When I was sick, I said, "Yahweh, act mercifully toward me and heal me; I know that I am sick because I have sinned against you."

<u>Psalms 42:11</u> Why art thou cast down, O my soul? and why art thou disquieted within me? hope thou in God: for I shall yet praise him, **who is the health of my countenance, and my God**.

[CEB] <u>Psalms 42:11</u> Why, I ask myself, are you so depressed? Why are you so upset inside? Hope in God! Because I will again give him thanks, **my saving presence and my God**.

[CWB] <u>Psalms 42:11</u> Why am I so discouraged? Why do I take these insults personally? I must trust God. He has not forsaken me. I will trust and praise Him, no matter how I feel. **He is my health and life**, my Savior and my God!

[Douay-Rheims] <u>Psalms 42:11</u> Why art thou cast down, O my soul? and why dost thou disquiet me? Hope thou in God, for I will still give praise to him: **the salvation of my countenance, and my God**.

[Goode-Ps] <u>Psalms 42:11</u> But my soul, with fears distressing, why to anxious thoughts resign'd? Why, disquietude oppressing, whelm'd in grief my downcast mind? Hope in God—His light and favour shall my lips to praise recall; He my everlasting SAVIOUR! **GOD my HEALTH! My GOD! My ALL!**

[Hawley-Ps] <u>Psalms 42:11</u> Why then, my soul, art thou cast down? Why bowed beneath the foe's dread frown? Hope thou in God, and sing his praise; **His presence will prolong my days**.

[Horsley-OT] <u>Psalms 42:11</u> Why wilt thou bow thyself down, O my soul, and disquiet thyself within me? Wait patiently for God, for I shall yet give him thanks, **The preserver of my person**, and my God.

[JMontgomery-Ps] <u>Psalms 42:11</u> Why are thou cast down, my soul? God, thy God, shall make thee whole; Why art thou disquieted? God shall lift thy fallen head; **And his countenance benign Be the saving health of thine**.

[Lyte-Ps] <u>Psalms 42:11</u> Why restless, why cast down, my soul? Trust God, and thou shalt sing His praise again, and **find Him still Thy health's eternal spring**!

<u>Psalms 43:5</u> Why art thou cast down, O my soul? and why art thou disquieted within me? hope in God: for I shall yet praise him, **who is the health of my countenance, and my God**.

[Goode-Ps] <u>Psalms 43:5</u> Why then should gloomy thoughts distress? Why inmost troubles roll? Why deep disquietude oppress My downcast, trembling soul? Hope thou in GOD, my grateful tongue Shall yet His praise recall: And own Him in my cheerful song. **My GOD, my HEALTH, my ALL!!**

[JUB] <u>Psalms 43:5</u> Why art thou cast down, O my soul? and why art thou disquieted within me? Wait for God, for I shall yet praise him, **who is the saving health of my countenance and my God**.

[Muhlenberg-Ps] <u>Psalms 43:5</u> Why, then, my soul, oppress'd with woes? Why thus cast down with anxious care? On God, thy **God, full trust repose, who will thy failing strength repair**.

[OANT] <u>Psalms 43:5</u> Why have you agitated me, my soul, and why have you perplexed me? Look for God, because I shall again praise him, **The Savior of my entire being, and my God.**

[TLB] <u>Psalms 43:5</u> O my soul, why be so gloomy and discouraged? Trust in God! I shall again praise him for his wondrous help; **he will make me smile again, for he is my God!**

[WEBBE] <u>Psalms 43:5</u> Why are you in despair, my soul? Why are you disturbed within me? Hope in God! For **I shall still praise him: my Saviour, my helper, and my God.**

<u>Psalms 67:2</u> That thy way may be known upon earth, thy saving health among all nations.

[CEB] <u>Psalms 67:2</u> so that your way becomes known on earth, so that your salvation becomes known among all the nations.

[CWB] <u>Psalms 67:2</u> so that the whole world will know the kind of God you are and what you can do to help them.

[Douay-Rheims] <u>Psalms 67:2</u> That we may know thy way upon earth: thy salvation in all nations.

[Jones-Ps] <u>Psalms 67:2</u> Show thy way to every nation, Show the earth thy health divine;

[Lyte-Ps] <u>Psalms 67:2</u> And Thy saving health extend, Unto earth's remotest end.

[NET] <u>Psalms 67:2</u> Then those living on earth will know what you are like; all nations will know how you deliver your people.

[Stow-Ps] <u>Psalms 67:2</u> That, O my GOD, Thy Way May upon Earth be known; And that all Nations of the World THY Saving Health may own!

[TLB] <u>Psalms 67:2</u> Send us around the world with the news of your saving power and your eternal plan for all mankind.

[UKJV] <u>Psalms 67:2</u> That your way may be known upon earth, your saving health among all nations.

[WBall-Ps] <u>Psalms 67:2</u> That thy power to save, and heal, Every realm, O God, may feel:

<u>Psalms 69:32</u> The humble shall see this, and be glad: and **your heart shall live that seek God.**

[Buttenwieser-OT] <u>Psalms 69:32</u> When the humble see it, they will rejoice; **When they that seek God behold it, Their hearts will revive.**

[Delitzsch-Ps] <u>Psalms 69:32</u> The afflicted seeing it, shall rejoice; **Ye who seek after Elohim—let your heart revive!**

[GNV-Zychal] <u>Psalms 69:32</u> The humble shall see this, and **they that seek God, shall be glad, and your heart shall live.**

[GW] <u>Psalms 69:32</u> Oppressed people will see this and rejoice. **May the hearts of those who look to God for help be refreshed.**

[LITV] <u>Psalms 69:32</u> The humble have seen and are glad; **you who seek God, your heart shall live.**

[NIRV] <u>Psalms 69:32</u> Poor people will see it and be glad. **The hearts of those who worship God will be strengthened.**

[NLV] <u>Psalms 69:32</u> Those without pride will see it and be glad. **You who look for God, let your heart receive new strength.**

[TLB] <u>Psalms 69:32</u> The humble shall see their God at work for them. No wonder they will be so glad! **All who seek for God shall live in joy.**

[TPT] <u>Psalms 69:32</u> All who seek you will see God do this for them, and they'll overflow with gladness. **Let this revive your hearts, all you lovers of God!**

<u>Psalms 73:26</u> My flesh and my heart faileth: **but God is the strength of my heart**, and my portion for ever.

[Alexander-OT] <u>Psalms 73:26</u> Spent is my flesh and my heart; **the rock of my heart and my portion (is) God to eternity.**

[Boothroyd] <u>Psalms 73:26</u> Although my flesh and my heart fail, **Yet the support of my heart and my portion shall God be for ever.**

[Delitzsch-Ps] <u>Psalms 73:26</u> My flesh and my heart may fail—**The refuge of my heart and my portion is Elohim** for ever.

[Driver-OT] <u>Psalms 73:26</u> My flesh and my heart faileth: (but) **God is the rock of my heart** and my portion for ever.

[EEBT] <u>Psalms 73:26</u> My heart and my body may fail, but **God will always make me strong.** He is all that I will ever need.

[Ewald-OT] <u>Psalms 73:26</u> though my body and heart fade away: **my heart's rock, my good is ever God!**

[GNT] <u>Psalms 73:26</u> My mind and my body may grow weak, **but God is my strength; he is all I ever need.**

[ICB] <u>Psalms 73:26</u> My mind and my body may become weak. **But God is my strength. He is mine forever.**

[Keble-Ps] <u>Psalms 73:26</u> My flesh, my heart, shall pine away; **God is my heart's sure Rock and Stay, My portion without end.**

[Sandys-OT] <u>Psalms 73:26</u> My Thoughts and flesh are fraile: yet **Lord, thou art My Portion, and the Vigour of my Heart.**

[T4T] <u>Psalms 73:26</u> My body and my mind may become very weak, but **God, you continue to enable me to be strong; I belong to you forever.**

[UDB] <u>Psalms 73:26</u> My body and my mind may become very weak, but, **God, you continue to enable me to be strong**; I belong to you forever.

<u>Psalms 80:18</u> So will not we go back from thee: **quicken us, and we will call upon thy name.**

[Berkeley] <u>Psalms 80:18</u> Then we shall not depart from Thee; **revive us and we shall call upon Thy name!**

[CE] <u>Psalms 80:18</u> Then we will no more withdraw from you; **give us new life, and we will call upon your name.**

[Ewald-OT] <u>Psalms 80:18</u> —We too will not depart from Thee, **let us live, we will call on Thy name!**

[Koren-OT] <u>Psalms 80:18</u> So shall we not turn back from Thee: **revive us and we will call upon Thy name.**

[LEB] <u>Psalms 80:18</u> Then we will not turn back from you. **Restore us to life, and we will proclaim your name.**

[MSG] <u>Psalms 80:18</u> We will never turn our back on you; **breathe life into our lungs so we can shout your name!**

[NLV] <u>Psalms 80:18</u> Then we will not turn away from You. **Give us new life again, and we will call on Your name.**

[OANT] <u>Psalms 80:18</u> **Give us life** so that we will not turn from you, **and we will call upon your Name.**

[RSV] <u>Psalms 80:18</u> Then we will never turn back from thee; **give us life, and we will call on thy name!**

[SAAS-OT] <u>Psalms 80:18</u> Then we will not turn away from You; **You will give us life, and we will call upon Your name.**

[Sandys-OT] <u>Psalms 80:18</u> **Reviv'd, we will thy Name adore**; Nor ever from thy Pleasure swerve.

<u>Psalms 84:5-7</u> **Blessed is the man whose strength is in thee**; in whose heart are the ways of them. [6]Who passing through the valley of Baca make it a well; the rain also filleth the pools. [7]**They go from strength to strength**, every one of them in Zion appeareth before God.

[AMPC] <u>Psalms 84:5-7</u> **Blessed (happy, fortunate, to be envied) is the man whose strength is in You**, in whose heart are the highways to Zion. [6]Passing through the Valley of Weeping (Baca), they make it a place of springs; the early rain also fills [the pools] with blessings. [7]**They go from strength to strength [increasing in victorious power]**; each of them appears before God in Zion.

[BLE] <u>Psalms 84:5-7</u> **Happy are men who have strength in you**, who have highways at heart, [6]Those who pass through Baca Vale making it a region of springs, even pools that fall rain overspreads. [7]**They go on from good times to good times**; Deity, God, is to be seen at Sion.

[CWB] <u>Psalms 84:5-7</u> **Blessed are those who find strength in you** and who travel the road to Zion! [6]When they pass through the Valley of Weeping, they will find springs of comfort. Blessings will fall on them like gentle autumn rains. [7]**They will go from strength to strength** until they see you face to face.

[EEBT] <u>Psalms 84:5-7</u> **The people that you make strong are very happy**. They want to come to you (in Zion). [6]As they pass through a dry valley, it (seems) to become a place with wells of water in it. The autumn rains cover (the valley) with pools. [7]**The people become stronger as they go**, (until) each one appears before God in Zion.

[Grail-Ps] <u>Psalms 84:5-7</u> **Blessed the people whose strength is in you**, whose heart is set on pilgrim ways. [6]As they go through the Baca Valley, they make it a place of springs; the autumn rain covers it with pools. [7]**They walk with ever-growing strength**; the God of gods will appear in Sion.

[GW] <u>Psalms 84:5-7</u> **Blessed are those who find strength in you**. Their hearts are on the road that leads to you. [6]As they pass through a valley where balsam trees grow, they make it a place of springs. The early rains cover it with blessings. [7]**Their strength grows as they go along** until each one of them appears in front of God in Zion.

[Haupt] <u>Psalms 84:5-7</u> **Happy the men, of whom Thou art the strength**, To whom a pilgrimage is never out of their mind. [6]When they go through the Valley of Baca, He makes it for them full of springs, He clothes Moreh with blessings. [7]**At every step their strength increases**, They appear before God in Zion.

[Jones-Ps] <u>Psalms 84:5-7</u> **How blest whose strength and hope thou art.** Who have highways within their heart: [6]While through the vale of tears they go, They make fresh springs of water flow; [7]**With growing strength their path is trod** To Zion's hill and Zion's God.

[Moffatt] <u>Psalms 84:5-7</u> **Happy are they who, nerved by thee**, set out on pilgrimage! [6]When they pass through Weary-glen, fountains flow for their refreshing, blessings rain upon them; [7]**they are the stronger as they go**, till God at last reveals himself in Sion.

[MOTB] <u>Psalms 84:5-7</u> **Nay, but happy, too, are those whose strength is in Jehovah**, and whose hearts are filled with thoughts of pilgrimage; [6]for even the hot and dusty valleys, where only the balsam grows, seem in their sight as though smiling with green, blest by fountains or rain. [7]**On they march, gathering strength as they go**, sustained by the assurance that the God of gods will reveal himself to them in Zion.

[NET] <u>Psalms 84:5-7</u> **How blessed are those who find their strength in you,** and long to travel the roads that lead to your temple! [6]As they pass through the Baca Valley, he provides a spring for them. The rain even covers it with pools of water. [7]**They are sustained as they travel along**; each one appears before God in Zion.

[NLT] <u>Psalms 84:5-7</u> **What joy for those whose strength comes from the Lord**, who have set their minds on a pilgrimage to Jerusalem. [6]When they walk through the Valley of Weeping, it will become a place of refreshing springs. The autumn rains will clothe it with blessings. [7]**They will continue to grow stronger**, and each of them will appear before God in Jerusalem.

[TLB] <u>Psalms 84:5-7</u> **Happy are those who are strong in the Lord**, who want above all else to follow your steps. [6]When they walk through the Valley of Weeping, it will become a place of springs where pools of blessing and refreshment collect after rains! [7]**They will grow constantly in strength**, and each of them is invited to meet with the Lord in Zion.

[TPT] <u>Psalms 84:5-7</u> **How enriched are they who find their strength in the Lord**; within their hearts are the highways of holiness! [6]Even when their paths wind through the dark valley of tears, they dig deep to find a pleasant pool where others find only pain. He gives to them a brook of blessing filled from the rain of an outpouring. [7]**They grow stronger and stronger with every step forward**, and the God of all gods will appear before them in Zion.

[VW] <u>Psalms 84:5-7</u> **Blessed is the man whose strength is in You**, whose heart is upon Your highways. [6]As they pass through the Valley of Baca, they make it a spring; the early rain also covers it with blessings. [7]**They go from strength to strength**, appearing before God in Zion.

<u>Psalms 89:21</u> With whom my hand shall be established: mine arm also shall strengthen him.

[Allen-Ps-Third] <u>Psalms 89:21</u> Thy strong right hand, thy mighty arm Strikes down the proudest of thy foes, But shields thy servants from all harm; And thus thy truth and mercy shows.

[Anchor] <u>Psalms 89:21</u> My hand shall supply his power, and my arm shall keep him strong.

[BBE] <u>Psalms 89:21</u> My hand will be his support; my arm will give him strength.

[CCB] <u>Psalms 89:21</u> My hand will be ever with him and my arm will sustain him,

[CJB] <u>Psalms 89:21</u> My hand will always be with him, and my arm will give him strength.

[Cottle-Ps] <u>Psalms 89:21</u> My hand, upon his head shall rest, I will establish long his power; strength will I give, and cheer his breast, in every dark and adverse hour.

[EEBT] <u>Psalms 89:21</u> My hand will make him strong and, Yes! My arm will make him powerful.

[EXB] <u>Psalms 89:21</u> I will steady him with my hand and strengthen him with my arm.

[Fenton] <u>Psalms 89:21</u> My hand shall be firmly with Him, Yes! he shall be strong by My arm.

[Grail-Ps] <u>Psalms 89:21</u> My hand shall always be with him, and my arm shall make him strong.

[ICB] <u>Psalms 89:21</u> I will steady him with my hand. I will strengthen him with my arm.

[JPS-OT 1985] <u>Psalms 89:21</u> My hand shall be constantly with him, and My arm shall strengthen him.

[Marson-Ps] <u>Psalms 89:21</u> My hand shall hold him fast: and my arm shall strengthen him.

[NIRV] <u>Psalms 89:21</u> My powerful hand will keep him going. My mighty arm will give him strength.

[NOG] <u>Psalms 89:21</u> My hand is ready to help him. My arm will also give him strength.

[TVB] <u>Psalms 89:21</u> My strong hand will stay with him and sustain him, regardless of trial or foe. My mighty arm will be his strength and shield.

[UDB] <u>Psalms 89:21</u> My strength will always be with him; with my power, I will make him strong.

<u>Psalms 91:3</u> Surely he shall deliver thee from the snare of the fowler, and from the noisome pestilence.

[Alexander-OT] <u>Psalms 91:3</u> For lo, he will free thee from the fowler's snare, from the plague of mischiefs.

[Beck] <u>Psalms 91:3</u> He is the One who will rescue you from the snare and from the deadly plague.

[Benisch-OT] <u>Psalms 91:3</u> Surely he shall deliver thee from the snare of a fowler, and from a destroying pestilence.

[Berkeley] <u>Psalms 91:3</u> Certainly it is He who rescues you from the hunter's trap and from the fatal pestilence.

[Boothroyd] <u>Psalms 91:3</u> Surely, he shall deliver thee From the snare of the fowler, And from all mischievous designs.

[CAB] <u>Psalms 91:3</u> For He shall deliver you from the snare of the fowler, from every troublesome matter.

[CEB] <u>Psalms 91:3</u> God will save you from the hunter's trap and from deadly sickness.

[CEV] <u>Psalms 91:3</u> The Lord will keep you safe from secret traps and deadly diseases.

[CJB] <u>Psalms 91:3</u> he will rescue you from the trap of the hunter and from the plague of calamities;

[CLV] <u>Psalms 91:3</u> For He Himself shall rescue you from the snare of the trapper, From the plague of woes.

[Cotton-Ps] <u>Psalms 91:3</u> Surely He shall deliver thee out of the Fowler's snare; He shall deliver thee from the malignant pestilence.

[Driver-OT] <u>Psalms 91:3</u> For he shall deliver thee from the trap of the fowler, from the engulfing pestilence.

[EEBT] <u>Psalms 91:3</u> He (God) really will save you from the trap that the bird-catcher (hid). And (God will save you) from illnesses that cause death.

[ERV] <u>Psalms 91:3</u> God will save you from hidden dangers and from deadly diseases.

[Farr-Ps] <u>Psalms 91:3</u> He shall, by his tender care, Save thee from the fowler's snare; He shall be thy sure defence, From the noisome pestilence.

[Horsley-OT] <u>Psalms 91:3</u> Truly he shall deliver thee from the snare of the fowler, From the noxious pestilence.

[HRB] <u>Psalms 91:3</u> For He delivers you from the fowlers snare, from destruction's plague.

[Keble-Ps] <u>Psalms 91:3</u> For He shall free thee from the net The wily hunter set; From plague and all her loathsome woes, God is thy sure repose.

[McFadyen-OT] <u>Psalms 91:3</u> For He saves thee from fowler's snare, From the yawning pit of destruction.

[McSwiney-Ps-V] <u>Psalms 91:3</u> For HE shall-deliver me from the snare of the hunters: And from the slanderous report.

[MOTB] <u>Psalms 91:3</u> For he is mighty to deliver from perils of every kind. He can save thee from the snare and deadly pestilence:

[MSG] <u>Psalms 91:3</u> That's right—he rescues you from hidden traps, shields you from deadly hazards.

[Perowne-Ps] <u>Psalms 91:3</u> For He shall deliver thee from the snare of the hunter, From the devouring pestilence.

[T4T] <u>Psalms 91:3</u> He will rescue you from all hidden traps and save you from deadly diseases.

[Thomson] Psalms 91:3 Because he will deliver thee from the snare of hunters; and tumultuous accusation—

[TPT] Psalms 91:3 He will rescue you from every hidden trap of the enemy, and he will protect you from false accusation and any deadly curse.

Psalms 91:5-6 Thou shalt not be afraid for the terror by night; nor for the arrow that flieth by day; ⁶Nor for the pestilence that walketh in darkness; nor for the destruction that wasteth at noonday.

[BBE] Psalms 91:5-6 You will have no fear of the evil things of the night, or of the arrow in flight by day, ⁶Or of the disease which takes men in the dark, or of the destruction which makes waste when the sun is high.

[CLV] Psalms 91:5-6 You shall not fear the alarm at night, Or the arrow that flies by day, ⁶Neither the plague that walks in gloom, Nor the sting that devastates at high noon.

[De Witt-Ps] Psalms 91:5-6 Thou shalt not be afraid for the terror by night, or the arrow that flies by day; ⁶For the pestilence walking in darkness, Or the sickness that wasteth at noonday;

[Douay-Rheims] Psalms 91:5-6 His truth shall compass thee with a shield: thou shalt not be afraid of the terror of the night. ⁶Of the arrow that flieth in the day, of the business that walketh about in the dark: of invasion, or of the noonday devil.

[EEBT] Psalms 91:5-6 Do not be afraid of: bad spirits at night, or the arrow that flies in the day, ⁶or illnesses that come when it is dark, or something bad that may destroy you at midday.

[ERV] Psalms 91:5-6 You will have nothing to fear at night and no need to be afraid of enemy arrows during the day. ⁶You will have no fear of diseases that come in the dark or terrible suffering that comes at noon.

[GNT] Psalms 91:5-6 You need not fear any dangers at night or sudden attacks during the day ⁶or the plagues that strike in the dark or the evils that kill in daylight.

[Haupt] Psalms 91:5-6 Thou needest not be afraid of terror at night, Of arrows which fly by daylight, ⁶Of pestilence which creeps in darkness, Of sudden death which surprises at noonday.

[McFadyen-OT] Psalms 91:5-6 Thou needst not be afraid for the terror of night, Nor for the arrow that flieth by day, ⁶Nor for the plague that stalketh in darkness, No yet for the pest or the demon of noon.

[NCV] Psalms 91:5-6 You will not fear any danger by night or an arrow during the day. ⁶You will not be afraid of diseases that come in the dark or sickness that strikes at noon.

[NIRV] Psalms 91:5-6 You won't have to be afraid of the terrors that come during the night. You won't have to fear the arrows that come at you during the day. ⁶You won't have to be afraid of the sickness that attacks in the darkness. You won't have to fear the plague that destroys at noon.

[Orton-OT] Psalms 91:5-6 Thou shalt not be afraid for the terror by night; nor for the arrow that flieth by day; ⁶Nor for the pestilence that walketh in darkness; nor for the destruction that wasteth at noon day; thou shalt be safe from wicked men, from storms and tempests, and the diseases which are occasioned by the coldness of the night or the heat of the day.

[Perowne-Ps] Psalms 91:5-6 Thou shalt not be afraid for any terror by night, (Nor) for the arrow that flight by day, ⁶Nor for the pestilence that walketh in darkness, (Nor) for the sickness that wasteth at noon-day.

[T4T] Psalms 91:5-6 You will not be afraid of things that happen during the night that could terrorize you/cause you to be very afraid, or of arrows that your enemies will shoot at you during the day. ⁶You will not be afraid of plagues/widespread sicknesses that demons cause when they attack people at night, or of other evil forces that kill people at midday.

OUR HEALING COVENANT

[TPT] <u>Psalms 91:5-6</u> You will never worry about an attack of demonic forces at night nor have to fear a spirit of darkness coming against you. ⁶Don't fear a thing! Whether by night or by day, demonic danger will not trouble you, nor will the powers of evil launched against you.

<u>Psalms 91:10-16</u> **There shall no evil befall thee, neither shall any plague come nigh thy dwelling**. ¹¹For he shall give his angels charge over thee, to keep thee in all thy ways. ¹²**They shall bear thee up in their hands**, lest thou dash thy foot against a stone. ¹³Thou shalt tread upon the lion and adder: the young lion and the dragon shalt thou trample under feet. ¹⁴Because he hath set his love upon me, **therefore will I deliver him**: I will set him on high, because he hath known my name. ¹⁵He shall call upon me, and **I will answer him**: I will be with him in trouble; **I will deliver him**, and honour him. ¹⁶**With long life will I satisfy him, and shew him my salvation.**

[AMPC] <u>Psalms 91:10-16</u> **There shall no evil befall you, nor any plague or calamity come near your tent**. ¹¹For He will give His angels [especial] charge over you to accompany and defend and preserve you in all your ways [of obedience and service]. ¹²**They shall bear you up on their hands**, lest you dash your foot against a stone. ¹³You shall tread upon the lion and adder; the young lion and the serpent shall you trample underfoot. ¹⁴Because he has set his love upon Me, **therefore will I deliver him**; I will set him on high, because he knows and understands My name [has a personal knowledge of My mercy, love, and kindness—trusts and relies on Me, knowing I will never forsake him, no, never]. ¹⁵He shall call upon Me, and **I will answer him**; I will be with him in trouble, **I will deliver him** and honor him. ¹⁶**With long life will I satisfy him and show him My salvation.**

[BBE] <u>Psalms 91:10-16</u> **No evil will come on you, and no disease will come near your tent**. ¹¹For he will give you into the care of his angels to keep you wherever you go. ¹²**In their hands they will keep you up**, so that your foot may not be crushed against a stone. ¹³You will put your foot on the lion and the snake; the young lion and the great snake will be crushed under your feet. ¹⁴Because he has given me his love, **I will take him out of danger**: I will put him in a place of honour, because he has kept my name in his heart. ¹⁵When his cry comes up to me, **I will give him an answer**: I will be with him in trouble; **I will make him free from danger** and give him honour. ¹⁶**With long life will he be rewarded; and I will let him see my salvation.**

[Besorah] <u>Psalms 91:10-16</u> **No evil befalls you and a plague does not come near your tent**; ¹¹For He commands His messengers concerning you, To guard you in all your ways. ¹²**They bear you up in their hands**, Lest you dash your foot against a stone. ¹³You tread upon lion and cobra, Young lion and serpent you trample under foot. ¹⁴"Because he cleaves to Me in love, **Therefore I deliver him**; I set him on high because he has known My Name. ¹⁵"When he calls on Me, **I answer him**; I am with him in distress; **I deliver him** and esteem him. ¹⁶"**With long life I satisfy him and show him My deliverance.**"

[BLE] <u>Psalms 91:10-16</u> **No harm will come upon you nor blight draw near your home**, ¹¹Because he will give his angels orders for you, to guard you in all your courses; ¹²**They shall take you up in their hands** to keep you from stubbing your toe on a stone. ¹³You shall tread on lion and viper, trample down two-year-old lion and reptile. ¹⁴Because he is in love with me **I will see him through**, will set him out of reach of harm because he knows my name. ¹⁵He shall call on me and **I will answer him**; I am with him in distress, **I will rescue him** and show him honor. ¹⁶**Of long life I will give him his fill, and will let him feast his eyes on my salvation.**

[BrownKrueger] <u>Psalms 91:10-16</u> **There shall none evil come unto thee, neither shall any plague come near thy tabernacle**. ¹¹For he shall give his angels charge over thee to keep thee in all thy ways. ¹²**They shall bear thee in their hands**, that thou hurt not thy foot against a stone. ¹³Thou shalt walk upon the lion and asp: the young lion and the dragon shalt thou tread under feet. ¹⁴Because he hath loved me, **therefore will I deliver him**: I will exalt him because he hath known my name. ¹⁵He shall call upon me, and **I will hear him**: I will be with him in trouble: **I will deliver him**, and glorify him. [16]**With long life will I satisfy him, and show him my salvation**.

[Burgess-Ps] <u>Psalms 91:10-16</u> **No ill shall strike thy guarded head, no plague approach thy home**. [11]For he shall charge his angel bands to keep thy pathway lone; [12]and, **lifted on their gentle hands**, thou shalt not touch a stone. [13]The lion's lair, the adder's brake, thy fearless heel shall tread, and trample down the coiling snake, and spurn the monster's bed. [14]"Because to mine own name he gave His steadfast fear and love, **I, in his need, will speed to save, and plant his feet above**. [15]**My ear shall hear his suppliant voice**, [16]**in length of days shall such rejoice, and my salvation see**."

[CEB] <u>Psalms 91:10-16</u> **no evil will happen to you; no disease will come close to your tent**. [11]Because he will order his messengers to help you, to protect you wherever you go. [12]**They will carry you with their own hands** so you don't bruise your foot on a stone. [13]You'll march on top of lions and vipers; you'll trample young lions and serpents underfoot. [14]God says, "Because you are devoted to me, **I'll rescue you**. I'll protect you because you know my name. [15]Whenever you cry out to me, **I'll answer**. I'll be with you in troubling times. **I'll save you** and glorify you. [16]**I'll fill you full with old age. I'll show you my salvation**.

[CEV] <u>Psalms 91:10-16</u> **and no terrible disasters will strike you or your home**. [11]God will command his angels to protect you wherever you go. [12]**They will carry you in their arms**, and you won't hurt your feet on the stones. [13]You will overpower the strongest lions and the most deadly snakes. [14]The Lord says, "If you love me and truly know who I am, **I will rescue you** and keep you safe. [15]When you are in trouble, call out to me. **I will answer** and **be there to protect** and honor you. [16]**You will live a long life and see my saving power**."

[CJB] <u>Psalms 91:10-16</u> **No disaster will happen to you, no calamity will come near your tent**; [11]for he will order his angels to care for you and guard you wherever you go. [12]**They will carry you in their hands**, so that you won't trip on a stone. [13]You will tread down lions and snakes, young lions and serpents you will trample underfoot. [14]"Because he loves me, **I will rescue him**; because he knows my name, I will protect him. [15]He will call on me, and **I will answer him**. I will be with him when he is in trouble. **I will extricate him** and bring him honor. [16]**I will satisfy him with long life and show him my salvation**."

[CLV] <u>Psalms 91:10-16</u> **Evil shall not be your fate, And contagion, it shall not approach into your tent**. [11]For He shall enjoin His messengers concerning you, To keep you in all your ways. [12]**On their palms shall they lift you**, Lest you should strike your foot against a stone. [13]Upon the black lion and the cobra shall you tread; You shall tramp down the sheltered lion and the snake. [14]Because he is attached to Me, **I shall deliver him; I shall make him impregnable**, for he knows My Name. [15]He shall call on Me, and **I shall answer him**; I am with him in distress; **I shall liberate him** and glorify him. [16]**With length of days shall I satisfy him, And I shall show him My salvation**.

[Cottle-Ps] <u>Psalms 91:10-16</u> **No evil on thy head shall light, through all thy mortal road; neither shall any plague affright, or reach thy calm abode**. [11]For o'er thy steps, with ceaseless care, His angels shall preside; they shall thy every path prepare, and be thy constant guide. [12]**They shall uphold thy feet**, alone, through God's Almighty power; lest thou should'st dash, against a stone, thy foot, in evil hour. [13]Thou shalt, the Lion, fierce, defeat, the adder, dreadless, view; and trample underneath thy feet, Satan, and all his crew. [14]"Because his heart is turn'd to me, He hath my favour found; hence, **his Deliverer, I will be from all his foes around**. [15]On me he calls, the Lord, supreme! Therefore, **his voice, I hear**; in trouble, **I will succour him**, and him, in sorrow, cheer. [16]**My honor, on his head, shall rest, he shall, in me, delight; and taste salvation, with the blest, in heave, that world of light**."

[Davis-Ps] <u>Psalms 91:10-16</u> **No foe shall enter where you dwell, or if the plague come nigh, and sweep the wicked down to hell, 'twill raise his saints on high**. [11]He gives his angels charge to keep

Your feet in all his ways, to watch your pillow while you sleep, and guard your happy days. [12]Our Father knows his sons are rash when left to walk alone, **His angels bear them** lest they dash the foot against a stone. [13]Tho lions roar, and serpents hiss, and dragons fierce engage, yet angels guide them safe to bliss, in spite of Satan's rage. [14]Thus saith the Lord, "because on me My children set their love, **I will their great salvation be**, and bring them all above. [15]My grace shall answer when they call, in trouble I'll be near, **My power shall raise them when they fail**, and they shall persevere. [16]**The saints, who here my name have known, in heaven shall be mine heirs; there my salvation shall be shown, and endless life be theirs**."

[Douay-Rheims] <u>Psalms 91:10-16</u> **There shall no evil come to thee: nor shall the scourge come near thy dwelling**. [11]For he hath given his angels charge over thee; to keep thee in all thy ways. [12]**In their hands they shall bear thee up**: lest thou dash thy foot against a stone. [13]Thou shalt walk upon the asp and the basilisk: and thou shalt trample under foot the lion and the dragon. [14]Because he hoped in me **I will deliver him**: I will protect him because he hath known my name. [15]He shall cry to me, and **I will hear him**: I am with him in tribulation, **I will deliver him**, and I will glorify him. [16]**I will fill him with length of days; and I will shew him my salvation**.

[Fenton] <u>Psalms 91:10-16</u> **So sickness will not approach you, Contagion not enter your Rest**, [11]For you He will order His Angels To keep guard upon all your paths, [12]**Who will in their hands hold you up**, From striking your foot on a stone. [13]You may tread on a lion or asp, Your feet may descend on a snake. — [14]"He trusted on me, —**I deliver**; He knew my name, —So I hold up! [15]He calls, —I reply **I am with You**; **I deliver** and help in distress. [16]**I content with extension of days, And will let him see that I can save**.

[GAC-Ps-Fourth] <u>Psalms 91:10-16</u> **No ill shall enter where you dwell; or if the plague come nigh, and sweep the wicked down to hell, 'T'will raise his saints on high**. [11]He'll give his angels charge to keep your feet in all their ways; to watch your pillow while you sleep, and guard your happy days. [12][**Their hands shall bear you** lest you fall and dash against the stones: are they not servants at his call, and sent to attend his sons?] [14]Because on me they set their love, **I'll save them**,' saith the Lord; 'I'll bear their joyful souls above destruction, and the sword. [15]My grace shall answer when they call; in trouble **I'll be nigh**; My power shall help them when they fall, And raise them when they die. Those that on earth my name have known, I'll honor them in heaven; [16]**there my salvation shall be shown, and endless life by given.'**

[JPS-OT 1985] <u>Psalms 91:10-16</u> **no harm will befall you, no disease touch your tent**. [11]For He will order His angels to <u>guard</u> you wherever you go. [12]**They will carry you in their hands** lest you hurt your foot on a stone. [13]You will tread on cubs and vipers; you will trample lions and asps. [14]"Because he is devoted to Me **I will deliver him**; I will keep him safe, for he knows My name. [15]When he calls on Me, **I will answer him**; I will be with him in distress; **I will rescue him** and make him honored; [16]**I will let him live to a ripe old age, and show him My salvation**."

[JUB] <u>Psalms 91:10-16</u> **no evil shall befall thee, neither shall any plague come near thy dwelling**. [11]For he shall give his angels charge over thee to keep thee in all thy ways. [12]**They shall bear thee up in their hands** lest thy foot stumble against a stone. [13]Thou shalt tread upon the lion and adder; the young lion and the dragon shalt thou trample under feet. [14]Because he has set his will upon me, therefore **I will deliver him**; I will set him on high because he has known my name. [15]He shall call upon me, and **I will answer him**; I will be with him in trouble; **I will deliver him** and glorify him. [16]**With long life I will satisfy him and show him my saving health**.

[MSG] <u>Psalms 91:10-16</u> **Evil can't get close to you, harm can't get through the door**. [11]He ordered his angels to guard you wherever you go. [12]**If you stumble, they'll catch you**; their job is to keep you from falling. [13]You'll walk unharmed among lions and snakes, and kick young lions and serpents from the path. [14]"If you'll hold on to me for dear life," says God, "**I'll get you out of any trouble**. I'll give you the best of care if you'll only get to know and trust me. [15]Call me and **I'll answer**, be at your side in bad times; **I'll rescue you**, then throw you a party. [16]**I'll give you a long life, give you a long drink of salvation!**"

[NAB] <u>Psalms 91:10-16</u> **No evil shall befall you, no affliction come near your tent**. [11]For God commands the angels to guard you in all your ways. [12]**With their hands they shall support you**, lest you strike your foot against a stone. [13]You shall tread upon the asp and the viper, trample the lion and the dragon. [14]Whoever clings to me **I will deliver**; whoever knows my name I will set on high. [15]All who call upon me **I will answer**; I will be with them in distress; I will deliver them and give them honor. [16]**With length of days I will satisfy them and show them my saving power**.

[NCV] <u>Psalms 91:10-16</u> **Nothing bad will happen to you; no disaster will come to your home**. [11]He has put his angels in charge of you to watch over you wherever you go. [12]**They will catch you in their hands** so that you will not hit your foot on a rock. [13]You will walk on lions and cobras; you will step on strong lions and snakes. [14]The Lord says, "Whoever loves me, I will save. **I will protect those who know me**. [15]They will call to me, and **I will answer them**. I will be with them in trouble; **I will rescue them** and honor them. [16]**I will give them a long, full life, and they will see how I can save**.

[NET] <u>Psalms 91:10-16</u> **No harm will overtake you; no illness will come near your home**. [11]For he will order his angels to protect you in all you do. [12]**They will lift you up in their hands**, so you will not slip and fall on a stone. [13]You will subdue a lion and a snake; you will trample underfoot a young lion and a serpent. [14]The Lord says, "Because he is devoted to me, **I will deliver him**; I will protect him because he is loyal to me. [15]When he calls out to me, **I will answer him**. I will be with him when he is in trouble; **I will rescue him** and bring him honor. [16]**I will satisfy him with long life, and will let him see my salvation**.

[NIRV] <u>Psalms 91:10-16</u> **Then no harm will come to you. No terrible plague will come near your tent**. [11]The Lord will command his angels to take good care of you. [12]**They will lift you up in their hands**. Then you won't trip over a stone. [13]You will walk on lions and cobras. You will crush mighty lions and poisonous snakes. [14]The Lord says, "I will save the one who loves me. **I will keep him safe**, because he trusts in me. [15]He will call out to me, and **I will answer him**. I will be with him in times of trouble. **I will save him** and honor him. [16]**I will give him a long and full life. I will save him**.

[NLT] <u>Psalms 91:10-16</u> **no evil will conquer you; no plague will come near your home**. [11]For he will order his angels to protect you wherever you go. [12]**They will hold you up with their hands** so you won't even hurt your foot on a stone. [13]You will trample upon lions and cobras; you will crush fierce lions and serpents under your feet! [14]The Lord says, "**I will rescue those who love me**. I will protect those who trust in my name. [15]When they call on me, **I will answer**; I will be with them in trouble. **I will rescue** and honor them. [16]**I will reward them with a long life and give them my salvation**."

[NOG] <u>Psalms 91:10-16</u> **No harm will come to you. No sickness will come near your house**. [11]He will put his angels in charge of you to protect you in all your ways. [12]**They will carry you in their hands** so that you never hit your foot against a rock. [13]You will step on lions and cobras. You will trample young lions and snakes. [14]**Because you love me, I will rescue you**. I will protect you because you know my name. [15]When you call to me, **I will answer you**. I will be with you when you are in trouble. **I will save you** and honor you. [16]**I will satisfy you with a long life. I will show you how I will save you**.

[Parkhurst-Ps] <u>Psalms 91:10-16</u> **No evil shall happen to thee, nor plague approach thy tent**. [11]For his angels have orders concerning thee, to keep thee in all thy ways. [12]**Upon their hands they shall bear thee up**, lest thou strike thy foot against a stone. [13]Thou shalt tread upon a lion and an adder: thou shalt trample upon a young lion and a dragon. [14]**For he shall be attached to me, and I will deliver him:** I will exalt him because he knows my name. [15]He will call upon me, and **I will answer him**: I will be with him in trouble; **I will deliver him**, and will honour him. [16]**With length of days I will satisfy him, and will shew him my salvation**.

[Thomson] <u>Psalms 91:10-16</u> **no evils shall come upon thee, nor shall a scourge approach thy dwelling**. [11]For he will give his angels a charge concerning thee; to keep thee in all thy ways; [12]**with their hands they shall bear thee up**; shouldst thou chance to strike thy foot against a stone. [13]Upon an asp and a basilisk thou shalt tread: and trample down a lion and a dragon. [14][JJ] **Because he trusted in me, I will deliver him**: I will protect him because he knew my name. [15]He will call on me, and **I will answer him**: I am with him in affliction: **I will deliver him** and honour him. [16]**With length of days I will satisfy him; and I will shew him my salvation**.

[TPT] <u>Psalms 91:10-16</u> **we will always be shielded from harm. How then could evil prevail against us or disease infect us?** [11]God sends angels with special orders to protect you wherever you go, defending you from all harm. [12]If you walk into a trap, they'll be there for you and **keep you from stumbling**. [13]You'll even walk unharmed among the fiercest powers of darkness, trampling every one of them beneath your feet! [14]For here is what the Lord has spoken to me: "**Because you have delighted in me as my great lover, I will greatly protect you**. I will set you in a high place, safe and secure before my face. [15]**I will answer your cry for help** every time you pray, and you will find and feel my presence even in your time of pressure and trouble. **I will be your glorious hero** and give you a feast. [16]**You will be satisfied with a full life and with all that I do for you. For you will enjoy the fullness of my salvation!**"

[Wrangham-Ps] <u>Psalms 91:10-16</u> For Thou, Jehovah, shelterest me: Since thou hast chosen God Most High Thy castle of defence to be, There shall no evil chance to thee, No plague approach thy dwelling nigh. [11]For to His angels God will say, 'Guard ye his footsteps round about: [12]And in their mighty hands shall they Uphold thee safe upon thy way; Lest 'gainst a stone thou strike thy foot. [13]On asp and lion shalt thou tread; Snake and young lion trample down: [14]Because he loves God hath said, 'Him will I free; and lift his head, Because by him My name is known. [15]'I will reply, whene'er he prays; I will be with him in his woe, Save him, and to high honour raise; [16]Fulfilling him with length of days; And to him My salvation show.'

<u>Psalms 103:2-5</u> Bless the LORD, O my soul, and forget not all his benefits: [3]Who forgiveth all thine iniquities; **who healeth**[raphah] **all thy diseases**; [4]Who redeemeth thy life from destruction; who crowneth thee with lovingkindness and tender mercies; [5]Who satisfieth thy mouth with good things; so that **thy youth is renewed like the eagle's**.

[Allen-Ps-First] <u>Psalms 103:2-5</u> Bless, O my soul, the living God; Call home thy thoughts, that rove abroad. Let all the powers within me join In work and worship so divine. [3]'Tis He, my soul, who sent his Son To die for crimes, which thou hast done; He owns the ransom and forgives The hourly follies of our lives. The vices of the mind **He heals and cures the pains, that nature feels**, [4]Redeems the soul from hell, and saves Our wasting life from threatening graves.

[Aston-Ps] <u>Psalms 103:2-5</u> O never unremembered be The benefits he poured on thee: [3]Whose pardon does all sins release, And **keep thy body from disease**; [4]Who thee redeemed, to death cast down, And doth thy life with mercies crown. [5]Who with good things shall fill thy mouth, And **eagle-like renew thy youth**.

[BBE] <u>Psalms 103:2-5</u> Give praise to the Lord, O my soul; let not all his blessings go from your memory. [3]He has forgiveness for all your sins; **he takes away all your diseases**; [4]He keeps back your life from destruction, crowning you with mercy and grace. [5]He makes your mouth full of good things, so that **your strength is made new again like the eagle's**.

[Beck] <u>Psalms 103:2-5</u> My soul, praise the Lord, and don't forget all the good He does: [3]He forgives all my wrongs, **heals all my sicknesses,** [4]saves my life from being destroyed, crowns me with love and mercies, [5]and satisfies me with good things as long as I live so that **like an eagle my youth is renewed.**

[BLE] <u>Psalms 103:2-5</u> Bless Jehovah, my soul, and do not forget all he has done for you, [3]He who forgives all your guilt, **who cures all your diseases,** [4]Who protects your life from being swallowed up in the depths below, who crowns you with his friendship and sympathy, [5]Who satisfies your lifetime with good things, letting **you renew your youth like the great vulture.**

[Cayley-Ps] <u>Psalms 103:2-5</u> Bless, O my soul, the Lord, and let thou not His bounties be forgot; [3]Who pardoneth all thy guilt; **whate'er in thee Is frail, that healeth he;** [4]Who ransoms from the pit thy life; whose grace And pity thee embrace; [5]Who fills thy lot with goodness; **who renews Thy youth like eagles' thewes [power / might];**

[CBC] <u>Psalms 103:2-5</u> Bless the Lord, O my soul, And forget not any of His dealings: [3]Who passeth over all thine iniquity; **Who healeth all thy diseases;** [4]Who redeemeth [as a kinsman] thy life from destruction; Who crowneth thee with lovingkindness and compassions; [5]Who satisfieth thy mouth with good things; So that **thy youth is renewed like the eagle's.**

[Collier-Ps] <u>Psalms 103:2-5</u> Awake, my soul, and bless the Lord, His countless benefits proclaim; [3]Who cleanses every guilty stain, **Who heals thy sickness, soothes thy pain.** [4]Thy life from death His love redeems, and, like a sun, He crowns thy days with loving-kindness' gentle beams, and tender mercy's warmer rays; [5]thy heart's desire he satisfies, and **strength of youth anew supplies.**

[Cotton-Ps] <u>Psalms 103:2-5</u> O my awakened Soul, Do thou Bless always the Eternal God; and O forget not any one of all His precious benefits. [3]'Tis He who gives a pardon to all thy most vile iniquities; **'Tis He who gives an healing to all thy most sad infirmities.** [4]'Tis He who doth redeem thy Life from the dark Grave's corrupting pit; 'Tis He who thee with Mercy doth and with tender compassions crown. [5]'Tis He who with the thing that's good doth satisfy thy craving mouth; thy Youth it is renew'd; **Then like the souring Eagle shalt thou be.**

[CWB] <u>Psalms 103:2-5</u> Praise the Lord, O my soul, and don't forget all the benefits He's given you. [3]He forgives your sins and **heals your diseases.** [4]He has kept you from an early grave and treats you with love and compassion. [5]He gives you the comforts of life so **your strength is renewed like an eagle's.**

[Davis-Ps] <u>Psalms 103:2-5</u> O, bless the Lord, my soul, and tell how God redeem'd the world from hell, His wond'rous love recall to mind, and ne'er forget a friend so kind. [3]'Twas God, my soul, who sent his Son, to die for crimes which thou hast done; **'tis God, who breath and being gives, and by his grace the sinner lives. The vices of the mind he heals, relieves our pains,** our pardon seals, [4]redeems our soul from hell, and saves our wasting lives from threat'ning graves. Our health decay'd his power repairs, [5]His mercy crowns our hoary hairs; **our youth renew'd, like eagles, oft we stretch our wings and soar aloft.**

[FAA] <u>Psalms 103:2-5</u> Bless, the Lord, O my being, And do not forget any of the recompenses of him, [3]Who forgives all my iniquity, **Who cures all my diseases,** [4]Who redeems my life from the pit, Who crowns me with kindness and mercy, [5]And who satiates my years with goodness; **My youth is renewed like an eagle.**

[Geddes-Ps] <u>Psalms 103:2-5</u> Bless Jehovah, O my soul! And forget none of his bounties. [3]It is he who forgive the thine iniquities: **It is he who healeth thy diseases;** [4]who rescueth thy life from destruction; who crowned thee with bounty and kindnesses: [5]who filleth thee with the best of aliments; so that **thy youth is renewed, like an eagle's.**

[Goode-Ps] <u>Psalms 103:2-5</u> Arise, my soul. His praise repeat. Nor e'er ungratefully forget The gifts which from His mercy flow. The bounties which His hands bestow. [3]His mercy all thy sins forgives, He speaks—and dying nature lives; **At His command diseases fly, And health beams cheerful from the eye**. ⁴When pain arrests thy lab'ring breath, 'Tis He redeems thy life from death His loving-kindness crowns thy days. And mercy spreads thro' all thy ways, ⁵His lib'ral hand thy food supplies. What streams of goodness round thee rise! And, **as the new-fledged Eagle soars, Thy youth, and health, and strength restores**.

[ICB] <u>Psalms 103:2-5</u> My whole being, praise the Lord. Do not forget all his kindnesses. ³The Lord forgives me for all my sins. **He heals all my diseases**. ⁴He saves my life from the grave. He loads me with love and mercy. ⁵He satisfies me with good things. **He makes me young again, like the eagle**.

[JPS-Ps 1972] <u>Psalms 103:2-5</u> Bless the Lord, O my soul and do not forget all His bounties. ³He forgives all your sins, **heals all your diseases**. ⁴He redeems your life from the Pit, surrounds you with steadfast love and mercy. ⁵He satisfies you with good things in the prime of life, so that **your youth is renewed like the eagle's**.

[Muhlenberg-Ps] <u>Psalms 103:2-5</u> O bless the Lord, my soul! His mercies bear in mind; Forget not all his benefits, Who is to thee so kind. ³He pardons all thy sins, **prolongs thy feeble breath; He healeth thine infirmities**, ⁴and ransoms thee from death. ⁵He feeds thee with his love, upholds thee with his truth, and **like the eagle's he renews the vigour of thy youth.**

[NEB] <u>Psalms 103:2-5</u> Bless the Lord, my soul, and forget none of his benefits. ³He pardons all my guilt and **heals all my suffering**. ⁴He rescues me from the pit of death and surrounds me with constant love, with tender affection; he contents me with all good in the prime of life, and **my youth is ever new like an eagles.**

[NIRV] <u>Psalms 103:2-5</u> I will praise the Lord. I won't forget anything he does for me. ³He forgives all my sins. **He heals all my sicknesses**. ⁴He saves my life from going down into the grave. His faithful and tender love makes me feel like a king. ⁵He satisfies me with the good things I desire. Then **I feel young and strong again, just like an eagle.**

[NJB] <u>Psalms 103:2-5</u> bless Yahweh, my soul, never forget all his acts of kindness. ³He forgives all your offences, **cures all your diseases**, ⁴he redeems your life from the abyss, crowns you with faithful love and tenderness; ⁵he contents you with good things all your life, **renews your youth like an eagle's.**

[NOG] <u>Psalms 103:2-5</u> Praise Yahweh, my soul, and never forget all the good he has done: ³He is the one who forgives all your sins, the one **who heals all your diseases**, ⁴the one who rescues your life from the pit, the one who crowns you with mercy and compassion, ⁵the one who fills your life with blessings so that **you become young again like an eagle**.

[Parkhurst-Ps] <u>Psalms 103:2-5</u> O my soul, bless Jehovah, and do not forget any of his rewards. ³He forgiveth all thy iniquities; and **healeth all thy ulcerations**. ⁴Who delivereth thy life from destruction; and whose abundant mercy encompasseth thee. ⁵Who moreover satisfieth even thee with good things; **thy youth is renewed like an eagle's.**

[REAL] <u>Psalms 103:2-5</u> Kneel before Ya-HoVaH's face, my soul, and do not forget all his benefits. ³He forgives all your perversions. **He heals all your diseases**. ⁴He buys back your life from destruction. He crowns you with kindness and acts of compassion. ⁵He satisfies your mouth with good. **Your youth is renewed like the eagle's.**

[Sandys-OT] <u>Psalms 103:2-5</u> Nor ever let the memory Of his surpassing Favours die. ³He gently pardons our misdeeds, And **cures the Wound which inward bleeds**. ⁴Hath from the Chains of Death unbound; With Clemency and Mercy crown'd. ⁵With Food our Hunger he subdues: **And Eagle-like our Youth renews**.

[Slavitt-Ps] <u>Psalms 103:2-5</u> Let the soul of my soul praise His name, exalt, laud, and extol His kindness, remembering all the ways ³He has forgiven our sins and **healed our sickness to save our lives**. ⁴Wherever we look, there is revealed His generous bounty. His people thrives. We are weak, we stagger and fall, but He snatches us back from the pit. ⁵We rise to a new day's bounty, surprised to be **sustained like the eagle that soars and flies on powerful updrafts of air, effortless, beautiful there**.

[TLB] <u>Psalms 103:2-5</u> Yes, I will bless the Lord and not forget the glorious things he does for me. ³He forgives all my sins. **He heals me**. ⁴He ransoms me from hell. He surrounds me with loving-kindness and tender mercies. ⁵He fills my life with good things! **My youth is renewed like the eagle's!**

[TVB] <u>Psalms 103:2-5</u> O my soul, come, praise the Eternal; sing a song from a grateful heart; sing and never forget all the good He has done. ³Despite all your many offenses, He forgives and releases you. **More than any doctor, He heals your diseases**. ⁴He reaches deep into the pit to deliver you from death. He crowns you with unfailing love and compassion like a king. ⁵When your soul is famished and withering, He fills you with good and beautiful things, satisfying you as long as you live. **He makes you strong like an eagle, restoring your youth**.

[UDB] <u>Psalms 103:2-5</u> I tell myself that I should praise Yahweh and never forget all the kind things he has done for me. ³He forgives all my sins, and **he heals me from all my diseases**; ⁴he keeps me from dying, and he blesses me by faithfully loving me and acting mercifully to me as he promised to do. ⁵He gives me good things during my entire life. **He makes me feel young and strong like eagles**.

[YLT] <u>Psalms 103:2-5</u> Bless, O my soul, Jehovah, And forget not all His benefits, ³Who is forgiving all thine iniquities, **Who is healing all thy diseases**, ⁴Who is redeeming from destruction thy life, Who is crowning thee—kindness and mercies, ⁵Who is satisfying with good thy desire, Renew itself as an eagle doth thy youth.

<u>Psalms 105:37</u> He brought them forth also with silver and gold: and **there was not one feeble person among their tribes**.

[Berkeley] <u>Psalms 105:37</u> He then led them out with silver and gold, **there were no invalids among His tribes**.

[BLE] <u>Psalms 105:37</u> And he brought them out with silver and gold, with **no one among his tribes stumbling**;

[Coles-Ps] <u>Psalms 105:37</u> Laden with silver and gold He brought them forth at length. **Among the tribes there was not one That feebleness betrayed**:

[CPDV] <u>Psalms 105:37</u> And he led them out with silver and gold, and **there was not an infirm one among their tribes**.

[De Witt-Ps] <u>Psalms 105:37</u> But He brought forth His people with silver and gold, **Not a man in His tribes became faint**.

[ERV] <u>Psalms 105:37</u> He led his people out of Egypt. They were carrying gold and silver, and **none of them stumbled or fell behind**.

[Farr-Ps] <u>Psalms 105:37</u> From Egypt he his people brought, Enrich'd with Egypt's wealth; **Not one was left behind forgot, For all were bless'd with health**.

[LTPB] <u>Psalms 105:37</u> He led them out with silver and gold. **There was not a sick one among their tribes**.

[Ming-Ps] <u>Psalms 105:37</u> He brought his servants forth, enriched with Egypt's borrowed wealth; And, what transcends all treasure else, **enriched with vigorous heath**.

[NAB] <u>Psalms 105:37</u> He brought his people out, laden with silver and gold; **no stragglers among the tribes.**

[NETS-OT] <u>Psalms 105:37</u> And he brought them out with silver and gold, and **there was no one among their tribes who was weak.**

[NLV] <u>Psalms 105:37</u> Then He brought Israel out with silver and gold. And **there was not one weak person among their families.**

[Rotherham] <u>Psalms 105:37</u> Thus brought he them forth, with silver and gold, **Nor was there, throughout his tribes, one that faltered**;

[Sandys-OT] <u>Psalms 105:37</u> Then He the Hebrews out of Goshen brought, **In able health**, with Gold, and Silver fraught.

[Smith] <u>Psalms 105:37</u> And he will bring them forth with silver and gold, and **none being weak in their tribes.**

[TVB] <u>Psalms 105:37</u> Then He brought His people out of slavery, weighed down with silver and gold; and of all His tribes, **not one of them stumbled, not one was left behind.**

[Wycliffe-Noble] <u>Psalms 105:37</u> And he led out them with silver and gold; and **none was sick in the lineages of them**. (And he led them out with silver and gold; and **no one was weak, or feeble, in all their tribes.**)

<u>Psalms 106:30</u> Then stood up Phinehas, and executed judgment: and so **the plague was stayed.**

[AMP] <u>Psalms 106:30</u> Then Phinehas [the priest] stood up and interceded, And so **the plague was halted.**

[BBE] <u>Psalms 106:30</u> Then Phinehas got up, and made prayer for them; and **the disease went no farther.**

[Besorah] <u>Psalms 106:30</u> Then Pinehas stood up and intervened, And **the plague was stopped.**

[BLE] <u>Psalms 106:30</u> Pinehas stood firm and intervened, and **the plague was checked,**

[CEB] <u>Psalms 106:30</u> Then Phinehas stood up and prayed, and **the plague was contained.**

[Lamsa] <u>Psalms 106:30</u> Then Phinehas stood up and prayed, and so **the plague was stopped.**

[NWT] <u>Psalms 106:30</u> But when Phin e·has stood up and intervened, **The scourge was halted.**

[Priest-Ps] <u>Psalms 106:30</u> Then stood up Phineas and prayed: and so **the plague ceased.**

[Sullivan-OT] <u>Psalms 106:30</u> But Phinehas pleaded and **the plague disappeared**

[VW] <u>Psalms 106:30</u> Then Phinehas stood up and intervened, and **the plague was restrained.**

[YLT] <u>Psalms 106:30</u> And Phinehas standeth, and executeth judgment, And **the plague is restrained,**

<u>Psalms 107:20</u> He sent his word, and healed[raphah] them, and delivered them from their destructions.

[Barton-Ps] <u>Psalms 107:20</u> He sent his word of power supreme, and did them heal and save; and graciously delivered them, even from the very grave.

[BBE] <u>Psalms 107:20</u> He sent his word and made them well, and kept them safe from the underworld.

[Beck] <u>Psalms 107:20</u> He sends His word and makes them well and rescues them from the grave.

[BLE] <u>Psalms 107:20</u> Sends his word and cures them and brings them clear of their blights,

[BWilliams-Ps] <u>Psalms 107:20</u> No med'cines could effect the Cure, so quick, so easy, or so sure: the deadly sentence God repeals, He sends his sov'reign Word and heals.

[CE] <u>Psalms 107:20</u> He sent forth his word to heal them and to snatch them from destruction.

[CEV] <u>Psalms 107:20</u> By the power of his own word, he healed you and saved you from destruction.

[CLV] <u>Psalms 107:20</u> He sent forth His word and healed them, And He provided escape from their graves.

[Coles-Ps] <u>Psalms 107:20</u> He sends forth His healing word, Pain and weakness to dispel: With new life the frame is stirred, And the sick again are well.

[CPDV] <u>Psalms 107:20</u> He sent his word, and he healed them, and he rescued them from their utter destruction.

[CWB] <u>Psalms 107:20</u> He spoke and they were healed. He delivered them from the pit of death.

[Davis-Ps] <u>Psalms 107:20</u> The deadly sentence God repeals, He sends his sovereign word and heals, inspires the souls with new desires, nature revives and death retires.

[EXB] <u>Psalms 107:20</u> God ·gave the command [sent forth his word] and healed them, so they were ·saved [rescued] from ·dying [destruction; or their pits].

[Fenton] <u>Psalms 107:20</u> He sent out His word, and it healed, and from their corruption it freed!

[Haupt] <u>Psalms 107:20</u> He sent forth His word for their healing, And let them escape from the pits wherein they lay.

[Hawley-Ps] <u>Psalms 107:20</u> And he deliverance kindly gave. He came to them, rebuked their pain, And them restored to health again.

[ISV] <u>Psalms 107:20</u> He issued his command and healed them; he delivered them from their destruction.

[JPS-Ps 1972] <u>Psalms 107:20</u> He gave an order and healed them; He delivered them from the pits.

[Keble-Ps] <u>Psalms 107:20</u> He sent His Word, and healed them all, He snatched them from their woe and thrall:

[Knox] <u>Psalms 107:20</u> uttered the word of healing, and saved them from their peril.

[Leeser-OT] <u>Psalms 107:20</u> He sendeth his word and healeth them, and delivereth them from their graves.

[LTPB] <u>Psalms 107:20</u> He sent His word and healed them, and rescued them from their destroyers.

[Moffatt] <u>Psalms 107:20</u> he sent his word to heal them and preserve their life.

[NIRV] <u>Psalms 107:20</u> He gave his command and healed them. He saved them from the grave.

[Norlie-NT] <u>Psalms 107:20</u> He issued a command, and healed them, saving them from destruction.

[REB] <u>Psalms 107:20</u> he sent his word to heal them and snatch them out of the pit of death.

[TLB] <u>Psalms 107:20</u> He spoke, and they were healed—snatched from the door of death.

[TPT] <u>Psalms 107:20</u> God spoke the words "Be healed," and we were healed, delivered from death's door!

[Watts-Ps] <u>Psalms 107:20</u> The deadly sentence God repeals, He sends his sovereign word, and heals.

<u>Psalms 113:9</u> He maketh the barren woman to keep house, and to be a joyful mother of children. Praise ye the LORD.

[Bartholomew-Ps] <u>Psalms 113:9</u> He, the sterile woman gladdens with a mother's sacred joys; By a numerous offspring blessing, her deep-felt reproach destroys!

[Buchanan-Ps] <u>Psalms 113:9</u> Who of the barren hears the prayers, and grants them children dear, that many young, joyless abodes with happiness may cheer.

[CCB] <u>Psalms 113:9</u> He gives a home to the barren woman, and makes her a joyful mother. Praise the Lord!

[EEBT] <u>Psalms 113:9</u> He makes the woman that is barren in her home into a happy mother of children. Hallelujah!

[ERV] <u>Psalms113:9</u> He gives children to the woman whose home is empty. He makes her a happy mother. Praise the Lord!

[EXB] <u>Psalms 113:9</u> He gives ·children to the woman who has none [the barren woman a home] and makes her ·a happy mother [joyful with children]. Praise the Lord!

[Grail-Ps] <u>Psalms 113:9</u> To the childless wife he gives a home as a joyful mother of children.

[ICB] <u>Psalms 113:9</u> He gives children to the woman who has none. He makes her a happy mother. Praise the Lord!

[Mitchell] <u>Psalms 113:9</u> who gives the barren wife children and overwhelms her with joy.

[MOTB] <u>Psalms 113:9</u> He assures the barren woman of a home, and makes her the happy mother of children.

[NCV] <u>Psalms 113:9</u> He gives children to the woman who has none and makes her a happy mother. Praise the Lord!

[NOG] <u>Psalms 113:9</u> He makes a woman who is in a childless home a joyful mother. Hallelujah!

[OEB-NT] <u>Psalms 113:9</u> He gives the childless woman a home, and makes her the happy mother of children. Hallelujah.

[T4T] <u>Psalms 113:9</u> He also enables women who have no children to have a family; he causes them to be happy mothers. Praise Yahweh!

[Thomson] <u>Psalms 113:9</u> Who settleth the barren woman in a family making her a joyful mother of children.

[TVB] <u>Psalms 113:9</u> Into the home of the childless bride, He sends children who are, for her, a cause of happiness beyond measure. Praise the Eternal!

[UDB] <u>Psalms 113:9</u> He also enables women who have no children to live in their houses as happy as mothers with children. Praise Yahweh!

[Watts-Ps] <u>Psalms 113:9</u> With joy the mother views her son, And tells the wonders God has done: Faith may grow strong when sense despairs; If nature fails, the promise bears.

<u>Psalms 118:14</u> **The Lord is my strength** and song, and is become my salvation.

[Bartholomew-Ps] <u>Psalms 118:14</u> **Hark! The voice of joy and health echoes through the righteous' dwelling: Providence**, though as by stealth working, is in might excelling!

[Bay-Ps] <u>Psalms 118:14</u> **The Lord my fortitude** & song: & **saving health is he.**

[EEBT] <u>Psalms 118:14</u> **The Lord makes me strong** and gives me psalms to sing. He has saved me.

[ERV] <u>Psalms 118:14</u> **The Lord is my strength** and my reason for singing. He saved me!

[LTPB] <u>Psalms 118:14</u> **The Lord is my strength** and my praise, and has become salvation for me.

[NET] <u>Psalms 118:14</u> **The Lord gives me strength** and protects me; he has become my deliverer."

[T4T] <u>Psalms 118:14</u> **Yahweh is the one who makes me strong**, and he is the one about whom I always sing; he has saved me from my enemies.

[TLB] <u>Psalms 118:14</u> **He is my strength** and song in the heat of battle, and now he has given me the victory.

[TPT] <u>Psalms 118:14</u> **Lord, you are my true strength** and my glory-song, my champion, my Savior!

[TVB] <u>Psalms 118:14</u> **He is my strength**, and He is the reason I sing; He has been there to save me in every situation.

[ULB] <u>Psalms 118:14</u> **Yahweh is my strength** and joy, and he is the one who rescues me.

[Wither-Ps] <u>Psalms 118:14</u> The Lord, my gracious aide became, **My strength, my health**, my joyful song.

<u>Psalms 118:17</u> **I shall not die, but live**, and declare the works of the LORD.

[AMPC] <u>Psalms 118:17</u> **I shall not die but live**, and shall declare the works and recount the illustrious acts of the Lord.

[BBE] <u>Psalms 118:17</u> **Life and not death will be my part**, and I will give out the story of the works of the Lord.

[Beaumont-Ps] <u>Psalms 118:17</u> **I shall not die, I know it well**, But be by grace restored; I shall be spared, that I may tell The mercies of the Lord.

[Boothroyd] <u>Psalms 118:17</u> **I shall not die: I shall surely live**, And shall still rehearse the works of Jehovah.

[CJB] <u>Psalms 118:17</u> **I will not die; no, I will live** and proclaim the great deeds of Yah!

[Cradock-Ps] <u>Psalms 118:17</u> **Fruitless thy insults, death; thy shafts I dare; long shall I live**, and heav'n's high pow'r declare;

[Hawley-Ps] <u>Psalms 118:17</u> **And now I know I shall not die**, But live God's works to show;

[ICB] <u>Psalms 118:17</u> **I will not die, but live**. And I will tell what the Lord has done.

[Ming-Ps] <u>Psalms 118:17</u> **God will not suffer me to fall, but still prolongs my days**; That, by declaring all his works, I may advance his praise.

[NETS-OT] <u>Psalms 118:17</u> **I shall not die, but I shall live** and recount the deeds of the Lord.

[NIRV] <u>Psalms 118:17</u> **I will not die but live**. I will talk about what the Lord has done.

[Norlie-NT] <u>Psalms 118:17</u> **I shall not die, but will survive** to tell of the Lord's doings.

[Sandys-OT] <u>Psalms 118:17</u> **I shall not die, but live to praise** The Lord, who hath prolong'd my Days.

[Sternhold-Ps] <u>Psalms 118:17</u> **I shall not die, but ever live** to utter and declare the mighty power of the Lord, his works, and what they are.

[Street-Ps] <u>Psalms 118:17</u> **That I might not die, but live**, and recount the works of Jehovah.

[TNIV] <u>Psalms 118:17</u> **I will not die but live**, and will proclaim what the LORD has done.

[YLT] <u>Psalms 118:17</u> **I do not die, but live**, And recount the works of Jah,

<u>Psalms 119:17</u> **Deal bountifully with thy servant, that I may live,** and keep thy word.

[Barton-Ps] <u>Psalms 119:17</u> **Deal bounteously in gifts of grace with me thy servant, Lord: that I may live** and run my race, and keep thy holy word.

[CWB] <u>Psalms 119:17</u> **Bless me with life** so I can keep your commandments.

[Ewald-OT] <u>Psalms 119:17</u> **Do well by Thy servant, that I may live** and hold fast Thy word!

[Farr-Ps] <u>Psalms 119:17</u> **Be gracious to thy servant, Lord, Extend to me thy grace That I may live** and keep thy word Throughout my mortal race.

[Moffatt] <u>Psalms 119:17</u> **Deal kindly with thy servant, till I live to do thy bidding.**

[MOTB] <u>Psalms 119:17</u> **Graciously suffer thy servant to live**, and I will keep thy word.

[NCV] <u>Psalms 119:17</u> **Do good to me, your servant, so I can live**, so I can obey your word.

[NJB] <u>Psalms 119:17</u> **Be generous to your servant** and I shall live, and shall keep your words.

[NWT] <u>Psalms 119:17</u> **Deal kindly with your servant, So that I may live** and observe your word.

[REAL] <u>Psalms 119:17</u> **Reward your slave, so I can live** and so I can put a boundary fence around your Word to guard it.

[Rotherham] <u>Psalms 119:17</u> **Bestow thy bounties upon thy servant—let me live**, That I may observe thy word.

[TLB] <u>Psalms 119:17</u> **Bless me with life** so that I can continue to obey you.

[TPT] <u>Psalms 119:17</u> **Let me, your servant, walk in abundance of life** that I may always live to obey your truth.

<u>Psalms 119:40</u> Behold, I have longed after thy precepts: **quicken me in thy righteousness.**

  [BBE] <u>Psalms 119:40</u> See how great is my desire for your orders: **give me life in your righteousness.**

  [Beck] <u>Psalms 119:40</u> I long for Your precepts; **by your righteousness give me life.**

  [Berkeley] <u>Psalms 119:40</u> Truly, I yearn for Thy precepts; **give me life according to Thy righteousness.**

  [Boothroyd] <u>Psalms 119:40</u> Behold! I long after thy precepts: **According to thy righteousness revive me.**

  [GW] <u>Psalms 119:40</u> I long for your guiding principles. **Give me a new life in your righteousness.**

  [KJ3] <u>Psalms 119:40</u> Behold, I have longed for Your precepts; **grant to me life in Your righteousness.**

  [NAB] <u>Psalms 119:40</u> See how I long for your precepts; **in your justice give me life.**

  [SAAS-OT] <u>Psalms 119:40</u> Behold, I long for Your commandments; **Give me life in Your righteousness.**

  [TPT] <u>Psalms 119:40</u> See how I long with cravings for more of your ways? **Let your righteousness revive my spirit!**

<u>Psalms 119:50</u> This is my comfort in my affliction: **for thy word hath quickened me.**

  [Anchor] <u>Psalms 119:50</u> This is my comfort during my affliction, that **your word sustains my life.**

  [Beck] <u>Psalms 119:50</u> This is my comfort in my misery: that **Your word gives me life.**

  [Berkeley] <u>Psalms 119:50</u> This is my comfort in my affliction; **what Thou hast said has brought life to me.**

  [Boothroyd] <u>Psalms 119:50</u> This is my comfort in my affliction, —That **thy word reviveth me.**

  [Buttenwieser-OT] <u>Psalms 119:50</u> It is my comfort in my misery: Verily, **thy promise keeps me alive.**

  [CBC] <u>Psalms 119:50</u> This is my comfort in my affliction: **For thy word hath kept me alive.**

[CEB] <u>Psalms 119:50</u> My comfort during my suffering is this: **your word gives me new life.**

[CJB] <u>Psalms 119:50</u> In my distress my comfort is this: that **your promise gives me life.**

[ICB] <u>Psalms 119:50</u> When I suffer, this comforts me: **Your promise gives me life.**

[ISV] <u>Psalms 119:50</u> This is what comforts me in my troubles: that **what you say revives me.**

[JGC-Ps-Zain] <u>Psalms 119:50</u> My comfort in my grief, **Thy word Gave life to heart and eyes.**

[JPS-Ps 1972] <u>Psalms 119:50</u> This is my comfort in my affliction, that **Your promise has preserved me.**

[JUB] <u>Psalms 119:50</u> This is my comfort in my affliction; for **thy spoken word has caused me to live.**

[Moffatt] <u>Psalms 119:50</u> this comforts me in trouble, **thy promise puts life into me.**

[MSG] <u>Psalms 119:50</u> These words hold me up in bad times; yes, **your promises rejuvenate me.**

[NEB] <u>Psalms 119:50</u> In time of trouble my consolation is this, that **thy promise has given me life.**

[NJB] <u>Psalms 119:50</u> It is my comfort in distress, that **your promise gives me life.**

[Noyes] <u>Psalms 119:50</u> This is my comfort in my affliction; **For thy promise reviveth me.**

[OANT] <u>Psalms 119:50</u> By it I have been comforted in my affliction, **because your word has given me life!**

[T4T] <u>Psalms 119:50</u> When I have been suffering, you comforted me; **you did what you promised me, and that revived me.**

[TPT] <u>Psalms 119:50</u> In all of my affliction I find great comfort in your promises, **for they have kept me alive!**

[UDB] <u>Psalms 119:50</u> When I have been suffering, you comforted me; **you did what you promised me, and that kept me alive.**

[Wither-Ps] <u>Psalms 119:50</u> For, thence in my afflictions I have aide: **it is thy Word that still revive the me.**

<u>Psalms 119:88</u> **Quicken me after thy lovingkindness**; so shall I keep the testimony of thy mouth.

[Barton-Ps] <u>Psalms 119:88</u> **Thy loving kindness let be sent to quicken up many fainting mind:** so shall I keep the testament which thy most holy mouth hath sign'd.

[BBE] <u>Psalms 119:88</u> **Give me life in your mercy**; so that I may be ruled by the unchanging word of your mouth.

[Berkeley] <u>Psalms 119:88</u> **Revive me according to Thy loving-kindness**; then I shall keep the testimony of Thy mouth.

[Buttenwieser-OT] <u>Psalms 119:88</u> **Keep me alive in thy love** That I may keep the law of thy mouth.

[CWB] <u>Psalms 119:88</u> **Spare my life, Lord, because of your enduring love** that I may keep your words.

[ERV] <u>Psalms 119:88</u> **Show me your faithful love and let me live.** I will do whatever you say.

[Ewald-OT] <u>Psalms 119:88</u> **Let me live according to Thy grace,** that I may keep Thy mouth's exhortation!

[HRB] <u>Psalms 119:88</u> **Give me life according to Your mercy,** and I will keep the Testimonies of Your mouth.

[NET] <u>Psalms 119:88</u> **Revive me with your loyal love,** that I might keep the rules you have revealed.

[NJB] <u>Psalms 119:88</u> **True to your faithful love, give me life**, and I shall keep the instructions you have laid down.

[NLT] <u>Psalms 119:88</u> **In your unfailing love, spare my life**; then I can continue to obey your laws.

[TPT] <u>Psalms 119:88</u> **Revive me with your tender love and spare my life by your kindness**, and I will continue to obey you.

[ULB] <u>Psalms 119:88</u> **By your steadfast love, keep me alive**, so that I may obey your commands.

<u>Psalms 119:93</u> I will never forget thy precepts: for with them thou hast quickened me.

[Berkeley] <u>Psalms 119:93</u> I will never forget Thy precepts; with them Thou hast granted me life.

[Boothroyd] <u>Psalms 119:93</u> I will never forget thy precepts; For by them thou revivest me.

[CT-OT] <u>Psalms 119:93</u> I shall never forget Your precepts for through them You have sustained me.

[CWB] <u>Psalms 119:93</u> I will not forget your word because they have given me life.

[ERV] <u>Psalms 119:93</u> I will never forget your commands, because through them you gave me new life.

[Fenton] <u>Psalms 119:93</u> I forgot not Your Precepts, by which I have life.

[GAC-Ps-Sixteenth] <u>Psalms 119:93</u> O that thy statutes every hour, might dwell upon my mind! Thence I derive a quickening power and daily peace I find.

[GNT] <u>Psalms 119:93</u> I will never neglect your instructions, because by them you have kept me alive.

[Grail-Ps] <u>Psalms 119:93</u> I will never forget your precepts, for with them you give me life.

[ICB] <u>Psalms 119:93</u> I will never forget your orders because you have given me life by them.

[Jones-Ps] <u>Psalms 119:93</u> Thy precepts shall within me dwell, With them dost thou restore me;

[JPS-OT 1985] <u>Psalms 119:93</u> I will never neglect Your precepts, for You have preserved my life through them.

[Lamsa] <u>Psalms 119:93</u> I will never forget thy commandments, because they are my very life.

[McFadyen-OT] <u>Psalms 119:93</u> I will never forget Thy precepts, For through them Thou hast put life in me.

[OANT] <u>Psalms 119:93</u> I shall never forget your commandments because my life is in them.

[SG] <u>Psalms 119:93</u> I shall never forget thy precepts; For by them thou didst keep my alive.

[TLB] <u>Psalms 119:93</u> I will never lay aside your laws, for you have used them to restore my joy and health.

[TPT] <u>Psalms 119:93</u> I can never forget the profound revelations you've taught me, for they have kept me alive more than once.

[ULB] <u>Psalms 119:93</u> I will never forget your instructions, for through them you have kept me alive.

[VW] <u>Psalms 119:93</u> I will never forget Your Precepts, for by them You have given me life.

<u>Psalms 119:116</u> **Uphold me according unto thy word, that I may live**: and let me not be ashamed of my hope.

[Boswell-Ps] <u>Psalms 119:116</u> **According to thy faithful word, uphold and stablish me, That I may live**, and of my hope ashamed may not be.

[CWB] <u>Psalms 119:116</u> **Give me physical and moral strength as you promised**. Don't let me be ashamed of the hope I have in your word.

[EEBT] <u>Psalms 119:116</u> **Give me help and life, as your word promises**. And do not make me ashamed, because I hope in you.

[MOTB] <u>Psalms 119:116</u> **Sustain me according to thy promise, that I may live**, and that my hope may not be put to shame.

[NIRV] <u>Psalms 119:116</u> **My God, keep me going as you have promised. Then I will live**. Don't let me lose all hope.

[OANT] <u>Psalms 119:116</u> **Lead me in your word and I shall live** and you will not disappoint me of my hope.

[Thomson] <u>Psalms 119:116</u> **Uphold me according to thy word and keep me alive**; and let me not be shamed for mine expectation.

[TLB] <u>Psalms 119:116</u> **Lord, you promised to let me live!** Never let it be said that God failed me.

[TNIV] <u>Psalms 119:116</u> Sustain me according to your promise, and I will live; do not let my hopes be dashed.

[TPT] <u>Psalms 119:116</u> **Lord, strengthen my inner being by the promises of your word so that I may live faithful** and unashamed for you.

<u>Psalms 119:144</u> The righteousness of thy testimonies is everlasting: **give me understanding, and I shall live**.

[Alexander-OT] <u>Psalms 119:144</u> Right (are) thy testimonies to eternity; **make me understand, and I shall live**.

[AMP] <u>Psalms 119:144</u> Your righteous testimonies are everlasting; **Give me understanding [the ability to learn and a teachable heart] that I may live.**

[Beck] <u>Psalms 119:144</u> The truths You wrote are always right, **make me understand them that I might live.**

[Boothroyd] <u>Psalms 119:144</u> Righteous are thy testimonies for ever: **Instruct me by them, that I may live.**

[CEB] <u>Psalms 119:144</u> Your laws are righteous forever. **Help me understand so I can live!**

[CEV] <u>Psalms 119:144</u> Your rules are always fair. **Help me to understand them and live.**

[CWB] <u>Psalms 119:144</u> Your law is always right. **Give me understanding so I may live.**

[Fenton] <u>Psalms 119:144</u> Your Proofs are right for ever, **they give sense and life.**

[FHV-NT] <u>Psalms 119:144</u> Your testimonies are always righteous. **Give me understanding that I may live.**

[Goode-Ps] <u>Psalms 119:144</u> Thy promises, O Lord, Both grace and glory give. **Grant me the knowledge of Thy Word, And I shall live.**

[MSG] <u>Psalms 119:144</u> The way you tell me to live is always right; **help me understand it so I can live to the fullest.**

[NIRV] <u>Psalms 119:144</u> Your covenant laws are always right. **Help me to understand them. Then I will live.**

[Smyth-Ps] <u>Psalms 119:144</u> Thy justice still endures; O **make Me wise, and I shall live.**

[TPT] <u>Psalms 119:144</u> **Give me more revelation so that I can live for you**, for nothing is more pure and eternal than your truth.

<u>Psalms 119:154</u> Plead my cause, and deliver me: **quicken me according to thy word.**

[AMP] <u>Psalms 119:154</u> Plead my cause and redeem me; **Revive me and give me life according to [the promise of] Your word.**

[Berkeley] <u>Psalms 119:154</u> Plead my cause and redeem me; **revive me according to Thy word.**

[CEB] <u>Psalms 119:154</u> Argue my case and redeem me. **Make me live again by your word.**

[EEBT] <u>Psalms 119:154</u> Fight my fight for me and redeem me. Keep me alive as your sayings promise me.

[NEB] <u>Psalms 119:154</u> Be thou my advocate and win release for me; **true to thy promise, give me life.**

[NIRV] <u>Psalms 119:154</u> Stand up for me and set me free. **Keep me alive as you have promised.**

[NLV] <u>Psalms 119:154</u> Stand by me and set me free. **Give me life again because of Your Word.**

[SAAS-OT] <u>Psalms 119:154</u> Plead my cause and redeem me; **Give me life because of Your word.**

[T4T] <u>Psalms 119:154</u> Defend me when others accuse me and rescue me from them; **allow me to continue to live, as you promised/said that you would.**

[TLB] <u>Psalms 119:154</u> Yes, rescue me and **give me back my life again just as you have promised.**

[TLV] <u>Psalms 119:154</u> Defend my cause and redeem me. **Restore my life through Your word.**

[TNIV] <u>Psalms 119:154</u> Defend my cause and redeem me; **preserve my life according to your promise.**

<u>Psalms 119:156</u> Great are thy tender mercies, O Lᴏʀᴅ: **quicken me according to thy judgments.**

[Berkeley] <u>Psalms 119:156</u> Great is Thy compassion, O Lord; **revive me according to Thy ordinances.**

[Besorah] <u>Psalms 119:156</u> Your compassions are many, O HWHY; **Revive me according to Your right-rulings.**

[CCB] <u>Psalms 119:156</u> Great is your compassion, O Lord; **renew my life according to your word.**

[CT-OT] <u>Psalms 119:156</u> Your mercies, O Lord, are abundant; **according to Your custom, sustain me.**

[De Witt-Ps] <u>Psalms 119:156</u> Thy compassions are many, Jehovah, **Give me new life, as Thou hast ordained.**

[GNT] <u>Psalms 119:156</u> But your compassion, Lord, is great; **show your mercy and save me!**

[NIRV] <u>Psalms 119:156</u> Lord, you have deep concern for me. **Keep me alive as you have promised.**

[NIVUK] <u>Psalms 119:156</u> Your compassion, Lord, is great; **preserve my life according to your laws.**

[NOG] <u>Psalms 119:156</u> Your acts of compassion are many in number, **O Yahweh. Give me a new life guided by your regulations.**

[Parkhurst-Ps] <u>Psalms 119:156</u> Thy compassion is great: **according to thy custom strengthen me, O Jehovah.**

[RSV] <u>Psalms 119:156</u> Great is thy mercy, O Lord; **give me life according to thy justice.**

<u>Psalms 119:159</u> Consider how I love thy precepts: **quicken me, O Lᴏʀᴅ, according to thy lovingkindness.**

[Berkeley] <u>Psalms 119:159</u> See how I love Thy precepts; **revive me, O Lord, according to Thy loving-kindness.**

[CAB] <u>Psalms 119:159</u> Behold, I have loved Your commandments, **O Lord; revive me in Your mercy.**

[CBC] <u>Psalms 119:159</u> Consider how I love Thy precepts: **Keep me alive, O Lord, according to Thy lovingkindness.**

[De Witt-Ps] <u>Psalms 119:159</u> Behold how I love Thy commandments, O Jehovah, **in Thy kindness give me life**.

[LTPB] <u>Psalms 119:159</u> See, Lord, because I loved Your precepts! **Revive me in Your mercy!**

[MEMS-Ps] <u>Psalms 119:159</u> Yet, while they slight, consider, Lord, How I Thy precepts love; **O! therefore, quicken me with beams Of mercy from above.**

[NIRV] <u>Psalms 119:159</u> See how I love your rules! Lord, **keep me alive, because you love me.**

[NLT] <u>Psalms 119:159</u> See how I love your commandments, Lord. **Give back my life because of your unfailing love.**

[OANT] <u>Psalms 119:159</u> See that I have loved your commandments, Lord Jehovah, and **give me life in your kindness**.

[UKLV] <u>Psalms 119:159</u> Consider how I love your precepts: **restore life in me, O Lord, according to your loving kindness.**

<u>Psalms 138:7</u> **Though I walk in the midst of trouble, thou wilt revive me**: thou shalt stretch forth thine hand against the wrath of mine enemies, and thy right hand shall save me.

[Anchor] <u>Psalms 138:7</u> **When I march amid my adversaries, keep me alive before the fury of my foes.** Stretch forth your left hand, and give me victory with your right hand.

[Beck] <u>Psalms 138:7</u> **Even though I live in the middle of trouble, You keep me alive.** You stretch out Your hand against my angry enemies, and Your right hand saves me.

[Berkeley] <u>Psalms 138:7</u> **When I walk through the midst of trouble, Thou bringest me through alive**; against the wrath of my foes, Thou doest stretch forth Thy hand, and Thy right hand saves me.

[Burgess-Ps] <u>Psalms 138:7</u> **Though I must walk mid thronging woes, Thy love shall give me life**: Thy strong right hand shall crush my foes, and end their stormy strife.

[CCB] <u>Psalms 138:7</u> **If I walk in the midst of trouble, you give me life.** With outstretched arm, you save me from the wrath of my foes, with your right hand you deliver me.

[CEB] <u>Psalms 138:7</u> **Whenever I am in deep trouble, you make me live again;** you send your power against my enemies' wrath; you save me with your strong hand.

[Cotton-Ps] <u>Psalms 138:7</u> **Although my walk be lying in the midst of much distress, yet thou with sweet revivals wilt enable me to live:** Thou'lt use thy hand against the rage of my fierce enemies; and thy Right hand shall unto me give a deliverance.

[CSB] <u>Psalms 138:7</u> **If I walk into the thick of danger, you will preserve my life from the anger of my enemies.** You will extend your hand; your right hand will save me.

[CWB] <u>Psalms 138:7</u> **When I'm in trouble, He is there to save my life.** He takes a stand against my enemies and with His right hand He delivers me.

[FHV-NT] <u>Psalms 138:7</u> **Though I walk close to trouble, you will keep me alive.** Against the wrath of my enemies you will extend your hand, and your right hand will deliver me.

[GNT] <u>Psalms 138:7</u> **When I am surrounded by troubles, you keep me safe.** You oppose my angry enemies and save me by your power.

[GW] <u>Psalms 138:7</u> **Even though I walk into the middle of trouble, you guard my life against the anger of my enemies.** You stretch out your hand, and your right hand saves me.

[HRB] <u>Psalms 138:7</u> If I walk in the midst of distress, You give me life; You send out Your hand against the wrath of my enemies, and Your right hand delivers me.

[ICB] <u>Psalms 138:7</u> Lord, even when I have trouble all around me, you will keep me alive. When my enemies are angry, you will reach down and save me by your power.

[MEMS-Ps] <u>Psalms 138:7</u> Though I with troubles am oppressed, He shall my foes disarm, relieve my soul when most distressed, and keep me safe from harm.

[MSTC] <u>Psalms 138:7</u> Though I walk in the midst of trouble, yet shalt thou refresh me; thou shalt stretch forth thine hand upon the furiousness of mine enemies, and thy righthand shall save me.

[NAB] <u>Psalms 138:7</u> Though I walk in the midst of dangers, you guard my life when my enemies rage. You stretch out your hand; your right hand saves me.

[NLV] <u>Psalms 138:7</u> Even if I walk into trouble, You will keep my life safe. You will put out Your hand against the anger of those who hate me. And Your right hand will save me.

[Priest-Ps] <u>Psalms 138:7</u> Though I walk in the midst of trouble, yet shalt Thou refresh me: Thou shalt stretch forth Thy hand upon the furiousness of mine enemies, and Thy right hand shall save me.

[Sidney-Ps] <u>Psalms 138:7</u> On ev'ry side, though tribulations grieve me, Yet shalt thou aid, yet shalt thou still relieve me. From angry foe thy succor shall me save. Thou Lord shalt finish what in hand I have.

[UDB] <u>Psalms 138:7</u> When I am in the middle of many troubles, you save me. With your hand you rescue me from my enemies who are angry at me.

<u>Psalms 143:11</u> **Quicken me, O Lord, for thy name's sake**: for thy righteousness' sake bring my soul out of trouble.

[AMP] <u>Psalms 143:11</u> Save my life, O Lord, for Your name's sake; In Your righteousness bring my life out of trouble.

[Berkeley] <u>Psalms 143:11</u> For the glory of Thy name, O Lord, preserve my life; in Thy righteousness remove my soul from distress.

[De Witt-Ps] <u>Psalms 143:11</u> For Thy Name's sake, Jehovah, let me live; In Thy justice deliver my soul from sore pressure;

[ERV] <u>Psalms 143:11</u> Lord, let me live so that people will praise your name. Show me how good you are and save me from my trouble.

[ISV] <u>Psalms 143:11</u> For the sake of your name, Lord, preserve my life. Because you are righteous, bring me out of trouble.

[NLT] <u>Psalms 143:11</u> For the glory of your name, O Lord, preserve my life. Because of your faithfulness, bring me out of this distress.

[REB] <u>Psalms 143:11</u> Revive me, Lord, for the honour of your name; be my deliverer; release me from distress.

[RNV] <u>Psalms 143:11</u> Restore my life, Yahuwah, for Your name's sake! For Your righteousness' sake bring my soul out of trouble.

[TLB] <u>Psalms 143:11</u> Lord, saving me will bring glory to your name. Bring me out of all this trouble because you are true to your promises.

[UDB] <u>Psalms 143:11</u> Yahweh, restore me when I am close to dying as you promised to do because you are righteous!

[UKJV] <u>Psalms 143:11</u> **Restore life in me, O Lᴏʀᴅ, for your name's sake**: for your righteousness' sake bring my soul out of trouble.

<u>Psalms 146:8</u> **The Lᴏʀᴅ openeth the eyes of the blind: the Lᴏʀᴅ raiseth them that are bowed down**: the Lᴏʀᴅ loveth the righteous:

[Allen-Ps-Third] <u>Psalms 146:8</u> **The film from darkened eye The Lord doth well remove: To humbled souls his grace is nigh**, The righteous He doth love.

[AMP] <u>Psalms 146:8</u> **The Lord opens the eyes of the blind; The Lord lifts up those who are bowed down**; The Lord loves the righteous [the upright in heart].

[Burgess-Ps] <u>Psalms 146:8</u> **The Lord unseals the sightless eyes**, and gives the weary strength to rise:

[BWilliams-Ps] <u>Psalms 146:8</u> **The Lord hath eyes to give the blind; the Lord supports the sinking mind**; He helps the stranger in distress, the widow and the fatherless.

[CEB] <u>Psalms 146:8</u> **The Lord: who makes the blind see. The Lord: who straightens up those who are bent low**. The Lord: who loves the righteous.

[Cottle-Ps] <u>Psalms 146:8</u> **The Lord from realms of light above, shall ope the blind-man's eye**; the Lord, the righteous man will love, and all his wants supply.

[CSB] <u>Psalms 146:8</u> **The Lord opens the eyes of the blind. The Lord raises up those who are oppressed**. The Lord loves the righteous.

[CT-OT] <u>Psalms 146:8</u> **The Lord gives sight to the blind; the Lord straightens the bent**; the Lord loves the righteous.

[ERV] <u>Psalms 146:8</u> **The Lord makes the blind see again. The Lord helps those who are in trouble**. The Lord loves those who do right.

[FAA] <u>Psalms 146:8</u> **The Lord who opens the eyes of the blind, The Lord who straightens up those bent double**, The Lord who loves the righteous.

[Fenton] <u>Psalms 146:8</u> **The Lord gives the blind renewed sight, The Lord helps the lame**; The Lord loves the good;

[GNT] <u>Psalms 146:8</u> and **gives sight to the blind. He lifts those who have fallen**; he loves his righteous people.

[GW] <u>Psalms 146:8</u> **The Lord gives sight to blind people. The Lord straightens the backs of those who are bent over.** The Lord loves righteous people.

[ICB] <u>Psalms 146:8</u> **The Lord gives sight to the blind. The Lord lifts up people who are in trouble.** The Lord loves those who do right.

[ISV] <u>Psalms 146:8</u> the **Lord gives sight to the blind. The Lord lifts up those who are weighed down.** The Lord loves the righteous.

[JPS-OT 1985] <u>Psalms 146:8</u> **The Lᴏʀᴅ restores sight to the blind; the Lᴏʀᴅ makes those who are bent stand straight**; the Lᴏʀᴅ loves the righteous;

[Muhlenberg-Ps] <u>Psalms 146:8</u> **The Lord gives eye-sight to the blind; the Lord supports the fainting mind**, and whispers to the mourner peace;

[NEB] <u>Psalms 146:8</u> **The Lᴏʀᴅ restores sight to the blind and straightens backs which are bent**; the Lᴏʀᴅ loves the righteous

[Smyth-Ps] <u>Psalms 146:8</u> **He to the eyes in darkness sealed, Restores the cheerful light: Lifts up the bowed down**, and loves All those whose hearts are right.

[Thomson] <u>Psalms 146:8</u> **The Lord looseth them who were bound. The Lord causeth the blind to see clearly. The Lord raiseth up them who were broken down**. The Lord loveth the righteous.

[TNIV] <u>Psalms 146:8</u> **the LORD gives sight to the blind, the LORD lifts up those who are bowed down**, the LORD loves the righteous.

[TPT] <u>Psalms 146:8</u> **You open the eyes of the blind and you fully restore those bent over with shame**. You love those who love and honor you.

[TVB] <u>Psalms 146:8</u> **He makes the blind see. He lifts up those whose backs are bent in labor**; He cherishes those who do what is right.

[UDB] <u>Psalms 146:8</u> **Yahweh enables those who are blind to see again. He lifts up those who have fallen down**. He loves the righteous people.

[Woodd-Ps] <u>Psalms 146:8</u> **By Him the blind receive their sight, the weak and fall'n He rears**; with kind regard and tender love He for the righteous cares.

<u>Psalms 147:3</u> He healeth[raphah] the broken in heart, and bindeth up their wounds.

[BLE] <u>Psalms 147:3</u> He who heals men broken at the heart and bandages their aches,

[CEV] <u>Psalms 147:3</u> He renews our hopes and heals our bodies.

[CWB] <u>Psalms 147:3</u> He heals the brokenhearted and binds up the wounds of those who are hurt.

[Fenton] <u>Psalms 147:3</u> Heal the broken in heart, And set their broken bones.

[Hawkins-Ps] <u>Psalms 147:3</u> He healeth those that are broken in heart: and giveth medicine to heal their sickness.

[HBIV] <u>Psalms 147:3</u> The physician for the broken in heart; And he binds up their pains.

[Kent-OT] <u>Psalms 147:3</u> He healeth the broken-hearted, And bindeth up their painful wounds.

[MP1650] <u>Psalms 147:3</u> Those that are broken in their heart, and grieved in their minds, He healeth, and their painful wounds he tenderly up-binds.

[NLV] <u>Psalms 147:3</u> He heals those who have a broken heart. He heals their sorrows.

[Rusling-Ps] <u>Psalms 147:3</u> The broken hearts are kindly bound; He healeth every open wound.

[Sidney-Ps] <u>Psalms 147:3</u> And now by him their broken hearts made sound, And now by him their bleeding wounds are bound.

[T4T] <u>Psalms 147:3</u> He enables those who were very discouraged to be encouraged again; it is as though they have wounds and he bandages them.

[TPT] <u>Psalms 147:3</u> He heals the wounds of every shattered heart.

[YLT] <u>Psalms 147:3</u> Who is giving healing to the broken of heart, And is binding up their griefs.

PROVERBS

<u>Proverbs 3:8</u> It shall be health to thy navel, and marrow to thy bones.

[ABU-Proverbs] <u>Proverbs 3:8</u> It shall be health to thy sinews, and moisture to thy bones.

[AMP] <u>Proverbs 3:8</u> It will be health to your body [your marrow, your nerves, your sinews, your muscles— all your inner parts] And refreshment (physical well-being) to your bones.

[AMPC] <u>Proverbs 3:8</u> It shall be health to your nerves and sinews, and marrow and moistening to your bones.

[BBE] <u>Proverbs 3:8</u> This will give strength to your flesh, and new life to your bones.

[Beck] <u>Proverbs 3:8</u> Then your body will be healthy, and your bones will be refreshed.

[Berkeley] <u>Proverbs 3:8</u> it will be healing to your body and nourishment to your bones.

[BLE] <u>Proverbs 3:8</u> It will be medicine for your navel and juice for your bones.

[CSB] <u>Proverbs 3:8</u> This will be healing for your body and strengthening for your bones.

[FHV-NT] <u>Proverbs 3:8</u> It will be healing for your muscles and refreshment for your bones.

[GNT] <u>Proverbs 3:8</u> If you do, it will be like good medicine, healing your wounds and easing your pains.

[JUB] <u>Proverbs 3:8</u> It shall be medicine to thy navel and marrow to thy bones.

[Knox] <u>Proverbs 3:8</u> here is health for the midmost of thy being, here is sap for the marrow of thy bones.

[Miller-Pr] <u>Proverbs 3:8</u> Let there be healing to thy muscles, and moisture to thy bones.

[Moffatt] <u>Proverbs 3:8</u> that will mean health for your body and fresh life to your frame.

[MSG] <u>Proverbs 3:8</u> Your body will glow with health, your very bones will vibrate with life!

[NCV] <u>Proverbs 3:8</u> Then your body will be healthy, and your bones will be strong.

[NEB] <u>Proverbs 3:8</u> Let that be the medicine to keep you in health, the liniment for your limbs.

[NETS-OT] <u>Proverbs 3:8</u> Then it will be a healing to your body and treatment for your bones.

[NLV] <u>Proverbs 3:8</u> It will be healing to your body and medicine to your bones.

[Noyes] <u>Proverbs 3:8</u> It shall be health to thy muscles, And moisture to thy bones.

[Orton-OT] <u>Proverbs 3:8</u> It shall be health to thy navel, or to thy flesh, and marrow to thy bones; it is the way to obtain health of body and cheerfulness of mind.

[T4T] <u>Proverbs 3:8</u> If you do that, your body will be healthy/strong; it will be like medicine for you.

[Thomson] <u>Proverbs 3:8</u> then shall thy body have health and thy bones a cure.

[TVB] <u>Proverbs 3:8</u> If you depend on Him, your body and mind will be free from the strain of a sinful life, will experience healing and health, and will be strengthened at their core.

<u>Proverbs 3:18</u> **She is a tree of life to them that lay hold upon her**: and happy is every one that retaineth her.

[AMP] <u>Proverbs 3:18</u> **She is a tree of life to those who take hold of her**, And happy [blessed, considered fortunate, to be admired] is everyone who holds her tightly.

[ERV] <u>Proverbs 3:18</u> **Wisdom is like a life-giving tree to those who hold on to her**; she is a blessing to those who keep her close.

[EXB] <u>Proverbs 3:18</u> **As a tree produces fruit, wisdom gives life to those who use it**, and everyone who uses it will be happy.

[FAA] <u>Proverbs 3:18</u> **It is a tree of life to those who take hold of it**, And those who obtain it are content.

[ICB] <u>Proverbs 3:18</u> **As a tree makes fruit, wisdom gives life to those who use it**. Everyone who uses wisdom will be happy.

[UDB] <u>Proverbs 3:18</u> **Wisdom is like a tree whose fruit gives life to those who hold on to it**, and Yahweh gives happiness to those who hold on to it.

<u>Proverbs 4:4</u> He taught me also, and said unto me, Let thine heart retain my words: **keep my commandments, and live**.

[CEB] <u>Proverbs 4:4</u> he taught me and said to me: "Let your heart hold on to my words: **Keep my commands and live."**

[ERV] <u>Proverbs 4:4</u> my father taught me this: "Pay attention to what I say. **Obey my commands and you will have a good life."**

[NCV] <u>Proverbs 4:4</u> my father taught me and said, "Hold on to my words with all your heart. **Keep my commands and you will live."**

[NIVUK] <u>Proverbs 4:4</u> Then he taught me, and he said to me, 'Take hold of my words with all your heart; **keep my commands, and you will live**.

[NJB] <u>Proverbs 4:4</u> This was what he used to teach me, 'Let your heart treasure what I have to say, keep my principles and you will live;

[REAL] <u>Proverbs 4:4</u> Also, he taught me, and he told me, "Your heart must retain my words. **Put a boundary fence around my commands to guard them, and live**.

[T4T] <u>Proverbs 4:4</u> my father told me, "Keep my words in your inner being; if you **obey my commandments, you will live a long time**.

[UDB] <u>Proverbs 4:4</u> my father told me, "Put my words deep within you, **obey my orders to you, and you will have life**.

<u>Proverbs 4:13</u> Take fast hold of instruction; let her not go: keep her; for she is thy life.

[AMP] <u>Proverbs 4:13</u> Take hold of instruction; [actively seek it, grip it firmly and] do not let go. Guard her, for she is your life.

[AMPC] <u>Proverbs 4:13</u> Take firm hold of instruction, do not let go; guard her, for she is your life.

[Boothroyd] <u>Proverbs 4:13</u> Firmly retain instruction; let her not go; Preserve her; for she is thy life.

[CWB] <u>Proverbs 4:13</u> So hold on to what I'm telling you. Don't let go. Grasp wisdom and understanding because they are your life.

[EEBT] <u>Proverbs 4:13</u> Always remember what you have learnt. Do not forget it. The things that you have learnt will give you life. So keep them well.

[EXB] <u>Proverbs 4:13</u> ·Always remember what you have been taught [Be determined/resolute in our instruction], and don't ·let go of it [slack off]. ·Keep all that you have learned [Protect it]; it is ·the most important thing in [your] life.

[FHV-NT] <u>Proverbs 4:13</u> Take hold of instruction. Do not let it slip away. Guard it, for it is your life.

[ICB] <u>Proverbs 4:13</u> Always remember what you have been taught. Don't let go of it. Keep safe all that you have learned. It is the most important thing in your life.

[McFadyen-OT] <u>Proverbs 4:13</u> Keep unceasing hold of instruction; Guard her, for she is thy life.

[NET] <u>Proverbs 4:13</u> Hold on to instruction, do not let it go; protect it, because it is your life.

[T4T] <u>Proverbs 4:13</u> Hold fast to the things I have taught you to do and do not let them go. Guard them, because they will be the source of a good life.

[TPT] <u>Proverbs 4:13</u> So receive my correction no matter how hard it is to swallow, for wisdom will snap you back into place—her words will be invigorating life to you.

<u>Proverbs 4:20-22</u> My son, attend to my words; incline thine ear unto my sayings. [21]Let them not depart from thine eyes; keep them in the midst of thine heart. **[22]For they are life unto those that find them, and health to all their flesh.**

The word "health" in verse 22 comes from the same word as raphah—the covenant name of the Lord as our healer. The definition from the Strong's says that it comes from two words— "incurable" plus health from the word "raphah". In other words, we have an incurable health disease that no amount of sickness can "cure"!

[BBE] <u>Proverbs 4:20-22</u> My son, give attention to my words; let your ear be turned to my sayings. [21]Let them not go from your eyes; keep them deep in your heart. **[22]For they are life to him who gets them, and strength to all his flesh.**

[Besorah] <u>Proverbs 4:20-22</u> My son, listen to my words; Incline your ear to my sayings. [21]Let them not depart from your eyes; Guard them in the midst of your heart; **[22]For they are life to those who find them, And healing to all their flesh.**

[BLE] <u>Proverbs 4:20-22</u> My son, listen to my words; bend your ear to my sayings; [21]Do not let them get away from your eyes; guard them in the core of your heart, **[22]Because they are life for him who finds them and soundness for all his flesh.**

[CEB] <u>Proverbs 4:20-22</u> My son, pay attention to my words. Bend your ear to my speech. [21]Don't let them slip from your sight. Guard them in your mind. **[22]They are life to those who find them, and healing for their entire body.**

[CLV] <u>Proverbs 4:20-22</u> My son, do attend to my words; To my sayings stretch out your ear; [21]Let them not steal away from before your eyes; Keep them in the midst of your heart; **[22]For they are life to those finding them, And to one's entire flesh, they are health.**

[CWB] <u>Proverbs 4:20-22</u> My son, listen to what I'm telling you; open your ears to what I have to say. [21]Don't let wisdom out of your sight; keep understanding close to your heart. **[22]They are life to those who find them; they bring health to a man's body.**

[EEBT] <u>Proverbs 4:20-22</u> Listen to what I say, my son. Listen to my words. [21]Never let my words leave you. Think about them and obey them. **[22]They will give life to anyone who understands them. And they will give health to their whole body.**

[ERV] <u>Proverbs 4:20-22</u> My son, pay attention to what I say. Listen closely to my words. [21]Don't let them out of your sight. Never stop thinking about them. **[22]These words are the secret of life and health to all who discover them.**

[HRB] <u>Proverbs 4:20-22</u> My son, pay attention to my words; stretch your ear to what I say; [21]let them not depart from your eyes; keep them in the center of your heart; **[22]for they are life to those who find them, and healing to all his flesh.**

[ICB] <u>Proverbs 4:20-22</u> My child, pay attention to my words. Listen closely to what I say. [21]Don't ever forget my words. Keep them deep within your heart. **[22]These words are the secret to life for those who find them. They bring health to the whole body.**

[Jerusalem] <u>Proverbs 4:20-22</u> My son, pay attention to my words, listen carefully to the words I say; [21]do not let them out of your sight, keep them deep in your heart. **[22]They are life to those who grasp them, health for the entire body.**

[JPS-OT 1985] <u>Proverbs 4:20-22</u> My son, listen to my speech; Incline your ear to my words. [21]Do not lose sight of them; Keep them in your mind. [22]**They are life to him who finds them, Healing for his whole body.**

[Knox] <u>Proverbs 4:20-22</u> Hear then and heed, my son, these words of warning; [21]never lose sight of them, cherish them in thy inmost heart; [22]**let a man master them, they will bring life and healing to his whole being.**

[MSG] <u>Proverbs 4:20-22</u> Dear friend, listen well to my words; tune your ears to my voice. [21]Keep my message in plain view at all times. Concentrate! Learn it by heart! [22]**Those who discover these words live, really live; body and soul, they're bursting with health.**

[NABRE] <u>Proverbs 4:20-22</u> My son, to my words be attentive, to my sayings incline your ear; [21]Let them not slip from your sight, keep them within your heart; [22]**For they are life to those who find them, bringing health to one's whole being.**

[NCV] <u>Proverbs 4:20-22</u> My child, pay attention to my words; listen closely to what I say. [21]Don't ever forget my words; keep them always in mind. [22]**They are the key to life for those who find them; they bring health to the whole body.**

[NET] <u>Proverbs 4:20-22</u> My child, pay attention to my words; listen attentively to my sayings. [21]Do not let them depart from your sight, guard them within your heart; [22]**for they are life to those who find them and healing to one's entire body.**

[NOG] <u>Proverbs 4:20-22</u> My son, pay attention to my words. Open your ears to what I say. [21]Do not lose sight of these things. Keep them deep within your heart [22]**because they are life to those who find them and they heal the whole body.**

[OANT] <u>Proverbs 4:20-22</u> My son, give ear to my words and incline your ear to my speech. [21]Do not let them depart before your eyes but keep them within your heart. [22]**Because he who finds them has life, and all healing in his flesh.**

[T4T] <u>Proverbs 4:20-22</u> My son, pay attention to what I am saying. Listen to my words carefully. [21]Keep them close to you; let them penetrate your inner being, [22]**because you will have a good life and good health if you search for them and find them.**

[TLB] <u>Proverbs 4:20-22</u> Listen, son of mine, to what I say, Listen carefully. [21]Keep these thoughts ever in mind; let them penetrate deep within your heart, [22]**For they will mean real life for you, and radiant health.**

[TPT] <u>Proverbs 4:20-22</u> Listen carefully, my dear child, to everything that I teach you, and pay attention to all that I have to say. [21]Fill your thoughts with my words until they penetrate deep into your spirit. [22]**Then, as you unwrap my words, they will impart true life and radiant health into the very core of your being.**

[WSP-OT] <u>Proverbs 4:20-22</u> My son, attend to my words; Incline thine ear to my sayings; [21]Let them not depart from thine eyes; Keep them within thy heart; [22]**For they are life to those who find them, And healing medicine to all their flesh.**

<u>Proverbs 7:2</u> Keep my commandments, and live; and my law as the apple of thine eye.

[CCB] <u>Proverbs 7:2</u> Hold fast to my instruction and you will have life; treasure my teachings as the apple of your eye.

[CEV] <u>Proverbs 7:2</u> Obey me, and you will live! Let my instructions be your greatest treasure.

[CSB] <u>Proverbs 7:2</u> Keep my commands and live, and guard my instructions as you would the pupil of your eye.

[CWB] <u>Proverbs 7:2</u> Practice what I've told you and live. Protect and value my teachings as you would your own eyes.

[ERV] <u>Proverbs 7:2</u> Consider my teaching as precious as your own eyes. Obey my commands, and you will have a good life.

[ICB] <u>Proverbs 7:2</u> Obey my commands, and you will live. Protect my teachings as you would your own eyes.

[NET] <u>Proverbs 7:2</u> Keep my commands so that you may live, and obey my instruction as your most prized possession.

[T4T] <u>Proverbs 7:2</u> Obey my commands, and as a result you will live a good life. Consider the things that I teach you to be very precious to you; guard them, just like you protect your eyes.

[UDB] <u>Proverbs 7:2</u> If you obey my commands, you will live. Consider my commands to be the most precious thing you possess, and obey them.

<u>Proverbs 12:18</u> There is that speaketh like the piercings of a sword: **but the tongue of the wise is health.**

[Beck] <u>Proverbs 12:18</u> A man's careless talk stabs like a sword, but **what a wise man says heals.**

[Berkeley] <u>Proverbs 12:18</u> Some speak rashly like the piercing of a sword, **but the tongue of the wise heals.**

[CCB] <u>Proverbs 12:18</u> The one who speaks thoughtlessly pierces like a sword; **but the words of the wise bring healing.**

[CEB] <u>Proverbs 12:18</u> Some chatter on like a stabbing sword, **but a wise tongue heals.**

[CEV] <u>Proverbs 12:18</u> Sharp words cut like a sword, **but words of wisdom heal.**

[EEBT] <u>Proverbs 12:18</u> Careless words can cut like a sharp knife. **But to speak wise words can make people well.**

[ESV] <u>Proverbs 12:18</u> There is one whose rash words are like sword thrusts, **but the tongue of the wise brings healing.**

[FAA] <u>Proverbs 12:18</u> There is one who speaks recklessly like the piercings of a sword, **But the tongue of the wise brings healing.**

[FrenchSkinner-OT] <u>Proverbs 12:18</u> There is, who speaketh rashly, like the piercing of a sword; **But the tongue of the wise healeth.**

[ICB] <u>Proverbs 12:18</u> Careless words stab like a sword. **But wise words bring healing.**

[JUB] <u>Proverbs 12:18</u> There are those that speak like the piercings of a sword, **but the tongue of the wise is medicine.**

[Moffatt] <u>Proverbs 12:18</u> A reckless tongue wounds like a sword, **but there is healing power in thoughtful words.**

[NCV] <u>Proverbs 12:18</u> Careless words stab like a sword, **but wise words bring healing.**

[NKJV] <u>Proverbs 12:18</u> There is one who speaks like the piercings of a sword, **But the tongue of the wise promotes health.**

[T4T] <u>Proverbs 12:18</u> What some people say hurts people badly, as much as a sword can; **but what wise people say heals others' souls/comforts others.**

[Thomson] <u>Proverbs 12:18</u> They who wound with their speeches are swords: **but the tongues of the wise are healing**.

[TLB] <u>Proverbs 12:18</u> Some people like to make cutting remarks, **but the words of the wise soothe and heal.**

[TPT] <u>Proverbs 12:18</u> Reckless words are like the thrusts of a sword, cutting remarks meant to stab and to hurt. But the **words of the wise soothe and heal.**

[WSP-OT] <u>Proverbs 12:18</u> There is who rashly uttereth as the piercings of a sword; But the **tongue of the wise is healing medicine.**

<u>Proverbs 13:17</u> A wicked messenger falleth into mischief: but **a faithful ambassador is health**.

[Berkeley] <u>Proverbs 13:17</u> An unreliable messenger precipitates trouble, but **a faithful envoy brings healing.**

[CE] <u>Proverbs 13:17</u> A wicked messenger brings on disaster, but **a trustworthy envoy is a healing remedy.**

[CWB] <u>Proverbs 13:17</u> An unreliable messenger brings nothing but trouble, but **a trustworthy messenger brings healing.**

[NIRV] <u>Proverbs 13:17</u> An evil messenger gets into trouble. But **a trusted messenger brings healing**.

[TPT] <u>Proverbs 13:17</u> An undependable messenger causes a lot of trouble, but the trustworthy and **wise messengers release healing wherever they go.**

[WSP-OT] <u>Proverbs 13:17</u> A wicked messenger causeth men to fall into evil; But **a faithful ambassador is a healing medicine.**

<u>Proverbs 14:30</u> **A sound heart is the life of the flesh**: but envy the rottenness of the bones.

[AMP] <u>Proverbs 14:30</u> **A calm and peaceful and tranquil heart is life and health to the body**, But passion and envy are like rottenness to the bones.

[CLV] <u>Proverbs 14:30</u> **A healing heart is life to the flesh**, Yet jealousy is rottenness to the bones.

[Elzas-OT] <u>Proverbs 14:30</u> **A contented heart giveth soundness to the flesh;** But envy is rottenness to the bones.

[Fenton] <u>Proverbs 14:30</u> **A contented heart strengthens the frame**, But envy is a rot in the bones!

[Hall] <u>Proverbs 14:30</u> **A heart, that is clearly free from envy and all vicious affections, is a comfortable preserver of the body**; but envy the rottenness of the bones.

[Harkavy-OT] <u>Proverbs 14:30</u> **A soft heart is the life of the flesh:** but envy is the rottenness of the bones.

[HRV] <u>Proverbs 14:30</u> **A tranquil heart is the life of the flesh**: but envy is the rottenness of the bones.

[Moffatt] <u>Proverbs 14:30</u> **A mind at ease is life and health**, but passion makes man rot away.

[NHEB] <u>Proverbs 14:30</u> **The life of the body is a heart at peace**, but envy rots the bones.

[NIRV] <u>Proverbs 14:30</u> **A peaceful heart gives life to the body**. But jealousy rots the bones.

[NJB] <u>Proverbs 14:30</u> **The life of the body is a tranquil heart**, but envy is a cancer in the bones.

[NLT] <u>Proverbs 14:30</u> **A peaceful heart leads to a healthy body**; jealousy is like cancer in the bones.

[REB] <u>Proverbs 14:30</u> **Peace of mind gives health to the body,** but envy is a canker in the bones.

[SG] <u>Proverbs 14:30</u> **A tranquil mind is health for the body**; But passion is a rot in the bones.

[UDB] <u>Proverbs 14:30</u> **Being at peace is good for the whole body,** but having evil within, rots the bones.

[WSP-OT] <u>Proverbs 14:30</u> **A healthful heart is the life of the flesh**; But jealousy is rottenness of the bones.

<u>Proverbs 15:4</u> **A wholesome tongue is a tree of life**: but perverseness therein is a breach in the spirit.

[Benisch-OT] <u>Proverbs 15:4</u> **Gentleness of tongue is a tree of life**: but perverseness therein is a breach in the spirit.

[CLV] <u>Proverbs 15:4</u> **A healing tongue is a tree of life**, Yet words of subversion in it are a breaking of the spirit.

[ERV] <u>Proverbs 15:4</u> **Kind words are like a life-giving tree**, but lying words will crush your spirit.

[EXB] <u>Proverbs 15:4</u> ·**As a tree gives fruit, healing words give life [A healthy/healing tongue is a tree of life]**, but ·dishonest [deceitful; perverse] words crush the spirit.

[FAA] <u>Proverbs 15:4</u> **A calming tongue is a tree of life**, But perverseness with the tongue is spiritual shipwreck.

[ICB] <u>Proverbs 15:4</u> **As a tree gives us fruit, healing words give us life**. But evil words crush the spirit.

[Kenrick] <u>Proverbs 15:4</u> **A peaceable tongue is a tree of life**: but that which is immoderate, shall crush the spirit.

[McFadyen-OT] <u>Proverbs 15:4</u> **A soothing tongue is life**, But violent words break the spirit.

[Miller-Pr] <u>Proverbs 15:4</u> **The tongue, as a healing thing, is a tree of life**; but, as a subverting thing, it is ruin like the wind.

[T4T] <u>Proverbs 15:4</u> **Those who speak kindly to people are like trees whose fruit gives life**; speaking what is false causes people to despair/feel very discouraged.

[TPT] <u>Proverbs 15:4</u> **When you speak healing words, you offer others fruit from the tree of life**. But unhealthy, negative words do nothing but crush their hopes.

[UDB] <u>Proverbs 15:4</u> **A person who can give healing with what they say is like a tree that gives life**; when someone lies to you, it can feel like they have crushed you.

<u>Proverbs 15:30</u> The light of the eyes rejoiceth the heart: and **a good report maketh the bones fat.**

[Beck] <u>Proverbs 15:30</u> Shining eyes delight the heart; **good news refreshes the body.**

[CEB] <u>Proverbs 15:30</u> Bright eyes give joy to the heart; **good news strengthens the bones**.

[CJB] <u>Proverbs 15:30</u> A cheerful glance brings joy to the heart, and **good news invigorates the bones.**

[CLV] <u>Proverbs 15:30</u> The luminosity of the eyes rejoices the heart; **a good report confers richness on the bones.**

[CWB] <u>Proverbs 15:30</u> A cheerful countenance makes others happy and good news refreshes the body.

[EEBT] <u>Proverbs 15:30</u> A face that smiles makes you happy. Good news makes you feel better.

[ERV] <u>Proverbs 15:30</u> A smile makes people happy. **Good news makes them feel better.**

[ICB] <u>Proverbs 15:30</u> Good news makes you feel better. **Your happiness will show in your eyes.**

[LXX-1844] <u>Proverbs 15:30</u> The eye that sees rightly rejoices the heart; and a **good report fattens the bones.**

[Moffatt] <u>Proverbs 15:30</u> Good-fortune is the joy of life, **good news is health and vigour.**

[NIRV] <u>Proverbs 15:30</u> The cheerful look of a messenger brings joy to your heart. And good news **gives health to your body.**

[NJB] <u>Proverbs 15:30</u> A kindly glance gives joy to the heart, good news lends strength to the bones.

[NKJV] <u>Proverbs 15:30</u> The light of the eyes rejoices the heart, And **a good report makes the bones healthy.**

[TPT] <u>Proverbs 15:30</u> Eyes that focus on what is beautiful bring joy to the heart, and **hearing a good report refreshes and strengthens the inner being.**

[UDB] <u>Proverbs 15:30</u> When people smile, it makes them happy, and **good news brings healing to the body.**

<u>Proverbs 16:24</u> Pleasant words are as an honeycomb, sweet to the soul, and **health to the bones.**

[AMPC] <u>Proverbs 16:24</u> Pleasant words are as a honeycomb, sweet to the mind and **healing to the body.**

[BBE] <u>Proverbs 16:24</u> Pleasing words are like honey, sweet to the soul and **new life to the bones.**

[CBC] <u>Proverbs 16:24</u> Pleasant sayings are as an honeycomb, Sweet to the soul, and **healing to the whole body.**

[CEB] <u>Proverbs 16:24</u> Pleasant words are flowing honey, sweet to the taste and **healing to the bones.**

[GNT] <u>Proverbs 16:24</u> Kind words are like honey—sweet to the taste and **good for your health.**

[ICB] <u>Proverbs 16:24</u> Pleasant words are like a honeycomb. **They make a person happy and healthy.**

[Jerusalem] <u>Proverbs 16:24</u> Kindly words are sweet to the taste, **wholesome to the body.**

[Knox] <u>Proverbs 16:24</u> Honey itself cannot vie with well-framed words, for heart's comfort and **body's refreshment.**

[NABRE] <u>Proverbs 16:24</u> Pleasing words are a honeycomb, sweet to the taste and **invigorating to the bones.**

[NIRV] <u>Proverbs 16:24</u> Kind words are like honey. They are sweet to the spirit and **bring healing to the body.**

[NOG] <u>Proverbs 16:24</u> Pleasant words are like honey from a honeycomb—**sweet to the spirit and healthy for the body.**

[Orton-OT] <u>Proverbs 16:24</u> Pleasant words, such words of wisdom as before described, are as an honeycomb, sweet to the soul, and **health to the bones**, are not only pleasant, but wholesome; like honey, they have an agreeable taste, **and a medicinal virtue.**

[T4T] <u>Proverbs 16:24</u> Kind words are like honey: We enjoy them both, and **both cause our bodies to be healthy/strong.**

[UDB] <u>Proverbs 16:24</u> Kind words are like a honeycomb; they are sweet for us to take in, and **they give healing to our bodies.**

<u>Proverbs 17:22</u> **A merry heart doeth good like a medicine**: but a broken spirit drieth the bones.

[BBE] <u>Proverbs 17:22</u> **A glad heart makes a healthy body,** but a crushed spirit makes the bones dry.

[Berkeley] <u>Proverbs 17:22</u> **A cheerful heart makes a good cure**, but a broken spirit makes the bones dry up.

The footnote for this verse says that a good cure is, "Up-to-date therapy, unsurpassed."

[CCB] <u>Proverbs 17:22</u> **A joyful heart gives health to the body**, while a sad spirit dries up the bones.

[Fenton] <u>Proverbs 17:22</u> **The best medicine is a cheerful heart;** But a loaded mind exhausts the frame.

[GNT] <u>Proverbs 17:22</u> **Being cheerful keeps you healthy.** It is slow death to be gloomy all the time.

[Holdens-Pr] <u>Proverbs 17:22</u> **A merry heart maketh a good medicine;** But a broken spirit drieth the bones.

[ICB] <u>Proverbs 17:22</u> **A happy heart is like good medicine.** But a broken spirit drains your strength.

[Jerusalem] <u>Proverbs 17:22</u> **A glad heart is excellent medicine**, a spirit depressed wastes the bones away.

[JPS-OT 1985] <u>Proverbs 17:22</u> **A joyful heart makes for good health;** Despondency dries up the bones.

[Kenrick] <u>Proverbs 17:22</u> **A joyful mind maketh age flourishing**: a sorrowful spirit drieth up the bones.

[Knox] <u>Proverbs 17:22</u> **A cheerful heart makes a quick recovery**, it is crushed spirits that waste a man's frame.

[LEB] <u>Proverbs 17:22</u> **A cheerful heart is good medicine**, but a downcast spirit will dry out bones.

[Miller-Pr] <u>Proverbs 17:22</u> **A glad heart helps forward a cure;** but an upbraiding spirit dries the bones.

[Moffatt] <u>Proverbs 17:22</u> **A glad heart is a healing medicine;** But a broken spirit dries up the bones.

[MSG] <u>Proverbs 17:22</u> **A cheerful disposition is good for your health;** gloom and doom leave you bone-tired.

[NCV] <u>Proverbs 17:22</u> **A happy heart is like good medicine**, but a broken spirit drains your strength.

[NOG] <u>Proverbs 17:22</u> **A joyful heart is good medicine**, but depression drains one's strength.

[NWT] <u>Proverbs 17:22</u> **A joyful heart is good medicine**, But a crushed spirit saps one's strength.

[REB] <u>Proverbs 17:22</u> **A glad heart makes for good health,** but low spirits sap one's strength.

[Rotherham] <u>Proverbs 17:22</u> **A joyful heart, worketh an excellent cure**, —but, a stricken spirit, drieth up the bone.

[SAAS-OT] <u>Proverbs 17:22</u> **A cheerful heart makes a man healthy,** But the bones of a sorrowful man dry him up.

[SG] <u>Proverbs 17:22</u> **A happy heart is a healing medicine;** But a broken spirit dries up the bones.

[T4T] <u>Proverbs 17:22</u> **Being cheerful is like swallowing good medicine;** being discouraged/gloomy all the time will drain away your energy/cause you to become weak.

[Thomson] <u>Proverbs 17:22</u> **A cheerful heart promoteth health;** but the bones of a heart wounded man are dried up.

[TLB] <u>Proverbs 17:22</u> **A cheerful heart does good like medicine**, but a broken spirit makes one sick.

[WSP-OT] <u>Proverbs 17:22</u> **A joyful heart bringeth healing;** But a wounded spirit drieth the bones.

Proverbs 24:5 A wise man is strong; yea, a man of knowledge increaseth strength.

[AMP] **Proverbs 24:5** A wise man is strong, And a man of knowledge strengthens his power;

[CEV] **Proverbs 24:5** Wisdom brings strength, and knowledge gives power.

[CLV] **Proverbs 24:5** A wise master is one with strength, and a man of knowledge is resolute with vigor;

[ERV] **Proverbs 24:5** Wisdom makes a man more powerful. Knowledge gives a man strength.

[FHV-NT] **Proverbs 24:5** A man of wisdom is strong, and with knowledge he adds to his strength.

[Kenrick] **Proverbs 24:5** A wise man is strong: and a knowing man stout and valiant.

[NAB] **Proverbs 24:5** A wise man is more powerful than a strong man, and a man of knowledge than a man of might;

[SECT] **Proverbs 24:5** A wise man is powerful in strength; Yea, a man of knowledge more than one of great might.

[TPT] **Proverbs 24:5** Wisdom can make anyone into a mighty warrior, and revelation-knowledge increases strength.

[UDB] **Proverbs 24:5** A man who has wisdom has strength, and a person with knowledge is mightier than the one who is strong,

ECCLESIASTES

Ecclesiastes 7:12 For wisdom is a defence, and money is a defence: but the excellency of knowledge is, that **wisdom giveth life to them that have it.**

[ASV-2014] **Ecclesiastes 7:12** For wisdom is a defense, even as money is a defense; but the excellency of knowledge is, that **wisdom preserveth the life of him that hath it.**

[Beck] **Ecclesiastes 7:12** Wisdom protects us like money protects us. **The advantage of wisdom is that it gives life to those who have it.**

[Besorah] **Ecclesiastes 7:12** For wisdom protects as silver protects, but the advantage of knowledge is that **wisdom gives life to those who have it.**

[EB] **Ecclesiastes 7:12** For wisdom is a shelter, And wealth is a shelter; But **the advantage of wisdom is That it fortifieth the heart of them that have it.**

[ERV] **Ecclesiastes 7:12** Wisdom and money can protect you. **But knowledge gained through wisdom is even better—it can save your life.**

[FAA] **Ecclesiastes 7:12** For one may be under the protection of wisdom, Or under the protection of money, **But the advantage of knowledge Is that wisdom gives life to its owners.**

[Ginsburg-OT] **Ecclesiastes 7:12** For to be in the shelter of wisdom is to be under the shelter of riches, and **the advantage of wisdom is, that wisdom enliveneth the possessor thereof.**

[Harrison-Ecc] **Ecclesiastes 7:12** For wisdom is a shelter as wealth is a shelter; **But wisdom has preeminence, As it procures long life to its possessor.**

[ICB] **Ecclesiastes 7:12** Wisdom is like money. They both help a person. **But wisdom is better than money, because it can save a person's life.**

[LEB] **Ecclesiastes 7:12** For wisdom offers protection like money offers protection. **But knowledge has an advantage—wisdom restores life to its possessor.**

[McFadyen-OT] <u>Ecclesiastes 7:12</u> Wisdom defends, even as money defends; But herein is the greater gain of knowledge, **That wisdom is life unto those that possess her.**

[NET] <u>Ecclesiastes 7:12</u> For wisdom provides protection, just as money provides protection. **But the advantage of knowledge is this: Wisdom preserves the life of its owner.**

[NLT] <u>Ecclesiastes 7:12</u> Wisdom and money can get you almost anything, **but only wisdom can save your life.**

[NOG] <u>Ecclesiastes 7:12</u> Wisdom protects us just as money protects us, **but the advantage of wisdom is that it gives life to those who have it.**

[Purver] <u>Ecclesiastes 7:12</u> For Wisdom is for Shelter, as well as Money; and **the Profit of Knowledge is, that Wisdom keeps the Owners of it alive.**

[TNIV] <u>Ecclesiastes 7:12</u> Wisdom is a shelter as money is a shelter, but the advantage of knowledge is this: **Wisdom preserves the life of its possessor.**

[ULB] <u>Ecclesiastes 7:12</u> For wisdom provides protection as money can provide protection, but the advantage of knowledge is that **wisdom gives life to whoever has it.**

[Ycard-Ecc] <u>Ecclesiastes 7:12</u> For under the shadow of wisdom, under the shadow of money: for all that thou sayest, one lives undisturbed under the shadow of money and of wisdom; but with this difference, that **the advantage is all on the side of the knowledge of wisdom, which alone makes him live who possesses it**; for besides that, there is not a more sure defence, it is when one is truly wise, that one can say that one lives; the life of fools not being a life.

<u>Ecclesiastes 7:17</u> Be not over much wicked, neither be thou foolish: **why shouldest thou die before thy time?**

[BBE] <u>Ecclesiastes 7:17</u> Be not evil overmuch, and be not foolish. **Why come to your end before your time?**

[CEV] <u>Ecclesiastes 7:17</u> **Don't die before your time** by being too evil or acting like a fool.

[CLV] <u>Ecclesiastes 7:17</u> Do not be abundantly wicked, and do not be frivolous; **Why should you die when it is not your time?**

[Coleman-OT] <u>Ecclesiastes 7:17</u> Be not overmuch wicked, Neither by thou foolish; **Why shouldest thou die eternally?**

[Garstang-OT] <u>Ecclesiastes 7:17</u> Do not enormously make wilful mistakes, and do not be an incorrigible: **why shalt thou die! at thine inopportune time.**

[GNT] <u>Ecclesiastes 7:17</u> But don't be too wicked or too foolish, either—**why die before you have to?**

[Greenaway-OT] <u>Ecclesiastes 7:17</u> Do not, to avoid the fault of being stupidly careless, and indifferent about thy affairs be too harsh, and rigorous in the management of them. **Why shouldst thou expose thyself to a violent, and untimely death?**

[GW] <u>Ecclesiastes 7:17</u> Don't be too wicked, and don't be a fool. **Why should you die before your time is up?**

[Haupt-Ecc] <u>Ecclesiastes 7:17</u> Be thou not over-wicked, neither be thou a fool.

[ICB] <u>Ecclesiastes 7:17</u> Don't be too wicked. And don't be a foolish person. **You will die young if you do so.**

[JUB] <u>Ecclesiastes 7:17</u> Do not be hasty to condemn, neither be thou foolish: **why should thou die in the midst of thy labours?**

[NIRV] <u>Ecclesiastes 7:17</u> Don't be too sinful. And don't be foolish. **Why die before your time comes?**

[REAL] <u>Ecclesiastes 7:17</u> Do not increase evil, or be stupid. **Why should you die before your season?**

[T4T] <u>Ecclesiastes 7:17</u> If you do what is evil or do what is foolish, **you might die while you are still young.**

[Thomson] <u>Ecclesiastes 7:17</u> Run not into an excess of wickedness nor become hardened, **that thou mayst not die untimely.**

[ULB] <u>Ecclesiastes 7:17</u> Do not be too wicked or foolish. **Why should you die before your time?**

[YLT] <u>Ecclesiastes 7:17</u> Do not much wrong, neither be thou a fool, **why dost thou die within thy time?**

SON OF SOLOMON

<u>Song of Solomon 2:4</u> He brought me to the banqueting house, and **his banner over me was love.**

[AMP] <u>Song of Solomon 2:4</u> "He has brought me to his banqueting place, **And his banner over me is love** [waving overhead to protect and comfort me].

[AMPC] <u>Song of Solomon 2:4</u> He brought me to the banqueting house, and **his banner over me was love** [for love waved as a protecting and comforting banner over my head when I was near him].

[REAL] <u>Song of Solomon 2:4</u> He brought me to the banqueting house, and **his battle flag over me was love.**

<u>Song of Solomon 8:6</u> Set me as a seal upon thine heart, as a seal upon thine arm: **for love is strong as death;** jealousy is cruel as the grave: the coals thereof are coals of fire, which hath a most vehement flame.

The Love of God is sufficient to overcome death.

[Glickman-Sos] <u>Song of Solomon 8:6</u> O, my darling lover, make me your most precious possession held securely in your arms, held close to your heart. **True love is as strong and irreversible as the onward march of death.** True love never ceases to care, and it would no more give up the beloved than the grave would give up the dead. The fires of true love can never be quenched because the source of its flame is God himself.

[MSTC] <u>Song of Solomon 8:6</u> O set me as a seal upon thine heart, and as a seal upon thine arm: **for love is mighty as the death,** and jealousy as the hell. Her coals are of fire, and a very flame of the LORD:

[TPT] <u>Song of Solomon 8:6</u> Fasten me upon your heart as a seal of fire forevermore. This living, consuming flame will seal you as my prisoner of love. **My passion is stronger than the chains of death and the grave,** all consuming as the very flashes of fire from the burning heart of God. Place this fierce, unrelenting fire over your entire being.

[UDB] <u>Song of Solomon 8:6</u> Keep me close to you, like a seal on your heart, or like a bracelet on your arm. **Our love for each other is as powerful as death;** it is as strong as the grave. It is as though our love for each other bursts into flames and burns like a hot fire.

ISAIAH

<u>Isaiah 5:27</u> **None shall be weary nor stumble among them**; none shall slumber nor sleep; neither shall the girdle of their loins be loosed, nor the latchet of their shoes be broken:

[ICB] <u>Isaiah 5:27</u> **Not one of them becomes tired or falls down**. Not one of them gets sleepy and falls asleep. Their weapons are close at hand. Their sandal straps are not broken.

[MSTC] <u>Isaiah 5:27</u> There is not one faint or feeble among them, no not a sluggish nor slippery person. There shall not one of them put off the girdle from his loins, nor loose the latchet of his shoe.

[NIRV] <u>Isaiah 5:27</u> **None of them grows tired. None of them falls down**. None of them sleeps or even takes a nap. All of them are ready for battle. Every belt is pulled tight. Not a single sandal strap is broken.

[UDB] <u>Isaiah 5:27</u> **They will not get tired or stumble**. They will not stop to rest or to sleep. None of their belts will be loose, and none of them will have sandals with broken straps, so they will all be ready to fight in battles.

<u>Isaiah 10:27</u> And it shall come to pass in that day, that his burden shall be taken away from off thy shoulder, and his yoke from off thy neck, and **the yoke shall be destroyed because of the anointing**.

[AMPC] <u>Isaiah 10:27</u> And it shall be in that day that the burden of [the Assyrian] shall depart from your shoulders, and his yoke from your neck. **The yoke shall be destroyed because of fatness [which prevents it from going around your neck]**.

[Besorah] <u>Isaiah 10:27</u> And in that day it shall be that his burden is removed from your shoulder and his yoke from your neck and **the yoke shall be destroyed because of the anointing oil**.

[CE] <u>Isaiah 10:27</u> On that day, his burden shall be taken from your shoulder, and **his yoke shattered from your neck**.

[CJB] <u>Isaiah 10:27</u> On that day his burden will fall from your shoulders and his yoke from your neck; **the yoke will be destroyed by your prosperity**.

[CLV] <u>Isaiah 10:27</u> And it will come to be in that day, His burden shall withdrawal from your back, And His yoke from your neck; **The yolk will be broken apart because a stoutness**.

[CPDV] <u>Isaiah 10:27</u> And this shall be in that day: his burden will be taken away from your shoulder, and his yoke will be taken away from your neck, and **the yoke will decay at the appearance of the oil**.

[Douay-Rheims] <u>Isaiah 10:27</u> And it shall come to pass in that day, that his burden shall be taken away from off thy shoulder, and his yoke from off thy neck, and **the yoke shall putrify at the presence of the oil**.

[GW] <u>Isaiah 10:27</u> At that time their burden will be removed from your shoulders. Their yoke will be removed from your neck. **The yoke will be torn away because you have grown fat**.

[Jenour-Isa] <u>Isaiah 10:27</u> And it shall come to pass in that day, his burden shall be removed from off thy shoulder, And his yoke from off thy neck; yea, **the yoke shall be destroyed by the anointing**.

[JUB] <u>Isaiah 10:27</u> And it shall come to pass in that day that his burden shall be taken away from off thy shoulder and his yoke from off thy neck, and **the yoke shall be consumed in the presence of the anointing**.

[NIRV] <u>Isaiah 10:27</u> People of Zion, in days to come he will help you. He will lift the heavy load of the Assyrians from your shoulders. He will remove their yokes from your necks. **Their yokes will be broken because you have become so strong**.

[NIV] <u>Isaiah 10:27</u> In that day their burden will be lifted from your shoulders, their yoke from your neck; **the yoke will be broken because you have grown so fat**.

[TVB] <u>Isaiah 10:27</u> When that time comes, all the weight of Assyria will be lifted off of your shoulders; its yoke will be removed from your neck, and **the burden of their assault and demands will evaporate, and you'll be free**.

<u>Isaiah 25:8</u> **He will swallow up death in victory**; and the Lord GOD will wipe away tears from off all faces; and the rebuke of his people shall he take away from off all the earth: for the LORD hath spoken it.

[AMP] <u>Isaiah 25:8</u> **He will swallow up death [and abolish it] for all time**. And the Lord God will wipe away tears from all faces, And He will take away the disgrace of His people from all the earth; For the Lord has spoken.

[BBE] <u>Isaiah 25:8</u> **He has put an end to death for ever**; and the Lord God will take away all weeping; and he will put an end to the shame of his people in all the earth: for the Lord has said it.

[Beck] <u>Isaiah 25:8</u> **He will swallow up death forever**, and the Lord GOD will wipe away tears from all faces. He will remove the disgrace of His people from the whole world; for the LORD has said so.

[Benisch-OT] <u>Isaiah 25:8</u> **He will swallow up the death everlastingly**; and the Lord God will wipe away a tear from off all faces; and the disgrace of his people shall he remove from off all the earth: for the Eternal hath spoken it.

[Box-OT] <u>Isaiah 25:8</u> **He has annihilated death for ever** And the Lord Jahveh will wipe away tears from all faces, And the reproach of His people will He remove from off all the earth. Jahveh has decreed it.

[CEV] <u>Isaiah 25:8</u> **The Lord All-Powerful will destroy the power of death** and wipe away all tears. No longer will his people be insulted everywhere. The Lord has spoken!

[HBIV] <u>Isaiah 25:8</u> **He will destroy death forever**; Yea, the Lord Jehovah will wipe tears from all faces; And the reproach of his people will he take away from the whole earth: For Jehovah has spoken.

[Henderson-OT] <u>Isaiah 25:8</u> **He shall utterly destroy death**; And the Lord Jehovah shall wipe away the tears from all faces, And shall remove the reproach of his people from the whole earth:

[Kenrick] <u>Isaiah 25:8</u> **He will cast death down headlong forever**: and the Lord God will wipe away tears from every face: and the reproach of His people He will take away from off the whole earth: for the Lord hath spoken it.

[LitProph-OT] <u>Isaiah 25:8</u> **He shall utterly destroy death for ever;** And the Lord Jehovah shall wipe away the tear from off all faces; And the reproach of his people shall he remove from off the whole earth: For Jehovah hath spoke it.

[MOTB] <u>Isaiah 25:8</u> **Even death, the most fertile source of grief, shall cease to be**. Then will he also remove completely the ignominy which has so long bowed down his chosen people. This new and glorious regime shall surely be a reality, because Jehovah has decreed it.

[Noyes] <u>Isaiah 25:8</u> **He will destroy death forever**; The Lord Jehovah will wipe away the tears from all faces, And the reproach of his people will he take away from the whole earth; For Jehovah hath said it.

[Purver] Isaiah 25:8 **He will devour Death eternally**, and the Sovereign Lord will wipe off the Tears from all Faces, and take away the Reproach of his People from the whole Earth; for the Lord has spoken it.

[TVB] Isaiah 25:8 **God will swallow up death forever**. The Lord, the Eternal, will wipe away the tears from each and every face And deflect the scorn and shame His people endure from the whole world, for the Eternal determined that it should be so.

[UDB] Isaiah 25:8 **He will get rid of death forever**! Yahweh our God will cause people to no longer mourn because someone has died. And he will stop other people insulting and making fun of his land and us his people. That will surely happen because Yahweh has said it!

[WEBBE] Isaiah 25:8 **He has swallowed up death forever!** The Lord GOD will wipe away tears from off all faces. He will take the reproach of his people away from off all the earth, for the Lord has spoken it.

[WGCIB] Isaiah 25:8 **He shall cast death down headlong forever**: and the Lord God shall wipe away tears from every face, and the reproach of his people he shall take away from off the whole earth: for the Lord has spoken it.

Isaiah 29:18 And in that day shall the deaf hear the words of the book, and the eyes of the blind shall see out of obscurity, and out of darkness.

[CWB] Isaiah 29:18 The day will come when the deaf will hear the word of the Lord, and the blind who have lived in darkness and gloom will be able to see and read.

[JPS-OT 1963] Isaiah 29:18 In that day, the deaf shall hear even written words, And the eyes of the blind shall see Even in the darkness and obscurity.

[NASB] Isaiah 29:18 On that day the deaf will hear words of a book, And out of their gloom and darkness the eyes of the blind will see.

[NEB] Isaiah 29:18 On that day deaf men shall hear when a book is read, and the eyes of the blind shall see out of impenetrable darkness.

[TLV] Isaiah 29:18 In that day the deaf will hear words of a book, and out of gloom and darkness the eyes of the blind will see.

Isaiah 30:26 Moreover the light of the moon shall be as the light of the sun, and the light of the sun shall be sevenfold, as the light of seven days, in the day that **the LORD bindeth up the breach of his people, and healeth**[raphah] **the stroke of their wound**.

[HOB-OT] Isaiah 30:26 And the light of the moon will be like the light of the sun, and the light of the sun will be sevenfold on the day when **the Lord will heal the destruction of His people, and will heal the pain of thy wound**.

[Leeser-OT] Isaiah 30:26 And the light of the moon shall be as the light of the sun, and the light of the sun shall be sevenfold, as the light of the seven days, on the day that **the Lord bindeth up the broken limbs of his people, and healeth the bruise of their wound**.

[NHEB] Isaiah 30:26 Moreover the light of the moon will be like the light of the sun, and the light of the sun will be seven times brighter, like the light of seven days, in the day that **the LORD binds up the fracture of his people, and heals the wound they were struck with**.

[SAAS-OT] Isaiah 30:26 In that day, the light of the moon will be as the light of the sun, and the light of the sun will be sevenfold, when **the Lord heals the wound of His people and the pain of your plague**.

<u>Isaiah 32:3-4</u> **And the eyes of them that see shall not be dim, and the ears of them that hear shall hearken**. [4]The heart also of the rash shall understand knowledge, and **the tongue of the stammerers shall be ready to speak plainly.**

[BLE] <u>Isaiah 32:3-4</u> **And the eyes of men who see will not be gummed over, and the ears of men who hear will be alert**, [4]and the brains of reckless men will have sense to know, and **the tongues of stammering men will be quick to speak clearly.**

[CE] <u>Isaiah 32:3-4</u> **The eyes of those who see will not be closed; the ears of those who hear will be attentive.** [4]The flighty will become wise and capable, and **the stutterers will speak fluently and clearly.**

[CEB] <u>Isaiah 32:3-4</u> **Then the eyes of those who can see will no longer be blind, the ears of those who can hear will listen**, [4]the minds of the rash will know and comprehend, and **the tongues of those who stammer will speak fluently and plainly.**

[CLV] <u>Isaiah 32:3-4</u> **And the eyes of the seers shall not squint, and the ears of the hearers shall be attentive,** [4]and the heart of the hasty shall understand knowledge, and **the tongue of the stammerers shall hasten to speak elegancies.**

[CSB] <u>Isaiah 32:3-4</u> **Then the eyes of those who see will not be closed, and the ears of those who hear will listen.** [4]The reckless mind will gain knowledge, and **the stammering tongue will speak clearly and fluently.**

[CWB] <u>Isaiah 32:3-4</u> **The eyes of those who saw things dimly will be opened. The ears of those who could not hear what was said will be unplugged.** [4]Those who were rash will have sound judgment, and **those who stammered will speak clearly and distinctly.**

[GW] <u>Isaiah 32:3-4</u> **Then the vision of those who can see won't be blurred, and the ears of those who can hear will pay attention.** [4]Then those who are reckless will begin to understand, and **those who stutter will speak quickly and clearly.**

[HRV] <u>Isaiah 32:3-4</u> **And the eyes of them that see, shall not be closed, and the ears of them that hear, shall attend.** [4]The heart also of the rash shall understand knowledge, and the tongue of **the stammerers shall be ready to speak plainly.**

[JPS-OT 1963] <u>Isaiah 32:3-4</u> **Then the eyes of those who have sight shall not be sealed, And the ears of those who have hearing shall listen**; [4]And the minds of the thoughtless shall attend and note, And **the tongues of mumblers shall shall speak with fluent eloquence.**

[LTPB] <u>Isaiah 32:3-4</u> **The seers' eyes will not be shadowed, and the hearers' ears will hear carefully.** [4]The fools' heart will understand knowledge, and **the stammerers' tongue will speak quickly and plainly.**

[NIRV] <u>Isaiah 32:3-4</u> **Then the eyes of those who see won't be closed anymore. The ears of those who hear will listen to the truth.** [4]People who are afraid will know and understand. **Tongues that stutter will speak clearly.**

[NLV] <u>Isaiah 32:3-4</u> **Then the eyes of those who see will be able to see. And the ears of those who hear will listen.** [4]The mind of those who act in a hurry will understand the truth. And **the tongue of those who have trouble speaking will hurry to speak well.**

[Sawyer-7590] <u>Isaiah 32:3-4</u> **The eyes of those that see shall not be blinded, and the ears of those that hear shall attend,** [4]and the mind of the hasty shall understand knowledge, and **the tongue of the stammering shall speak rapidly and plainly.**

A SURVEY OF HEALING SCRIPTURES

[VW] <u>Isaiah 32:3-4</u> **And the eyes of those who see shall not be dim, and the ears of those who hear shall listen.** [4]And the heart of the rash shall understand knowledge, and **the tongue of those who stutter shall be ready to speak plainly.**

<u>Isaiah 33:24</u> **And the inhabitant shall not say, I am sick**: the people that dwell therein shall be forgiven their iniquity.

[AMP] <u>Isaiah 33:24</u> **And no inhabitant [of Zion] will say, "I am sick"**; The people who dwell there will be forgiven their wickedness [their sin, their injustice, their wrongdoing].

[CEV] <u>Isaiah 33:24</u> The Lord will forgive your sins, and **none of you will say, "I feel sick."**

[CWB] <u>Isaiah 33:24</u> **No one will say, "I'm sick."** And the sins of those who dwell there will be forgiven.

[GNT] <u>Isaiah 33:24</u> **No one who lives in our land will ever again complain of being sick**, and all sins will be forgiven.

[Hall] <u>Isaiah 33:24</u> **But my people shall, in the meantime, be kept in safety and health**; forasmuch as the very cause of their suffering, which is their iniquity, shall be removed and forgiven.

[JosephStock-Isa] <u>Isaiah 33:24</u> **No inhabitant shall say, I am sick; The people that dwell therein shall be free from disease.**

[Kenrick] <u>Isaiah 33:24</u> **Neither shall he that is near, say: I am feeble.** The people that dwell therein, shall have their iniquity taken away from them.

[LitProph-OT] <u>Isaiah 33:24</u> **Neither shall the inhabitant say, I am disabled with sickness**: The people, that dwelleth therein, is freed from the punishment of their iniquity.

[MOTB] <u>Isaiah 33:24</u> **There shall be in her no more sickness**, for all shall have their sins forgiven.

[Ottley-Isa-LXX] <u>Isaiah 33:24</u> And **the people that dwelleth among them shall not say, I am faint**; for their sin is forgiven.

[TVB] <u>Isaiah 33:24</u> **And nobody who lives in God's city will say he doesn't feel well.** For everyone will be washed clean and forgiven for their wrongdoing.

[UDB] <u>Isaiah 33:24</u> **And the people in Jerusalem will no longer say, "We are sick,"** because Yahweh will forgive the sins that have been committed by the people who live there.

<u>Isaiah 35:3</u> Strengthen ye the weak hands, and confirm the feeble knees.

[Beck] <u>Isaiah 35:3</u> Strengthen the weak hands, and make firm the stumbling knees.

[Berkeley] <u>Isaiah 35:3</u> Strengthen the feeble hands; make firm the tottering knees.

[Besorah] <u>Isaiah 35:3</u> Strengthen the weak hands and make firm the weak knees.

[ERV] <u>Isaiah 35:3</u> Make the weak arms strong again. Strengthen the weak knees.

[ICB] <u>Isaiah 35:3</u> Make the weak hands strong. Make the weak knees strong.

[Moffatt] <u>Isaiah 35:3</u> Put heart into the listless, and brace all weak-kneed souls,

[NETS-OT] <u>Isaiah 35:3</u> Be strong, you weak hands and feeble knees!

[VW] <u>Isaiah 35:3</u> Make the weak hands strong, and make the feeble knees secure.

<u>Isaiah 35:5-6</u> Then the eyes of the blind shall be opened, and the ears of the deaf shall be unstopped. [6]Then shall the lame man leap as an hart, and the tongue of the dumb sing: for in the wilderness shall waters break out, and streams in the desert.

OUR HEALING COVENANT

[BBE] <u>Isaiah 35:5-6</u> Then the eyes of the blind will see, and the ears which are stopped will be open. ⁶Then will the feeble-footed be jumping like a roe, and the voice which was stopped will be loud in song: for in the waste land streams will be bursting out, and waters in the dry places.

[CWB] <u>Isaiah 35:5-6</u> He will open the eyes of the blind and unstop the ears of the deaf. ⁶The lame will leap like a deer and the dumb will shout for joy. Water will break forth in the wilderness and streams will flow in the desert.

[EEBT] <u>Isaiah 35:5-6</u> Then he will open the eyes of people who are cannot see. And he will make well the ears of people who cannot hear. ⁶Then people who cannot walk now will jump like deer. And people who cannot speak now will shout. That will be because they are very happy. Yes! God will pour water into the wild, dry places. And he will pour streams of water into the sandy places.

[ERV] <u>Isaiah 35:5-6</u> Then the eyes of the blind will be opened so that they can see, and the ears of the deaf will be opened so that they can hear. ⁶Crippled people will dance like deer, and those who cannot speak now will use their voices to sing happy songs. This will happen when springs of water begin to flow in the dry desert.

[EXB] <u>Isaiah 35:5-6</u> Then the blind ·people [eyes] will see again, and the ·deaf [deaf ears] will hear. ⁶Crippled people [Then the lame] will ·jump [leap] like deer, and ·those who can't talk now [the tongue of the mute] will shout with joy. Water will ·flow [burst forth] in the ·desert [wilderness], and streams will flow in the ·dry land [arid plain; or Arabah].

[JPS-OT 1985] <u>Isaiah 35:5-6</u> Then the eyes of the blind shall be opened, And the ears of the deaf shall be unstopped. ⁶Then the lame shall leap like a deer, And the tongue of the dumb shall shout aloud; For waters shall burst forth in the desert, Streams in the wilderness.

[NLV] <u>Isaiah 35:5-6</u> Then the eyes of the blind will be opened. And the ears of those who cannot hear will be opened. ⁶Then those who cannot walk will jump like a deer. And the tongue of those who cannot speak will call out for joy. For waters will break out in the wilderness, and rivers in the desert.

[TLB] <u>Isaiah 35:5-6</u> And when he comes, he will open the eyes of the blind and unstop the ears of the deaf. ⁶The lame man will leap up like a deer, and those who could not speak will shout and sing! Springs will burst forth in the wilderness, and streams in the desert.

[TVB] <u>Isaiah 35:5-6</u> Then, such healing, such repair: the eyes of the blind will be opened; the ears of the deaf will be clear. ⁶The lame will leap like deer excited; they will run and jump tirelessly and gracefully. The stutterer, the stammerer, and the tongue of the mute will sing out loud and clear in joyful song. Waters will pour through the deserts; streams will flow in godforsaken lands.

[WEBBE] <u>Isaiah 35:5-6</u> Then the eyes of the blind will be opened, and the ears of the deaf will be unstopped. ⁶Then the lame man will leap like a deer, and the tongue of the mute will sing; for waters will break out in the wilderness, and streams in the desert.

<u>Isaiah 38:9</u> The writing of Hezekiah king of Judah, when **he had been sick, and was recovered of his sickness**:

[NOG] <u>Isaiah 38:9</u> King Hezekiah of Judah wrote this after **he was sick and became well again**:

[Ottley-Isa-Heb] <u>Isaiah 38:9</u> A writing of Hezekiah, king of Judah, **when he had been sick, and come to life from his sickness**:

[Pauli-Isa] <u>Isaiah 38:9</u> The writing of the thanksgiving for the miracle, which had been done for Hezekiah, the king of the tribe of the house of Judah, **when he had been sick, and was healed of his sickness**.

A SURVEY OF HEALING SCRIPTURES

[TNIV] <u>Isaiah 38:9</u> A writing of Hezekiah king of Judah **after his illness and recovery**:

<u>Isaiah 38:16</u> O Lord, by these things men live, and in all these things is the life of my spirit: so wilt thou recover me, and make me to live.

[Beck] <u>Isaiah 38:16</u> Lord, by these things men live, and by all of them my spirit is kept alive. You make me healthy and alive.

[Berkeley] <u>Isaiah 38:16</u> O Lord, by these things men live, through them may my spirit revive; restore me to health and make me to live!

[Boothroyd] <u>Isaiah 38:16</u> "Yea this, O Jehovah, shall be declared of thee; That thou hast revived my spirit—Hast restored my health, and prolonged my life."

[EEBT] <u>Isaiah 38:16</u> Lord, by these things, people have life. By all these things, my spirit has life. You gave my health back to me and you have let me live.

[FAA] <u>Isaiah 38:16</u> O Lord, by these things men live, And in all of them is my spiritual life, And you are restoring me to health And reviving me.

[Fenton] <u>Isaiah 38:16</u> Now my spirit will live through them all, For You have revived me to strength,

[ICB] <u>Isaiah 38:16</u> Lord, because of you, men live. Because of you, my spirit also lives. You made me well and let me live.

[KJ3] <u>Isaiah 38:16</u> O Lord, on them they live, and for all in them is the life of my spirit. And You heal me, and make me live.

[LitProph-OT] <u>Isaiah 38:16</u> For this cause shall it be declared, O Jehovah, concerning thee, That thou hast revived my spirit; That thou hast restored my health, and prolonged my life.

[NIRV] <u>Isaiah 38:16</u> Lord, people find the will to live because you keep your promises. And my spirit also finds life in your promises. You brought me back to health. You let me live.

[NIVUK] <u>Isaiah 38:16</u> Lord, by such things people live; and my spirit finds life in them too. You restored me to health and let me live.

[Ottley-Isa-LXX] <u>Isaiah 38:16</u> O Lord; yea, it was told thee concerning it, and thou didst rouse up my breath, and I was comforted, and came to life.

[WSP-OT] <u>Isaiah 38:16</u> O Lord, by these thy promises and deeds men live, And the life of my spirit is altogether in them: Therefore wilt thou strengthen me, and make me to live.

<u>Isaiah 38:21</u> For Isaiah had said, Let them take a lump of figs, and lay it for a plaister upon the boil, and he shall recover.

[CT-OT] <u>Isaiah 38:21</u> And Isaiah said, "Let them take a cake of pressed figs and lay it for a plaster on the boil, and it will heal."

[ICB] <u>Isaiah 38:21</u> Then Isaiah said, "Make a paste from figs. Put it on Hezekiah's boil. Then he will get well."

[NOG] <u>Isaiah 38:21</u> Then Isaiah said, "Take a fig cake, and place it over the boil so that the king will get well."

[TLB] <u>Isaiah 38:21</u> (For Isaiah had told Hezekiah's servants, "Make an ointment of figs and spread it over the boil, and he will get well again."

[WGCIB] <u>Isaiah 38:21</u> Now Isaiah had ordered that they should take a lump of figs, and lay it as a plaster upon the wound, and that he should be healed.

Isaiah 39:1 At that time Merodachbaladan, the son of Baladan, king of Babylon, sent letters and a present to Hezekiah: **for he had heard that he had been sick, and was recovered.**

[CAB] <u>Isaiah 39:1</u> At that time Merodach-Baladan, the son of Baladan, the king of Babylon, sent letters and ambassadors and gifts to Hezekiah; for **he had heard that he had been sick, even unto death, and had recovered.**

[Haak] <u>Isaiah 39:1</u> At that time Merodach Baladan the son of Baladan, King of Babel, sent letters and a present to Hezekiah; **for he had heard, that he had been sick, and was (again) grown strong.**

[HRB] <u>Isaiah 39:1</u> At that time Merodach-Baladan, the son of Baladan, king of Babylon, sent letters and a present to Hezekiah; **for he had heard that he was ill, and was made strong.**

[ISV] <u>Isaiah 39:1</u> At that time Merodach-baladan, the son of Baladan, king of Babylon, sent letters and a gift to Hezekiah, when **he heard he had been sick and had survived.**

[Lamsa] <u>Isaiah 39:1</u> AT that time Merodach-baladan, the son of Baladan, king of Babylon, sent letters and presents to Hezekiah; **for he had heard that he had been sick and was healed.**

[NIVUK] <u>Isaiah 39:1</u> At that time Marduk-Baladan son of Baladan king of Babylon sent Hezekiah letters and a gift, because **he had heard of his illness and recovery.**

[TLB] <u>Isaiah 39:1</u> Soon afterwards, the king of Babylon (Merodach-baladan, the son of Baladan) sent Hezekiah a present and his best wishes, **for he had heard that Hezekiah had been very sick and now was well again.**

[YLT] <u>Isaiah 39:1</u> At that time hath Merodach-Baladan, son of Baladan, king of Babylon, sent letters and a present unto Hezekiah, when **he heareth that he hath been sick, and is become strong.**

Isaiah 40:29 He giveth power to the faint; and to them that have no might he increaseth strength.

[Abegg-OT] <u>Isaiah 40:29</u> The one who gives might to the faint will make power abound in those without strength.

[AMP] <u>Isaiah 40:29</u> He gives strength to the weary, And to him who has no might He increases power.

[BBE] <u>Isaiah 40:29</u> He gives power to the feeble, increasing the strength of him who has no force.

[Berkeley] <u>Isaiah 40:29</u> He imparts vigor to the fainting, and to those who have no might He increases strength.

[Box-OT] <u>Isaiah 40:29</u> To the weary, strength He imparts, He makes the feeble powerful;

[CEB] <u>Isaiah 40:29</u> giving power to the tired and reviving the exhausted.

[Cheyne-OT] <u>Isaiah 40:29</u> He give the strength to the weary, and maketh the feeble powerful.

[CJB] <u>Isaiah 40:29</u> He invigorates the exhausted, he gives strength to the powerless.

[CPDV] <u>Isaiah 40:29</u> It is he who gives strength to the weary, and it is he who increases fortitude and strength in those who are failing.

[CT-OT] <u>Isaiah 40:29</u> Who gives the tired strength, and to him who has no strength, He increases strength.

[ERV] <u>Isaiah 40:29</u> He helps tired people be strong. He gives power to those without it.

[Haak] <u>Isaiah 40:29</u> He giveth power to the weary one, and he multiplieth strength to him that hath no power.

[JPS-OT 1963] <u>Isaiah 40:29</u> He gives strength to the weary, Fresh vigor to the spent.

[Kenrick] <u>Isaiah 40:29</u> It is He that giveth strength to the weary, and increaseth force and might to them that are not.

[Kent-OT] <u>Isaiah 40:29</u> He giveth vigor to the fainting, And upon the powerless he lavisheth strength.

[Koren-OT] <u>Isaiah 40:29</u> He gives power to the faint; and to the powerless he increases strength.

[Lamsa] <u>Isaiah 40:29</u> He gives power to the weary, and to them that are stricken with disease he increases strength.

[LitProph-OT] <u>Isaiah 40:29</u> He giveth strength to the faint, And to the infirm he multiplieth force.

[Moffatt] <u>Isaiah 40:29</u> into the weary he puts power, and adds new strength to the weak.

[NCV] <u>Isaiah 40:29</u> He gives strength to those who are tired and more power to those who are weak.

[NEB] <u>Isaiah 40:29</u> He gives vigour to the weary, new strength to the exhausted.

[NJB] <u>Isaiah 40:29</u> He gives strength to the weary, he strengthens the powerless.

[Noyes] <u>Isaiah 40:29</u> He giveth power to the faint; To the feeble abundant strength.

[Pauli-Isa] <u>Isaiah 40:29</u> Who give the wisdom to the righteous that long for the words of the law; and to those who have no strength, he multiplies strength.

[T4T] <u>Isaiah 40:29</u> He strengthens those who feel weak and tired.

[TLB] <u>Isaiah 40:29</u> He gives power to the tired and worn out, and strength to the weak.

[TVB] <u>Isaiah 40:29</u> God strengthens the weary and gives vitality to those worn down by age and care.

[ULB] <u>Isaiah 40:29</u> He gives strength to the tired; and to the weak he gives renewed energy.

[WSP-OT] <u>Isaiah 40:29</u> He giveth strength to the faint; And to them that are feeble he increaseth vigour.

<u>Isaiah 40:31</u> But they that wait upon the LORD shall renew their strength; they shall mount up with wings as eagles; they shall run, and not be weary; and they shall walk, and not faint.

[AMP] <u>Isaiah 40:31</u> But those who wait for the Lord [who expect, look for, and hope in Him] Will gain new strength and renew their power; They will lift up their wings [and rise up close to God] like eagles [rising toward the sun]; They will run and not become weary, They will walk and not grow tired.

[BLE] <u>Isaiah 40:31</u> but those who hope in Jehovah will have freshening strength, take wing like eagles, run without tiring, walk without fainting.

[CLV] <u>Isaiah 40:31</u> Yet those stretching toward Yahweh will vary their vigor, and they shall ascend on pinions as vultures. They shall run, and not be weary. They shall go, and not faint.

[CT-OT] <u>Isaiah 40:31</u> But those who put their hope in the Lord shall renew [their] vigor, they shall raise wings as eagles; they shall run and not weary, they shall walk and not tire.

[Douay-Rheims-Peters] <u>Isaiah 40:31</u> But they that hope in our Lord shall change their strength, they shall take wings as eagles, they shall run and not labor, they shall walk and not faint.

[ERV] <u>Isaiah 40:31</u> But those who trust in the Lord will become strong again. They will be like eagles that grow new feathers. They will run and not get weak. They will walk and not get tired.

[FAA] <u>Isaiah 40:31</u> But those who confide in the Lord Will revive in strength; They will soar in flight like eagles. They will run and not grow weary, They will proceed And not become exhausted.

[Henderson-OT] <u>Isaiah 40:31</u> For they that wait upon Jehovah shall gain fresh strength; They shall soar on pinions like eagles: They shall run and not become weary; They shall walk and not faint.

[JUB] <u>Isaiah 40:31</u> but those that wait for the Lord shall have new strength; they shall mount up with wings as eagles; they shall run and not be weary; and they shall walk, and not faint.

[Moffatt] <u>Isaiah 40:31</u> but those who wait for the Eternal shall renew their strength, they put out wings like eagles, they run and never weary, they walk and never faint.

[MSG] <u>Isaiah 40:31</u> But those who wait upon God get fresh strength. They spread their wings and soar like eagles, They run and don't get tired, they walk and don't lag behind.

[MSTC] <u>Isaiah 40:31</u> But unto them that have the Lord before their eyes, shall strength be increased, Eagles wings shall grow upon them; When they run, they shall not fall; and when they go, they shall not be weary."

[NASB] <u>Isaiah 40:31</u> Yet those who wait for the Lord Will gain new strength; They will mount up with wings like eagles, They will run and not get tired, They will walk and not become weary.

[NCV] <u>Isaiah 40:31</u> But the people who trust the Lord will become strong again. They will rise up as an eagle in the sky; they will run and not need rest; they will walk and not become tired.

[NWT] <u>Isaiah 40:</u>31 But those hoping in Jehovah will regain power. They will soar on wings like eagles. They will run and not grow weary; They will walk and not tire out.

[Smith] <u>Isaiah 40:31</u> And they waiting for Jehovah shall change power; they shall go up on the wing as eagles; they shall run and not be weary; they shall go and not faint.

[Thomson] <u>Isaiah 40:31</u> but they who wait upon God shall have new strength; they shall put forth fresh feathers like eagles; they shall run and not be wearied; they shall march on and shall not faint.

<u>Isaiah 41:10</u> Fear thou not; for I am with thee: be not dismayed; for I am thy God: **I will strengthen thee; yea, I will help thee**; yea, I will uphold thee with the right hand of my righteousness.

[AMP] <u>Isaiah 41:10</u> 'Do not fear [anything], for I am with you; Do not be afraid, for I am your God. **I will strengthen you, be assured I will help you**; I will certainly take hold of you with My righteous right hand [a hand of justice, of power, of victory, of salvation].'

[AMPC] <u>Isaiah 41:10</u> Fear not [there is nothing to fear], for I am with you; do not look around you in terror and be dismayed, for I am your God. **I will strengthen and harden you to difficulties, yes, I will help you**; yes, I will hold you up and retain you with My [victorious] right hand of rightness and justice.

[BLE] <u>Isaiah 41:10</u> do not be alarmed, because I am your God; **I have been invigorating you, yes, helping you**, yes, holding you up with my fair-dealing right hand.

[CEV] <u>Isaiah 41:10</u> Don't be afraid. I am with you. Don't tremble with fear. I am your God. **I will make you strong**, as I protect you with my arm and give you victories.

[CLV] <u>Isaiah 41:10</u> You must not fear, for I am with you, and you must not take heed for yourself, for I am your Elohim. **I make you resolute; indeed, I help you**. Indeed, I uphold you with the right hand of My righteousness.'

[EEBT] <u>Isaiah 41:10</u> So do not be afraid, because I am with you. Do not be sad, because I am your God. **I will make you strong and I will help you**. Really, I will hold you with my right hand. It is strong and it wins wars."

[ERV] <u>Isaiah 41:10</u> Don't worry—I am with you. Don't be afraid—I am your God. **I will make you strong and help you**. I will support you with my right hand that brings victory.

[ISV] <u>Isaiah 41:10</u> Don't be afraid, because I'm with you; don't be anxious, because I am your God. **I keep on strengthening you; I'm truly helping you.** I'm surely upholding you with my victorious right hand.

[Knox] <u>Isaiah 41:10</u> Have no fear, I am with thee; do not hesitate, am I not thy God? **I am here to strengthen and protect thee**; faithful the right hand that holds thee up.

[LEB] <u>Isaiah 41:10</u> You must not fear, for I am with you; you must not be afraid, for I am your God. **I will strengthen you, indeed I will help you**, indeed I will take hold of you with the right hand of my salvation.

[NABRE] <u>Isaiah 41:10</u> Do not fear: I am with you; do not be anxious: I am your God. **I will strengthen you, I will help you**, I will uphold you with my victorious right hand.

[NCV] <u>Isaiah 41:10</u> So don't worry, because I am with you. Don't be afraid, because I am your God. **I will make you strong and will help you**; I will support you with my right hand that saves you.

[NOG] <u>Isaiah 41:10</u> Don't be afraid, because I am with you. Don't be intimidated; I am your Elohim. **I will strengthen you. I will help you.** I will support you with my victorious right hand.

[NWT] <u>Isaiah 41:10</u> Do not be afraid, for I am with you. Do not be anxious, for I am your God. **I will fortify you, yes, I will help you**, I will really hold on to you with my right hand of righteousness.'

[Pauli-Isa] <u>Isaiah 41:10</u> Fear not, for my Word shall be thy support; be not dismayed, for I am thy God: **I will strengthen thee; yea, I will help thee**; yea, I will uphold thee with the right hand of my truth.

[Rotherham] <u>Isaiah 41:10</u> Do not fear, for, with thee, I am! Look not around, for, I, am thy God, —**I have emboldened thee, Yea I have helped thee**, Yea I have upheld thee, with my righteous, right-hand.

[T4T] <u>Isaiah 41:10</u> Do not be afraid, because I will be with/help you. Do not be discouraged, because I am your God. **I will enable you to be strong, and I will help you**; I will hold you up with my powerful arm by which you will be rescued.

[UDB] <u>Isaiah 41:10</u> Do not be afraid, because I will be with you. Do not be discouraged, because I am your God. **I will enable you to be strong, and I will help you**; I will hold you up with my powerful arm by which I will rescue you, and I will be completely right to do so!

<u>Isaiah 42:5-7</u> Thus saith God the Lᴏʀᴅ, he that created the heavens, and stretched them out; **he that spread forth the earth, and that which cometh out of it; he that giveth breath unto the people upon it**, and spirit to them that walk therein: [6]**I the Lᴏʀᴅ** have called thee in righteousness, and will hold thine hand, and **will keep thee**, and give thee for a covenant of the people, for a light of the Gentiles; [7]**To open the blind eyes**, to bring out the prisoners from the prison, and them that sit in darkness out of the prison house.

[CEV] <u>Isaiah 42:5-7</u> I am the Lord God. I created the heavens like an open tent above. **I made the earth and everything that grows on it. I am the source of life for all who live on this earth**, so listen to what I say. [6]I chose you to bring justice, and **I am here at your side.** I selected you and sent you to bring light and my promise of hope to the nations. [7]**You will give sight to the blind**; you will set prisoners free from dark dungeons.

[CT-OT] <u>Isaiah 42:5-7</u> So said God the Lord, the Creator of the heavens and the One Who stretched them out, **Who spread out the earth and what springs forth from it, Who gave a soul to the people upon it** and a spirit to those who walk thereon. [6]**I am the Lord**; I called you with righteousness and **I will strengthen your hand**; and I formed you, and I made you for a people's covenant, for a light to nations. ⁷**To open blind eyes**, to bring prisoners out of a dungeon, those who sit in darkness out of a prison.

[CWB] <u>Isaiah 42:5-7</u> This is what the God of Israel says, the One who created the heavens and stretched out the universe, **who made the earth and everything in it, who gives life to all people** and breath to those who walk here: ⁶**"I, the God of heaven and earth**, have called you to be my Servant, to come and live out my righteousness. Day by day **I will take you by the hand and guide you**. Through you I will confirm my covenant for all people. Through you I will bring light to all nations. ⁷**You will open the eyes of the blind**. You will set free those who are in prison.

[Darby] <u>Isaiah 42:5-7</u> Thus saith God, Jehovah, he that created the heavens and stretched them out, **he that spread forth the earth and its productions, he that giveth breath unto the people upon it**, and spirit to them that walk therein: ⁶**I, Jehovah**, have called thee in righteousness, and will take hold of thy hand; and I **will preserve thee**, and give thee for a covenant of the people, for a light of the nations, ⁷**to open the blind eyes**, to bring forth the prisoner from the prison, them that sit in darkness out of the house of restraint.

[EEBT] <u>Isaiah 42:5-7</u> God is the Lᴏʀᴅ. This is what he says. He is the God who created the skies. He hung them up like a curtain. **He made the shape of the whole earth. He made everything that grows in it. He gives air to its people so that they can breathe**. And he has given a spirit to everyone who walks on the earth. ⁶He says, 'I am the Lᴏʀᴅ. I have asked you to work for Righteousness. I will hold your hand. **I will keep you safe**. And I will cause you to be a Covenant for the people. You will be like a light for the countries that are not Jewish. ⁷**You will cause blind eyes to see**. You will make the prisoners free from their prison. And you will make free those people who sit in a dark prison, deep in the ground.

[ERV] <u>Isaiah 42:5-7</u> The Lord, the true God, said these things. (He created the sky and spread it out over the earth. **He formed the earth and everything it produced. He breathes life into all the people on earth**. He gives a spirit to everyone who walks on the earth.) ⁶**"I, the Lord**, was right to call you. **I will hold your hand and protect you**. You will be the sign of my agreement with the people. You will be a light for the other nations. ⁷**You will make the blind able to see**. You will free those who are held as captives. You will lead those who live in darkness out of their prison.

[FAA] <u>Isaiah 42:5-7</u> This is what God, the Lord—Who created the heavens and stretched them out, **Who pitched the earth and what it brings forth, Who gives breath to the people upon it**, And spirit to those who walk on it—says, ⁶**I, the Lord**, have called you in righteousness, And I **will hold your hand, And I will guard you**, And I will make you into a covenant of the people—A light of the Gentiles— ⁷**To open blind eyes**, To take prisoners out of confinement, And those who dwell in darkness Out of their prison.

[GNT] <u>Isaiah 42:5-7</u> God created the heavens and stretched them out; **he fashioned the earth and all that lives there; he gave life and breath to all its people**. And now the Lord God says to his servant, ⁶**"I, the Lord**, have called you and **given you power** to see that justice is done on earth. Through you I will make a covenant with all peoples; through you I will bring light to the nations. ⁷**You will open the eyes of the blind** and set free those who sit in dark prisons.

[GNV] <u>Isaiah 42:5-7</u> Thus saith God the Lord (he that created the heavens and spread them abroad: he that stretched forth the earth, and the buds thereof: **he that giveth breath unto the people upon it**, and spirit to them that walk therein) ⁶**I the Lord** have called thee in righteousness, and will hold thine hand, and I **will keep thee**, and give thee for a covenant of the people, and for a light of the Gentiles, ⁷**That thou mayest open the eyes of the blind**, and bring out the prisoners from the prison: and them that sit in darkness, out of the prison house.

[LEB] <u>Isaiah 42:5-7</u> Thus says the God, Yahweh, who created the heavens and stretched them out, who spread out the earth and its offspring, **who gives breath to the people upon it** and spirit to those who walk in it. [6]"I am Yahweh; I have called you in righteousness, and I have grasped your hand and **watched over you**; and I have given you as a covenant of the people, as a light of the nations, [7]**to open the blind eyes**, to bring the prisoner out from the dungeon, those who sit in darkness from the house of imprisonment.

[LTPB] <u>Isaiah 42:5-7</u> The Lord God says this: creating skies and stretching them out; **establishing the earth and** what springs up from it; **giving air to the people who are on it**, and breath to those walking on it. [6]**I am the Lord**. I called you in righteousness, and have taken your hand. **I saved you**, and have given you as the people's covenant, as the nations' light, [7]**so you may open the blind's eyes**, and lead the chained from custody, those sitting in shadows from the prison's house.

[NET] <u>Isaiah 42:5-7</u> This is what the true God, the Lord, says—the one who created the sky and stretched it out, **the one who fashioned the earth and everything that lives on it, the one who gives breath to the people on it**, and life to those who live on it: [6]"I, the Lord, officially commission you; I take hold of your hand. I **protect you** and make you a covenant mediator for people, and a light to the nations, [7]**to open blind eyes,** to release prisoners from dungeons, those who live in darkness from prisons.

[NLT] <u>Isaiah 42:5-7</u> God, the Lord, created the heavens and stretched them out. He created the earth and everything in it. **He gives breath to everyone, life to everyone who walks the earth.** And it is he who says, [6]"**I, the Lord**, have called you to demonstrate my righteousness. I **will take you by the hand and guard you**, and I will give you to my people, Israel, as a symbol of my covenant with them. And you will be a light to guide the nations. [7]**You will open the eyes of the blind**. You will free the captives from prison, releasing those who sit in dark dungeons.

[NOG] <u>Isaiah 42:5-7</u> Yahweh El created the heavens and stretched them out. He shaped the earth and all that comes from it. **He gave life to the people who are on it and breath to those who walk on it**. This is what Yahweh El says: [6]I, Yahweh, have called you to do what is right. I will take hold of your hand. I will protect you. I will appoint you as my promise to the people, as my light to the nations. [7]**You will give sight to the blind**, bring prisoners out of prisons, and bring those who live in darkness out of dungeons.

[REAL] <u>Isaiah 42:5-7</u> This is what El-ohim Ya-HoVaH, says who created the heavens and stretched them out, the one **who spread out the Earth** and what comes out of it, the one **who gives breath to the people on it** and Ru-ah to those who walk on it. [6]I, Ya-HoVaH, have called you in justice, and I shall hold your hand, and **I shall guard you**, and I shall give you as a Binding Contract for the people, for Light of the nations, [7]**to open the blind eyes**, to bring the prisoners out from the jail, and those who sit down in darkness out of the jail.

[SAAS-OT] <u>Isaiah 42:5-7</u> Thus says the Lord God, who made heaven and established it, **who made firm the earth** and the things in it, and **who gives breath to the people in it**, and spirit to those who walk on it: [6]"I, the Lord God, called You in righteousness, and will hold Your hand. **I will strengthen You**, and give You as the covenant of a race, as the light of the Gentiles, [7]**to open the eyes of the blind**, to bring out prisoners who are bound, and those who sit in darkness from the prison house.

[Thomson] <u>Isaiah 42:5-7</u> Thus saith the Lord, the God who made the heaven and fixed it; who established the earth and the things therein and **who giveth vital air to the people on it, and breath to them who tread thereon**; [6]I the Lord God have called thee for saving mercy, and I **will take hold of thy hand and strengthen thee;** for I have given thee for the covenant of a race—for the light of nations: [7]**to open the eyes of the blind**; to lead out from chains them who are bound, and out of prison, them who are sitting in darkness.

OUR HEALING COVENANT

[TLB] <u>Isaiah 42:5-7</u> The Lord God who created the heavens and stretched them out, who created the earth and everything in it, **who gives life and breath and spirit to everyone in all the world**, he is the one who says to his Servant, the Messiah: [6]**"I the Lord** have called you to demonstrate my righteousness. I **will guard and support you**, for I have given you to my people as the personal confirmation of my covenant with them. You shall also be a light to guide the nations unto me. [7]**You will open the eyes of the blind** and release those who sit in prison darkness and despair.

[TVB] <u>Isaiah 42:5-7</u> God, the Eternal One, who made the starry skies, stretched them tight above and around; **Who cast the shimmering globe of earth and filled it with life**; who gives breath and animates the people; Who walks and talks with life-giving spirit has this to say: [6]Eternal One: I am the Eternal One. By righteousness I have called you. **I will take you by the hand and keep you safe.** You are given as a covenant between Me and the people: a light for the nations, a shining beacon to the world. [7]**You will open blind eyes so they will see again.** You will lead prisoners, blinking, out from caverns of captivity, from cells pitch black with despair.

<u>Isaiah 53:3-5</u> He is despised and rejected of men; a man of sorrows, and acquainted with grief: and we hid as it were our faces from him; he was despised, and we esteemed him not. [4]**Surely he hath borne our griefs, and carried our sorrows**: yet we did esteem him stricken, smitten of God, and afflicted. [5]**But he was wounded for our transgressions, he was bruised for our iniquities: the chastisement of our peace was upon him; and with his stripes we are healed**[raphah].

[AMP] <u>Isaiah 53:3-5</u> He was despised and rejected by men, A Man of sorrows and pain and acquainted with grief; And like One from whom men hide their faces He was despised, and we did not appreciate His worth or esteem Him. [4]**But [in fact] He has borne our griefs, And He has carried our sorrows and pains**; Yet we [ignorantly] assumed that He was stricken, Struck down by God and degraded and humiliated [by Him]. [5]**But He was wounded for our transgressions, He was crushed for our wickedness [our sin, our injustice, our wrongdoing]; The punishment [required] for our well-being fell on Him, And by His stripes (wounds) we are healed.**

[AMPC] <u>Isaiah 53:3-5</u> He was despised and rejected and forsaken by men, a Man of sorrows and pains, and acquainted with grief and sickness; and like One from Whom men hide their faces He was despised, and we did not appreciate His worth or have any esteem for Him. [4]**Surely He has borne our griefs (sicknesses, weaknesses, and distresses) and carried our sorrows and pains [of punishment]**, yet we [ignorantly] considered Him stricken, smitten, and afflicted by God [as if with leprosy]. [5]**But He was wounded for our transgressions, He was bruised for our guilt and iniquities; the chastisement [needful to obtain] peace and well-being for us was upon Him, and with the stripes [that wounded] Him we are healed and made whole.**

[Anchor] <u>Isaiah 53:3-5</u> He was despised, the lowest of men: a man of pains, familiar with disease, One from whom men avert their gaze—despised, and we reckoned him as nothing. [4]**But it was our diseases that he bore, our pains that he carried**, While we counted him as one stricken, touched by God with affliction. [5]**He was wounded for our rebellions, crushed for our transgressions; The chastisement that reconciled us fell upon him, and we were healed by his bruises.**

[BBE] <u>Isaiah 53:3-5</u> Men made sport of him, turning away from him; he was a man of sorrows, marked by disease; and like one from whom men's faces are turned away, he was looked down on, and we put no value on him. [4]**But it was our pain he took, and our diseases were put on him**: while to us he seemed as one diseased, on whom God's punishment had come. [5]**But it was for our sins he was wounded, and for our evil doings he was crushed: he took the punishment by which we have peace, and by his wounds we are made well.**

[BLE] <u>Isaiah 53:3-5</u> He was despised and avoided by men, a man of pains and familiar with sickness; like one from whom people screen their faces we despised him and did not count him for anything. **⁴But in fact it was our sicknesses he was carrying, our pains he was loaded with**—while we all the time thought he was a smitten one, struck by God and disciplined. **⁵But he was being stabbed by our crimes, felled by our guilt; the chastisement to give us soundness came on him, and by his stripes we got healing.**

[Cheyne-OT] <u>Isaiah 53:3-5</u> Despised (was he) and forsaken of men, a man of pains and acquainted with sickness, and as one from whom we hide the face—despised, and we esteemed him not. **⁴But surely it was he who bare our sickness, and our pains—he carried them,** while we—we esteemed him as stricken, as smitten of God, and afflicted. **⁵But he was dishonored because of our rebellions, crushed because of our iniquities; the chastisement of our peace was upon him, and through his stripes healing came unto us.**

[CT-OT] <u>Isaiah 53:3-5</u> Despised and rejected by men, a man of pains and accustomed to illness, and as one who hides his face from us, despised and we held him of no account. **⁴Indeed, he bore our illnesses, and our pains-he carried them,** yet we accounted him as plagued, smitten by God and oppressed. **⁵But he was pained because of our transgressions, crushed because of our iniquities; the chastisement of our welfare was upon him, and with his wound we were healed.**

[GNT] <u>Isaiah 53:3-5</u> We despised him and rejected him; he endured suffering and pain. No one would even look at him—we ignored him as if he were nothing. **⁴But he endured the suffering that should have been ours**, the pain that we should have borne. All the while we thought that his suffering was punishment sent by God. **⁵But because of our sins he was wounded, beaten because of the evil we did. We are healed by the punishment he suffered, made whole by the blows he received.**

[Haak] <u>Isaiah 53:3-5</u> He was despised, and the unworthiest among men, a man of sorrows, that hath experience of sickness in sickness and (every one) as it were hiding then his face from him; he was despised, and we esteemed him not. **⁴Verily he hath taken our sicknesses upon him, and our sorrows them hath he carried**: yet we esteemed that he was plagued, smitten of God and humbled. **⁵But he was wounded for our transgression, he was bruised for our iniquities: the punishment that bringeth peace unto us, was upon him, and by his stripes healing is made unto us.**

[Haupt] <u>Isaiah 53:3-5</u> Despised was he, and forsaken of men, A man of many pains, and familiar with sickness, Yea, like one from whom men hide the face, Despised, and we esteemed him not. **⁴But our sickness, alone, he bore,** And our pains—he carried them, Whilst we esteemed him stricken, Smitten of God, and afflicted. **⁵But alone he was humiliated because of our rebellions, Alone he was crushed because of our iniquities; A chastisement, all for our peace, was upon him, And to us came healing through his stripes.**

[HRB] <u>Isaiah 53:3-5</u> He is despised and abandoned of men, a Man of pains, and acquainted with sickness. And as it were hiding our faces from Him, He being despised, and we did not value Him. **⁴Surely He has borne our sicknesses, and He carried our pain**; yet we esteemed Him plagued, smitten by Elohim, and afflicted. **⁵But He was wounded for our transgressions; He was bruised for our iniquities; the chastisement of our peace was upon Him; and with His wounds we ourselves are healed.**

[JPS-OT 1917] <u>Isaiah 53:3-5</u> He was despised, and forsaken of men, a man of pains, and acquainted with disease, and as one from whom men hide their face: he was despised, and we esteemed him not. **⁴Surely our diseases he did bear, and our pains he carried**; whereas we did esteem him stricken, smitten of God, and afflicted. **⁵But he was wounded because of our transgressions, he was crushed**

because of our iniquities: the chastisement of our welfare was upon him, and with his stripes we were healed.

[LEB] <u>Isaiah 53:3-5</u> He was despised and rejected by men, a man of suffering, and acquainted with sickness, and like one from whom others hide their faces, he was despised, and we did not hold him in high regard. [4]**However, he was the one who lifted up our sicknesses, and he carried our pain**, yet we ourselves assumed him stricken, struck down by God and afflicted. [5]**But he was pierced because of our transgressions, crushed because of our iniquities; the chastisement for our peace was upon him, and by his wounds we were healed.**

[Leeser-OT] <u>Isaiah 53:3-5</u> He was despised and shunned by men; a man of pains, and acquainted with disease; and as one who hid his face from us was he despised, and we esteemed him not. [4]**But only our diseases did he bear himself, and our pains he carried**: while we indeed esteemed him stricken, smitten of God, and afflicted. [5]**Yet he was wounded for our transgressions, he was bruised for our iniquities: the chastisement for our peace was upon him; and through his bruises was healing granted to us.**

[McFadyen-OT] <u>Isaiah 53:3-5</u> He was spurned and forsaken of men, Familiar with suffering and pain; As one from whom men hide their faces, He was spurned and we heeded him not. [4]**But ours was the pain that he bore, And the sorrows he carried were ours**; Yet by us he was counted as smitten And tortured by God's own hand. [5]**But ours was the sin that pierced him, The guilt that crushed him was ours: Yea, he was chastised for our welfare, And his stripes brought healing to us.**

[Moffatt] <u>Isaiah 53:3-5</u> He was despised and shunned by men, a man of pain, who knew what sickness was; like one from whom men turn with shuddering, he was despised, we took no heed of him. [4]**And yet ours was the pain he bore, the sorrow he endured!** We thought him suffering from a stroke at God's own hand; [5]**yet he was wounded because we had sinned, 'twas our misdeeds that crushed him; 'twas for our welfare that he chastised, the blows that fell to him have brought us healing.**

[MOTB] <u>Isaiah 53:3-5</u> The victim of adverse circumstances, he possessed no external attractions. Abandoned by his fellows, afflicted with wasting disease, avoided as an outcast, we despised him, never suspecting his true character and the nature of the service which he was performing for us all. [4]**And yet it is now clear that he whom we regarded as the especial object of Jehovah's righteous wrath, was afflicted that we might thereby be delivered from pain and disease. [5]The repeated disasters that fell upon him were the consequences, not of his, but our, crimes. Peace came to us instead of judgment, because our punishment fell upon him.**

[MSTC] <u>Isaiah 53:3-5</u> He was despised and cast out of men's company; and one that had suffered sorrow, and had experience of infirmity. And we were as one that had hid his face from him. [4]He was so despisable, that we esteemed him not. **Truly, he took upon him our diseases, and bare our sorrows.** And yet we counted him plagued, and beaten, and humbled of God. [5]**He was wounded for our transgressions, and bruised for our iniquities. The correction that brought us peace was on him, and with his stripes we were healed.**

[NABRE] <u>Isaiah 53:3-5</u> He was spurned and avoided by men, a man of suffering, knowing pain, Like one from whom you turn your face, spurned, and we held him in no esteem. [4]**Yet it was our pain that he bore, our sufferings he endured.** We thought of him as stricken, struck down by God and afflicted, [5]**But he was pierced for our sins, crushed for our iniquity. He bore the punishment that makes us whole, by his wounds we were healed.**

[NCV] <u>Isaiah 53:3-5</u> He was hated and rejected by people. He had much pain and suffering. People would not even look at him. He was hated, and we didn't even notice him. [4]**But he took our suffering on him and felt our pain for us.** We saw his suffering and thought God was punishing him. [5]**But he**

was wounded for the wrong we did; he was crushed for the evil we did. **The punishment, which made us well, was given to him, and we are healed because of his wounds**.

[NEB] <u>Isaiah 53:3-5</u> He was despised, he shrank from the sight of men, tormented and humbled by suffering; we despised him, we held him of no account, a thing from which men turn away their eyes. [4]**Yet on himself he bore our sufferings**, our torments he endured, which we counted him smitten by God, struck down by disease and misery; [5]**but he was pierced for our transgressions, tortured for our iniquities; the chastisement he bore is health for us and by his scourging we are healed.**

[NIRV] <u>Isaiah 53:3-5</u> People looked down on him. They didn't accept him. He knew all about pain and suffering. He was like someone people turn their faces away from. We looked down on him. We didn't have any respect for him. [4]**He suffered the things we should have suffered**. He took on himself the pain that should have been ours. But we thought God was punishing him. We thought God was wounding him and making him suffer. [5]**But the servant was pierced because we had sinned. He was crushed because we had done what was evil. He was punished to make us whole again. His wounds have healed us**.

[NWT] <u>Isaiah 53:3-5</u> He was despised and was avoided by men, A man who was meant for pains and was familiar with sickness. It was as if his face were hidden from us. He was despised, and we held him as of no account. [4]**Truly he himself carried our sicknesses, And he bore our pains**. But we considered him as plagued, stricken by God and afflicted. [5]**But he was pierced for our transgression; He was crushed for our errors. He bore the punishment for our peace, And because of his wounds we were healed**.

[Ottley-Isa-Heb] <u>Isaiah 53:3-5</u> Despised and avoided of men; a man of pains, and one that knew sickness; and as one from whom faces are hid; despised, and we esteemed him not. [4]**Surely he bore our sicknesses; and our pains, he supported them**; and we, (on our part,) did esteem him stricken, smitten of God, and afflicted. [5]**And he was pierced for our rebellions, bruised for our iniquities; the chastisement of our peace was upon him; and in his stripes was there healing for us**.

[Ottley-Isa-LXX] <u>Isaiah 53:3-5</u> But his form was unhonoured, and failing among all men; a man under a stroke, and one that knew how to bear sickness; for his face is turned away, he was dishonoured and not esteemed. [4]**This is he that beareth our sins, and sorroweth for us and we esteemed him to be in trouble, and under a stroke, and calamity. [5]But he was wounded for our transgressions, and was sick because of our sins; the discipline of our peace was upon him with his stripe we were healed**.

[Rotherham] <u>Isaiah 53:3-5</u> Despised was he, and forsaken of men, Man of pains, and familiar with sickness, —Yea, like one from whom the face is hidden, Despised, and we esteemed him not. [4]**Yet surely, our sicknesses, he, carried, And, as for our pains, he bare the burden of them**, —But, we, accounted him stricken, Smitten of God, and humbled. [5]**Yet, he, was pierced for transgressions that were ours, was crushed for iniquities that were ours, —The chastisement for our well-being, was upon him, And, by his stripes, there is healing for us**.

[SG] <u>Isaiah 53:3-5</u> He was despised, and avoided by men, A man of sorrows, and acquainted with pain; And like one from whom men hide their faces, He was despised, and we esteemed him not. [4]**Yet it was our pains that he bore, Our sorrows that he carried**; While we accounted him stricken, Smitten by God, and afflicted. [5]**He was wounded for our transgressions, He was crushed for our iniquities; The chastisement of our welfare was upon him, And through his stripes we were healed**.

[TLB] <u>Isaiah 53:3-5</u> We despised him and rejected him—a man of sorrows, acquainted with bitterest grief. We turned our backs on him and looked the other way when he went by. He was despised, and we didn't care. [4]**Yet it was our grief he bore, our sorrows that weighed him down**. And we thought his troubles were a punishment from God, for his own sins! **⁵But he was wounded and bruised for our sins. He was beaten that we might have peace; he was lashed—and we were healed!**

[UDB] <u>Isaiah 53:3-5</u> People will despise and reject him. He will endure much pain, and he will suffer much. Because his face will be very disfigured, people will not want to look at him; he will not even look human any more; people will despise him and think that he is not worth paying any attention to. **⁴But he will be punished for the sicknesses within our lives; he will endure great pain for us.** But we will think that he is being punished by God, afflicted for his own sins. **⁵But people will pierce him through and kill him because of the evil things that we did; they will wound him because of our sins. They will beat him in order that things may go well with us; because they will whip him, we will be healed.**

[YLT] <u>Isaiah 53:3-5</u> He is despised, and left of men, A man of pains, and acquainted with sickness, And as one hiding the face from us, He is despised, and we esteemed him not. **⁴Surely our sicknesses he hath borne, And our pains—he hath carried them,** And we—we have esteemed him plagued, Smitten of God, and afflicted. **⁵And he is pierced for our transgressions, Bruised for our iniquities, The chastisement of our peace [is] on him, And by his bruise there is healing to us.**

<u>Isaiah 53:10</u> **Yet it pleased the L**ORD **to bruise him; he hath put him to grief: when thou shalt make his soul an offering for sin,** he shall see his seed, he shall prolong his days, and the pleasure of the L ORD shall prosper in his hand.

[Benisch-OT] <u>Isaiah 53:10</u> **Yet it pleased the Eternal to crush him, he caused him to sicken: if thou lay guilt on his soul,** he shall see seed, he shall prolong his days; and the pleasure of the Eternal shall prosper in his hand.

[CCB] <u>Isaiah 53:10</u> **Yet it was the will of Yahweh to crush him with grief. When he makes himself an offering for sin,** he will have a long life and see his descendants. Through him the will of Yahweh is done.

[CEV] <u>Isaiah 53:10</u> **The Lord decided his servant would suffer as a sacrifice to take away the sin and guilt of others.** Now the servant will live to see his own descendants. He did everything the Lord had planned.

[CWB] <u>Isaiah 53:10</u> **It was the will of the Lord for Him to die. And though God made Him to be an offering for our sins,** He will rise again and complete what God wants Him to do. He will see the fruit of His labor, and His offspring will live forever.

[GNT] <u>Isaiah 53:10</u> The Lord says, "**It was my will that he should suffer; his death was a sacrifice to bring forgiveness.** And so he will see his descendants; he will live a long life, and through him my purpose will succeed.

[HBIV] <u>Isaiah 53:10</u> **But it has pleased Jehovah to crush him with grievous sickness [With the purpose that] if he were to make himself an offering for guilt,** He would see [his] seed, he would prolong his days, And the pleasure of Jehovah would prosper in his hand.

[JPS-OT 1985] <u>Isaiah 53:10</u> **But the L**ORD **chose to crush him by disease, That, if he made himself an offering for guilt,** He might see offspring and have long life, And that through him the LORD's purpose might prosper.

[Kenrick] <u>Isaiah 53:10</u> **And the Lord was pleased to bruise Him in infirmity: if he lay down His life for sin,** He shall see a long-lived seed, and the will of the Lord shall be prosperous in His hand.

[Leeser-OT] Isaiah 53:10 But **the Lord was pleased to crush him through disease: when now his soul hath brought the trespass-offering**, then shall he see his seed, live many days, and the pleasure of the Lord shall prosper in his hand.

[NLV] Isaiah 53:10 But **it was the will of the Lord to crush Him, causing Him to suffer. Because He gives His life as a gift on the altar for sin**, He will see His children. Days will be added to His life, and the will of the Lord will do well in His hand.

[Ottley-Isa-Heb] Isaiah 53:10 **And the Lord was pleased to bruise him; he laid sickness on him; if his soul should make a guilt-offering,** he should see a seed, he should prolong days, and the pleasure of the Lord should prosper in his hand.

[REB] Isaiah 53:10 **Yet the LORD took thought for his oppressed servant and healed him who had given himself as a sacrifice for sin**. He will enjoy long life and see his children's children, and in his hand the LORD's purpose will prosper.

[Rodwell-Isa] Isaiah 53:10 **Yet did it please Yahveh to bruise Him—He made Him sick: —** If Thou make His soul a sin-offering. He would see a seed, would prolong His days, And Yahveh's purpose would prosper in His Hand:

[TVB] Isaiah 53:10 Yet **the Eternal One planned to crush him all along, to bring him to grief, this innocent servant of God. When he puts his life in sin's dark place**, in the pit of wrongdoing, this servant of God will see his children and have his days prolonged. For in His servant's hand, the Eternal's deepest desire will come to pass and flourish.

[UDB] Isaiah 53:10 But **it will be Yahweh's will that he be afflicted and caused to suffer. When he dies as an offering for your own sin**, he will benefit many, many people, as if they were his children; he will live a long time after he dies and becomes alive again, and he will accomplish everything that Yahweh has planned.

Isaiah 54:1 Sing, O barren, thou that didst not bear; break forth into singing, and cry aloud, thou that didst not travail with child: **for more are the children of the desolate than the children of the married wife, saith the LORD.**

[AMP] Isaiah 54:1 "Shout for joy, O barren one, she who has not given birth; Break forth into joyful shouting and rejoice, she who has not gone into labor [with child]! **For the [spiritual] sons of the desolate one will be more numerous Than the sons of the married woman,"** says the Lord.

[EXB] Isaiah 54:1 The Lord says, "Sing, ·Jerusalem [barren one]. ·You are like a woman who [...who] never gave birth to children. Start singing and shout for joy. You never ·felt the pain of giving birth [were in labor], ·but **you will have more children [for more are the children of the desolate one] than the woman who has a husband.**

[MSG] Isaiah 54:1 "Sing, barren woman, who has never had a baby. Fill the air with song, you who've never experienced childbirth! **You're ending up with far more children than all those childbearing women." God says so!**

[NCV] Isaiah 54:1 The Lord says, "Sing, Jerusalem. You are like a woman who never gave birth to children. Start singing and shout for joy. You never felt the pain of giving birth, but **you will have more children than the woman who has a husband.**

Isaiah 54:17 **No weapon that is formed against thee shall prosper**; and every tongue that shall rise against thee in judgment thou shalt condemn. This is the heritage of the servants of the LORD, and their righteousness is of me, saith the LORD.

[Abegg-OT] <u>Isaiah 54:17</u> **No weapon that is forged against you will be effective.** This is the heritage of the Lord's servants, and their righteousness from me, says the Lord.

[ABP] <u>Isaiah 54:17</u> **Every weapon concocted against you shall not be prosperous**; and every voice that shall rise up against you for judgment, all of them you shall vanquish. And the ones liable of you shall be in her; it is the inheritance to the ones attending the Lord, and you shall be righteous to me, says the Lord.

[Anchor] <u>Isaiah 54:17</u> "**The weapon that will succeed against you has not been forged**, And the tongue that rises in court against you shall be proved guilty; This is the portion of the servants of Yahweh, And their victory is from me" —the oracle of Yahweh.

[BBE] <u>Isaiah 54:17</u> **No instrument of war which is formed against you will be of any use**; and every tongue which says evil against you will be judged false. This is the heritage of the servants of the Lord, and their righteousness comes from me, says the Lord.

[CAB] <u>Isaiah 54:17</u> **I will not allow any weapon formed against you to prosper**; and every voice that shall rise up against you for judgment, you shall vanquish them all; and your adversaries shall be condemned thereby. There is an inheritance to them that serve the Lord, and you shall be righteous before Me, says the Lord.

[CCB] <u>Isaiah 54:17</u> **No weapon forged against you will succeed**, and all who speak against you will be silenced. Such is the lot of the servants of Yahweh, and such is the right I grant them—says Yahweh.

[CPDV] <u>Isaiah 54:17</u> **No object which has been formed to use against you will succeed**. And every tongue that resists you in judgment, you shall judge. This is the inheritance of the servants of the Lord, and this is their justice with me, says the Lord.

[CWB] <u>Isaiah 54:17</u> But **no weapon forged against you will prevail**. No army that attacks you will succeed. I will help you answer those who accuse you. I will protect you and defend you. This is the rightful heritage of the servants of the Lord. I will vindicate my servants in the eyes of all the people."

[ERV] <u>Isaiah 54:17</u> "**People will make weapons to fight against you, but their weapons will not defeat you**. Some people will say things against you, but anyone who speaks against you will be proved wrong." The Lord says, "That is what my servants get! They get the good things that come from me, their Lord.

[FAA] <u>Isaiah 54:17</u> **No weapon produced against you will be successful**, And you will condemn every tongue which confronts you in law. This is the inheritance of the Lord's servants, Whose righteousness comes from me", Says the Lord.

[GNT] <u>Isaiah 54:17</u> But **no weapon will be able to hurt you**; you will have an answer for all who accuse you. I will defend my servants and give them victory." The Lord has spoken.

[Haupt] <u>Isaiah 54:17</u> **No weapon formed against thee will succeed**, And against every tongue that contends with thee thou wilt gain thy cause. This is the inheritance of the Servants of Jhvh, And their justification that is of me, says Jhvh.

[JosephStock-Isa] <u>Isaiah 54:17</u> **Every weapon, that is forged against thee, shall miscarry**; And every tongue, that riseth up against thee in judgment, thou shalt prove guilty.

[JPS-OT 1985] <u>Isaiah 54:17</u> **No weapon formed against you Shall succeed**, And every tongue that contends with you at law You shall defeat. Such is the lot of the servants of the Lord, Such their triumph through Me—declares the Lord.

[Moffatt] <u>Isaiah 54:17</u> **No weapon forged against you shall succeed**, no tongue raised against you shall win its plea. Such is the lot of the Eternal's servants; thus, the Eternal promises, do I maintain their cause.

[MOTB] <u>Isaiah 54:17</u> "**The arms of your enemies shall be raised in vain against you**. From every contest you will emerge victors. These shall be the rewards and permanent possessions of those who have proved themselves my true servants, for this will I vindicate them."

[MSG] <u>Isaiah 54:17</u> **but no weapon that can hurt you has ever been forged**. Any accuser who takes you to court will be dismissed as a liar. This is what God's servants can expect. I'll see to it that everything works out for the best." God's Decree.

[NLV] <u>Isaiah 54:17</u> **No tool that is made to fight against you will do well**. And you will prove wrong every tongue that says you are guilty. This is the gift given to the servants of the Lord. I take away their guilt and make them right," says the Lord.

[Ottley-Isa-LXX] <u>Isaiah 54:17</u> **Every instrument is corruptible, but against thee I will not approve it**; and every voice that shall stand up against thee for judgment, all them shalt thou vanquish, and they that are subject to thee shall be therein. There is an inheritance for them that attend on the Lord, and ye shall be righteous in my sight, saith the Lord.

[SAAS-OT] <u>Isaiah 54:17</u> **I will not prosper any instrument of destruction used against you**, and every voice raised against you in judgment, you shall overcome them all; and your adversaries shall be judged guilty. This is the inheritance for those who serve the Lord, and you shall be my righteous ones," says the Lord.

[TLB] <u>Isaiah 54:17</u> But in that coming day, **no weapon turned against you shall succeed**, and you will have justice against every courtroom lie. This is the heritage of the servants of the Lord. This is the blessing I have given you, says the Lord.

[TVB] <u>Isaiah 54:17</u> **But no instrument forged against you will be allowed to hurt you**, and no voice raised to condemn you will successfully prosecute you. It's that simple; this is how it will be for the servants of the Eternal; I will vindicate them.

[ULB] <u>Isaiah 54:17</u> **No weapon that is formed against you will succeed**; and you will condemn everyone who accuses you. This is the heritage of the servants of Yahweh, and their vindication from me—this is Yahweh's declaration."

<u>Isaiah 55:3</u> **Incline your ear, and come unto me: hear, and your soul shall live**; and I will make an everlasting covenant with you, even the sure mercies of David.

[EXB] <u>Isaiah 55:3</u> **Come to me and ·listen [extend your ear]; listen to me so you may live**. I will make an ·agreement with you that will last forever [everlasting covenant/treaty with you]. I will give you the ·blessings [covenant love; loyalty; lovingkindness; sure mercies] I promised to David.

[GNT] <u>Isaiah 55:3</u> "**Listen now, my people, and come to me; come to me, and you will have life!** I will make a lasting covenant with you and give you the blessings I promised to David."

[Haupt] <u>Isaiah 55:3</u> **Incline your ear, and come to me; hear, that your soul may be revived!** I will give you an everlasting covenant, the sure promises of lovingkindness to David;

[ICB] <u>Isaiah 55:3</u> **Come to me and listen. Listen to me so you may live**. I will make an agreement with you that will last forever. I will give you the blessings I promised to David.

[NJB] <u>Isaiah 55:3</u> **Pay attention, come to me; listen, and you will live**. I shall make an everlasting covenant with you in fulfilment of the favours promised to David.

[T4T] <u>Isaiah 55:3</u> **Listen to me and come to me; pay attention to me, and if you do that, you will have new life in your soul**. I will make an agreement with you that will last forever to faithfully love you like I loved King David.

[Thomson] <u>Isaiah 55:3</u> **Incline your ears and follow in my paths; hearken to me and your soul shall live on good things**; and I will make with you an everlasting covenant—the gracious promises to David which are faithful.

[TNIV] <u>Isaiah 55:3</u> **Give ear and come to me; listen, that you may live**. I will make an everlasting covenant with you, my faithful love promised to David.

[TVB] <u>Isaiah 55:3</u> **Listen closely, and come even closer. My words will give life,** for I will make a covenant with you that cannot be broken, a promise Of My enduring presence and support like I gave to David.

[ULB] <u>Isaiah 55:3</u> **Turn your ears and come to me! Listen, that you may live!** I will make an everlasting covenant with you: My reliable, faithful love promised to David.

<u>Isaiah 55:11</u> So shall my word be that goeth forth out of my mouth: it shall not return unto me void, but it shall accomplish that which I please, and it shall prosper in the thing whereto I sent it.

[AMP] <u>Isaiah 55:11</u> So will My word be which goes out of My mouth; It will not return to Me void (useless, without result), Without accomplishing what I desire, And without succeeding in the matter for which I sent it.

[Beck] <u>Isaiah 55:11</u> so will My word be that I speak. It will not come back to Me with nothing done but do what I want it to do and accomplish what I sent it for.

[BLE] <u>Isaiah 55:11</u> so shall be my word that goes out of my mouth: it shall not come back to me empty-handed, but do what I please that it should and succeed in what I sent it for.

[CEV] <u>Isaiah 55:11</u> That's how it is with my words. They don't return to me without doing everything I send them to do."

[CJB] <u>Isaiah 55:11</u> so is my word that goes out from my mouth—it will not return to me unfulfilled; but it will accomplish what I intend, and cause to succeed what I sent it to do."

[CWB] <u>Isaiah 55:11</u> so the word that goes out of my mouth will not return to me empty but will carry out my wishes and succeed in doing what I sent it out to do.

[ERV] <u>Isaiah 55:11</u> In the same way, my words leave my mouth, and they don't come back without results. My words make the things happen that I want to happen. They succeed in doing what I send them to do.

[JPS-OT 1985] <u>Isaiah 55:11</u> So is the word that issues from My mouth: It does not come back to Me unfulfilled, But performs what I purpose, Achieves what I sent it to do.

[LitProph-OT] <u>Isaiah 55:11</u> So shall be the word which goeth forth from my mouth; It shall not return unto me fruitless; But it shall effect what I have willed; And make the purpose succeed, for which I have sent it.

[NET] <u>Isaiah 55:11</u> In the same way, the promise that I make does not return to me, having accomplished nothing. No, it is realized as I desire and is fulfilled as I intend."

[NLT] <u>Isaiah 55:11</u> It is the same with my word. I send it out, and it always produces fruit. It will accomplish all I want it to, and it will prosper everywhere I send it.

[Ottley-Isa-LXX] <u>Isaiah 55:11</u> So shall be my word, whatsoever goeth forth from my mouth; it shall not return until all that I willed be fulfilled, and I prosper thy ways and my commandments.

[Pauli-Isa] <u>Isaiah 55:11</u> Thus shall be the word of my kindness, which proceeds from my presence, it is not possible that it shall return to my presence void, but it shall accomplish that which I please, and shall prosper in the thing where to I sent it.

[Plaisted] <u>Isaiah 55:11</u> So shall my word be that goes forth out of my mouth: it shall not return to me empty, but it shall accomplish that which I please, and it shall prosper in the thing for which I sent it.

[Spurrell-OT] <u>Isaiah 55:11</u> So shall My word be which proceedeth from My mouth; It shall not return unto Me profitless, But it shall accomplish the very thing which I desire, And shall effect that for which I have commissioned it.

[T4T] <u>Isaiah 55:11</u> And similarly the things that I promise to do, I will always cause to happen; my promises will always be fulfilled. They will accomplish the things that I gave them to accomplish.

[Thomson] <u>Isaiah 55:11</u> so shall it be with my word: when it hath proceeded from my mouth, it shall not be reversed, till all are accomplished which I willed; and till I prosper thy ways and my commandments.

<u>Isaiah 57:18-19</u> **I have seen his ways, and will heal**[raphah] **him**: I will lead him also, and restore comforts unto him and to his mourners. [19]I create the fruit of the lips; Peace, peace to him that is far off, and to him that is near, saith the LORD; and **I will heal**[raphah] **him**.

[BBE] <u>Isaiah 57:18-19</u> **I have seen his ways, and I will make him well**: I will give him rest, comforting him and his people who are sad. [19]I will give the fruit of the lips: Peace, peace, to him who is near and to him who is far off, says the Lord; and **I will make him well**.

[BrownKrueger] <u>Isaiah 57:18-19</u> I have seen his ways, and will heal him: I will lead him also, and restore comfort unto him, and to those that lament him. [19]I create the fruit of the lips, to be peace: peace unto them that are far off, and to them that are near, saith the Lord: for I will heal him.

[CWB] <u>Isaiah 57:18-19</u> **"I have seen what they have done, but I will offer them forgiveness and healing**. I will bring them back home and give them peace. I will comfort those who mourn. [19]I will give peace to those far and near. **I will heal my people**, and praise will be on their lips.

[Douay-Rheims] <u>Isaiah 57:18-19</u> **I saw his ways, and I healed him**, and brought him back, and restored comforts to him, and to them that mourn for him. [19]I created the fruit of the lips, peace, peace to him that is far off, and to him that is near, said the Lord, and **I healed him**.

[EEBT] <u>Isaiah 57:18-19</u> **I have seen what he is doing. But I will give health to him again**. Then I will be a guide to him and I will make him strong again. And I will cause those among my people who are sad to feel better.' [19]God will cause his people to speak words of praise. The LORD says, 'I will give peace. There will be peace for the people who are a long way from here. And there will be peace for those who are near. **And I will give health to them**.

[ERV] <u>Isaiah 57:18-19</u> **I have seen their way of life, but I will heal them**. I will guide and comfort them and those who mourn for them. [19]I will teach them a new word: peace. I will give peace to those who are near and to those who are far away. **I will heal them**. The Lord himself said this.

[EXB] <u>Isaiah 57:18-19</u> **I have seen ·what they have done [their ways], but I will heal them**. I will guide them and comfort them and those who ·felt sad for them [mourn]. ·They will all praise me [I will create praise on their lips; …creating fruit of lips]. [19]·I will give peace, real peace [Peace, peace], to those far and near, and **I will heal them**," says the Lord.

[FAA] <u>Isaiah 57:18-19</u> **I have seen his ways But I will heal him and lead him, And I will restore comfort to him** And to those of his company who mourn. [19]I create the fruit of the lips: Peace, peace to him who is far off And to him who is near", Says the Lord, **"And I will heal him**."

[GW] <u>Isaiah 57:18-19</u> **I've seen their sinful ways, but I'll heal them**. I'll guide them and give them rest. I'll comfort them and their mourners. [19]I'll create praise on their lips: "Perfect peace to those both far and near." **"I'll heal them**," says the Lord.

[ICB] <u>Isaiah 57:18-19</u> **I have seen what they have done, but I will heal them**. I will guide them and comfort them. And those who were sad will praise me. ¹⁹I will give peace, real peace, to those far and near. And **I will heal them,"** says the Lord.

[Knox] <u>Isaiah 57:18-19</u> **Now to pity his plight, now to bring him remedy**! Home-coming at last, consolation at last, for him and all that bemoan him! ¹⁹The harvest of men's thanks, it is I that bring it to the birth. Peace, the Lord says, peace to those who are far away, and to those who are near at hand; **I have brought him remedy**.

[NCV] <u>Isaiah 57:18-19</u> "**I have seen what they have done, but I will heal them**. I will guide them and comfort them and those who felt sad for them. They will all praise me. ¹⁹I will give peace, real peace, to those far and near, and **I will heal them,"** says the Lord.

[NEB] <u>Isaiah 57:18-19</u> **Then I considered his ways, I cured him and gave him relief**, and I brought him comfort in full measure, ¹⁹brought peace for all men, both near and far, and **so I cured him**, says the LORD.

[NLT] <u>Isaiah 57:18-19</u> **I have seen what they do, but I will heal them anyway**! I will lead them. I will comfort those who mourn, ¹⁹bringing words of praise to their lips. May they have abundant peace, both near and far," says **the Lord, who heals them**.

[NWT] <u>Isaiah 57:18-19</u> "**I have seen his ways, But I will heal him** and lead him And restore comfort to him and to his mourning ones. ¹⁹I am creating the fruit of the lips. Continuous peace will be given to the one who is far away and the one who is near," says Jehovah, "**And I will heal him**."

[T4T] <u>Isaiah 57:18-19</u> **I have seen the evil things that they continually do, but I will restore them and lead them**. I will encourage/comfort them. And to those who are mourning, ¹⁹I will enable them to sing songs to praise me. I will restore all my people, those who live near Jerusalem and those who live far away, and **I will cause things to go well for them**.

[TLB] <u>Isaiah 57:18-19</u> **I have seen what they do, but I will heal them anyway**! I will lead them and comfort them, helping them to mourn and to confess their sins. ¹⁹Peace, peace to them, both near and far, for I will heal them all.

[TVB] <u>Isaiah 57:18-19</u> **I have seen how they act, but I will still bind them up and make them well again**. I will show them the way, comfort and console them. ¹⁹I will create in them a desire to praise. "Peace, peace, to those far away. All will be well, wherever you are." And I will heal them.

<u>Isaiah 58:8</u> Then shall thy light break forth as the morning, and **thine health shall spring forth speedily**: and thy righteousness shall go before thee; the glory of the LORD shall be thy rereward.

[AMPC] <u>Isaiah 58:8</u> Then shall your light break forth like the morning, and **your healing (your restoration and the power of a new life) shall spring forth speedily**; your righteousness (your rightness, your justice, and your right relationship with God) shall go before you [conducting you to peace and prosperity], and the glory of the Lord shall be your rear guard.

[BBE] <u>Isaiah 58:8</u> Then will light be shining on you like the morning, and **your wounds will quickly be well**: and your righteousness will go before you, and the glory of the Lord will come after you.

[Beck] <u>Isaiah 58:8</u> Then your light will break through like the dawn, and **you will quickly be healed**. Your righteousness will go ahead of you, and the LORD's glory will protect you from behind.

[Benisch-OT] <u>Isaiah 58:8</u> Then shall thy light break forth as the dawn, and **thy cure shall spring forth speedily**; and thy righteousness shall go before thee: the glory of the Eternal shall be thy rereward.

[BLE] <u>Isaiah 58:8</u> Then your light would break like the dawn and **your wounds would quickly grow whole**, and the rightness of your cause would go before you and Jehovah's glory would bring up your rear;

[CCB] <u>Isaiah 58:8</u> Then will your light will break forth as the dawn and **your healing come in a flash**. Your righteousness will be your vanguard, the Glory of Yahweh your rearguard.

[CEB] <u>Isaiah 58:8</u> Then your light will break out like the dawn, and **you will be healed quickly**. Your own righteousness will walk before you, and the Lord's glory will be your rear guard.

[CJB] <u>Isaiah 58:8</u> Then your light will burst forth like the morning, **your new skin will quickly grow over your wound**; your righteousness will precede you, and Adonai's glory will follow you.

[CLV] <u>Isaiah 58:8</u> Then your light shall be rent as the dawn, and **your longevity with haste shall sprout**. And there goes before you your righteousness. And the glory of Yahweh shall gather about you.

[CSB] <u>Isaiah 58:8</u> Then your light will appear like the dawn, and **your recovery will come quickly**. Your righteousness will go before you, and the Lord's glory will be your rear guard.

[CT-OT] <u>Isaiah 58:8</u> Then your light shall break forth as the dawn, and **your healing shall quickly sprout**, and your righteousness shall go before you; the glory of the Lord shall gather you in.

[CWB] <u>Isaiah 58:8</u> If you do this, my light will shine on you like the morning sun and **your healing will be quickly evident**. I will go before you and my glory will be your rear guard.

[EEBT] <u>Isaiah 58:8</u> Then your light will shine like the light at dawn. And **soon everyone will see that you are well again**. Then your righteous God will go in front of you. And the glory of the LORD at your backs will make you safe.

[Haupt] <u>Isaiah 58:8</u> Then will thy light break forth as the dawn, **thy wounds will be quickly healed over**, They righteousness will go before thee, and JHVH's glory will be thy rearward.

[HRB] <u>Isaiah 58:8</u> Then your light shall break as the dawn, and **your healing shall spring up quickly**; and your righteousness shall go before you; the glory of YAHWEH shall gather you.

[JPS-OT 1985] <u>Isaiah 58:8</u> Then shall your light burst through like the dawn And **your healing spring up quickly**; Your Vindicator shall march before you, The Presence of the LORD shall be your rear guard.

[Knox] <u>Isaiah 58:8</u> Then, sudden as the dawn, the welcome light shall break on thee, in a moment **thy health shall find a new spring**; divine favour shall lead thee on thy journey, brightness of the Lord's presence close thy ranks behind.

[NCV] <u>Isaiah 58:8</u> Then your light will shine like the dawn, and **your wounds will quickly heal**. Your God will walk before you, and the glory of the Lord will protect you from behind.

[NEB] <u>Isaiah 58:8</u> Then shall your light break forth like the dawn and **soon you will grow healthy like a wound newly healed**; your own righteousness shall be your vanguard and the glory of the LORD your rearguard.

[NET] <u>Isaiah 58:8</u> Then your light will shine like the sunrise; **your restoration will quickly arrive**; your godly behavior will go before you, and the Lord's splendor will be your rear guard.

[NIRV] <u>Isaiah 58:8</u> Then the light of my blessing will shine on you like the rising sun. **I will heal you quickly**. I will march out ahead of you. And my glory will follow behind you and guard you. That's because I always do what is right.

[NOG] <u>Isaiah 58:8</u> Then your light will break through like the dawn, and **you will heal quickly**. Your righteousness will go ahead of you, and the glory of Yahweh will guard you from behind.

[Noyes] <u>Isaiah 58:8</u> Then shall thy light break forth like the morning, **And thy health shall spring forth speedily**; Thy salvation shall go before thee, And the glory of Jehovah shall bring up thy rear.

[Rotherham] <u>Isaiah 58:8</u> Then, shall break forth, as the dawn, thy light, **And, thy new flesh, shall, speedily, grow**, —Then shall go, before thee, thy righteousness, The glory of Yahweh, shall bring up thy rear:

[Thomson] <u>Isaiah 58:8</u> then shall thy light break forth like the morning, and **thy remedies shall spring up speedily**: and thy righteousness shall go before thee, and the glory of the Lord will surround thee.

[TVB] <u>Isaiah 58:8</u> Then, oh then, your light will break out like the warm, golden rays of a rising sun; **in an instant, you will be healed**. Your rightness will precede and protect you; the glory of the Eternal will follow and defend you.

<u>Isaiah 58:11</u> And the LORD shall guide thee continually, and satisfy thy soul in drought, and **make fat thy bones**: and thou shalt be like a watered garden, and like a spring of water, whose waters fail not.

[Alexander-OT] <u>Isaiah 58:11</u> And Jehovah will guide thee ever, and satisfy thy soul in drought, and **thy bones shall he invigorate**, and thou shalt be like a watered garden, and like a spring of water, whose waters shall not fail.

[BBE] <u>Isaiah 58:11</u> And the Lord will be your guide at all times; in dry places he will give you water in full measure, and **will make strong your bones**; and you will be like a watered garden, and like an ever-flowing spring.

[Beck] <u>Isaiah 58:11</u> And the LORD will guide you continually and satisfy you even in times of drought. **Your bodies will be vigorous**. You will be like a watered garden and a spring whose waters don't fail.

[Berkeley] <u>Isaiah 58:11</u> The Lord shall guide you continually and shall satisfy your soul in dry places; **your strength shall be renewed**, and you shall be like a well-watered garden, like a spring whose waters never disappoint.

[CBC] <u>Isaiah 58:11</u> And the LORD shall gently guide thee continually, and satisfy thy soul in great drought, and **invigorate thy bones**: and thou shalt be like a watered garden, and like a spring of water, whose waters fail not.

[CLV] <u>Isaiah 58:11</u> Yahweh will guide you continually, and He will satisfy your soul in sun-glaring places; **He shall invigorate your bones**, And you will become like a well-watered garden, And like a flowing well of water whose waters are not defaulting.

[CPDV] <u>Isaiah 58:11</u> And the Lord will give you rest continually, and he will fill your soul with splendor, and **he will free your bones**, and you will be like a watered garden and like a fountain of water whose waters will not fail.

[CSB] <u>Isaiah 58:11</u> The Lord will always lead you, satisfy you in a parched land, and **strengthen your bones**. You will be like a watered garden and like a spring whose water never runs dry.

[Douay-Rheims] <u>Isaiah 58:11</u> And the Lord will give thee rest continually, and will fill thy soul with brightness, and **deliver thy bones**, and thou shalt be like a watered garden, and like a fountain of water whose waters shall not fail.

[FAA] <u>Isaiah 58:11</u> And the Lord will always lead you, And he will satisfy your appetite in dry places, And **make your joints pliant**, And you will become like a well-watered garden, And like a fount of water Whose water does not fail.

[HBIV] <u>Isaiah 58:11</u> And Jehovah will guide thee continually, And satisfy thy soul in dry places, And **make strong thy bones**; And thou will be like a watered garden, And like a spring of water, whose waters deceive not.

[KJ3] <u>Isaiah 58:11</u> And Jehovah shall always guide you, and satisfy your soul in dry places, and **make strong your bones**. And you shall be like a watered garden, and like a spring of waters which do not prove to be deceiving.

[MSTC] <u>Isaiah 58:11</u> The LORD shall ever be thy guide, and satisfy the desire of thine heart, and **fill thy bones with marrow.** Thou shalt be like a fresh watered garden, and like the fountain of water, that never leaveth running.

[NETS-OT] <u>Isaiah 58:11</u> And your God will be with you continually, and you shall be satisfied exactly as your soul desires, and **your bones shall be enriched**, and they shall be like a soaked garden and like a spring whose water has never failed.

[REB] <u>Isaiah 58:11</u> the LORD will be your guide continually and will satisfy your needs in the bare desert; **he will give you strength of limb**; you will be like a well-watered garden, like a spring whose waters never fail.

[T4T] <u>Isaiah 58:11</u> I, Yahweh, will guide you continually, and I will give you good things to satisfy you. **I will enable you to remain strong and healthy.** You will be like a garden that is well watered, like a spring that never dries up.

[TLB] <u>Isaiah 58:11</u> And the Lord will guide you continually, and satisfy you with all good things, **and keep you healthy too**; and you will be like a well-watered garden, like an ever-flowing spring.

[ULB] <u>Isaiah 58:11</u> Then Yahweh will lead you continually and satisfy you in regions where there is no water, and **he will strengthen your bones**. You will be like a watered garden, and like a spring of water, whose waters never fail.

<u>Isaiah 66:14</u> And when ye see this, your heart shall rejoice, and **your bones shall flourish like an herb**: and the hand of the LORD shall be known toward his servants, and his indignation toward his enemies.

[AMP] <u>Isaiah 66:14</u> When you see this, your heart will rejoice; **Your bones will flourish like new grass**. And the [powerful] hand of the Lord will be revealed to His servants, But His indignation will be toward His enemies.

[BBE] <u>Isaiah 66:14</u> And you will see it and your heart will be glad, and **your bones will get new strength, like young grass**: and the hand of the Lord will be seen at work for his servants, and his wrath against his haters.

[CWB] <u>Isaiah 66:14</u> When you see what the Lord will do for His servants you'll be glad. Your heart will rejoice and **your bones will grow strong**. Everyone will see the merciful hand of God on His people and His indignation carried out against His enemies.

[Ewald-OT] <u>Isaiah 66:14</u> then you will see—and your heart leapeth and **your bones become fresh as the young grass**, how Yahvé hand is revealed with his servants, but he is angry with his enemies.

[Fenton] <u>Isaiah 66:14</u> You shall see, and be glad in your hearts, And **your vigour shall grow like the grass**, And the Lord's hand be shown to His Servants, And His wrath to His foes, —

[NETS-OT] <u>Isaiah 66:14</u> You shall see, and your heart shall rejoice, and **your bones shall grow like grass**, and the hand of the Lord shall be known to those who worship him, and he shall threaten those who disobey him.

[T4T] <u>Isaiah 66:14</u> When you see those things happen, you will rejoice. **Your old bones will become strong again like grass that grows quickly/well in the springtime.** When that happens, everyone will know that Yahweh has power to help those who worship and obey him, but that he is angry with his enemies.

[TLB] <u>Isaiah 66:14</u> When you see Jerusalem, your heart will rejoice; **vigorous health will be yours.** All the world will see the good hand of God upon his people and his wrath upon his enemies.

JEREMIAH

<u>Jeremiah 1:12</u> Then said the LORD unto me, Thou hast well seen: for **I will hasten my word to perform it.**

[ACV] <u>Jeremiah 1:12</u> Then LORD said to me, Thou have well seen. For **I watch over my word to perform it.**

[AMP] <u>Jeremiah 1:12</u> Then the Lord said to me, "You have seen well, for **I am [actively] watching over My word to fulfill it."**

[CEV] <u>Jeremiah 1:12</u> "That's right," the Lord replied, "and **I always rise early to keep a promise."**

[CPDV] <u>Jeremiah 1:12</u> And the Lord said to me: "You have seen well. For **I will keep watch over my word, so that I may accomplish it."**

[CSB] <u>Jeremiah 1:12</u> The Lord said to me, "You have seen correctly, for **I watch over my word to accomplish it."**

[Driver-OT] <u>Jeremiah 1:12</u> Then said Yahweh unto me, 'Thou hast well seen: for **I am wakeful over my word to perform it.'**

[EEBT] <u>Jeremiah 1:12</u> 'Yes, that is correct', he said. '**I am watching my words. And I will cause them to happen.'**

[Ewald-OT] <u>Jeremiah 1:12</u> and Yahvé said unto me: "thou hast well seen! for **I will ever guard my word to perform it."**

[Henderson-OT] <u>Jeremiah 1:12</u> Then Jehovah said to me: Thou has rightly seen; **for I will be early awake with respect to my word, to perform it.**

[Kenrick] <u>Jeremiah 1:12</u> And the Lord said to me: Thou has seen well: for **I watch over My word to perform it.**

[LitProph-OT] <u>Jeremiah 1:12</u> And Jehovah said unto me, Thou hast rightly seen: for **I am intent upon my word to perform it.**

[NIV] <u>Jeremiah 1:12</u> The Lord said to me, "You have seen correctly, for **I am watching to see that my word is fulfilled."**

[NWT] <u>Jeremiah 1:12</u> Jehovah said to me: "You have seen correctly, for **I am wide awake concerning my word to carry it out."**

[SAAS-OT] <u>Jeremiah 1:12</u> Then the Lord said to me, "You see well, for **I keep watch to perform the works of my words."**

[SG] <u>Jeremiah 1:12</u> Then the LORD said to me, "You have seen aright; for **I am watching over my word to put it into effect."**

A SURVEY OF HEALING SCRIPTURES

[Thomson] Jeremiah 1:12 And the Lord said to me, Thou hast seen well: for **I have watched over my words to perform them.**

[ULB] Jeremiah 1:12 Yahweh said to me, "You have seen well, for **I am watching over my word to carry it out.**"

[Wycliffe-Noble] Jeremiah 1:12 And the Lord said to me, Thou hast seen well, for **I shall wake on my word, to do it.** (And the Lord said to me, Thou hast seen well, for **I am on watch, to carry out my word.**)

Jeremiah 8:22 Is there no balm in Gilead; is there no physician[raphah] there? **why then is not the health of the daughter of my people recovered?**

[CCB] Jeremiah 8:22 Is there no balm in Gilead? Is there no healer there? **Why is no remedy given to my people?**

[CSB] Jeremiah 8:22 Is there no balm in Gilead? Is there no physician there? So **why has the healing of my dear people not come about?**

[CT-OT] Jeremiah 8:22 Is there no balm in Gilead? Is there no physician there? **Why then, has the health of the daughter of my people not been restored?**

[GNT] Jeremiah 8:22 Is there no medicine in Gilead? Are there no doctors there? **Why, then, have my people not been healed?**

[ICB] Jeremiah 8:22 Surely there is a balm in the land of Gilead. Surely there is a doctor there. So **why aren't the hurts of my people healed?**

[Kenrick] Jeremiah 8:22 Is there no balm in Galaad? or is there no physician there? **Why then is not the wound of the daughter of my people closed?**

[Moffatt] Jeremiah 8:22 Surely Gilead has balsam! **Surely there are healers there!**

[MSG] Jeremiah 8:22 Are there no healing ointments in Gilead? Isn't there a doctor in the house? So **why can't something be done to heal and save my dear, dear people?**

[NLV] Jeremiah 8:22 Is there no healing oil in Gilead? Is there no doctor there? **Why then have my people not been healed?**

[TVB] Jeremiah 8:22 Is there no healing medicine in Gilead, no balm that could help my people? Is there no physician who can help? **Why is there no healing for the wounds inflicted on my people?**

Jeremiah 17:14 Heal[raphah] **me, O Lord, and I shall be healed**[raphah]; save me, and I shall be saved: for thou art my praise.

[CAB] Jeremiah 17:14 Heal me, O Lord, and I shall be healed. Save me, and I shall be saved; for You are my boast.

[CEB] Jeremiah 17:14 Heal me, Lord, and I'll be healed. Save me and I'll be saved, for you are my heart's desire.

[ICB] Jeremiah 17:14 Lord, heal me, and I will truly be healed. Save me, and I will truly be saved. Lord, you are the one I praise.

[NLT] Jeremiah 17:14 O Lord, if you heal me, I will be truly healed; if you save me, I will be truly saved. My praises are for you alone!

[TLB] Jeremiah 17:14 Lord, you alone can heal me, you alone can save, and my praises are for you alone.

OUR HEALING COVENANT

[UDB] Jeremiah 17:14 Yahweh, please heal me, because if you heal me, I will truly be healed. If you rescue me, I will truly be safe, because you are the only one whom I praise.

Jeremiah 30:17 For I will restore health unto thee, and I will heal[raphah] thee of thy wounds, saith the LORD; because they called thee an Outcast, saying, This is Zion, whom no man seeketh after.

[BBE] Jeremiah 30:17 For I will make you healthy again and I will make you well from your wounds, says the Lord; because they have given you the name of an outlaw, saying, It is Zion cared for by no man.

[CT-OT] Jeremiah 30:17 For I will bring healing to you, and of your wounds I will heal you, says the Lord, for they called you an outcast, that is Zion whom no one seeks out.

[CWB] Jeremiah 30:17 "But I will heal your wounds and restore your health. I will care for you and plead your cause. They have called you an outcast, but you are still my son.

[Darby] Jeremiah 30:17 For I will apply a bandage unto thee, and I will heal thee of thy wounds, saith Jehovah; for they have called thee an outcast: This is Zion that no man seeketh after.

[Douay-Rheims] Jeremiah 30:17 For I will close up thy scar, and will heal thee of thy wounds, saith the Lord. Because they have called thee, O Sion, an outcast: This is she that hath none to seek after her.

[ERV] Jeremiah 30:17 "And I will bring your health back and heal your wounds," says the Lord, "because other people said you were outcasts. They said, 'No one cares about Zion.'"

[GNT] Jeremiah 30:17 I will make you well again; I will heal your wounds, though your enemies say, 'Zion is an outcast; no one cares about her.' I, the Lord, have spoken.

[HBIV] Jeremiah 30:17 For I will restore sound flesh to thee, and I will heal thee of thy wounds, says Jehovah; Because men call thee Outcast, This is Zion, whom no one cares for.

[HRB] Jeremiah 30:17 For I will give health back to you, and I will heal you of your wounds, says YAHWEH, because they called you, Outcast; saying, This is Zion; no one is seeking for her.

[ICB] Jeremiah 30:17 I will bring back your health. And I will heal your injuries," says the Lord. "This is because other people forced you out from among them. Those people said about you, 'No one cares about Jerusalem!'"

[JUB] Jeremiah 30:17 For I will cause healing to come for thee, and I will heal thee of thy wounds, said the LORD; because they called thee an Outcast, saying, This is Zion, whom no man seeks after.

[McFadyen-OT] Jeremiah 30:17 I will cause new flesh to grow over thy wound, I will heal thy scars, saith Jehovah; For men have called thee an outcast, "Our quarry" —for whom none careth.

[NCV] Jeremiah 30:17 "I will bring back your health and heal your injuries," says the Lord, "because other people forced you away. They said about you, 'No one cares about Jerusalem!'"

[NEB] Jeremiah 30:17 I will cause new skin to grow and heal your wounds, says the LORD, although men call you the Outcast, Zion, nobody's friend.

[NLV] Jeremiah 30:17 'For I will heal you. I will heal you where you have been hurt,' says the Lord, 'because they have said that you are not wanted. They have said, "It is Zion. No one cares for her."'

[SAAS-OT] Jeremiah 30:17 For I will bring about your healing from a painful wound. I will heal you,' says the Lord. 'For you were called Dispersed, for they said, "She is your prey, because no one seeks her."'

[Sawyer-7590] <u>Jeremiah 30:17</u> **for I will restore soundness to you, and heal your wounds**, says Jehovah, though they call you Zion the outcast, whom no man inquires for.

[Thomson] <u>Jeremiah 30:17</u> **Because I will bring up the cure for thee I will cure thee, saith the Lord, of thy painful wound**; because thou wast called the Outcast, the hunt is up after thee; because there is none who seeketh this outcast,

[TVB] <u>Jeremiah 30:17</u> **For I will make you well again and heal your wounds** I, the Eternal One, declare to you, Because they have called you an outcast: "Look, it is Zion, the one for whom no one cares."

[UDB] <u>Jeremiah 30:17</u> Everyone says that you are outcasts, and that you live in Jerusalem, a city that no one cares about." But Yahweh says, "**I will heal your injuries and cause you to be healthy again.**"

[YLT] <u>Jeremiah 30:17</u> **For I increase health to thee, And from thy strokes I do heal thee**, An affirmation of Jehovah, For 'Outcast' they have called to thee, 'Zion it [is], there is none seeking for her.'

<u>Jeremiah 33:6</u> **Behold, I will bring it health and cure, and I will cure**[raphah] **them**, and will reveal unto them the abundance of peace and truth.

[AMPC] <u>Jeremiah 33:6</u> **Behold, [in the future restored Jerusalem] I will lay upon it health and healing**, and I will cure them and will reveal to them the abundance of peace (prosperity, security, stability) and truth.

[BBE] <u>Jeremiah 33:6</u> **See, I will make it healthy and well again, I will even make them well**; I will let them see peace and good faith in full measure.

[Beck] <u>Jeremiah 33:6</u> **I'm going to restore and heal them. When I have healed them**, I will show them a very happy and secure life.

[Berkeley] <u>Jeremiah 33:6</u> **Look, I will bring to her restoration and health; and I will heal them** and reveal to them an abundance of peace and prosperity.

[CWB] <u>Jeremiah 33:6</u> "But **I will turn trials into blessings and bring health and healing to my people.** They will enjoy an abundance of peace and security.

[Darby] <u>Jeremiah 33:6</u> **Behold, I will apply a healing dressing to it and cure, and I will heal them**, and will reveal unto them an abundance of peace and truth.

[ERV] <u>Jeremiah 33:6</u> 'But then **I will heal the people** in that city. I will let them enjoy peace and safety.'

[HBIV] <u>Jeremiah 33:6</u> **Behold, I am about to bring her sound flesh and healing, and I will heal them**; And I will open to them an abundance of peace and permanence.

[HCSB] <u>Jeremiah 33:6</u> **Yet I will certainly bring health and healing to it and will indeed heal them.** I will let them experience the abundance of peace and truth.

[Jerusalem] <u>Jeremiah 33:6</u> **But look, I will hasten their recovery and their cure; I will cure them** and let them know peace and security in full measure.

[JPS-OT 1985] <u>Jeremiah 33:6</u> **I am going to bring her relief and healing.** I will heal them and reveal to them abundance of true favor.

[Kent-OT] <u>Jeremiah 33:6</u> 'Behold, **I will make new flesh to grow on her, and healing so that I will heal her**, and I will reveal to them treasures of peace and stability.'

[LitProph-OT] <u>Jeremiah 33:6</u> **Behold, I will make it perfectly sound and whole, and will heal them**; I will also grant their prayer for peace and truth:

[NABRE] <u>Jeremiah 33:6</u> **Look! I am bringing the city recovery and healing; I will heal them** and reveal to them an abundance of lasting peace.

[NCV] <u>Jeremiah 33:6</u> **But then I will bring health and healing to the people there. I will heal them** and let them enjoy great peace and safety.

[NOG] <u>Jeremiah 33:6</u> **"But I will heal this city and restore it to health. I will heal its people,** and I will give them peace and security."

[Noyes] <u>Jeremiah 33:6</u> **Behold, I will bind up her wounds, and heal them,** And I will reveal to them abundance of peace and stability.

[SG] <u>Jeremiah 33:6</u> 'Behold, **I will bring them complete recovery and healing,** and will reveal to them abundance of peace and security.'

[Spurrell-OT] <u>Jeremiah 33:6</u> **Behold, I will restore unto her soundness and health**; And I will heal them, and I will encircle them With abundance of peace and truth.

[TNIV] <u>Jeremiah 33:6</u> "'Nevertheless, **I will bring health and healing to it; I will heal my people** and will let them enjoy abundant peace and security.'"

[TVB] <u>Jeremiah 33:6</u> Nevertheless, keep watching! **I will restore this city and heal the wounds of My people**. I will lavish them with peace and stability.

[UKJV] <u>Jeremiah 33:6</u> **Behold, I will bring it health and cure, and I will cure them,** and will reveal unto them the abundance of peace and truth.

[ULB] <u>Jeremiah 33:6</u> But see, **I am about to bring healing and a cure, for I will heal them** and will bring to them abundance, peace, and faithfulness.

[YLT] <u>Jeremiah 33:6</u> **Lo, I am increasing to it health and cure, And have healed them,** and revealed to them The abundance of peace and truth.

<u>Jeremiah 38:20</u> But Jeremiah said, They shall not deliver thee. Obey, I beseech thee, the voice of the Lord, which I speak unto thee: so it shall be well unto thee, **and thy soul shall live.**

[CCB] <u>Jeremiah 38:20</u> Jeremiah said, "They will not hand you over. Listen to what Yahweh says to you through me; **it will be well with you and you will live.**

[CEB] <u>Jeremiah 38:20</u> "That won't happen," Jeremiah replied, "if you obey the Lord, whose message I bring. You will survive, and **all will go well for you.**"

[CWB] <u>Jeremiah 38:20</u> I said, "The Babylonians will not hand you over to these Jews. Don't worry about it. Obey the Lord by doing what He tells you to do, and He'll be with you. Your life will be spared and **all will go well.**

[EXB] <u>Jeremiah 38:20</u> But Jeremiah answered, "·The Babylonians will not hand you over to the Jews [You will not be given up]. ·Obey [Listen to the voice of] the Lord by doing what I tell you. Then things will go well for you, and **your life will be saved.**"

[McFadyen-OT] <u>Jeremiah 38:20</u> "No," said Jeremiah, "you will not be handed over. But I entreat you to listen to what I say—it is the voice of Jehovah: **your happiness and your life depend upon it.**"

[MSG] <u>Jeremiah 38:20</u> Jeremiah assured him, "They won't get hold of you. Listen, please. Listen to God's voice. I'm telling you this for your own good **so that you'll live.**

[NOG] <u>Jeremiah 38:20</u> Jeremiah said, "You will not be handed over to them. Obey Yahweh by doing what I'm telling you. Then everything will go well for you, and **you will live.**

LAMENTATIONS

Lamentations 3:22-23 It is of the Lord's mercies that we are not consumed, because his compassions fail not. ²³They are new every morning: great is thy faithfulness.

[AMPC] **Lamentations 3:22-23** It is because of the Lord's mercy and loving-kindness that we are not consumed, because His [tender] compassions fail not. ²³They are new every morning; great and abundant is Your stability and faithfulness.

[CSB] **Lamentations 3:22-23** Because of the Lord's faithful love we do not perish, for his mercies never end. ²³They are new every morning; great is your faithfulness!

[CT-OT] **Lamentations 3:22-23** Verily, the kindnesses of the Lord never cease! Indeed, His mercies never fail! ²³They are new every morning; great is Your faithfulness.

[EEBT] **Lamentations 3:22-23** God is good and he never stops being kind to us. That is why we are alive at all. ²³Each new day we can remember that God's promises will certainly happen.

[JPS-OT 1985] **Lamentations 3:22-23** The kindness of the Lord has not ended, His mercies are not spent. ²³They are renewed every morning—Ample is Your grace!

[MOTB] **Lamentations 3:22-23** I will take this to heart and build my hope upon it—that the love of my God never ceases, and his pity never fails. ²³Every morning thy love is new, and tokens of thy faithfulness abundant.

[NASB] **Lamentations 3:22-23** The Lord's lovingkindnesses indeed never cease, For His compassions never fail. ²³They are new every morning; Great is Your faithfulness.

[Smith] **Lamentations 3:22-23** The mercies of Jehovah are that we were not consumed, for his compassions were not finished. ²³New for the mornings: great thy faithfulness.

[T4T] **Lamentations 3:22-23** Yahweh never stops faithfully loving us, and he never stops acting kindly toward us. ²³He is the one whom we can always trust/lean on. Every morning he acts mercifully toward us again.

[TVB] **Lamentations 3:22-23** How enduring is God's loyal love; the Eternal has inexhaustible compassion. ²³Here they are, every morning, new! Your faithfulness, God, is as broad as the day.

Lamentations 3:58 O Lord, thou hast pleaded the causes of my soul; **thou hast redeemed my life.**

[CCB] **Lamentations 3:58** O Lord, you took up my case and **redeemed my life.**

[CSB] **Lamentations 3:58** You championed my cause, Lord; **you redeemed my life.**

[CWB] **Lamentations 3:58** You took up my case and came to my rescue. **You saved my life.**

[EEBT] **Lamentations 3:58** Lord, you have given me help. You have paid the price to **keep me alive.**

[ERV] **Lamentations 3:58** You defended me and **brought me back to life.**

[GNT] **Lamentations 3:58** You came to my rescue, Lord, **and saved my life.**

[Knox] **Lamentations 3:58** Thine, Lord, to take my part; **thine to rescue me from death;**

[NIRV] **Lamentations 3:58** Lord, you stood up for me in court. **You saved my life and set me free.**

[TLV] **Lamentations 3:58** Lord, You pled my soul's case, **You redeemed my life.**

[TVB] **Lamentations 3:58** Taking up my cause, Lord, You've been my champion. You've paid the price; **You saved my life.**

EZEKIEL

Ezekiel 3:21 Nevertheless if thou warn the righteous man, that the righteous sin not, **and he doth not sin, he shall surely live, because he is warned**; also thou hast delivered thy soul.

[AMP] **Ezekiel 3:21** However, if you have warned the righteous man not to sin **and he does not sin, he will surely live because he took warning**; also you have freed yourself [from responsibility]."

[CT-OT] **Ezekiel 3:21** But you, if you warn him-the righteous man-that a righteous man should not sin, and **he does not sin-he will live because he took heed**, and you-you will have saved your soul."

Ezekiel 18:19 Yet say ye, Why? doth not the son bear the iniquity of the father? **When the son hath done that which is lawful and right, and hath kept all my statutes, and hath done them, he shall surely live.**

[CCB] **Ezekiel 18:19** You may say, 'Why does the son not bear the guilt of his father?' But **the son did what was just and right, observing and practicing my decrees; he will live!**

[CSB] **Ezekiel 18:19** But you may ask, 'Why doesn't the son suffer punishment for the father's iniquity?' **Since the son has done what is just and right, carefully observing all my statutes, he will certainly live.**

[ERV] **Ezekiel 18:19** "You might ask, 'Why will the son not be punished for his father's sins?' **The reason is that the son was fair and did good things. He very carefully obeyed my laws, so he will live.**

[FAA] **Ezekiel 18:19** But you will say, 'Why does the son not bear the iniquity of the father?' **If the son executes justice and righteousness and keeps all my statutes, and does them, he will surely live.**

[GNT] **Ezekiel 18:19** "But you ask, 'Why shouldn't the son suffer because of his father's sins?' **The answer is that the son did what was right and good. He kept my laws and followed them carefully, and so he will certainly live.**

[TVB] **Ezekiel 18:19** So why do you ask, "Why is the son not also punished for his father's guilt?" **Don't you see? The son did not commit his father's sins. The son chose to do what is just and right by remembering and following My laws, so he will surely live.**

[UDB] **Ezekiel 18:19** If you ask, 'Why should the man's son not suffer for the evil things that his father did?', I will answer that **the son has done what is fair and right and has obeyed all my laws, so he will surely remain alive.**

Ezekiel 18:21 But if the wicked will turn from all his sins that he hath committed, and keep all my statutes, and do that which is lawful and right, he shall surely live, he shall not die.

[AMPC] **Ezekiel 18:21** But if the wicked man turns from all his sins that he has committed and keeps all My statutes and does that which is lawful and right, he shall surely live; he shall not die.

[CAB] **Ezekiel 18:21** And if the transgressor shall turn away from all his iniquities which he has committed, and keep all My commandments, and do justice and mercy, he shall surely live, and shall no means die.

[MSG] **Ezekiel 18:21** "But a wicked person who turns his back on that life of sin and keeps all my statutes, living a just and righteous life, he'll live, really live. He won't die.

[NOG] **Ezekiel 18:21** "But suppose a wicked person turns away from all the sins that he has done. He obeys all my laws and does what is fair and right. He will certainly live. He will not die.

[REAL] <u>Ezekiel 18:21</u> but if the evil guy turns away from all his habitual sins that he has carried out, and he puts a boundary fence around all my laws to guard them, and he does what is lawful and right, for sure, he shall live. He shall not die!

<u>Ezekiel 18:23</u> Have I any pleasure at all that the wicked should die? saith the Lord God: and not that he should return from his ways, and live?

[Beck] <u>Ezekiel 18:23</u> "Do I want the wicked to die?" asks the Lord God. "Don't I want him to return from his ways and live?"

[ERV] <u>Ezekiel 18:23</u> The Lord God says, "I don't want evil people to die. I want them to change their lives so that they can live!

[Fenton] <u>Ezekiel 18:23</u> "Have I any pleasure in the death of the wicked?" the Mighty Lord asks, — "I would rather he should turn from his wicked course and live."

[MSG] <u>Ezekiel 18:23</u> Do you think I take any pleasure in the death of wicked men and women? Isn't it my pleasure that they turn around, no longer living wrong but living right—really living?

[NIRV] <u>Ezekiel 18:23</u> When sinful people die, it does not give me any joy," announces the Lord and King. "But when they turn away from their sins and live, that makes me very happy.

[NOG] <u>Ezekiel 18:23</u> I don't want wicked people to die." declares Adonay Yahweh. "I want them to turn from their evil ways and live.

[SAAS-OT] <u>Ezekiel 18:23</u> Do I ever will the death of a lawless man," says the Lord, "since My will is for him to turn from the evil way and live?

[Sawyer-7590] <u>Ezekiel 18:23</u> Do I delight at all in the death of the wicked, says the Lord Jehovah, [and] not in his turning from his way, that he may live?

[T4T] <u>Ezekiel 18:23</u> I, Yahweh the Lord, declare that I certainly am not happy about wicked people dying. Instead, I am happy when they turn away from their wicked behavior, and because of that, they remain alive.

[TVB] <u>Ezekiel 18:23</u> Do I enjoy watching the wicked die? No. I, the Eternal One, would prefer for the wicked to stop doing the wrong things they do and live.

[UDB] <u>Ezekiel 18:23</u> I, Yahweh the Lord, declare that I certainly am not happy about wicked people dying. Instead, I am happy when they stop doing wicked things and remain alive as a result.

<u>Ezekiel 18:27</u> Again, when the wicked man turneth away from his wickedness that he hath committed, and doeth that which is lawful and right, he shall save his soul alive.

[CCB] <u>Ezekiel 18:27</u> And if the wicked man does what is good and right, after turning from the sins he committed, he will save his life.

[CJB] <u>Ezekiel 18:27</u> And when the wicked person turns away from all the wickedness he has committed and does what is lawful and right, he will save his life.

[GNT] <u>Ezekiel 18:27</u> When someone evil stops sinning and does what is right and good, he saves his life.

[Haupt] <u>Ezekiel 18:27</u> And if a wicked man turn from the wickedness which he does, and do justice and righteousness, he shall save his life.

[NASB] <u>Ezekiel 18:27</u> Again, when a wicked man turns away from his wickedness which he has committed and practices justice and righteousness, he will save his life.

[NJB] <u>Ezekiel 18:27</u> Similarly, when the wicked abandons wickedness to become law-abiding and upright, he saves his own life.

[NOG] <u>Ezekiel 18:27</u> When a wicked person turns away from the wicked things that he has done and does what is fair and right, he will live.

[SAAS-OT] <u>Ezekiel 18:27</u> Again when a lawless man turns away from the lawlessness he commits and does judgment and righteousness, then he guards his life;

<u>Ezekiel 18:32</u> For I have no pleasure in the death of him that dieth, saith the Lord GOD: wherefore turn yourselves, and live ye.

[CSB] <u>Ezekiel 18:32</u> For I take no pleasure in anyone's death." This is the declaration of the Lord God. "So repent and live!

[EXB] <u>Ezekiel 18:32</u> I ·do not want anyone to die [take no pleasure/delight in anyone's death], says the Lord God, so ·change your hearts and lives so you may [repent and] live.

[GNT] <u>Ezekiel 18:32</u> I do not want anyone to die," says the Sovereign Lord. "Turn away from your sins and live."

[JPS-OT 1985] <u>Ezekiel 18:32</u> For it is not My desire that anyone shall die—declares the Lord GOD. Repent, therefore, and live!

[NOG] <u>Ezekiel 18:32</u> I don't want anyone to die," declares Adonay Yahweh. "Change the way you think and act!"

[REB] <u>Ezekiel 18:32</u> I have no desire for the death of anyone. This is the word of the Lord GOD.

[Sawyer-7590] <u>Ezekiel 18:32</u> For I have no pleasure in the death of mortal, says the Lord Jehovah. Therefore turn and live.

[T4T] <u>Ezekiel 18:32</u> I, Yahweh the Lord, declare that I am not pleased about your dying. So repent, and remain alive!"

[TLB] <u>Ezekiel 18:32</u> I do not enjoy seeing you die," the Lord God says. "Turn, turn and live!"

[TVB] <u>Ezekiel 18:32</u> I don't enjoy watching anyone die, so turn back to Me and live!

[UDB] <u>Ezekiel 18:32</u> I, Yahweh the Lord, declare that I am not pleased if you die. So turn away from your sins and stay alive!"

[ULB] <u>Ezekiel 18:32</u> For I do not rejoice in the death of the one who dies—this is Lord Yahweh's declaration—so repent and live!"

<u>Ezekiel 20:11</u> And I gave them my statutes, and shewed them my judgments, which if a man do, he shall even live in them.

[BBE] <u>Ezekiel 20:11</u> And I gave them my rules and made clear to them my orders, which, if a man keeps them, will be life to him.

[Beck] <u>Ezekiel 20:11</u> I gave them My laws and taught them My rules in which there is life for those who keep them.

[Berkeley] <u>Ezekiel 20:11</u> I gave them My statutes and taught them My judgments, by obedience to which man shall live.

[CEB] <u>Ezekiel 20:11</u> I gave them my regulations and made known to them my case laws, which bring life to all who observe them.

[CWB] <u>Ezekiel 20:11</u> There I gave them my laws and my commandments which bring life to those who keep them.

[ICB] <u>Ezekiel 20:11</u> I gave them my rules. I told them about my laws. If a person obeys them, he will live.

[NLT] <u>Ezekiel 20:11</u> There I gave them my decrees and regulations so they could find life by keeping them.

[WSP-OT] <u>Ezekiel 20:11</u> And I gave them my statutes, And shewed them my judgments, Which if a man do, he shall even live by them.

<u>Ezekiel 33:11</u> Say unto them, As I live, saith the Lord God, I have no pleasure in the death of the wicked; **but that the wicked turn from his way and live**: turn ye, turn ye from your evil ways; for why will ye die, O house of Israel?

[CEV] <u>Ezekiel 33:11</u> Tell them that as surely as I am the living Lord God, I don't like to see wicked people die. **I enjoy seeing them turn from their sins and live**. So if the Israelites want to live, they must stop sinning and turn back to me.

[MOTB] <u>Ezekiel 33:11</u> Not so, fellow Israelites; you misapprehend the divine purpose. **Jehovah wishes that all should live**, and ever holds forth the possibility of redemption.

[MSG] <u>Ezekiel 33:11</u> "Tell them, 'As sure as I am the living God, I take no pleasure from the death of the wicked. **I want the wicked to change their ways and live.** Turn your life around! Reverse your evil ways! Why die, Israel?'

[NCV] <u>Ezekiel 33:11</u> Say to them: 'The Lord God says: As surely as I live, I do not want any who are wicked to die. **I want them to stop doing evil and live.** Stop! Stop your wicked ways! You don't want to die, do you, people of Israel?'

[NIRV] <u>Ezekiel 33:11</u> Tell them, 'When sinful people die, it does not give me any joy. **But when they turn away from their sins and live, that makes me very happy.** And that is just as sure as I am alive,' announces the Lord and King. 'So turn away from your sins! Change your evil ways! Why should you die, people of Israel?'

[NLT] <u>Ezekiel 33:11</u> As surely as I live, says the Sovereign Lord, I take no pleasure in the death of wicked people. **I only want them to turn from their wicked ways so they can live.** Turn! Turn from your wickedness, O people of Israel! Why should you die?

[Thomson] <u>Ezekiel 33:11</u> Say unto them, As I live, saith the Lord, I desire not the death of the wicked, but that **the wicked should turn from his way and live**. Turn ye, turn ye from your way. Why do you die, O house of Israel.

[UDB] <u>Ezekiel 33:11</u> Say to them, 'Yahweh the Lord says, "As surely as I am alive, I am not happy when wicked people die; **I would prefer that they turn away from their wicked behavior and continue to live**. So repent! Turn away from your evil behavior! You Israelite people, do you really want to die?"'

[UKJV] <u>Ezekiel 33:11</u> Say unto them, As I live, says the Lord God, I have no pleasure in the death of the wicked; but that **the wicked turn from his way and live**: turn all of you, turn all of you from your evil ways; for why will all of you die, O house of Israel?

<u>Ezekiel 33:15-16</u> If the wicked restore the pledge, give again that he had robbed, walk in the statutes of life, without committing iniquity; he shall surely live, he shall not die. [16]None of his sins that he hath committed shall be mentioned unto him: he hath done that which is lawful and right; he shall surely live.

[AMP] <u>Ezekiel 33:15-16</u> if a wicked man returns [what he took as] a pledge, pays back what he had taken by robbery, walks in the statutes which ensure life, without committing injustice, he will certainly live; he will not die. [16]None of his sins that he has committed will be remembered against him. He has practiced that which is just (fair) and right; he will most certainly live.

[CJB] <u>Ezekiel 33:15-16</u> if the wicked person restores pledged property and returns what he stole, so that he lives by the laws that give life and does not commit evil deeds; then he will live, he will not die. [16]None of the sins he committed will be remembered against him; he has done what is lawful and right; he will surely live.'

[NCV] <u>Ezekiel 33:15-16</u> For example, they may return what somebody gave them as a promise to repay a loan, or pay back what they stole. If they live by the rules that give life and do not sin, then they will surely live, and they will not die. [16]They will not be punished for any of their sins. They now do what is right and fair, so they will surely live.

[NJB] <u>Ezekiel 33:15-16</u> if he returns pledges, restores what he has stolen, keeps the laws that give life and no longer does wrong, he will live and will not die. [16]None of his previous sins will be remembered against him; having done what is lawful and upright, he will live.

[ULB] <u>Ezekiel 33:15-16</u> if he restores the loan guarantee that he wickedly demanded, or if he makes restitution for what he has stolen, and if he walks in the statutes that give life and no longer commits sin—then he will surely live. He will not die. [16]None of the sins that he has committed will be called to mind for him. He has acted justly and rightly, and so, he will surely live!

<u>Ezekiel 33:19</u> But if the wicked turn from his wickedness, and do that which is lawful and right, he shall live thereby.

[BBE] <u>Ezekiel 33:19</u> And when the evil man, turning away from his evil-doing, does what is ordered and right, he will get life by it.

[CAB] <u>Ezekiel 33:19</u> And when the sinner turns from his iniquity, and shall do judgment and righteousness, he shall live by them.

[CJB] <u>Ezekiel 33:19</u> And when the wicked person turns from his wickedness and does what is lawful and right, he will live because of it.

[NET] <u>Ezekiel 33:19</u> When the wicked turns from his sin and does what is just and right, he will live because of it.

[NETS-OT] <u>Ezekiel 33:19</u> And when the sinner turns back from his lawlessness and performs judgment and righteousness, in them he shall live.

[SAAS-OT] <u>Ezekiel 33:19</u> But when the sinner turns from his lawlessness and does judgment and righteousness, he shall live because of it.

[Smith] <u>Ezekiel 33:19</u> And in the turning back of the unjust from his injustice and doing judgment and justice upon them, he shall live.

[VW] <u>Ezekiel 33:19</u> But when the wicked turns from his wickedness and does justice and righteousness, he shall live because of it.

<u>Ezekiel 34:16</u> I will seek that which was lost, and bring again that which was driven away, and will **bind up that which was broken, and will strengthen that which was sick**: but I will destroy the fat and the strong; I will feed them with judgment.

A SURVEY OF HEALING SCRIPTURES

[AMPC] <u>Ezekiel 34:16</u> I will seek that which was lost and bring back that which has strayed, and **I will bandage the hurt and the crippled and will strengthen the weak and the sick**, but I will destroy the fat and the strong [who have become hardhearted and perverse]; I will feed them with judgment and punishment.

[CEB] <u>Ezekiel 34:16</u> I will seek out the lost, bring back the strays, **bind up the wounded, and strengthen the weak**. But the fat and the strong I will destroy, because I will tend my sheep with justice.

[CWB] <u>Ezekiel 34:16</u> I will look for the lost and bring back the ones who have strayed. **I will bind up the brokenhearted, strengthen the weak and heal those who are sick**. But I will destroy all those who got fat on my sheep. I will do what is right and I will administer justice.

[GNT] <u>Ezekiel 34:16</u> I will look for those that are lost, bring back those that wander off, **bandage those that are hurt, and heal those that are sick**; but those that are fat and strong I will destroy, because I am a shepherd who does what is right.

[JPS-OT 1985] <u>Ezekiel 34:16</u> I will look for the lost, and I will bring back the strayed; **I will bandage the injured, and I will sustain the weak**; and the fat and healthy ones I will destroy. I will tend them rightly.

[Knox] <u>Ezekiel 34:16</u> The lost sheep I will find, the strayed sheep I will bring home again; **bind up the broken limb, nourish the wasted frame**, keep the well-fed and the sturdy free from harm; they shall have a true shepherd at last.

[LXX-1844] <u>Ezekiel 34:16</u> I will seek that which is lost, and I will recover the stray one, and **will bind up that which was broken, and will strengthen the fainting**, and will guard the strong, and will feed them with judgment.

[MSG] <u>Ezekiel 34:16</u> I'll go after the lost, I'll collect the strays, **I'll doctor the injured, I'll build up the weak ones** and oversee the strong ones so they're not exploited.

[NIRV] <u>Ezekiel 34:16</u> I will search for the lost. I will bring back those who have wandered away. **I will bandage the ones who are hurt. I will make the weak ones stronger**. But I will destroy those who are fat and strong. I will take good care of my sheep. I will treat them fairly.

[NLV] <u>Ezekiel 34:16</u> I will look for the lost, bring back those that have gone away, **help those who have been hurt, and give strength to the sick**. But I will destroy the fat and the strong. I will feed them with punishment.

[NOG] <u>Ezekiel 34:16</u> I will look for those that are lost, bring back those that have strayed away, **bandage those that are injured, and strengthen those that are sick**. I will destroy those that are fat and strong. I will take care of my sheep fairly.

[Noyes] <u>Ezekiel 34:16</u> I will seek that which was lost, and bring back that which was driven away, and **will bind up that which was broken, and will strengthen the sick**; but the fat and the strong will I destroy; I will feed them as they deserve.

[REB] <u>Ezekiel 34:16</u> I shall search for the lost, recover the straggler, **bandage the injured, strengthen the sick**, leave the healthy to play, and give my flock their proper food.

[Rotherham] <u>Ezekiel 34:16</u> That which is straying, will I seek out, And, that which hath been driven away, will I bring back, And, **that which is torn, will I bind up, And, the weak, will I strengthen**, — But, the fat and the strong, will I watch, I will feed them with justice.

[RSV] <u>Ezekiel 34:16</u> I will seek the lost, and I will bring back the strayed, and **I will bind up the crippled, and I will strengthen the weak**, and the fat and the strong I will watch over; I will feed them in justice.

[Sawyer-7590] <u>Ezekiel 34:16</u> and will seek the lost, and bring back the driven away, and **bind up the bruised, and strengthen the weak**, and keep the fat and strong, and feed them with justice.

[TNIV] <u>Ezekiel 34:16</u> I will search for the lost and bring back the strays. **I will bind up the injured and strengthen the weak**, but the sleek and the strong I will destroy. I will shepherd the flock with justice.

[UDB] <u>Ezekiel 34:16</u> I will search for those who are lost; I will bring back the ones who have strayed away. **I will bandage those who have been injured and strengthen those who are weak**. But I will destroy those who are fat and powerful. I will act fairly toward my sheep, my people.

[ULB] <u>Ezekiel 34:16</u> I will seek the lost and restore the outcast. **I will bind up the broken sheep and heal the sick sheep**, but the fat and the strong I will destroy. I will shepherd with justice.

[YLT] <u>Ezekiel 34:16</u> The lost I seek, and the driven away bring back, And **the broken I bind up, and the sick I strengthen**, And the fat and the strong I destroy, I feed it with judgment.

<u>Ezekiel 37:5-6,14</u> Thus saith the Lord G O D unto these bones; Behold, **I will cause breath to enter into you, and ye shall live**: [6]**And I will lay sinews upon you, and will bring up flesh upon you, and cover you with skin, and put breath in you, and ye shall live**; and ye shall know that I am the L O R D. [14]**And shall put my spirit in you, and ye shall live**, and I shall place you in your own land: then shall ye know that I the L O R D have spoken it, and performed it, saith the L O R D.

[AMP] <u>Ezekiel 37:5-6,14</u> Thus says the Lord G O D to these bones, 'Behold, **I will make breath enter you so that you may come to life. [6]I will put sinews on you, make flesh grow back on you, cover you with skin, and I will put breath in you so that you may come alive**; and you will know that I am the L O R D.'" [14]**I will put My Spirit in you and you will come to life**, and I will place you in your own land. Then you will know that I the Lord have spoken, and fulfilled it," says the L O R D.'"

[BBE] <u>Ezekiel 37:5-6,14</u> This is what the Lord has said to these bones: See, **I will make breath come into you so that you may come to life; [6]And I will put muscles on you and make flesh come on you, and put skin over you, and breath into you, so that you may have life**; and you will be certain that I am the Lord. [14]**And I will put my spirit in you, so that you may come to life**, and I will give you a rest in your land: and you will be certain that I the Lord have said it and have done it, says the Lord.

[CEV] <u>Ezekiel 37:5-6,14</u> "**I, the Lord God, will put breath in you, and once again you will live. [6]I will wrap you with muscles and skin and breathe life into you**. Then you will know that I am the Lord." [14]**My Spirit will give you breath, and you will live again**. I will bring you home, and you will know that I have kept my promise. I, the Lord, have spoken."

[CSB] <u>Ezekiel 37:5-6,14</u> This is what the Lord God says to these bones: **I will cause breath to enter you, and you will live. [6]I will put tendons on you, make flesh grow on you, and cover you with skin. I will put breath in you so that you come to life**. Then you will know that I am the Lord." [14]**I will put my Spirit in you, and you will live**, and I will settle you in your own land. Then you will know that I am the Lord. I have spoken, and I will do it. This is the declaration of the Lord.'"

[Fenton] <u>Ezekiel 37:5-6,14</u> The Mighty Lord proclaims, "**I will bring a wind to you, and you shall revive! [6]I will also put sinews on you, and cause flesh to cover you, and cover you with skin, and put breath into you, when you will revive**, —and learn that I am the Life. [14]**And I will put My breath into you, and revive you**, —I, the Life, have promised, and I will perform it!" said the Ever-Living.

[GNT] <u>Ezekiel 37:5-6,14</u> Tell them that I, the Sovereign Lord, am saying to them: **I am going to put breath into you and bring you back to life. [6]I will give you sinews and muscles, and cover you with skin. I will put breath into you and bring you back to life**. Then you will know that I am the

Lord. **¹⁴I will put my breath in them, bring them back to life**, and let them live in their own land. Then they will know that I am the Lord. I have promised that I would do this—and I will. I, the Lord, have spoken.

[GW] Ezekiel 37:5-6,14 This is what the Almighty Lord says to these bones: **I will cause breath to enter you, and you will live. ⁶I will put ligaments on you, place muscles on you, and cover you with skin. I will put breath in you, and you will live.** Then you will know that I am the Lord.'" **¹⁴I will put my Spirit in you, and you will live.** I will place you in your own land. Then you will know that I, the Lord, have spoken, and I have done it, declares the Lord.'"

[LXX-1844] Ezekiel 37:5-6,14 Thus saith the Lord to these bones; Behold, **I will bring upon you the breath of life: ⁶and I will lay sinews upon you, and will bring up flesh upon you, and will spread skin upon you, and will put my Spirit into you, and ye shall live**; and ye shall know that I am the Lord. **¹⁴And I will put my Spirit within you, and ye shall live**, and I will place you upon your own land: and ye shall know that I am the Lord; I have spoken, and will do it, saith the Lord.

[NAB] Ezekiel 37:5-6,14 Thus says the Lord GOD to these bones: See! **I will bring spirit into you, that you may come to life. ⁶I will put sinews upon you, make flesh grow over you, cover you with skin, and put spirit in you so that you may come to life** and know that I am the LORD. **¹⁴I will put my spirit in you that you may live**, and I will settle you upon your land; thus you shall know that I am the LORD. I have promised, and I will do it, says the LORD.

[NET] Ezekiel 37:5-6,14 This is what the sovereign Lord says to these bones: Look, **I am about to infuse breath into you and you will live. ⁶I will put tendons on you and muscles over you and will cover you with skin; I will put breath in you and you will live**. Then you will know that I am the Lord. **¹⁴I will place my breath in you and you will live**; I will give you rest in your own land. Then you will know that I am the Lord—I have spoken and I will act, declares the Lord.

[SAAS-OT] Ezekiel 37:5-6,14 Thus says the Lord to these bones: "Behold, **I will bring the Spirit of life upon you. ⁶I will put muscles on you and bring flesh upon you. I will cover you with skin and put my Spirit into you. Then you shall live** and know that I am the Lord.'"" **¹⁴I will put My Spirit in you, and you will live**; and I will place you in your own land. Then you will know that I am the Lord. I have spoken, and I will do it," says the Lord.'"

[T4T] Ezekiel 37:5-6,14 This is what Yahweh the Lord says to you bones: **I will put my breath into each of you, and you will become alive again. ⁶I will fasten tendons to your bones, and cause your bones to be covered with flesh. I will cover the flesh with skin. Then I will breathe into you, and you will become alive.** When that happens, you will know that I, Yahweh, have the power to do what I say that I will do.'" **¹⁴I will put my Spirit in you, and it will be as though you will become alive again**, and I will enable you to live in your own land again. Then you will know that it is I, Yahweh, who said that it would happen and who has caused it to happen. That is what I, Yahweh, declare.'"

[TLB] Ezekiel 37:5-6,14 for the Lord God says, **'See! I am going to make you live and breathe again! ⁶I will replace the flesh and muscles on you and cover you with skin. I will put breath into you, and you shall live** and know I am the Lord.'" **¹⁴I will put my Spirit into you, and you shall live** and return home again to your own land. Then you will know that I, the Lord, have done just what I promised you.'"

[UDB] Ezekiel 37:5-6,14 This is what Yahweh the Lord says to you bones: **I am going to put my breath into each of you, and you will become alive again. ⁶I will fasten tendons to your bones and cause your bones to be covered with flesh. I will cover the flesh with skin. Then I will breathe into you, and you will become alive.** When that happens, you will know that I, Yahweh, have the power to do what I say that I will do.'" **¹⁴I will put my spirit in you, and it will be as though you**

will become alive again, and I will enable you to live in your own land again. Then you will know that it is I, Yahweh, who said that it would happen and who has caused it to happen. That is what I, Yahweh, declare."'

DANIEL

Daniel 1:15 And at the end of ten days **their countenances appeared fairer and fatter in flesh** than all the children which did eat the portion of the king's meat.

[AMP] **Daniel 1:15** At the end of ten days it seemed that **they were looking better and healthier** than all the young men who ate the king's finest food.

[CWB] **Daniel 1:15** At the end of ten days **they looked healthier and were stronger** than all those who were on the king's diet.

[GW] **Daniel 1:15** After ten days **they looked healthier and stronger** than the young men who had been eating the king's rich food.

[Jerusalem] **Daniel 1:15** When the ten days were over **they looked and were in better health** than any of the boys who had eaten their allowance from the royal table;

[LEB] **Daniel 1:15** And at the end of ten days **their appearances appeared better and they were healthier of body** than all the young men who were eating the fine food of the king.

[Spurrell-OT] **Daniel 1:15** And at the expiration of ten days **their appearance was perceived better and more plump in flesh** than any of the young men who eat of the king's allowance.

[VW] **Daniel 1:15** And at the end of ten days **their appearance looked better and fatter of flesh** than all the boys who were eating the king's food.

Daniel 4:34 And at the end of the days **I Nebuchadnezzar lifted up mine eyes unto heaven, and mine understanding returned unto me**, and I blessed the most High, and I praised and honoured him that liveth for ever, whose dominion is an everlasting dominion, and his kingdom is from generation to generation:

[AMPC] **Daniel 4:34** And at the end of the days [seven years], **I, Nebuchadnezzar, lifted up my eyes to heaven, and my understanding and the right use of my mind returned to me**; and I blessed the Most High [God] and I praised and honored and glorified Him Who lives forever, Whose dominion is an everlasting dominion; and His kingdom endures from generation to generation.

[BBE] **Daniel 4:34** And at the end of the days, **I, Nebuchadnezzar, lifting up my eyes to heaven, got back my reason**, and, blessing the Most High, I gave praise and honour to him who is living for ever, whose rule is an eternal rule and whose kingdom goes on from generation to generation.

[CLV] **Daniel 4:34** And at the end of the days, **I, Nebuchadnezzar, lifted my eyes to the heavens, and my knowledge is returning to me**. Then I blessed the Supreme, and I lauded and honored Him Who is living for the eon, seeing that His jurisdiction is an eonian jurisdiction, and His kingdom is with generation after generation.

[CSB] **Daniel 4:34** But at the end of those days, **I, Nebuchadnezzar, looked up to heaven, and my sanity returned to me**. Then I praised the Most High and honored and glorified him who lives forever: For his dominion is an everlasting dominion, and his kingdom is from generation to generation.

[CT-OT] **Daniel 4:34** And at the end of the days, **I, Nebuchadnezzar, raised my eyes toward heaven, and my understanding was restored to me**, and I blessed the Most High, and I praised and glorified

Him Who lives to Eternity, Whose dominion is an eternal dominion, and Whose kingdom is with every generation.

[Douay-Rheims] <u>Daniel 4:34</u> Now at the end of the days, **I Nabuchodonosor lifted up my eyes to heaven, and my sense was restored to me**: and I blessed the most High, and I praised and glorified him that liveth for ever: for his power is an everlasting power, and his kingdom is to all generations.

[EEBT] <u>Daniel 4:34</u> At the end of that time, I, Nebuchadnezzar, looked up towards heaven and I prayed. **I got my proper mind back** and I thanked the true God. I gave honour to him who never dies. His kingdom will never end because he rules always and for all time.

[ERV] <u>Daniel 4:34</u> Then at the end of that time, **I, Nebuchadnezzar, looked up toward heaven, and I was in my right mind again**. Then I gave praise to God Most High. I gave honor and glory to him who lives forever. God rules forever! His kingdom continues for all generations.

[GNT] <u>Daniel 4:34</u> "When the seven years had passed," said the king, "**I looked up at the sky, and my sanity returned**. I praised the Supreme God and gave honor and glory to the one who lives forever. He will rule forever, and his kingdom will last for all time.

[NCV] <u>Daniel 4:34</u> At the end of that time, **I, Nebuchadnezzar, looked up toward heaven, and I could think normally again**! Then I gave praise to the Most High God; I gave honor and glory to him who lives forever. God's rule is forever, and his kingdom continues for all time.

[NET] <u>Daniel 4:34</u> But at the end of the appointed time **I, Nebuchadnezzar, looked up toward heaven, and my sanity returned to me**. I extolled the Most High, and I praised and glorified the one who lives forever. For his authority is an everlasting authority, and his kingdom extends from one generation to the next.

[NIRV] <u>Daniel 4:34</u> At the end of that time **I, Nebuchadnezzar, looked up toward heaven. My mind became clear again**. Then I praised the Most High God. I gave honor and glory to the God who lives forever. His rule will last forever. His kingdom will never end.

[UDB] <u>Daniel 4:34</u> After those seven years ended, **I, Nebuchadnezzar, looked up toward heaven and acknowledged that what God said was true. Then I could think correctly again, and my sanity was restored**. I praised and worshiped the Most High, and I honored him, the one who lives forever. He rules forever; his ruling power is an everlasting authority.

[Wycliffe-Noble] <u>Daniel 4:34</u> Therefore after the end of days, **I, Nebuchadnezzar, raised mine eyes to heaven, and my wit was yielded to me**; and I blessed the Highest, and I praised, and glorified him that liveth without end; for why his power is everlasting power, and his realm is in generation and into generation. (And so at the end of these days, **I, Nebuchadnezzar, raised up my eyes to heaven, and my mind, or my sanity, was restored to me;** and I blessed the Most High God, and I praised, and glorified him who liveth forever; because his power is everlasting power, and his kingdom is forever and ever.)

<u>Daniel 10:18</u> Then there came again and **touched me** one like the appearance of a man, **and he strengthened me,**

[BLE] <u>Daniel 10:18</u> And once more what had the look of a **man touched me and put strength into me,**

[CJB] <u>Daniel 10:18</u> Then, again someone who looked human **touched me and revived me.**

[CWB] <u>Daniel 10:18</u> He touched me again, and I felt new strength flow into me.

[ERV] <u>Daniel 10:18</u> The one who looked like a man touched me again. **When he touched me, I felt better**.

[GNT] <u>Daniel 10:18</u> Once more **he took hold of me, and I felt stronger**.

[ICB] <u>Daniel 10:18</u> The one who looked like a man **touched me again. And he gave me strength**.

[Knox] <u>Daniel 10:18</u> Once again a hand seemed to **touch me, and words came to hearten me**;

[Koren-OT] <u>Daniel 10:18</u> Then again came one in the likeness of a man, and touched me and strengthened me,

[LITV] <u>Daniel 10:18</u> And again one in form as a man **touched me and made me strong**.

[NCV] <u>Daniel 10:18</u> The one who looked like a man **touched me again and gave me strength**.

[NLT] <u>Daniel 10:18</u> Then the one who looked like a man **touched me again, and I felt my strength returning**.

[NOG] <u>Daniel 10:18</u> Again, the person who looked like a human **touched me, and I became stronger**.

[TVB] <u>Daniel 10:18</u> Again the one who looked like a man reached out and **touched me. With that I felt my strength begin to return**.

[UDB] <u>Daniel 10:18</u> But **he took hold of me again, and enabled me to become stronger again**.

<u>Daniel 10:19</u> And said, O man greatly beloved, fear not: peace be unto thee, be strong, yea, be strong. **And when he had spoken unto me, I was strengthened**, and said, Let my lord speak; for thou hast strengthened me.

[CPDV] <u>Daniel 10:19</u> And he said, "Fear not, O man of longing. May peace be with you. Take courage and be strong." **And when he spoke to me, I recovered**, and I said, "Speak, my lord, for you have strengthened me."

[CSB] <u>Daniel 10:19</u> He said, "Don't be afraid, you who are treasured by God. Peace to you; be very strong!" As **he spoke to me, I was strengthened** and said, "Let my lord speak, for you have strengthened me."

[EEBT] <u>Daniel 10:19</u> 'Do not be afraid, man', he said to me, 'because God loves you very much. I want your mind to rest. I want you to be strong, very strong.' **When he said this, I felt stronger**. So I spoke again. 'My lord, speak to me, because you have made me strong again', I said.

[ICB] <u>Daniel 10:19</u> He said, "Daniel, don't be afraid. God loves you very much. Peace be with you. Be strong now, be strong." When **he spoke to me, I became stronger**. Then I said, "Master, speak, since you have given me strength."

[JPS-OT 1985] <u>Daniel 10:19</u> He said, "Have no fear, precious man, all will be well with you; be strong, be strong!" As he spoke with me, I was strengthened, and said, "Speak on, my lord, for you have strengthened me!"

[MKJV] <u>Daniel 10:19</u> and said, O man greatly beloved, do not fear. Peace to you; be strong; yes, be strong. **And when he had spoken to me, I was made stronger**, and said, Let my lord speak; for you have made me stronger.

[NLT] <u>Daniel 10:19</u> "Don't be afraid," he said, "for you are very precious to God. Peace! Be encouraged! Be strong!" **As he spoke these words to me, I suddenly felt stronger** and said to him, "Please speak to me, my lord, for you have strengthened me."

[NOG] <u>Daniel 10:19</u> He said, "Don't be afraid. You are highly respected. Everything is alright! Be strong! Be strong!" As **he talked to me, I became stronger**. I said, "Sir, tell me what you came to say. You have strengthened me."

[T4T] <u>Daniel 10:19</u> He said to me, "You human, God loves you very much. So do not be afraid. I desire/want that things will go well for you and that you will be encouraged." **When he had said that, I felt even stronger**, and I said, "Sir, tell me what you want to tell me. You have enabled me to feel stronger."

[Thomson] <u>Daniel 10:19</u> and said to me, Man much beloved, fear not: peace be to thee. Take courage and be strong. **And when he had spoken to me I recovered strength** and said, Let my lord speak, for thou hast strengthened me.

[TVB] <u>Daniel 10:19</u> Messenger: Do not be afraid, you who are highly regarded by God. May peace rest on you and make you whole; be strong; be brave. **At his words, I grew even stronger**. Daniel: Please continue, my lord, for your words have given me strength.

[UDB] <u>Daniel 10:19</u> He said to me, "Man, God loves you very much. So do not be afraid. I desire that things will go well for you and that you will be encouraged." **When he had said that, I felt even stronger**, and I said, "Sir, tell me what you want to tell me. You have enabled me to feel stronger."

[WGCIB] <u>Daniel 10:19</u> He said: Fear not, O man of desires, peace be to thee: take courage, and be strong. **When he spoke to me, I grew strong**, and I said: Speak, O my lord, for thou hast strengthened me.

<u>Daniel 11:32</u> And such as do wickedly against the covenant shall he corrupt by flatteries: **but the people that do know their God shall be strong**, and do exploits.

[ESV] <u>Daniel 11:32</u> He shall seduce with flattery those who violate the covenant, **but the people who know their God shall stand firm** and take action.

[GW] <u>Daniel 11:32</u> With flattery he will corrupt those who abandon the promise. **But the people who know their God will be strong** and take action.

[NIVUK] <u>Daniel 11:32</u> With flattery he will corrupt those who have violated the covenant, **but the people who know their God will firmly resist him**.

[Thomson] <u>Daniel 11:32</u> which they who break covenant will bring in by flatteries. **But the people who acknowledge their God will take courage and act**.

[TLB] <u>Daniel 11:32</u> He will flatter those who hate the things of God and win them over to his side. **But the people who know their God shall be strong** and do great things.

[ULB] <u>Daniel 11:32</u> As for those who acted wickedly against the covenant, he will deceive them and corrupt them. But **the people who know their God will be strong** and will take action.

HOSEA

<u>Hosea 11:3</u> I taught Ephraim also to go, taking them by their arms; **but they knew not that I healed**[raphah] **them**.

[CWB] <u>Hosea 11:3</u> "Yet, I was the One who took Israel by the hand and taught him to walk. I was the One who watched over him. But **the people of Israel don't seem to know that I did all this for them and healed them**.

[EEBT] <u>Hosea 11:3</u> But it was I who taught this child to walk! I took my people up in my arms! **I gave them health. But they did not know this**.

[ERV] <u>Hosea 11:3</u> "But I was the one who taught Ephraim to walk. I took the Israelites in my arms. **I healed them, but they don't know that.**

[Haak] <u>Hosea 11:3</u> I nevertheless, taught Ephraim to go; he took them upon his arms, but **they acknowledged not, that I healed them.**

[JPS-OT 1963] <u>Hosea 11:3</u> I have pampered Ephraim, Taking them in My arms; But **they have ignored My healing care.**

[MOTB] <u>Hosea 11:3</u> When they were weary and discouraged, I comforted them, although **they were too obtuse to realize that it was I who healed their bruises when they fell.**

[NOG] <u>Hosea 11:3</u> I was the one who taught the people of Ephraim to walk. I took them by the hand. But **they didn't realize that I had healed them.**

[NWT] <u>Hosea 11:3</u> But it was I who taught E phra·im to walk, taking them in my arms; **And they did not acknowledge that I had healed them.**

[TLV] <u>Hosea 11:3</u> Yet it was I who taught Ephraim to walk. I took them on My arms. But **they never acknowledged that I had healed them.**

<u>Hosea 13:14</u> I will ransom them from the power of the grave; I will redeem them from death: O death, I will be thy plagues; O grave, I will be thy destruction: repentance shall be hid from mine eyes.

[Bassett] <u>Hosea 13:14</u> From the hand of Hades I will redeem them, from death I will avenge them; where (are) thy plagues, O death, where thy sting, O Hades, compassion (on them) shall be hid from my eyes.

[BBE] <u>Hosea 13:14</u> I will give the price to make them free from the power of the underworld, I will be their saviour from death: O death! where are your pains? O underworld! where is your destruction? my eyes will have no pity.

[Beck] <u>Hosea 13:14</u> I want to free them from the grave and redeem them from death. I want to be a plague to you, death and a pest to you, grave, and I will not think of changing My mind.

[CPDV] <u>Hosea 13:14</u> I will free them from the hand of death; from death I will redeem them. Death, I will be your death. Hell, I will be your deadly wound. Consolation is hidden from my eyes.

[ERV] <u>Hosea 13:14</u> I will save them from the grave. I will rescue them from death. Death, where are your diseases? Grave, where is your power? I am not looking for revenge.

[Ewald-OT] <u>Hosea 13:14</u> (From the hand of hell I will redeem them, from death deliver them! where are thy plagues O death, where is thy sting thou hell? resentment shall be hid from mine eyes!)

[GNV] <u>Hosea 13:14</u> I will redeem them from the power of the grave: I will deliver them from death: O death, I will be thy death: O grave, I will be thy destruction: repentance is hid from mine eyes.

[GW] <u>Hosea 13:14</u> I want to free them from the power of the grave. I want to reclaim them from death. Death, I want to be a plague to you. Grave, I want to destroy you. I won't even think of changing my plans.

[Hall] <u>Hosea 13:14</u> Let them repent, and I will deliver them from all their distresses; yea, even from death itself, and from the power of the grave: O death, I will vanquish and consume thee; O grave, I will destroy thee for ever, and will never repent me of that victory.

[Horsley-OT] <u>Hosea 13:14</u> From the power of HELL I will redeem them. From DEATH I will reclaim them. DEATH! I will be thy Pestilence. HELL! I will be thy Burning Plague. No repentance is discoverable to my eye.

[NIRV] <u>Hosea 13:14</u> I will set these people free from the power of the grave. I will save them from death. Death, where are your plagues? Grave, where is your power to destroy? I will no longer pity Ephraim.

[NIVUK] <u>Hosea 13:14</u> 'I will deliver this people from the power of the grave; I will redeem them from death. Where, O death, are your plagues? Where, O grave, is your destruction? 'I will have no compassion,

[Sawyer-7590] <u>Hosea 13:14</u> I will redeem them from the hand of Hades, and save them from death. I will be your destruction, death; I will be your destruction, Hades; compassion shall be hid from my eyes.

[TNIV] <u>Hosea 13:14</u> "I will deliver them from the power of the grave; I will redeem them from death. Where, O death, are your plagues? Where, O grave, is your destruction? "I will have no compassion,

[WGCIB] <u>Hosea 13:14</u> I will deliver them out of the hand of death. I will redeem them from death: O death, I will be thy death; O hell, I will be thy bite: comfort is hidden from my eyes.

<u>Hosea 14:7</u> **They that dwell under his shadow shall return; they shall revive as the corn, and grow as the vine**: the scent thereof shall be as the wine of Lebanon.

[CEB] <u>Hosea 14:7</u> **They will again live beneath my shadow, they will flourish like a garden; they will blossom like the vine,** their fragrance will be like the wine of Lebanon.

[GNT] <u>Hosea 14:7</u> **Once again they will live under my protection. They will grow crops of grain and be fruitful like a vineyard.** They will be as famous as the wine of Lebanon.

[HBIV] <u>Hosea 14:7</u> **Again shall they dwell under his shadow, And they shall live well-watered like a garden**: Their renown will be like wine of Lebanon.

[ICB] <u>Hosea 14:7</u> **The people of Israel will again live under my protection. They will grow like the grain. They will bloom like a vine.** They will be as famous as the wine of Lebanon.

[MSG] <u>Hosea 14:7</u> **Those who live near him will be blessed by him, be blessed and prosper like golden grain. Everyone will be talking about them,** spreading their fame as the vintage children of God.

JOEL

<u>Joel 2:25</u> **And I will restore to you the years that the locust hath eaten**, the cankerworm, and the caterpiller, and the palmerworm, my great army which I sent among you.

[FV] <u>Joel 2:25</u> **And I will restore to you the years which the swarming locust has eaten**, the locust larvae, and the destroying locust, and the cutting locust, My great army which I sent among you.

[NIV] <u>Joel 2:25</u> "**I will repay you for the years the locusts have eaten**—the great locust and the young locust, the other locusts and the locust swarm—my great army that I sent among you."

[NKJV] <u>Joel 2:25</u> "**So I will restore to you the years that the swarming locust has eaten**, The crawling locust, The consuming locust, And the chewing locust, My great army which I sent among you."

<u>Joel 3:10</u> Beat your plowshares into swords, and your pruninghooks into spears: **let the weak say, I am strong**.

[AMPC] <u>Joel 3:10</u> Beat your plowshares into swords, and your pruning hooks into spears; **let the weak say, I am strong [a warrior]!**

[BBE] <u>Joel 3:10</u> Get your plough-blades hammered into swords, and your vine-knives into spears: **let the feeble say, I am strong**.

[BLE] <u>Joel 3:10</u> Pound your hoes into swords and your pruning-hooks into lances; **let the weakling declare himself a champion.**

[CEB] <u>Joel 3:10</u> Beat the iron tips of your plows into swords and your pruning tools into spears; **let the weakling say, "I am mighty."**

[CLV] <u>Joel 3:10</u> Pound your mattocks into swords and your pruning hooks into lances! **The defeatist shall say, a master am I!**

[EEBT] <u>Joel 3:10</u> Make your digging tools into sharp knives. Make the tools that you use on the farm into pointed fighting sticks. **The weak man must say, 'I am strong!'**

[ERV] <u>Joel 3:10</u> Beat your plows into swords. Make spears from your pruning hooks. **Let the weak man say, "I am a strong soldier."**

[FAA] <u>Joel 3:10</u> Beat your ploughshares into swords, And your pruning shears into spears. **Let him who is weak say, "I am a warrior."**

[GW] <u>Joel 3:10</u> Hammer your plowblades into swords and your pruning shears into spears. **Weaklings should say that they are warriors.**

[Haak] <u>Joel 3:10</u> Beat your spades into swords, and your sickles into spears: **let the weak say, I am a valiant man.**

[Jerusalem] <u>Joel 3:10</u> Hammer your ploughshares into swords, your sickles into spears, **let the weakling say, 'I am a fighting man'.**

[Knox] <u>Joel 3:10</u> Ploughshare beat into sword, spade into spear; **weakling is none but must summon up his manhood now!**

[LEB] <u>Joel 3:10</u> Beat your cutting tools of iron into swords and your pruning hooks into spears; **let the weakling say, 'I am a mighty warrior!'**

[Leeser-OT] <u>Joel 3:10</u> Beat your plough-shares into swords, and your pruning-knives into spears: **let the weak say, I am a hero.**

[MSG] <u>Joel 3:10</u> Turn your shovels into swords, turn your hoes into spears. **Let the weak one throw out his chest and say, "I'm tough, I'm a fighter."**

[NET] <u>Joel 3:10</u> Beat your plowshares into swords, and your pruning hooks into spears! **Let the weak say, 'I too am a warrior!'**

[NLV] <u>Joel 3:10</u> Beat your plows into swords, and your vine hooks into spears. **Let the weak say, "I am a powerful soldier."**

[NWT] <u>Joel 3:10</u> Beat your plowshares into swords and your pruning shears into spears. **Let the weak one say: "I am powerful."**

AMOS

<u>Amos 5:4,6</u> For thus saith the Lord unto the house of Israel, **Seek ye me, and ye shall live:** [6]**Seek the Lord, and ye shall live;** lest he break out like fire in the house of Joseph, and devour it, and there be none to quench it in Bethel.

A SURVEY OF HEALING SCRIPTURES

[AMP] <u>Amos 5:4,6</u> For thus says the Lord to the house of Israel, "**Seek Me [search diligently for Me and regard Me as more essential than food] so that you may live.** ⁶**"Seek the Lord [search diligently for Him and long for Him as your most essential need] so that you may live**, Or He will rush down like a [devouring] fire, O house of Joseph, And there will be no one to quench the flame for [idolatrous] Bethel,

[AMPC] <u>Amos 5:4,6</u> For thus says the Lord to the house of Israel: **Seek Me [inquire for and of Me and require Me as you require food] and you shall live!** ⁶**Seek the Lord [inquire for and of Him and require Him] and you shall live**, lest He rush down like fire upon the house of Joseph [representing the ten tribes] and devour it, and there be none to quench it in Bethel [the center of their idol hopes].

[BLE] <u>Amos 5:4,6</u> For the Lord Jehovah says to the house of Israel, **Resort to me and live, ⁶Resort to Jehovah and live**, for fear he should strike in with fire in the house of Joseph and Bethel have nobody to quench it,

[CJB] <u>Amos 5:4,6</u> For here is what Adonai says to the house of Isra'el: **If you seek me, you will survive; ⁶If you seek Adonai, you will survive**. Otherwise, he will break out against the house of Yosef like fire, devouring Beit-El, with no one to quench the flames.

[CLV] <u>Amos 5:4,6</u> For thus says Yahweh to the house of Israel; **Inquire of Me and live. ⁶Inquire of Yahweh and live**, lest He should prosper as fire in the house of Joseph, and it devours, and no one is quenching it for the house of Israel.

[ERV] <u>Amos 5:4,6</u> The Lord says this to the nation of Israel: "**Come looking for me and live. ⁶Come to the Lord and live**. If you don't go to him, a fire will start at Joseph's house, and no one in Bethel can stop it.

[NIRV] <u>Amos 5:4,6</u> The Lord speaks to the people of Israel. He says, "**Look to me and live. ⁶Israel, look to the Lord and live**. If you don't, he will sweep through the tribes of Joseph like a fire. It will burn everything up. And Bethel won't have anyone to put it out.

[NLT] <u>Amos 5:4,6</u> Now this is what the Lord says to the family of Israel: "**Come back to me and live! ⁶Come back to the Lord and live**! Otherwise, he will roar through Israel like a fire, devouring you completely. Your gods in Bethel won't be able to quench the flames.

[NWT] <u>Amos 5:4,6</u> For this is what Jehovah says to the house of Israel: '**Search for me and keep living. ⁶Search for Jehovah, and keep living**, So that he does not burst out like a fire on the house of Joseph, Consuming Beth el, with no one to extinguish it.

<u>Amos 5:14</u> **Seek good, and not evil, that ye may live**: and so the Lᴏʀᴅ, the God of hosts, shall be with you, as ye have spoken.

[AMP] <u>Amos 5:14</u> **Seek (long for, require) good and not evil, that you may live**; And so may the Lord God of hosts be with you, Just as you have said!

[BBE] <u>Amos 5:14</u> **Go after good and not evil, so that life may be yours**: and so the Lord, the God of armies, will be with you, as you say.

[CEB] <u>Amos 5:14</u> **Seek good and not evil, that you may live;** and so the Lord, the God of heavenly forces, will be with you just as you have said.

[CSB] <u>Amos 5:14</u> **Pursue good and not evil so that you may live**, and the Lord, the God of Armies, will be with you as you have claimed.

[MSG] <u>Amos 5:14</u> **Seek good and not evil—and live!** You talk about God, the God-of-the-Angel-Armies, being your best friend. Well, live like it, and maybe it will happen.

[TVB] <u>Amos 5:14</u> **Search for good and not for evil so that you may live**; That way the Eternal God, the Commander of heavenly armies, will be at your side, as you yourselves have even said.

[UDB] <u>Amos 5:14</u> **In order to remain alive, you must stop doing what is wrong, and start doing what is right**. If you do that, Yahweh, Commander of the angel armies, will be with you as you claim that he always is.

OBADIAH

<u>Obadiah 1:17</u> **But upon mount Zion shall be deliverance**, and there shall be holiness; and the house of Jacob shall possess their possessions.

[BBE] <u>Obadiah 1:17</u> **But in Mount Zion some will be kept safe**, and it will be holy; and the children of Jacob will take their heritage.

[CAB] <u>Obadiah 1:17</u> **But on Mount Zion there shall be deliverance**, and there shall be a sanctuary; and the house of Jacob shall take for an inheritance those that took them for an inheritance.

[CWB] <u>Obadiah 1:17</u> **"But from Mount Zion deliverance will come** to the house of Jacob. My mountain will become a sacred place and my people will possess the land that is rightfully theirs.

[ERV] <u>Obadiah 1:17</u> **But there will be survivors on Mount Zion.** They will be my special people. The nation of Jacob will take back what belongs to it.

[ISV] <u>Obadiah 1:17</u> **"But there will be a delivered remnant on Mount Zion.** There will be holiness, and the house of Jacob will take back their possessions."

[JPS-OT 1985] <u>Obadiah 1:17</u> **But on Zion's mount a remnant shall survive**, And it shall be holy. The House of Jacob shall dispossess Those who dispossessed them.

[Kenrick] <u>Obadiah 1:17</u> **And in mount Sion shall be salvation**, and it shall be holy: and the house of Jacob shall possess those that possessed them.

[Leeser-OT] <u>Obadiah 1:17</u> **But upon mount Zion shall be deliverance**, and it shall be holy: and the house of Jacob shall again possess their inheritances.

[NET] <u>Obadiah 1:17</u> **But on Mount Zion there will be a remnant of those who escape**, and it will be a holy place once again. The descendants of Jacob will conquer those who had conquered them.

[NJB] <u>Obadiah 1:17</u> **But on Mount Zion will be those who have escaped**—it will be a sanctuary- and the House of Jacob will recover what is rightfully theirs.

[NLV] <u>Obadiah 1:17</u> **"But on Mount Zion there will be a way to be set free**, and it will be holy. The people of Jacob will own what belongs to them."

[Noyes] <u>Obadiah 1:17</u> **But upon mount Zion shall be deliverance**, and it shall be holy; And the house of Jacob shall regain their possessions.

[SAAS-OT] <u>Obadiah 1:17</u> **"But deliverance will come to Mount Zion**, and it will be holy. And the house of Jacob shall obtain their inheritance as their rightful inheritance.

JONAH

Jonah 2:6 I went down to the bottoms of the mountains; the earth with her bars was about me for ever: yet hast thou brought up my life from corruption, O Lord my God.

[AMP] Jonah 2:6 "I descended to the [very] roots of the mountains. The earth with its bars closed behind me [bolting me in] forever, Yet You have brought up my life from the pit (death), O Lord my God.

[CB] Jonah 2:6 The Earth swallowed me, dragging me to the bottom of the mountains, and its bars closed behind me. But you, my Lord, rescued me from the grave.

[CLV] Jonah 2:6 I go down to the fashioning points of the mountains; the earth, its bars are about me for the eon, yet You wilt bring up my life from ruin, Yahweh, my Elohim."

[EXB] Jonah 2:6 When I ·went [sank] down to ·where the mountains of the sea start to rise [the roots of the mountains], ·I thought I was locked in this prison [the earth's bars held me] forever, but you ·saved me [brought up my life] from the pit of death, Lord my God.

[GNT] Jonah 2:6 I went down to the very roots of the mountains, into the land whose gates lock shut forever. But you, O Lord my God, brought me back from the depths alive.

[HCSB] Jonah 2:6 I sank to the foundations of the mountains; the earth with its prison bars closed behind me forever! But You raised my life from the Pit, Lord my God!

[NLT] Jonah 2:6 I sank down to the very roots of the mountains. I was imprisoned in the earth, whose gates lock shut forever. But you, O Lord my God, snatched me from the jaws of death!

[UDB] Jonah 2:6 I sank down to where the mountains start rising from the bottom of the sea. I thought that forever it would be as though my body would be in a prison inside the earth below me. But you, Yahweh God, whom I worship, rescued me from going down to the place of the dead!

MICAH

Micah 7:8 Rejoice not against me, O mine enemy: when I fall, I shall arise; when I sit in darkness, the Lord shall be a light unto me.

[CEV] Micah 7:8 My enemies, don't be glad because of my troubles! I may have fallen, but I will get up; I may be sitting in the dark, but the Lord is my light.

[CSB] Micah 7:8 Do not rejoice over me, my enemy! Though I have fallen, I will stand up; though I sit in darkness, the Lord will be my light.

[CWB] Micah 7:8 Don't rejoice, O my enemy, over the fall of Israel and her people! For though we have fallen, we will rise again. Though we sit in darkness, the Lord will be our light.

[JSharpe-Mic] Micah 7:8 Rejoice not at me, O my enemy; because I have fallen, I have risen: for though I may sit in darkness, Jehovah is a light to me.

[MOTB] Micah 7:8 Although my oppressor exults over my destruction as if final, and I seem to be in the darkness of despair, still Jehovah will bring me to the light;

[T4T] <u>Micah 7:8</u> You who are our enemies, do not gloat/rejoice about what has happened to us, because even if we have experienced disasters, those disasters will end and we will be restored. Even if it is as though we are sitting in the darkness, Yahweh will be our light.

[Thomson] <u>Micah 7:8</u> Rejoice not over me, O mine enemy, because I have fallen. I shall rise again, for though I sit in darkness the Lord will give me light.

[UDB] <u>Micah 7:8</u> You who are our enemies, do not gloat about what has happened to us, because even if we have experienced disasters, those disasters will end, and we will be prosperous again. Even if it is as though we are sitting in the darkness, Yahweh will be our light.

NAHUM

<u>Nahum 1:13</u> For now will I break his yoke from off thee, and will burst thy bonds in sunder.

[BBE] <u>Nahum 1:13</u> And now I will let his yoke be broken off you, and your chains be parted.

[BLE] <u>Nahum 1:13</u> And now I will break his yoke-bow off from you and snap your tether.

[CEB] <u>Nahum 1:13</u> Now I will break off his yoke from you and tear off your chains.

[CJB] <u>Nahum 1:13</u> Now I will break his yoke from your necks and snap the chains that bind you.

[Douay-Rheims] <u>Nahum 1:13</u> And now I will break in pieces his rod with which he struck thy back, and I will burst thy bonds asunder.

[ERV] <u>Nahum 1:13</u> Now I will set you free from the power of Assyria. I will take the yoke off your neck and tear away the chains holding you.

[HCSB] <u>Nahum 1:13</u> For I will now break off his yoke from you and tear off your shackles.

[JCB] <u>Nahum 1:13</u> Now I will free you from their control. And I will tear away the chains with which they hold you."

[Jerusalem] <u>Nahum 1:13</u> And now I am going to break that yoke of his that weighs you down, and I will burst your chains.

[Knox] <u>Nahum 1:13</u> and now I mean to shatter that yoke of his that lies on thy back, tear thy chains asunder

[LTPB] <u>Nahum 1:13</u> Now I will shatter his rod from your back, and I will break your chains."

[MSG] <u>Nahum 1:13</u> From now on I'm taking the yoke from your neck and splitting it up for kindling. I'm cutting you free from the ropes of your bondage.

[NCV] <u>Nahum 1:13</u> Now I will free you from their control and tear away your chains.

[NEB] <u>Nahum 1:13</u> Now I will break his yoke from your necks and snap the cords that bind you.

[NWT] <u>Nahum 1:13</u> And now I will break his yoke bar from off you, And I will tear your bonds in two.

[Rotherham] <u>Nahum 1:13</u> Now, therefore, will I break his yoke from off thee, —and, thy fetters, will I tear off.

[THS-Nah] <u>Nahum 1:13</u> And now will I shiver his yoke from upon thee, And thy bonds will I tear off.

[TVB] <u>Nahum 1:13</u> Now I will break their yoke of slavery and death from your shoulders and tear their chains of religious and political oppression away from you.

[UKJV] <u>Nahum 1:13</u> For now will I break his yoke from off you, and will burst your bonds in two.

[ULB] <u>Nahum 1:13</u> Now will I break that people's yoke from off you; I will break your chains."

[YLT] <u>Nahum 1:13</u> And now I break his rod from off thee, And thy bands I do draw away.

HABAKKUK

<u>Habakkuk 2:4</u> Behold, his soul which is lifted up is not upright in him: **but the just shall live by his faith.**

[Berkeley] <u>Habakkuk 2:4</u> Look, his soul is puffed up; it is not upright in him! **But the righteous shall live by his faith.**

[CSB] <u>Habakkuk 2:4</u> Look, his ego is inflated; he is without integrity. **But the righteous one will live by his faith.**

[CWB] <u>Habakkuk 2:4</u> This is the message I want you to write: The nation that is proud will not survive. But **those who are righteous will, because they live by faith in their God.**

[Eakin-Hab] <u>Habakkuk 2:4</u> Behold! the wicked man shall not save himself, **But the righteous shall survive by his steadfastness.**

[Hall] <u>Habakkuk 2:4</u> In any case, give thou full believe to this word of the Lord; for, behold, that man, which withdraweth his soul from trusting unto God, and will be raising to himself projects of his own, as he is unsound and faithless to God, so is he accordingly displeasing to him: **but the just and upright man will depend upon the promises of God, and speed thereafter; for his faith in God shall both uphold his life here, and crown it with glory hereafter.**

[JPS-OT 1963] <u>Habakkuk 2:4</u> Lo, his spirit within him is puffed up, not upright. **But the righteous man is rewarded with life For his fidelity.**

[Leeser-OT] <u>Habakkuk 2:4</u> Behold, disturbed, not at rest is the soul of the wicked in him; **but the righteous ever liveth in his trustful faith.**

[MOTB] <u>Habakkuk 2:4</u> "Pride dominates these rapacious Chaldeans, therefore their ultimate downfall is certain; **but the righteous, because of their moral integrity and believing fidelity, which are the absolute essentials of life, though now crushed and oppressed, shall surely survive the present crisis."**

[MSG] <u>Habakkuk 2:4</u> "Look at that man, bloated by self-importance—full of himself but soul-empty. **But the person in right standing before God through loyal and steady believing is fully alive, really alive.**

[NABRE] <u>Habakkuk 2:4</u> See, the rash have no integrity; **but the just one who is righteous because of faith shall live.**

[REB] <u>Habakkuk 2:4</u> The reckless will lack an assured future, while **the righteous will live by being faithful.**

[Sharpe] <u>Habakkuk 2:4</u> Behold, his soul which is puffed up is not upright in him: but **he that is righteous, in his faithfulness shall he live.**

[Thomson] <u>Habakkuk 2:4</u> If any one draw back my soul hath no pleasure in him. **But the just shall live by faith in me.**

[TLB] <u>Habakkuk 2:4</u> "Note this: Wicked men trust themselves alone as these Chaldeans do, and fail; **but the righteous man trusts in me and lives!**

[TLV] <u>Habakkuk 2:4</u> Behold, the puffed up one—his soul is not right within him, **But the righteous will live by his trust.**

<u>Habakkuk 3:19</u> **The Lord God is my strength, and he will make my feet like hinds' feet**, and he will make me to walk upon mine high places. To the chief singer on my stringed instruments.

[AMP] <u>Habakkuk 3:19</u> **The Lord God is my strength [my source of courage, my invincible army]; He has made my feet [steady and sure] like hinds' feet** And makes me walk [forward with spiritual confidence] on my high places [of challenge and responsibility]. For the choir director, on my stringed instruments.

[AMPC] <u>Habakkuk 3:19</u> **The Lord God is my Strength, my personal bravery, and my invincible army; He makes my feet like hinds' feet** and will make me to walk [not to stand still in terror, but to walk] and make [spiritual] progress upon my high places [of trouble, suffering, or responsibility]!

[EEBT] <u>Habakkuk 3:19</u> **The Lord, who is my master, will make me safe. He makes my feet like the feet of a deer** so that I can climb mountains. The music leader must use things that have strings to make music.

[GNT] <u>Habakkuk 3:19</u> **The Sovereign Lord gives me strength. He makes me sure-footed as a deer** and keeps me safe on the mountains.

[MSG] <u>Habakkuk 3:19</u> **Counting on God's Rule to prevail, I take heart and gain strength. I run like a deer.** I feel like I'm king of the mountain! (For congregational use, with a full orchestra.)

[NET] <u>Habakkuk 3:19</u> **The sovereign Lord is my source of strength. He gives me the agility of a deer;** he enables me to negotiate the rugged terrain. (This prayer is for the song leader. It is to be accompanied by stringed instruments.)

[NIRV] <u>Habakkuk 3:19</u> **The Lord and King gives me strength. He makes my feet like the feet of a deer.** He helps me walk on the highest places. This prayer is for the director of music. It should be sung while being accompanied by stringed instruments.

[UDB] <u>Habakkuk 3:19</u> **Yahweh the Lord is the one who gives me strength, and he enables me to climb safely like a deer does**, he makes me walk on my high hills. (This message is for the choir director: When this prayer is sung, it is to be accompanied by people playing stringed instruments.

ZEPHANIAH

<u>Zephaniah 3:19</u> Behold, at that time I will undo all that afflict thee: and **I will save her that halteth**, and gather her that was driven out; and I will get them praise and fame in every land where they have been put to shame.

[AMPC] <u>Zephaniah 3:19</u> Behold, at that time I will deal with all those who afflict you; **I will save the limping [ones]** and gather the outcasts and will make them a praise and a name in every land of their shame.

[ASV] <u>Zephaniah 3:19</u> Behold, at that time I will deal with all them that afflict thee; and **I will save that which is lame**, and gather that which was driven away; and I will make them a praise and a name, whose shame hath been in all the earth.

[CCB] <u>Zephaniah 3:19</u> On that day I will face your oppressors; **I will save the lame sheep** and bring the lost back into the fold. I will give them renown and honor in all the lands where humiliation was your lot.

[FAA] <u>Zephaniah 3:19</u> I will deal with all your oppressors at that time, And **I will save her who is limping**. I will gather her who has been cast out, And make them a recipient of praise and renown In all the land Where their shame was.

[GNT] <u>Zephaniah 3:19</u> The time is coming! I will punish your oppressors; **I will rescue all the lame** and bring the exiles home. I will turn their shame to honor, and all the world will praise them.

[LEB] <u>Zephaniah 3:19</u> Behold, at that time I will deal with all your oppressors; **I will save the lame** and gather the outcast. I will change them from shame to glory and renown throughout the whole world.

[MOTB] <u>Zephaniah 3:19</u> "I will then do all that I have ever promised. **I will heal and restore my afflicted ones**, and will make them respected and renowned wherever they have been humiliated."

[MSG] <u>Zephaniah 3:19</u> At the same time, I'll get rid of all those who've made your life miserable. **I'll heal the maimed**; I'll bring home the homeless. In the very countries where they were hated they will be venerated.

[NCV] <u>Zephaniah 3:19</u> At that time I will punish all those who harmed you. **I will save my people who cannot walk** and gather my people who have been thrown out. I will give them praise and honor in every place where they were shamed.

[NJB] <u>Zephaniah 3:19</u> I am taking action here and now against your oppressors. When that time comes **I will rescue the lame**, and gather the strays, and I will win them praise and renown when I restore their fortunes.

[SG] <u>Zephaniah 3:19</u> Lo, I will deal with all your oppressors at that time. And **I will deliver the lame**, and gather the outcast. And I will make them renowned and praised in all the earth.

[Thomson] <u>Zephaniah 3:19</u> Behold here am I—I am dealing with thee for thy sake at that time, saith the Lord, and **I will save her who hath been trodden down**; and take back her who hath been put away; and I will make them a boast and renowned in every land.

[YLT] <u>Zephaniah 3:19</u> Lo, I am dealing with all afflicting thee at that time, And **I have saved the halting one**, And the driven out ones I do gather, And have set them for a praise and for a name, In all the land of their shame.

HAGGAI

<u>Haggai 2:4</u> Yet now **be strong**, O Zerubbabel, saith the Lord; and **be strong**, O Joshua, son of Josedech, the high priest; and **be strong**, all ye people of the land, saith the Lord, and work: **for I am with you**, saith the Lord of hosts:

[AMPC] <u>Haggai 2:4</u> Yet now **be strong**, alert, and courageous, O Zerubbabel, says the Lord; **be strong**, alert, and courageous, O Joshua son of Jehozadak, the high priest; and **be strong**, alert, and courageous, all you people of the land, says the Lord, and work! **For I am with you**, says the Lord of hosts.

[CPDV] <u>Haggai 2:4</u> And now **be strengthened**, Zerubbabel, says the Lord. And **be strengthened**, Jesus the son of Jehozadak, the high priest. And **be strengthened**, all people of the land, says the Lord of hosts. **For I am with you**, says the Lord of hosts.

[LTPB] <u>Haggai 2:4</u> Now, **be strengthened**, Zerubbabel, and **be strengthened**, Jesus, Josedech's son, High Priest, and **be strengthened**, all the land's people, the Lord of armies says! Work, **because I am with you**, the Lord of armies says!

[NIRV] <u>Haggai 2:4</u> But **be strong**, Zerubbabel,' announces the Lord. '**Be strong**, Joshua. **Be strong**, all of you people in the land,' announces the Lord. 'Start rebuilding. **I am with you**,' announces the Lord who rules over all.

[UDB] <u>Haggai 2:4</u> But now Yahweh, Commander of the angel armies, says to all of you, to Zerubbabel, Jeshua, and the rest of you people who live in this nation, 'Do not be discouraged; **instead be strong**!

ZECHARIAH

<u>Zechariah 10:12</u> And I will strengthen them in the Lᴏʀᴅ; and they shall walk up and down in his name, saith the Lᴏʀᴅ.

[BBE] <u>Zechariah 10:12</u> And their strength will be in the Lord; and their pride will be in his name, says the Lord.

[EEBT] <u>Zechariah 10:12</u> 'I will make my people strong. They will obey me because they love my name.'

[HBIV] <u>Zechariah 10:12</u> And their strength will be in Jehovah; And in his name they will boast themselves, It is the oracle of Jehovah.

[ICB] <u>Zechariah 10:12</u> I will make my people strong. And they will live as I say," says the Lord.

[LitProph-OT] <u>Zechariah 10:12</u> And I will strengthen them through Jehovah [their God;] And in his name shall they walk, saith Jehovah.

[MEV] <u>Zechariah 10:12</u> I will make them strong in the Lord, and they will go to and fro in His name, says the Lord.

[NIRV] <u>Zechariah 10:12</u> I will make my people strong. They will live in safety because of me," announces the Lord.

[TLB] <u>Zechariah 10:12</u> The Lord says, "I will make my people strong with power from me! They will go wherever they wish, and wherever they go they will be under my personal care."

[TVB] <u>Zechariah 10:12</u> I will give strength to My people, and in My name will they live. So says the Eternal One.

[UDB] <u>Zechariah 10:12</u> I will enable my people to be strong, and they will honor me and obey me. That will surely happen because I, Yahweh, have said it."

MALACHI

<u>Malachi 4:2</u> But unto you that fear my name shall the Sun of righteousness arise with **healing in his wings**; and ye shall go forth, and grow up as calves of the stall.

[Berkeley] <u>Malachi 4:2</u> But for you, who revere My name, the sun of righteousness will arise with **healing in its beams**, and you will go forth and leap like calves from the stall.

[CEV] <u>Malachi 4:2</u> But for you that honor my name, victory will shine like the sun with **healing in its rays**, and you will jump around like calves at play.

[CSB] <u>Malachi 4:2</u> But for you who fear my name, the sun of righteousness will rise with **healing in its wings**, and you will go out and playfully jump like calves from the stall.

[Douay-Rheims-Peters] <u>Malachi 4:2</u> And there shall rise to you that fear my name the Sun of justice, and **health in his wings**: and you shall go forth, and shall leap as calves of the heard.

[ERV] <u>Malachi 4:2</u> But, for my followers, goodness will shine on you like the rising sun. And it will **bring healing power like the sun's rays**. You will be free and happy, like calves freed from their stalls.

[GNV] <u>Malachi 4:2</u> But unto you that fear my name, shall the sun of righteousness arise, and **health shall be under his wings**, and ye shall go forth and grow up as fat calves.

[Jerusalem] <u>Malachi 4:2</u> But for you who fear my name, the sun of righteousness will shine out **with healing in its rays**; you will leap like calves going out to pasture.

[JUB] <u>Malachi 4:2</u> But unto you that fear my name shall the Sun of righteousness be born, and **in his wings he shall bring saving health**; and ye shall go forth and jump like calves of the herd.

[UDB] <u>Malachi 4:2</u> But for you who honor me, I, who always act righteously, will come to you and **heal you, as the sun rises in the morning.** You will be as happy as young calves when they leave their stalls to play in the fields.

MATTHEW

<u>Matthew 4:4</u> But he answered and said, It is written, Man shall not live by bread alone, but by every word that proceedeth out of the mouth of God.

[AMP] <u>Matthew 4:4</u> But Jesus replied, "It is written and forever remains written, 'Man shall not live by bread alone, but by every word that comes out of the mouth of God.'"

[Authentic-NT] <u>Matthew 4:4</u> To this Jesus replied, 'It is stated, "Not by bread alone shall a man live, but by every utterance that proceeds from the mouth of God."'

[AUV-NT 2005] <u>Matthew 4:4</u> But Jesus answered, "It is written, 'A person is not to live by [eating] bread only, but [instead] by [believing and obeying] every statement spoken by God.'"

[Barclay-NT] <u>Matthew 4:4</u> Jesus answered, 'Scripture says: "It takes more than bread to keep a man alive; man's life depends on every word that God speaks."'

[Campbell-Gs] <u>Matthew 4:4</u> Jesus answering said, It is written, "Man liveth not by bread only, but by every thing which God is pleased to appoint."

[CWB] <u>Matthew 4:4</u> But as famished as Jesus was, He recognized who was tempting Him. So He answered, "The Scripture teaches that man is not to put survival before obedience to God's word."

[ECB] <u>Matthew 4:4</u> But he answers, saying, It is scribed, Humanity lives, not by bread alone, but by every rhema proceeding through the mouth of Yah Veh.

[ERV] <u>Matthew 4:4</u> Jesus answered him, "The Scriptures say, 'It is not just bread that keeps people alive. Their lives depend on what God says.'"

[GNC-NT] <u>Matthew 4:4</u> "This is what is written in scripture," was Jesus' reply, "'Man cannot live with bread as his only support; what he stands in need of is every word which proceeds from the mouth of the Lord.'"

[Hall] <u>Matthew 4:4</u> It is not the very material substance of bread, that can or doth maintain the life of man; but the blessing of God, giving power to that bread to nourish: neither is Almighty God tied to the ordinary means of bread, as if without that he could not sustain man's life; but he is able, by his infinite power, either to create new means, or to work without or against the means.

[Johnson-NT] <u>Matthew 4:4</u> Jesus responded, "A human being cannot exist on the physical necessities alone, but must be sustained by spiritual resources."

[Knox] <u>Matthew 4:4</u> He answered, It is written, Man cannot live by bread only; there is life for him in all the words which proceed from the mouth of God.

[KNT] <u>Matthew 4:4</u> 'The Bible says', replied Jesus, 'that it takes more than bread to keep you alive. You actually live on every word that comes out of God's mouth.'

[LDB-NT] <u>Matthew 4:4</u> But Jesus responded, "The Scriptures declare, It is not possible for man to survive on bread alone. He must also feast and meditate upon every word that comes from God."

[Mace-NT] <u>Matthew 4:4</u> but Jesus answered him, It is written, "Man shall not live by bread alone, but by every thing that God shall prescribe."

[MSG] <u>Matthew 4:4</u> Jesus answered by quoting Deuteronomy: "It takes more than bread to stay alive. It takes a steady stream of words from God's mouth."

[NOG] <u>Matthew 4:4</u> Yeshua answered, "Scripture says, 'A person cannot live on bread alone but on every word that God speaks.'"

[Sindlinger-NT] <u>Matthew 4:4</u> Quoting God's spokesman Moses who lived long ago, Jesus replied, "Following God's advice is more important than satisfying my hunger."

[TLB] <u>Matthew 4:4</u> But Jesus told him, "No! For the Scriptures tell us that bread won't feed men's souls: obedience to every word of God is what we need."

[TTNT] <u>Matthew 4:4</u> Jesus replied: "It is written: 'Man is not to live only on bread, but he is to feed on every word that comes from God's mouth.'"

[Wuest-NT] <u>Matthew 4:4</u> But answering He said, It has been written and is at present on record, Not upon the basis of bread only shall the individual live, but upon the basis of every word proceeding out of God's mouth.

<u>Matthew 4:23-24</u> And Jesus went about all Galilee, teaching in their synagogues, and preaching the gospel of the kingdom, and **healing all manner of sickness and all manner of disease among the people**. [24]And his fame went throughout all Syria: and they brought unto him all sick people that were taken with divers diseases and torments, and those which were possessed with devils, and those which were lunatick, and those that had the palsy; and **he healed them**.

[Barclay-NT] <u>Matthew 4:23-24</u> Jesus made a circular tour of the whole of Galilee, teaching in their synagogues, and proclaiming the Good News of the Kingdom and **healing all kinds of illness and all kinds of sickness among the people**. [24]Reports of what he was doing spread all over Syria. So they brought to him all those who were ill, in the grip of the most varied diseases and pains, those who were possessed by demons, epileptics and paralysed people, **and he cured them**.

[BBE] <u>Matthew 4:23-24</u> And Jesus went about in all Galilee, teaching in their Synagogues and preaching the good news of the kingdom, and **making well those who were ill with any disease among the people**. [24]And news of him went out through all Syria; and they took to him all who were ill with different diseases and pains, those having evil spirits and those who were off their heads, and those who had no power of moving. **And he made them well**.

[BLE] <u>Matthew 4:23-24</u> And he went around in all Galilee, teaching in their synagogues and proclaiming the gospel of the Reign and **curing every disease and every ailment among the people**. [24]And the report about him went to all Syria; and they brought to him all who were ill with various diseases and suffering agonies, demoniacs and epileptics and paralytics, and **he cured them;**

[CB] <u>Matthew 4:23-24</u> And Jesus traveled throughout the whole of Galilee, teaching in their synagogues and preaching the gospel of the Kingdom, and **healing every kind of chronic illness and every kind of germ among the people.** [24]And the news of him spread throughout the whole of Syria (Province), and people brought to him the sick people having various diseases and torments, all demon-oppressed people, and mentally disturbed people, and paralyzed people, and **He healed them.**

[ClarkePyle] <u>Matthew 4:23-24</u> With these Men Jesus travelled over all Galilee, preaching, not only privately, but also openly in all their Places of public Worship; teaching them his true Religion; and proving the Authority and the Goodness of his Doctrine, **by the beneficial Miracles of healing all manner of Diseases and Infirmities.** [24]By this means his Fame presently spread over Syria: So that all sorts of diseased Persons, and Lunaticks, and Men possessed with Devils, were brought to him from all Parts; and **he healed them with a Word.**

[CLV] <u>Matthew 4:23-24</u> And Jesus led them about in the whole of Galilee, teaching in their synagogues and heralding the evangel of the kingdom, and **curing every disease and every debility among the people.** [24]And forth came the tidings of Him into the whole of Syria. And they bring to Him all who have an ill ness, those with various diseases and pressing torments, also demoniacs and epileptics and paralytics, and **He cures them.**

[CPDV] <u>Matthew 4:23-24</u> And Jesus traveled throughout all of Galilee, teaching in their synagogues, and preaching the Gospel of the kingdom, and **healing every sickness and every infirmity among the people.** [24]And reports of him went out to all of Syria, and they brought to him all those who had maladies, those who were in the grasp of various sicknesses and torments, and those who were in the hold of demons, and the mentally ill, and paralytics. And **he cured them.**

[CWB] <u>Matthew 4:23-24</u> Jesus went on foot throughout the country of Galilee, spreading the good news of the presence of God's kingdom by teaching in the synagogues, preaching in the open air and **healing people of every kind of sickness.** [24]He became known almost overnight. From as far away as Syria, people with all kinds of diseases came to be healed, including those suffering from devil possession, seizures and paralysis. **He healed them all.**

[GT] <u>Matthew 4:23-24</u> Jesus was going all around the Galilee, teaching the Good News of the kingdom in their houses of worship. **Jesus was also healing people of all types of diseases and sicknesses.** [24]The news about Jesus went all over the land of Syria. They brought him all the people who were sick. These people had all kinds of diseases; they were suffering with much pain. Some of them had demons inside them. Some were epileptics and some were paralyzed. **Jesus healed them all.**

[NLV] <u>Matthew 4:23-24</u> Jesus went over all Galilee. He taught in their places of worship and preached the Good News of the holy nation. **He healed all kinds of sickness and disease among the people.** [24]The news about Him went over all the country of Syria. They brought all the sick people to Him with many kinds of diseases and pains. They brought to Him those who had demons. They brought those who at times lose the use of their minds. They brought those who could not use their hands and legs. **He healed them.**

[Phillips] <u>Matthew 4:23-24</u> Jesus now moved about through the whole of Galilee, teaching in their synagogues and preaching the good news about the kingdom, and **healing every disease and disability among the people.** [24]His reputation spread throughout Syria, and people brought to him all those who were ill, suffering from all kinds of diseases and pains—including the devil-possessed, the insane and the paralysed. **He healed them,**

[PNT] <u>Matthew 4:23-24</u> And Jesus went about all Galilee, teaching in their synagogues, and preaching the gospel of the kingdom, and **healing all manner of sickness, and all manner of disease among the people.** ²⁴And his fame went throughout all Syria: and they brought unto him all sick people that were ill of divers diseases, and torments, and those who were possessed with dæmons, and those who were lunatick, and those who had the palsie; and **he healed them all.**

[REM-NT] <u>Matthew 4:23-24</u> Jesus traveled throughout Galilee, teaching the truth about God's kingdom of love, distributing the Remedy for selfishness and sin, and demonstrating God's ultimate healing plan by **curing every physical disease and alleviating every malady among the people.** ²⁴The news about him spread like wildfire all over Syria, and the crowds flocked to him, bringing to him all who were sick with disease—those with chronic pain, the mentally ill, the demon-possessed, those with seizures, and the paralyzed—and **he healed them all.**

[Sacred-NT] <u>Matthew 4:23-24</u> Then Jesus went over all Galilee, teaching in their synagogues, and proclaiming the glad tidings of the Reign, and **curing every sort of disease and malady among the people.** ²⁴And his fame spread all through Syria, and they brought to him all their sick, seized and tormented with various distempers, demoniacs, and lunatics, and paralytics, and **he healed them.**

[SENT] <u>Matthew 4:23-24</u> Jesus went around all of Galilee. He taught in their synagogues, preached the good news of God's Reign, and **healed all sorts of illnesses and disabilities among the people.** ²⁴And the news about him spread through all of Syria. People brought him all the sick, whatever kind of illness they had. Whether they were suffering with terrible chronic pain, afflicted with demons, mentally unstable, or paralyzed, **he healed them.**

[TLB] <u>Matthew 4:23-24</u> Jesus traveled all through Galilee teaching in the Jewish synagogues, everywhere preaching the Good News about the Kingdom of Heaven. And **he healed every kind of sickness and disease.** ²⁴The report of his miracles spread far beyond the borders of Galilee so that sick folk were soon coming to be healed from as far away as Syria. And whatever their illness and pain, or if they were possessed by demons, or were insane, or paralyzed—**he healed them all.**

[TNT] <u>Matthew 4:23-24</u> He went all through Galilee, teaching in the synagogues, proclaiming the Good New of the Kingdom, and **healing every kind of disease and sickness among the people.** ²⁴The news of him went into the whole of Syria, and they brought to him all who were sick with various diseases and in agony, demoniacs, lunatics and paralytics, and **he healed them.**

[TPT] <u>Matthew 4:23-24</u> Jesus ministered from place to place throughout all of the province of Galilee. He taught in the synagogues, preaching the hope of the kingdom realm and **healing every kind of sickness and disease among the people.** ²⁴His fame spread everywhere! Many people who were in pain and suffering with every kind of illness were brought to Jesus for their healing—epileptics, paralytics, and those tormented by demonic powers were all set free. **Everyone who was brought to Jesus was healed!**

[TVB] <u>Matthew 4:23-24</u> And so Jesus went throughout Galilee. He taught in the synagogues. He preached the good news of the Kingdom, and **He healed people, ridding their bodies of sickness and disease.** ²⁴Word spread all over Syria, as more and more sick people came to Him. The innumerable ill who came before Him had all sorts of diseases, they were in crippling pain; they were possessed by demons; they had seizures; they were paralyzed. But **Jesus healed them all.**

[TWTY-RCT-NT-V1] <u>Matthew 4:23-24</u> Then He went and wandered, revolved and passed, walked and travelled around and through the whole of and the entirety of Galiylah, teaching, explaining and instructing, holding discourses and discussions within and inside their Synagogues, their gatherings and assemblies, congregations and places of meeting, and announcing and declaring, publically pronouncing and publishing, openly preaching and teaching the good news, glad tiding and message, proclamation and victorious declaration of the kingdom and royal power, dominion and rule, kingship, reign and authority, and willingly serving, **healing and curing each and every individual and collective illness and sickness, disease and pain, plague and distress, anguish and physical malady, epidemic and calamity, and every individual and collective debility and bodily weakness, infirmity and ailment within and among the people and tribe, populace and nation, restoring them to health.** [24]And the rumour and fame, report and news, message and proclamation, account and information about Him went forth and departed, left and proceeded to go into and among the whole of and the entirety of Syria, and they brought and led, presented and offered to Him every individual and collective person that had and held, acquired and received, owned and possessed sickness and severe illnesses, bodily suffering and physical distress of various and diverse, intricate and complex, difficult and abstruse, manifold and unstable, foreign and alien, new, unknown and unheard of illnesses and sicknesses, diseases and pains, plagues and distresses, anguishes and physical maladies, epidemics and calamities, and those surrounded and held, constrained and seized, gripped and absorbed by testing and afflictions of the soul; the demon-possessed, those who had a fallen messenger and envoy in power and control over them, and the epileptic and lunatic, and the paralytic and disabled, paralysed and lame, those unable to walk, and **He willingly served and healed, cured and restored them to health.**

<u>Matthew 7:11</u> If ye then, being evil, know how to give good gifts unto your children, **how much more shall your Father which is in heaven give good things to them that ask him**?

[Authentic-NT] <u>Matthew 7:11</u> If you then, bad as you are, know how to give good gifts to your children, **how much more shall your heavenly Father give what is good to those who ask him.**

[Berkeley] <u>Matthew 7:11</u> If you then, mean as you are, know enough to give your children what is good, **how much more surely will your heavenly Father give what is good to those who ask Him!**

[ClarkePyle] <u>Matthew 7:11</u> If Men, I say, who are wicked and perverse and ill-natured, cannot but give good things to the Children; **How much more shall God, who is infinitely good and merciful, the gracious Creator and Preserver of all things, give such things as are needful to those who earnestly pray for them?**

[Doddridge-NT] <u>Matthew 7:11</u> If therefore you, imperfect and evil as you are, and some of you perhaps tenacious, froward, and unkind, yet know how to give good gifts to your children; if you find your hearts disposed and ready to communicate the best of what you have for their relief and sustenance, **how much more will your almighty and all-bountiful Father in heaven, who has a perfect sight of all your wants, and who himself has wrought into your hearts these benevolent affections, be ready to exceed you in expressing his kindness, so as freely to give good things to those that ask them of him by fervent and constant prayer?**

[HRB] <u>Matthew 7:11</u> Therefore, if you, who are imperfect, know how to give good gifts to your children, **how much more will your Father in Heaven give good things to those that ask Him**?

[LDB-NT] <u>Matthew 7:11</u> "If you, then, evil as you are, know how to give good gifts to your children, **how much more will your Father in Heaven give good things to those who earnestly persevere in asking Him for them!**"

[REM-NT] <u>Matthew 7:11</u> If you, who are selfish, know how to give good gifts to your children, **how much more will your Father in heaven give good gifts to those who ask him!**

[Spencer-NT] <u>Matthew 7:11</u> If you, then, who are sinful, know how to bestow good gifts upon your children, **how much more will your Father who is in heaven bestow benefits on those who ask Him!**

[TPT] <u>Matthew 7:11</u> If you, imperfect as you are, know how to lovingly take care of your children and give them what's best, **how much more ready is your heavenly Father to give wonderful gifts to those who ask him?**"

[TTT-NT] <u>Matthew 7:11</u> So if you, evil as you are, know how to give good gifts to your children, **how much greater gifts shall your father in heaven give if you ask him!**

<u>Matthew 8:2-3</u> And, behold, there came a leper and worshipped him, saying, Lord, **if thou wilt, thou canst make me clean.** ³And Jesus put forth his hand, and touched him, saying, **I will; be thou clean.** And immediately his leprosy was cleansed.

[Authentic-NT] <u>Matthew 8:2-3</u> Now there came a leper and prostrated himself before him saying, 'Sir, **if you will you can make me clean.**' ³Then Jesus put out his hand and touched him and said, '**I do will it. Be clean!**' At once he was cleansed of his leprosy,

[Ballentine-NT] <u>Matthew 8:2-3</u> And a leper came to him and worshipped him, and said: "Lord **if you wish you can cure me.**" ³He stretched out his hand and touched him: "**It is my wish,**" he said. "**Be cured.**" His leprosy was at once cured.

[BBE] <u>Matthew 8:2-3</u> And a leper came and gave him worship, saying, Lord, **if it is your pleasure, you have power to make me clean.** ³And he put his hand on him, saying, **It is my pleasure; be clean.** And straight away he was made clean.

[CEB] <u>Matthew 8:2-3</u> A man with a skin disease came, kneeled before him, and said, "Lord, **if you want, you can make me clean.**" ³Jesus reached out his hand and touched him, saying, "**I do want to. Become clean.**" Instantly his skin disease was cleansed.

[EEBT] <u>Matthew 8:2-3</u> Then a man with an illness of the skin came to meet Jesus. The illness was called leprosy. The man went down on his knees in front of him. '**Sir, if you want**', he said, '**you can make me well. Please do it.**' ³Jesus put out his hand towards him and touched him. '**I do want to help you. Be well**', he said. Immediately, the illness left the man.

[ERV] <u>Matthew 8:2-3</u> Then a man sick with leprosy came to him. The man bowed down before Jesus and said, "Lord, **you have the power to heal me if you want.**" ³Jesus touched the man. He said, "**I want to heal you. Be healed!**" Immediately the man was healed from his leprosy.

[GT] <u>Matthew 8:2-3</u> Then a man with leprosy came to him. He bowed down in front of Jesus. The leper said, "**Lord, you can heal me if you want to.**" ³Jesus said, "**I do want to heal you-be healed!**" Then Jesus stretched out his hand and touched the man. Immediately the man's leprosy was healed.

[Guyse-NT] <u>Matthew 8:2-3</u> And as he preached to them, so he frequently took opportunities of confirming his doctrine by miracles: Among these, we have a remarkable instance of one wrought on a man over-run with a leprosy, which the Jews used to look upon as an unclean distemper that was inflicted by the immediate hand of God, in token of his displeasure, and could not be cured by human art. This leprous person came to Jesus; and, throwing himself at his feet for mercy, begged that he would take pity on him, saying, Lord, I verily believe that, **if thou pleasest, thou art able to cleanse me from this otherwise incurable disease.** ³And he no sooner applied to Christ with this faith, but he effectually answered it; and, touching him with his hand, said, with the majesty and authority of a God, **I am as ready as thy faith can be; I will; what thou askest is granted; I say unto thee, Be thou clean:** And so powerful were his words, that the man was in that very instant cleansed of his leprosy: He spake, and it was done; he said, Let it be so, and it was so.

[ICB] <u>Matthew 8:2-3</u> Then a man sick with a harmful skin disease came to Jesus. The man bowed down before him and said, "**Lord, you have the power to heal me if you want.**" ³Jesus touched the man and said, "**I want to heal you. Be healed!**" And immediately the man was healed from his skin disease.

[JMNT] <u>Matthew 8:2-3</u> And then—look and consider! —a leper approaching began doing obeisance to (paying homage to; worshiping) Him, repeatedly saying, "**O Lord (Master), if you should want to, You are able and continue having power to at once cleanse me!**" ³So, stretching out His hand, He touched him, while saying, "**I am habitually wanting to: Be cleansed at once!**" And immediately his leprosy was cleansed!

[Jordan-NT] <u>Matthew 8:2-3</u> And then here comes this guy in bad shape, begging and pleading, "Sir, **if you really wanted to, you could heal me.**" ³Jesus put out his hand, hugged him, and said, "**I really do want to. BE HEALED.**" And that quick, his disease was gone.

[Knox] <u>Matthew 8:2-3</u> and now, a leper came and knelt before him, and said, Lord, **if it be thy will, thou hast power to make me clean**. ³Jesus held out his hand and touched him, and said, **It is my will; be thou made clean**. Whereupon his leprosy was immediately cleansed.

[KNT] <u>Matthew 8:2-3</u> Suddenly someone with a virulent skin disease approached, and knelt down in front of him. '**Master,' he said, 'if you want, you can make me clean!**' ³Jesus stretched out his hand and touched him. '**I do want to,' he said. 'Be clean!**' At once his disease was cured.

[Madsen-NT] <u>Matthew 8:2-3</u> And see, a leper came up to him, fell down before him and said, '**Lord, if only you will you can make me clean.**' ³And he stretched out his hand, touched him, and said, '**It is my will; be clean**!' And at once he was cleansed of his leprosy.

[Moffatt] <u>Matthew 8:2-3</u> Up came a leper and knelt before him, saying, "**If you only choose, sir, you can cleanse me**"; ³so he stretched his hand out and touched him, with the words, "**I do choose, be cleansed**." And his leprosy was cleansed at once.

[MSG] <u>Matthew 8:2-3</u> Then a leper appeared and went to his knees before Jesus, praying, "Master, **if you want to, you can heal my body**." ³Jesus reached out and touched him, saying, "**I want to. Be clean**." Then and there, all signs of the leprosy were gone.

[NEB] <u>Matthew 8:2-3</u> And now a leper approached him, bowed low, and said, 'Sir, **if only you will, you can cleanse me**.' ³Jesus stretched out his hand, touched him, and said, '**Indeed I will; be clean again**.' And his leprosy was cured immediately.

[NLV] <u>Matthew 8:2-3</u> A man with a bad skin disease came and got down before Him and worshiped Him. He said, "Lord, **if You will, You can heal me!**" ³Then Jesus put His hand on him and said, "**I will. You are healed!**" At once the man was healed.

[Phillips] <u>Matthew 8:2-3</u> There was a leper who came and knelt in front of him. 'Sir,' he said, '**if you want to, you can make me clean**.' ³Jesus stretched out his hand and placed it on the leper saying, '**Of course I want to. Be clean**!' And at once he was clear of the leprosy.

[REM-NT] <u>Matthew 8:2-3</u> An outcast suffering with leprosy came and humbled himself before Jesus and said, "**Lord, I know you can make me clean if you are willing**." ³Jesus gently reached out and touched the man whom no one else would touch, and said, "**I am very willing. Be clean!**" Immediately he was cured, the leprosy disappeared, and his skin became healthy and normal again.

[Rieu-Gs] <u>Matthew 8:2-3</u> And there suddenly appeared a leper, who approached him and did obeisance, saying, 'Lord, **if you will, you can cleanse me**.' ³Jesus stretched out his hand, touched him and said: '**I will it. Be cleansed**.' And his leprosy was cleansed immediately.

[SENT] <u>Matthew 8:2-3</u> Suddenly a leper came up and bowed down in front of him. He said, "**Sir, if you want to, you have the power to make me clean**." [3]And Jesus reached out his hand and touched him. He said, "**I do want to. Be clean**." Right away his leprosy was cleansed.

[TCNT] <u>Matthew 8:2-3</u> And he saw a leper who came up, and bowed to the ground before him, and said: "Master, **if only you are willing, you are able to make me clean**." [3]Stretching out his hand, Jesus touched him, saying as he did so: "**I am willing; become clean**." Instantly he was made clean from his leprosy;

[TPT] <u>Matthew 8:2-3</u> Suddenly, a leper walked up to Jesus and threw himself down before him in worship and said, "**Lord, you have the power to heal me … if you really want to**." [3]Jesus reached out his hand and touched the leper and said, "**Of course I want to heal you—be healed!**" And instantly, all signs of leprosy disappeared!

[Wade] <u>Matthew 8:2-3</u> And there was seen a leper approaching, who did Him reverence, saying, "Sir, **if you have the will, you have the power, to cleanse me**." [3]And He, stretching out His hand, touched him, saying, "**I have the will; be cleansed**."

[Wuest-NT] <u>Matthew 8:2-3</u> And behold, a leper having come, fell upon his knees and touched the ground with his forehead in an expression of profound reverence before Him, saying, Master, **in the event that you may be having a heartfelt desire, you are able to cleanse me**. [3]And having stretched out His hand He touched him saying, **I am desiring it from all my heart. Be cleansed at once**. And immediately his leprosy was cured by being cleansed away.

<u>Matthew 8:5-7</u> And when Jesus was entered into Capernaum, there came unto him a centurion, beseeching him, [6]And saying, Lord, my servant lieth at home sick of the palsy, grievously tormented. [7]And Jesus saith unto him, **I will come and heal him**.

[Ainslie-NT] <u>Matthew 8:5-7</u> And on his entering into Capernaum, there came to him a centurion, beseeching him, [6]And saying, my child lieth in the house a paralytic suffering severely. [7]And he saith to him, **Follow me: I will come and heal him**.

[AMPC] <u>Matthew 8:5-7</u> As Jesus went into Capernaum, a centurion came up to Him, begging Him, [6]And saying, Lord, my servant boy is lying at the house paralyzed and distressed with intense pains. [7]And Jesus said to him, **I will come and restore him**.

[BBE] <u>Matthew 8:5-7</u> And when Jesus was come into Capernaum, a certain captain came to him with a request, [6]Saying, Lord, my servant is ill in bed at the house, with no power in his body, and in great pain. [7]And he said to him, **I will come and make him well**.

[BLE] <u>Matthew 8:5-7</u> And when he came into Capernaum a centurion approached him, appealing to him with the words [6]"Sir, my boy is in the house down with paralysis and suffering frightful tortures." [7]He said to him "**I will come and cure him**."

[BV-KJV-NT] <u>Matthew 8:5-7</u> When Jesus went into Capernaum, a lieutenant came forward to Him encouraging Him [6]and saying, "Master, my servant boy has been bedridden in the house, disabled, being tortured dreadfully." [7]And Jesus says to him, "**When I come, I will heal him**."

[D'Onston-GS] <u>Matthew 8:5-7</u> And when he was entered into Capernaum, there came unto him a centurion, beseeching him, [6]and saying, My servant is thrown down at home paralysed, grievously tormented. [7]Jesus saith unto him, **I will come and heal him**.

[EEBT] <u>Matthew 8:5-7</u> When Jesus went into Capernaum, an officer in the army came to meet him. He asked Jesus to help him. [6]"Sir, my servant is lying in bed at home. He cannot move and he has a lot of pain.' ⁷Jesus said to the officer, '**I will go with you to your house and I will make your servant well again**.'

[Jerusalem] <u>Matthew 8:5-7</u> When he went into Capernaum a centurion came up and pleaded with him. ⁶'Sir,' he said 'my servant is lying at home paralysed, and in great pain.' ⁷'**I will come myself and cure him**' said Jesus.

[Johnson-NT] <u>Matthew 8:5-7</u> As he entered Capernaum, where he had made his headquarters, a Roman army officer came to him with an urgent request. ⁶"Sir, I have a servant at my house who is paralyzed, and he is suffering beyond description." ⁷"**Then I will come and make him whole**," replied Jesus.

[NCV] <u>Matthew 8:5-7</u> When Jesus entered the city of Capernaum, an army officer came to him, begging for help. ⁶The officer said, "Lord, my servant is at home in bed. He can't move his body and is in much pain." ⁷Jesus said to the officer, "**I will go and heal him**."

[NEB] <u>Matthew 8:5-7</u> When he had entered Capernaum a centurion came up to ask his help. ⁶'Sir,' he said, 'a boy of mine lies at home paralysed and racked with pain.' ⁷Jesus said, '**I will come and cure him**.'

[NLV] <u>Matthew 8:5-7</u> Jesus came to the city of Capernaum. A captain of the army came to Him. He asked for help, ⁶saying, "Lord, my servant is sick in bed. He is not able to move his body. He is in much pain." ⁷Jesus said to the captain, "**I will come and heal him**."

[TVB] <u>Matthew 8:5-7</u> Eventually Jesus came to the little town of Capernaum. In Capernaum a military officer came to Him and asked Him for help. ⁶Officer: Lord, I have a servant who is lying at home in agony, paralyzed. ⁷Jesus: **I will come to your house, and I will heal him**.

<u>Matthew 8:13</u> And Jesus said unto the centurion, Go thy way; and as thou hast believed, so be it done unto thee. And his servant was healed in the selfsame hour.

[AMPC] <u>Matthew 8:13</u> Then to the centurion Jesus said, Go; it shall be done for you as you have believed. And the servant boy was restored to health at that very moment.

[Barclay-NT] <u>Matthew 8:13</u> 'Go,' Jesus said to the centurion. 'Because you have a faith like this, your prayer is granted.' And the servant was cured at that very hour.

[BBE] <u>Matthew 8:13</u> And Jesus said to the captain, Go in peace; as your faith is, so let it be done to you. And the servant was made well in that hour.

[Berkeley] <u>Matthew 8:13</u> Then Jesus said to the centurion, Go home! As you have believed so shall it be for you. And at that exact moment the boy was cured.

[BV-KJV-NT] <u>Matthew 8:13</u> And Jesus said to the lieutenant, "Go, and as you trusted, it must happen to you." And his servant boy was cured in that hour.

[BWE-NT] <u>Matthew 8:13</u> Jesus said to the officer, 'Go home. What you have believed, will be done.' At that very same time the officer's servant was healed.

[Campbell-Gs] <u>Matthew 8:13</u> Then Jesus said to the centurion, Go home; be it to thee according to thy faith. That instant his servant was cured.

[CWB] <u>Matthew 8:13</u> Then Jesus turned to the Roman officer and said, "Go home, and it will be just as you believed." When the officer arrived home, he found that his servant had been healed the same hour that Jesus had spoken to him.

[ERV] <u>Matthew 8:13</u> Then Jesus said to the officer, "Go home. Your servant will be healed the way you believed he would." Right then his servant was healed.

[GNC-NT] <u>Matthew 8:13</u> And to the centurion Jesus spoke thus: "Go on your way, and may that be done for you which your faith has deserved." And it was at that very moment that the servant's health was restored.

[GNT] <u>Matthew 8:13</u> Then Jesus said to the officer, "Go home, and what you believe will be done for you." And the officer's servant was healed that very moment.

[Harwood-NT] <u>Matthew 8:13</u> Jesus then turned to the officer and told him that the divine power, with which he believed him to be endowed, was already exerted in the recovery of his servant—and at that very instant he found himself in perfect health.

[ICB] <u>Matthew 8:13</u> Then Jesus said to the officer, "Go home. Your servant will be healed just as you believed he would." And at that same time his servant was healed.

[JMNT] <u>Matthew 8:13</u> So Jesus said to the centurion, "Go! In the same way that you trusted, let it come to be for you (or: Just as you believe, let it be birthed and happen with you)!" And so the orderly (manservant; servant boy) was healed and made whole in that hour.

[LDB-NT] <u>Matthew 8:13</u> Then Jesus said to the Roman captain, "Be on your way, because what you have believed would happen has already happened." And his servant was healed that very moment.

[Martin-NT] <u>Matthew 8:13</u> And Jesus said to the centurion, "Go! As you have trusted, it must happen for you." And his child [servant] was healed at that hour.

[NJB] <u>Matthew 8:13</u> And to the centurion Jesus said, 'Go back, then; let this be done for you, as your faith demands.' And the servant was cured at that moment.

[Rieu-Gs] <u>Matthew 8:13</u> To the centurion, Jesus said: 'Go now; and your reward shall be equal to your faith.' And in that very hour his boy was cured.

[Shadwell-Gs] <u>Matthew 8:13</u> And Jesus said unto the centurion: Go, receive according to thy belief. And the lad was healed in that hour.

[TVB] <u>Matthew 8:13</u> Then Jesus turned to the Centurion. Jesus: You may go home. For it is as you say it is; it is as you believe. And the officer's servant was healed, right then.

[Wade] <u>Matthew 8:13</u> And Jesus said to the Army Captain, "Go; the result shall be as you have believed it can be." And the man-servant recovered at that moment.

[Wells-NT] <u>Matthew 8:13</u> And what Jesus said unto them that were sent from the Centurion, may be represented (more short, and according to the Maxim that One's Proxy is One's Self) to this Effect, Go thy way, and as thou hast believed that I am able to heal thy Servant by a Word's Speaking, so be it done unto thee. And his Servant was healed in the self-same hour.

<u>Matthew 8:15</u> And he touched her hand, and the fever left her: and she arose, and ministered unto them.

[AUV-NT 2003] <u>Matthew 8:15</u> He touched her hand and [immediately] her fever subsided and she got up [out of bed] and waited on Him.

[BBE] <u>Matthew 8:15</u> And he put his hand on hers and the disease went from her, and she got up and took care of his needs.

[BWE-NT] <u>Matthew 8:15</u> Jesus took hold of her hand and the fever left her. She got up and began to do things for Jesus.

[ClarkePyle] <u>Matthew 8:15</u> And he took her by the Hand and helped her up; and the Fever was immediately cured so entirely, that her Strength returned to her, and she made Provision for them, and they say down to Meat, and she served them.

[CWB] <u>Matthew 8:15</u> Jesus went over to her bed and gently touched her. Immediately her temperature returned to normal and her sickness was gone. Then she got up and helped care for the guests.

[ICB] <u>Matthew 8:15</u> Jesus touched her hand, and the fever left her. Then she stood up and began to serve Jesus.

[NLV] <u>Matthew 8:15</u> He touched her hand and the sickness left her. She got up and cared for Jesus.

[Smith] <u>Matthew 8:15</u> And he touched her hand, and the fever let her go: and she arose, and served them.

[T4T] <u>Matthew 8:15</u> He touched her hand, and as a result, immediately she no longer had a fever. Then she got up and served them some food.

[TLB] <u>Matthew 8:15</u> But when Jesus touched her hand, the fever left her; and she got up and prepared a meal for them!

[TPT] <u>Matthew 8:15</u> The moment Jesus touched her hand she was healed! Immediately she got up and began to make dinner for them.

<u>Matthew 8:16-17</u> When the even was come, they brought unto him many that were possessed with devils: and **he cast out the spirits with his word, and healed all that were sick**: [17]That it might be fulfilled which was spoken by Esaias the prophet, saying, **Himself took our infirmities, and bare our sicknesses**.

[AMPC] <u>Matthew 8:16-17</u> When evening came, they brought to Him many who were under the power of demons, and **He drove out the spirits with a word and restored to health all who were sick**. [17]And thus He fulfilled what was spoken by the prophet Isaiah, He **Himself took [in order to carry away] our weaknesses and infirmities and bore away our diseases**.

[Barclay-NT] <u>Matthew 8:16-17</u> When evening came, they brought many demon-possessed people to him, and **he ejected the spirits with a word, and cured all those who were ill**. [17]This happened that the statement made through the prophet Isaiah might come true: **'He took upon himself our weaknesses and carried the burden of our diseases.'**

[Berkeley] <u>Matthew 8:16-17</u> At eventide they brought to Him many demoniacs and with a word **He cast out the spirits, and He healed all who had diseases**, [17]so that the word spoken though the prophet Isaiah became fulfilled, **"He Himself took our weaknesses and carried off our diseases."**

[BWE-NT] <u>Matthew 8:16-17</u> That evening, many people who had bad spirits were brought to Jesus. **He spoke to the bad spirits and drove them out. And he healed all the people who were sick**. [17]What the prophet Isaiah said came true. He said, **'He took away the things that made us weak. He took away the things that made us sick.'**

[Campbell-Gs] <u>Matthew 8:16-17</u> In the evening, they presented to him many demoniacs; and **he expelled the spirits with a word, and cured all the sick**; [17]thus verifying the saying of the Prophet Isaiah, **"He hath himself carried off our infirmities and borne our distresses."**

[CWB] <u>Matthew 8:16-17</u> As soon as it was sundown and Sabbath restrictions were lifted, people came from everywhere wanting to be healed, including many who were devil possessed. **Jesus cast out the demons simply by speaking to them and healed all the people who were sick**. [17]This was a direct fulfillment of Isaiah's prophecy: **"He will take upon Himself our infirmities and He will take away our sicknesses."**

[ICB] <u>Matthew 8:16-17</u> That evening people brought to Jesus many who had demons. **Jesus spoke and the demons left them. Jesus healed all the sick**. [17]He did these things to make come true what Isaiah the prophet said: **"He took our suffering on him. And he felt our pain for us."**

[Madsen-NT] <u>Matthew 8:16-17</u> When it was evening, many who were possessed were brought to him, and **through the power of his word he drove out the demons and healed all the sick.** [17]So the word of the prophet Isaiah was fulfilled: **He has taken our sickness from us, he has borne all our infirmities.**

[Moffatt] <u>Matthew 8:16-17</u> Now when evening came they brought him many demoniacs, **and he cast out the spirits with a word of and healed all the invalids—** [17]that the word spoken by the prophet Isaiah might be fulfilled, **He took away our sicknesses and our diseases he removed.**

[NEB] <u>Matthew 8:16-17</u> When evening fell, they brought to him many who were possessed by devils; and **he drove the spirits out with a word and healed all who were ill,** [17]to make good the prophecy of Isaiah: '**He took away our illnesses and lifted our diseases from us.**'

[Newcome] <u>Matthew 8:16-17</u> Now when evening was come, many that had demons were brought unto him: and **he cast out the spirits with a word, and cured all who were sick:** [17]so that it was fulfilled which was spoken by the prophet Isaiah, saying, "**He took away our infirmities, and removed our diseases.**"

[Original-NT] <u>Matthew 8:16-17</u> When evening came many demoniacs were brought up to him, and **he expelled the spirits by a command, and cured all who were ill.** [17]Thereby was fulfilled what was announced by the prophet Isaiah, "**Himself took our infirmities and bore our diseases.**"

[REAL] <u>Matthew 8:16-17</u> When evening came, they brought him many who were demonized, and **he threw out the spirits with a word, and he healed all who were sick,** [17]so what was spoken by the revealer Isaiah could be fulfilled— "**He took our infirmities on himself and he carried diseases.**"

[TLB] <u>Matthew 8:16-17</u> That evening several demon-possessed people were brought to Jesus; and **when he spoke a single word, all the demons fled; and all the sick were healed.** [17]This fulfilled the prophecy of Isaiah, "**He took our sicknesses and bore our diseases.**"

[TPT] <u>Matthew 8:16-17</u> That evening the people brought to him many who were demonized. And **by Jesus only speaking a word of healing over them, they were totally set free from their torment, and everyone who was sick received their healing!** [17]In doing this, Jesus fulfilled the prophecy of Isaiah: **He put upon himself our weaknesses, and he carried away our diseases and made us well.**

[TWTY-RCT-NT-V1] <u>Matthew 8:16-17</u> As evening came to be and exist, arise and appear, when the sun had set and had gone down, many numerous and large amounts of people who were demon-possessed, those who had a fallen messenger and envoy in power and control over them, were brought and handed over, presented and offered to Him, and He threw out and expelled, drove out and repudiated, pulled and tore out, brought and sent out, cast and extracted out, disposed of and ejected, banished and got rid of the spirits with a word and saying, message and statement, declaration and thought, instruction and teaching, decree, mandate and matter, and **He willingly served and healed, cured and restored all those, individually and collectively, who had and held, acquired and received, owned and possessed sickness and severe illnesses, bodily suffering and physical distress to health.** [17]This happened for the purpose of, so that and in order for that which was put forth and uttered by Yasha'Yahu the prophet, the man who declared the thoughts of the Supreme One before and in the presence of mankind, would be completed and fulfilled, perfected and celebrated, executed and carried out, finished and concluded, ratified and satisfied, realised and effected, performed and accomplished; saying and teaching, maintaining and affirming, directing and exhorting, advising and pointing out, "**He Himself received and accepted, took and seized, acquired and collected, grasped and obtained, chose and selected, claimed and procured, apprehended and admitted our weaknesses and frailties, feebleness's and inadequacies, powerlessness's, poorness's and neediness's; and He carried off and endured, bore and took up, raised and lifted our illnesses and sicknesses, diseases and**

pains, plagues and distresses, anguish and physical maladies, epidemics and calamities from us."

Matthew 8:31-32 So the devils besought him, saying, If thou cast us out, suffer us to go away into the herd of swine. ³²**And he said unto them, Go. And when they were come out, they went into the herd of swine**: and, behold, the whole herd of swine ran violently down a steep place into the sea, and perished in the waters.

[ERV] **Matthew 8:31-32** The demons begged Jesus, "If you make us leave these men, please send us into that herd of pigs." ³²**Jesus said to them, "Go!" So the demons left the men and went into the pigs.** Then the whole herd of pigs ran down the hill into the lake, and all were drowned.

[FBV-NT] **Matthew 8:31-32** The demons pleaded with him, "If you're going to drive us out, send us into the herd of pigs." ³²**"Go!" said Jesus. The demons left the men and went into the pigs.** The whole herd ran down the steep hillside into the sea and drowned.

[Lingard-Gs] **Matthew 8:31-32** And the fiends besought him, saying: "If thou cast us out, suffer us to go into the herd of swine." ³²**And he said to them: "Get you gone." And they went out, and entered into the herd of swine.** And behold, the whole herd of swine rushed down the precipice into the sea, and perished in the waters.

[LTPB] **Matthew 8:31-32** The demons begged him, saying, "If you throw us out, send us into the herd of pigs!" ³²**He said to them, "Go!" Going out, they went into the pigs**, and look! The whole herd went away violently headlong into the sea, and they died in the waters.

[TTNT] **Matthew 8:31-32** The demons in the men pleaded with Jesus: "If You drive us out, send us into the herd of pigs." ³²**Jesus spoke just one word: "Go!" The demons immediately came out of the men and entered the pigs.** The whole herd rushed down the steep bank into the lake where they were all drowned.

Matthew 9:6 But that ye may know that the Son of man hath power on earth to forgive sins, (then saith he to the sick of the palsy,) **Arise, take up thy bed, and go unto thine house**.

[AMP] **Matthew 9:6** But so that you may know that the Son of Man has authority and the power on earth to forgive sins" —then He said to the paralytic, "**Get up, pick up your stretcher and go home.**"

[EEBT] **Matthew 9:6** But I want you to know this. The Son of Man has authority on earth. He can forgive people for all the wrong things that they have done.' Then he said to the man who could not move his legs, '**Stand up. Pick up the bed where you are lying. And go home.**'

[FV] **Matthew 9:6** But I speak these words so that you may understand that the Son of man has authority on earth to forgive sins." Then He said to the paralytic, "**Arise, take up your bed, and go to your house.**"

[Original-NT] **Matthew 9:6** "But so that you may know that the Son of Man is entitled on earth to forgive sins" —he said to the paralytic, "**Rise, pick up your mattress, and go to your home!**"

[REM-NT] **Matthew 9:6** But I will make it simple for you to understand: My mission is to heal humanity from all the damage of sin—mental, physical, and spiritual. Just so there will be no doubt that I have authority to forgive sin" —turning to the paralyzed man, Jesus continued— "**stand up, take your mat, and walk home.**"

[Rieu-Gs] **Matthew 9:6** However, to teach you that the Son of Man has authority on earth to forgive sins—and he turned to the paralytic— '**Get up, take your bed and go home.**'

[T4T] <u>Matthew 9:6</u> So I am going to do something in order that you may know that God has authorized me, the one who came from heaven, to forgive the sins of people while I am on the earth, as well as to heal people." Then he said to the paralyzed man, "**Get up, pick up your sleeping pad, and go home!**"

<u>Matthew 9:12</u> But when Jesus heard that, he said unto them, **They that be whole need not a physician, but they that are sick.**

[AMPC] <u>Matthew 9:12</u> But when Jesus heard it, He replied, **Those who are strong and well (healthy) have no need of a physician, but those who are weak and sick.**

[Authentic-NT] <u>Matthew 9:12</u> Jesus overheard this and replied, '**It is not the healthy who need a doctor, but those who are ill.**'

[BBE] <u>Matthew 9:12</u> But on hearing this he said, **Those who are well have no need of a medical man, but those who are ill.**

[BLE] <u>Matthew 9:12</u> But he, hearing it, said "**Not the able-bodied, but the ill, need a physician.**

[CB] <u>Matthew 9:12</u> But when Jesus heard that, He told them, "**The well do not need to see the doctor, but the sick do.**

[CEB] <u>Matthew 9:12</u> When Jesus heard it, he said, "**Healthy people don't need a doctor, but sick people do.**

[CLV] <u>Matthew 9:12</u> Now hearing, He said, "**No need have the strong of a physician, but those having an illness.**

[Douay-Rheims] <u>Matthew 9:12</u> But Jesus hearing it, said: **They that are in health need not a physician, but they that are ill.**

[Knox] <u>Matthew 9:12</u> Jesus heard it, and said, **It is not those who are in health that have need of the physician, it is those who are sick.**

[Murdock-NT] <u>Matthew 9:12</u> And as Jesus heard [it], he said to them: **They who are in health have no need of a physician, but they that are very sick.**

[Phillips] <u>Matthew 9:12</u> But Jesus heard this and replied, '**It is not the fit and flourishing who need the doctor, but those who are ill!**'

[REM-NT] <u>Matthew 9:12</u> Jesus heard their question and answered: "**Those who think they are healthy don't recognize their need for a doctor, but those who know they are sick do recognize their need.**

[TPT] <u>Matthew 9:12</u> When Jesus overheard this, he spoke up and said, "**Healthy people don't need to see a doctor, but the sick will go for treatment.**"

<u>Matthew 9:20-22</u> And, behold, a woman, which was diseased with an issue of blood twelve years, came behind him, and touched the hem of his garment: [21]**For she said within herself, If I may but touch his garment, I shall be whole**[sozo]. [22]But Jesus turned him about, and when he saw her, he said, Daughter, be of good comfort; **thy faith hath made thee whole**[sozo]. **And the woman was made whole**[sozo] from that hour.

[AMP] <u>Matthew 9:20-22</u> Then a woman who had suffered from a hemorrhage for twelve years came up behind Him and touched the [tassel] fringe of His outer robe; [21]**for she had been saying to herself, "If I only touch His outer robe, I will be healed.**" [22]But Jesus turning and seeing her said, "Take courage, daughter; **your [personal trust and confident] faith [in Me] has made you well.**" **And at once the woman was [completely] healed.**

[AMPC] <u>Matthew 9:20-22</u> And behold, a woman who had suffered from a flow of blood for twelve years came up behind Him and touched the fringe of His garment; **²¹For she kept saying to herself, If I only touch His garment, I shall be restored to health.** ²²Jesus turned around and, seeing her, He said, Take courage, daughter! **Your faith has made you well. And at once the woman was restored to health.**

[ClarkePyle] <u>Matthew 9:20-22</u> and as he was in the Way, a Woman that had been twelve Years troubled with a bloody Flux, and was ashamed to confess her Disease publicly before the Multitude, came behind him privately, and touched the Hem of his Coat. **²¹For she verily persuaded her self, that if she could but touch his Clothes, she should be healed.** ²²Accordingly as soon as she touched his Coat, **she was immediately healed.** But Jesus by his Divine Power knowing what was done, and not being willing that so excellent an Instance of Faith should pass undiscovered, turned himself to the Woman, and said unto her; Daughter, be of good Courage, **your great Faith hath obtained the Cure of your Disease.**

[FBV-NT] <u>Matthew 9:20-22</u> At that moment a woman who had been sick with bleeding for twelve years came up behind him and touched the hem of his of his cloak. **²¹She had told herself, "If I can just touch his cloak, I'll be healed."** ²²Jesus turned and saw her. "Be happy, for your trust in me has healed you," he told her. **The woman was immediately healed.**

[Godbey-NT] <u>Matthew 9:20-22</u> And behold, a woman, having an issue of blood twelve years, and coming to Him behind, touched the hem of His garment. **²¹For she continued to say within herself, If I may only touch His garment, I will be saved. ²²And the woman was saved from that hour.** And Jesus turning and seeing her said, Be of good cheer, daughter; **thy faith hath saved thee.**

[HNT] <u>Matthew 9:20-22</u> And behold, a woman who had had a hemorrhage for twelve years, came behind him and touched the tassel of his cloak; **²¹for she kept saying to herself, "If only I touch his cloak, I shall be restored."** ²²When Jesus turned and saw her, he said, "Be of good cheer, daughter; **thy faith has restored thee."**

[Kenrick] <u>Matthew 9:20-22</u> And behold, a woman having an issue of blood twelve years, came behind Him, and touched the fringe of His garment. **²¹For she said within herself: If I may but touch His garment, I shall be healed.** ²²But Jesus turned about, and seeing her, said: Be of good heart, daughter, **thy faith has healed thee. And the woman was healed from that hour.**

[MSG] <u>Matthew 9:20-22</u> Just then a woman who had hemorrhaged for twelve years slipped in from behind and lightly touched his robe. **²¹She was thinking to herself, "If I can just put a finger on his robe, I'll get well."** Jesus turned—caught her at it. Then he reassured her: **"Courage, daughter. You took a risk of faith, and now you're well." ²²The woman was well from then on.**

[Original-NT] <u>Matthew 9:20-22</u> Now a woman who had suffered twelve years with a haemorrhage came up behind and touched the fringe of his cloak, **²¹for she said to herself, "If only I can touch his cloak I shall get well."** ²²But Jesus turned round and saw her and said, "Courage, daughter! **Your faith has cured you." From that moment the woman was cured.**

[Phillips] <u>Matthew 9:20-22</u> And on the way a woman who had had a haemorrhage for twelve years approached him from behind and touched the edge of his cloak. **²¹'If I can only touch his cloak,' she kept saying to herself, 'I shall be all right.'** ²²But Jesus turned round and saw her. **'Cheer up, my daughter,' he said, 'your faith has made you well!' And the woman was completely cured from that moment.**

[Spencer-NT] <u>Matthew 9:20-22</u> And, behold, a woman who had suffered from hemorrhage for twelve years, approaching from behind, touched the fringe of His robe; **²¹for she said to herself, "If I merely touch His robe I shall be saved."** ²²Jesus, however, turned, and seeing her said, **"Take heart, daughter; thy faith hath saved thee." And the woman was cured from that moment.**

[SPV] <u>Matthew 9:20-22</u> And behold, a woman who had been suffering from a hemorrhage for twelve years came up from behind [and] touched the edge of his cloak, **²¹for she kept saying to herself, "If I should only touch his cloak, I will be restored to health."** ²²But Jesus, when [he] turned around and saw her, said, "Have courage, daughter; **your faith has restored you to health." And the woman was restored to health from that time on**.

[TCNT] <u>Matthew 9:20-22</u> But meanwhile a woman, who had been suffering from hemorrhage for twelve years, came up behind and touched the tassel of his cloak. ²¹**"If I only touch his cloak," she said to herself, "I shall get well."** ²²Turning and seeing her, Jesus said: "Courage, Daughter! **your faith has delivered you." And the woman was delivered from her malady from that very hour.**

[TPT] <u>Matthew 9:20-22</u> Suddenly, a woman came from behind Jesus and touched the tassel of his prayer shawl for healing. She had been suffering from continual bleeding for twelve years, but had faith that Jesus could heal her. ²¹**For she kept saying to herself, "If I could only touch his prayer shawl I would be healed."** ²²Just then Jesus turned around and looked at her and said, "My daughter, be encouraged. **Your faith has healed you." And instantly she was healed!**

<u>Matthew 9:25</u> But when the people were put forth, he went in, and **took her by the hand, and the maid arose**.

[Authentic-NT] <u>Matthew 9:25</u> But when the crowd had been ejected he went in and **took her by the hand, and the little girl rose up**.

[AUV-NT 2003] <u>Matthew 9:25</u> But after the crowd was sent outside, Jesus entered [her room, along with her parents and three of His disciples] and **took her by the hand, and the young lady rose up [from the dead]**.

[Berkeley] <u>Matthew 9:25</u> but after the crowd had been expelled, He went in and **took her hand and the girl rose up**.

[EEBT] <u>Matthew 9:25</u> But the family sent the crowd out of the house. Then Jesus went into the room where the girl was lying. **He held her hand, and she stood up**.

[GNT] <u>Matthew 9:25</u> But as soon as the people had been put out, Jesus went into the girl's room and **took hold of her hand, and she got up**.

[GW] <u>Matthew 9:25</u> When the crowd had been put outside, Jesus went in, **took her hand, and the girl came back to life**.

[Lewis-Gs] <u>Matthew 9:25</u> And when he had put out the crowd, he came and **touched her hand, and immediately she arose**.

[NCV] <u>Matthew 9:25</u> After the crowd had been thrown out of the house, Jesus went into the girl's room and **took hold of her hand, and she stood up**.

[Palmer] <u>Matthew 9:25</u> And when the crowd was put out, he went in and **took hold of her hand, and the maiden was raised from the dead**.

[Sindlinger-NT] <u>Matthew 9:25</u> After he asked them to leave, he went inside and **brought the girl back to life**.

[UDB] <u>Matthew 9:25</u> But Jesus told them to get out of the house. Then he went into the room where the girl was lying. **He took hold of her hand and she became alive again and got up**.

<u>Matthew 9:29-30</u> Then touched he their eyes, saying, **According to your faith be it unto you**. ³⁰And their eyes were opened; and Jesus straitly charged them, saying, See that no man know it.

A SURVEY OF HEALING SCRIPTURES

[AMP] <u>Matthew 9:29-30</u> Then He touched their eyes, saying, "**According to your faith [your trust and confidence in My power and My ability to heal] it will be done to you**." [30]And their eyes were opened. And Jesus sternly warned them: "See that no one knows this!"

[AMPC] <u>Matthew 9:29-30</u> Then He touched their eyes, saying, **According to your faith and trust and reliance [on the power invested in Me] be it done to you**; [30]And their eyes were opened. And Jesus earnestly and sternly charged them, See that you let no one know about this.

[AUV-NT 2005] <u>Matthew 9:29-30</u> Then He touched their eyes and said, "**Let what you expect be done for you**." [30]And [immediately] they were able to see. Jesus then strongly urged them, saying, "Make sure that no one knows [what I have done for you]."

[Barclay-NT] <u>Matthew 9:29-30</u> He touched their eyes. '**Let your prayer be answered in proportion to your faith**,' he said. [30]Their sight was restored. Jesus sternly ordered them: 'See that no one gets to know about this.'

[Beck] <u>Matthew 9:29-30</u> Then He touched their eyes and said, "**As you believed, so it must by done to you!**" [30]Then they could see again. "See that nobody finds out about this!" He sternly ordered them.

[Berkeley] <u>Matthew 9:29-30</u> He then touched their eyes and said, **To the measure of your faith it shall be to you**. [30]And their eyes were opened. Jesus charged them strictly, See that no one learns of this.

[BLE] <u>Matthew 9:29-30</u> Then he touched their eyes, saying "**Have it as you have faith for**"; [30]and their eyes were opened. And Jesus said to them sternly "See that nobody finds it out."

[BWE-NT] <u>Matthew 9:29-30</u> Then Jesus touched their eyes. He said, '**As you believed, so will it happen to you**.' [30]Then they were able to see. Jesus said to them, 'Take care, do not tell anyone about this.'

[CEB] <u>Matthew 9:29-30</u> Then Jesus touched their eyes and said, "**It will happen for you just as you have believed**". [30]Their eyes were opened. Then Jesus sternly warned them, "Make sure nobody knows about this."

[CJB] <u>Matthew 9:29-30</u> Then he touched their eyes and said, "**Let it happen to you according to your trust**"; [30]and their sight was restored. Yeshua warned them severely, "See that no one knows about it."

[ERV] <u>Matthew 9:29-30</u> Then Jesus touched their eyes and said, "**You believe that I can make you see again, so it will happen**." [30]Then the men were able to see. Jesus gave them a strong warning. He said, "Don't tell anyone about this."

[Etheridge-NT] <u>Matthew 9:29-30</u> Then he touched their eyes, and said, **As you believe be it to you**. [30]And immediately their eyes were opened. And Jeshu forbad them and said, Beware lest any man know.

[Fenton] <u>Matthew 9:29-30</u> He touched their eyes, remarking, "**As your faith, so shall the result be**." [30]And their eyes were opened; and Jesus enjoined them to "Take care and inform no one about it."

[Goodspeed-NT] <u>Matthew 9:29-30</u> Then he touched their eyes and said, "**You shall have what your faith expects**." [30]And their sight was restored. Jesus warned them sternly not to let anyone hear of it.

[GW] <u>Matthew 9:29-30</u> He touched their eyes and said, "**What you have believed will be done for you!**" [30]Then they could see. He warned them, "Don't let anyone know about this!"

[Jerusalem] <u>Matthew 9:29-30</u> Then he touched their eyes saying, '**Your faith deserves it, so let this be done for you**'. [30]And their sight returned. Then Jesus sternly warned them, 'Take care that no one learns about this'.

[Johnson-NT] <u>Matthew 9:29-30</u> He then touched their eyes with the tips of his fingers, saying, "**What you have believed in the depths of your being will be true in your body**." [30]Their eyes were healed and they could see again. Immediately Jesus carefully instructed them, "Don't tell anyone what I have done. I don't want anyone to know about it."

[MSG] <u>Matthew 9:29-30</u> He touched their eyes and said, "**Become what you believe.**" [30]It happened. They saw. Then Jesus became very stern. "Don't let a soul know how this happened."

[NCV] <u>Matthew 9:29-30</u> Then Jesus touched their eyes and said, "**Because you believe I can make you see again, it will happen.**" [30]Then the men were able to see. But Jesus warned them strongly, saying, "Don't tell anyone about this."

[NIRV] <u>Matthew 9:29-30</u> Then he touched their eyes. He said, "**It will happen to you just as you believed.**" [30]They could now see again. Jesus strongly warned them, "Be sure that no one knows about this."

[NLV] <u>Matthew 9:29-30</u> Then Jesus put His hands on their eyes and said, "**You will have what you want because you have faith.**" [30]Their eyes were opened. Jesus told them to tell no one.

[Phillips] <u>Matthew 9:29-30</u> Then he touched their eyes, saying, '**You have believed and so it shall be.**' [30]Then their sight returned, but Jesus sternly warned them, 'Don't let anyone know about this.'

[Rieu-Gs] <u>Matthew 9:29-30</u> Then he touched their eyes and said: '**Your reward shall be equal to your faith.**' [30]And their eyes were opened.

[TTNT] <u>Matthew 9:29-30</u> "Then Jesus reached out His hand, touched their eyes and said: "**It will now be done to you exactly as you have believed.**" [30]And their sight was restored immediately. Then Jesus spoke strictly to them: "Be sure that no-one knows about this."

<u>Matthew 9:33</u> **And when the devil was cast out, the dumb spake**: and the multitudes marvelled, saying, It was never so seen in Israel.

[CEB] <u>Matthew 9:33</u> **When Jesus had thrown out the demon, the man who couldn't speak began to talk.** The crowds were amazed and said, "Nothing like this has ever been seen in Israel."

[CWB] <u>Matthew 9:33</u> **After Jesus cast out the demon, the man could talk again.** The people were amazed and said, "Never did things like this happen in Israel before!"

[JMNT] <u>Matthew 9:33</u> **And then, upon the demon being thrown out, the "mute man" spoke!** And the crowds were amazed and filled with wonder, one after another saying, "Never was it thus seen (or: was it shown in light to be made visible in this way) within Israel!"

[Lingard-Gs] <u>Matthew 9:33</u> **And when the fiend was cast out, the dumb man spake.** And the crowds marvelled, saying: "Nothing like this was ever seen in Israel."

[REM-NT] <u>Matthew 9:33</u> And **when Jesus overruled the work of the devils and healed the mute man, the man spoke.** The crowd was stunned with awe and said, "Nothing like this has ever been seen in all Israel."

[Smith] <u>Matthew 9:33</u> **And the demon being cast out, the dumb, spake**, and the crowd admired, saying, It was never so brought to light in Israel.

[T4T] <u>Matthew 9:33</u> **After Jesus had expelled the demon, the man who had been unable to speak began to speak!** The crowd who saw this marveled. They said, "Never before have we seen anything as marvelous as this happen in Israel!"

[Thomson] <u>Matthew 9:33</u> **and the demon being expelled, the dumb man spake**, and the crowds expressed their amazement, saying, Nothing like this was ever seen in Israel.

[TPT] <u>Matthew 9:33</u> **Jesus cast the demon out of him, and immediately the man began to speak plainly**. The crowds marveled in astonishment, saying, "We've never seen miracles like this in Israel!"

Matthew 9:35 And Jesus went about all the cities and villages, teaching in their synagogues, and preaching the gospel of the kingdom, and healing every sickness and every disease among the people.

[AMPC] **Matthew 9:35** And Jesus went about all the cities and villages, teaching in their synagogues and proclaiming the good news (the Gospel) of the kingdom and curing all kinds of disease and every weakness and infirmity.

[BBE] **Matthew 9:35** And Jesus went about all the towns and small places, teaching in their Synagogues and preaching the good news of the kingdom and making well all sorts of disease and pain.

[BWE-NT] **Matthew 9:35** Jesus went around to all the cities and towns. He taught people in their meeting houses and told them the good news of the kingdom of heaven. He healed all the sick and weak people.

[ERV] **Matthew 9:35** Jesus traveled through all the towns and villages. He taught in their synagogues and told people the Good News about God's kingdom. He healed all kinds of diseases and sicknesses.

[FAA] **Matthew 9:35** Then Jesus went around all the cities and the villages teaching in their synagogues and proclaiming the gospel of the kingdom and curing every sickness and every ailment among the people.

[GNT] **Matthew 9:35** Jesus went around visiting all the towns and villages. He taught in the synagogues, preached the Good News about the Kingdom, and healed people with every kind of disease and sickness.

[Goodspeed-NT] **Matthew 9:35** Jesus went round among all the towns and villages, teaching in their synagogues, and proclaiming the good news of the kingdom, and curing any disease or illness.

[Mace-NT] **Matthew 9:35** And Jesus went about all the towns and villages, teaching in their synagogues, preaching the gospel of the kingdom, and healing diseases and disorders of every kind.

[NCV] **Matthew 9:35** Jesus traveled through all the towns and villages, teaching in their synagogues, preaching the Good News about the kingdom, and healing all kinds of diseases and sicknesses.

[REM-NT] **Matthew 9:35** Jesus visited all the towns and villages in the region. He taught in their synagogues and preached the good news of his kingdom of love and of the Remedy he brought, demonstrating his mission by healing every disease and sickness.

[Sindlinger-NT] **Matthew 9:35** Jesus and his followers then traveled to a lot of other towns and villages. When people gathered in the local worship centers, he explained how they could enjoy a better life, and he healed a lot of people with a variety of illnesses.

[SPV] **Matthew 9:35** Then Jesus began going throughout all the cities and the villages for the purpose of teaching in their synagogues and proclaiming the gospel of the kingdom and healing every kind of disease and every kind of sickness among the people.

[Tackwall-NT] **Matthew 9:35** And Jesus went about all the cities and the villages, teaching in their synagogues and proclaiming the Good News of the Kingdom, and healing every disease and every infirmity.

[TLB] **Matthew 9:35** Jesus traveled around through all the cities and villages of that area, teaching in the Jewish synagogues and announcing the Good News about the Kingdom. And wherever he went he healed people of every sort of illness.

[TPT] **Matthew 9:35** Jesus walked throughout the region with the joyful message of God's kingdom realm. He taught in their meeting houses, and wherever he went he demonstrated God's power by healing every kind of disease and illness.

[Weymouth-NT] <u>Matthew 9:35</u> And Jesus continued His circuits through all the towns and the villages, teaching in their synagogues and proclaiming the Good News of the Kingdom, and curing every kind of disease and infirmity.

[Williams-NT] <u>Matthew 9:35</u> Jesus kept visiting all the towns and villages, teaching in their synagogues, preaching the good news of the kingdom, and curing every sort of sickness and ailment.

[YLT] <u>Matthew 9:35</u> And Jesus was going up and down all the cities and the villages, teaching in their synagogues, and proclaiming the good news of the reign, and healing every sickness and every malady among the people.

<u>Matthew 10:1</u> And when he had called unto him his twelve disciples, he gave them power against unclean spirits, to cast them out, and to **heal all manner of sickness and all manner of disease**.

[AUV-NT 2005] <u>Matthew 10:1</u> Jesus then called His twelve apostles to Him and gave them authority to drive out evil spirits and to **heal all kinds of diseases and illnesses**.

[Berkeley] <u>Matthew 10:1</u> Calling His twelve disciples to Him, He gave them power over depraved spirits to cast them out, and to **heal every disease and every malady**.

[Darby] <u>Matthew 10:1</u> And having called to [him] his twelve disciples, he gave them power over unclean spirits, so that they should cast them out, and **heal every disease and every bodily weakness**.

[EEBT] <u>Matthew 10:1</u> One day, Jesus asked 12 of his disciples to come to him. He gave them authority over bad spirits that were living in people. These disciples could then cause the spirits to leave people. Jesus also **gave them authority to cause sick people to become well again. They could remove all their illnesses.**

[Goodspeed-NT] <u>Matthew 10:1</u> Then he called his twelve disciples to him, and gave them power over the foul spirits so that they could drive them out, and **so that they could heal any disease or illness**.

[GW] <u>Matthew 10:1</u> Jesus called his twelve disciples and gave them authority to force evil spirits out of people and to **cure every disease and sickness**.

[Harwood-NT] <u>Matthew 10:1</u> After this Jesus collected his twelve disciples in a body, and communicated to them such miraculous endowments, as would empower them to **cure the most inveterate and stubborn disorders of every kind and degree, to which human nature is subjected.**

[LITV] <u>Matthew 10:1</u> And having called His twelve disciples, He gave them authority over unclean spirits, so as to throw them out, and to **heal every disease and every weakness of body**.

[OEB-NT] <u>Matthew 10:1</u> Calling his twelve Disciples to him, Jesus gave them authority over foul spirits, so that they could drive them out, as well as **the power of curing every kind of disease and every kind of sickness**.

[Original-NT] <u>Matthew 10:1</u> Then summoning his twelve disciples he gave them power over foul spirits to enable them to expel them and **to cure every kind of disease and infirmity**.

[Phillips] <u>Matthew 10:1</u> Jesus called his twelve disciples to him and gave them authority to expel evil spirits and **heal all kinds of disease and infirmity**.

[Rotherham] <u>Matthew 10:1</u> And, calling near his twelve disciples, he gave them authority over impure spirits, —so as to be casting them out, and **curing every disease and every infirmity**.

[TLB] <u>Matthew 10:1</u> Jesus called his twelve disciples to him and gave them authority to cast out evil spirits and to **heal every kind of sickness and disease**.

[TPT] <u>Matthew 10:1</u> Jesus gathered his twelve disciples and imparted to them authority to cast out demons and to **heal every sickness and every disease**.

[TVB] <u>Matthew 10:1</u> Jesus called His twelve disciples to Him. He endowed them with the authority to **heal sickness and disease** and to drive demons out of those who were possessed.

[Wuest-NT] <u>Matthew 10:1</u> And having called to Himself His twelve disciples, He gave them authority over unclean spirits to be ejecting them and **to be healing every disease and every sickness.**

<u>Matthew 10:7-8</u> And as ye go, preach, saying, The kingdom of heaven is at hand. **8Heal the sick, cleanse the lepers, raise the dead, cast out devils**: freely ye have received, freely give.

[Authentic-NT] <u>Matthew 10:7-8</u> As you travel proclaim, "The Kingdom of Heaven is at hand." **8Cure the ailing, raise the dead, cleanse the lepers, expel the demons**. You have received without payment, so give without payment.

[BWE-NT] <u>Matthew 10:7-8</u> As you go, tell people that the kingdom of heaven is here. **8Heal sick people. Bring dead people to life. Heal people who have leprosy. Drive bad spirits out of people.** You got it free, so give it free to others

[CWB] <u>Matthew 10:7-8</u> Tell them that the kingdom of God is near! 8Then give them a glimpse of that kingdom by **healing their sick, cleansing their lepers, raising their dead and casting out demons**. Do this graciously and freely as though you're giving gifts to people, because this power is also a gift to you.

[ECB] <u>Matthew 10:7-8</u> and preach as you go, wording, The sovereigndom of the heavens approaches. **8Cure the frail; purify the lepers; raise the dead; eject demons**: gratuitously you have taken; gratuitously give.

[ERV] <u>Matthew 10:7-8</u> When you go, tell them this: 'God's kingdom is now very near.' **8Heal the sick. Bring the dead back to life. Heal the people who have leprosy. And force demons out of people.** I give you these powers freely, so help others freely.

[ESV] <u>Matthew 10:7-8</u> And proclaim as you go, saying, 'The kingdom of heaven is at hand.' **8Heal the sick, raise the dead, cleanse lepers, cast out demons**. You received without paying; give without pay.

[Gilpin-NT] <u>Matthew 10:7-8</u> Explain the nature of the gospel to them; 8**and confirm your doctrine by miracles. Exercise liberally the divine power I have given you.** Freely communicate, what you have so freely received.

[GT] <u>Matthew 10:7-8</u> As you are going, preach this: 'The kingdom of heaven is very near!' 8"**Heal sick people. Raise people from death. Make lepers well. Throw out demons.** You received freely; give freely.

[GW] <u>Matthew 10:7-8</u> As you go, spread this message: 'The kingdom of heaven is near.' **8Cure the sick, bring the dead back to life, cleanse those with skin diseases, and force demons out of people**. Give these things without charging, since you received them without paying.

[KNT] <u>Matthew 10:7-8</u> As you go, declare publicly that the kingdom of heaven has arrived. **8Heal the sick, raise the dead, cleanse people with skin diseases, cast out demons.** 'It was all free when you got it; make sure it's free when you give it.

[Newcome] <u>Matthew 10:7-8</u> "And as ye go, preach, saying; 'The kingdom of heaven draweth near.' **8Cure the sick, cleanse the lepers, cast out demons:** ye have received of free bounty, give of free bounty."

[Phillips] <u>Matthew 10:7-8</u> As you go proclaim that the kingdom of Heaven has arrived. **8Heal the sick, raise the dead, cure the lepers, drive out devils**—give, as you have received, without any charge whatever.

OUR HEALING COVENANT

[REM-NT] <u>Matthew 10:7-8</u> Tell them, 'The Remedy from heaven is here' ⁸and then demonstrate my purpose to heal humanity from sin by **healing the sick, raising the dead, cleansing the lepers, and freeing minds from the influence of demons.** But don't accept payment. You have received the Remedy freely, so freely give it away,

[Wuest-NT] <u>Matthew 10:7-8</u> Moreover, as you go, make a public proclamation with such formality, gravity, and authority as must be listened to and obeyed, saying, The kingdom of heaven has come near and is imminent. ⁸**Be healing those who are sick. Be raising the dead. Lepers be cleansing. Demons be ejecting.** In a gratuitous manner you received, in a gratuitous manner give.

<u>Matthew 11:5</u> The blind receive their sight, and the lame walk, the lepers are cleansed, and the deaf hear, the dead are raised up, and the poor have the gospel preached to them.

[BBE] <u>Matthew 11:5</u> The blind see; those who were not able to, are walking; lepers are made clean; those who were without hearing, now have their ears open; the dead come to life again, and the poor have the good news given to them.

[CWB] <u>Matthew 11:5</u> You'll see the blind receiving their sight, the lame walking, lepers being healed and the deaf having their hearing restored. In fact, a dead girl has already been raised, and others will be raised also. And all the time, the good news is being preached, even to the most destitute.

[EEBT] <u>Matthew 11:5</u> People who could not see can see again. People who could not walk can now walk again. Some people who were ill with an illness of the skin are now well again. Some people who could not hear can now hear again. Some people who were dead now live again. Poor people are hearing the good news.

[HRB] <u>Matthew 11:5</u> The blind receive sight, and the lame walk; lepers are cleansed, and the deaf hear; the dead are raised, and the poor are given hope.

[Phillips] <u>Matthew 11:5</u> that blind men are recovering their sight, cripples are walking, lepers being healed, the deaf hearing, the dead being raised to life and the good news is being given to those in need.

[T4T] <u>Matthew 11:5</u> I am enabling blind people to see and lame people to walk. I am healing people who have leprosy. I am enabling deaf people to hear and dead people to become alive again. I am telling poor people God's good message.

[TPT] <u>Matthew 11:5</u> 'The blind see again, the crippled walk, lepers are cured, the deaf hear, the dead are raised back to life, and the poor and broken now hear of the hope of salvation!'

[TVB] <u>Matthew 11:5</u> Tell him you have seen the blind receive sight, the lame walk, the lepers cured, the deaf hear, the dead raised, and the good news preached to the poor.

[Williams-NT] <u>Matthew 11:5</u> the blind are seeing and the crippled are walking, the lepers are being healed and the deaf are hearing, the dead are being raised and the poor are having the good news preached to them.

<u>Matthew 11:28-29</u> Come unto me, all ye that labour and are heavy laden, and **I will give you rest.** ²⁹Take my yoke upon you, and learn of me; for I am meek and lowly in heart: and **ye shall find rest unto your souls.**

[AENT] <u>Matthew 11:28-29</u> Come to me all who labor and bear burdens, and **I will give you rest.** ²⁹Bear my yoke upon you and learn from me. That I am tranquil and I am meek, and in my heart **you will find tranquility in your souls.**

[AMPC] <u>Matthew 11:28-29</u> Come to Me, all you who labor and are heavy-laden and overburdened, and **I will cause you to rest. [I will ease and relieve and refresh your souls.]** ²⁹Take My yoke upon you and learn of Me, for I am gentle (meek) and humble (lowly) in heart, and **you will find rest (relief and ease and refreshment and recreation and blessed quiet) for your souls.**

[Authentic-NT] <u>Matthew 11:28-29</u> Come to me, all you who are weary and overburdened, and **I will relieve you**. [29]Take my yoke upon you, and learn from me; for I am gentle and of a quiet disposition, and **you will get relief;**

[AUV-NT 2005] <u>Matthew 11:28-29</u> Come to me, all of you who are overworked and overburdened and **I will give you rest [i.e., spiritual refreshment]**. [29]Accept my reins [on your life], and learn about me, because I am gentle and humble, and [in my service] **you will experience rest in your spirits.**

[BBE] <u>Matthew 11:28-29</u> Come to me, all you who are troubled and weighted down with care, and **I will give you rest**. [29]Take my yoke on you and become like me, for I am gentle and without pride, and **you will have rest for your souls;**

[EEBT] <u>Matthew 11:28-29</u> Come to me all of you who are tired. You are like people who have worked for a long time. You are like people who have carried heavy things. Come to me and **you will find a place to rest**. [29]Do what I teach you to do. Learn from me everything that is true. I am very kind and I obey God. Then you will have true life and **you will not be anxious.**

[FBV-NT] <u>Matthew 11:28-29</u> Come to me, all of you who struggle and who are burdened down. **I will give you rest**. [29]Accept my yoke, and learn from me. For I am kind and I have a humble heart, and in me **you will find the rest you need.**

[GNT] <u>Matthew 11:28-29</u> "Come to me, all of you who are tired from carrying heavy loads, and **I will give you rest**. [29]Take my yoke and put it on you, and learn from me, because I am gentle and humble in spirit; and **you will find rest.**

[Mace-NT] <u>Matthew 11:28-29</u> Believe in me, all ye that labour under oppression, and **I will give you relief**. [29]take my yoke upon you, and learn to be meek like me, and of an humble temper: and **ye shall enjoy tranquillity of mind.**

[Martin-NT] <u>Matthew 11:28-29</u> "Come to me, all who are exhausted and burdened, and **I will refresh you all**. [29]Pick up my yoke, upon yourselves, and learn from me, because I am gentle and my heart recognizes no status, and **you all will find refreshment for yourselves.**

[MCC-NT] <u>Matthew 11:28-29</u> Come unto Me, all Ye toiling and burdened, and **I will grant You Rest**. [29]Take Ye my Yoke upon You, and learn of Me; because I am gentle, and humble in Heart. Then **Ye shall find Relaxation for your Souls.**

[MSG] <u>Matthew 11:28-29</u> "Are you tired? Worn out? Burned out on religion? Come to me. Get away with me and you'll recover your life. **I'll show you how to take a real rest.** [29]Walk with me and work with me—watch how I do it. Learn the unforced rhythms of grace. **I won't lay anything heavy or ill-fitting on you.**

[NEB] <u>Matthew 11:28-29</u> 'Come to me, all whose work is hard, whose load is heavy; and **I will give you relief**. [29]Bend your necks to my yoke, and learn from me, for I am gentle and humble-hearted; and **your souls will find relief.**

[REM-NT] <u>Matthew 11:28-29</u> "So come to me, all who are tired, worn down and exhausted from fear, selfishness, and fighting to survive on your own, and **I will give you** operate—for I am gentle and humble in heart, and **you will find healing and rest for your souls.**

[TGNT] <u>Matthew 11:28-29</u> So come to me, all who labor under a heavy load, and **I will relieve you**. [29]Put my harness on you and learn from me, for I am gentle and considerate. Then **you will find rest for yourselves,**

[Tolstoy-Gs] <u>Matthew 11:28-29</u> And he said: Give yourselves to me, all you who are troubled, and who are burdened beyond their strength, and **I will give you rest.** [29]Take my yoke upon you, and learn from me. For I am meek and gentle in heart. And **you shall find rest in life.**

[TPT] <u>Matthew 11:28-29</u> "Are you weary, carrying a heavy burden? Then come to me. I will refresh your life, for **I am your oasis.** [29]Simply join your life with mine. Learn my ways and you'll discover that I'm gentle, humble, easy to please. **You will find refreshment and rest in me.**

[Wade] <u>Matthew 11:28-29</u> Come unto me, all who are toiling under exacting ordinances, and are burdened by oppressive rules, and it is **I that will relieve you.** [29]Take upon you my yoke, and learn from me, because I am meek and humble-minded, and **you will find relief for your souls.**

[Worsley-NT] <u>Matthew 11:28-29</u> Come unto me therefore all ye who are labouring and oppressed, and **I will give you ease.** [29]Take but my yoke upon you, and learn of me, (for I am meek and lowly in heart,) and **ye shall find refreshment to your souls:**

[Wuest-NT] <u>Matthew 11:28-29</u> Come here to me, all who are growing weary to the point of exhaustion, and who have been loaded with burdens and are bending beneath their weight, and I alone will cause you to cease from your labor and take away your burdens and thus **refresh you with rest.** [29]Take at once my yoke upon you and learn from me, because I am meek and lowly in heart, and **you will find cessation from labor and refreshment for your souls,**

[Wycliffe-Noble] <u>Matthew 11:28-29</u> All ye that travail, and be charged, come to me, and I shall fulfill you [and **I shall refresh, or fulfill, you**]. [29]Take ye my yoke on you [Take ye my yoke upon you], and learn ye of me, for I am mild and meek in heart; and **ye shall find rest to your souls.**

<u>Matthew 12:13</u> Then saith he to the man, Stretch forth thine hand. And he stretched it forth; and it was restored whole, like as the other.

[AUV-NT 2003] <u>Matthew 12:13</u> Then Jesus said to the man "Reach out your hand." And when he stretched it out, it became normal, just like the other one.

[CWB] <u>Matthew 12:13</u> Turning to the man, Jesus said, "Stretch out your arm." The man obeyed and in the attempt to stretch it out, his arm was healed.

[ERV] <u>Matthew 12:13</u> Then Jesus said to the man with the crippled hand, "Hold out your hand." The man held out his hand, and it became well again, the same as the other hand.

[FBV-NT] <u>Matthew 12:13</u> Then he said to the man, "Hold out your hand." The man held out his hand, and it was healed, just as healthy as the other hand.

[HBIV] <u>Matthew 12:13</u> Then he says to the man, Stretch forth thy hand. And he stretched it forth; and it was restored to health as the other.

[LDB-NT] <u>Matthew 12:13</u> "Stretch out your hand," He then said to the man. So he stretched it out, and it was restored, just as full of life and vigor as the other!

[NIV] <u>Matthew 12:13</u> Then he said to the man, "Stretch out your hand." So he stretched it out and it was completely restored, just as sound as the other.

[REM-NT] <u>Matthew 12:13</u> He turned to the man with a withered hand and said, "Use your arm normally," and he did, and his arm was completely restored to normal.

[TTNT] <u>Matthew 12:13</u> Then He said to the man: "Stretch out your hand." When he did so it was completely healed and was just as strong as the other hand.

[TVB] <u>Matthew 12:13</u> (to the man with the shriveled hand) Stretch out your hand. As the man did so, his hand was completely healed, as good as new.

<u>Matthew 12:15</u> But when Jesus knew it, he withdrew himself from thence: and great multitudes followed him, and **he healed them all;**

[AMPC] <u>Matthew 12:15</u> But being aware of this, Jesus went away from there. And many people joined and accompanied Him, and **He cured all of them,**

[ERV] <u>Matthew 12:15</u> Jesus knew what the Pharisees were planning. So he left that place, and many people followed him. **He healed all who were sick,**

[Knox] <u>Matthew 12:15</u> Jesus was aware of this, and withdrew from the place; great multitudes followed him, and **he healed all their diseases;**

[MCC-NT] <u>Matthew 12:15</u> But Jesus being aware, removed thence. And vast Multitudes followed him; and **He remedied Them all.**

[T4T] <u>Matthew 12:15</u> Because Jesus knew that the Pharisees were plotting to kill him, he took us disciples and went away from there. Crowds, including many sick people, followed him, wanting him to heal them, and **he healed them all.**

[TPT] <u>Matthew 12:15</u> Jesus knew what they were thinking, so he left by another way. Massive crowds followed him from there, and **he healed all who were sick.**

[TTNT] <u>Matthew 12:15</u> Aware of their plans, Jesus withdrew from there. But many followed Him and He healed all the sick among them,

[TWTY-RCT-NT-V1] <u>Matthew 12:15</u> But nevertheless, knowing and understanding, perceiving and realising, noticing and discerning, discovering and observing, experiencing and ascertaining, learning about and distinguishing, comprehending, acknowledging and recognising this, Yahushua, departed and retired, went away from and withdrew back from there, in that place. And many numerous and large amounts of crowds and multitudes, throngs and masses of people accompanied and followed after, obeyed and joined themselves to Him, and He willingly served and healed, cured and **restored all of them, individually and collectively, to health.**

<u>Matthew 12:22</u> Then was brought unto him one possessed with a devil, blind, and dumb: and **he healed him, insomuch that the blind and dumb both spake and saw.**

[Barclay-NT] <u>Matthew 12:22</u> It was after that that a demon-possessed man who was blind and dumb was brought to Jesus, and **he cured him so effectively that the dumb man was able to speak and see.**

[CCB] <u>Matthew 12:22</u> Then some people brought to him a possessed man who was blind and who could not talk. **Jesus healed the man, who was then able to speak and see.**

[ERV] <u>Matthew 12:22</u> Then some people brought a man to Jesus. This man was blind and could not talk, because he had a demon inside him. **Jesus healed the man, and he could talk and see.**

[Hammond-NT] <u>Matthew 12:22</u> Then was brought unto him one whom the devil had cast into a disease which deprived him of speech and sight, and **he healed him, insomuch that the blind and dumb both spake and saw.**

[Mace-NT] <u>Matthew 12:22</u> Then they brought to him a demoniac, who was both blind and dumb: and **he cured him so effectually, that he recovered both his speech and his sight;**

[T4T] <u>Matthew 12:22</u> One day when Jesus was at home, some men brought to Jesus a man who, because of being controlled by a demon {a demon controlled him}, was blind and unable to speak. **Jesus healed him by expelling the demon. As a result, the man began to talk and was able to see.**

[TPT] <u>Matthew 12:22</u> Then a man was brought before Jesus who had a demon spirit that made him both blind and unable to speak. **Jesus healed him instantly, and he could see and talk again!**

[TVB] <u>Matthew 12:22</u> Some of the faithful brought Jesus a man who was possessed by a demon, who was blind and mute, and **Jesus healed him. The man could see and talk , and demons no longer crawled around in him**.

[UDB] <u>Matthew 12:22</u> One day some men brought to Jesus a man who was blind and unable to speak because he had a demon. **Jesus drove out the demon and healed him. Then the man began to talk and was able to see**.

[Williams-NT] <u>Matthew 12:22</u> At that time some people brought to Him a man under the power of demons, who was blind and dumb, and **He cured him, so that the dumb man could talk and see.**

<u>Matthew 13:54</u> And when he was come into his own country, he taught them in their synagogue, insomuch that they were astonished, and said, **Whence hath this man this wisdom, and these mighty works**?

[AMPC] <u>Matthew 13:54</u> And coming to His own country [Nazareth], He taught in their synagogue so that they were amazed with bewildered wonder, and said, **Where did this Man get this wisdom and these miraculous powers**?

[Ballentine-NT] <u>Matthew 13:54</u> And coming into his own country he taught them in their synagogue so they were astonished, and said: **"Where did this man get this wisdom and the power to do these great things?"**

[BBE] <u>Matthew 13:54</u> And coming into his country, he gave them teaching in their Synagogue, so that they were greatly surprised and said, **Where did this man get this wisdom and these works of power**?

[CLV] <u>Matthew 13:54</u> And coming into His own country, He taught them in their synagogue, so that they are astonished, and are saying, **"Whence has this one this wisdom and powerful deeds**?"

[CWB] <u>Matthew 13:54</u> There He taught in the local synagogue and healed many people of all kinds of diseases. The townspeople were so amazed at His wisdom that they asked each other, **"Where did Joseph's son get all this wisdom and power to heal the sick**?

[ESB-NT] <u>Matthew 13:54</u> When He came to His hometown, He was teaching them in their synagogue, so that they were astonished, and said, **"Where did this wisdom and miraculous powers come from**?

[Montgomery-NT] <u>Matthew 13:54</u> and came into his own country, where he continued teaching the people in their synagogues, until they were amazed. **"Where did he get such wisdom?" they said, "and such wondrous powers?"**

[NRSV] <u>Matthew 13:54</u> He came to his hometown and began to teach the people in their synagogue, so that they were astounded and said, **"Where did this man get this wisdom and these deeds of power**?"

[OEB-NT] <u>Matthew 13:54</u> Going to his own part of the country, he taught the people in their synagogue in such a manner that they were deeply impressed. **"Where did he get this wisdom?" they said, "and the miracles**?

[TPT] <u>Matthew 13:54</u> When Jesus arrived in his hometown of Nazareth, he began teaching the people in the synagogue. Everyone was dazed, overwhelmed with astonishment over the depth of revelation they were hearing. They said to one another, **"Where did this man get such great wisdom and miraculous powers?"**

[UASV] <u>Matthew 13:54</u> After coming to his hometown, he began teaching them in their synagogue, so that they were astonished and said: "**Where did this man get this wisdom and these powerful works**?

<u>Matthew 14:14</u> And Jesus went forth, and saw a great multitude, and was moved with compassion toward them, and he healed their sick.

[AMP] <u>Matthew 14:14</u> When He went ashore, He saw a large crowd, and felt [profound] compassion for them and healed their sick.

[AMPC] <u>Matthew 14:14</u> When He went ashore and saw a great throng of people, He had compassion (pity and deep sympathy) for them and cured their sick.

[AUV-NT 2003] <u>Matthew 14:14</u> When Jesus came out [of His place of seclusion] and saw a large crowd, He felt a deep compassion for them and healed their sick people.

[BBE] <u>Matthew 14:14</u> And he came out and saw a great number of people and he had pity on them, and made well those of them who were ill.

[Darby] <u>Matthew 14:14</u> And going out he saw a great crowd, and was moved with compassion about them, and healed their infirm.

[DLNT] <u>Matthew 14:14</u> And having gone-out, He saw a large crowd and felt-deep-feelings [of compassion] for them. And He cured their sick ones.

[FHV-NT] <u>Matthew 14:14</u> As he stepped out of the boat, and looked on the large crowd, his heart went out to them, and he healed their sick.

[Harwood-NT] <u>Matthew 14:14</u> Jesus beholding such an immense crowd collected together, was affected with the tenderest sympathy and compassion, and healed all among them, who laboured under any indisposition.

[NEB] <u>Matthew 14:14</u> When he came ashore, he saw a great crowd; his heart went out to them, and he cured those of them who were sick.

[Spencer-NT] <u>Matthew 14:14</u> So on landing He saw a great throng; and He pitied them, and restored their sick to health.

[TTNT] <u>Matthew 14:14</u> When He saw such a vast crowd, His heart went out to them with compassion and He healed the sick among them.

[TVB] <u>Matthew 14:14</u> Though Jesus wanted solitude, when He saw the crowds, He had compassion on them, and He healed the sick and the lame.

[Wesley-NT] <u>Matthew 14:14</u> And coming forth he saw a great multitude, and was moved with tender compassion for them, and healed their sick.

[Weymouth-NT] <u>Matthew 14:14</u> So Jesus went out and saw an immense multitude, and felt compassion for them, and cured those of them who were out of health.

[YLT] <u>Matthew 14:14</u> And Jesus having come forth, saw a great multitude, and was moved with compassion upon them, and did heal their infirm;

<u>Matthew 14:36</u> And besought him that they might only touch the hem of his garment: and **as many as touched were made perfectly whole**.

[AMPC] <u>Matthew 14:36</u> And begged Him to let them merely touch the fringe of His garment; and **as many as touched it were perfectly restored**.

[Barclay-NT] <u>Matthew 14:36</u> They begged to be allowed to do no more than touch the tassel of his cloak. **All who touched it were completely cured**.

[BBE] <u>Matthew 14:36</u> With the request that they might only put their hands on the edge of his robe: and **all those who did so were made well.**

[Berkeley] <u>Matthew 14:36</u> They begged of Him that they might simply touch the fringes of His robe, and **all who touched Him were completely healed.**

[CEB] <u>Matthew 14:36</u> Then they begged him that they might just touch the edge of his clothes. **Everyone who touched him was cured.**

[CEV] <u>Matthew 14:36</u> They begged him just to let them touch his clothes, and **everyone who did was healed.**

[CJB] <u>Matthew 14:36</u> They begged him that the sick people might only touch the tzitzit on his robe, and **all who touched it were completely healed.**

[CLV] <u>Matthew 14:36</u> And they entreated Him that they should only be touching the tassel of His cloak. **And whoever touch it were brought safely through.**

[Etheridge-NT] <u>Matthew 14:36</u> and besought from him that they might touch only the border of his mantle; **and those who touched were healed.**

[HNT] <u>Matthew 14:36</u> beseeching him to let them touch only the tassel of his cloak; **and all who touched were quite restored.**

[JMNT] <u>Matthew 14:36</u> And they began calling Him to their side, and kept on begging and entreating Him—with the purpose that they themselves might only touch the ritual fringe (or: tassel) of His cloak— **and as many as touched [it] were thoroughly healed, restored to health, and made whole, through and through (or: were completely rescued; or: were brought safely through [their illness])!**

[JUB] <u>Matthew 14:36</u> and besought him that they might only touch the hem of his garment, and **as many as touched were made perfectly whole.**

[Knox] <u>Matthew 14:36</u> and they entreated him that they might be allowed to touch even the hem of his garments. And **everyone who touched him was restored to health.**

[Rotherham] <u>Matthew 14:36</u> and were beseeching [him], that they might, only, touch the border of his mantle, and, **as many as touched, were made quite well.**

[Sawyer-7590] <u>Matthew 14:36</u> and requested of him that they might only touch the fringe of his garment; and **as many as touched it were entirely cured.**

[TPT] <u>Matthew 14:36</u> So they brought him all their sick, begging him to let them touch the fringe of his robe. And **everyone who touched it was instantly healed!**

[Weymouth-NT] <u>Matthew 14:36</u> and they entreated Him that they might but touch the tassel of His outer garment; and **all who did so were restored to perfect health.**

[Williams-NT] <u>Matthew 14:36</u> and they continued to beg Him to let them touch just the tassel on His coat, and **all who barely touched it were completely cured.**

[Worrell-NT] <u>Matthew 14:36</u> and they were beseeching Him, that they might only touch the border of His garment; and **as many as touched it were made thoroughly well.**

<u>Matthew 15:26-28</u> But he answered and said, **It is not meet to take the children's bread, and to cast it to dogs.** [27]And she said, Truth, Lord: yet the dogs eat of the crumbs which fall from their masters' table. [28]Then Jesus answered and said unto her, **O woman, great is thy faith: be it unto thee even as thou wilt. And her daughter was made whole from that very hour.**

Children—refers to Israel; dogs—refers to gentiles; bread—refers to healing.

[Authentic-NT] <u>Matthew 15:26-28</u> He replied. '**It is not fair to take the children's food and throw it to puppies.**' [27]'Quite so, sir,' she said. 'But even puppies may eat the scraps that fall from their masters' table.' [28]Then Jesus said to her, '**Madam, you have great faith. Let it be as you wish.' From that moment her daughter was cured.**

[CEV] <u>Matthew 15:26-28</u> Jesus replied, "**It isn't right to take food away from children and feed it to dogs.**" [27]"Lord, this is true," the woman said, "but even puppies get the crumbs that fall from their owner's table." [28]Jesus answered, "**Dear woman, you really do have a lot of faith, and you will be given what you want.**" At that moment her daughter was healed.

[EOB-NT] <u>Matthew 15:26-28</u> But he answered, "**It is not right to take the children's bread and throw it to the little dogs.**" [27]But she replied, "Yes, Lord, but even the little dogs eat the crumbs which fall from their masters' table." [28]Then Jesus answered her, "**Woman, great is your faith! Let it be it done to you even as you desire.**" And her daughter was healed from that hour.

[GT] <u>Matthew 15:26-28</u> Jesus answered, "**It is not good to take the children's bread and throw it to the dogs.**" [27]But the woman said, "Yes, Lord, but even the dogs eat the crumbs which fall from their masters' table." [28]Then Jesus answered her, "**Woman, you have a strong faith. What you want will be done for you!**" At that moment her daughter was healed.

[Heylyn-Gs] <u>Matthew 15:26-28</u> He answered, **It is not right to take the Children's Bread and throw it to Dogs.** [27]She replied, True, Lord, yet the Dogs eat the Crumbs which fall from the Table of their Masters. [28]Then Jesus answered, **O Woman, great is thy Faith; Be it unto thee even as Thou willest; and her Daughter was instantly cured.**

[ICB] <u>Matthew 15:26-28</u> Jesus answered, "**It is not right to take the children's bread and give it to the dogs.**" [27]The woman said, "Yes, Lord, but even the dogs eat the pieces of food that fall from their masters' table." [28]Then Jesus answered, "**Woman, you have great faith! I will do what you asked me to do.**" And at that moment the woman's daughter was healed.

[Mace-NT] <u>Matthew 15:26-28</u> but he answered, **it is not just to take the childrens bread, and throw it to puppies.** [27]'tis true, Lord, said she: yet even puppies eat of the crumbs which fall from their master's table. [28]then Jesus answered her, **O woman, great is thy faith: as you desire, be it done. and her daughter was healed from that very hour.**

[MSG] <u>Matthew 15:26-28</u> He said, "**It's not right to take bread out of children's mouths and throw it to dogs.**" [27]She was quick: "You're right, Master, but beggar dogs do get scraps from the master's table." [28]Jesus gave in. "**Oh, woman, your faith is something else. What you want is what you get!**" Right then her daughter became well.

[REM-NT] <u>Matthew 15:26-28</u> He gently said, "**It isn't proper to take the food off the table before the children have eaten and give it to their puppies.**" [27]"You're right, Lord," she pressed, "but even the puppies eat the crumbs that fall from their master's table before his children are fed properly." [28]Jesus smiled and said, "**Young lady, your trust and determination are amazing. What you desire, you now have.**" And her daughter was healed at that very moment.

[TLB] <u>Matthew 15:26-28</u> "**It doesn't seem right to take bread from the children and throw it to the dogs,**" he said. [27]"Yes, it is!" she replied, "for even the puppies beneath the table are permitted to eat the crumbs that fall." [28]"Woman," Jesus told her, "**your faith is large, and your request is granted.**" And her daughter was healed right then.

[Wells-NT] <u>Matthew 15:26-28</u> But he answered and said, **As it is not meet to take the Children's Bread, and to cast it to the Dogs; so those Favours which God has sent me to bestow among his peculiar People the Jews, I must not dispose to the Gentiles and Strangers.** [27]And she said, Truth,

Lord: Yet as the Dogs are permitted to eat of the Crumbs which fall from their Master's Table; so I trust that I, though a Gentile, may be permitted to obtain this one request out of that bounteous Liberality, wherewith you dispense God's Favours among the Jews. [28]The Jesus answered and said unto her, **O woman, Great is thy Faith, Greater than I have ordinarily found, even among the Jews themselves: therefore be it unto thee even as thou wilt, or desirest. And her Daughter was made whole from that very hour**.

Matthew 15:30 And great multitudes came unto him, having with them those that were lame, blind, dumb, maimed, and many others, and cast them down at Jesus' feet; and he healed them:

[AUV-NT 2003] **Matthew 15:30** Large crowds came to Him, bringing crippled, blind, deaf-mute, disabled and many other [sick] people and laid them down at His feet. And He healed [all of] them,

[CEB] **Matthew 15:30** Large crowds came to him, including those who were paralyzed, blind, injured, and unable to speak, and many others. They laid them at his feet, and he healed them.

[CEVUK2012] **Matthew 15:30** Large crowds came and brought many people who were crippled or blind or lame or unable to talk. They placed them, and many others, in front of Jesus, and he healed them all.

[ERV] **Matthew 15:30** A large crowd of people came to him. They brought many other sick people and put them before him. There were people who could not walk, people who were blind, crippled, or deaf, and many others. Jesus healed them all.

[REM-NT] **Matthew 15:30** Large multitudes flocked to him, bringing their sick, paralyzed, blind, crippled, deaf, mute, and anyone else who was disabled, and presented them before Jesus. He healed every one of them.

[Stringfellow-NT] **Matthew 15:30** And there came to him many crowds, having with them lame, crooked, blind, dumb, and many others; and they cast them at his feet, and he healed them.

[TCNT] **Matthew 15:30** Great crowds of people came to him, bringing with them those who were lame, crippled, blind, or dumb, and many others. They put them down at his feet, and he cured them;

[TLB] **Matthew 15:30** And a vast crowd brought him their lame, blind, maimed, and those who couldn't speak, and many others, and laid them before Jesus, and he healed them all.

[TWTY-RCT-NT-V1] **Matthew 15:30** And many numerous and large amounts of crowds and multitudes, throngs and masses of people came and approached, turned towards and drew near to Him, having and holding, owning and possessing those that were lame and crippled, maimed and infirm, physically blind and unable to see, mutilated and crooked, bent and deformed, injured and disabled, dull and deaf and many numerous and large amounts of others together with them, and they cast and laid, threw and set them along, beside and by His feet, and He willingly served and healed, cured and restored them to health,

Matthew 17:18 And Jesus rebuked the devil; and he departed out of him: and the child was cured from that very hour.

[Authentic-NT] **Matthew 17:18** Then Jesus reprimanded the demon and it came out of him. And the boy was cured from that hour.

[AUV-NT 2003] **Matthew 17:18** Then Jesus spoke sternly to [the evil spirit in] the boy, and it left him, and he was immediately healed.

[Barclay-NT] **Matthew 17:18** Then Jesus spoke to him with a stern authority, and the demon came out of him, and there and then the boy was cured.

[Berkeley] Matthew 17:18 So Jesus rebuked the demon and it came out of him, and from that exact moment the boy was cured.

[Campbell-Gs] Matthew 17:18 Then Jesus rebuked the demon, and he came out; and the lad was instantly cured.

[CCB] Matthew 17:18 And Jesus commanded the evil spirit to leave the boy, and the boy was immediately healed.

[CT] Matthew 17:18 Jesus gave an order and the demon came out of him. The boy was healed from that moment on.

[Lingard-Gs] Matthew 17:18 And Jesus rebuked him, and the fiend went out from him. And the boy was healed from that hour.

[MSG] Matthew 17:18 He ordered the afflicting demon out—and it was out, gone. From that moment on the boy was well.

[Wade] Matthew 17:18 And Jesus checked the demon, and it left him; and the boy was cured from that moment.

Matthew 18:19-20 Again I say unto you, That if two of you shall agree on earth as touching any thing that they shall ask, it shall be done for them of my Father which is in heaven. [20]For where two or three are gathered together in my name, there am I in the midst of them.

[BBE] Matthew 18:19-20 Again, I say to you, that if two of you are in agreement on earth about anything for which they will make a request, it will be done for them by my Father in heaven. [20]For where two or three are come together in my name, there am I among them.

[Beck] Matthew 18:19-20 Again I tell you, if two of you here on earth agree to ask for anything, My Father in heaven will certainly do it for you. [20]Where two or three have come together to be with Me, there I am among them.

[CEV] Matthew 18:19-20 I promise that when any two of you on earth agree about something you are praying for, my Father in heaven will do it for you. [20]Whenever two or three of you come together in my name, I am there with you.

[Douay-Rheims] Matthew 18:19-20 Again I say to you, that if two of you shall consent upon earth, concerning any thing whatsoever they shall ask, it shall be done to them by my Father who is in heaven. [20]For where there are two or three gathered together in my name, there am I in the midst of them.

[ERV] Matthew 18:19-20 To say it another way, if two of you on earth agree on anything you pray for, my Father in heaven will do what you ask. [20]Yes, if two or three people are together believing in me, I am there with them."

[FBV-NT] Matthew 18:19-20 "I also tell you that if two of you agree here on earth about something you're praying for, then my heavenly Father will do it for you. [20]For where two or three gather together in my name, I'm there with them."

[Folsom-Gs] Matthew 18:19-20 Again, I say to you that if two of you shall agree on earth concerning every thing which they should ask, it shall come to pass to them from my Father who is in heaven. [20]For where two or three are gathered together for [the advancement of] my name, I am there in the midst of them.

[Hall] Matthew 18:19-20 The single prayers of faithful suppliants shall not want audience and respect from God; but when they are doubled, by the conjunction of the hearts of more suitors

and the united forces of many fervent desires, they cannot but be more effectual, and shall receive a gracious acceptation from my Father which is in heaven. [20]For, so highly do I respect the assemblies of my faithful servants, that, where any number of them shall be met together in a sincere desire to do me service, I will be there present with them by my Spirit, for the exciting, and directing, and accepting of their holy endeavors.

[Haweis-NT] Matthew 18:19-20 Again I say unto you, That if two of you are concurring upon earth, respecting any matter, which ye shall ask, it shall be done for them by my Father who is in heaven. [20]For where two or three are gathered together in my name, there am I in the midst of them.

[Jordan-NT] Matthew 18:19-20 Again I want to tell you that if two of you in the physical realm covenant together about any matter of concern, it will be acted on for them by my spiritual Father. [20]For where two or three are banded together as Christians, I am present with them.

[MCC-NT] Matthew 18:19-20 Moreover, I tell You that, if ever two of You on Earth apply with one Consent touching every Affair which Ye shall petition for, it shall accrue to Them from your Father who is in the Heavens. [20]For where Two or Three are assembled to profess My Name, there am I in the Midst of Them."

[Moffatt-NT 1917] Matthew 18:19-20 I tell you another thing: if two of you agree on earth about anything you pray for, it will be done for you by my Father in heaven. [20]For where two or three have gathered in my name, I am there among them."

[Original-NT] Matthew 18:19-20 I will go further, and say, that if any two of you agree among yourselves on earth about anything for which you need to ask, my heavenly Father will undertake it for you, [20]for 'in every place where two or three are assembled in my name I am there among them.'

[TLB] Matthew 18:19-20 "I also tell you this—if two of you agree down here on earth concerning anything you ask for, my Father in heaven will do it for you. [20]For where two or three gather together because they are mine, I will be right there among them."

[TPT] Matthew 18:19-20 Again, I give you an eternal truth: If two of you agree to ask God for something in a symphony of prayer, my heavenly Father will do it for you. [20]For wherever two or three come together in honor of my name, I am right there with them!"

[TTNT] Matthew 18:19-20 "I also tell you clearly that when two of you agree in faith about the outcome of any matter about which you pray, it will be done for you by My Father in heaven. [20]You see, whenever two or three of you gather together with faith in the authority of My name, I am there with you."

[TTT-NT] Matthew 18:19-20 "Again, I say to you, that if two of you shall consent upon the earth, of all things whatever they may ask for, it shall be done for them by my father who is in heaven. [20]For where two or three have gathered together in my name, I am there in their midst."

[WEB] Matthew 18:19-20 Again, assuredly I tell you, that if two of you will agree on earth concerning anything that they will ask, it will be done for them by my Father who is in heaven. [20]For where two or three are gathered together in my name, there I am in the middle of them."

Matthew 19:2 And great multitudes followed him; and he healed them there.

[AMPC] Matthew 19:2 And great throngs accompanied Him, and He cured them there.

[AUV-NT 2005] Matthew 19:2 Large crowds followed Him there and were healed by Him.

[HPAJ] Matthew 19:2 And large crowds came and followed after him, and he healed them there.

[Phillips] Matthew 19:2 Vast crowds followed him, and he healed them there.

[Sindlinger-NT] <u>Matthew 19:2</u> As usual, Jesus healed a lot of people who followed him.

[TPT] <u>Matthew 19:2</u> Massive crowds followed him and he healed all who were sick.

[TTNT] <u>Matthew 19:2</u> As usual, large crowds followed Him and He healed the sick among them.

[TVB] <u>Matthew 19:2</u> Large crowds followed Him, and when He got to Judea, He set about healing them.

[TWTY-RCT-NT-V1] <u>Matthew 19:2</u> And many numerous and large amounts of crowds and multitudes, throngs and masses of people accompanied and followed after, obeyed and joined themselves to Him, and He willingly served and healed, cured and restored them to health there, in that place.

<u>Matthew 20:32-34</u> And Jesus stood still, and called them, and said, What will ye that I shall do unto you? ³³They say unto him, Lord, that our eyes may be opened. ³⁴**So Jesus had compassion on them, and touched their eyes: and immediately their eyes received sight**, and they followed him.

[AMP] <u>Matthew 20:32-34</u> Jesus stopped and called them, and asked, "What do you want Me to do for you?" ³³They answered Him, "Lord, we want our eyes to be opened." ³⁴**Moved with compassion, Jesus touched their eyes; and immediately they regained their sight** and followed Him [as His disciples].

[Barclay-NT] <u>Matthew 20:32-34</u> Jesus stopped and called them. 'What to you want me to do for you?' he said. ³³'Sir,' they said to him, 'the only thing we want is to be able to see.' ³⁴**Jesus was heart-sorry for them. He touched their eyes, and there and then their sight returned**, and they followed him.

[BSB-NT] <u>Matthew 20:32-34</u> Jesus stopped and called them. "What do you want Me to do for you?" He asked. ³³"Lord," they answered, "let our eyes be opened." ³⁴**Moved with compassion, Jesus touched their eyes, and at once they received their sight** and followed Him.

[CEB] <u>Matthew 20:32-34</u> Jesus stopped in his tracks and called to them. "What do you want me to do for you?" he asked. ³³"Lord, we want to see," they replied. ³⁴**Jesus had compassion on them and touched their eyes. Immediately they were able to see**, and they followed him.

[CWB] <u>Matthew 20:32-34</u> Jesus heard them, and when He came to where they were, He stopped and asked, "What is it you would like me to do for you?" ³³They said, "Lord, please give us our sight." ³⁴**With tender compassion Jesus reached out and touched their eyes. Instantly they could see**. Then the two men followed Him as He continued on His way.

[JUB] <u>Matthew 20:32-34</u> And Jesus stood still and called them and said, What desire ye that I shall do unto you? ³³They say unto him, Lord, that our eyes may be opened. ³⁴**Then Jesus, having mercy on them, touched their eyes; and immediately their eyes received sight,** and they followed him.

[REM-NT] <u>Matthew 20:32-34</u> Jesus stopped and called out to them, "What would you have me do for you?" ³³They answered eagerly, "Lord, we want to see!" ³⁴**Jesus was merciful to them and touched their eyes. Immediately they were cured and could see**, and they followed him.

[TTNT] <u>Matthew 20:32-34</u> Hearing them, Jesus stopped and called them forward. "What is it that you want Me to do for you?" He asked them. ³³"Lord, we want our sight to be restored," they answered. ³⁴**With compassion Jesus touched their eyes, and immediately they received their sight** and then followed Him.

[Wuest-NT] <u>Matthew 20:32-34</u> And Jesus, having come to a stop, stood still, called them and said, What do you desire that I should do for you? ³³They say to Him, Lord, that our eyes may be opened. ³⁴**And Jesus, having been moved with compassion, touched their eyes, and immediately they received their sight** and followed with Him.

Matthew 21:14 And the blind and the lame came to him in the temple; and he healed them.

[AUV-NT 2005] Matthew 21:14 [Then] blind and crippled people came to Him in the Temple and He healed them.

[BBE] Matthew 21:14 And the blind and the broken in body came to him in the Temple, and he made them well.

[BV-KJV-NT] Matthew 21:14 And blind and crippled people came to Him on the temple grounds, and He healed them.

[CWB] Matthew 21:14 Then the blind and the lame came in to find Jesus. He responded to their requests by healing every one of them.

[Knox] Matthew 21:14 And there were blind and lame men who came up to him in the temple, and he healed them there.

[Newcome] Matthew 21:14 And the blind and the lame came near to him in the temple; and he restored them.

[NLV] Matthew 21:14 The blind and those who could not walk came to Jesus in the house of God and He healed them.

[TWTY-RCT-NT-V1] Matthew 21:14 And those that were blind, those who were unable to see, and those who were lame and crippled, maimed and infirm came and approached, turned and drew near to Him within and inside the Sacred Place and Temple, and He willingly served and healed, cured and restored them to health.

Matthew 21:21 Jesus answered and said unto them, Verily I say unto you, If ye have faith, and doubt not, ye shall not only do this which is done to the fig tree, but also if ye shall say unto this mountain, Be thou removed, and be thou cast into the sea; it shall be done.

[Barclay-NT] Matthew 21:21 'I tell you truly,' Jesus answered, 'if you have unquestioning faith, you will be able to do not only what was done to the fig tree, but even if you were to say to this hill: "Be picked up and flung into the sea," it will happen.

[BWE-NT] Matthew 21:21 Jesus said to them, 'I tell you the truth. Believe God. Do not doubt him. Then you can do what I did to this fig tree. But that is not all. You can even say to this hill, Go and jump into the sea and it will be done.

[Campbell-Gs] Matthew 21:21 Verily I say unto you, if ye have an unshaken faith, ye may not only do as much as is done to the fig-tree, but even if ye should say to this mountain, 'Be lifted, and thrown into the sea,' it shall be done.

[CPDV] Matthew 21:21 And Jesus responded to them by saying: "Amen I say to you, if you have faith and do not hesitate, not only shall you do this, concerning the fig tree, but even if you would say to this mountain, 'Take and cast yourself into the sea,' it shall be done.

[CWB] Matthew 21:21 Jesus turned to them and said, "Don't be surprised. If you have faith in God without doubting, you, too, will be able to do unusual things for Him. If God wanted you to, you could say to a mountain, 'Out of my way and disappear into the sea,' and it would.

[ERV] Matthew 21:21 Jesus answered, "The truth is, if you have faith and no doubts, you will be able to do the same as I did to this tree. And you will be able to do more. You will be able to say to this mountain, 'Go, mountain, fall into the sea.' And if you have faith, it will happen.

[Etheridge-NT] <u>Matthew 21:21</u> Jeshu answered and said to them, Amen I say to you, that if faith were in you, and you did not hesitate, you should not only do (as) to this fig-tree, but also were you to say to this mountain, Be thou lifted up and fall into the sea, it should be done.

[FHV-NT] <u>Matthew 21:21</u> Jesus replied, Indeed, I assure you, if you have faith, and do not waver, not only will you do as I did to this fig tree, but also you will say to this mountain, "Be removed and cast into the sea," and it will be so.

[GNC-NT] <u>Matthew 21:21</u> And this is the reply Jesus made them: "Indeed, I can give you solemn assurance of this: if you had faith, a never doubting faith, what has been done regarding this fig tree would by no means be all you could accomplish. Why, if you said to this mountain here, 'Lift yourself up and throw yourself into the sea,' that is what would happen.

[GW] <u>Matthew 21:21</u> Jesus answered them, "I can guarantee this truth: If you have faith and do not doubt, you will be able to do what I did to the fig tree. You could also say to this mountain, 'Be uprooted and thrown into the sea,' and it will happen.

[PalmerBz-NT] <u>Matthew 21:21</u> And in answer Jesus said to them, "Truly I say to you, if you have faith, and do not second guess, not only will you do something like the fig tree, but also should you say to this mountain, 'Be lifted up and thrown into the sea,' it would happen.

[Phillips] <u>Matthew 21:21</u> 'Believe me,' replied Jesus, 'if you have faith and have no doubts in your heart, you will not only do this to a fig-tree but even if you should say to this hill, "Be uprooted and thrown into the sea", it will happen!

[Spitsbergen] <u>Matthew 21:21</u> And Jesus replied and said to them I tell you most absolutely if you have faith and do not waver then not only will you do what has been done to this fig tree but even if you say to the mountain be lifted up and thrown into the sea it will be done!

[Stringfellow-NT] <u>Matthew 21:21</u> And Jesus answered and said to them, Verily I say to you, If you shall have faith and not entertain a doubt, you shall not only do this of the fig-tree, but even if you shall say to this mountain, Be taken up and cast into the sea, it shall happen.

[T4T] <u>Matthew 21:21</u> Jesus said to us, "Think about this: If you believe that God has power to do what you ask him to and you do not doubt that, you will be able to do things like what I have done to this fig tree. You will even be able to do marvelous deeds like saying to a nearby hill, 'Uproot yourself and throw yourself into the sea', and it will happen!

[TLB] <u>Matthew 21:21</u> Then Jesus told them, "Truly, if you have faith and don't doubt, you can do things like this and much more. You can even say to this Mount of Olives, 'Move over into the ocean,' and it will.

[TPT] <u>Matthew 21:21</u> Jesus replied, "Listen to the truth. If you have no doubt of God's power and speak out of faith's fullness, you can be the ones who speak to a tree and it will wither away. Even more than that, you could say to this mountain, 'Be lifted up and be thrown into the sea' and it will be done.

[UDB] <u>Matthew 21:21</u> Jesus said to them, "Think about this: If you believe that Yahweh has power to do what you ask him to and you do not doubt that, you will be able to do things like what I have done to this fig tree. You will even be able to do marvelous deeds like saying to that hill over there, 'Uproot yourself and throw yourself into the sea,' and it will happen!

[Weymouth-NT] <u>Matthew 21:21</u> "I solemnly tell you," said Jesus, "that if you have an unwavering faith, you shall not only perform such a miracle as this of the fig-tree, but that even if you say to this mountain, 'Be thou lifted up and hurled into the sea,' it shall be done;

[WGCIB] <u>Matthew 21:21</u> Jesus answered them, "Amen, I say to you, if you shall have faith and do not stagger, not only shall you do this with the fig tree, but if you shall say to this mountain, 'Pick yourself up and cast yourself into the sea,' it shall be done too.

MARK

Mark 1:25-26 And Jesus rebuked him, saying, Hold thy peace, and come out of him. [26]And when the unclean spirit had torn him, and cried with a loud voice, he came out of him.

[CWB] <u>Mark 1:25-26</u> Jesus rebuked the demon, "Stop shouting and come out of him!" [26]Immediately the demon threw the man down and into convulsions and then, with a shriek, left him.

[FBV-NT] <u>Mark 1:25-26</u> Jesus interrupted the evil spirit, telling him, "Be quiet! Come out of him." [26]The evil spirit screamed, threw the man into convulsions, and came out of him.

[GNC-NT] <u>Mark 1:25-26</u> Jesus administered a rebuke to him, exclaiming, "Be silent and come out of him!" [26]At that the tarnished spirit threw him into convulsions and, crying out in a loud voice, it came out of him.

[GNT] <u>Mark 1:25-26</u> Jesus ordered the spirit, "Be quiet, and come out of the man!" [26]The evil spirit shook the man hard, gave a loud scream, and came out of him.

[HNT] <u>Mark 1:25-26</u> And Jesus rebuked it, "Silence! Leave him!" [26]So after convulsing him and crying with a loud voice, the unclean spirit left him.

[KNT] <u>Mark 1:25-26</u> 'Be quiet!' ordered Jesus. 'And come out of him!' [26]The unclean spirit convulsed the man, gave a great shout, and came out of him.

[Lewis-Gs] <u>Mark 1:25-26</u> And Jesus rebuked him, saying unto him, Shut thy mouth, and come out of him. [26]And the unclean spirit threw him down, and when it had cried with a loud voice, it came out of him.

[NCV] <u>Mark 1:25-26</u> Jesus commanded the evil spirit, "Be quiet! Come out of the man!" [26]The evil spirit shook the man violently, gave a loud cry, and then came out of him.

[NENT] <u>Mark 1:25-26</u> And Jesus censured him, saying, "Be voiceless and come out of him." [26]And the unclean spirit gave him spasms, and it sounded with a loud voice and came out of him.

[Stringfellow-NT] <u>Mark 1:25-26</u> And Jesus rebuked him, saying, Be muzzled and come out of him. [26]And the unclean spirit, having convulsed him and having cried with a loud voice, came out of him.

[TNIV] <u>Mark 1:25-26</u> "Be quiet!" said Jesus sternly. "Come out of him!" [26]The evil spirit shook the man violently and came out of him with a shriek.

[Witham-NT] <u>Mark 1:25-26</u> And Jesus threatened him, saying: hold thy peace, and go out of the man. [26]And the unclean Spirit tearing him, and shouting out with a loud voice, went out of him.

[Worsley-NT] <u>Mark 1:25-26</u> And Jesus rebuked him, saying, Be silent, and come out of him: and the impure spirit threw him into convulsions, [26]and roaring with a loud voice, came out of him.

Mark 1:31 And he came and took her by the hand, and lifted her up; and immediately the fever left her, and she ministered unto them.

[AMP] <u>Mark 1:31</u> **Jesus went to her, and taking her by the hand, raised her up; and the fever left her**, and she began to serve them [as her guests].

[BWE-NT] <u>Mark 1:31</u> **Jesus went to her. He took her hand and helped her up. The fever left her right away**, and she began to do things to help them.

[EEBT] <u>Mark 1:31</u> So he went to her and he held her hand. Then he helped her to sit up and immediately she was well. Then she prepared food for Jesus and for his disciples.

[Guyse-NT] <u>Mark 1:31</u> **Thereupon, going into the room where she lay, he took hold of her hand, and raised her up; and his divine power wrought so effectually at the same time, that the fever immediately ceased, and she was in an instant restored** to such a degree of health and strength, that she went about the business of the house, and managed the entertainment which was made for him and the family, as if nothing had ailed her before.

[JMNT] <u>Mark 1:31</u> **So upon approaching and facing her, He, taking a strong hold on her hand, raised her up, and the fever suddenly flowed away and abandoned (or: left) her**, and she began giving attending service to them.

[MSG] <u>Mark 1:31</u> **He went to her, took her hand, and raised her up. No sooner had the fever left** than she was up fixing dinner for them.

[NLV] <u>Mark 1:31</u> **He went and took her by the hand and raised her up. At once her sickness was gone**. She got up and cared for them.

[REM-NT] <u>Mark 1:31</u> **He went to her, and when he touched her, the fever went away. She got up** and began to wait on them.

[Swendenborg-Gs] <u>Mark 1:31</u> **And He came and raised her up, having taken hold of her hand, and the fever instantly left her**, and she ministered unto them.

[TVB] <u>Mark 1:31</u> **Jesus went to her side, took her hand, and lifted her up. As soon as He touched her, the fever left her and she felt well again**—strong enough to bustle around the house taking care of her visitors.

<u>Mark 1:34</u> **And he healed many that were sick of divers diseases, and cast out many devils**; and suffered not the devils to speak, because they knew him.

[AMP] <u>Mark 1:34</u> And **Jesus healed many who were suffering with various diseases; and He drove out many demons,** but would not allow the demons to speak, because they knew Him [recognizing Him as the Son of God].

[CEV] <u>Mark 1:34</u> **Jesus healed all kinds of terrible diseases and forced out a lot of demons**. But the demons knew who he was, and he did not let them speak.

[CWB] <u>Mark 1:34</u> That evening **Jesus healed many people of all kinds of diseases and cast out many demons**, telling the demons to come out quietly, which they did.

[EEBT] <u>Mark 1:34</u> Jesus caused many sick people to become well. They had many different illnesses. **He also caused many bad spirits to leave people**. The spirits knew who he was. So Jesus did not let them speak.

[ERV] <u>Mark 1:34</u> **Jesus healed many of those who had different kinds of sicknesses. He also forced many demons out of people.** But he would not allow the demons to speak, because they knew who he was.

[Etheridge-NT] <u>Mark 1:34</u> and **he healed multitudes who were grievously affected with various diseases, and cast out many demons**, and would not permit the demons to speak; for they knew him.

[FBV-NT] <u>Mark 1:34</u> **He healed many people who had various diseases, and threw out many demons**. He did not permit the demons to speak, for they knew who he was.

[Murdock-NT] <u>Mark 1:34</u> **And he healed many who labored under divers diseases, and cast out many demons;** and he suffered not the demons to speak, because they knew him.

[REM-NT] <u>Mark 1:34</u> and **Jesus healed all their physical diseases. He also cleansed the minds of those controlled by demons, sending the demons away,** but he would not allow the demons to speak, because they knew who he was.

[TTNT] <u>Mark 1:34</u> **Jesus healed many from a whole variety of diseases. He also freed many who were in bondage to demonic powers.** However, He would not permit the demons to speak because they knew He was God's Son.

<u>Mark 1:39</u> And he preached in their synagogues throughout all Galilee, and cast out devils.

[Barclay-NT] <u>Mark 1:39</u> So he went all over Galilee, proclaiming his message in their synagogues, and ejecting demons.

[EEBT] <u>Mark 1:39</u> So Jesus travelled everywhere in Galilee. He taught the people in their meeting places. He caused bad spirits to come out of people.

[HRB] <u>Mark 1:39</u> And He was proclaiming in their synagogues in all Galilee, and casting out the demons.

[ICB] <u>Mark 1:39</u> So he traveled everywhere in Galilee. He preached in the synagogues and forced demons to leave people.

[JMNT] <u>Mark 1:39</u> And He came (or: went) into their synagogues—into [the] whole [region of] the Galilee [area] —constantly heralding (loudly publicly announcing) as well as repeatedly throwing out the demons.

[Lingard-Gs] <u>Mark 1:39</u> And he announced in their synagogues throughout all Galilee, and cast out the fiends.

[REM-NT] <u>Mark 1:39</u> So he went from town to town, all through Galilee, preaching and teaching in their churches, and driving out evil forces.

[SG] <u>Mark 1:39</u> So he went through Galilee, preaching in their synagogues and driving out the demons.

[TLB] <u>Mark 1:39</u> So he traveled throughout the province of Galilee, preaching in the synagogues and releasing many from the power of demons.

[TTNT] <u>Mark 1:39</u> So He journeyed throughout Galilee, preaching in the synagogues and setting people free from demonic powers.

<u>Mark 1:41</u> And Jesus, moved with compassion, put forth his hand, and touched him, and saith unto him, I will; be thou clean.

[Ballentine-NT] <u>Mark 1:41</u> Jesus pitied him and stretched out his hand and touched him: "It is my wish," he said. "Be cured."

[Berkeley] <u>Mark 1:41</u> Deeply sympathetic, He reached out His hand to touch him and said to him, I am willing! Be cleansed!

[CAB] <u>Mark 1:41</u> And Jesus, being moved with compassion, and reaching out His hand, touched him, and said to him, "I am willing, be cleansed."

[CWB] <u>Mark 1:41</u> When Jesus saw this man's condition, He was moved with compassion. He reached out and touched him and said, "Of course I want you to be clean! You're healed!"

[FBV-NT] <u>Mark 1:41</u> With compassion Jesus reached out and touched the man, and said, "I am willing. Be healed!"

[Hammond-NT] <u>Mark 1:41</u> And Jesus, moved with compassion, put forth his hand, and touched him, and saith unto him, It is my pleasure; be thou cured of thy leprosy.

[ISV] <u>Mark 1:41</u> Moved with compassion, Jesus reached out his hand, touched him, and told him, "I do want to. Be made clean!"

[JMNT] <u>Mark 1:41</u> Now Jesus, being instantly moved with compassion in His inward being, instantly stretching out His hand, touches him, even as He continues in saying to him, "I continually will it and am habitually intending to! Be at once cleansed and made clean!"

[MCC-NT] <u>Mark 1:41</u> But Jesus being wrung with Compassion, having extended a Hand, touched Him; then says He to Him, "I will, Be Thou purified."

[NEB] <u>Mark 1:41</u> In warm indignation Jesus stretched out his hand, touched him, and said, 'Indeed I will; be clean again.'

[NENT] <u>Mark 1:41</u> And he felt compassion, and he stretched out his hand, touched him, and said to him, "I want it. Be cleansed."

[Original-NT] <u>Mark 1:41</u> With deep pity Jesus put out his hand and touched him, saying, "I do will it. Be cleansed!"

[REB] <u>Mark 1:41</u> Jesus was moved to anger; he stretched our his hand, touched him, and said, 'I will; be clean.'

[REM-NT] <u>Mark 1:41</u> Jesus, his heart filled with tenderness and mercy, reached out and touched what others considered untouchable. As he touched the man, he said, "I am willing. Be clean!"

[TLB] <u>Mark 1:41</u> And Jesus, moved with pity, touched him and said, "I want to! Be healed!"

[TPT] <u>Mark 1:41</u> Being deeply moved with tender compassion, Jesus reached out and touched the skin of the leper and told him, "Of course I want you to be healed—so now, be cleansed!"

[TVB] <u>Mark 1:41</u> Jesus was powerfully moved. He reached out and actually touched the leper. Jesus: I do want to. Be clean.

[UDB] <u>Mark 1:41</u> Jesus felt compassion for him. He reached out his hand and touched the man. Then he said to him, "Since I am willing to heal you, be healed!"

[Wade] <u>Mark 1:41</u> And he was moved with sympathy, and stretching out His hand, He touched him and says to him, "I have the will: be cleansed."

[Wuest-NT] <u>Mark 1:41</u> And having been moved with compassion, having stretched out His hand, He touched him and says to him, I desire it. Be cleansed at once.

<u>Mark 2:10-12</u> But that ye may know that the Son of man hath power on earth to forgive sins, (he saith to the sick of the palsy,) **[11]I say unto thee, Arise, and take up thy bed, and go thy way into thine house. [12]And immediately he arose, took up the bed, and went forth before them all**; insomuch that they were all amazed, and glorified God, saying, We never saw it on this fashion.

[ACV] <u>Mark 2:10-12</u> But that ye may know that the Son of man has authority on earth to forgive sins (he says to the paralyzed man), **[11]I say to thee, Arise, and take up thy bed, and go to thy house. [12]And straightaway he arose, and having taken up the bed, he went forth before them all**, so as for all to be amazed, and to glorify God, saying, We never saw it like this.

[AENT] <u>Mark 2:10-12</u> But that you might know that it is Lawful for the Son of man to forgive sins on earth," he said to the paralytic, **[11]"I say to you, arise and take your pallet and go to your house." [12]And at once he arose and took his pallet and departed in the sight of everyone**, so that all of them were amazed. And they gave glory to Elohim while saying they had never seen such.

[AMPC] <u>Mark 2:10-12</u> But that you may know positively and beyond a doubt that the Son of Man has right and authority and power on earth to forgive sins—He said to the paralyzed man, **¹¹I say to you, arise, pick up and carry your sleeping pad or mat, and be going on home. ¹²And he arose at once and picked up the sleeping pad or mat and went out before them all**, so that they were all amazed and recognized and praised and thanked God, saying, We have never seen anything like this before!

[Barclay-NT] <u>Mark 2:10-12</u> Just to show you that the Son of Man actually has authority on earth to forgive sins' —with this he said to the paralysed man— **¹¹I tell you, Get up! Lift your stretcher, and away you go home!' ¹²On the spot, in front of them all, the man got up, lifted his stretcher, and went off**. This left them in such a state of astonishment that they kept on praising God. 'Never,' they kept on saying, 'have we seen anything like this.'

[BSB-NT] <u>Mark 2:10-12</u> But so that you may know that the Son of Man has authority on earth to forgive sins…" He said to the paralytic, **¹¹"I tell you, get up, pick up your mat, and go home." ¹²And immediately the man got up, picked up his mat, and walked out in front of them all**. As a result, everyone was amazed and glorified God, saying, "We have never seen anything like this!"

[BWE-NT] <u>Mark 2:10-12</u> I want you to know that the Son of Man has power on earth to forgive the wrong things people do.' So he said to the sick man, **¹¹I tell you, get up! Take up your mat and go home.' ¹²Right away the man stood up in front of them. He took up his mat and went home**. They were all very much surprised, and they praised God. They said, 'We have never seen anything like this before.'

[EEBT] <u>Mark 2:10-12</u> But I want you to know this. I, the Son of Man, have authority on earth. I can forgive people for the wrong things that they have done.' Then he spoke to the man who could not walk. **¹¹I am saying to you: Stand up! Pick up your small carpet and go to your home.' ¹²The man stood up. Immediately, he picked up the small carpet. Everyone watched him walk out of the house**. This surprised all the people very much. The people said that God had done this powerful thing. They said, 'We have never seen anything like this before.'

[GW] <u>Mark 2:10-12</u> I want you to know that the Son of Man has authority on earth to forgive sins." Then he said to the paralyzed man, **¹¹"I'm telling you to get up, pick up your cot, and go home!" ¹²The man got up, immediately picked up his cot, and walked away while everyone watched**. Everyone was amazed and praised God, saying, "We have never seen anything like this."

[Haweis-NT] <u>Mark 2:10-12</u> But that ye may know that the Son of man hath authority upon earth to forgive sins, he saith to the paralytic, **¹¹I say unto thee, Arise, and take up thy couch, and go into thy house. ¹²And he arose instantly, and taking up his couch, went out before them all**; so that they were all astonished, and glorified God, saying, We never before saw any thing like this.

[KNT] <u>Mark 2:10-12</u> 'You want to know that the son of man has authority on earth to forgive sins?' He turned to the paralytic. **¹¹'I tell you,' he said, 'Get up, take your stretcher, and go home.' ¹²He got up, picked up the stretcher in a flash, and went out before them all**. Everyone was astonished, and they praised God. 'We've never seen anything like this!' they said.

[Madsen-NT] <u>Mark 2:10-12</u> But you shall see that the Son of Man has the creative power to free Man from the burden of sin on the earth.' And so he said to the paralysed man, **¹¹I say to you, stand up, take your stretcher and return to your house.' ¹²And suddenly he was able to stand upright, and he took his stretcher and before their very eyes he walked out**. And they were all lifted out of themselves with wonder and they praised the revelation of God and said, 'Never have we seen anything like this!'

[Original-NT] <u>Mark 2:10-12</u> "But that you may know that the Son of Man is entitled to forgive sins on earth" —he addressed the paralytic— **¹¹"To you I say, rise, pick up your mattress, and go to your**

home!" **12He rose, and immediately picking up his mattress went out in front of them all**; so that they were all astounded and praised God, for, they said, "we have never see the like of this".

[Phillips] <u>Mark 2:10-12</u> But to prove to you that the Son of Man has full authority to forgive sins on earth, I say to you,'—and here he spoke to the paralytic— **11"Get up, pick up your bed and go home.'** **12At once the man sprang to his feet, picked up his bed and walked off in full view of them all.** Everyone was amazed, praised God and said, 'We have never seen anything like this before.'

[REM-NT] <u>Mark 2:10-12</u> Just so you will know for certain that the Son of Man has authority on earth to abolish and remove sin…" Jesus paused, looked at the paralyzed man, and continued, **11"Do as I say: stand up, pick up your stretcher and walk home." 12Instantly the man was healed. He stood up, picked up his stretcher and walked out in front of the entire crowd.** Everyone was absolutely awed and they shouted praises to God, proclaiming, "We have never seen such clear revelations of God's healing love!"

[Sindlinger-NT] <u>Mark 2:10-12</u> "I'll heal this man's physical condition to prove that I'm one of God's spokesmen. But restoring his physical condition is only part of helping him enjoy a better life." **11As soon as Jesus healed him, 12the man stood up, picked up the stretcher and began walking home.** The people who witnessed the event thanked God because they had never seen anything so amazing before.

[T4T] <u>Mark 2:10-12</u> So I will do something in order that you may know that God has authorized me, the one who came from heaven, to forgive sins on earth as well as to heal people." Then he said to the paralyzed man, **11"To you I say, 'Get up! Pick up your sleeping pad! And then go home!'" 12The man stood up immediately! He picked up the sleeping pad, and then he went away, while all the people there were watching.** They were all amazed, and they praised God and said, "We have never before seen anything like what happened just now!"

<u>Mark 3:5</u> And when he had looked round about on them with anger, being grieved for the hardness of their hearts, **he saith unto the man, Stretch forth thine hand. And he stretched it out: and his hand was restored whole as the other**.

[Anchor] <u>Mark 3:5</u> and looking at them with anger, but sorrowing for their obdurate stupidity, he said to the man, **"Stretch out your hand." He stretched it out, and it was restored**.

[Barclay-NT] <u>Mark 3:5</u> His gaze swept round them, and there was anger in his eyes, for he was saddened by the imperviousness of their hearts. **'Stretch out your hand!' he said to the man. He stretched it out, and his hand was restored to health**.

[Beck] <u>Mark 3:5</u> Looking around at them, He felt angry as well as sorry because their minds were closed. Then He told the man, **"Stretch out your hand." He stretched it out, and his hand was made healthy again**.

[CEB] <u>Mark 3:5</u> Looking around at them with anger, deeply grieved at their unyielding hearts, he said to the man, **"Stretch out your hand." So he did, and his hand was made healthy**.

[CLV] <u>Mark 3:5</u> And looking about on them with indignation, commiserating the callousness of their hearts, He is saying to the man, **"Stretch out your hand. And he stretches it out, and his hand was restored."**

[FBV-NT] <u>Mark 3:5</u> He looked around at them in exasperation, very upset by their hard-hearted attitude. Then he told the man, **"Hold out your hand." The man held out his hand, and it was healed**.

[Harwood-NT] <u>Mark 3:5</u> Jesus looked round about, and filled with indignation and grief at the determined malice and incorrigible obstinacy that lurked in their hearts, said to the man—**Extend thy hand—he extended it—and it was instantly restored to as perfect a state as the other.**

[JUB] <u>Mark 3:5</u> And looking round about on them with anger, being grieved for the blindness of their hearts, he said unto the man, **Stretch forth thine hand. And he stretched it out and his hand was restored whole as the other.**

[LDB-NT] <u>Mark 3:5</u> So after looking around at them in anger, but also deeply grief-stricken by the hardness of their hearts, He said to the man, **"Stretch out your hand." And as he did so, it was restored! It was now just as well and strong as the other.**

[Lewis-Gs] <u>Mark 3:5</u> being grieved about the deadness of their hearts, and he said unto the man, **Stretch forth thy hand. And he stretched it out: and it was restored like its fellow.**

[NIV] <u>Mark 3:5</u> He looked around at them in anger and, deeply distressed at their stubborn hearts, said to the man, **"Stretch out your hand." He stretched it out, and his hand was completely restored.**

[PNT] <u>Mark 3:5</u> And when he had looked round about on them with anger, being grieved for the deadness of their hearts, he saith unto the man, **Stretch forth thine hand. And he stretched it out: and his hand was restored presently.**

[REB] <u>Mark 3:5</u> and, looking round at them with anger and sorrow at their obstinate stupidity, he said to the man, **'Stretch out your arm.' He stretched it out and his arm was restored.**

[REM-NT] <u>Mark 3:5</u> Jesus looked at them, angry at the depth of selfishness infecting their hearts and distressed at their lack of compassion, then he turned to the man and said, **"Extend your hand and be well." The man immediately lifted his hand and used it normally, as it was completely healed.**

[TTNT] <u>Mark 3:5</u> Their stubbornness angered and upset Jesus deeply. **"Stretch out your hand," He said to the man. When he obeyed, his hand was healed completely.**

[Wuest-NT] <u>Mark 3:5</u> And having looked round about on them with a righteous indignation, being grieved at the callousness of their hearts, He says to the man, **Stretch out your hand at once. And he stretched it out. And his hand was restored to its former state.**

[Wycliffe-Noble] <u>Mark 3:5</u> And he beheld them about with wrath, and had sorrow on the blindness of their heart [having sorrow upon the blindness of their heart], and saith to the man, **Hold forth thine hand. And he held forth, and his hand was restored to him.**

<u>Mark 3:10</u> For he had healed many; insomuch that they pressed upon him for to touch him, as many as had plagues.

[AUV-NT 2003] <u>Mark 3:10</u> For He had healed so many people that large numbers of them who were plagued with serious illnesses were crowding around Him in hope of getting to touch Him.

[CEB] <u>Mark 3:10</u> He had healed so many people that everyone who was sick pushed forward so that they could touch him.

[Etheridge-NT] <u>Mark 3:10</u> for he had healed multitudes, until they were falling upon him to touch him.

[GT] <u>Mark 3:10</u> The people were trying to get as close to Jesus as they could because he had healed many people. People with diseases wanted to touch him.

[GW] <u>Mark 3:10</u> He had cured so many that everyone with a disease rushed up to him in order to touch him.

[Newcome] <u>Mark 3:10</u> For he had cured many; so that as many as had grievous diseases pressed upon him to touch him.

[NIRV] <u>Mark 3:10</u> Jesus had healed many people. So those who were sick were pushing forward to touch him.

[Original-NT] <u>Mark 3:10</u> For he had cured many, causing all who were afflicted with diseases to fling themselves on him to touch him.

[Phillips] <u>Mark 3:10</u> For he healed so many people that all those who were in pain kept pressing forward to touch him with their hands.

[REM-NT] <u>Mark 3:10</u> He had healed many people, and this caused those with sickness to press to the front of the crowd and try to get near enough to touch him.

[RJ Miller-Gs] <u>Mark 3:10</u> After all, he had healed so many, that all who had diseases were pushing forward to touch him.

[TPT] <u>Mark 3:10</u> For he had healed so many that the sick kept pushing forward just so they could touch Jesus.

[Wesley-NT] <u>Mark 3:10</u> For he had healed many, so that they rushed in upon him, as many as had plagues.

<u>Mark 3:14-15</u> And he ordained twelve, that they should be with him, and that he might send them forth to preach, **¹⁵And to have power to heal sicknesses, and to cast out devils**:

[AMPC] <u>Mark 3:14-15</u> And He appointed twelve to continue to be with Him, and that He might send them out to preach [as apostles or special messengers] **¹⁵And to have authority and power to heal the sick and to drive out demons:**

[Campbell-Gs] <u>Mark 3:14-15</u> And he selected twelve, that they might attend him, and that he might commission them to proclaim the reign, **¹⁵empowering them to cure diseases, and to expel demons.**

[Etheridge-NT] <u>Mark 3:14-15</u> And he chose twelve to be with him, and to send them to preach, **¹⁵and to have authority to heal diseases and to cast out devils.**

[FAA] <u>Mark 3:14-15</u> and he appointed twelve, for them to be with him, and to send them to preach, **¹⁵and to have authority to cure sicknesses and to cast out demons.**

[Mace-NT] <u>Mark 3:14-15</u> then he chose twelve of them to be near his person, and afterwards to be gospel-missionaries. **¹⁵with full power to heal diseases, and dispossess demons.**

[Spitsbergen] <u>Mark 3:14-15</u> And He appointed twelve, which were with Him that he might also send them to proclaim the message. **¹⁵And He gave them authority to cure sickness and to cast out demons.**

[TPT] <u>Mark 3:14-15</u> He appointed the Twelve, whom he named apostles. He wanted them to be continually at his side as his friends, and so that he could send them out to preach **¹⁵and have authority to heal the sick and to cast out demons.**

[TTNT] <u>Mark 3:14-15</u> He then appointed twelve of them to be apostles, those who would be with Him consistently and who He could send out to preach the gospel of God's Kingdom, **¹⁵with the authority to free people from the demonic spirits that oppose that Kingdom.**

[Wuest-NT] <u>Mark 3:14-15</u> And He appointed twelve in order that they might constantly be with Him, and in order that He might send them forth as ambassadors with credentials, representing Him, to accomplish a certain task, that of making a proclamation with such formality, gravity, and authority as must be heeded and obeyed, **¹⁵being equipped with delegated authority to be casting out the demons.**

<u>Mark 5:12-13</u> And all the devils besought him, saying, Send us into the swine, that we may enter into them. ¹³And forthwith Jesus gave them leave. **And the unclean spirits went out, and entered into the swine**: and the herd ran violently down a steep place into the sea, (they were about two thousand;) and were choked in the sea.

[CEB] <u>Mark 5:12-13</u> "Send us into the pigs!" they begged. "Let us go into the pigs!" [13]Jesus gave them permission, **so the unclean spirits left the man and went into the pigs**. Then the herd of about two thousand pigs rushed down the cliff into the lake and drowned.

[CEV] <u>Mark 5:12-13</u> So the evil spirits begged Jesus, "Send us into those pigs! Let us go into them." [13]Jesus let them go, and **they went out of the man and into the pigs**. The whole herd of about 2,000 pigs rushed down the steep bank into the lake and drowned.

[ERV] <u>Mark 5:12-13</u> The evil spirits begged Jesus, "Send us to the pigs. Let us go into them." [13]So Jesus allowed them to do this. **The evil spirits left the man and went into the pigs.** Then the herd of pigs ran down the hill and into the lake. They were all drowned. There were about 2000 pigs in that herd.

[Mace-NT] <u>Mark 5:12-13</u> and all the demons intreated him, saying, "send us to the swine, that we may enter into them." [13]Jesus immediately gave them leave, **and the impure spirits quitting the possessed, entered into the swine**, and the whole herd, which were about two thousand, ran down a precipice into the sea, and were there stifled.

[UDB] <u>Mark 5:12-13</u> So the evil spirits pleaded with Jesus, "Allow us to go to the pigs in order that we might enter them!" [13]Jesus permitted them to do that. So **the evil spirits left the man and entered the pigs**. The herd, which numbered about two thousand, rushed down the steep hill into the lake, where they drowned.

<u>Mark 5:28-29</u> For she said, If I may touch but his clothes, I shall be whole[sozo]. [29]And straightway the fountain of her blood was dried up; and she felt in her body that she was healed of that plague.

[AMPC] <u>Mark 5:28-29</u> For she kept saying, If I only touch His garments, I shall be restored to health. [29]And immediately her flow of blood was dried up at the source, and [suddenly] she felt in her body that she was healed of her [distressing] ailment.

[Barclay-NT] <u>Mark 5:28-29</u> for she said to herself: 'If I touch even his clothes, I will be cured'. [29]There and then her flow of blood was staunched, and she felt in her body that she was cured of the trouble which had been her scourge for so long.

[BSB-NT] <u>Mark 5:28-29</u> For she kept saying, "If I only touch His clothes, I will be healed." [29]At that instant, her bleeding stopped, and she sensed in her body that she was healed of her affliction.

[ClarkePyle] <u>Mark 5:28-29</u> Thinking within her self, that surely he who had done so many and great Miracles with only a Word speaking, could not but heal her Disease even with the least Touch of his Cloths. [29]And her Expectation did not deceive her. For as soon as she touched him, she found evidently such a Change within her self, and such a sudden Restoration of Strength and Vigour of Body, as satisfied her that her Disease was entirely cured.

[Doddridge-NT] <u>Mark 5:28-29</u> For, as she knew that many had before been healed by touching him, she had such a firm persuasion of the virtue that was in him, and of his power to cure her, that she said within herself, If I but touch any part of his clothes, I shall be recovered. [29]And immediately on her having done it, the fountain of her blood that issued from her was at once stanched and dried up, and she felt such an unusual vigour and flow of spirits, that she plainly perceived in her body that she was healed of that wasting and dangerous distemper with which she had been chastised for so long a time.

[FBV-NT] <u>Mark 5:28-29</u> She was telling herself, "If I can just touch his cloak, I'll be healed." [29]The bleeding stopped immediately, and she felt her body healed from her disease.

[Godbey-NT] <u>Mark 5:28-29</u> For she was saying, If I may touch His garment, I shall be saved. [29]And immediately the issue of her blood dried up: and she knew in her body that she is healed of her plague.

[Hammond-NT] <u>Mark 5:28-29</u> Being thus confidently persuaded in her mind that the least touch of his clothes would cure her. [29]And straightway the flux of her blood was dried up; and she felt in her body that she was healed of that plague.

[ISV] <u>Mark 5:28-29</u> because she had been saying, "If I can just touch his robe, I will get well." [29]Her bleeding stopped at once, and she felt in her body that she was healed from her illness.

[JMNT] <u>Mark 5:28-29</u> for she kept saying, "If I can just touch even His clothes, I will be restored to health (be healed; be saved; be rescued [from this condition])!". [29]And instantly the fountain (or: spring) of her blood was dried up, and she knew by experience that she had been healed and remained cured from the grievous illness (or: disorder) which had been like being scourged with a whip.

[Murdock-NT] <u>Mark 5:28-29</u> For she said: If I but touch his garment, I shall live. [29]And immediately the fountain of her blood dried up; and she felt in her body that she was healed of that plague.

[NWT] <u>Mark 5:28-29</u> for she kept saying: "If I touch just his outer garments, I will get well." [29]And immediately her flow of blood dried up, and she sensed in her body that she had been healed of the grievous sickness.

[Original-NT] <u>Mark 5:28-29</u> for she said, "If I can only touch his clothes I shall get better." [29]At once her flow of blood stopped at its source, and she was physically conscious that she was cured of her complaint.

[Pickering-NT] <u>Mark 5:28-29</u> (She had kept saying, "If I can just touch His clothes, I will be healed". [29]Immediately the flow of her blood was dried up, and she knew in her body that she was healed from the affliction.

[SPV] <u>Mark 5:28-29</u> for she kept saying, "If I should touch just his garments, I will be restored to health." [29]And immediately her flow of blood dried up, and she felt in [her] body that she was healed of the affliction.

[Wuest-NT] <u>Mark 5:28-29</u> for she kept saying, If I touch even His garments, I will be made whole. [29]And immediately there was dried up the fountain of her blood, and she suddenly came to feel in her body that she had been healed of her plague and was at that moment in a state of health.

Mark 5:34 And he said unto her, Daughter, thy faith hath made thee whole[sozo]; go in peace, and be whole of thy plague.

[AENT] <u>Mark 5:34</u> And he said to her, "My daughter, your faith has given you life. Go in peace and be healed from your sickness."

[AMP] <u>Mark 5:34</u> Then He said to her, "Daughter, your faith [your personal trust and confidence in Me] has restored you to health; go in peace and be [permanently] healed from your suffering."

[Barclay-NT] <u>Mark 5:34</u> 'Daughter,' he said, 'your faith has cured you. Go and God bless you! Go and enjoy your new health, free from the trouble that was your scourge.'

[CB] <u>Mark 5:34</u> Jesus said to her: "Daughter, your faith has saved you. Go with peace of mind, and live a life free from that terrible disease."

[CEV] <u>Mark 5:34</u> Jesus said to the woman, "You are now well because of your faith. May God give you peace! You are healed, and you will no longer be in pain."

[ClarkePyle] <u>Mark 5:34</u> Then Jesus spoke comfortably to her, saying; Be not afraid; your great Faith has purchased you this Cure; Go home in Peace, and your Disease shall return upon you no more.

[EEBT] <u>Mark 5:34</u> 'Young woman, do not have troubles in your mind', said Jesus. 'You are well again because you believed. Go now and be well.'

[ERV] <u>Mark 5:34</u> He said to her, "Dear woman, you are made well because you believed. Go in peace. You will not suffer anymore."

[FBV-NT] <u>Mark 5:34</u> "My daughter, your trust in me has healed you. Go in peace. You have been completely cured of your disease," Jesus told her.

[Folsom-Gs] <u>Mark 5:34</u> And he said to her, Daughter, thy faith has restored thee: go thy way into peace, and continue in health, [relieved] from thy complaint!

[GoodSpeed-NT] <u>Mark 5:34</u> And he said to her, "My daughter, it is your faith that has cured you. Go in peace and be free from your disease."

[Heylyn-Gs] <u>Mark 5:34</u> And he said to her, Daughter, your Faith has cured you. Go in Peace, and continue free from your Malady.

[Murdock-NT] <u>Mark 5:34</u> And he said to her: My daughter, thy faith hath made thee live: go in peace; and be thou healed of thy plague.

[NEB] <u>Mark 5:34</u> He said to her, 'My daughter, your faith has cured you. Go in peace, free for ever from this trouble.'

[Norlie-NT] <u>Mark 5:34</u> "Daughter," He then said, "your faith has brought the cure. Go in peace, and be free from your illness."

[REM-NT] <u>Mark 5:34</u> He smiled at her and said, "Child, your trust is what allowed you to be healed. Live healthy and happy, free from your suffering."

[RJ Miller-Gs] <u>Mark 5:34</u> He said to her, "Daughter, your trust has cured you. Go in peace, and farewell to your illness."

[TPT] <u>Mark 5:34</u> Then Jesus said to her, "Daughter, because you dared to believe, your faith has healed you. Go with peace in your heart, and be free from your suffering!"

[TTNT] <u>Mark 5:34</u> Jesus was not angry or upset. Far from it, for He said to her: "My daughter, you are healed because you showed such faith. You can go in peace and remain free, for your days of suffering are over."

[Whiting-NT] <u>Mark 5:34</u> And he said to her, Daughter, thy faith hath healed thee; go in peace, and remain cured of thy plague.

[Wilson-NT] <u>Mark 5:34</u> And He said to her, "Daughter, thy Faith has cured thee; go in peace, and be entirely free from thy Disease."

<u>Mark 5:41-42</u> And he took the damsel by the hand, and said unto her, Talitha cumi; which is, being interpreted, Damsel, I say unto thee, arise. [42]And straightway the damsel arose, and walked; for she was of the age of twelve years. And they were astonished with a great astonishment.

[AMP] <u>Mark 5:41-42</u> Taking the child's hand, He said [tenderly] to her, "Talitha kum!"—which translated [from Aramaic] means, "Little girl, I say to you, get up!" [42]The little girl immediately got up and began to walk, for she was twelve years old. And immediately they [who witnessed the child's resurrection] were overcome with great wonder and utter amazement.

[AMPC] <u>Mark 5:41-42</u> Gripping her [firmly] by the hand, He said to her, Talitha cumi—which translated is, Little girl, I say to you, arise [from the sleep of death]! [42]And instantly the girl got up and started walking around—for she was twelve years old. And they were utterly astonished and overcome with amazement.

[Doddridge-NT] <u>Mark 5:41-42</u> And, approaching the bed on which the corpse was laid out, he took hold of her hand: and, to express his power over death itself, called with a loud voice, saying to her, (as if she had indeed been only asleep,) Talitha cumi; which Syriac expression, being translated into our language, signifies, Maiden, (I say unto thee,) rise up. ⁴²And he had no sooner spoken these words, but presently her spirit came back again to animate the body which it had deserted, and she was so perfectly recovered that she arose and walked; which she was able to do, for she was twelve years old.

[ERV] <u>Mark 5:41-42</u> Then Jesus held the girl's hand and said to her, "Talitha, koum!" (This means "Little girl, I tell you to stand up!") ⁴²The girl immediately stood up and began walking. (She was twelve years old.) The father and mother and the followers were amazed.

[Moffatt-NT 1917] <u>Mark 5:41-42</u> then he took the child's hand and said to her, "Talitha koum"—which may be translated, "Little girl, I am telling you to rise." ⁴²The girl got up at once and began to walk (she was twelve years old); and at once they were lost in utter amazement.

[TPT] <u>Mark 5:41-42</u> He tenderly clasped the child's hand in his and said to her in Aramaic, "Talitha koum," which means, "Little girl, wake up from the sleep of death." ⁴²Instantly the twelve-year-old girl sat up, stood to her feet, and started walking around the room! Everyone was overcome with astonishment in seeing this miracle!

[Weekes-NT] <u>Mark 5:41-42</u> And he took the child by the hand, and said to her, "Taleitha, coum," (which is, being translated, "Darling, arise.") ⁴²And immediately the little girl arose and walked; for she was twelve years old: and they were greatly amazed.

<u>Mark 6:2</u> And when the sabbath day was come, he began to teach in the synagogue: and many hearing him were astonished, saying, From whence hath this man these things? and **what wisdom is this which is given unto him, that even such mighty works are wrought by his hands**?

[BBE] Mark 6:2 And when the Sabbath day had come, he was teaching in the Synagogue; and a number of people hearing him were surprised, saying, From where did this man get these things? and, **What is the wisdom given to this man, and what are these works of power done by his hands?**

[Berkeley] <u>Mark 6:2</u> and at the opening of Sabbath He began to teach in the synagogue. Many listeners were utterly amazed. "Where did he get all this?" they remarked. "**What wisdom has been given him and what miracles are these that happen by his hands?**"

[Besorah] <u>Mark 6:2</u> And Sabbath having come, He began to teach in the congregation. And many who heard Him were astonished, saying, "Where did He get all this? And **what wisdom is this which is given to Him, that such miracles are done through His hands**?

[CWB] <u>Mark 6:2</u> On the Sabbath, Jesus went to the synagogue and spoke. When the people heard Him they were amazed and inspired by what He said. They asked, "Where did He learn all this? Where did He get such insight? **Where does He get power to work the miracles that He does?**"

[Mace-NT] <u>Mark 6:2</u> when the sabbath was come, he preached in the synagogue, to the great astonishment of many, who upon hearing his discourse, said, how came he by all this? **what strange endowment of knowledge is this, that he should work such miracles?**

[NCV] <u>Mark 6:2</u> On the Sabbath day he taught in the synagogue. Many people heard him and were amazed, saying, "Where did this man get these teachings? **What is this wisdom that has been given to him? And where did he get the power to do miracles?**

[REM-NT] <u>Mark 6:2</u> On Sabbath, he went to the local worship center and began to teach. Those who heard him were astounded. "How does he know all this?" they asked. "**What he says makes sense and has power to actually change lives!**"

[TPT] <u>Mark 6:2</u> On the Sabbath, he went to teach in the synagogue. Everyone who heard his teaching was overwhelmed with astonishment. They said among themselves, "What incredible wisdom has been given to him! **Where did he receive such profound insights? And what mighty miracles flow through his hands**!

Mark 6:13 And they cast out many devils, and anointed with oil many that were sick, and healed them.

> **[AUV-NT 2003]** **Mark 6:13** And they drove out many evil spirits and applied [olive] oil to [the heads of] many sick people and healed them.

> **[CWB]** **Mark 6:13** They also cast out demons, anointed the sick with oil and prayed for people to be healed. And God healed them.

> **[JUB]** **Mark 6:13** And they cast out many demons and anointed with oil many that were sick, and they were healed.

> **[Palmer]** **Mark 6:13** And many demons they expelled, and many sick ones they anointed with oil and healed.

Mark 6:56 And whithersoever he entered, into villages, or cities, or country, they laid the sick in the streets, and besought him that they might touch if it were but the border of his garment: and **as many as touched him were made whole**[sozo].

> **[AMPC]** **Mark 6:56** And wherever He came into villages or cities or the country, they would lay the sick in the marketplaces and beg Him that they might touch even the fringe of His outer garment, and **as many as touched Him were restored to health.**

> **[CAB]** **Mark 6:56** And wherever He would enter into villages, or towns, or the country, they laid the sick in the marketplaces, and they would beg Him at least that they might touch the hem of His garment. And **as many as touched Him were healed**.

> **[CEB]** **Mark 6:56** Wherever he went—villages, cities, or farming communities—they would place the sick in the marketplaces and beg him to allow them to touch even the hem of his clothing. **Everyone who touched him was healed.**

> **[EEBT]** **Mark 6:56** Jesus went into villages, towns and fields. Everywhere that he went, they brought sick people into their market places to him. The sick people asked Jesus for help. They wanted to touch even the edge of his coat. And **every sick person who touched him became well.**

> **[Gilpin-NT]** **Mark 6:56** where Jesus being presently known, great crowds from all the towns, and villages in the neighborhood, came to him, bringing sick people; whom they laid down in the roads, and streets, wherever he passed, desiring only to touch his cloths. **Such instances of faith never passed unrewarded.**

> **[HPAJ]** **Mark 6:56** And wherever he entered into the villages and cities, those with illnesses were laid in the streets. They were begging him, that they might touch but the edge of his clothing. And **all those that touched him were healed.**

> **[Noyes]** **Mark 6:56** And wherever he entered into villages or cities or the open country, they laid the sick in the market-places, and besought him that they might touch if it were but the fringe of his garment; and **as many as touched him were made well.**

> **[REM-NT]** **Mark 6:56** No matter where he went—small hamlets, towns, cities, or out in the countryside—the people brought their sick. They begged to touch him—even just the edge of his coat—and **everyone who did, was healed.**

> **[T4T]** **Mark 6:56** In whatever village, town or other place where he entered, they would bring to the marketplaces those who were sick. Then the sick people would beg Jesus to let them touch him or even

the edge of his clothes in order that Jesus might heal them. **All those who touched him or his robe were healed**.

[Wakefield-NT] Mark 6:56 and into whatever village, or city, or country, he was going, they need to place the sick in the streets, and to beseech him that they might touch if it were but the border of his garment; and **as many as touched it were constantly made well.**

Mark 7:29-30 And he said unto her, For this saying go thy way; the devil is gone out of thy daughter. [30]And when she was come to her house, she found the devil gone out, and her daughter laid upon the bed.

[Ainslie-NT] Mark 7:29-30 And he said to her, On account of this speech go thy way; the demon is gone out of thy daughter. [30]And entering into her house, she found the child laid upon the bed and the demon gone out.

[AMP] Mark 7:29-30 And He said to her, "**Because of this answer [reflecting your humility and faith], go [knowing that your request is granted]; the demon has left your daughter [permanently].**" [30]And returning to her home, she found the child lying on the couch [relaxed and resting], the demon having gone.

[AUV-NT 2003] Mark 7:29-30 And He said to her, "**Because you have said this, go on your way; the evil spirit has left your daughter.**" [30]And she went away to her house and found her child lying on her bed with the evil spirit gone from her.

[BLE] Mark 7:29-30 And he said to her "Because of those words, go; the demon has gone out of your daughter." [30]And she went home and found the child down on the couch, and the demon gone out.

[CCB] Mark 7:29-30 Then **Jesus said to her, "You may go your way; because of such a reply the demon has gone out of your daughter."** [30]And when the woman went home, she found her child lying in bed and the demon gone.

[ClarkePyle] Mark 7:29-30 At this Answer, Jesus as it were surprised with the Woman's Faith, and vanquished by her modest Importunity, yielded to grant her Request, saying, Woman, your extraordinary Faith and Patience shall not go unrewarded; you Daughter's Disease is removed. [30]Whereupon the Woman, believing what was said, and joyful at her Success, went Home and found her Daughter perfectly well.

[Etheridge-NT] Mark 7:29-30 Jeshu saith to her, Go; on account of that word, the demon hath gone forth from thy daughter. [30]And she went to her house, and found her daughter lying on the couch, and the demon had gone out from her.

[EXB] Mark 7:29-30 Then Jesus said, "Because of your answer, you may go. The demon has left your daughter." [30]The woman went home and found her daughter lying in bed; the demon was gone.

[FBV-NT] Mark 7:29-30 Jesus told her, "For such an answer you may go-the demon has left your daughter." [30]She went home and found the child lying on the bed, the demon gone.

[Fenton] Mark 7:29-30 "Because of this expression," He answered her, "**you may go; the demon has left your daughter.**" [30]And returning home, she found the demon gone, and her daughter resting upon a couch.

[Godbey-NT] Mark 7:29-30 And He said to her, On account of this word go; the demon has already gone from thy daughter. [30]And having come into her house, she found the demon gone out, and the daughter lying on the bed.

[Hammond-NT] Mark 7:29-30 And he said, The faith expressed by this answer of thine is such, and so much beyond ordinary, that it shall not go unrewarded, and therefore go thy way; the

devil is gone out of thy daughter. [30]And when she was come to her house, she found the devil gone out, and her daughter laid upon the bed.

[LDB-NT] <u>Mark 7:29-30</u> "**For making that admirable and compelling statement you may go now,**" **Jesus responded. "The demon has left your daughter.**" [30]When she arrived home, she found that the demon had indeed left her daughter, and the girl was lying on the bed.

[Lingard-Gs] <u>Mark 7:29-30</u> **And he said to her; "In reward of that answer, go: the fiend hath left thy daughter."** [30]And returning to her house, she found the fiend gone, and her daughter lying on the bed.

[Palmer] <u>Mark 7:29-30</u> **And he said to her, "Because of this reply, go your way; the demon has left your daughter**." [30]And going away to her house, she found the child lying on the bed, and the demon gone.

[Phillips] <u>Mark 7:29-30</u> **'If you can answer like that,' Jesus said to her, 'you can go home! The evil spirit has left your daughter.'** [30]And she went back to her home and found the child lying quietly on her bed, and the evil spirit gone.

[SG] <u>Mark 7:29-30</u> He said to her, "**If you can say that, go home; the demon has left your daughter**." [30]And she went home and found the child lying on the bed, and the demon gone.

[TGNT] <u>Mark 7:29-30</u> "**Good answer!**" **Jesus said to her. "Because of it, you may go; the demon has come out of your daughter.**" [30]She went to her home and found the little one placed on a bed, free of the demon.

[TPT] <u>Mark 7:29-30</u> Then Jesus said to her, "**That's a good reply! Now, because you said this, you may go. The demon has permanently left your daughter.**" [30]And when she returned home, she found her daughter resting quietly on the couch, completely set free from the demon!

[TTNT] <u>Mark 7:29-30</u> "**For such a faith response, you may go,**" **Jesus told her. "The demon has now left your daughter.**" [30]The woman returned home to find her child lying on the bed, the demon gone.

[Weymouth-NT] <u>Mark 7:29-30</u> "**For those words of yours, go home,**" **He replied; "the demon has gone out of your daughter.**" [30]So she went home, and found the child lying on the bed, and the demon gone.

[Witham-NT] <u>Mark 7:29-30</u> **And he said to her: by reason of these words go thy way, the Devil is gone out of thy Daughter**. [30]And when she was returned to her house, she found the Girl lying on the Bed, and the devil gone out of her.

<u>Mark 7:34-35</u> And looking up to heaven, he sighed, and saith unto him, Ephphatha, that is, Be opened. [35]And straightway his ears were opened, and the string of his tongue was loosed, and he spake plain.

[AMP] <u>Mark 7:34-35</u> and looking up to heaven, He sighed deeply and said to the man, "Ephphatha," which [in Aramaic] means, "Be opened and released!" [35]And his ears were opened, his tongue was released, and he began speaking plainly.

[ERV] <u>Mark 7:34-35</u> Jesus looked up to the sky and with a loud sigh he said, "Ephphatha!" (This means "Open!") [35]As soon as Jesus did this, the man was able to hear. He was able to use his tongue, and he began to speak clearly.

[Fenton] <u>Mark 7:34-35</u> Then looking up to heaven, He sighed, and said to him, "Ephphatha!" which is, "Be opened!" [35]And his hearing was immediately restored, the defects of his tongue were remedied, and he spoke quite plainly.

[Folsom-Gs] <u>Mark 7:34-35</u> and looking up to heaven sighed deeply, and says to him, Ephphatha! which means, Be thoroughly opened! [35]And his organs of hearing were opened, and the ligature of his tongue was immediately loosened, and he spake correctly.

[Mace-NT] <u>Mark 7:34-35</u> then looking up to heaven, with a sigh, he said, Ephphata, that is, be open: [35]and his Ears were instantly opened, his tongue was loosened, and he spoke freely.

[MSG] <u>Mark 7:34-35</u> Then Jesus looked up in prayer, groaned mightily, and commanded, "Ephphatha!—Open up!" [35]And it happened. The man's hearing was clear and his speech plain—just like that.

[NENT] <u>Mark 7:34-35</u> And he looked up into the sky, groaned, and said to him, "Effatha," [that is, "Be fully opened"]. [35]And immediately his ears were opened, and the bond on his tongue was loosened, and he spoke properly.

[OANT] <u>Mark 7:34-35</u> And he gazed into Heaven and he groaned and he said to him, "Be opened." [35]And at that moment his ears were opened and a bond of his tongue was released and he spoke distinctly.

[Phillips] <u>Mark 7:34-35</u> Then, looking up to Heaven, he gave a deep sigh and said to him in Aramaic, 'Open!' [35]And his ears were opened and immediately whatever had tied his tongue came loose and he spoke quite plainly.

[REM-NT] <u>Mark 7:34-35</u> He looked heavenward, groaning at how far from God's design this man was, and said to him, "Ephphatha!" (which means "Be opened!"). [35]Immediately the man could hear and speak, and began talking normally.

[TLB] <u>Mark 7:34-35</u> Then, looking up to heaven, he sighed and commanded, "Open!" [35]Instantly the man could hear perfectly and speak plainly!

<u>Mark 7:37</u> And were beyond measure astonished, saying, He hath done all things well: **he maketh both the deaf to hear, and the dumb to speak.**

[Ainslie-NT] <u>Mark 7:37</u> And were beyond measure astonished, saying, He hath done all things well: **he maketh both the deaf to hear, and the speechless to speak.**

[AMP] <u>Mark 7:37</u> They were thoroughly astounded and completely overwhelmed, saying, "He has done everything well! **He even makes the deaf hear and the mute speak!"**

[BBE] <u>Mark 7:37</u> And they were overcome with wonder, saying, He has done all things well: **he even gives back the power of hearing and the power of talking to those who have been without them.**

[CEV] <u>Mark 7:37</u> They were completely amazed and said, "Everything he does is good! **He even heals people who cannot hear or talk."**

[ERV] <u>Mark 7:37</u> They were all completely amazed. They said, "Look at what he has done. It's all good. **He makes deaf people able to hear and gives a new voice to people who could not talk.**

[FBV-NT] <u>Mark 7:37</u> They were totally amazed and said, "Everything he does is marvelous. **He even makes the deaf hear, and the dumb speak."**

[KNT] <u>Mark 7:37</u> They were totally astonished. 'Everything he does is marvellous!' they said. **'He even makes the deaf hear and the mute speak!'**

[Madsen-NT] <u>Mark 7:37</u> They were beside themselves beyond all measure and said, 'He has done great deeds; **to the deaf he gives their hearing, to the dumb he gives their speech.'**

[Moffatt-NT 1917] <u>Mark 7:37</u> they were astounded in the extreme, saying, "How splendidly he has done everything! **He actually makes the deaf hear and the dumb speak!"**

[Montgomery-NT] <u>Mark 7:37</u> and people were amazed beyond measure saying. "How successfully he does things! **Even the deaf he makes to hear, and the dumb to speak."**

[NCV] <u>Mark 7:37</u> They were completely amazed and said, "Jesus does everything well. **He makes the deaf hear! And those who can't talk he makes able to speak.**

[Phillips] <u>Mark 7:37</u> People were absolutely amazed, and kept saying, 'How wonderfully he has done everything! **He even makes the deaf hear and the dumb speak.**'

[Tackwall-NT] <u>Mark 7:37</u> And they were most exceedingly astonished, saying, "He has done all things well. **He makes even the deaf to hear and the mute to speak.**"

[Thomson] <u>Mark 7:37</u> And being struck with inexpressible amazement, said, He hath done all things well, **he maketh the deaf hear, and the dumb speak.**

[TLB] <u>Mark 7:37</u> for they were overcome with utter amazement. Again and again they said, "Everything he does is wonderful; **he even corrects deafness and stammering!**"

[TPT] <u>Mark 7:37</u> The people were absolutely beside themselves and astonished beyond measure. And they began to declare, "Everything he does is wonderful! **He even makes the deaf hear and the mute speak!**"

[Tyndale21-NT] <u>Mark 7:37</u> And they were excessively astonished, saying, He has done all things excellently: **he makes both the deaf hear, and the dumb speak!**

[UDB] <u>Mark 7:37</u> People who heard about it were utterly amazed and were saying, "Everything he has done is wonderful! Besides doing other amazing things, **he enables deaf people to hear! And he enables those who cannot speak to speak!**"

[Wuest-NT] <u>Mark 7:37</u> And they were completely flabbergasted, and that in a superabundant degree which itself was augmented by the addition of more astonishment, saying, He has done all things well. **He makes both the deaf to be hearing and the dumb to be speaking.**

<u>Mark 8:23-25</u> And he took the blind man by the hand, and led him out of the town; and when he had spit on his eyes, and put his hands upon him, he asked him if he saw ought. [24]And he looked up, and said, I see men as trees, walking. [25]**After that he put his hands again upon his eyes, and made him look up: and he was restored, and saw every man clearly.**

[AMP] <u>Mark 8:23-25</u> Taking the blind man by the hand, He led him out of the village; and after spitting on his eyes and laying His hands on him, He asked him, "Do you see anything?" [24]And he looked up and said, "I see people, but [they look] like trees, walking around." [25]**Then again Jesus laid His hands on his eyes; and the man stared intently and [his sight] was [completely] restored, and he began to see everything clearly.**

[Madsen-NT] <u>Mark 8:23-25</u> And he took the blind man by the hand and led him outside the village, moistened his eyes with spittle and laid his hands upon him. Then he asked him, 'Do you see anything?' [24]And the blind man opened his eyes and said, 'I see people as though they were walking trees.' [25]**And he laid his hands upon his eyes again, and now when he looked about him he was completely restored and saw everything in clear outlines.**

[NABRE] <u>Mark 8:23-25</u> He took the blind man by the hand and led him outside the village. Putting spittle on his eyes he laid his hands on him and asked, "Do you see anything?" [24]Looking up he replied, "I see people looking like trees and walking." [25]**Then he laid hands on his eyes a second time and he saw clearly; his sight was restored and he could see everything distinctly.**

[OEB-NT] <u>Mark 8:23-25</u> Taking the blind man's hand, Jesus led him to the outskirts of the village, and, when he had put saliva on the man's eyes, he placed his hands on him, and asked him: "Do you see anything?" [24]The man looked up, and said: "I see the people, for, as they walk about, they look to me like trees." **²⁵Then Jesus again placed his hands on the man's eyes; and the man saw clearly, his sight was restored, and he saw everything with perfect distinctness.**

[T4T] <u>Mark 8:23-25</u> Jesus took the hand of the blind man, led him outside the town, he put his saliva on the man's eyes, he put his hands on the man, and then he asked him, "Do you see anything?" ²⁴The man looked up and then he said, "Yes, I see people! They are walking around, but I cannot see them clearly. They look like trees!" **²⁵Then Jesus again touched the eyes of the blind man. The man looked intently and at that moment he was completely healed! He could see everything clearly.**

[TLB] <u>Mark 8:23-25</u> Jesus took the blind man by the hand and led him out of the village, and spat upon his eyes, and laid his hands over them. "Can you see anything now?" Jesus asked him. ²⁴The man looked around. "Yes!" he said, "I see men! But I can't see them very clearly; they look like tree trunks walking around!" **²⁵Then Jesus placed his hands over the man's eyes again and as the man stared intently, his sight was completely restored, and he saw everything clearly, drinking in the sights around him.**

[TPT] <u>Mark 8:23-25</u> So Jesus led him, as his sighted guide, outside the village. He placed his saliva on the man's eyes and covered them with his hands. Then he asked him, "Now do you see anything?" ²⁴"Yes," he said. "My sight is coming back! I'm beginning to see people, but they look like trees—walking trees." **²⁵Jesus put his hands over the man's eyes a second time and made him look up. The man opened his eyes wide and he could see everything perfectly. His eyesight was completely restored!**

[TTNT] <u>Mark 8:23-25</u> He took the man by the hand and led him outside the village. He placed some of His spittle on the man's eyes, laid His hands on him and asked: "Are you able to see?" ²⁴The man looked up and said: "I can see people, but they are walking around looking like trees." **²⁵Jesus again placed His hands over the man's eyes. When he opened them, he could see perfectly; his sight was totally restored.**

<u>Mark 9:23</u> Jesus said unto him, If thou canst believe, all things are possible to him that believeth.

[AMP] <u>Mark 9:23</u> Jesus said to him, "[You say to Me,] 'If You can?' All things are possible for the one who believes and trusts [in Me]!"

[Authentic-NT] <u>Mark 9:23</u> 'Anything you can do?' echoed Jesus. 'Everything can be done for one who believes.'

[Baxter-NT] <u>Mark 9:23</u> If thy Faith make thee a Capable Receiver, thou shalt find that I want not Power.

[BBE] <u>Mark 9:23</u> And Jesus said to him, If you are able! All things are possible to him who has faith.

[CEV] <u>Mark 9:23</u> Jesus replied, "Why do you say 'if you can'? Anything is possible for someone who has faith!"

[CJB] <u>Mark 9:23</u> Yeshua said to him, "What do you mean, 'if you can'? Everything is possible to someone who has trust!"

[CLV] <u>Mark 9:23</u> Now Jesus said to him, "Why the if? You are able to believe. All is possible to him who is believing."

[Darby] <u>Mark 9:23</u> And Jesus said to him, The "if thou canst" is [if thou canst] believe. All things are possible to him that believes.

[Doddridge-NT] <u>Mark 9:23</u> And Jesus said unto him, The question is not at all concerning my power, but concerning the strength of thy faith; for if thou canst firmly and cheerfully believe, the deliverance will surely be effected, as all things of this kind [are] possible to him that believeth.

[GNC-NT] <u>Mark 9:23</u> "As for your words, 'If you are able'," Jesus said to them, "he who has faith is able to do anything."

[Guyse-NT] <u>Mark 9:23</u> Jesus answered, The only difficulty lies in your own unbelief: You put an if upon my ability; I return it upon your faith; if you are but as ready to believe in my power and mercy, as I am to exert them, all will be well, and nothing shall be found too difficult for me to do: What say you then? Do you really believe that I am able to do this great thing for your son?

[Johnson-NT] <u>Mark 9:23</u> Jesus said, "It is not a question of whether I can do anything; rather, it is a question of whether you can believe. Anything can happen if you can believe."

[KNT] <u>Mark 9:23</u> 'What d'you mean, "If you can"?' said Jesus. 'Everything is possible to someone who believes.'

[Lingard-Gs] <u>Mark 9:23</u> But Jesus said to him: "If thou canst believe; all things are possible in favour of him who believeth."

[Montefiore-Gs] <u>Mark 9:23</u> Jesus said unto him, 'If thou canst, sayest thou? All things are possible to him that believeth.'

[MSG] <u>Mark 9:23</u> Jesus said, "If? There are no 'ifs' among believers. Anything can happen."

[NEB] <u>Mark 9:23</u> 'If it is possible!' said Jesus. 'Everything is possible to one who has faith.'

[NLV] <u>Mark 9:23</u> Jesus said to him, "Why do you ask Me that? The one who has faith can do all things."

[Rieu-Gs] <u>Mark 9:23</u> 'If I can?' said Jesus. 'Everything is possible for one who has faith.'

[Stringfellow-NT] <u>Mark 9:23</u> And Jesus said to him, That, "If you are able! All things are possible to him that keeps on believing."

[TPT] <u>Mark 9:23</u> Jesus said to him, "What do you mean 'if'? If you are able to believe, all things are possible to the believer."

[TTNT] <u>Mark 9:23</u> "If I can?" said Jesus. "When you believe, everything becomes possible."

[Wade] <u>Mark 9:23</u> And Jesus said to him, "Why this 'If you can'? Everything can be done for him that has faith."

<u>Mark 9:26-27</u> And the spirit cried, and rent him sore, and came out of him: and he was as one dead; insomuch that many said, He is dead. [27]But Jesus took him by the hand, and lifted him up; and he arose.

[AUV-NT 2003] <u>Mark 9:26-27</u> The spirit shrieked and caused violent convulsions [in the boy], then came out of him. The boy appeared to be dead, so that most of the people were saying, "He is dead." [27]But Jesus grasped his hand and lifted him up, and he arose [fully healed].

[CEB] <u>Mark 9:26-27</u> After screaming and shaking the boy horribly, the spirit came out. The boy seemed to be dead; in fact, several people said that he had died. [27]But Jesus took his hand, lifted him up, and he arose.

[GoodSpeed-NT] <u>Mark 9:26-27</u> And it gave a cry and convulsed him terribly, and went out of him. And the boy was like a corpse, so that most of them said that he was dead. [27]But Jesus grasped his hand and made him rise, and he stood up.

[KIT-NT] <u>Mark 9:26-27</u> And having cried out and very much having convulsed it came out; and he became as if dead as-and the many to be saying that he died. [27]The but Jesus having laid hold of the hand of him he raised up him, and he stood up.

[Mace-NT] <u>Mark 9:26-27</u> and the spirit came out of him, having made him roar, and thrown him into such agonies, that he became like one that was dead, and many were of opinion he actually was so. [27]but Jesus taking him by the hand, raised him up, and he was perfectly recovered.

[Madsen-NT] <u>Mark 9:26-27</u> And with screams and convulsions it left him. And the boy lay there as if dead, so that many said, 'He has died.' [27]But Jesus took him by the hand and raised him up and life returned to him.

[T4T] <u>Mark 9:26-27</u> The evil spirit shouted, it shook the boy violently, and then it left the boy. The boy did not move. He seemed like a dead body. So many of the people there said, "He is dead!" [27]However, Jesus took him by the hand and helped him get up. Then the boy stood up. He was healed!

[TPT] <u>Mark 9:26-27</u> The demon shrieked and threw the boy into terrible seizures and finally came out of him! As the boy lay there, looking like a corpse, everyone thought he was dead. [27]But Jesus stooped down, gently took his hand, and raised him up to his feet, and he stood there completely set free!

[TTNT] <u>Mark 9:26-27</u> The spirit in the boy shrieked, caused him to have a violent seizure and then left him. At first the boy lay so still he appeared to be dead. Some thought he had died. [27]But Jesus took him by the hand and raised him to his feet and he stood up, completely free.

<u>Mark 10:51-52</u> And Jesus answered and said unto him, What wilt thou that I should do unto thee? The blind man said unto him, **Lord, that I might receive my sight**. [52]And Jesus said unto him, **Go thy way; thy faith hath made thee whole**[sozo]. **And immediately he received his sight**, and followed Jesus in the way.

[AMP] <u>Mark 10:51-52</u> And Jesus said, "What do you want Me to do for you?" The blind man said to Him, **"Rabboni (my Master), let me regain my sight."** [52]Jesus said to him, "Go; **your faith [and confident trust in My power] has made you well." Immediately he regained his sight** and began following Jesus on the road.

[AMPC] <u>Mark 10:51-52</u> And Jesus said to him, What do you want Me to do for you? And the blind man said to Him, **Master, let me receive my sight**. [52]And Jesus said to him, **Go your way; your faith has healed you. And at once he received his sight and accompanied Jesus on the road.**

[AUV-NT 2003] <u>Mark 10:51-52</u> Jesus said to him, "What do you want me to do for you?" And the blind man answered, **"Rabboni, I want to have my sight restored."** [52]And Jesus said to him, **"Go on your way, your faith [in me] has made you well." And immediately his sight was restored**, and he began following Jesus along the road.

[BWE-NT] <u>Mark 10:51-52</u> Jesus said, 'What do you want me to do for you?' The blind man said to him, **'Teacher, I want to see.'** [52]Jesus said, **'Go home. Because you believe in me, your faith has made you well.' Right then he was able to see.** He followed Jesus on the road.

[ERV] <u>Mark 10:51-52</u> Jesus asked the man, "What do you want me to do for you?" He answered, **"Teacher, I want to see again."** [52]Jesus said, **"Go. You are healed because you believed." Immediately the man was able to see again. He followed Jesus down the road.**

[Godbey-NT] <u>Mark 10:51-52</u> And Jesus responding said to him, What do you wish that I shall do to you? And the blind man said to Him, **Great Master, that I may look up.** [52]And Jesus said to him, **Go; thy faith hath saved thee: and immediately he looked up**, and followed Jesus in the way.

[HRB] <u>Mark 10:51-52</u> And answering, Yahshua said to him, What do you desire I should do to you? And the blind one said to Him, **My Rabboni that I may see again**. [52]And Yahshua said to him, **Go, your faith has healed you. And instantly he saw again**, and followed Yahshua in the highway.

[Mace-NT] <u>Mark 10:51-52</u> who thereupon spoke to him, and said, what would you have me do for you? the blind man replied, **Lord, I desire to have my sight**. [52]and Jesus said to him, **go your way, your faith has cured you, and immediately he had sight**, and followed Jesus in the road.

[Murdock-NT] <u>Mark 10:51-52</u> Jesus said to him: What wilt thou, that I do for thee? And the blind man said to him: **Rabbi, that I may have sight**. [52]And Jesus said to him: **Go; thy faith hath procured thee life. And immediately his sight was restored;** and he followed after him.

[SENT] <u>Mark 10:51-52</u> Jesus said to him, "What do you want me to do for you?" The blind man said to him, "**Teacher, I'd like to see again**!" [52]And Jesus said to him, "**Go—your faith has healed you." Right away he could see again**, and began following Jesus on the road.

[TLB] <u>Mark 10:51-52</u> "What do you want me to do for you?" Jesus asked. "O Teacher," the blind man said, "**I want to see!**" [52]And Jesus said to him, "**All right, it's done. Your faith has healed you.**" And instantly the blind man could see and followed Jesus down the road!

[TTNT] <u>Mark 10:51-52</u> Jesus asked him: "What is it you want? What can I do for you?" "**Rabbi, I want my sight restored**," the blind man said. [52]"**Go, because of your faith you are healed," Jesus said to him. Immediately he could see** and followed Jesus along with the crowd.

<u>Mark 11:23-24</u> For verily I say unto you, That whosoever shall say unto this mountain, Be thou removed, and be thou cast into the sea; and shall not doubt in his heart, but shall believe that those things which he saith shall come to pass; he shall have whatsoever he saith. [24]Therefore I say unto you, What things soever ye desire, when ye pray, believe that ye receive them, and ye shall have them.

[ABP] <u>Mark 11:23-24</u> For amen I say to you, that who ever should say to this mountain, Be lifted, and be thrown into the sea! and should not examine in his heart, but should trust that what he says takes place, it will be to him what ever he should say. [24]On account of this I say to you, All as much as [praying you ask], trust that you receive! and it will be to you.

[Ainslie-NT] <u>Mark 11:23-24</u> Verily I say to you, Whoever shall say to this mountain, Be thou removed, and cast into the sea, and shall not doubt in his heart, but shall believe that what he saith shall come to pass; it shall be to him. [24]On this account, I say to you, All things whatever ye pray and ask, believe that ye have received, and they shall be to you.

[AMP] <u>Mark 11:23-24</u> I assure you and most solemnly say to you, whoever says to this mountain, 'Be lifted up and thrown into the sea!' and does not doubt in his heart [in God's unlimited power], but believes that what he says is going to take place, it will be done for him [in accordance with God's will]. [24]For this reason I am telling you, whatever things you ask for in prayer [in accordance with God's will], believe [with confident trust] that you have received them, and they will be given to you.

[Authentic-NT] <u>Mark 11:23-24</u> 'I tell you positively, if anyone should say to this hill, "Go and hurl yourself into the sea," and should have not the slightest doubt, but fully believe that what he says will happen, he will bring it about. [24]That is why I tell you, whatever it may be you pray for or ask for, believe that you will obtain it and you will have it.'

[Barclay-NT] <u>Mark 11:23-24</u> 'I tell you truly, if anyone were to say to this hill: "Be picked up and flung into the sea," if there are no doubts in his mind, but if he really believes that what he is saying will happen, what he asks will be done. [24]That is why I tell you that you must believe that you have as good as received everything for which you pray and ask, and then you will receive it.

[BrownKrueger] <u>Mark 11:23-24</u> For verily I say unto you, that whosoever shall say unto this mountain, Take thyself away, and cast thyself into the sea, and shall not waver in his heart, but shall believe that those things which he saith, shall come to pass, whatsoever he saith, shall be done to him. [24]Therefore I say unto you, Whatsoever ye desire when ye pray, believe that ye shall have it, and it shall be done unto you.

[BV-KJV-NT] <u>Mark 11:23-24</u> You see, amen, I tell you that whoever might say to this mountain, 'Be picked up and thrown into the sea,' and in his heart does not consider it to be wrong, but trusts that what he speaks is happening, he will have whatever he said. [24]Because of this, I tell you, everything, however many things that you ask for as you pray, trust that you are receiving them, and you will have them.

[Condon-Mk] <u>Mark 11:23-24</u> Truly I say to you, if anyone says to this mountain: "Be lifted and thrown into the sea", without hesitation in his heart but with faith that what he says will come true, it will be done for him. [24]Therefore I say to you: Whatever you ask for in prayer, believe that you have received, and it will be done for you.

[Douay-Rheims-Peters] <u>Mark 11:23-24</u> Amen I say to you, that whosoever shall say to this mountain, Be taken up and be cast into the sea, and shall not stagger in his heart, but believe that whatsoever he saith, shall be done: it shall be done unto him. [24]Therefore I say to you, all things whatsoever you ask, praying, believe that you shall receive and they shall come unto you.

[Etheridge-NT] <u>Mark 11:23-24</u> Amen I say to you, That whosoever shall say to this mountain, Be lifted up, and fall into the sea, and shall not be divided in his heart, but shall believe that that thing which he speaketh is, he shall have the thing that he saith. [24]On this account I tell you, that every thing whatever you supplicate and ask, believe that you receive, and it shall be unto you.

[GW] <u>Mark 11:23-24</u> I can guarantee this truth: This is what will be done for someone who doesn't doubt but believes what he says will happen: He can say to this mountain, 'Be uprooted and thrown into the sea,' and it will be done for him. [24]That's why I tell you to have faith that you have already received whatever you pray for, and it will be yours.

[HRB] <u>Mark 11:23-24</u> For truly I say to you, that he who says to this mountain, "Be lifted up and fall into the sea." And does not become divided in his heart but believes that it will happen. That thing which he said it will happen. [24]Therefore I say to you, All things, whatever you ask, praying, believe that you will receive, and it will be to you.

[LTPB] <u>Mark 11:23-24</u> Amen, I say to you, whoever says to this mountain, 'Be taken up and thrown into the sea,' and doesn't hesitate in his heart, but believes that whatever he said can be done—it will be done for him! [24]"For this reason I'm saying to you, believe that you will receive all—whatever you ask, praying—and they will come to you!

[Montgomery-NT] <u>Mark 11:23-24</u> In solemn truth I tell you that if any one shall say to this mountain, 'Up and hurl yourself into the sea!' and shall not doubt in his heart, but on the contrary shall believe that what he says will happen, it will be granted him. [24]That is why I am telling you that whatever you ask for in prayer, believe that you have received it, and it shall be yours.

[MSG] <u>Mark 11:23-24</u> and nothing will be too much for you. This mountain, for instance: Just say, 'Go jump in the lake'—no shuffling or shilly-shallying—and it's as good as done. [24]That's why I urge you to pray for absolutely everything, ranging from small to large. Include everything as you embrace this God-life, and you'll get God's everything.

[NIRV] <u>Mark 11:23-24</u> What I'm about to tell you is true. Suppose someone says to this mountain, 'Go and throw yourself into the sea.' They must not doubt in their heart. They must believe that what they say will happen. Then it will be done for them. [24]So I tell you, when you pray for something, believe that you have already received it. Then it will be yours.

[Norlie-NT] <u>Mark 11:23-24</u> "I tell you," He continued, "if anyone would say to this mountain, 'Move! Throw yourself into the sea!' and have no doubt in his heart, but would be sure that what he said would come to pass, then it would so happen. ²⁴"Therefore, I say, whenever you ask for anything in prayer, believe that you will receive it, and you will."

[RVIC] <u>Mark 11:23-24</u> Truly I say unto you, Whosoever shall say unto this mountain, Be thou taken up and cast into the sea; and shall not doubt in his heart, but shall believe that what he saith cometh to pass; he shall have it. ²⁴Therefore I say unto you, All things whatsoever ye pray and ask for, believe that ye have as good as received it, and ye shall have it.

[TGNT] <u>Mark 11:23-24</u> I tell you truly that if you were to tell this mountain to lift up and throw itself into the sea, without second-guessing but being confident that what you're saying will happen, it will happen. ²⁴"What I'm saying here is that whatever you're praying about or requesting, believe that you have it, and it will be yours.

[TLB] <u>Mark 11:23-24</u> this is the absolute truth—you can say to this Mount of Olives, 'Rise up and fall into the Mediterranean,' and your command will be obeyed. All that's required is that you really believe and have no doubt! ²⁴Listen to me! You can pray for anything, and if you believe, you have it; it's yours!

[TPT] <u>Mark 11:23-24</u> Listen to the truth I speak to you: If someone says to this mountain with great faith and having no doubt, 'Mountain, be lifted up and thrown into the midst of the sea,' and believes that what he says will happen, it will be done. ²⁴This is the reason I urge you to boldly believe for whatever you ask for in prayer—believe that you have received it and it will be yours.

[Witham-NT] <u>Mark 11:23-24</u> Amen I say to you, that whosoever shall say to this mountain: be removed, and cast into the Sea: and if he shall not stagger in his Heart, but shall believe, that whatsoever he shall say, shall be done; the same shall be done for him. ²⁴Therefore I say to you, all things whatsoever you shall ask in Prayer, believe that you shall receive, and they shall happen to you.

<u>Mark 16:15-20</u> And he said unto them, Go ye into all the world, and preach the gospel to every creature. ¹⁶He that believeth and is baptized shall be saved^[sozo]; but he that believeth not shall be damned. **¹⁷And these signs shall follow them that believe; In my name shall they cast out devils**; they shall speak with new tongues; ¹⁸They shall take up serpents; and if they drink any deadly thing, it shall not hurt them; **they shall lay hands on the sick, and they shall recover**. ¹⁹So then after the Lord had spoken unto them, he was received up into heaven, and sat on the right hand of God. ²⁰And they went forth, and preached every where, **the Lord working with them, and confirming the word with signs following. Amen**.

[AMPC] <u>Mark 16:15-20</u> And He said to them, Go into all the world and preach and publish openly the good news (the Gospel) to every creature [of the whole human race]. ¹⁶He who believes [who adheres to and trusts in and relies on the Gospel and Him Whom it sets forth] and is baptized will be saved [from the penalty of eternal death]; but he who does not believe [who does not adhere to and trust in and rely on the Gospel and Him Whom it sets forth] will be condemned. **¹⁷And these attesting signs will accompany those who believe: in My name they will drive out demons**; they will speak in new languages; ¹⁸They will pick up serpents; and [even] if they drink anything deadly, it will not hurt them; **they will lay their hands on the sick, and they will get well**. ¹⁹So then the Lord Jesus, after He had spoken to them, was taken up into heaven and He sat down at the right hand of God. ²⁰And they went out and preached everywhere, while **the Lord kept working with them and confirming the message by the attesting signs and miracles that closely accompanied [it].** Amen (so be it).

[AUV-NT 2005] <u>Mark 16:15-20</u> Then He said to them, "You [men] go into the entire world and preach the good news to every person. ¹⁶The person who believes [i.e., the Gospel] and is immersed will be saved [i.e., from condemnation], but whoever does not believe it will be condemned. **¹⁷And these [miraculous] signs will attend [the conversion of] those who believe. In my name [i.e., by my authority], they will drive out evil spirits**; they will speak in languages [supernaturally]; ¹⁸they will pick up snakes [i.e., without being harmed]; and if they happen to drink anything poisonous, it will not harm them; **they will place hands on sick people [i.e., with prayer] and they will be healed.**" [19]So then, after the Lord Jesus had spoken to them He was taken up to heaven, where He sat down at the right side of God. [20]And the apostles went out and preached everywhere. **The Lord worked with them and confirmed the message [i.e., verified that it was true] by means of the [miraculous] signs which accompanied their ministry.** May it be so.

[Barclay-NT] Mark 16:15-20 'Go all over the world,' he said to them, 'and proclaim the Good News to the whole of creation. [16]He who believes and is baptized will be saved but he who refuses to believe will be condemned. [17]**These are the visible demonstrations of the action of God which will accompany the life of those who believe. By using my name they will eject demons.** They will speak in strange languages. [18]They will lift snakes in their bare hands. Even if they drink any deadly poison, it will not hurt them. **They will place their hands on the sick and they will be cured.**' [19]After he had spoken to them, the Lord Jesus was taken up into heaven, and took his seat at the right hand of God. [20]They went and preached everywhere, and **all the time the Lord worked with them, and confirmed their message by visible demonstrations of his power.**

[CJB] Mark 16:15-20 Then he said to them, "As you go throughout the world, proclaim the Good News to all creation. [16]Whoever trusts and is immersed will be saved; whoever does not trust will be condemned. [17]**And these signs will accompany those who do trust: in my name they will drive out demons,** speak with new tongues, [18]not be injured if they handle snakes or drink poison, and **heal the sick by laying hands on them.**" [19]So then, after he had spoken to them, the Lord Yeshua was taken up into heaven and sat at the right hand of God. [20]And they went out and proclaimed everywhere, **the Lord working with them and confirming the message by the accompanying signs.**

[CWB] Mark 16:15-20 Then He said to them, "Go and preach the good news of God's love to the whole world. [16]Anyone who believes and is baptized will be saved, but those who do not believe will be found guilty. [17]**Those who believe will be able to work miracles. They will cast out demons in my name** and will preach in languages they never learned. [18]When they're bitten by poisonous snakes or drink something poisonous, they won't be hurt. And **they will lay their hands on the sick and the sick will be healed.**" [19]After the Lord had stayed with them many days, He ascended to heaven to sit at the right hand of God the Father. [20]Then the disciples went everywhere preaching the good news, and **the Lord confirmed His word by the miracles He did through them.**

[ERV] Mark 16:15-20 He said to them, "Go everywhere in the world. Tell the Good News to everyone. [16]Whoever believes and is baptized will be saved. But those who do not believe will be judged guilty. [17]**And the people who believe will be able to do these things as proof: They will use my name to force demons out of people.** They will speak in languages they never learned. [18]If they pick up snakes or drink any poison, they will not be hurt. **They will lay their hands on sick people, and they will get well.**" [19]After the Lord Jesus said these things to his followers, he was carried up into heaven. There, Jesus sat at the right side of God. [20]The followers went everywhere in the world telling people the Good News, **and the Lord helped them. By giving them power to do miracles the Lord proved that their message was true.**

[EXB] Mark 16:15-20 Jesus said to them, "Go everywhere in the world, and ·tell [preach; proclaim] the ·Good News [Gospel] to ·everyone [all creation]. [16]Anyone who believes and is baptized will be saved, but anyone who does not believe will be ·punished [condemned]. [17]**And those who believe will be able to do these things as ·proof [signs]: They will use my name to ·force [drive; cast] out demons.** They will speak in new ·languages [tongues]. [18]They will pick up snakes and drink poison without being hurt. **They will ·touch [lay hands on] the sick, and the sick will ·be healed [recover].**" [19]After the Lord Jesus said these things to them, he was carried up into heaven, and he sat at the right ·side [hand] of

God. [20]The ·followers [disciples] went everywhere in the world and ·told [preached; proclaimed] the ·Good News [Gospel] to people, and the Lord helped them. **The Lord ·proved [confirmed] that the ·Good News [Gospel] they ·told [preached; proclaimed] was true by giving them power to work ·miracles [signs].**]

[GNT] Mark 16:15-20 He said to them, "Go throughout the whole world and preach the gospel to all people. [16]Whoever believes and is baptized will be saved; whoever does not believe will be condemned. [17]**Believers will be given the power to perform miracles: they will drive out demons in my name**; they will speak in strange tongues; [18]if they pick up snakes or drink any poison, they will not be harmed; **they will place their hands on sick people, and these will get well."** [19]After the Lord Jesus had talked with them, he was taken up to heaven and sat at the right side of God. [20]The disciples went and preached everywhere, and **the Lord worked with them and proved that their preaching was true by the miracles that were performed.**]

[Magiera-NT] Mark 16:15-20 And he said to them, "Go to all the world and preach my gospel in all of creation. [16]Whoever believes and is baptized will live, and whoever does not believe is condemned. [17]**And these signs will follow those who believe, in my name they will cast out demons** and they will speak with new tongues. [18]And they will capture snakes, and if they should drink a deadly poison, it will harm not them **and they will place their hands on the sick and they will be made whole."** [19]And Jesus, our Lord, after speaking with them, went up to heaven and sat on the right hand of God. [20]And they went out and preached in every place and **our Lord was helping them and establishing their words by the signs that they were doing**.

[MSG] Mark 16:15-20 Then he said, "Go into the world. Go everywhere and announce the Message of God's good news to one and all. [16]Whoever believes and is baptized is saved; whoever refuses to believe is damned. [17]**"These are some of the signs that will accompany believers: They will throw out demons in my name**, they will speak in new tongues, [18]they will take snakes in their hands, they will drink poison and not be hurt, **they will lay hands on the sick and make them well."** [19]Then the Master Jesus, after briefing them, was taken up to heaven, and he sat down beside God in the place of honor. [20]And the disciples went everywhere preaching, **the Master working right with them, validating the Message with indisputable evidence.**]

[NCV] Mark 16:15-20 Jesus said to his followers, "Go everywhere in the world, and tell the Good News to everyone. [16]Anyone who believes and is baptized will be saved, but anyone who does not believe will be punished. [17]**And those who believe will be able to do these things as proof: They will use my name to force out demons.** They will speak in new languages. [18]They will pick up snakes and drink poison without being hurt. **They will touch the sick, and the sick will be healed."** [19]After the Lord Jesus said these things to his followers, he was carried up into heaven, and he sat at the right side of God. [20]The followers went everywhere in the world and told the Good News to people, and **the Lord helped them. The Lord proved that the Good News they told was true by giving them power to work miracles.**]

[Original-NT] Mark 16:15-20 "Travel the world over," he told them, "and proclaim the News to all creation. Whoever believes and is immersed will be saved, but whoever does not believe will be condemned. [17]**And these signs shall attend those who have believed: they shall expel demons in my name**; they shall speak in tongues; [18]they shall take up snakes; if they drink anything poisonous it will not harm them; and **they shall lay hands on the sick and cure them."** [19]So then the Lord Jesus, after he had spoken to them, was taken up to heaven and sat at God's right hand. [20]But they set off and preached everywhere, **the Lord working with them and confirming the Message by the signs that authenticated it.**]

[Rotherham] <u>Mark 16:15-20</u> and he said unto them—Go ye into all the world, and proclaim the glad-message, to the whole creation: [16]He that hath believed, and been immersed, shall be saved; but, he that hath disbelieved, shall be condemned: [17]**Signs, moreover, shall follow, them who have believed, — these: —In my name, shall they cast, demons, out**, with tongues, shall they speak, —[and, in their hands,] they shall take up, serpents; [18]And, if, any deadly thing, they have drunk, in nowise, shall it, hurt, them: **Upon sick persons, shall they lay, hands, and, well, shall they remain**. [19]The Lord [Jesus], therefore, on the one hand, after talking with them, was taken up into heaven, and sat down on the right hand of God: [20]They, on the other hand, going forth, proclaimed on every side, **the Lord, co-working, and confirming, the word, through, the closely following signs.]**

[TPT] <u>Mark 16:15-20</u> And he said to them, "As you go into all the world, preach openly the wonderful news of the gospel to the entire human race! [16]Whoever believes the good news and is baptized will be saved, and whoever does not believe the good news will be condemned. [17]**And these miracle signs will accompany those who believe: They will drive out demons in the power of my name.** They will speak in tongues. [18]They will be supernaturally protected from snakes and from drinking anything poisonous. **And they will lay hands on the sick and heal them.**" [19]After saying these things, Jesus was lifted up into heaven and sat down at the place of honor at the right hand of God! [20]And the apostles went out announcing the good news everywhere, as **the Lord himself consistently worked with them, validating the message they preached with miracle-signs that accompanied them!**

[TTNT] <u>Mark 16:15-20</u> Jesus gave them this commission: "Go to every part of the world and preach the good news everywhere. [16]Whoever believes in Me and is then baptised will be saved and will be given eternal life; but whoever does not believe will remain condemned. [17]**Those who believe will perform signs to verify the truth of what they believe. They will drive out demons in My name from those who are in such bondage.** They will speak in new languages given them by the Holy Spirit. [18]Some will even pick up deadly snakes with their hands without being harmed: others will be given deadly poison to drink, but it will have no effect on them. **They will lay their hands on the sick and they will be healed.**" [19]When the Lord Jesus had finished speaking to them, they watched as He was taken up into heaven, where He took His place at God's right hand. [20]Then the disciples began to obey the commission Jesus had given them. Everywhere they went they preached the good news of all Jesus had said and done. **The Lord Himself worked with them performing the miraculous signs that verified that what they preached was the truth!**

LUKE

<u>Luke 1:13</u> But the angel said unto him, Fear not, Zacharias: **for thy prayer is heard; and thy wife Elisabeth shall bear thee a son**, and thou shalt call his name John.

[AUV-NT 2005] <u>Luke 1:13</u> But the angel said to him, "Do not be afraid Zacharias, **for your earnest prayer has been heard. Your wife Elizabeth will give birth to a son** and you will name him John.

[BWE-NT] <u>Luke 1:13</u> But the angel said, 'Do not be afraid, Zechariah. **You have been talking to God. He has heard you. Your wife Elizabeth will have a son**. Name him John.

[EEBT] <u>Luke 1:13</u> 'Zechariah, do not be afraid', the angel said to him. '**God has heard what you prayed. He will give you what you asked for. Your wife Elizabeth will have a baby boy**. You will call him John.

[NWT] <u>Luke 1:13</u> However, the angel said to him: "Do not be afraid, Zech·a·ri ah, **because your supplication has been favorably heard, and your wife Elizabeth will bear you a son**, and you are to name him John.

[Rotherham] <u>Luke 1:13</u> But the messenger said unto him—Do not fear, Zachariah! Inasmuch as **thy supplication hath been hearkened to, —and, thy wife Elizabeth, shall bring forth a son to thee**, and thou shalt call his name, John;

[TPT] <u>Luke 1:13</u> But the angel reassured him, saying, "Don't be afraid, Zechariah! God is showing grace to you. For I have come to tell you that **your prayer for a child has been answered. Your wife, Elizabeth, will bear you a son** and you are to name him John.

[TTNT] <u>Luke 1:13</u> but the angel told him: "Don't be afraid, Zechariah, for **God has heard your prayer. Your wife Elizabeth will bear you a son** who you are to call John.

[UDB] <u>Luke 1:13</u> But the angel said to him, "Zechariah, do not be afraid! When you prayed, **Yahweh heard your request. So your wife Elizabeth will bear a son for you**. You must name him John.

<u>Luke 1:37</u> For with God nothing shall be impossible.

[AMP] <u>Luke 1:37</u> For with God nothing [is or ever] shall be impossible."

[AMPC] <u>Luke 1:37</u> For with God nothing is ever impossible and no word from God shall be without power or impossible of fulfillment.

[ASV-2014] <u>Luke 1:37</u> For no word from God shall be void of power.

[AUV-NT 2003] <u>Luke 1:37</u> For nothing that God says [will happen] is impossible."

[Ballentine-NT] <u>Luke 1:37</u> For no word from God will be powerless.

[Berkeley] <u>Luke 1:37</u> For nothing is ever impossible with God.

[BWE-NT] <u>Luke 1:37</u> But God can do anything.'

[ClarkePyle] <u>Luke 1:37</u> For to God all things are equally possible and easy.

[CPDV] <u>Luke 1:37</u> For no word will be impossible with God."

[DLNT] <u>Luke 1:37</u> because no word from God will be impossible".

[EEBT] <u>Luke 1:37</u> There is nothing that God cannot do.'

[Fenton] <u>Luke 1:37</u> because no event is impossible with God!

[Folsom-Gs] <u>Luke 1:37</u> Because no word from God will be impossible.

[Harwood-NT] <u>Luke 1:37</u> For the divine power is able to effect the greatest impossibilities.

[ISV] <u>Luke 1:37</u> "Nothing is impossible with respect to any of God's promises."

[Martin-NT] <u>Luke 1:37</u> Because nothing is impossible before God. [None of God's declarations can fail.]" [can be without power].

[Moffatt] <u>Luke 1:37</u> for with God nothing is ever impossible.

[Montgomery-NT] <u>Luke 1:37</u> "For no word of God shall be void of power."

[Murdock-NT] <u>Luke 1:37</u> Because nothing is difficult for God.

[NEB] <u>Luke 1:37</u> 'for God's promises can never fail.'

[NIRV] <u>Luke 1:37</u> That's because what God says will always come true."

[NIV] <u>Luke 1:37</u> "For no word from God will ever fail."

[Original-NT] <u>Luke 1:37</u> Nothing whatever is impossible to God.

[Spencer-NT] <u>Luke 1:37</u> for with God no word shall be devoid of power.

[TPT] <u>Luke 1:37</u> "Not one promise from God is empty of power, for nothing is impossible with God!"

[TVB] <u>Luke 1:37</u> So the impossible is possible with God.

[Wilson-NT] <u>Luke 1:37</u> For "No Declaration is impossible with God."

[WMB] <u>Luke 1:37</u> "For nothing spoken by God is impossible."

[Worrell-NT] <u>Luke 1:37</u> because no word from God shall be without power.

<u>Luke 1:64</u> And his mouth was opened immediately, and his tongue loosed, and he spake, and praised God.

[Authentic-NT] <u>Luke 1:64</u> Instantly his mouth and tongue were freed of impediment and he spoke, blessing God.

[Etheridge-NT] <u>Luke 1:64</u> And immediately his mouth and his tongue were opened, and he spake, and blessed Aloha.

[GoodSpeed-NT] <u>Luke 1:64</u> And they were all amazed. Then his voice and the use of his tongue were immediately restored, and he blessed God aloud.

[ISV] <u>Luke 1:64</u> Suddenly, Zechariah could open his mouth, his tongue was set free, and he began to speak and to praise God.

[NIRV] <u>Luke 1:64</u> Right away Zechariah could speak again. Right away he praised God.

[NJB] <u>Luke 1:64</u> At that instant his power of speech returned and he spoke and praised God.

[Phillips] <u>Luke 1:64</u> Then his power of speech suddenly came back, and his first words were to thank God.

[TGNT] <u>Luke 1:64</u> Instantly his mouth was opened and his tongue [was freed], and he began to speak praises to God.

[TNT] <u>Luke 1:64</u> Immediately his speech came back and he talked freely, praising God.

[TPT] <u>Luke 1:64</u> Instantly Zechariah could speak again. And his first words were praises to the Lord.

[TVB] <u>Luke 1:64</u> They were even more surprised when, at that moment, Zacharias was able to talk again, and he shouted out praises to God.

<u>Luke 4:18</u> The Spirit of the Lord is upon me, because he hath anointed me to preach the gospel to the poor; he hath sent me to heal the brokenhearted, to preach deliverance to the captives, and recovering of sight to the blind, to set at liberty them that are bruised,

[AMPC] <u>Luke 4:18</u> The Spirit of the Lord [is] upon Me, because He has anointed Me [the Anointed One, the Messiah] to preach the good news (the Gospel) to the poor; He has sent Me to announce release to the captives and recovery of sight to the blind, to send forth as delivered those who are oppressed [who are downtrodden, bruised, crushed, and broken down by calamity],

[AUV-NT 2005] <u>Luke 4:18</u> "The Holy Spirit of the Lord is upon me, because He anointed me [i.e., specially chose me] to preach good news to poor people. He has sent me to proclaim freedom to those who are captives [i.e., to sin]; recovery of sight to the [spiritually as well as physically] blind; to set free those who are oppressed [i.e., by Satan] and

[CJB] <u>Luke 4:18</u> The Spirit of Adonai is upon me; therefore he has anointed me to announce Good News to the poor; he has sent me to proclaim freedom for the imprisoned and renewed sight for the blind, to release those who have been crushed,

[EXB] <u>Luke 4:18</u> ·The Lord has put his Spirit in me [The Spirit of the Lord is on me], because he ·appointed [anointed; at Jesus' baptism he was anointed by the Spirit as the Messiah, meaning the Anointed One] me to ·tell [proclaim; preach] the ·Good News [Gospel] to the poor. He has sent me to ·tell the captives they are free [proclaim liberty/release for the captives/prisoners] and to tell the blind that they can see again. God sent me to free ·those who have been treated unfairly [the oppressed]

[Heylyn-Gs] <u>Luke 4:18</u> "The Spirit of the Lord is upon me, because he has anointed me: he has sent me to declare glad Tidings to the Poor, to heal the Broken-hearted, to preach deliverance to the Captives, to restore Sight to the Blind, to set at liberty them who are bruised with their Chains."

[KNT] <u>Luke 4:18</u> The spirit of the Lord is upon me because he has anointed me to tell the poor the good news. He has sent me to announce release to the prisoners and sight to the blind, to set the wounded victims free,

[NLV] <u>Luke 4:18</u> The Spirit of the Lord is on Me. He has put His hand on Me to preach the Good News to poor people. He has sent Me to heal those with a sad heart. He has sent Me to tell those who are being held that they can go free. He has sent Me to make the blind to see and to free those who are held because of trouble.

[NOG] <u>Luke 4:18</u> "The Spirit of the Lord is with me. He has anointed me to tell the Good News to the poor. He has sent me to announce forgiveness to the prisoners of sin and the restoring of sight to the blind, to forgive those who have been shattered by sin,

[REM-NT] <u>Luke 4:18</u> "God's Spirit is on me because I am his anointed One to bring the Remedy to the afflicted. He has sent me to bring freedom to those held in the bondage of fear and selfishness, and a clear understanding to those blinded by Satan's lies, to exterminate oppression, to remove human brokenness,

[Rieu-Gs] <u>Luke 4:18</u> 'The Spirit of the Lord is on me, For He anointed me to bring good tidings to the poor. He has sent me to proclaim deliverance to captives, And new eyes for the blind, Setting the shattered free, And heralding an age acceptable to God.'

[Stringfellow-NT] <u>Luke 4:18</u> The Spirit of the Lord is upon me, Because he anointed me to preach good news to the poor people. He has sent me to herald release to captives and recovery of sight to blind people, To send away in a state of release shattered men,

[TGNT] <u>Luke 4:18</u> "The Spirit of the Master is upon me, because he has anointed me to announce good news to the destitute; he has commissioned me to proclaim release to the prisoners of war and recovery of sight to the blind; he has dispatched me to cancel charges against the oppressed

[Thomson] <u>Luke 4:18</u> The spirit of the Lord is upon me, for the business for which he anointed me. He hath sent me to publish glad tidings to the poor; to heal them who are broken hearted; to proclaim a deliverance to captives; and a recovery of sight, to the blind; to set at liberty the bruised;

[TPT] <u>Luke 4:18</u> "The Spirit of the Lord is upon me, and he has anointed me to be hope for the poor, freedom for the brokenhearted, and new eyes for the blind, and to preach to prisoners, 'You are set free!'

[TVB] <u>Luke 4:18</u> The Spirit of the Lord the Eternal One is on Me. Why? Because the Eternal designated Me to be His representative to the poor, to preach good news to them. He sent Me to tell those who are held captive that they can now be set free, and to tell the blind that they can now see. He sent Me to liberate those held down by oppression.

[Weymouth-NT] <u>Luke 4:18</u> [The Spirit of the Lord is upon me, because He has anointed me to proclaim Good News to the poor; He has sent me to announce release to the prisoners of war and recovery of sight to the blind: to send away free those whom tyranny has crushed,]

[Wuest-NT] <u>Luke 4:18</u> The Lord's Spirit is upon me because He anointed me, to announce good news to the poor. He has sent me on a mission to proclaim release to those held captive and recovery of sight to those who are blind, to send away in release those who are broken by calamity,

[YLT] <u>Luke 4:18</u> 'The Spirit of the Lord [is] upon me, Because He did anoint me; To proclaim good news to the poor, Sent me to heal the broken of heart, To proclaim to captives deliverance, And to blind receiving of sight, To send away the bruised with deliverance,

<u>Luke 4:35</u> And Jesus rebuked him, saying, Hold thy peace, and come out of him. And when the devil had thrown him in the midst, he came out of him, and hurt him not.

[AUV-NT 2005] <u>Luke 4:35</u> Then Jesus spoke sternly to the evil spirit [in the man], saying, "Be quiet, and come out of him." And when the evil spirit had thrown the man down in front of them, it came out of him, without causing any harm.

[BOOKS-NT] <u>Luke 4:35</u> "Be quiet!" Jesus said sternly. "Come out of him!" Then the demon threw the man down before them all and came out without injuring him.

[BSB-NT] <u>Luke 4:35</u> But Jesus rebuked the demon. "Be silent!" He said. "Come out of him!" Then the demon threw the man down before them all and came out without harming him.

[CCB] <u>Luke 4:35</u> Then Jesus said to him sharply, "Be silent and leave this man!" The evil spirit then threw the man down in front of them and came out of him without doing him harm.

[EEBT] <u>Luke 4:35</u> 'Be quiet!' Jesus replied. 'Come out of the man.' At this, the bad spirit caused the man to fall to the ground in front of the people. Then it came out without hurting him.

[EXB] <u>Luke 4:35</u> Jesus ·commanded [reprimanded; rebuked] the evil spirit, "Be quiet! Come out of the man!" The ·evil spirit [demon] threw the man down to the ground before all the people and then left the man without ·hurting [injuring] him.

[FBV-NT] <u>Luke 4:35</u> Jesus interrupted him, saying. "Be quiet!" Then he ordered the demon, "Come out of him!" Throwing him to the ground right before them, the demon left the man without injuring him.

[Fenton] <u>Luke 4:35</u> Jesus, however, repelled him, saying, "Keep silent! and go out of him!" And when the demon had thrown him down among them in convulsions, he came out of him, leaving him uninjured.

[NENT] <u>Luke 4:35</u> And Jesus censured him, saying, "Muzzle yourself and come out from him." And after tossing him out into the middle, the spirit being came out from him without hurting him.

[REM-NT] <u>Luke 4:35</u> "Silence!" Jesus said and commanded, "Leave him!" Then the demon caused the man to fall down and left him without harming him.

[TLB] <u>Luke 4:35</u> Jesus cut him short. "Be silent!" he told the demon. "Come out!" The demon threw the man to the floor as the crowd watched, and then left him without hurting him further.

<u>Luke 4:39</u> And he stood over her, and rebuked the fever; and it left her: and immediately she arose and ministered unto them.

[AMP] <u>Luke 4:39</u> Standing over her, He rebuked the fever, and it left her; and immediately she got up and began serving them [as her guests].

[AUV-NT 2003] <u>Luke 4:39</u> So, He stood over her and spoke sternly to the fever. It left her and she got up [out of bed] and began serving them.

[BV-KJV-NT] <u>Luke 4:39</u> And when He stood over her, He forbid the fever, and it left her. At once, after standing up, she was serving them.

[CB] <u>Luke 4:39</u> Jesus stood over her, and ordered the fever to leave, and it did. Immediately she got up and waited on them.

[ClarkePyle] <u>Luke 4:39</u> Then Jesus, standing by her Bed-side, commanded the Fever to depart from her. And she recovered, not slowly and by degrees, as in the course of Nature or Medicine; but immediately and at once she received her full strength, so that she arose and attended upon them at Supper.

[Fenton] <u>Luke 4:39</u> And standing over her, He arrested the fever, and it left her: and getting up at once, she attended to them.

[GNC-NT] <u>Luke 4:39</u> He drew near, bent over her, and reprimanded the fever, which thereupon left her. And all at once she rose up and waited on them.

[ICB] <u>Luke 4:39</u> He stood very close to her and commanded the fever to leave. It left her immediately, and she got up and began serving them.

[Madsen-NT] <u>Luke 4:39</u> And he went and stood by the head of her bed and commanded the fever to cease, and she was freed of it. At once she arose to serve them.

[REM-NT] <u>Luke 4:39</u> So he leaned over her and ordered her body to be well, and the fever went away. She immediately got up and began serving them.

[TNT] <u>Luke 4:39</u> Standing over her he spoke sternly to the fever, and it left her. She got up at once and attended to their needs.

[TVB] <u>Luke 4:39</u> Jesus stands over her, and just as He had rebuked the demon, He rebukes the fever, and the woman's temperature returns to normal. She feels so much better that she gets right up and cooks them all a big meal.

[UDB] <u>Luke 4:39</u> So he bent over her and commanded the fever to leave her. Immediately she became well! She got up and served them some food.

<u>Luke 4:40-41</u> Now when the sun was setting, all they that had any sick with divers diseases brought them unto him; and **he laid his hands on every one of them, and healed them.** [41]**And devils also came out of many,** crying out, and saying, Thou art Christ the Son of God. And he rebuking them suffered them not to speak: for they knew that he was Christ.

[AMPC] <u>Luke 4:40-41</u> Now at the setting of the sun [indicating the end of the Sabbath], all those who had any [who were] sick with various diseases brought them to Him, and **He laid His hands upon every one of them and cured them.** [41]**And demons even came out of many people,** screaming and crying out, You are the Son of God! But He rebuked them and would not permit them to speak, because they knew that He was the Christ (the Messiah).

[AUV-NT 2003] <u>Luke 4:40-41</u> And when the sun was setting, everyone who had friends or relatives who were sick with various diseases brought them to Jesus and **He placed His hands on each one of them and healed them.** [41]**And evil spirits also came out of many people,** shouting [at Him], "You are the Son of God." And Jesus spoke sternly to them and would not allow them to speak [anymore] because they knew He was the Christ.

[Barclay-NT] <u>Luke 4:40-41</u> When the sun was setting, everyone who had friends who were ill with all kinds of troubles brought them to Jesus, and **he laid his hands on each of them, and cured them.** [41]**Demons too went out of many people,** shouting: 'You are the Son of God.' He reprimanded them, and would not allow them to speak, because they knew that he was the Messiah.

[Dillard-NT] <u>Luke 4:40-41</u> Now when the sun was setting, all they that had any sick with divers diseases brought them unto him; and **he laid his hands on every one of them, and healed them.** [41]**And devils**

also came out of many, crying out, and saying, Thou art the Anointed Son of God. And he rebuking them suffered them not to speak: for they knew that he was the Anointed.

[ICB] <u>Luke 4:40-41</u> When the sun went down, the people brought their sick to Jesus. They had many different diseases. **Jesus put his hands on each sick person and healed every one of them.** [41]Demons **came out of many people.** The demons would shout, "You are the Son of God." But Jesus gave a strong command for the demons not to speak. They knew Jesus was the Christ.

[Mace-NT] <u>Luke 4:40-41</u> As soon as the sun was set, all sorts of diseased persons were brought before him by their friends, and **he healed them all, by laying his hands upon them.** [41]many were **dispossessed of the demons,** who cried aloud, you are the Messiah, the son of God. but he rebuked them, and would not suffer them to declare, that they knew him to be the Messiah.

[MSG] <u>Luke 4:40-41</u> When the sun went down, everyone who had anyone sick with some ailment or other brought them to him. **One by one he placed his hands on them and healed them.** [41]Demons **left in droves,** screaming, "Son of God! You're the Son of God!" But he shut them up, refusing to let them speak because they knew too much, knew him to be the Messiah.

[NLT] <u>Luke 4:40-41</u> As the sun went down that evening, people throughout the village brought sick family members to Jesus. **No matter what their diseases were, the touch of his hand healed every one.** [41]**Many were possessed by demons; and the demons came out at his command,** shouting, "You are the Son of God!" But because they knew he was the Messiah, he rebuked them and refused to let them speak.

[Phillips] <u>Luke 4:40-41</u> Then, as the sun was setting, all those who had friends suffering from every kind of disease brought them to Jesus and **he laid his hands on each one of them separately and healed them.** [41]**Evil spirits came out of many of these people,** shouting, 'You are the Son of God!' But he spoke sharply to them and would not allow them to say any more, for they knew perfectly well that he was Christ.

[REM-NT] <u>Luke 4:40-41</u> At sunset the people brought to Jesus those suffering with a variety of illnesses and disabilities. **He laid hands on them and healed them all.** [41]**Not only that, but from many he commanded demons to leave** and they left shouting, "You are God the Son!" But he gave them firm instructions to be silent and would not grant them permission to speak, because they knew he was the Messiah.

[T4T] <u>Luke 4:40-41</u> When the sun was setting that day, and the restriction about not traveling on the Sabbath/on the Jewish rest day was ended, many people whose friends or relatives were sick or who had various diseases brought them to Jesus. **He put his hands on them and healed all of them.** [41]**He also was expelling demons from many people.** As the demons left those people, they shouted to Jesus, "You are the Son of God/the one who is God and man!" But he rebuked those demons and would not allow them to tell people about him, because they knew that he was the Messiah, and for various reasons he did not want everyone to know that yet.

[TPT] <u>Luke 4:40-41</u> At sunset, the people brought all those who were sick to Jesus to be healed. **Jesus laid his hands on them one by one, and they were all healed of different ailments and sicknesses.** [41]**Demons also came out of many of them.** The demons knew that Jesus was the Anointed One, so they shouted while coming out, "You are the Messiah, the Son of El Shaddai!" But Jesus rebuked them and commanded them to be silent.

[TVB] <u>Luke 4:40-41</u> By this time, it's just before nightfall, and as the sun sets, groups of families, friends, and bystanders come until a huge crowd has gathered. Each group has brought along family members or friends who are sick with any number of diseases. One by one, **Jesus lays His hands on**

them and heals them. [41]On several occasions, demonic spirits are expelled from these people, after shouting at Jesus, "You are the Son of God!" Jesus always rebukes them and tells them to be quiet. They know He is the Anointed One, but He doesn't want to be acclaimed in this way.

[TWTY-RCT-NT-V1] <u>Luke 4:40-41</u> Moreover, at the time when the sun was setting and going down, everyone, individually and collectively, who had and held, acquired and received, owned and possessed any person who was sick and weak, ill and feeble with various and diverse, intricate and complex, difficult and abstruse, manifold and unstable, foreign and alien, new, unknown and unheard of sicknesses and severe illnesses, bodily suffering and physical distresses, took and led, guided and directed them to Him for His advantage. And **having laid and set, placed and put His hands on each and every single one of them, He willingly served, healed and cured them. [41]Not only that, but demons, the fallen messengers and envoys, were also coming out from and departed, leaving and proceeding to go from many numerous and a large amount of people, becoming separated from them,** crying out loud and shouting, screaming and yelling loudly, exclaiming and shrieking, and saying and teaching, maintaining and exhorting, advising and directing, affirming and pointing out that concerning this, "You are and exist as the Son of God!" And He was rebuking and admonishing, rating and chiding, reproving and censuring, punishing and warning, charging, evaluating and denouncing them, not suffering or letting, allowing or permitting them to speak, chatter or babble, for concerning this, they had seen and perceived, observed and witnessed, knew and experienced, recognised and respected, understood and took note of, comprehended and discerned, paid attention to and discovered, noticed and examined, inspected and beheld that He was and existed as the Anointed Messiah.

[Wuest-NT] <u>Luke 4:40-41</u> Now, when the sun was setting, all, as many as had those who were sick with various kinds of diseases, chronic cases, brought them to Him. **And having laid His hands upon one after another separately, He healed them. [41]And there also came out demons from many,** shouting out and saying, As for you, you are the Son of God. And rebuking them with a rebuke that did not elicit an acknowledgment of guilt or repentance, He was not permitting them to be speaking, because they knew Him to be the Christ.

<u>Luke 5:13</u> And he put forth his hand, and touched him, saying, I will: be thou clean. And immediately the leprosy departed from him.

[BBE] <u>Luke 5:13</u> And he put out his hand to him and said, It is my pleasure; be clean. And straight away his disease went from him.

[BWE-NT] <u>Luke 5:13</u> Jesus put out his hand and touched the man. He said, 'I want you to be healed.' Right away the man was free from leprosy.

[CWB] <u>Luke 5:13</u> Jesus reached out, touched him and said, "I do want to heal you. Be clean." Immediately the leprosy left him.

[Etheridge-NT] <u>Luke 5:13</u> And Jeshu extended his hand, touched him, and said to him, I am willing; be clean. And in an instant his leprosy went from him.

[GT] <u>Luke 5:13</u> Jesus said, "I do want to heal you—be healed!" Then Jesus stretched out his hand and touched the man. The leprosy disappeared immediately.

[ICB] <u>Luke 5:13</u> Jesus said, "I want to. Be healed!" And Jesus touched the man. Immediately the disease disappeared.

[Jerusalem] <u>Luke 5:13</u> Jesus stretched out his hand, touched him and said, 'Of course I want to! Be cured!' And the leprosy left him at once.

[Johnson-NT] <u>Luke 5:13</u> Contrary to popular practice, Jesus touched the leper with his hand, saying, "I want you to become whole." At once the leprosy disappeared.

[NEB] <u>Luke 5:13</u> Jesus stretched out his hand, touched him, and said, 'Indeed I will; be clean again.' The leprosy left him immediately.

[NENT] <u>Luke 5:13</u> And stretching out his hand, he touched him, saying, "I want it. Be cleansed." And immediately the leprosy left him.

[NLT] <u>Luke 5:13</u> Jesus reached out and touched him. "I am willing," he said. "Be healed!" And instantly the leprosy disappeared.

[Original-NT] <u>Luke 5:13</u> Stretching out his hand he touched him saying, "I do will it. Be cleansed!" At once his leprosy left him.

[REM-NT] <u>Luke 5:13</u> Jesus didn't hesitate but touched the man and said, "I am glad to. Be clean!" And instantly the leprosy was gone.

[T4T] <u>Luke 5:13</u> Then Jesus, disregarding the religious law that forbade people to come close to lepers, reached out his hand and touched the man. He said, "I am willing to heal you; and I heal you now!" Immediately the man was healed. He was no longer a leper!

[TLB] <u>Luke 5:13</u> Jesus reached out and touched the man and said, "Of course I will. Be healed." And the leprosy left him instantly!

[TPT] <u>Luke 5:13</u> Jesus reached out and touched him and said, "Of course I am willing to heal you, and now you will be healed." Instantly the leprous sores were healed and his skin became smooth.

[TTNT] <u>Luke 5:13</u> Jesus reached out and laid His hand on the man and said: "Of course I want to: Be healed!" And immediately he was cleansed from his leprosy.

[TVB] <u>Luke 5:13</u> Jesus reaches out His hand and touches the man, something no one would normally do for fear of being infected or of becoming ritually unclean. Jesus: I want to heal you. Be cleansed! Immediately the man is cured.

[Tyndale21-NT] <u>Luke 5:13</u> And he put out his hand, and touched him, saying, I want you to be healthy. And immediately the leprosy left him.

[WMB] <u>Luke 5:13</u> He stretched out his hand, and touched him, saying, "I want to. Be made clean." Immediately the leprosy left him.

[Wuest-NT] <u>Luke 5:13</u> And having stretched forth His hand, He touched him, saying at the same time, My heart desires it. Be cleansed at once. And instantly the leprosy left him.

<u>Luke 5:15</u> But so much the more went there a fame abroad of him: and **great multitudes came together to hear, and to be healed by him of their infirmities**.

[AUV-NT 2003] <u>Luke 5:15</u> But the news about what Jesus had done spread all the more widely, so that **large crowds assembled to listen to Him and to be healed of their sicknesses**.

[BBE] <u>Luke 5:15</u> But news of him went out all the more, in every direction, and **great numbers of people came together to give hearing to his words and to be made well from their diseases**.

[BOOKS-NT] <u>Luke 5:15</u> Yet the news about him spread all the more, so that **crowds of people came to hear him and to be healed of their sicknesses**.

[CEV] <u>Luke 5:15</u> News about Jesus kept spreading. **Large crowds came to listen to him teach and to be healed of their diseases**.

[CPDV] <u>Luke 5:15</u> Yet word of him traveled around all the more. And **great crowds came together, so that they might listen and be cured by him from their infirmities.**

[NLT] <u>Luke 5:15</u> But despite Jesus' instructions, the report of his power spread even faster, and **vast crowds came to hear him preach and to be healed of their diseases.**

[T4T] <u>Luke 5:15</u> But many people heard the man's report of what Jesus had done. The result was that **large crowds came to Jesus to hear his message and to be healed of their sicknesses {so that he would heal their sicknesses}.**

[TLB] <u>Luke 5:15</u> Now the report of his power spread even faster and **vast crowds came to hear him preach and to be healed of their diseases.**

[TTNT] <u>Luke 5:15</u> Nevertheless, the news of this event spread rapidly. As a result, **crowds came to hear Jesus preach and to be healed of their afflictions.**

[UDB] <u>Luke 5:15</u> But many people heard about how Jesus had healed the man. The result was that **large crowds came to Jesus to hear him teach and to have him heal them from their sicknesses.**

<u>Luke 5:17</u> And it came to pass on a certain day, as he was teaching, that there were Pharisees and doctors of the law sitting by, which were come out of every town of Galilee, and Judaea, and Jerusalem: and **the power of the Lord was present to heal them.**

[AMP] <u>Luke 5:17</u> One day as He was teaching, there were Pharisees and teachers of the Law sitting there who had come from every village of Galilee and Judea and from Jerusalem. And **the power of the Lord was present with Him to heal.**

[AUV-NT 2005] <u>Luke 5:17</u> And it happened on one of those days [in Capernaum.], as Jesus was teaching, that some Pharisees [i.e., a strict sect of the Jewish religion] and teachers of the Law of Moses, who had come from every village of Galilee and Judea and from Jerusalem, were sitting around [i.e., listening to Him]. And **the power of the Lord was with Him, enabling Him to heal people.**

[BSB-NT] <u>Luke 5:17</u> One day Jesus was teaching, and the Pharisees and teachers of the law were sitting there. People had come from Jerusalem and from every village of Galilee and Judea, and **the power of the Lord was present for Him to heal the sick.**

[CSB] <u>Luke 5:17</u> On one of those days while he was teaching, Pharisees and teachers of the law were sitting there who had come from every village of Galilee and Judea, and also from Jerusalem. And **the Lord's power to heal was in him.**

[Etheridge-NT] <u>Luke 5:17</u> And it was on one of the days, while Jeshu was teaching, (certain) Pharishee and doctors of the law were sitting. And they had come from all the villages of Galila and of Jehud, and from Urishlem: and **the power of the Lord was (there) to heal them.**

[Moffatt-NT 1917] <u>Luke 5:17</u> One day he was teaching, and near him sat Pharisees and doctors of the Law who had come from every village of Galilee and Judaea as well as from Jerusalem. Now **the power of the Lord was present for the work of healing.**

[MSG] <u>Luke 5:17</u> One day as he was teaching, Pharisees and religion teachers were sitting around. They had come from nearly every village in Galilee and Judea, even as far away as Jerusalem, to be there. **The healing power of God was on him.**

[NASB] <u>Luke 5:17</u> One day He was teaching; and there were some Pharisees and teachers of the law sitting there, who had come from every village of Galilee and Judea and from Jerusalem; and **the power of the Lord was present for Him to perform healing.**

[Original-NT] <u>Luke 5:17</u> It happened one day when he was teaching that there were Pharisees and doctors of the Law sitting there, who had come from various Galilean villages, and from Judea and Jerusalem. **He was exercising the Lord's curative power**.

[Rieu-Gs] <u>Luke 5:17</u> One day, surrounded by Pharisees and Lawyers from Jerusalem and every town in Galilee and Judaea, he was teaching and **in full possession of the healing power of God**, when some men arrived, carrying on a couch a paralytic whom they wanted to bring in and lay down before him.

[SPV] <u>Luke 5:17</u> Now it happened on one of the days, that he was teaching, and Pharisees and teachers of the law were sitting [there], who had come from every village of Galilee and [from] Judea and Jerusalem; and **[the] power of [the] Lord was present for the purpose of healing them**.

[TCNT] <u>Luke 5:17</u> On one of those days, when Jesus was teaching, some Pharisees and Doctors of the Law were sitting near by. (They had come from all the villages in Galilee and Judea, and from Jerusalem; and **the power of the Lord was upon Jesus, so that he could work cures.)**

[TTNT] <u>Luke 5:17</u> One day while Jesus was teaching, a number of Pharisees and teachers of the religious law were present. They had come from all over Galilee and from Judea and Jerusalem. **The anointing of God's power was obviously present for Jesus to heal the sick**.

[Wilson-NT] <u>Luke 5:17</u> And it occurred on one of the Days, he was teaching, and the Pharisees and Teachers of the Law were sitting near, having come out of Every Village of Galilee, and of Judea, and from Jerusalem; **and the Mighty Power of the Lord was on him to Cure**.

<u>Luke 5:24-25</u> But that ye may know that the Son of man hath power upon earth to forgive sins, (he said unto the sick of the palsy,) **I say unto thee, Arise, and take up thy couch, and go into thine house.** [25]**And immediately he rose up before them**, and took up that whereon he lay, and departed to his own house, glorifying God.

[ASV] <u>Luke 5:24-25</u> But that ye may know that the Son of man hath authority on earth to forgive sins (he said unto him that was palsied), **I say unto thee, Arise, and take up thy couch, and go unto thy house.** [25]**And immediately he rose up before them,** and took up that whereon he lay, and departed to his house, glorifying God.

[BOOKS-NT] <u>Luke 5:24-25</u> But I want you to know that the Son of Man has authority on earth to forgive sins." So he said to the paralyzed man, **"I tell you, get up, take your mat and go home."** [25]**Immediately he stood up in front of them**, took what he had been lying on and went home praising God.

[CEV] <u>Luke 5:24-25</u> But now you will see that the Son of Man has the right to forgive sins here on earth." Jesus then said to the man, **"Get up! Pick up your mat and walk home."** [25]**At once the man stood up in front of everyone**. He picked up his mat and went home, giving thanks to God.

[EEBT] <u>Luke 5:24-25</u> Now I will show you that I, the Son of Man, have authority on earth. I can forgive people for the bad things that they have done. I will show you that I can forgive them.' Then he turned to the man that could not move his legs. **'I say to you', he said, 'stand up. Take up your carpet and go home!'** [25]**Immediately, the man stood up in front of them**. He took the carpet that he had used to lie on. He went home. 'How great and powerful God is', he was saying.

[GNC-NT] <u>Luke 5:24-25</u> Things turned out the way they did in order that you should be made to realize that the Son of Man, while he is on the earth, has the authority granted to him to forgive sins. He then turned to the paralyzed man. **"I am telling you,"** he said, **"to rise to your feet, to lift your bed, and to make your way home."** [25]**Without the least delay the man got up**, in full view of them all, lifted up his bedding, and went home, praising God.

[Madsen-NT] <u>Luke 5:24-25</u> But you shall see that the Son of Man has the power to release Man from sin here on the earth.' And so he said to the paralysed man, '**I say to you, stand up, take your stretcher and go home.'** ²⁵**And at once he stood up in the sight of them all**, took the pallet on which he had been lying and went home, praising God.

[REM-NT] <u>Luke 5:24-25</u> So that there can be no confusion and that you may know without a doubt that the Son of Man has the authority to abolish and remove sin…"—turning to the paralyzed man, he continued—"**follow my instructions: Stand up, pick up your mat, and walk home."** ²⁵**Instantly he was healed and jumped up in front of them**, picked up the mat he had been lying upon, and went home praising God.

[T4T] <u>Luke 5:24-25</u> But as a result of my healing this man you will know that God has authorized me, the one who came from heaven, to forgive the sins of people while I am on the earth, **as well as to heal people." Then he said to the man who was paralyzed, "To you I say, 'Get up, pick up your sleeping pad, and go home!'"** ²⁵**Immediately the man was healed He got up in front of them**. He picked up the sleeping pad on which he had been lying, and he went home, praising God.

[TGNT] <u>Luke 5:24-25</u> But just so you can see that the Human One has jurisdiction on earth to release faults…" Jesus turned to the paralyzed person: "**I tell you, get up, pick up your stretcher and go home!"** ²⁵**Instantly he got up in front of them**, picked up the stretcher he had been put upon, and went home praising God.

[TPT] <u>Luke 5:24-25</u> "To prove to you all that I, the Son of Man, have the lawful authority on earth to forgive sins, **I say to you now, stand up! Carry your stretcher and go on home, for you are healed."** ²⁵**In an instant, the man rose right before their eyes**. He stood, picked up his stretcher, and went home, giving God all the glory with every step he took.

[TVB] <u>Luke 5:24-25</u> Just so you'll know that the Son of Man is fully authorized to forgive sins on earth (He turned to the paralyzed fellow lying on the pallet), **I say, get up, take your mat, and go home.** ²⁵**Then, right in front of their eyes, the man stood up**, picked up his bed, and left to go home—full of praises for God!

<u>Luke 6:10</u> And looking round about upon them all, he said unto the man, **Stretch forth thy hand. And he did so: and his hand was restored whole as the other**.

[AUV-NT 2003] <u>Luke 6:10</u> Then He looked around at all of them [there] and said to the man, "**Reach out your hand." And [when] he did this, his hand was restored [to normal use]**.

[Barclay-NT] <u>Luke 6:10</u> His gaze swept round them all. '**Stretch out your hand,' he said to the man. The man did so, and his hand was restored to health**.

[CWB] <u>Luke 6:10</u> After looking around and waiting for an answer, He turned back to the man and said, "**Stretch out your shriveled arm." As the man made an effort to obey, suddenly his arm was completely healed**.

[GW] <u>Luke 6:10</u> He looked around at all of them and then said to the man, "**Hold out your hand." The man did so, and his hand became normal again**.

[Harwood-NT] <u>Luke 6:10</u> Jesus looking around them with a mixture of pity and indignation at their perverseness and obstinacy, said to the man, **extend thine hand—He extended it—and it was instantly restored to the same perfect state as the other**.

[LDB-NT] <u>Luke 6:10</u> After looking around at each one of them, He said to the man, "**Stretch out your hand." And when he did so, it was restored, just as full of life and strength as the other!**

[NCV] <u>Luke 6:10</u> Jesus looked around at all of them and said to the man, **"Hold out your hand." The man held out his hand, and it was healed.**

[TLB] <u>Luke 6:10</u> He looked around at them one by one and then said to the man, "**Reach out your hand." And as he did, it became completely normal again.**

[TPT] <u>Luke 6:10</u> One by one Jesus looked into the eyes of each person in the room. Then he said to the man, "**Stretch out your arm and open your hand!" With everyone watching intently, he stretched out his arm, and his hand was completely healed!**

[TVB] <u>Luke 6:10</u> He turned His gaze to each of them, one at a time. Then He spoke to the man. Jesus: **Stretch your hand out. As the man did, his deformed hand was made normal again.**

[Worsley-NT] <u>Luke 6:10</u> And looking round upon them all, He said to the man, **Stretch out thine hand: and he did so, and his hand was made as sound as the other.**

<u>Luke 6:17-19</u> And he came down with them, and stood in the plain, and the company of his disciples, and a great multitude of people out of all Judaea and Jerusalem, and from the sea coast of Tyre and Sidon, which came to hear him, and to be healed of their diseases; [18]And they that were vexed with unclean spirits: and they were healed. [19]And the whole multitude sought to touch him: for there went virtue out of him, and healed them all.

[AMP] <u>Luke 6:17-19</u> Then Jesus came down with them and stood on a level place; and there was a large crowd of His disciples, and a vast multitude of people from all over Judea and Jerusalem and the coastal region of Tyre and Sidon, [18]who had come to listen to Him and to be healed of their diseases. Even those who were troubled by unclean spirits (demons) were being healed. [19]All the people were trying to touch Him, because [healing] power was coming from Him and healing them all.

[Bowes-NT] <u>Luke 6:17-19</u> And descending with them, he stood upon a level place, and a crowd of his disciples, and a great number of the people from all Judea, and Jerusalem, and the maritime coasts of Tyre and Sidon, who came to hear him, and to be healed of their diseases. [18]And those that were harassed with unclean spirits were cured. [19]And all the crowd sought to touch him: for power went out from him and healed all.

[Campbell-Gs] <u>Luke 6:17-19</u> Afterward, Jesus coming down with them, stopped in the plain, whither a company of his disciples, with a vast multitude from all parts of Judea, Jerusalem, and the maritime country of Tyre and Sidon, were come to hear him, and to be healed of their diseases. [18]Those also who were infested with unclean spirits, came and were cured. [19]And every one strove to touch him, because a virtue came from him, which healed them all.

[CWB] <u>Luke 6:17-19</u> After Jesus had commissioned them, they came down from the hill country to the plains below. Soon they were surrounded by great crowds of people who had come from Judea, Jerusalem, and as far away as Tyre and Sidon on the coast to see and hear Jesus. Many of them wanted to be healed. [18]Among them were some who were demon possessed. They, too, wanted Jesus to heal them, and He did. [19]Many believed that if they could just touch Him, they would be healed, and they were. In fact, before the day was over there was not a sick person in the whole crowd.

[ICB] <u>Luke 6:17-19</u> Jesus and the apostles came down from the mountain. Jesus stood on level ground where there was a large group of his followers. Also, there were many people from all around Judea, Jerusalem, and the seacoast cities of Tyre and Sidon. [18]They all came to hear Jesus teach and to be healed of their sicknesses. He healed those who were troubled by evil spirits. [19]All the people were trying to touch Jesus, because power was coming from him and healing them all!

[Lamsa] <u>Luke 6:17-19</u> And Jesus went down with them and stood up in the plain; and a large group of his disciples and a large crowd of people from all over Judea and from Jerusalem and from the sea coast of Tyre and Sidon came to hear his word and to be healed of their diseases; [18]And those who were suffering from unclean spirits were healed. [19]And all the people wanted to touch him, because power proceeded from him, and he healed them all.

[Mace-NT] <u>Luke 6:17-19</u> At length he came down the hill with them, and stayed with the rest of his disciples in the plain, where a great multitude of people from all Judea, from Jerusalem, and the maritime country of Tyre and Sidon, came to hear him, and to have their diseases cured. [18]many that were tormented by evil spirits came likewise, and were cured. [19]so that all the people strove to touch him: for a divine virtue flowed from him, which healed them all.

[Madsen-NT] <u>Luke 6:17-19</u> Then he came down with them until he was standing on a level place. A great number of his disciples surrounded him, together with a large crowd from the whole of Judea and Jerusalem and from the coastal regions of Tyre and Sidon who had come to hear him and to be healed of their diseases. [18]Those who were plagued by unclean spirits were also cured. [19]And the whole crowd yearned to touch him because living power radiated from him, and he healed them all.

[Moffatt] <u>Luke 6:17-19</u> With them he came down the hill and stood on a level spot. There was a great company of his disciples with him, and a large multitude of people from all Judea, from Jerusalem, and from the coast of Tyre and Sidon, who had come to hear him and to get cured of their diseases. [18]Those who were annoyed with unclean spirits also were healed. [19]Indeed the whole of the crowd made efforts to touch him, for power issued from him and cured everybody.

[Montgomery-NT] <u>Luke 6:17-19</u> With these he came down till he reached a level place, where there was a great crowd of his disciples and a great many people from all Judea and Jerusalem and from the seacoast of Tyre and Sidon. These came to hear him, and to be healed of their diseases. [18]Those who were tormented by unclean spirits were healed also. [19]The whole crowd were trying to touch him, because power emanated from him and cured them all.

[Original-NT] <u>Luke 6:17-19</u> Descending with them he stood on a level space with a large body of his disciples, and a mass of the people drawn from all over Judea, from Jerusalem, and from the seaboard of Tyre and Sidon, who had come to hear him and to be cured of their diseases; [18]and those who were troubled with foul spirits were given relief. [19]Indeed, the whole crowd tried to touch him, because power emanated from him and cured everyone.

[TPT] <u>Luke 6:17-19</u> Jesus and his apostles came down from the hillside to a level field, where a large number of his disciples waited, along with a massive crowd of people who had gathered from all over Judea, Jerusalem, and the coastal district of Tyre and Sidon. [18]They had all come to listen to the Manifestation so that they could be healed of their diseases and be set free from the demonic powers that tormented them. [19]The entire crowd eagerly tried to come near Jesus so they could touch him and be healed, because a tangible supernatural power emanated from him, healing all who came close to him.

[TTNT] <u>Luke 6:17-19</u> When Jesus came down from the hillside with them, He stood on a level area to address a crowd of His disciples and a large number of people who had come from all over Judea, including Jerusalem, and from the coastal region of Tyre and Sidon. [18]They went to hear Him preach and to be healed from their various diseases. Those who had been afflicted by evil spirits were set free and healed. [19]Everyone wanted to touch Him because God's power flowed out of Him and healed them all.

<u>Luke 7:9-10</u> When Jesus heard these things, he marvelled at him, and turned him about, and said unto the people that followed him, I say unto you, **I have not found so great faith, no, not in Israel. [10]And they that were sent, returning to the house, found the servant whole that had been sick.**

[Barclay-NT] <u>Luke 7:9-10</u> Jesus was astonished to hear this. He turned to the crowd which was following him. 'I tell you,' he said, '**not even in Israel have I met a faith like this.**' [10]**When those who had been sent returned to the house, they found the slave in perfect health.**

[Beck] <u>Luke 7:9-10</u> Surprised to hear him say this, Jesus turned to the crowd following Him. "I tell you," He said, "**not even in Israel have I found such faith.**" [10]**When the men who had been sent went back to the house, they found the slave well again.**

[ERV] <u>Luke 7:9-10</u> When Jesus heard this, he was amazed. He turned to the people following him and said, "**I tell you, this is the most faith I have seen anywhere, even in Israel.**" [10]**The group that was sent to Jesus went back to the house. There they found that the servant was healed.**

[Fenton] <u>Luke 7:9-10</u> When Jesus heard this, He was astonished at it; and, turning round to the crowd who followed Him, He said, "**Not even in Israel, I tell you, have I found faith so strong.**" [10]**The messengers, returning then to the house, found the boy quite well.**

[ICB] <u>Luke 7:9-10</u> When Jesus heard this, he was amazed. He turned to the crowd following him and said, "**I tell you, this is the greatest faith I have seen anywhere, even in Israel.**" [10]**The men who had been sent to Jesus went back to the house. There they found that the servant was healed.**

[IRENT] <u>Luke 7:9-10</u> And when Yeshua heard these things, he was appalled at the centurion. He turned to the crowd that followed him, And said: "**I am telling you: No, not even in the whole Yisrael have I found such deep trust!**" [10]**And the centurion's friends who had been sent out returned to the house and found the servant in good health.**

[KNT] <u>Luke 7:9-10</u> When Jesus heard this he was astonished. 'Let me tell you,' he said, turning to the crowd that was following him, '**I haven't found faith of this kind, even in Israel.**' [10]**The people who had been sent to him went back to the house. There they found the slave in good health.**

[Mace-NT] <u>Luke 7:9-10</u> when Jesus heard this, he admired the man, and turning about, he said to the people, that followed him, **I assure you, I have not met with such an instance of faith even among the Jews themselves.** [10]**and they that were sent, being returned to the house, they found the servant, who had been sick, in good health.**

[MSG] <u>Luke 7:9-10</u> Taken aback, Jesus addressed the accompanying crowd: "**I've yet to come across this kind of simple trust anywhere in Israel, the very people who are supposed to know about God and how he works.**" [10]**When the messengers got back home, they found the servant up and well.**

[REM-NT] <u>Luke 7:9-10</u> When Jesus heard the confidence in him, he was deeply moved, and turning to the crowd, said, "**I tell you plainly, I haven't found another person in Israel whose confidence in me is as great as his.**" [10]**Then the men who had been sent went back to the house and found the servant completely well.**

[T4T] <u>Luke 7:9-10</u> When the officer's friends arrived and told that to Jesus, he marveled at what the officer had said. Then he turned and said to the crowd that was going with him, "**I tell you, I have never before found anyone who trusted in me like this non-Jewish man does. No one from Israel, where I would expect people to believe in me, has trusted in me like he has!**" [10]**When those men returned to the officer's house, they found that the slave was well.**

[TLB] <u>Luke 7:9-10</u> Jesus was amazed. Turning to the crowd he said, "**Never among all the Jews in Israel have I met a man with faith like this.**" [10]**And when the captain's friends returned to his house, they found the slave completely healed.**

[TPT] <u>Luke 7:9-10</u> Jesus marveled at this. He turned around and said to the crowd who had followed him, "**Listen, everyone! Never have I found even one among the people of God a man like this**

who believes so strongly in me." [10]Jesus then spoke the healing word from a distance. When the man's friends returned to the home, they found the servant completely healed and doing fine.

[TVB] <u>Luke 7:9-10</u> Jesus was deeply impressed when He heard this. He turned to the crowd that followed Him. Jesus: Listen, everyone. **This outsider, this Roman, has more faith than I have found even among our own Jewish people. [10]The friends of the Centurion returned home, and they found the slave was completely healed.**

[UDB] <u>Luke 7:9-10</u> When Jesus heard what the officer had said, he was amazed at him. Then he turned to the crowd that was with him and said, "**I tell you, I have not found any Israelite who trusts me as much as this Gentile does!" [10]When those people who had come from the centurion returned to his house, they found out that the slave was in good health again.**

<u>Luke 7:12-15</u> Now when he came nigh to the gate of the city, behold, there was a dead man carried out, the only son of his mother, and she was a widow: and much people of the city was with her. [13]And when the Lord saw her, he had compassion on her, and said unto her, Weep not. [14]And he came and touched the bier: and they that bare him stood still. **And he said, Young man, I say unto thee, Arise. [15]And he that was dead sat up, and began to speak.** And he delivered him to his mother.

[BOOKS-NT] <u>Luke 7:12-15</u> As he approached the town gate, a dead person was being carried out— the only son of his mother, and she was a widow. And a large crowd from the town was with her. [13]When the Lord saw her, his heart went out to her and he said, "Don't cry." [14]Then he went up and touched the bier they were carrying him on, and the bearers stood still. He said, "**Young man, I say to you, get up!**" [15]**The dead man sat up and began to talk**, and Jesus gave him back to his mother.

[ECB] <u>Luke 7:12-15</u> and he approaches the gate of the city, and behold, a dead man being carried out— the only birthed son of his mother; and she is a widow: and a sufficient multitude of the city is with her. [13]And Adonay sees her, and has a sympathetic spleen on her, and says to her, Weep not! [14]—and he comes and touches the coffin and they who bear him stand. And he says, **Youth, I word to you, Rise! [15]—and the dead sits, and begins to speak**: and he gives him to his mother.

[Elkhazen-NT] <u>Luke 7:12-15</u> And when he came near to the gate of the city, behold a dead man was carried out, the only son of his mother; and she was a widow: and a great multitude of the city was with her. [13]Whom when the Lord had seen, being moved with mercy toward her, he said to her: Weep not. [14]And he came near and touched the coffin. And they who carried it, stood still. **And he said: Young man, I say to you, arise. [15]And he who was dead, sat up, and began to speak.** And he gave him to his mother.

[FHV-NT] <u>Luke 7:12-15</u> He came near the gate of the village, and look! A mother's only son had died, and was being carried out. She was a widow, and a large crowd was with her. [13]When the Lord saw her, his heart went out to her, and he said, "Do not weep." [14]He approached the coffin, and touched it, while the ones carrying it stood still. **Jesus commanded, "Young man, arise." [15]He sat up and began to talk,** and Jesus gave him to his mother.

[T4T] <u>Luke 7:12-15</u> As they approached the town gate, the corpse of a young man who had just died was being carried out on a stretcher {people were carrying out on a stretcher the corpse of a young man who had just died}. His mother was a widow, and he was her only son. A large group of people from the town were accompanying them. [13]When the Lord saw her, he pitied her. He said to her, "Do not cry!" [14]Then, ignoring the Jewish laws about not coming near a corpse, he came close and touched the stretcher on which the body was lying. So the men carrying it stood still. He said, "**Young man, I say to you, get up!" [15]The man sat up and began to talk!** Jesus returned him to his mother to care for her.

[TCNT] <u>Luke 7:12-15</u> Just as he approached the gate of the town, there was a dead man being carried out for burial—an only son, and his mother was a widow. A large number of the people of the town were with her. [13]When he saw her, the Master was moved with compassion for her, and he said to her: "Do not weep." [14]Then he went up and touched the bier, and the bearers stopped; and Jesus said: **"Young man, I am speaking to you—Rise!" [15]The dead man sat up and began to talk**, and Jesus restored him to his mother.

[TPT] <u>Luke 7:12-15</u> As he approached the village, he met a multitude of people in a funeral procession, who were mourning as they carried the body of a young man to the cemetery. The boy was his mother's only son and she was a widow. [13]When the Lord saw the grieving mother, his heart broke for her. With great tenderness he said to her, "Please don't cry." [14]Then he stepped up to the coffin and touched it. When the pallbearers came to a halt, Jesus said to the corpse, **"Young man, I say to you, arise and live!" [15]Immediately, the young man moved, sat up, and spoke to those nearby**. Jesus presented the son to his mother, alive!

[TTNT] <u>Luke 7:12-15</u> The funeral procession of a widow's only son was passing through the town gate as Jesus approached. [13]When the Lord saw the woman, His heart was filled with compassion for her and He said to her: "Don't cry." [14]Then He went to the coffin and touched it. Shocked, those carrying it stood still. "Young man," **Jesus said, "I command you to rise up!" [15]Immediately the dead man sat up and began speaking**. Then Jesus restored him to his mother.

[TVB] <u>Luke 7:12-15</u> He was coming near the gate of the city as a corpse was being carried out. This man was the only child and support of his widowed mother, and she was accompanied by a large funeral crowd. [13]As soon as the Lord saw her, He felt compassion for her. Jesus: Don't weep. [14]Then He came to the stretcher, and those carrying it stood still. Jesus: **Young man, listen! Get up! [15]The dead man immediately sat up and began talking**. Jesus presented him to his mother,

<u>Luke 7:21</u> And in that same hour he cured many of their infirmities and plagues, and of evil spirits; and unto many that were blind he gave sight.

[AMPC] <u>Luke 7:21</u> In that very hour Jesus was healing many [people] of sicknesses and distressing bodily plagues and evil spirits, and to many who were blind He gave [a free, gracious, joy-giving gift of] sight.

[AUV-NT 2003] <u>Luke 7:21</u> At that very time Jesus was healing many people from diseases, those plagued with serious illnesses and those dominated by evil spirits. He [also] restored sight to many blind people.

[CEB] <u>Luke 7:21</u> Right then, Jesus healed many of their diseases, illnesses, and evil spirits, and he gave sight to a number of blind people.

[FBV-NT] <u>Luke 7:21</u> Right at that time Jesus healed many people of their diseases, illnesses, evil spirits, and made blind people see.

[Folsom-Gs] <u>Luke 7:21</u> In that hour he cured many of diseases, and complaints, and evil spirits, and on many blind he bestowed the favor to see.

[HNT] <u>Luke 7:21</u> At that hour he healed many people of diseases and plagues and hurtful spirits, and bestowed sight on many blind people.

[ICB] <u>Luke 7:21</u> At that time, Jesus healed many people of their sicknesses, diseases, and evil spirits. He healed many blind people so that they could see again.

[Lingard-Gs] <u>Luke 7:21</u> Now at that time he was healing many from diseases, and pains, and evil spirits, and giving site to many blind persons.

OUR HEALING COVENANT

[MEV] <u>Luke 7:21</u> In that same hour He cured many of their infirmities and afflictions and evil spirits. And to many who were blind He gave sight.

[MW-NT] <u>Luke 7:21</u> In that hour he healed many people of sicknesses, infectious diseases, and evil spirits. And he gave sight to many who were blind.

[Original-NT] <u>Luke 7:21</u> He was engaged at the time in curing many of the diseases, plagues, and evil spirits, and blessing with sight many who were blind.

[REM-NT] <u>Luke 7:21</u> As they stood watching, Jesus demonstrated God's methods: he cured many people of disease, infections and mental oppression, and to those who were blind, he gave sight.

[Thomson] <u>Luke 7:21</u> Now at that very time he was curing many of diseases, and maladies, and evil spirits, and graciously bestowing sight to many who were blind.

[Weymouth-NT] <u>Luke 7:21</u> He immediately cured many of diseases, severe pain, and evil spirits, and to many who were blind He gave the gift of sight.

[Wuest-NT] <u>Luke 7:21</u> In that hour He healed many of chronic diseases and of acute, distressing illnesses and of pernicious spirits, and to many blind people He gave as a free, gracious, joy-giving gift the restoration of their eyesight.

[Wycliffe-Noble] <u>Luke 7:21</u> And in that hour he healed many men of their sicknesses, and wounds, and [of] evil spirits; and he gave sight to many blind men.

<u>Luke 7:22</u> Then Jesus answering said unto them, Go your way, and tell John what things ye have seen and heard; how that **the blind see, the lame walk, the lepers are cleansed, the deaf hear, the dead are raised**, to the poor the gospel is preached.

[BBE] <u>Luke 7:22</u> And answering them he said, Go back and give news to John of what you have seen, and the things which have come to your ears; **the blind now see, those who had no power in their legs are walking, lepers are made clean, those who had no hearing now have their ears open, dead men come to life again,** and the poor have the good news given to them.

[CB] <u>Luke 7:22</u> Jesus replied to them, "Carry on, and tell John what you have seen and heard: that the blind see, the lepers are cleansed, the deaf hear, and the dead rise to life, and the gospel is taught to the powerless.

[NCV] <u>Luke 7:22</u> Then Jesus answered John's followers, "Go tell John what you saw and heard here. **The blind can see, the crippled can walk, and people with skin diseases are healed. The deaf can hear, the dead are raised to life,** and the Good News is preached to the poor.

[T4T] <u>Luke 7:22</u> So he answered those two men, "Go back and report to John what you have seen me doing and what you have heard me telling people. **I am enabling blind people to see. I am enabling lame people to walk. I am healing people who have leprosy. I am enabling deaf people to hear. I am causing dead people to become alive again,** and I am telling God's good message to poor people.

[TLB] <u>Luke 7:22</u> this was his reply: "Go back to John and tell him all you have seen and heard here today: **how those who were blind can see. The lame are walking without a limp. The lepers are completely healed. The deaf can hear again. The dead come back to life**. And the poor are hearing the Good News.

[TPT] <u>Luke 7:22</u> Only then did Jesus answer the question posed by John's disciples. "Now go back and tell John what you have just seen and heard here today. **The blind are now seeing. The crippled are now walking. Those who were lepers are now cured. Those who were deaf are now hearing.**

Those who were dead are now raised back to life. The poor and broken are given the hope of salvation.

[TVB] Luke 7:22 Jesus (to John's disciples): Go and tell John what you've witnessed with your own eyes and ears: **the blind are seeing again, the lame are walking again, the lepers are clean again, the deaf hear again, the dead live again**, and good news is preached to the poor.

Luke 8:2 And certain women, which had been healed of evil spirits and infirmities, Mary called Magdalene, **out of whom went seven devils,**

[Barnstone-NT] Luke 8:2 And some women were cured of crafty spirits and sicknesses: Miryam who was called Miryam of Magdala **from whom seven demons had gone out,**

[CB] Luke 8:2 Also with Him were several women He had sent The Devil out of and healed: Mary Magdalene, **from whom He had expelled seven devils,**

[EEBT] Luke 8:2 Some women were also travelling with them. These women had been ill, but Jesus had made them well again. One of the women was Mary Magdalene. **Jesus had sent 7 bad spirits away from her**.

[GNT] Luke 8:2 and so did some women who had been healed of evil spirits and diseases: Mary (who was called Magdalene), **from whom seven demons had been driven out;**

[Thomson] Luke 8:2 and by certain women who had been delivered from evil spirits and diseases, particularly Mary, called Magdalene, **Out of whom had gone seven demons;**

[TPT] Luke 8:2 and also a number of women who had been healed of many illnesses under his ministry and set free from demonic power. **Jesus had cast out seven demons from one woman**. Her name was Mary Magdalene, for she was from the village of Magdala. Among the women were Susanna and

[TTNT] Luke 8:2 and a group of women who had been healed and set free from demonic spirits. This group included Mary Magdalene, **who had been delivered from seven demons,**

Luke 8:32-36 And there was there an herd of many swine feeding on the mountain: and they besought him that he would suffer them to enter into them. And he suffered them. [33]**Then went the devils out of the man, and entered into the swine**: and the herd ran violently down a steep place into the lake, and were choked. [34]When they that fed them saw what was done, they fled, and went and told it in the city and in the country. [35]Then they went out to see what was done; and came to Jesus, and found the man, **out of whom the devils were departed, sitting at the feet of Jesus, clothed, and in his right mind**: and they were afraid. [36]They also which saw it told them by what means **he that was possessed of the devils was healed**[sozo].

[AMP] Luke 8:32-36 Now a large herd of pigs was feeding there on the mountain. The demons begged Jesus to allow them to enter the pigs, and He gave them permission. [33]**Then the demons came out of the man and entered the pigs**; and the herd rushed down the steep bank into the lake and was drowned. [34]When the herdsmen saw what had happened, they ran away and told it in the city and out in the country. [35]And people came out to see what had happened. They came to Jesus, and found the man **from whom the demons had gone out, sitting at Jesus' feet, clothed and in his right mind (mentally healthy)**; and they were frightened. [36]Those who had seen it told them how **the man who had been demon-possessed had been healed**.

[AUV-NT 2005] Luke 8:32-36 Now a herd of many [wild (?)] hogs was grazing on a [nearby] mountain, so the evil spirits begged Jesus to give them permission to enter [the bodies of] the hogs. So, He gave them permission [to do it]. [33]**Then the evil spirits went out of the man and entered the hogs**. The herd [immediately] rushed down the cliff into the lake and was drowned. [34]And when those who had been grazing the hogs saw what had happened, they ran and told it in the town and [around] the country. [35]People went out to see [i.e., to find out] what had happened. And [when] they came to Jesus and found the man **from whom the evil spirits had been driven out sitting down at Jesus' feet with his clothes on and perfectly sane**, they were afraid. [36]Those who saw this told others **how the man dominated by evil spirits was restored.**

[BWE-NT] <u>Luke 8:32-36</u> Many pigs were feeding on the hill there. The spirits begged Jesus to let them go into the pigs. Jesus let them. [33]**The spirits came out of the man and went into the pigs.** They ran fast down the steep hill into the sea. They died in the water. [34]The men who cared for the pigs saw what happened. They ran and told it to the people in the town and in the country. [35]The people went out to see what had happened. They came to Jesus. They saw the man **from whom the bad spirits had gone. He was sitting near the feet of Jesus. He had clothes on and was not crazy any more.** The people were afraid. [36]Those who had seen it told the people how **the man had been saved from the bad spirits.**

[CB] <u>Luke 8:32-36</u> And there was a herd of pigs feeding on the mountain, and the devils begged Jesus to permit them to enter the pigs, and He gave them permission to do so. [33]**Then all of the devils left the man and possessed the pigs**, and the herd of pigs jumped off a cliff, falling into the lake and drowning. [34]When the pig farmers saw what Jesus had done, they ran away, and went and told the story in the city, and throughout the country. [35]So then the inhabitants of the city went out to see what had happened, and when they found Jesus, the man **from whom He had expelled the devils was sitting at His feet, properly dressed and sane**, and the people were afraid. [36]The eyewitnesses told the people **how Jesus had healed the possessed man.**

[CEB] <u>Luke 8:32-36</u> A large herd of pigs was feeding on the hillside. The demons begged Jesus to let them go into the pigs. Jesus gave them permission, [33]**and the demons left the man and entered the pigs.** The herd rushed down the cliff into the lake and drowned. [34]When those who tended the pigs saw what happened, they ran away and told the story in the city and in the countryside. [35]People came to see what had happened. They came to Jesus and found the man **from whom the demons had gone. He was sitting at Jesus' feet, fully dressed and completely sane.** They were filled with awe. [36]Those people who had actually seen what had happened told them how **the demon-possessed man had been delivered.**

[CWB] <u>Luke 8:32-36</u> He begged Jesus to let them go into a nearby herd of swine feeding on the mountainside. Jesus agreed and gave them permission. [33]**So the demons came out of the man and rushed into the pigs.** Suddenly the pigs began running madly down the hill, straight into the lake where they all drowned. [34]When the herdsmen saw what had happened, they ran back to town to tell their masters. And on the way, they told everyone they met what had taken place. [35]Then the owners came out to see for themselves what had happened. When they got there, **the madman was dressed, sitting at the feet of Jesus, free of demons, and once more in his right mind.** Seeing this, they were afraid of what Jesus might do next. [36]The herdsmen had told everyone they met **how the man was healed** and who had done it.

[ECB] <u>Luke 8:32-36</u> And there is an ample drove of swine grazing on the mountain: and they beseech him to allow them to enter them.—and he allows them. [33]And **the demons come from the human and enter the swine**: and violently the drove runs down a cliff into the lake and choke. [34]And they who graze them see what becomes, and they flee, and go and evangelize in the city and in the field. [35]And they go to see what became; and come to Yah Shua and **find the human from whom the demons departed sitting at the feet of Yah Shua, clothed, and sound minded**: and they are awestricken: [36]and they who see also evangelize them how **the demonized was saved.**

[EEBT] <u>Luke 8:32-36</u> There was a large group of pigs and they were eating their food on the side of the hill. 'Let us go into the pigs', they asked Jesus. 'You can go into them', he replied. ³³**So the bad spirits came out of the man and they went into the pigs**. All the pigs rushed together down the high hill. They ran into the lake and all of them died in the water. ³⁴The men that were taking care of the pigs saw this happen. They ran away to tell other people about the pigs. They went to all the towns and villages that were near. ³⁵So the people came out from all these places to see what had happened. When they arrived, they found the man. **He was sitting at the feet of Jesus. The bad spirits had gone out of him. He was now quiet and his mind was well again**. He was also wearing clothes. When the people saw this, they were afraid. ³⁶Some people had seen Jesus make the man well. **They told the other people how he had done this**.

[NIRV] <u>Luke 8:32-36</u> A large herd of pigs was feeding there on the hillside. The demons begged Jesus to let them go into the pigs. And he allowed it. ³³**When the demons came out of the man, they went into the pigs**. Then the herd rushed down the steep bank. They ran into the lake and drowned. ³⁴Those who were tending the pigs saw what had happened. They ran off and reported it in the town and countryside. ³⁵The people went out to see what had happened. Then they came to Jesus. **They found the man who was now free of the demons. He was sitting at Jesus' feet. He was dressed and thinking clearly**. All this made the people afraid. ³⁶Those who had seen it told the others how **the man who had been controlled by demons was now healed**.

[TPT] <u>Luke 8:32-36</u> On the hillside nearby, there was a large herd of pigs, and the demons pled with Jesus, "Let us enter into the pigs." ³³**So Jesus ordered all the "mob" of demons to come out of the man and enter the pigs**. The crazed herd of swine stampeded over the cliff into the lake and all of them drowned. ³⁴When the herders tending the pigs saw what had happened, they ran off in fear and reported it to the nearby town and throughout the countryside. ³⁵Then the people of the region came out to see for themselves what had happened. When they came to where Jesus was, **they discovered the notorious madman totally set free. He was clothed, speaking intelligently, and sitting at the feet of Jesus**. They were shocked! ³⁶Then eyewitnesses to the miracle reported all that they had seen and how **the demonized man was completely delivered from his torment**. After hearing about such amazing power, the townspeople became frightened.

[TTNT] <u>Luke 8:32-36</u> A large heard of pigs was feeding on the hillside nearby. So the demons begged Jesus to allow them to enter the pigs. ³³When Jesus gave them permission **they came out of the man, entered the pigs** and the whole herd rushed down the steep hillside into the lake and were drowned. ³⁴When those who cared for the pigs saw what had happened, they ran and spread the news in neighbouring towns and the surrounding countryside. ³⁵People came to see for themselves what had happened. When they arrived at the place **they found the man completely set free from the demons, sitting and listening to Jesus. He was now clothed and in his right mind**, yet the people felt afraid. ³⁶Those who had witnessed the miracle explained **how the demon-possessed man had been completely liberated**.

[UDB] <u>Luke 8:32-36</u> There was a large herd of pigs grazing on the hillside nearby. The demons begged Jesus to allow them to enter the pigs, and he allowed them. ³³**So the demons left the man and entered the pigs**, and the herd of pigs rushed down the steep bank into the lake and drowned. ³⁴When the men who were taking care of the pigs saw what happened, they ran away! They reported what they had seen to people in the town and in the countryside. ³⁵Then the people went out to see what had happened. When they came to where Jesus was, they saw that **the man from whom the demons had gone out was sitting at the feet of Jesus, listening to him. They saw that he had clothes on, and that his mind was normal again**, and they became afraid. ³⁶The men who had seen what had happened told the people who had just arrived how **Jesus had healed the man who had been controlled by demons**.

<u>Luke 8:47-48</u> And when the woman saw that she was not hid, she came trembling, and falling down before him, she declared unto him before all the people for what cause she had touched him, and how **she was healed immediately**. [48]And he said unto her, Daughter, be of good comfort: **thy faith hath made thee whole**[sozo]; go in peace.

[AMPC] <u>Luke 8:47-48</u> And when the woman saw that she had not escaped notice, she came up trembling, and, falling down before Him, she declared in the presence of all the people for what reason she had touched Him and how **she had been instantly cured**. [48]And He said to her, Daughter, **your faith (your confidence and trust in Me) has made you well!** Go (enter) into peace (untroubled, undisturbed well-being).

[BV-KJV-NT] <u>Luke 8:47-48</u> When the woman saw that she was not unnoticed, she came trembling and got down close to Him. She announced to Him in the sight of the entire group the reason why she touched Him and how **she was cured at once**. [48]He said to her, "Daughter, be courageous. **Your trust has rescued you**. Travel into peace."

[EEBT] <u>Luke 8:47-48</u> The woman knew that she could not hide it. So she was very afraid, when she came to Jesus. She went down on the ground in front of him. She spoke so that all the people could hear her. 'I wanted to be well', she told them, 'so I touched the edge of his clothes. As soon as I touched him, **I became well**.' [48]'Daughter', Jesus said to her, '**you are well again, because you believed in me**. Do not have troubles in your mind any longer.'

[EHV] <u>Luke 8:47-48</u> When the woman saw that she did not escape his notice, she came trembling and fell down before Jesus. In the presence of all the people she told him why she had touched him and how **she was healed immediately**. [48]And he said to her, "Daughter, **your faith has saved you**. Go in peace."

[ERV] <u>Luke 8:47-48</u> When the woman saw that she could not hide, she came forward, shaking. She bowed down before Jesus. While everyone listened, she told why she touched him. Then she said that **she was healed immediately** when she touched him. [48]Jesus said to her, "My daughter, **you are made well because you believed**. Go in peace."

[GNC-NT] <u>Luke 8:47-48</u> When the woman realized that the matter had come into the open, a trembling seized her and, falling down at Jesus' feet, she declared in front of all the people what had been the reason for her touching him, and how **she had found instant healing**. [48]"My daughter," Jesus said to her, "**it is by your faith that your health has been restored**. Go on your way in peace."

[HRB] <u>Luke 8:47-48</u> And seeing that she was not hidden, the woman came trembling and kneeled down before Him and told Him before all the people for what reason she touched Him, and how **she was instantly cured**. [48]And He said to her, Daughter, be comforted. **Your faith has given you life**. Go in peace.

[ICB] <u>Luke 8:47-48</u> When the woman saw that she could not hide, she came forward, shaking. She bowed down before Jesus. While all the people listened, she told why she had touched him. Then, she said, **she was healed immediately**. [48]Jesus said to her, "Dear woman, **you are healed because you believed**. Go in peace."

[IRENT] <u>Luke 8:47-48</u> And the woman, seeing she could not go unnoticed, came up to him trembling and fell down before him. She disclosed before all the people why she came to touch him and how **she was healed instantly**. [48]And he said to her, "Have courage, daughter! **it is by your faith that you have been restored**. Go on your way in peace."

[Original-NT] <u>Luke 8:47-48</u> Seeing that she had not escaped notice the woman came forward trembling, and prostrating herself before him declared in front of all the people why she had touched him and how **she was instantly cured**. [48]"Daughter", he told her, "**your faith has cured you**. Go in peace."

[Phillips] <u>Luke 8:47-48</u> When the woman realised that she had not escaped notice she came forward trembling, and fell at his feet and admitted before everybody why she had had to touch him, and how **she had been instantly cured**. [48]'Daughter,' said Jesus, **'It is your faith that has healed you**—go in peace.'

[REM-NT] <u>Luke 8:47-48</u> Then the woman, realizing she could not escape unnoticed, came forward trembling and fell down at his feet. In front of the crowd, she explained why she had touched him and how **she had been instantly healed**. [48]He smiled and said, "Daughter, **your trust in me has healed you**. Live in peace."

[TPT] <u>Luke 8:47-48</u> When the woman realized she couldn't hide any longer, she came and fell trembling at Jesus' feet. Before the entire crowd she declared, "I was desperate to touch you, Jesus, for I knew if I could just touch even the fringe of your robe **I would be healed**." [48]Jesus responded, "Beloved daughter, **your faith in me has released your healing**. You may go with my peace."

[TWTY-RCT-NT-V1] <u>Luke 8:47-48</u> So, when the woman had seen and perceived, observed and witnessed, known and experienced, recognised and respected, understood, comprehended and paid attention to fact that concerning this, she did not escape notice or remain hidden, be unaware of or ignored, go unnoticed or unknown, move secretly or escape His knowledge, detection or sight, she came, arose and appeared, trembling, quaking and shaking in fear. And having fallen down before and prostrated herself at His feet, expressing reference and respect to Him, she publically told and informed, proclaimed and declared, confessed and professed, reported and recited before and in the presence of, in the judgement of and in the sight of all the individual and collective people, crowd and populace through the means of and on the grounds of, on account of and for the reason of, on the basis of and because of what cause and matter, reason and ground she had touched and taken hold of, grabbed and fastened herself to Him, and how, in **what manner and way she had been healed and cured, restored and made whole suddenly and instantly, immediately and at that very moment**. [48]But nevertheless, He, Yahushua, said to her, "Daughter, **your trust and reliance, obedience and confidence, certainty and guarantee, assurance and dependence has delivered and preserved, saved and kept you from danger and destruction, ruin and annihilation**. Go away and depart, withdraw and proceed on your journey with peace and tranquillity, harmony and concord, security and safety, prosperity and freedom, exemption from chaos, felicity and the assurance of salvation."

[Tyndale21-NT] <u>Luke 8:47-48</u> And when the woman saw that she was not hidden from him, she came trembling, and fell down at his feet and told him in front of all the people why she had touched him, and how **she was healed immediately**. [48]And he said to her, Daughter, be of good comfort! **Your faith has made you healthy**. Go in peace.

<u>Luke 8:54-55</u> And he put them all out, and took her by the hand, and **called, saying, Maid, arise. [55]And her spirit came again, and she arose straightway**: and he commanded to give her meat.

[AENT] <u>Luke 8:54-55</u> And he put everyone outside and took her by the hand and called her and said, **"Arise young girl!"** [55]**And her spirit returned immediately and she arose**. And he commanded that they give her something to eat.

[CEV] <u>Luke 8:54-55</u> Jesus took hold of the girl's hand and **said, "Child, get up!"** [55]**She came back to life and got right up**. Jesus told them to give her something to eat.

[CWB] <u>Luke 8:54-55</u> So He asked them to leave and wait outside. Then He went to the room where the little girl's body was, took her by the hand and said, **"My child, it's time to get up."** [55]**Immediately, life returned to her body. She opened her eyes, sat up and looked around**. Then Jesus asked the parents to give her something to eat.

[GW] <u>Luke 8:54-55</u> But Jesus took her hand and **called out, "Child, get up!"** ⁵⁵**She came back to life and got up at once.** He ordered her parents to give her something to eat.

[NKJV] <u>Luke 8:54-55</u> But He put them all outside, took her by the hand and **called, saying, "Little girl, arise."** ⁵⁵**Then her spirit returned, and she arose immediately**. And He commanded that she be given something to eat.

[NLT] <u>Luke 8:54-55</u> Then Jesus took her by the hand and **said in a loud voice, "My child, get up!"** ⁵⁵**And at that moment her life returned, and she immediately stood up!** Then Jesus told them to give her something to eat.

<u>Luke 9:1-2</u> Then he called his twelve disciples together, and gave them power and authority over all devils, and to cure diseases. ²And he sent them to preach the kingdom of God, and to heal the sick.

[AMP] <u>Luke 9:1-2</u> Now Jesus called together the twelve [disciples] and gave them [the right to exercise] power and authority over all the demons and to heal diseases. ²Then He sent them out [on a brief journey] to preach the kingdom of God and to perform healing.

[BBE] <u>Luke 9:1-2</u> And getting the twelve together, he gave them power and authority over all evil spirits and over diseases, to make them well. ²And he sent them out to be preachers of the kingdom of God, and to make well those who were ill.

[Bowes-NT] <u>Luke 9:1-2</u> And having called the twelve together, he gave them power and authority over all the demons, and to heal diseases. ²And he sent them to proclaim the reign of God, and to heal the afflicted.

[Fenton] <u>Luke 9:1-2</u> Afterwards, calling the twelve together, He endowed them with power and authority over all the demons and to cure mental diseases. ²And sending them out to proclaim the Kingdom of God, and to restore the suffering,

[Lingard-Gs] <u>Luke 9:1-2</u> Now, calling to him the twelve apostles, he gave to them power and authority over all fiends, and to heal distempers. ²And he sent them to announce the 'kingdom of God,' and to cure the infirm.

[NLT] <u>Luke 9:1-2</u> One day Jesus called together his twelve disciples and gave them power and authority to cast out all demons and to heal all diseases. ²Then he sent them out to tell everyone about the Kingdom of God and to heal the sick.

[NLV] <u>Luke 9:1-2</u> Jesus called His twelve followers to Him. He gave them the right and the power over all demons and to heal diseases. ²He sent them to preach about the holy nation of God and to heal the sick.

[REM-NT] <u>Luke 9:1-2</u> Jesus called the Twelve together and empowered them to cure diseases, and gave them the authority to drive out all evil forces. ²He sent them out to reveal God's kingdom of love, demonstrating how it works by healing the sick.

[T4T] <u>Luke 9:1-2</u> One day Jesus summoned his twelve apostles, and gave them power to expel all kinds of demons and to heal people with diseases. He gave them authority to do that. ²Before he sent them out to heal people and to tell people what it meant to let God rule/have complete control over their lives,

[TPT] <u>Luke 9:1-2</u> Jesus summoned together his twelve apostles and imparted to them authority over every demon and the power to heal every disease. ²Then he commissioned them to preach God's kingdom realm and to heal the sick to demonstrate that the kingdom had arrived. As he sent them out, he gave them these instructions:

[TTNT] <u>Luke 9:1-2</u> On one occasion, Jesus called together the twelve and gave them the power and authority to drive out every demon and to heal people from their diseases. ²He sent them out to preach the gospel of God's Kingdom and to heal the sick,

[Wuest-NT] <u>Luke 9:1-2</u> Then, having called together the Twelve, He gave them power and authority over all the demons, and over diseases, to be healing them. ²And He sent them off on a mission to be heralding forth the kingdom of God with that formality, gravity, and authority which must be listened to and obeyed, and to be healing.

<u>Luke 9:6</u> And they departed, and went through the towns, preaching the gospel, and healing every where.

[AENT] <u>Luke 9:6</u> Then the Shlichim departed and were going around in the villages and in the cities and preaching hope and were healing in every place.

[Anderson-NT] <u>Luke 9:6</u> And they departed, and went through every village, preaching the gospel, and performing cures everywhere.

[BBE] <u>Luke 9:6</u> And they went away, journeying through all the towns, preaching the good news and making people free from diseases in all places.

[Douay-Rheims-Peters] <u>Luke 9:6</u> And going forth they went a circuit from town to town evangelizing and curing everywhere.

[NLV] <u>Luke 9:6</u> They went out, going from town to town. They preached the Good News and healed the sick everywhere.

[Original-NT] <u>Luke 9:6</u> So on their departure they went from village to village proclaiming the News and effecting cures everywhere.

[T4T] <u>Luke 9:6</u> Then they left and traveled through many villages. Everywhere they went, they told people God's good message and healed sick people.

<u>Luke 9:11</u> And the people, when they knew it, followed him: and he received them, and spake unto them of the kingdom of God, and **healed them that had need of healing**.

[AMPC] <u>Luke 9:11</u> But when the crowds learned of it, [they] followed Him; and He welcomed them and talked to them about the kingdom of God, and **healed those who needed restoration to health**.

[ASV] <u>Luke 9:11</u> But the multitudes perceiving it followed him: and he welcomed them, and spake to them of the kingdom of God, and **them that had need of healing he cured**.

[Barnstone-NT] <u>Luke 9:11</u> When the crowds learned of it, they followed him. After welcoming them, he spoke to them about the kingdom of God, and **those in need of treatment he healed**.

[BBE] <u>Luke 9:11</u> But the people, getting news of it, went after him: and he was pleased to see them, and gave them teaching about the kingdom of God, and **made those well who were in need of it**.

[BWE-NT] <u>Luke 9:11</u> But the people found out and they followed him. He was glad to see them and talked to them about God's kingdom. **He healed those who were sick**.

[CWB] <u>Luke 9:11</u> But the people followed them and found Jesus and His disciples. He welcomed them, taught them things about the kingdom of God and **healed as many as needed to be healed**.

[Haak] <u>Luke 9:11</u> And the multitudes understanding (that) followed him; and he received them and spake unto them of the kingdom of God, and **those that had need of healing, he made whole**.

[Montgomery-NT] <u>Luke 9:11</u> But when the crowd learned this they followed him. He received them kindly and spoke to them concerning the kingdom of God, and **healed those who needed restored to good health**.

[Original-NT] <u>Luke 9:11</u> But the populace, becoming aware of it, followed him, and welcoming them he spoke to them of the Kingdom of God and **cured those who stood in need of healing**.

[REM-NT] <u>Luke 9:11</u> but it didn't stay private for long. Soon the crowds found out where he was and flocked to him. He was gracious and made them welcome. He spoke to them about God's kingdom of love, and he demonstrated this kingdom by **healing all who needed it**.

[Rieu-Gs] <u>Luke 9:11</u> But the people came to know this and went after him. He made them welcome, spoke to them about the Kingdom of God, and **cured those who were in need of healing.**

[TLB] <u>Luke 9:11</u> But the crowds found out where he was going and followed. And he welcomed them, teaching them again about the Kingdom of God and **curing those who were ill**.

[TPT] <u>Luke 9:11</u> But the crowds soon found out about it and took off after him. When they caught up with Jesus, he graciously welcomed them all, taught them more about God's kingdom realm, and **healed all who were sick**.

[Wuest-NT] <u>Luke 9:11</u> And the crowds having come to know it, followed with Him. And having welcomed them, He went to speaking to them concerning the kingdom of God, and **He continued healing those who had need of healing**.

<u>Luke 9:42</u> And as he was yet a coming, the devil threw him down, and tare him. **And Jesus rebuked the unclean spirit, and healed the child**, and delivered him again to his father.

[Barclay-NT] <u>Luke 9:42</u> When the boy was coming to Jesus, the spirit tore him and convulsed him. **Jesus spoke to the unclean spirit with stern authority, and cured the boy**, and gave him back to his father.

[Beck] <u>Luke 9:42</u> While the boy was coming, the devil dashed him on the ground and threw him into convulsions. **Jesus talked sharply to the unclean spirit, made the boy well**, and gave him back to his father.

[BSB-NT] <u>Luke 9:42</u> Even while the boy was approaching, the demon slammed him to the ground in a convulsion. But **Jesus rebuked the unclean spirit, healed the boy**, and gave him back to his father.

[Fenton] <u>Luke 9:42</u> And while he was on the way, the demon threw him down and convulsed him painfully. But **Jesus restrained the foul spirit, cured the boy**, and returned him to his father.

[GNC-NT] <u>Luke 9:42</u> Now even as the boy was drawing near, the demon spirit rent him and threw him into convulsions. But **Jesus administered a rebuke to the tarnished spirit, brought healing to the boy**, and gave him back to his father.

[GNT] <u>Luke 9:42</u> As the boy was coming, the demon knocked him to the ground and threw him into a fit. **Jesus gave a command to the evil spirit, healed the boy**, and gave him back to his father.

[Hanson-NT] <u>Luke 9:42</u> And while he was approaching, the demon dashed him down, and violently convulsed him. **But Jesus reproved the impure spirit, and cured the boy**, and delivered him to his father.

[ICB] <u>Luke 9:42</u> While the boy was coming, the demon threw him on the ground. The boy lost control of himself. But **Jesus gave a strong command to the evil spirit. Then the boy was healed**, and Jesus gave him back to his father.

[MSG] <u>Luke 9:42</u> While he was coming, the demon slammed him to the ground and threw him into convulsions. **Jesus stepped in, ordered the vile spirit gone, healed the boy**, and handed him back to his father.

[NIRV] <u>Luke 9:42</u> Even while the boy was coming, the demon threw him into a fit. The boy fell to the ground. But **Jesus ordered the evil spirit to leave the boy. Then Jesus healed him** and gave him back to his father.

[REM-NT] <u>Luke 9:42</u> As the boy approached Jesus, the evil agency caused the boy to have a seizure and he convulsed on the ground; but **Jesus ordered the evil force to leave, healed the boy**, and restored him back to his father.

[TPT] <u>Luke 9:42</u> As the boy approached, the demon slammed him to the ground, throwing him into violent convulsions. **Jesus sternly commanded the demon to come out of the boy, and immediately it left. Jesus healed the boy of his injuries** and returned him to his father, saying, "Here is your son."

[TTNT] <u>Luke 9:42</u> While the boy was being brought forward, the demon threw him to the ground in a convulsion. **Jesus immediately commanded the spirit to leave him. He healed the boy** and returned him to his father.

<u>Luke 10:9</u> **And heal the sick that are therein**, and say unto them, The kingdom of God is come nigh unto you.

[BSB-NT] <u>Luke 10:9</u> **Heal the sick who are there** and tell them, 'The kingdom of God is near you.'

[CPDV] <u>Luke 10:9</u> And **cure the sick who are in that place**, and proclaim to them, 'The kingdom of God has drawn near to you.'

[FBV-NT] <u>Luke 10:9</u> and **heal those who are sick**. Tell them, 'God's kingdom has come to you.'

[Montgomery-NT] <u>Luke 10:9</u> "**Heal the sick in that town** and tell them, The kingdom of God draws near to you."

[MSG] <u>Luke 10:9</u> **heal anyone who is sick**, and tell them, 'God's kingdom is right on your doorstep!'

[NET] <u>Luke 10:9</u> **Heal the sick in that town** and say to them, 'The kingdom of God has come upon you!'

[Original-NT] <u>Luke 10:9</u> **and cure the sick people in it**, and tell them, 'For you the Kingdom of God is at hand.'

[REM-NT] <u>Luke 10:9</u> and then **give to them by healing the sick among them**, and telling them that this is how God's kingdom operates.

[TTNT] <u>Luke 10:9</u> Then **heal the sick in that place** and tell them, 'God's Kingdom is now within your reach.'

[ULB] <u>Luke 10:9</u> and **heal the sick that are there**. Say to them, 'The kingdom of God has come close to you.'

[Weymouth-NT] <u>Luke 10:9</u> **Cure the sick in that town**, and tell them, "'The Kingdom of God is now at your door.'

<u>Luke 10:17</u> And the seventy returned again with joy, saying, Lord, **even the devils are subject unto us through thy name**.

[BOOKS-NT] <u>Luke 10:17</u> The seventy-two returned with joy and said, "Lord, **even the demons submit to us in your name**."

[CWB] <u>Luke 10:17</u> When the seventy finished their mission, they came back rejoicing and said, "Lord, even **the demons obeyed us when we rebuked them in your name**."

[GNT] Luke 10:17 The seventy-two men came back in great joy. "Lord," they said, "**even the demons obeyed us when we gave them a command in your name!**"

[Godbey-NT] Luke 10:17 And the seventy returned with joy, saying, Lord **even the demons are subordinated to us in thy name.**

[GW] Luke 10:17 The 70 disciples came back very happy. They said, "Lord, **even demons obey us when we use the power and authority of your name!**"

[Mace-NT] Luke 10:17 At length the seventy returned with great joy, saying, Lord, **even the demons have been made subject to us by virtue of your name.**

[REAL] Luke 10:17 and the seventy returned back with joy. They said, "Lord even **the demons are under our authority through your Name.**"

[REM-NT] Luke 10:17 When the seventy-two returned, they were jubilant, saying, "Lord, **even evil angels obeyed our commands issued in your name.**"

[SG] Luke 10:17 The seventy-two came back delighted, and said, "Master, **when we use your name the very demons submit to us!**"

[TNT] Luke 10:17 The seventy-two returned with joy, saying, 'Lord, **even the demons are made obedient to us in your name.**'

[Tolstoy-Gs] Luke 10:17 And the seventy returned filled with joy, that he had sent them, and said: **Through thy power, evil has been made subject to us.**

[Tomson-NT] Luke 10:17 And the seventy turned again with joy, saying, Lord, **even the devils are subdued to us through thy Name.**

[TTNT] Luke 10:17 When the seventy-two returned they were filled with joy and told Jesus: "Lord, **even the demons obeyed us when we addressed them in Your name.**"

[TVB] Luke 10:17 When the 70 completed their mission and returned to report on their experiences, they were elated. Seventy: It's amazing, Lord! **When we use Your name, the demons do what we say**!

[UDB] Luke 10:17 The seventy people whom Jesus appointed went and did as he told them to. When they returned, they were very joyful. They said, "Lord, **even the demons obeyed us when by your authority we commanded them to leave people!**"

Luke 10:19 Behold, **I give unto you power** to tread on serpents and scorpions, and **over all the power of the enemy**: and nothing shall by any means hurt you.

[AMPC] Luke 10:19 Behold! **I have given you authority and power** to trample upon serpents and scorpions, and [physical and mental strength and ability] **over all the power that the enemy [possesses]**; and nothing shall in any way harm you.

[Authentic-NT] Luke 10:19 **I have indeed invested you with power to stamp** on snakes and scorpions, and **on every minion of the Enemy**; and nothing whatever shall harm you.

[BWE-NT] Luke 10:19 **I have given you power over all the power of the enemy.** Nothing will hurt you.

[Fenton] Luke 10:19 Now **I have given you the authority to tread upon** serpents and scorpions, and upon **all the might of the enemy**; and none can resist you.

[FHV-NT] Luke 10:19 **I have given you the authority** to walk on snakes and scorpions, and **on all the power of the enemy**, and you will not be injured at all.

[Green-NT] <u>Luke 10:19</u> Lo, I have given the free right of **treading over** serpents and scorpions and on **all the power of the foe**, and nothing shall harm you.

[Harwood-NT] <u>Luke 10:19</u> Behold! **I endow you with power to vanquish** your most fell and implacable adversaries—and **all their determined rage and rancor** shall not be able to injure you or your cause.

[ICB] <u>Luke 10:19</u> Listen! **I gave you power** to walk on snakes and scorpions. **I gave you more power than the Enemy has.** Nothing will hurt you.

[Jordan-NT] <u>Luke 10:19</u> Look here, **I've given you the ability to trample** on 'snakes and scorpions,' and **on the power-structure of the opposition**, and nothing will be able to stop you.

[Norlie-NT] <u>Luke 10:19</u> Now listen! **I have given you authority to trample on** serpents and scorpions and **all the might of the satanic foe**, and nothing will harm you in any way.

[OEB-NT] <u>Luke 10:19</u> Remember, **I have given you the power** to 'trample on snakes and scorpions,' and **to meet all the strength of the Enemy**. Nothing will ever harm you in any way.

[Phillips] <u>Luke 10:19</u> It is true that **I have given you the power to tread on** snakes and scorpions and to overcome **all the enemy's power**—there is nothing at all that can do you any harm.

[Pickering-NT] <u>Luke 10:19</u> Take note, **I am giving you the authority** to trample on snakes and scorpions, and **over all the power of the enemy**, and nothing at all may harm you.

[T4T] <u>Luke 10:19</u> Listen! I have given you authority so that if you oppose evil spirits they will not hurt you. **I have given you authority to defeat our enemy**, Satan. Nothing shall hurt you.

[TGNT] <u>Luke 10:19</u> So now **I have given you the jurisdiction** to trample serpents and scorpions, and **over all the forces of the enemy**, and not one of you will be harmed.

[TPT] <u>Luke 10:19</u> Now you understand that **I have imparted to you all my authority** to trample over his kingdom. **You will trample upon every demon before you and overcome every power Satan possesses.** Absolutely nothing will be able to harm you as you walk in this authority.

[TTNT] <u>Luke 10:19</u> **I have given you authority** to trample on demonic spirits and **to overcome every power the enemy has**. Nothing will be able to harm you as you exercise that authority.

[Wade] <u>Luke 10:19</u> Listen! **I have given to you the authority needed for trampling upon the agencies of evil**, poisonous as serpents and scorpions—yes, **authority over all the power of the Enemy**; and nothing shall harm you.

[Worsley-NT] <u>Luke 10:19</u> Behold **I give you power to trample upon** serpents and scorpions, and over **all the might of the enemy**; and nothing shall at all hurt you.

<u>Luke 11:14</u> And he was casting out a devil, and it was dumb. And it came to pass, **when the devil was gone out, the dumb spake**; and the people wondered.

[AMP] <u>Luke 11:14</u> And [at another time] Jesus was casting out a demon, and it was [controlling a man so as to make him] mute; **when the demon had gone out, the mute man spoke**. And the crowds were awed.

[AUV-NT 2003] <u>Luke 11:14</u> [Once] Jesus was driving out an evil spirit from a [man who was] mute. And it happened **when the evil spirit left [him] that the [former] mute began to speak**. And the crowds were amazed.

[EEBT] <u>Luke 11:14</u> One day, Jesus was ordering a bad spirit to come out of a man. Because of the bad spirit, the man could not speak. But **after it had gone out of him, the man could speak**. All the people that were watching were surprised at this.

[GW] <u>Luke 11:14</u> Jesus was forcing a demon out of a man. The demon had made the man unable to talk. **When the demon had gone out, the man began to talk**. The people were amazed.

[Phillips] <u>Luke 11:14</u> Another time, Jesus was expelling an evil spirit which was preventing a man from speaking, and **as soon as the evil spirit left him, the dumb man found his speech**, to the amazement of the crowds.

[TPT] <u>Luke 11:14</u> One day there was a crowd gathered around Jesus, and among them was a man who was mute. Jesus drove out of the man the spirit that made him unable to speak. **Once the demon left him, the mute man's tongue was loosed and he was able to speak again**. The stunned crowd saw it all and marveled in amazement over this miracle!

[UDB] <u>Luke 11:14</u> One day a man came to Jesus who was not able to speak because a demon controlled him. **After Jesus forced out the demon, the man began to talk**, and crowds of people were amazed.

<u>Luke 13:13</u> And he laid his hands on her: and immediately she was made straight, and glorified God.

[BV-KJV-NT] <u>Luke 13:13</u> And He placed His hands on her, and at once she was straightened up and was admitting that God is magnificent.

[BWE-NT] <u>Luke 13:13</u> Jesus put his hands on her, and right away she stood up straight. And she praised God.

[ERV] <u>Luke 13:13</u> He laid his hands on her, and immediately she was able to stand up straight. She began praising God.

[HCSB] <u>Luke 13:13</u> Then He laid His hands on her, and instantly she was restored and began to glorify

[Noyes] <u>Luke 13:13</u> And he laid his hands on her; and immediately she stood upright, and gave glory to God.

[TTNT] <u>Luke 13:13</u> Then He laid hands on her and immediately her back was straightened and she praised God.

[TWTY-RCT-NT-V1] <u>Luke 13:13</u> And so He laid and set, placed and put His hands upon her, and suddenly and instantly, immediately and at that very moment, she was straightened up, restored to health and was able to stand up straight, and so she gave glory and splendour, magnificence and excellence, pre-eminence and dignity, brightness, favour and majesty to God.

<u>Luke 13:16</u> And ought not this woman, being a daughter of Abraham, whom Satan hath bound, lo, these eighteen years, be loosed from this bond on the sabbath day?

[Ballentine-NT] <u>Luke 13:16</u> So this daughter of Abraham, who Satan has kept bound eighteen years, must she not be freed from this bond on the Sabbath?

[Barclay-NT] <u>Luke 13:16</u> 'This woman is a daughter of Abraham. For eighteen years Satan has fettered her. Is it not right that she should be liberated from her fetters, Sabbath though it is?'

[Berkeley] <u>Luke 13:16</u> Ought not then this woman, a daughter of Abraham whom Satan held tied up, mind you, these eighteen years, to be untied of her bond on the Sabbath day?

[ERV] <u>Luke 13:16</u> This woman that I healed is a true descendant of Abraham. But Satan has held her for 18 years. Surely it is not wrong for her to be made free from her sickness on a Sabbath day!

[Etheridge-NT] <u>Luke 13:16</u> But this daughter of Abraham, whom, behold, the Accuser hath bound eighteen years, is it not lawful to loose from this binding on the day of shabath?

[EXB] Luke 13:16 This woman that I healed, a daughter of Abraham, has been held by Satan for eighteen years. ·Surely it is not wrong [Was it not necessary…?] for her to be freed from ·her sickness [this bond / imprisonment] on a Sabbath day!

[Fenton] Luke 13:16 And this woman, who is a daughter of Abraham, whom his enemy has been around for eighteen years, ought she not to be loosed from this bond on the Day of Rest?

[GW] Luke 13:16 Now, here is a descendant of Abraham. Satan has kept her in this condition for 18 years. Isn't it right to free her on the day of rest—a holy day?

[ICB] Luke 13:16 This woman that I healed is our Jewish sister. But Satan has held her for 18 years. Surely it is not wrong for her to be freed from her sickness on a Sabbath day!"

[Montefiore-Gs] Luke 13:16 'And ought not this woman, being a daughter of Abraham, whom Satan has bound, lo, these eighteen years, to be loosed from this chain on the sabbath day?'

[NKJV] Luke 13:16 So ought not this woman, being a daughter of Abraham, whom Satan has bound—think of it—for eighteen years, be loosed from this bond on the Sabbath?

[Norlie-NT] Luke 13:16 But this women, a daughter of Abraham, who has been in the bondage of Satan—think of it! —for eighteen years, should not have the right to be released from her bonds because it is the sabbath?

[REB] Luke 13:16 'And here is this woman, a daughter of Abraham, who has been bound by Satan for eighteen long years: was it not right for her to be loosed from her bonds on the sabbath?'

[REM-NT] Luke 13:16 Then should not this poor lady—a daughter of Abraham, one of God's children—who has been bound by Satan for eighteen miserable years, be set free of what bound her, on the Sabbath day?"

[Sindlinger-NT] Luke 13:16 Jesus heard this, so he responded, "Some of your rules don't make sense. You allow people to give their animals water on the weekly day of rest, but you don't want someone to heal this Jewish woman who has been suffering for 18 years."

[T4T] Luke 13:16 This woman is more important than an animal; she is a Jew, descended from Abraham! But Satan has kept her crippled for eighteen years, as though he had tied her and not let her escape! So it is certainly right that she be freed {that I free her}, even if this is a Sabbath day! /was it not right that she be freed {that I free her}, even if this is a Jewish rest day?"

[TLB] Luke 13:16 And is it wrong for me, just because it is the Sabbath day, to free this Jewish woman from the bondage in which Satan has held her for eighteen years?"

[TTNT] Luke 13:16 So this woman, one of Abraham's descendants, who has been locked up by satan for eighteen years should surely be freed from her bondage on the Sabbath!"

[TVB] Luke 13:16 Do you care more about your farm animals than you care about this woman, one of Abraham's daughters, oppressed by Satan for 18 years? Can't we untie her from her oppression on the Sabbath?

[UDB] Luke 13:16 This woman is a Jew, descended from Abraham! But Satan has kept her crippled for eighteen years, as though he had tied her up! Certainly you would agree that it is right that I free her from Satan, even if I do it on a day of rest!

[Wuest-NT] Luke 13:16 And this woman, being a daughter of Abraham, whom Satan bound, just think of it, eighteen years, was it not a necessity in the nature of the case that she be released from this binding restriction on the sabbath?

[YLT] Luke 13:16 and this one, being a daughter of Abraham, whom the Adversary bound, lo, eighteen years, did it not behove to be loosed from this bond on the sabbath-day?

Luke 14:2-4 And, behold, there was a certain man before him which had the dropsy. ³And Jesus answering spake unto the lawyers and Pharisees, saying, Is it lawful to heal on the sabbath day? ⁴And they held their peace. **And he took him, and healed him**, and let him go;

[**Anderson-Sinaitic NT**] <u>Luke 14:2-4</u> And behold, there was before him a man that had the dropsy. ³And Jesus answered and spoke to the lawyers and Pharisees, saying: Is it lawful to cure on the sabbath or not? But they were silent. ⁴**And he took him and restored him to health** and let him go.

[**BBE**] <u>Luke 14:2-4</u> And a certain man was there who had a disease. ³And Jesus, answering, said to the scribes and Pharisees, Is it right to make people well on the Sabbath or not? ⁴But they said nothing. **And he made him well** and sent him away.

[**BOOKS-NT**] <u>Luke 14:2-4</u> There in front of him was a man suffering from abnormal swelling of his body. ³Jesus asked the Pharisees and experts in the law, "Is it lawful to heal on the Sabbath or not?" ⁴But they remained silent. **So taking hold of the man, he healed him** and sent him on his way.

[**CWB**] <u>Luke 14:2-4</u> There was a man among the guests who was suffering from swollen arms and legs caused by excessive body fluid. He asked Jesus to heal him. ³Jesus turned to the lawyers and Pharisees sitting there and said, "Is it right to heal someone on the Sabbath?" ⁴Nobody answered. **So Jesus healed him**, and the man went away rejoicing.

[**MSG**] <u>Luke 14:2-4</u> Right before him there was a man hugely swollen in his joints. ³So Jesus asked the religion scholars and Pharisees present, "Is it permitted to heal on the Sabbath? Yes or no?" ⁴They were silent. **So he took the man, healed him**, and sent him on his way.

[**REM-NT**] <u>Luke 14:2-4</u> Right in front of him was a man suffering from heart failure, with very swollen legs. ³Jesus asked the Pharisees and lawyers, both of whom promoted a legal religion, "What is your opinion: is it lawful to heal on the Sabbath, or let people suffer and die?" ⁴But they refused to answer, **so Jesus put his hands on the man, healed him**, and sent him home.

[**T4T**] <u>Luke 14:2-4</u> Unexpectedly, there was a man in front of Jesus whose arms and legs were swollen. ³Jesus said to them, "Is it permitted in our Jewish laws to heal someone on our Jewish rest day/on the Sabbath, or not?" ⁴They knew that their laws permitted it, but they thought that healing was work, which they thought was wrong to do on the Sabbath/on the Jewish rest day (OR, they knew that their laws permitted it, but they did not want to admit it). So they did not reply. **Then Jesus put his hands on the man and healed him**. Then he told him to go home.

[**TPT**] <u>Luke 14:2-4</u> Just then, standing right in front of him was a man suffering with his limbs swollen with fluid. ³Jesus asked the experts of the law and the Pharisees who were present, "Is it permitted within the law to heal a man on the Sabbath day? Is it right or wrong?" ⁴No one dared to answer. **So Jesus turned to the sick man, took hold of him, and released healing to him**, then sent him on his way.

[**TVB**] <u>Luke 14:2-4</u> Jesus noticed a man suffering from a swelling disorder. ³He questioned the religious scholars and Pharisees. Jesus: Is it permitted by traditions and the Hebrew Scriptures to heal people on the Sabbath, or is it forbidden? ⁴They didn't reply. **Then Jesus healed the man** and sent him on his way.

Luke 17:12-14 And as he entered into a certain village, there met him ten men that were lepers, which stood afar off: ¹³And they lifted up their voices, and said, Jesus, Master, have mercy on us. ¹⁴And when he saw them, he said unto them, **Go shew yourselves unto the priests. And it came to pass, that, as they went, they were cleansed**.

[**CBC**] <u>Luke 17:12-14</u> And as He was about to enter into a certain village, there met Him ten men that were lepers, which stood afar off: ¹³And they lifted up their voices, and said, Jesus, Commander, have compassion on us. ¹⁴And when He saw them, He said unto them, "**Go shew yourselves unto the priests." And it came to pass, that, in their going, they were cleansed**.

[CWB] <u>Luke 17:12-14</u> As He approached a certain village, ten lepers came to meet him, stopped some distance away [13]and called out to Him, "Master, have mercy on us!" [14]Jesus could see their leprosy and simply said, **"Go show yourselves to the priest." They left, and on the way they were healed.**

[EEBT] <u>Luke 17:12-14</u> When he was going into a village, 10 men came towards him. These men had an illness of the skin. They stopped some way away from Jesus [13]and they shouted, 'Jesus, Master, please be kind to us.' [14]Jesus saw them standing there. **'Go and show yourselves to the priests',** he answered. **While they were going there, they became well again.**

[REM-NT] <u>Luke 17:12-14</u> As he was entering one village, ten lepers came to him. They stayed a respectable distance away [13]and shouted, "Lord Jesus, have mercy on us!" [14]When he saw them, he smiled and said, **"Go to the priests and let them examine you." And as they went, they were healed.**

[RNT] <u>Luke 17:12-14</u> As he was approaching a certain village, ten leprous men met him. They stood at a distance, [13]and, raising their voices, called, "Jesus, Master, have compassion on us." [14]When Jesus saw them, he said, **"Go and show yourselves to the priests." While they were going, they became clean.**

[TLB] <u>Luke 17:12-14</u> and as they entered a village there, ten lepers stood at a distance, [13]crying out, "Jesus, sir, have mercy on us!" [14]He looked at them and said, **"Go to the Jewish priest and show him that you are healed!" And as they were going, their leprosy disappeared.**

[TPT] <u>Luke 17:12-14</u> As he entered one village, ten men approached him, but they kept their distance, for they were lepers. [13]They shouted to him, "Mighty Lord, our wonderful Master! Won't you have mercy on us and heal us?" [14]When Jesus stopped to look at them, he spoke these words: **"Go to be examined by the Jewish priests." They set off, and they were healed while walking along the way.**

[TTNT] <u>Luke 17:12-14</u> When He entered a particular village ten lepers met Him. They remained a safe distance away [13]but called out to Him: "Jesus, Master, have mercy on us." [14]When He noticed them, Jesus said to them: **"Go and show yourselves to the priests (to have your healing verified)." On the way they were cleansed of their leprosy**!

[Wuest-NT] <u>Luke 17:12-14</u> And as He was entering a certain village there met Him ten lepers, men, who stood at a distance, [13]and they themselves raised their voice, saying, Jesus, Master, you who have power and authority, be sympathetic with our affliction and do something to help us. [14]And having seen them He said to them, **Having gone on your way, show yourselves as proof to the priests. And it came to pass that while they were going, they were cleansed.**

<u>Luke 17:19</u> And he said unto him, Arise, go thy way: **thy faith hath made thee whole**[sozo].

[ClarkePyle] <u>Luke 17:19</u> Then turning himself to the Man; he said, Go in peace; **your exemplary Faith has obtained the Cure of your Disease.**

[CWB] <u>Luke 17:19</u> Then He said, "Get up and be on your way; **your faith in me made it possible for you to be healed."**

[EOB-NT] <u>Luke 17:19</u> Then Jesus said to him, "Get up and go your way. Your faith has healed you!"

[ERV] <u>Luke 17:19</u> Then Jesus said to the man, "Stand up! You can go. **You were healed because you believed."**

[Folsom-Gs] <u>Luke 17:19</u> And he said to him, Rise up, and go thy way: **thy faith has restored thee.**

[GNC-NT] <u>Luke 17:19</u> Then he turned to the man and said, "Rise up and be on your way. **It is your faith that has given you back your health."**

[ICB] <u>Luke 17:19</u> Then Jesus said to him, "Stand up and go on your way. **You were healed because you believed."**

[JMNT] <u>Luke 17:19</u> And so He said to him, "After arising (or: standing up), continue going your way. **Your trust and faith has made you healthy and left you whole (or: has healed, delivered and saved you so that you are now rescued from your prior condition)."**

[Knox] <u>Luke 17:19</u> And he said to him, Arise and go on thy way, **thy faith has brought thee recovery.**

[NIRV] <u>Luke 17:19</u> Then Jesus said to him, "Get up and go. **Your faith has healed you."**

[NLV] <u>Luke 17:19</u> Then Jesus said to him, "Get up and go on your way. **Your trust in God has healed you."**

[Phillips] <u>Luke 17:19</u> And he said to the man, 'Stand up now, and go on your way. **It is your faith that has made you well.'**

[Sacred-NT] <u>Luke 17:19</u> And he said to him, Arise, go your way; **your faith has cured you.**

[Wuest-NT] <u>Luke 17:19</u> And He said to him, Having arisen, be going on your way. **Your faith has restored your body to soundness of health.**

<u>Luke 18:41-43</u> Saying, What wilt thou that I shall do unto thee? And he said, Lord, that I may receive my sight. ⁴²And Jesus said unto him, **Receive thy sight: thy faith hath saved**[sozo] **thee.** ⁴³**And immediately he received his sight**, and followed him, glorifying God: and all the people, when they saw it, gave praise unto God.

[AMP] <u>Luke 18:41-43</u> "What do you want Me to do for you?" He said, "Lord, let me regain my sight!" ⁴²Jesus said to him, **"Regain your sight; your [personal trust and confident] faith [in Me] has made you well."** ⁴³**Immediately he regained his sight** and began following Jesus, glorifying and praising and honoring God. And all the people, when they saw it, praised God.

[AMPC] <u>Luke 18:41-43</u> What do you want Me to do for you? He said, Lord, let me receive my sight! ⁴²And Jesus said to him, **Receive your sight! Your faith (your trust and confidence that spring from your faith in God) has healed you.** ⁴³**And instantly he received his sight** and began to follow Jesus, recognizing, praising, and honoring God; and all the people, when they saw it, praised God.

[Barclay-NT] <u>Luke 18:41-43</u> 'What do you want me to do for you?' The man said: 'Master, the only thing I want is to see again!' ⁴²**"See again!' Jesus said to him. 'Your faith has cured you!'** ⁴³**Immediately his sight returned**, and he followed Jesus praising God, and, when the people saw it, they all gave praise to God.

[CEV] <u>Luke 18:41-43</u> "What do you want me to do for you?" "Lord, I want to see!" he answered. ⁴²Jesus replied, **"Look and you will see! Your eyes are healed because of your faith."** ⁴³**At once the man could see**, and he went with Jesus and started thanking God. When the crowds saw what happened, they praised God.

[EEBT] <u>Luke 18:41-43</u> 'What do you want me to do for you?' 'Sir', he replied, 'please cause me to see again.' ⁴²**'See again', said Jesus. 'You are well now because you believed in me.'** ⁴³**Immediately the man could see again**. He started to follow Jesus. He was saying, 'God, you are very great and powerful.' Many people saw what had happened. 'God, how great and important you are', they also said.

[EXB] <u>Luke 18:41-43</u> "What do you want me to do for you?" He said, "Lord, I want to see." ⁴²Jesus said to him, **"Then see. ·You are healed because you believed [Your faith has healed/saved you]."** ⁴³**At once the man was able to see,** and he followed Jesus, thanking God. All the people who saw this praised God.

[GT] <u>Luke 18:41-43</u> "What do you want of me?" The blind man said, "Lord, heal me! Let me be able to see again." ⁴²Jesus said to him, **"See again! You are made well because you believed."** ⁴³Immediately

the man was able to see again. He followed Jesus, giving glory to God. All of the people who saw this praised God for what had occurred.

[ICB] <u>Luke 18:41-43</u> "What do you want me to do for you?" He said, "Lord, I want to see again." ⁴²Jesus said to him, "**Then see! You are healed because you believed.**" ⁴³**At once the man was able to see**, and he followed Jesus, thanking God. All the people who saw this praised God.

[Johnson-NT] <u>Luke 18:41-43</u> "What do you want me to do for you?" Instantly he said, "Lord, I want to see." ⁴²"**Then see." Jesus said simply. Your trust has made you whole.**" ⁴³**In that instant, the man could see** and he followed Jesus, worshipping and praising God. When all the people saw what had happened, they, too, praise God.

[Lee-NT] <u>Luke 18:41-43</u> What do you want Me to do for you? And he said, Lord, that I may receive my sight! ⁴²**And Jesus said to him, Receive your sight; your faith has healed you.** ⁴³**And instantly he received his sight** and followed Him, glorifying God. And all the people, seeing it, gave praise to God.

[Mace-NT] <u>Luke 18:41-43</u> what would you have me do for you? he said, Lord, I desire to have sight. ⁴²**have sight, said Jesus, your faith has obtained you a cure.** ⁴³**and immediately he saw**: and followed Jesus, glorifying God: and all the people, who were eye-witnesses, gave praise unto God.

[REM-NT] <u>Luke 18:41-43</u> "What would you have me do for you?" "Lord, I want to see!" the man cried. ⁴²**Jesus smiled and said, "Then see! Your trust in me has healed you."** ⁴³**Immediately his sight was restored**, and he followed Jesus, shouting praises to God. When the crowd saw it, they also praised God.

[Smith] <u>Luke 18:41-43</u> Saying, What wilt thou I shall do to thee? And he said, Lord, that I might see again. ⁴²And Jesus said to him, **See again: thy faith has saved thee.** ⁴³**And he immediately saw again**, and followed him, honouring God: and all the people having seen, gave praise to God.

[Stanhope-NT] <u>Luke 18:41-43</u> Saying, What wilt thou that I shall do unto thee? And he said, Lord, that I may receive my sight. ⁴²And Jesus said unto him, **Thy Faith hath rendered thee a proper Object of this Mercy.** ⁴³**And immediately he received his sight**, and followed him, glorifying God: and all the people, when they saw it, gave praise unto God.

[TGNT] <u>Luke 18:41-43</u> "What is it that you want me to do?" "Master," he replied, "I want to see!" ⁴²"**All right, see!" said Jesus, "Your faith has restored you."** ⁴³**Instantly he could see**, and he followed him, giving honor to God. And all the people who saw this praised God as well.

<u>Luke 22:50-51</u> And one of them smote the servant of the high priest, and cut off his right ear. ⁵¹And Jesus answered and said, Suffer ye thus far. **And he touched his ear, and healed him**.

[EEBT] <u>Luke 22:50-51</u> One of them hit the servant of the leader of the priests. He cut off his right ear. ⁵¹'Enough!' said Jesus, 'Stop doing this!' **He then touched the man and made his ear well again**.

[GW] <u>Luke 22:50-51</u> One of the disciples cut off the right ear of the chief priest's servant. ⁵¹But Jesus said, "Stop! That's enough of this." **Then he touched the servant's ear and healed him.**

[NKJV] <u>Luke 22:50-51</u> And one of them struck the servant of the high priest and cut off his right ear. ⁵¹But Jesus answered and said, "Permit even this." **And He touched his ear and healed him.**

[Original-NT] <u>Luke 22:50-51</u> One of them did strike the high priest's servant and severed his right ear. ⁵¹"Leave this to me", Jesus replied, **and touching the ear healed him.**

[PNT] <u>Luke 22:50-51</u> And one of them smote the servant of the high priest, and cut off his right ear. ⁵¹And he answered and said, Suffer ye thus far, And he streched out his hand, and **touched his ear, and his ear was restored**.

[T4T] <u>Luke 22:50-51</u> One of them drew his sword and struck the servant of the high priest to kill him, but only cut off his right ear. ⁵¹But Jesus said, "Do not do any more of that!" **He touched the servant's ear and healed him.**

[TGNT] <u>Luke 22:50-51</u> And one of them struck the ruling priest's deputy, cutting off his right ear. ⁵¹But Jesus said, "Enough of this!" Then **he touched the ear and instantly healed him.**

[TPT] <u>Luke 22:50-51</u> Just then, one of the disciples swung his sword at the high priest's servant and slashed off his right ear. ⁵¹Jesus stopped the incident from escalating any further by shouting, "Stop! That's enough of this!" **Then he touched the right side of the injured man's head and the ear grew back—he was healed!**

[TVB] <u>Luke 22:50-51</u> Before Jesus could answer, one of them had swung his sword at the high priest's slave, cutting off his right ear. ⁵¹Jesus: Stop! No more of this! Then **He reached out to touch—and heal—the man's ear.**

JOHN

<u>John 1:1</u> In the beginning was the Word, and the Word was with God, and the Word was God.

[AMP] <u>John 1:1</u> In the beginning [before all time] was the Word (Christ), and the Word was with God, and the Word was God Himself.

[Barclay-NT] <u>John 1:1</u> When the world began, the Word was already there. The Word was with God, and the nature of the Word was the same as the nature of God.

[ERV] <u>John 1:1</u> Before the world began, the Word was there. The Word was with God, and the Word was God.

[GNC-NT] <u>John 1:1</u> It was the Word that was at the very beginning; and the Word was by the side of God, and the Word was the very same as God.

[GT] <u>John 1:1</u> The Word was in the beginning, and the Word was with God, and the Word is the essence of God.

[ICB] <u>John 1:1</u> Before the world began, there was the Word. The Word was with God, and the Word was God.

[Lamsa] <u>John 1:1</u> THE Word was in the beginning, and that very Word was with God, and God was that Word.

[NEB] <u>John 1:1</u> WHEN ALL THINGS BEGAN, the Word already was. The Word dwelt with God, and what God was, the Word was.

[Original-NT] <u>John 1:1</u> In the beginning was the Word. And the Word was with God. So the Word was divine.

[REB] <u>John 1:1</u> In the beginning the Word already was. The Word was in God's presence, and what God was, the Word was.

[Stanhope-NT] <u>John 1:1</u> Before Time or the World was, the Word (a Title understood by the generality of the Jews, and many Heathen of that and former Ages, to denote a Divine Person) had a Being; and did exist inseparably with God, yea and was himself literally and truly God.

[Stringfellow-NT] <u>John 1:1</u> In the beginning was the Word, and the Word was face to face with God, and the Word was Divine.

[TNT] John 1:1 When everything began the Word already existed. The Word was with God and shared his nature.

[TTNT] John 1:1 Jesus is the Word. He existed in the beginning, before time began. This Word was with God and, indeed, the Word was God.

[Wuest-NT] John 1:1 In the beginning the Word was existing. And the Word was in fellowship with God the Father. And the Word was as to His essence absolute deity.

John 1:4 In him was life[zoé]; and the life[zoé] was the light of men.

[AMP] John 1:4 In Him was life [and the power to bestow life], and the life was the Light of men.

[Anderson-Sinaitic NT] John 1:4 In him is life, and the life was the light of men.

[AUV-NT 2003] John 1:4 Life existed in Him; and that Life [was what] enlightened mankind [spiritually].

[Ballentine-NT] John 1:4 What has made its appearance in him was Life, and the Life was the Light of men.

[BWE-NT] John 1:4 Life was in the Word. That life was Light for people.

[CEB] John 1:4 through the Word was life, and the life was the light for all people.

[Etheridge-NT] John 1:4 In him was life, and the life is the light of the sons of man;

[GT] John 1:4 He was the Source of life and that life was the light for people.

[GW] John 1:4 He was the source of life, and that life was the light for humanity.

[Jordan-NT] John 1:4 In him was life, and the life was humanity's light.

[KNT] John 1:4 Life was in him, and this life was the light of the human race.

[Macrae] John 1:4 In him was (the fountain of life and light, natural, spiritual, and eternal), and (he) the life was the light of men.

[MSG] John 1:4 What came into existence was Life, and the Life was Light to live by.

[NLT] John 1:4 The Word gave life to everything that was created, and his life brought light to everyone.

[NLV] John 1:4 Life began by Him. His Life was the Light for men.

[Norton-Gs] John 1:4 In him was the source of blessedness; and the source of blessedness was the light for man.

[TLB] John 1:4 Eternal life is in him, and this life gives light to all mankind.

[Tolstoy-Gs] John 1:4 In it was the power of life, and the life became the light of men.

[TPT] John 1:4 Life came into being because of him, for his life is light for all humanity.

[TTNT] John 1:4 In Jesus, in this Word, was the life that brought God's light into people's lives.

[TWTY-RCT-NT-V1] John 1:4 In, by and with Him was, is and exists life and continued existence; and this life and continued existence was, is and exists as the Light, Radiance and Illumination of mankind.

John 1:14 And the Word was made flesh, and dwelt among us, (and we beheld his glory, the glory as of the only begotten of the Father,) full of grace and truth.

[Authentic-NT] John 1:14 The Word took bodily form and dwelt with us. And we beheld his glory. Glory as of the Father's Only-begotten. Full of loving-kindness and truth.

OUR HEALING COVENANT

[CEV] John 1:14 The Word became a human being and lived here with us. We saw his true glory, the glory of the only Son of the Father. From him the complete gifts of undeserved grace and truth have come down to us.

[CEVUK2012] John 1:14 The Word became a human being and lived here with us. We saw his true glory, the glory of the only Son of the Father. From him all the kindness and all the truth of God have come down to us.

[CJB] John 1:14 The Word became a human being and lived with us, and we saw his Sh'khinah, the Sh'khinah of the Father's only Son, full of grace and truth.

[CWB] John 1:14 So **the Word of God became a man and lived among us**. We saw that Light with our own eyes and knew He was from God. Jesus was gracious, kind and full of light and truth.

[ERV] John 1:14 The Word became a man and lived among us. We saw his divine greatness—the greatness that belongs to the only Son of the Father. The Word was full of grace and truth.

[GT] John 1:14 The Word became human and lived among us. We saw his glory, the glory of the Father's one and only son—who came from the Father, full of help in time of need and truth.

[HRB] John 1:14 And **the Word became flesh and tabernacled among us**. And we beheld His glory, glory as of an only begotten one from the Father, full of grace and of truth.

[MLV] John 1:14 And **the Word became flesh and resided among us** (and we saw his glory, glory like that of the only begotten from the Father), full of favor and truth.

[MSG] John 1:14 The Word became flesh and blood, and moved into the neighborhood. We saw the glory with our own eyes, the one-of-a-kind glory, like Father, like Son, Generous inside and out, true from start to finish.

[NIRV] John 1:14 The Word became a human being. He made his home with us. We have seen his glory. It is the glory of the One and Only, who came from the Father. And the Word was full of grace and truth.

[NLT] John 1:14 So **the Word became human and made his home among us**. He was full of unfailing love and faithfulness. And we have seen his glory, the glory of the Father's one and only Son.

[NLV] John 1:14 Christ became human flesh and lived among us. We saw His shining-greatness. This greatness is given only to a much-loved Son from His Father. He was full of loving-favor and truth.

[Palmer] John 1:14 And **the Word became flesh, and moved his tent in among us**; and we beheld his glory, the glory as of an only begotten from a Father, full of grace and truth.

[REM-NT] John 1:14 Jesus became a real human being, and he established his temple—the temple of his body—among us. We have seen the glory of his character—the character of the One and Only true God. He came from God, and perfectly revealed the Father who is the source of all grace and truth.

[T4T] John 1:14 The one who expresses God's character/what God is like became a human being, and he lived among us for a while. As a result, we saw how wonderful he is. He came from God his father, and there was no other person as wonderful as he. He was wonderful because he always acted kindly toward us/in ways we did not deserve, and he always spoke truthfully to us about God.

[Thomson] John 1:14 Now the Word became incarnate, and dwelt as in a tent among us, and we beheld his glory—a glory as of an only begotten from the father. He was full of grace and truth.

[TVB] John 1:14 The Voice took on flesh and became human and chose to live alongside us. We have seen Him, enveloped in undeniable splendor—the one true Son of the Father—evidenced in the perfect balance of grace and truth.

[TWTY-RCT-NT-V1] John 1:14 And so the Word and saying, message and statement, declaration and thought, instruction and teaching, decree, mandate and matter came to be and exist, arose, appeared and originated as mortal flesh, and He tented and took up His residence, pitched His abode and Tabernacled among us. And so we saw and beheld, gazed at and attentively viewed, contemplated, perceived and watched His glory and splendour, magnificence and excellence, pre-eminence and dignity, brightness, favour and majesty, a glory and splendour, magnificence and excellence, pre-eminence and dignity, brightness, favour and majesty as, like and similar to that of one and only unique child from the presence of and the immediate proximity of a father, completely filled and imbued, perfect and solid, whole, abounding and thoroughly endowed with undeserved favour and joy, delight and thanks, glory and charm, goodwill and sweetness, pleasure and the gift of merciful and loving kindness, as well as the reality and disclosure, expression and certainty, uprightness and dependableness, genuineness and reliability, fact, sincerity and honesty of truth.

[Wuest-NT] John 1:14 And the Word, entering a new mode of existence, became flesh, and lived in a tent [His physical body] among us. And we gazed with attentive and careful regard and spiritual perception at His glory, a glory such as that of a uniquely-begotten Son from the Father, full of grace and truth.

John 3:14-15 And as Moses lifted up the serpent in the wilderness, even so must the Son of man be lifted up: [15]That whosoever believeth in him should not perish, but have eternal life[zoé].

These verses refer to the story in Numbers 21:9 where Moses lifted up the serpent in the wilderness to heal the people. Now Jesus is lifted up as the serpent. Because He is now lifted up, we get the same benefits the children of Israel did—healing—in addition to the great blessings of forgiveness of sins and salvation.

[AMPC] John 3:14-15 And just as Moses lifted up the serpent in the desert [on a pole], so must [so it is necessary that] the Son of Man be lifted up [on the cross], [15]In order that everyone who believes in Him [who cleaves to Him, trusts Him, and relies on Him] may not perish, but have eternal life and [actually] live forever!

[AUV-NT 2003] John 3:14-15 And [just] like Moses lifted up the snake [on the pole] in the wilderness, so the Son of man must be lifted up [on the cross] [15]so that whoever believes in Him would have never ending life."

[BLE] John 3:14-15 And as Moses raised the snake aloft in the desert, so the Son of Man must be raised aloft, [15]that everyone who believes in him may have eternal life.

[BV-KJV-NT] John 3:14-15 And just as Moses put the snake up high in the backcountry, so it is necessary for the Human Son to be put up high [15]so that everyone who trusts in Him might not be ruined, but may have life that spans all time.

[EXB] John 3:14-15 Just as Moses lifted up the ·snake [serpent] in the ·desert [wilderness; Moses put a bronze snake statue on a pole, and those who looked at it were healed of snake bites], the Son of Man must also be lifted up [an allusion to the cross and resurrection]. [15]So that everyone who ·believes can have eternal life in him [or believes in him can have eternal life].

[Hall] John 3:14-15 And, as the brazen serpent was erected by Moses in the wilderness, for the cure of those Israelites, that were stung with the fiery serpents, there; so must of the Son of Man be lifted up, on the cross, [15]that all they, who are envenomed by that old serpent the Devil, and stung with the conscience of their sins, looking up unto him, by a true faith, maybe healed and live for ever.

[NEB] John 3:14-15 This Son of Man must be lifted up as the serpent was lifted up by Moses in the wilderness, [15]so that everyone who has faith in him may in him possess eternal life.

[REM-NT] <u>John 3:14-15</u> Just as Moses lifted up the snake in the desert in order to bring healing to those who would look at it and trust, so also I—the Son of Man—must be lifted up ¹⁵so that everyone who looks to me and trusts in me may be healed and live eternally.

[Rotherham] <u>John 3:14-15</u> And, just as, Moses, lifted up the serpent in the desert, so, must, the Son of Man, be lifted up, — ¹⁵That, whosoever believeth in him, may have life age-abiding.

[TCNT] <u>John 3:14-15</u> And, as Moses lifted up the serpent in the desert, so must the Son of Man be lifted up; ¹⁵That every one who believes in him may have Immortal Life.

[Weymouth-NT] <u>John 3:14-15</u> And just as Moses lifted high the serpent in the Desert, so must the Son of Man be lifted up, ¹⁵in order that every one who trusts in Him may have the Life of the Ages.

[Wuest-NT] <u>John 3:14-15</u> And just as Moses elevated the snake in the uninhabited region, in like manner is it necessary in the nature of the case for the Son of Man to be lifted up, ¹⁵in order that everyone who places his trust in Him may be having life eternal.

[YLT] <u>John 3:14-15</u> And as Moses did lift up the serpent in the wilderness, so it behoveth the Son of Man to be lifted up, ¹⁵that every one who is believing in him may not perish, but may have life age-during,

<u>John 4:49-50</u> The nobleman saith unto him, Sir, come down ere my child die. ⁵⁰Jesus saith unto him, **Go thy way; thy son liveth**. And the man believed the word that Jesus had spoken unto him, and he went his way.

[AMPC] <u>John 4:49-50</u> The king's officer pleaded with Him, Sir, do come down at once before my little child is dead! ⁵⁰Jesus answered him, **Go in peace; your son will live**! And the man put his trust in what Jesus said and started home.

[BOOKS-NT] <u>John 4:49-50</u> The royal official said, "Sir, come down before my child dies." ⁵⁰**"Go,"** **Jesus replied, "your son will live."** The man took Jesus at his word and departed.

[FBV-NT] <u>John 4:49-50</u> "Lord, just come before my child dies," the official pleaded. ⁵⁰**"Go on home,"** **Jesus told him. "Your son will live!"** The man trusted what Jesus told him and left for home.

[GoodSpeed-NT] <u>John 4:49-50</u> The official said to him, "Come down, sir, before my child is dead!" ⁵⁰Jesus said to him, **"You can go home. Your son is going to live."** The man believed what Jesus said to him and went home.

[GT] <u>John 4:49-50</u> The government official said to Jesus, "Lord, please go to my house before my little boy dies!" ⁵⁰Jesus answered him, **"Go, your son lives."** The man believed. He took Jesus at his word and left.

[HRV] <u>John 4:49-50</u> That servant of the king said to Him, My Adon, come down before the boy dies. ⁵⁰Yeshua said to him: **Go, your son is alive**. And that man had trust in the word that Yeshua spoke to him, and went away.

[Madsen-NT] <u>John 4:49-50</u> Then the courtier said to him, 'Sir, come down before my child dies!' ⁵⁰Then Jesus said, **'Go now, your son lives!'** And the man put his faith in the word that Jesus spoke to him, and he went.

[Rieu-Gs] <u>John 4:49-50</u> 'Sir,' said the nobleman, 'come down before my child is dead.' ⁵⁰**'You can go back,' said Jesus. 'Your son is living.'** And the man set out, convinced that he had heard the truth from Jesus.

[TLB] <u>John 4:49-50</u> The official pled, "Sir, please come now before my child dies." ⁵⁰Then Jesus told him, **"Go back home. Your son is healed!"** And the man believed Jesus and started home.

[TPT] <u>John 4:49-50</u> But the man continued to plead, "You have to come with me to Capernaum before my little boy dies!" ⁵⁰Then Jesus looked him in the eyes and said, "**Go back home now. I promise you, your son will live and not die.**" The man believed in his heart the words of Jesus and set off for home.

[TTT-NT] <u>John 4:49-50</u> The ruler said to him, "Lord, come down, before my son dies." ⁵⁰Jesus said to him, "**Go. Your son lives.**" The man believed the word that Jesus said, and he went.

[Weymouth-NT] <u>John 4:49-50</u> "Sir," pleaded the officer, "come down before my child dies." ⁵⁰"**You may return home,**" **replied Jesus; "your son has recovered**." He believed the words of Jesus, and started back home;

<u>John 5:6-9</u> When Jesus saw him lie, and knew that he had been now a long time in that case, he saith unto him, Wilt thou be made whole? ⁷The impotent man answered him, Sir, I have no man, when the water is troubled, to put me into the pool: but while I am coming, another steppeth down before me. ⁸**Jesus saith unto him, Rise, take up thy bed, and walk.** ⁹**And immediately the man was made whole**, and took up his bed, and walked: and on the same day was the sabbath.

[Anderson-Sinaitic NT] <u>John 5:6-9</u> Jesus saw him lying, and knowing that he had already been sick a long time, said to him: Wilt thou be restored to health? ⁷The sick man answered him: Sir, I have no man, that when the water is stirred he may put me into the pool; but while I am coming another goes down before me. ⁸**Jesus says to him: Arise, take up thy bed, and walk.** ⁹**And the man was restored to health, and took up his bed and walked**; but a sabbath was on that day.

[BBE] <u>John 5:6-9</u> When Jesus saw him there on the floor it was clear to him that he had been now a long time in that condition, and so he said to the man, Is it your desire to get well? ⁷The ill man said in answer, Sir, I have nobody to put me into the bath when the water is moving; and while I am on the way down some other person gets in before me. ⁸**Jesus said to him, Get up, take your bed and go.** ⁹**And the man became well straight away**, and took up his bed and went. Now that day was the Sabbath.

[CWB] <u>John 5:6-9</u> As Jesus walked beside the columns of the porches around the pool, He saw this man lying on a mat. Jesus knew by looking at him that he had been sick for a long time. So He stopped and said to him, "Would you like to be healed?" ⁷The sick man barely looked up, but straining his voice to talk, said, "Sir, there is no one here to help me into the water at the right time. When I try to make it to the pool by myself, the others push and shove and always get in before I do. So there's no use. I'm ready to give up." ⁸Jesus looked at him and said, "**I'm not here to help you into the water. I'm here to tell you to stand up on your feet. Then roll up your mat and go on home.**" ⁹**The man didn't even question Jesus. He just willed to do what Jesus said, put forth the effort to stand, and as he did, he found that he was healed.** He reached down, rolled up his mat and turned to thank Jesus. But Jesus had disappeared into the crowd. So the man tucked his mat under his arm and left for home. This was on the Sabbath day.

[FBV-NT] <u>John 5:6-9</u> "Do you want to be healed?" ⁷"Sir," the sick man answered," I don't have anyone to help me get into the pool when the water is stirred. While I'm trying to get there, someone always gets in before me" ⁸**"Stand up, pick up your mat, and start walking!" Jesus told him.** ⁹**Immediately the man was healed.** He picked up his mat and started walking. Now the day that this happened was the Sabbath.

[MCC-NT] <u>John 5:6-9</u> ⁶Jesus seeing this Man lying down, and knowing that He had been already a long Time affected; says to Him, "Art Thou willing to become sound?" ⁷The infirm Man replied to Him, "O, Sir! I have no Man-that, when the Water is stirred, might put Me into the Pond; but at the Time that I am coming, Another before Me gets down." ⁸**Jesus tells Him, "Arise, take up thy Couch and walk along."** ⁹**And presently the Man became sound**, and took up his Couch, and walked along; but the Sabbath was on that Day.

[REM-NT] <u>John 5:6-9</u> When Jesus saw him lying there, and learned that he had been in this condition for such a long time, he asked him, "Do you want to get well?" [7]"Sir," the paralyzed man replied, "I have no one to help me into the water when it is stirred. While I am trying to get in, those who are quicker and faster enter before me." [8]Then Jesus said to him, **"Get up! Pick up your mat and walk." [9]Immediately the man was completely cured**: he jumped up, picked up his mat, and walked. This happened on the Sabbath,

[RSV] <u>John 5:6-9</u> When Jesus saw him and knew that he had been lying there a long time, he said to him, "Do you want to be healed?" [7]The sick man answered him, "Sir, I have no man to put me into the pool when the water is troubled, and while I am going another steps down before me." [8]**Jesus said to him, "Rise, take up your pallet, and walk." [9]And at once the man was healed**, and he took up his pallet and walked. Now that day was the sabbath.

[TLB] <u>John 5:6-9</u> When Jesus saw him and knew how long he had been ill, he asked him, "Would you like to get well?" [7]"I can't," the sick man said, "for I have no one to help me into the pool at the movement of the water. While I am trying to get there, someone else always gets in ahead of me." [8]**Jesus told him, "Stand up, roll up your sleeping mat and go on home!" [9]Instantly, the man was healed**! He rolled up the mat and began walking! But it was on the Sabbath when this miracle was done.

[TPT] <u>John 5:6-9</u> When Jesus saw him lying there, he knew that the man had been crippled for a long time. So Jesus said to him, "Do you truly long to be healed?" [7]The sick man answered him, "Sir, there's no way I can get healed, for I have no one who will lower me into the water when the angel comes. As soon as I try to crawl to the edge of the pool, someone else jumps in ahead of me." [8]**Then Jesus said to him, "Stand up! Pick up your sleeping mat and you will walk!" [9]Immediately he stood up—he was healed!** So he rolled up his mat and walked again! Now this miracle took place on the Jewish Sabbath.

[TVB] <u>John 5:6-9</u> He knew this man had been waiting here a long time. Jesus (to the disabled man): Are you here in this place hoping to be healed? [7]Disabled Man: Kind Sir, I wait, like all of these people, for the waters to stir; but I cannot walk. If I am to be healed in the waters, someone must carry me into the pool. Without a helping hand, someone else beats me to the water's edge each time it is stirred. [8]Jesus: **Stand up, carry your mat, and walk. [9]At the moment Jesus uttered these words, a healing energy coursed through the man and returned life to his limbs**—he stood and walked for the first time in 38 years. But this was the Sabbath Day; and any work, including carrying a mat, was prohibited on this day.

[VW] <u>John 5:6-9</u> When Jesus saw him lying there, and knew that he already had been there a long time, He said to him, Do you want to be made well? [7]The sick man answered Him, Sir, I have no man to throw me into the pool when the water is stirred up; but while I am coming, another goes down before me. [8]**Jesus said to him, Rise up, take up your bed and walk. [9]And immediately the man was made well**, took up his bed, and walked. And that day was the Sabbath.

[Williams-NT] <u>John 5:6-9</u> Jesus saw him lying there, and when He found out that he had been in that condition for a long time, He asked him, "Do you want to get well?" [7]The sick man answered, "Sir, I have no one to put me into the pool when the water is moved, but while I am trying to get down, somebody else steps down ahead of me." [8]**Jesus said to him, "Get up, pick up your pallet, and go to walking." [9]And at once the man was well,** and picked up his pallet, and went to walking. Now it was the Sabbath.

[Wuest-NT] <u>John 5:6-9</u> Jesus, having seen this one lying prostrate, and knowing that for a long time already he had been in that condition, says to him, Do you have a longing to become well? [7]The man who was infirm answered Him, Sir, a man I do not have in order that whenever the waters are stirred up, he might throw me at once into the pool. But during the time I am coming, another steps down before me.

[8]Jesus says to him, Be arising. Snatch up your pallet, and start walking and keep on walking. [9]And immediately the man became well. And he snatched up his pallet and went to walking about. Now, there was a sabbath on that day.

<u>John 6:2</u> And a great multitude followed him, because they saw his miracles which he did on them that were diseased.

[AMP] <u>John 6:2</u> A large crowd was following Him because they had seen the signs (attesting miracles) which He continually performed on those who were sick.

[CCB] <u>John 6:2</u> and large crowds followed him because of the miraculous signs they saw when he healed the sick.

[EEBT] <u>John 6:2</u> A large crowd of people followed him, because of the miracles that he had done. They had seen him make sick people well.

[ERV] <u>John 6:2</u> A great crowd of people followed him because they saw the miraculous signs he did in healing the sick.

[Godbey-NT] <u>John 6:2</u> And a great multitude followed Him, because they saw the miracles He was doing in behalf of the sick.

[Montgomery-NT] <u>John 6:2</u> A great crowd were following him, because they witnessed the signs which he was continually performing among those who were ill.

[MSG] <u>John 6:2</u> A huge crowd followed him, attracted by the miracles they had seen him do among the sick.

[Torrey-Gs] <u>John 6:2</u> And a crowd followed him, for they had seen his marvellous healing of the sick.

[TPT] <u>John 6:2</u> And a massive crowd of people followed him everywhere. They were attracted by his miracles and the healings they watched him perform.

<u>John 6:63</u> It is the spirit that quickeneth; the flesh profiteth nothing: the words that I speak unto you, they are spirit, and they are life[zoé].

[AMPC] <u>John 6:63</u> It is the Spirit Who gives life [He is the Life-giver]; the flesh conveys no benefit whatever [there is no profit in it]. The words (truths) that I have been speaking to you are spirit and life.

[BBE] <u>John 6:63</u> The spirit is the life giver; the flesh is of no value: the words which I have said to you are spirit and they are life.

[Brichto] <u>John 6:63</u> The Spirit gives life; the flesh gives nothing of any worth. The words I have spoken are of Spirit: they are life!

[CEB] <u>John 6:63</u> The Spirit is the one who gives life and the flesh doesn't help at all. The words I have spoken to you are spirit and life.

[CEV] <u>John 6:63</u> The Spirit is the one who gives life! Human strength can do nothing. The words that I have spoken to you are from that life-giving Spirit.

[EEBT] <u>John 6:63</u> It is the Spirit that causes you to live. The body alone is worth nothing. The words that I have spoken to you are spirit. They cause you to live.

[ERV] <u>John 6:63</u> It is the Spirit that gives life. The body is of no value for that. But the things I have told you are from the Spirit, so they give life.

[GNT] <u>John 6:63</u> What gives life is God's Spirit; human power is of no use at all. The words I have spoken to you bring God's life-giving Spirit.

[GW] John 6:63 Life is spiritual. Your physical existence doesn't contribute to that life. The words that I have spoken to you are spiritual. They are life.

[MKJV] John 6:63 It is the Spirit that makes alive, the flesh profits nothing. The words that I speak to you are spirit and are life.

[Moffatt] John 6:63 What gives life is the Spirit: flesh is of no avail at all. The words I have uttered to you are spirit and life.

[MOTB] John 6:63 Is it not always the spirit and the spirit alone, that is life-giving? "Flesh," without it has no abiding value; it is like manna. All the words through which I have offered myself to you are meant to be channels of the spirit and of life to you, since in believing those words you would be brought into contact with the life in me.

[MSG] John 6:63 The Spirit can make life. Sheer muscle and willpower don't make anything happen. Every word I've spoken to you is a Spirit-word, and so it is life-making.

[Norton-Gs] John 6:63 What is spiritual gives life. The flesh profits nothing. The words which I speak to you are spiritual, and give life.

[Original-NT] John 6:63 The Spirit is the life-giving agency: the physical counts for nothing. The words I have addressed to you are Spirit, and they are Life.

[Phillips] John 6:63 It is the Spirit which gives life. The flesh will not help you. The things which I have told you are spiritual and are life.

[REM-NT] John 6:63 The Spirit of God is the Spirit of love, truth and freedom, who brings life; humanity is currently infected with selfishness, which brings death and counts for nothing good. The words I have spoken to you are the truth; they heal and bring life.

[Spencer-NT] John 6:63 It is the Spirit that imparts life; the flesh can give no help whatever. The words I have spoken to you are spirit and life.

[T4T] John 6:63 God's Spirit is the one who gives people eternal life. Human efforts are no help at all for giving people eternal life. The message I have spoken to you gives spiritual life (OR, comes from God's Spirit and gives eternal life.)

[TCNT] John 6:63 It is the Spirit that gives Life; mere flesh is of no avail. In the teaching that I have been giving you there is Spirit and there is Life.

[TPT] John 6:63 "The Holy Spirit is the one who gives life, that which is of the natural realm is of no help. The words I speak to you are Spirit and life. But there are still some of you who won't believe."

[TTT-NT] John 6:63 "It is the spirit that gives life; flesh has no gain. The words which I have spoken to you are spirit and life.

[Webster] John 6:63 It is the spirit that reviveth; the flesh profiteth nothing: the words that I speak to you, [they] are spirit, and [they] are life.

[Wuest-NT] John 6:63 The Spirit is He who makes alive. The flesh is not of any use at all. The words which I have spoken to you, spirit are they and life.

John 9:6-7 When he had thus spoken, he spat on the ground, and made clay of the spittle, and he anointed the eyes of the blind man with the clay, [7]And said unto him, Go, wash in the pool of Siloam, (which is by interpretation, Sent.) **He went his way therefore, and washed, and came seeing**.

[AMP] John 9:6-7 When He had said this, He spat on the ground and made mud with His saliva, and He spread the mud [like an ointment] on the man's eyes. [7]And He said to him, "Go, wash in the pool of Siloam" (which is translated, Sent). So **he went away and washed, and came back seeing**.

[Authentic-NT] John 9:6-7 Having said this, he spat on the ground and made clay with the saliva, and dabbed the clay on the man's eyes, ⁷and said to him, 'Go and wash in the Pool of Siloam.' **So he went away and washed, and returned with his sight.**

[CB] John 9:6-7 As He said these things, He spat on the ground, made clay with His spit, and spread the clay on the eyes of the blind man. ⁷He told the man, "Go wash this off in the pool of Siloam (which means, 'Having been Set Apart')." **So he went there, washed himself, and his eyesight returned.**

[GT] John 9:6-7 After Jesus said these things, he spit on the ground and made some mud with it. Then he rubbed it on the blind man's eyes. ⁷Jesus said to him, "Go, wash yourself in the pool of Siloam." (This word means 'Sent'.) Then **the blind man went away and washed himself and came back with sight**!

[Lewis-Gs] John 9:6-7 When he had spoken these things, he spat on the ground, and formed clay of his spittle, and taking it up, painted it upon the eyes of that blind man, ⁷and said unto him, Go, wash thy face in the pool of Shiloah. And **when he had washed his face, his eyes were opened.**

[Lingard-Gs] John 9:6-7 Having said this, he spat on the ground, made clay with the spittle, and rubbed the clay on his eyes. ⁷Then he said to him, "Go thy way, and wash them in the pool of Siloe," which word is translated sent. **He went therefore, washed, and returned with the power of sight.**

[Sindlinger-NT] John 9:6-7 Jesus made mud with his spit and applied it to the man's eyes, a common manner of healing at the time. ⁷He then told the man to go to the nearby reservoir named Siloam and wash the mud off. When he did, **he was able to see for the first time in his life.**

[TTNT] John 9:6-7 After saying this, Jesus spat on the ground and made some mud with His spittle before putting it on the man's eyes. ⁷He told him: "Go and wash in the Pool of Siloam" (meaning 'Sent'). **The man went and washed and then went home with his sight restored.**

[UDB] John 9:6-7 When he said this, he spit on the ground. He made mud with his saliva, and applied it like a medicine to the man's eyes. ⁷Then Jesus said to him, "Go and wash in the pool of Siloam!" (The name of the pool means 'sent'). **So the man went and washed in the pool. When he came back, he was able to see.**

John 10:10 The thief cometh not, but for to steal, and to kill, and to destroy: I am come that they might have life[zoé], and that they might have it more abundantly.

The thief or the devil is the one stealing, killing, and destroying. If it looks like death, theft, or destruction, the source is the devil. All sickness and disease is one of these, and so all sickness and disease would have to come from the devil.

[AMPC] John 10:10 The thief comes only in order to steal and kill and destroy. I came that they may have and enjoy life, and have it in abundance (to the full, till it overflows).

[AUV-NT 2005] John 10:10 The thief comes only to steal and kill and destroy; I came so that people could have life to its fullest.

[Barclay-NT] John 10:10 The thief comes only to kill and destroy. I have come that they might have life and overflowing life.

[BBE] John 10:10 The thief comes only to take the sheep and to put them to death: he comes for their destruction: I have come so that they may have life and have it in greater measure.

[Beck] John 10:10 A thief comes only to steal and kill and destroy. I came so that they will have life and have it overflowing in them.

[Berkeley] John 10:10 The thief's only purpose in coming is to steal, to butcher and to spoil. I have come so they may have life and have it abundantly.

[Besorah] <u>John 10:10</u> "The thief does not come except to steal, and to slaughter, and to destroy. I have come that they might possess life, and that they might possess it beyond measure.

[BLE] <u>John 10:10</u> The thief comes only to steal and kill and waste; I came that they may have life and plenty of it.

[BV-KJV-NT] <u>John 10:10</u> The thief doesn't come except to steal, kill, and ruin. I came so that they may have life and have much more.

[BWE-NT] <u>John 10:10</u> The thief comes only to steal the sheep and to kill them and spoil them. I have come so that people may live and that they may enjoy life to the full.

[Campbell-Gs] <u>John 10:10</u> The thief cometh only to steal, to slay, and to destroy. I am come that they may have life, and more than life.

[CEB] <u>John 10:10</u> The thief enters only to steal, kill, and destroy. I came so that they could have life—indeed, so that they could live life to the fullest.

[Doddridge-NT] <u>John 10:10</u> For whereas the thief only comes that he may steal, and kill, and destroy, —I am come for the benefit of all my sheep, that they may have true life, and that at length they may have it yet more abundantly; a most plentiful provision being made for their everlasting comfort and happiness, even far beyond what has ever been known before.

[ERV] <u>John 10:10</u> A thief comes to steal, kill, and destroy. But I came to give life—life that is full and good.

[Green-NT] <u>John 10:10</u> The thief comes not but to steal and slaughter and destroy: I came that they may have life and have it plenteously.

[GW] <u>John 10:10</u> A thief comes to steal, kill, and destroy. But I came so that my sheep will have life and so that they will have everything they need.

[ICB] <u>John 10:10</u> A thief comes to steal and kill and destroy. But I came to give life—life in all its fullness.

[JMNT] <u>John 10:10</u> "The thief does not constantly come, except to the end that he may steal, slaughter (slay for food—as for a feast—or, for a sacrifice) and destroy (utterly loose away). I Myself come so that they can progressively possess (would continuously have; could habitually hold) Life, and may continue possessing [it] in superabundance (or: and may have a surplus surrounding them in excessive amounts)."

[Johnson-NT] <u>John 10:10</u> Burglars are dishonest, murderous, and destructive. I am here to offer life, even life beyond what you have ever known.

[KNT] <u>John 10:10</u> The thief only comes to steal, and kill, and destroy. I came so that they could have life—yes, and have it full to overflowing.'

[LDB-NT] <u>John 10:10</u> "The thief's only purpose in coming is to steal, kill, and destroy. I have come so that mankind may have Life, and have it in unimagined abundance.

[Mace-NT] <u>John 10:10</u> the thief comes only to steal, to kill, and destroy: but I am come that they might have life, and have it with all its advantages.

[MSG] <u>John 10:10</u> A thief is only there to steal and kill and destroy. I came so they can have real and eternal life, more and better life than they ever dreamed of.

[Murdock-NT] <u>John 10:10</u> The thief cometh not, but that he may steal, and kill, and destroy. I have come, that they may have life, and may have that which is excellent.

[NIRV] <u>John 10:10</u> A thief comes only to steal and kill and destroy. I have come so they may have life. I want them to have it in the fullest possible way.

[NLT] <u>John 10:10</u> The thief's purpose is to steal and kill and destroy. My purpose is to give them a rich and satisfying life.

[NLV] <u>John 10:10</u> The robber comes only to steal and to kill and to destroy. I came so they might have life, a great full life.

[Original-NT] <u>John 10:10</u> The thief only comes to steal and kill and destroy. I have come that they may have life, and ever more life.

[PLAWL] <u>John 10:10</u> The thief cometh not, but for to steal, and to kill, and to destroy: I am come that they (who are my sheep) might have life, and that they might have it more abundantly and that they might have abundance of pasture.

[Rotherham] <u>John 10:10</u> The thief, cometh not, save that he may thieve and slay and destroy: I, came, that, life, they might have, and, above measure, might have.

[TGNT] <u>John 10:10</u> The thief only comes to steal and execute and destroy; I came that they may have life, and have it to the extreme!

[TPT] <u>John 10:10</u> A thief has only one thing in mind—he wants to steal, slaughter, and destroy. But I have come to give you everything in abundance, more than you expect—life in its fullness until you overflow!

[TTNT] <u>John 10:10</u> "The purpose of the thief, the devil, is to steal, kill and destroy. But I have come to give the fullness of God's life to those who believe in Me.

[TVB] <u>John 10:10</u> The thief approaches with malicious intent, looking to steal, slaughter, and destroy; I came to give life with joy and abundance.

[Wakefield-NT] <u>John 10:10</u> The thief only cometh to steal, and to kill, and to destroy: I am come, that the sheep may have life, and abundance of all good things.

[Wuest-NT] <u>John 10:10</u> The thief does not come except to steal and to kill and to destroy. I alone came in order that they might be possessing life, and that they might be possessing it in superabundance.

<u>John 11:25</u> Jesus said unto her, I am the resurrection, and the life[zoé]: he that believeth in me, though he were dead, yet shall he live:

[AUV-NT 2003] <u>John 11:25</u> Jesus said to her, "I am the resurrection and the life; the person who believes in me will live on, even though he dies [physically].

[Baxter-NT] <u>John 11:25</u> I am the principle and cause of Life and Resurrection. The dead that believe in me shall be raised: And the living that believe in me shall live for ever, their Souls, first and their Bodies after, raised to blessedness.

[BV-KJV-NT] <u>John 11:25</u> Jesus said to her, "I am the Return back to life and the Life. The person trusting in Me, even if he were dead, he will live.

[CJB] <u>John 11:25</u> Yeshua said to her, "I AM the Resurrection and the Life! Whoever puts his trust in me will live, even if he dies;

[GW] <u>John 11:25</u> Jesus said to her, "I am the one who brings people back to life, and I am life itself. Those who believe in me will live even if they die.

[NLV] <u>John 11:25</u> Jesus said to her, "I am the One Who raises the dead and gives them life. Anyone who puts his trust in Me will live again, even if he dies.

[Norton-Gs] <u>John 11:25</u> Jesus said to her, I am the resurrection and eternal life. He who has faith in me, though he die, will live; and whoever lives and has faith in me will never die.

[NWT] <u>John 11:25</u> Jesus said to her: "I am the resurrection and the life. The one who exercises faith in me, even though he dies, will come to life;

[T4T] <u>John 11:25</u> Jesus said to her, "I am the one who enables people to become alive again and who causes people to live eternally. Those who believe in me, even if they die, they will live again.

[TLB] <u>John 11:25</u> Jesus told her, "I am the one who raises the dead and gives them life again. Anyone who believes in me, even though he dies like anyone else, shall live again.

[Tolstoy-Gs] <u>John 11:25</u> I am the quickener and the life. He that believes in me, though he die, shall live.

[TPT] <u>John 11:25</u> "Martha," Jesus said, "You don't have to wait until then. I am the Resurrection, and I am Life Eternal. Anyone who clings to me in faith, even though he dies, will live forever.

[TVB] <u>John 11:25</u> Jesus: I am the resurrection and the source of all life; those who believe in Me will live even in death.

[YLT] <u>John 11:25</u> Jesus said to her, 'I am the rising again, and the life; he who is believing in me, even if he may die, shall live;'

<u>John 11:43-44</u> And when he thus had spoken, **he cried with a loud voice, Lazarus, come forth.** [44]**And he that was dead came forth**, bound hand and foot with graveclothes: and his face was bound about with a napkin. Jesus saith unto them, Loose him, and let him go.

[BOOKS-NT] <u>John 11:43-44</u> When he had said this, **Jesus called in a loud voice, "Lazarus, come out!"** [44]**The dead man came out**, his hands and feet wrapped with strips of linen, and a cloth around his face. Jesus said to them, "Take off the grave clothes and let him go."

[CEV] <u>John 11:43-44</u> When Jesus had finished praying, **he shouted, "Lazarus, come out!"** [44]**The man who had been dead came out**. His hands and feet were wrapped with strips of burial cloth, and a cloth covered his face. Jesus then told the people, "Untie him and let him go."

[ESV] <u>John 11:43-44</u> When he had said these things, **he cried out with a loud voice, "Lazarus, come out."** [44]**The man who had died came out**, his hands and feet bound with linen strips, and his face wrapped with a cloth. Jesus said to them, "Unbind him, and let him go."

[LGV-NT] <u>John 11:43-44</u> And having said these things, **He shouted with a loud voice, "Lazarus, come out here!"** [44]**And the one having died came out**, having been wrapped feet and hands with a burial cloth and his face had been wrapped with a cloth. Jesus says to them, "Loose him and let him go."

[Montgomery-NT] <u>John 11:43-44</u> When he had said this **he cried with a great voice, "Lazarus, come forth!"** [44]**Out came the dead man**, wrapped hand and foot with grave-clothes, and his face bound up in a napkin. Jesus said to them, "Untie him, and let him go."

[OEB-NT] <u>John 11:43-44</u> Then, after saying this, **Jesus called in a loud voice: "Lazarus! Come out!"** [44]**The dead man came out**, wrapped hand and foot in a winding-sheet; his face, too, had been wrapped in a cloth. "Set him free," said Jesus, "and let him go."

[Phillips] <u>John 11:43-44</u> And when he had said this, **he called out in a loud voice, 'Lazarus, come out!'** [44]**And the dead man came out**, his hands and feet bound with grave-clothes and his face muffled with a handkerchief. 'Now unbind him,' Jesus told them, 'and let him go home.'

[REM-NT] <u>John 11:43-44</u> After he had said this, **Jesus called in a clear and loud voice, "Lazarus, arise and come forth!"** [44]**Then the dead man arose from the dead and came out**, with his hands and feet still wrapped in the grave clothes, and his face also covered with a cloth. Jesus instructed them, "Take off the burial clothes and set him free."

[Spencer-NT] John 11:43-44 Having said this **He called with a loud voice, "Lazarus, come forth!"** **⁴⁴And he who was dead came forth**, bound hand and foot with grave-cloths, and his face bound up in a napkin. Jesus said to them, "Unbind him and **leave him free to move."**

[TWTY-RCT-NT-V1] John 11:43-44 And having said these certain specific things, **He shouted and cried out, clamoured and screamed in a great and mighty, powerful and strong, intense and outstanding sound, tone and voice, "'El'azar: come out here, to this place!" ⁴⁴The one who had died and perished, who had his soul separated from his body, came out and showed himself, arose and appeared, became established and walked forth**, with His feet and hands bound and tied up, restricted and fastened with bandages, swathes and grave clothes, and His face and countenance bound about and bandaged, wrapped around and tied over with a facecloth, kerchief and burial towel. Yahushua says and teaches, maintains and affirms, directs and exhorts, advises and point out to them, "Untie and loosen, set free and release, set aside and unbind, undo and unfasten him, and permit and allow, do not hinder and release, accord and authorise, approve and sanction, endorse and let him go off and depart, leave, withdraw and proceed on his way."

[UDB] John 11:43-44 After he said that, **he cried out with a loud voice, "Lazarus, come out!" ⁴⁴The man who had died came out!** His hands were still wrapped and his feet were still bound with linen strips of cloth, and there was a cloth wrapped around his face as well. Jesus said to them, "Take off the strips of cloth that bind him and untie him. Let him go."

John 14:12-14 Verily, verily, I say unto you, He that believeth on me, the works that I do shall he do also; and greater works than these shall he do; because I go unto my Father. ¹³And whatsoever ye shall ask in my name, that will I do, that the Father may be glorified in the Son. ¹⁴If ye shall ask any thing in my name, I will do it.

[AMPC] John 14:12-14 I assure you, most solemnly I tell you, if anyone steadfastly believes in Me, he will himself be able to do the things that I do; and he will do even greater things than these, because I go to the Father. ¹³And I will do [I Myself will grant] whatever you ask in My Name [as presenting all that I Am], so that the Father may be glorified and extolled in (through) the Son. ¹⁴[Yes] I will grant [I Myself will do for you] whatever you shall ask in My Name [as presenting all that I Am].

[Anchor] John 14:12-14 "Let me firmly assure you, the man who has faith in me will perform the same works that I perform. In fact, he will perform far greater than these, because I am going to the Father, ¹³and whatever you ask in my name I will do, so that the Father may be glorified in the Son. ¹⁴If you ask anything of me in my name, I will do it."

[AUV-NT 2003] John 14:12-14 Truly, truly, I tell you, the person who believes in me will perform the deeds that I do also; and he will perform even greater deeds than these, because I am going to the Father. ¹³And I will do [for you] whatever you ask in my name, so that the Father may be honored through the Son. ¹⁴I will do anything [for you], if you ask [for it] in my name.

[BBE] John 14:12-14 Truly I say to you, He who puts his faith in me will do the very works which I do, and he will do greater things than these, because I am going to my Father. ¹³And whatever request you make in my name, that I will do, so that the Father may have glory in the Son. ¹⁴If you make any request to me in my name, I will do it.

[BV-KJV-NT] John 14:12-14 Amen, amen, I tell you, the person trusting in Me, the actions that I do, that person will also do, and he will do greater things than these because I am traveling to My Father. ¹³And whatever you ask for in My name, this I will do so that the Father might be made magnificent in the Son. ¹⁴If you ask for anything in My name, I will do it.

OUR HEALING COVENANT

[BWE-NT] John 14:12-14 'I tell you the truth. The person who believes in me will do the big work that I do. And he will do even bigger work because I go to my Father. ¹³I will do anything you ask of my Father in my name. In that way the Son will make my Father's name great. ¹⁴If you ask anything in my name, I will do it.'

[CLV] John 14:12-14 Verily, verily, I am saying to you, he who is believing in Me, the works which I am doing he also will be doing, and greater than these will he be doing, for I am going to the Father. ¹³And whatever you should be requesting in My name, this I will be doing, that the Father should be glorified in the Son. ¹⁴If you should ever be requesting anything of Me in My name, this I will be doing.

[CWB] John 14:12-14 Jesus turned to the rest of the disciples and said, "If you really believe that I am who I say I am, you will do the same things that I have done. In fact, you'll do these things in many more places than I have, because I'm going back to the Father. ¹³Whatever you ask me to do for you, I'll do it, as long as you ask for it in the same spirit that I would. Then your actions will glorify the Father just as mine have. ¹⁴So ask for what you need in order to accomplish my mission and I'll do it for you.

[EEBT] John 14:12-14 I am telling you what is true. Anyone who believes me will do the same things as me. That person will do the same things that I have done. Yes, he will do even greater things than these, because I go to my Father. ¹³Ask for things in my name (because you are mine). If you ask anything in my name, I will do it. So then the Son will show everyone how great and how good the Father is. ¹⁴If you ask me for anything in my name, I will do it.'

[Goodspeed-NT] John 14:12-14 I tell you, whoever believes in me will do such things as I do, and things greater yet, because I am going to the Father. ¹³Anything you ask for as followers of mine I will grant, so that the Father may be honored through the Son. ¹⁴I will grant anything you ask me for as my followers.

[IRENT] John 14:12-14 Yes, indeed! I say to you, whoever put trust on me will also do the works that I, I am doing, indeed, will do bigger tasks than these; now that I, I am going to my Father: ¹³Besides, anything you-all ask for in my name, I'll bring it about so that the Father may be glorified in the Son. ¹⁴If anything you should ask for {from me} in my name, I, I will bring it about.

[Mace-NT] John 14:12-14 I assure you, he that believeth on me, shall likewise perform the works that I do; nay, greater works than these shall he do; because for that end am I going to my father. ¹³and if in my name ye shall ask any thing of the father, whereby he may be glorified by the son, I will effect it. ¹⁴when ye shall ask any thing in my name, I will do it.

[NOG] John 14:12-14 "I can guarantee this truth: Those who believe in me will do the things that I am doing. They will do even greater things because I am going to the Father. ¹³I will do anything you ask the Father in my name so that the Father will be given glory because of the Son. ¹⁴If you ask me to do something, I will do it.

[REM-NT] John 14:12-14 I tell you the truth: Anyone who genuinely trusts me will also be in unity with the Father and will reveal his character—just as I have been doing. His life will be a further revelation of the life-giving power of God and the healing power of his methods. My life reveals the truth of God's character and methods; but those who trust in me will reveal that God's methods, when applied in trust via the Spirit of God, actually heal and transform those who are deformed by sin. I am going to the Father. ¹³And I will do whatever you ask—that is in harmony with my character, methods, and principles—so that the Son may bring honor and glory to the Father by revealing the healing and life-giving power of his methods. ¹⁴You may ask me for anything in harmony with my character and methods, and I will do it.

[Sindlinger-NT] John 14:12-14 "I've shared God's advice with you and God has helped me demonstrate it, so you just need to follow my example. ¹³If you do, you'll be able to help a lot more people than I was able to. I want everyone to realize how much God cares about them, ¹⁴so don't hesitate to ask me for help.

[TLB] <u>John 14:12-14</u> "In solemn truth I tell you, anyone believing in me shall do the same miracles I have done, and even greater ones, because I am going to be with the Father. [13]You can ask him for anything, using my name, and I will do it, for this will bring praise to the Father because of what I, the Son, will do for you. [14]Yes, ask anything, using my name, and I will do it!

[TPT] <u>John 14:12-14</u> "I tell you this timeless truth: The person who follows me in faith, believing in me, will do the same mighty miracles that I do—even greater miracles than these because I go to be with my Father! [13]For I will do whatever you ask me to do when you ask me in my name. And that is how the Son will show what the Father is really like and bring glory to him. [14]Ask me anything in my name, and I will do it for you!"

<u>John 15:7</u> If ye abide in me, and my words abide in you, ye shall ask what ye will, and it shall be done unto you.

[ACV] <u>John 15:7</u> If ye dwell in me, and my sayings dwell in you, ye will ask whatever ye may want, and it will be done to you.

[AMPC] <u>John 15:7</u> If you live in Me [abide vitally united to Me] and My words remain in you and continue to live in your hearts, ask whatever you will, and it shall be done for you.

[AUV-NT 2003] <u>John 15:7</u> If you remain in [fellowship with] me and my teaching remains in your hearts, [you can] ask for whatever you want, and it will be done for you.

[BBE] <u>John 15:7</u> If you are in me at all times, and my words are in you, then anything for which you make a request will be done for you.

[Brichto] <u>John 15:7</u> If you live in me and my teaching lives in you, Ask for whatever you require and it shall be.

[BV-NT] <u>John 15:7</u> If you stay in Me and My statements stay in you, whatever you want, ask for it, and it will happen to you.

[CEB] <u>John 15:7</u> If you remain in me and my words remain in you, ask for whatever you want and it will be done for you.

[Greaves-NT] <u>John 15:7</u> If you abide in me, and my words abide in you, whatever ye shall desire ye shall ask, and it shall be done for you.

[GT] <u>John 15:7</u> If you stay in me and my words stay in you, then you may ask for whatever you want and it will happen for you.

[Hanson-NT] <u>John 15:7</u> If you dwell in me, and my words dwell in you, ask whatever you wish, and it shall be given you.

[Knox] <u>John 15:7</u> As long as you live on in me, and my words live on in you, you will be able to make what request you will, and have it granted.

[LGV-NT] <u>John 15:7</u> If you should continue in Me and My sayings should continue in you whatever you desire you will ask and it will happen to you.

[MSG] <u>John 15:7</u> But if you make yourselves at home with me and my words are at home in you, you can be sure that whatever you ask will be listened to and acted upon.

[NOG] <u>John 15:7</u> If you live in me and what I say lives in you, then ask for anything you want, and it will be yours.

[Norton-Gs] <u>John 15:7</u> If you remain united to me, and my words abide in you, you shall ask whatever you will, and it will be granted.

[OEB-NT] <u>John 15:7</u> If you remain united to me, and my teaching remains in your hearts, ask whatever you wish, and it will be yours.

[Palmer] <u>John 15:7</u> If you abide in me, and my sayings abide in you, ask whatever you will, and it will happen for you.

[Phillips] <u>John 15:7</u> But if you live your life in me, and my words live in your hearts, you can ask for whatever you like and it will come true for you.

[REV-NT] <u>John 15:7</u> If you live in union with me, and my words live in you, ask whatever you want and it will be done for you.

[Thomson] <u>John 15:7</u> If you continue in me, and my words continue in you, ask what you will and it will be done for you:

[Williams-NT] <u>John 15:7</u> If you remain in union with me and my words remain in you, you may ask whatever you please and you shall have it.

[Wuest-NT] <u>John 15:7</u> If you maintain a living communion with me and my words are at home in you, I command you to ask, at once, something for yourself, whatever your heart desires, and it will become yours.

<u>John 16:23-24</u> And in that day ye shall ask me nothing. Verily, verily, I say unto you, **Whatsoever ye shall ask the Father in my name, he will give it you**. [24]Hitherto have ye asked nothing in my name: **ask, and ye shall receive**, that your joy may be full.

[AMP] <u>John 16:23-24</u> In that day you will not [need to] ask Me about anything. I assure you and most solemnly say to you, **whatever you ask the Father in My name [as My representative], He will give you**. [24]Until now you have not asked [the Father] for anything in My name; but now **ask and keep on asking and you will receive**, so that your joy may be full and complete.

[AUV-NT 2003] <u>John 16:23-24</u> At that time, you will not be asking me [for] anything. Truly, truly, I tell you, **if you will ask the Father for anything [then], in my name, He will give it to you**. [24]Up until now you have not asked for anything in my name. **[So now] ask, and you will receive**, that your joy may be complete.

[Barclay-NT] <u>John 16:23-24</u> When that time comes, you will not ask me for anything. I tell you, and it is true, **the Father will give you anything you ask for in my name**. [24]Up to now you have asked nothing in my name. **Keep on asking and you will keep on receiving**, and so your joy will be complete.

[FBV-NT] <u>John 16:23-24</u> "When that time comes you won't need to ask me for anything. I tell you the truth, **the Father will give you whatever you ask in my name**. [24]Until now you haven't asked for anything in my name, **so ask and you shall receive**, and your happiness will be complete.

[Knox] <u>John 16:23-24</u> When that day comes, you will not need to ask anything of me. Believe me, **you have only to make any request of the Father in my name, and he will grant it to you**. [24]Until now, you have not been making any requests in my name; **make them, and they will be granted**, to bring you gladness in full measure.

[MSG] <u>John 16:23-24</u> You'll no longer be so full of questions. [24]Ask in my name, according to my will, and **he'll most certainly give it to you**. Your joy will be a river overflowing its banks!

[Original-NT] <u>John 16:23-24</u> When that time comes you will not need to ask me for anything. I tell you for a positive fact, **whatever you ask the Father he will grant you for my sake**. [24]So far you have asked nothing in my name. **Ask, and you shall receive**, that your joy may be complete.

[Thomson] John 16:23-24 Now in that day you will not ask me any thing. Verily, verily, I say to you, **whatever you shall ask of the Father in my name, he will give you**. [24]Hitherto you have asked nothing in my name. **Ask and ye shall receive**, that your joy may be complete.

[TLB] John 16:23-24 At that time you won't need to ask me for anything, for you can go directly to the Father and **ask him, and he will give you what you ask for** because you use my name. [24]You haven't tried this before, but begin now. **Ask, using my name, and you will receive**, and your cup of joy will overflow.

[TPT] John 16:23-24 For here is eternal truth: When that time comes you won't need to ask me for anything, but instead you will go directly to the Father and **ask him for anything you desire and he will give it to you**, because of your relationship with me. [24]Until now you've not been bold enough to ask the Father for a single thing in my name, but **now you can ask, and keep on asking him! And you can be sure that you'll receive what you ask for**, and your joy will have no limits!

[TTNT] John 16:23-24 "At that time you will no longer question Me about anything. I tell you the truth, you will speak directly to the Father and **He will give you whatever you ask in My name**. [24]Until now you have not asked for anything using the authority of My name, the authority I have given you. But now **when you ask in this way you will receive** and this will give you great joy.

[UDB] John 16:23-24 On that day, you will have no more questions to ask me. I am telling you the truth: **Whatever you ask the Father, he will give it to you** when you ask because you are joined to me. [24]Up until now, you have not asked for anything like that. **Ask and you will receive it**, and Yahweh will give you such joy that fills everything.

[Wuest-NT] John 16:23-24 And in that day you shall ask me no question about anything. Most assuredly, I am saying to you, **Whatever you shall request of the Father, He will give it to you** in view of all that I am in His estimation. [24]Up to this time you requested not even one thing in my Name. **Be constantly making request**, and you shall receive, in order that your joy, having been filled completely full, might persist in that state of fulness in present time.

ACTS

Acts 2:43 And fear came upon every soul: and many wonders and signs were done by the apostles.

[AMP] Acts 2:43 A sense of awe was felt by everyone, and many wonders and signs (attesting miracles) were taking place through the apostles.

[Authentic-NT] Acts 2:43 Every individual was awed, and many signs and wonders occurred through the envoys.

[CCB] Acts 2:43 A holy fear came upon all the people, for many wonders and miraculous signs were done by the apostles.

[CEB] Acts 2:43 A sense of awe came over everyone. God performed many wonders and signs through the apostles.

[CWB] Acts 2:43 The apostles also worked miracles and healed all kinds of diseases, and everyone who saw them do these things was amazed at what was happening.

[ERV] Acts 2:43 Many wonders and miraculous signs were happening through the apostles, and everyone felt great respect for God.

OUR HEALING COVENANT

[Madsen-NT] <u>Acts 2:43</u> All souls were filled by the awareness of the nearness of God. Many wonders and signs were done through the apostles.

[NET] <u>Acts 2:43</u> Reverential awe came over everyone, and many wonders and miraculous signs came about by the apostles.

[REM-NT] <u>Acts 2:43</u> Everyone was filled with awe at the miracles performed and signs shown by Christ's ambassadors.

[T4T] <u>Acts 2:43</u> All the people who were in Jerusalem were greatly reverencing God because the apostles were frequently doing many kinds of miraculous things.

[TLB] <u>Acts 2:43</u> A deep sense of awe was on them all, and the apostles did many miracles.

<u>Acts 3:6-7</u> Then Peter said, Silver and gold have I none; but such as I have give I thee: In the name of Jesus Christ of Nazareth rise up and walk. ⁷And he took him by the right hand, and lifted him up: and **immediately his feet and ankle bones received strength.**

[AMP] <u>Acts 3:6-7</u> But Peter said, "Silver and gold I do not have; but what I do have I give to you: In the name (authority, power) of Jesus Christ the Nazarene—[begin now to] walk and go on walking!" ⁷Then he seized the man's right hand with a firm grip and raised him up. **And at once his feet and ankles became strong and steady,**

[AUV-NT 2003] <u>Acts 3:6-7</u> But instead, Peter said, "I do not have any money, but I will give you what I do have. In the name of Jesus from Nazareth, get up and walk." ⁷And Peter took him by his right hand and lifted him up. **Immediately the man's feet and ankles became strong [enough to walk on].**

[Ballentine-NT] <u>Acts 3:6-7</u> "Silver and gold are not mine. But what is mine I give you. In the name of Jesus Christ the Nazarene walk." ⁷And he took him by the right hand and raised him up. And his feet and ankle bones **at once received strength.**

[BWE-NT] <u>Acts 3:6-7</u> Then Peter said, 'I have no money. But I will give you what I have. In the name of Jesus Christ of Nazareth, get up and walk!' ⁷He took the man's right hand and raised him up. **Right away his feet and ankles became strong.**

[CPDV] <u>Acts 3:6-7</u> But Peter said: "Silver and gold is not mine. But what I have, I give to you. In the name of Jesus Christ the Nazarene, rise up and walk." ⁷And taking him by the right hand, he lifted him up. And **immediately his legs and feet were strengthened.**

[CWB] <u>Acts 3:6-7</u> Peter said, "We don't have money to give you, but we'll give you what we do have. In the name of Jesus Christ of Nazareth, stand up and walk." ⁷Then he reached down and took the man's right hand to help him up. **Instantly the man's feet and ankles straightened out and his muscles strengthened.**

[Doddridge-NT] <u>Acts 3:6-7</u> But Peter, under the divine impulse, intended him a far more important favour; and therefore said, As for silver and gold, I have none of either to impart to thee, were I ever so free to do it; but what I have in my power I willingly give thee, and thou shalt find it not less valuable; I say unto thee, therefore, in the great and prevailing name of Jesus Christ of Nazareth, and as proof that he is indeed the Messiah, rise up and walk. ⁷And Peter taking him by the right hand, encouraged him to do as he had said, and raised him up; and **immediately on his speaking this, and touching him, his feet and his ankle-bones, which had before been disabled, were in an extraordinary manner strengthened, and reduced to their proper situation.**

[ERV] <u>Acts 3:6-7</u> But Peter said, "I don't have any silver or gold, but I do have something else I can give you. By the power of Jesus Christ from Nazareth—stand up and walk!" ⁷Then Peter took the man's right hand and lifted him up. **Immediately his feet and legs became strong.**

[Godbey-NT] <u>Acts 3:6-7</u> Peter said, Silver and gold do not belong to me; but I give thee that which I have. In the name of Jesus Christ the Nazarene, walk about. [7]And taking him by the right hand he raised him up; and **immediately the bottoms of his feet and his ankle bones were strengthened**.

[Madsen-NT] <u>Acts 3:6-7</u> But Peter said, 'I own no silver or gold, but what I have, that I will give you: in the name of Jesus Christ the Nazarene, walk!' [7]And he grasped him by the right hand and lifted him upright. And **at once strength flowed into his feet, and his ankles became firm**.

[NLT] <u>Acts 3:6-7</u> But Peter said, "I don't have any silver or gold for you. But I'll give you what I have. In the name of Jesus Christ the Nazarene, get up and walk!" [7]Then Peter took the lame man by the right hand and helped him up. And as he did, **the man's feet and ankles were instantly healed and strengthened**.

[Original-NT] <u>Acts 3:6-7</u> "I have no silver or gold," Peter told him, "but what I have I will give you. In the name of Jesus Christ the Nazarene, walk!" [7]And he took him by the hand and raised him up. **Immediately his feet and ankles acquired strength**.

[REM-NT] <u>Acts 3:6-7</u> When he had the man's attention, Peter said, "I don't have money, but what I do have I give you: In accordance with the character of Jesus Christ of Nazareth, be healed and walk." [7]Reaching down and taking his right hand, Peter helped him up, and **immediately the man's feet and legs went from being shriveled, weak and deformed to a normal size and strength**.

[TTNT] <u>Acts 3:6-7</u> Peter said to him: "I don't have any silver or gold to give you, but what I do have I give you now. Walk, in the name of Jesus Christ of Nazareth." [7]He took the man by the right hand and began to pull him to his feet. **Immediately his ankles were healed and were made strong**.

[VW] <u>Acts 3:6-7</u> Then Peter said, Silver and gold I do not have, but what I do have I give you: In the name of Jesus Christ of Nazareth, rise up and walk. [7]And he took him by the right hand and lifted him up, and **immediately his feet and ankle bones received strength**.

<u>Acts 3:16</u> And his name through faith in his name hath made this man strong, whom ye see and know: yea, the faith which is by him hath given him this perfect soundness in the presence of you all.

[AMP] <u>Acts 3:16</u> And on the basis of faith in His name, it is the name of Jesus which has strengthened this man whom you see and know; and the faith which comes through Him has given him this perfect health and complete wholeness in your presence.

[AUV-NT 2005] <u>Acts 3:16</u> And by [means of] the name [of Jesus], that is, by faith in the [power of His] name, this [crippled] man, whom you now see and know, was healed. Yes, it is the faith that comes through Jesus that is responsible for this man's perfect health, as you now all see.

[Barclay-NT] <u>Acts 3:16</u> It is the name of Jesus and faith in that name which have given strength to this man whom you see and know. It is the faith which this name awakens that has given him perfect health as all of you can see.

[BLE] <u>Acts 3:16</u> And upon faith in his name he has put firmness into the limbs of this man whom you see and know; and the faith that comes through him has given him this absolute soundness before you all.

[CB] <u>Acts 3:16</u> "Faith in the name of Jesus has healed this man, who is known to you. His sturdy faith has given him his stability in your presence."

[CEB] <u>Acts 3:16</u> His name itself has made this man strong. That is, because of faith in Jesus' name, God has strengthened this man whom you see and know. The faith that comes through Jesus gave him complete health right before your eyes.

[CJB] <u>Acts 3:16</u> And it is through putting trust in his name that his name has given strength to this man whom you see and know. Yes, it is the trust that comes through Yeshua which has given him this perfect healing in the presence of you all.

[CWB] <u>Acts 3:16</u> It was the power of Jesus Christ that healed this man and made him whole. What happened to him came through faith in Jesus, the source of all life and power. That's why the man stands in front of you now, perfectly well and strong. You can see this with your own eyes.

[Goodspeed-NT] <u>Acts 3:16</u> It is by his power and through faith in him that this man whom you see and recognize has been made strong again, and it is faith inspired by him that has given him the perfect health you all see.

[GT] <u>Acts 3:16</u> "It was the authority of Jesus which made this crippled man well. This happened because we trusted in the power of Jesus. You can see this man and you know him. He was made completely well because of trusting in Jesus. You all saw it happen!

[ICB] <u>Acts 3:16</u> It was the power of Jesus that made this crippled man well. This happened because we trusted in the power of Jesus. You can see this man, and you know him. He was made completely well because of trust in Jesus. You all saw it happen!

[JUB] <u>Acts 3:16</u> And in the faith of his name, unto this man whom ye see and know, has confirmed his name; and the faith which is by him has given this man this perfect soundness in the presence of you all.

[Mace-NT] <u>Acts 3:16</u> it is the faith which we have in him, that has procured strength to this man whom ye see and know: yea, the faith which is by him, hath given him this perfect soundness in the presence of you all.

[Madsen-NT] <u>Acts 3:16</u> And because this man, whom you see and know, trusted in his name, this name has become a power in him, and the inner connection with him has brought him renewed health before the eyes of you all.

[Montgomery-NT] <u>Acts 3:16</u> And his name, on the ground of faith in his name, has made strong this man, whom you now see and know; yes, the faith that is through him has made this man sound and strong again, in the presence of you all.

[MOUNCE] <u>Acts 3:16</u> And on the basis of faith in his name—his name itself has made this man strong, whom you see and know. The faith that is through Jesus has given him this wholeness before all of you.

[NCV] <u>Acts 3:16</u> It was faith in Jesus that made this crippled man well. You can see this man, and you know him. He was made completely well because of trust in Jesus, and you all saw it happen!

[NEB] <u>Acts 3:16</u> And the name of Jesus, by awakening faith, has strengthened this man, whom you see and know, and this faith has made him completely well, as you can all see for yourselves.

[NWT] <u>Acts 3:16</u> And through his name, and by our faith in his name, this man whom you see and know has been made strong. The faith that is through him has made this man completely healthy in front of all of you.

[Original-NT] <u>Acts 3:16</u> and by virtue of his name this man whom you see and know has been set on his feet. It is his name and the confidence it inspires which has given him his soundness of limb in the presence of you all.

[Phillips] <u>Acts 3:16</u> It is the name of this same Jesus, it is faith in that name, which has cured this man whom you see and recognise. Yes, it was faith in Christ which gave this man perfect health and strength in full view of you all.

[TLB] <u>Acts 3:16</u> "Jesus' name has healed this man—and you know how lame he was before. Faith in Jesus' name—faith given us from God—has caused this perfect healing.

[TPT] <u>Acts 3:16</u> Faith in Jesus' name has healed this man standing before you. It is the faith that comes through believing in Jesus' name that has made the crippled man walk right in front of your eyes!

[TTNT] <u>Acts 3:16</u> "So by faith in the person of Jesus this man has been healed and he is someone you clearly recognise. It is by the name of Jesus and the faith that comes from knowing Him that this complete healing has been given to this man, as you can all see clearly for yourselves.

[TVB] <u>Acts 3:16</u> So that's how this miracle happened: we have faith in the name of Jesus, and He is the power that made this man strong—this man who is known to all of you. It is faith in Jesus that has given this man his complete health here today, in front of all of you.

[Weymouth-NT] <u>Acts 3:16</u> It is His name—faith in that name being the condition—which has strengthened this man whom you behold and know; and the faith which He has given has made this man sound and strong again, as you can all see.

<u>Acts 4:29-30</u> And now, Lord, behold their threatenings: and grant unto thy servants, that with all boldness they may speak thy word, [30]By stretching forth thine hand to heal; and that signs and wonders may be done by the name of thy holy child Jesus.

[AMP] <u>Acts 4:29-30</u> And now, Lord, observe their threats [take them into account] and grant that Your bond-servants may declare Your message [of salvation] with great confidence, [30]while You extend Your hand to heal, and signs and wonders (attesting miracles) take place through the name [and the authority and power] of Your holy Servant and Son Jesus."

[AMPC] <u>Acts 4:29-30</u> And now, Lord, observe their threats and grant to Your bond servants [full freedom] to declare Your message fearlessly, [30]While You stretch out Your hand to cure and to perform signs and wonders through the authority and by the power of the name of Your holy Child and Servant Jesus.

[AUV-NT 2005] <u>Acts 4:29-30</u> So, now Lord, take account of the threats [of these Jewish leaders] and give your servants all the boldness [we need] to speak your message, [30]while you perform [miraculous] healings and signs and wonders through the name [i.e., by the authority] of your Holy Servant Jesus."

[BBE] <u>Acts 4:29-30</u> And now, Lord, take note of their cruel words, and give your servants power to be preachers of your word without fear, [30]While your hand is stretched out to do works of mercy; so that signs and wonders may be done through the name of your holy servant Jesus.

[CEB] <u>Acts 4:29-30</u> Now, Lord, take note of their threats and enable your servants to speak your word with complete confidence. [30]Stretch out your hand to bring healing and enable signs and wonders to be performed through the name of Jesus, your holy servant.

[CEV] <u>Acts 4:29-30</u> Lord, listen to their threats! We are your servants. So make us brave enough to speak your message. [30]Show your mighty power, as we heal people and work miracles and wonders in the name of your holy Servant Jesus.

[ERV] <u>Acts 4:29-30</u> "And now, Lord, listen to what they are saying. They are trying to make us afraid. We are your servants. Help us to say what you want us to say without fear. [30]Help us to be brave by showing us your power. Make sick people well. Cause miraculous signs and wonders to happen by the authority of Jesus, your holy servant."

[GNT] <u>Acts 4:29-30</u> And now, Lord, take notice of the threats they have made, and allow us, your servants, to speak your message with all boldness. [30]Reach out your hand to heal, and grant that wonders and miracles may be performed through the name of your holy Servant Jesus.

OUR HEALING COVENANT

[GT] Acts 4:29-30 And now, Lord, listen to what they are saying. They are trying to make us afraid! Lord, we are Your slaves. Help us to speak the things You want us to say without fear. ³⁰Show your power: make sick people well, give proofs, and cause miracles to take place by the power of Jesus, Your holy servant."

[GW] Acts 4:29-30 Lord, pay attention to their threats now, and allow us to speak your word boldly. ³⁰Show your power by healing, performing miracles, and doing amazing things through the power and the name of your holy servant Jesus.

[Madsen-NT] Acts 4:29-30 And now, Lord, look upon their threats and give your servants the strength to proclaim your word with courage. ³⁰Stretch out your hand and let deeds of healing, signs and wonders be performed in the name and in the power of Jesus, your holy servant.'

[MSG] Acts 4:29-30 "And now they're at it again! Take care of their threats and give your servants fearless confidence in preaching your Message, ³⁰as you stretch out your hand to us in healings and miracles and wonders done in the name of your holy servant Jesus."

[Original-NT] Acts 4:29-30 And now, Lord, regard their threatenings, and grant to thy servants to declare thy Message with all eloquence, ³⁰with the stretching forth of thy hand to heal, and with signs and wonders to be performed through the name of thy devoted servant Jesus.

[REM-NT] Acts 4:29-30 So now, dear Lord, make note of their threats and overrule their opposition, and enable us, your agents, to speak the truth with clarity and distribute the Remedy with boldness. ³⁰Pour forth your life-giving power to heal and perform miracles, signs and wonders in harmony with the character of your holy Son Jesus."

[Thomson] Acts 4:29-30 Now with regard to present occurrences, look down, O Lord, on their threatenings, and enable thy servants to speak thy word with all freedom ³⁰when thou stretchest forth thy hand for healing; and signs and wonders are done by the name of thy holy child, Jesus.

[TPT] Acts 4:29-30 So now, Lord, listen to their threats to harm us. Empower us, as your servants, to speak the word of God freely and courageously. ³⁰Stretch out your hand of power through us to heal, and to move in signs and wonders by the name of your holy Son, Jesus!"

[TVB] Acts 4:29-30 And now, Lord, take note of their intimidations intended to silence us. Grant us, Your servants, the courageous confidence we need to go ahead and proclaim Your message ³⁰while You reach out Your hand to heal people, enabling us to perform signs and wonders through the name of Your holy servant Jesus.

[Wade] Acts 4:29-30 And now, Lord, pay heed to their threats, and enable Thy servants to tell with all boldness Thy message, ³⁰by exerting Thy Active Power to bring about Healing and attesting Signs and Wonders through the Name of Thy Holy Servant Jesus.

[Weymouth-NT] Acts 4:29-30 And now, Lord, listen to their threats, and enable Thy servants to proclaim Thy Message with fearless courage, ³⁰whilst Thou stretchest out Thine arm to cure men, and to give signs and marvels through the name of Thy holy Servant Jesus.

[Wuest-NT] Acts 4:29-30 And as to the present circumstances, Lord, look upon their threatenings and grant at once to your bondslaves the ability to be speaking your word with all fearless confidence and freedom of speech ³⁰while you stretch out your hand to heal, and grant that attesting miracles and miracles which arouse wonder may be done through the Name of your holy servant Jesus.

Acts 5:12 And by the hands of the apostles were many signs and wonders wrought among the people; (and they were all with one accord in Solomon's porch.

[AMPC] <u>Acts 5:12</u> **Now by the hands of the apostles (special messengers) numerous and startling signs and wonders were being performed among the people.** And by common consent they all met together [at the temple] in the covered porch (walk) called Solomon's.

[AUV-NT 2003] <u>Acts 5:12</u> **And many [miraculous] signs and wonders were performed through the apostles' hands** in front of the people. And all [the disciples] were united together in "Solomon's Portico".

[Beck] <u>Acts 5:12</u> **Many miracles and startling wonders were done among the people by the apostles' hands.** And there were all together in Solomon's Porch.

[CWB] <u>Acts 5:12</u> **In addition to this witness of the Holy Spirit's presence among them, the apostles also worked numerous miracles, healing the sick of all kinds of diseases.** Every day the believers met together to pray in the shaded walk around the Temple called Solomon's Porch.

[MW-NT] <u>Acts 5:12</u> **Many signs and wonders were done among the people by the hands of the ambassadors.** They were all with a common purpose in Solomon's porch.

[Palmer] <u>Acts 5:12</u> And **through the hands of the apostles many signs and wonders were happening among the people**, and they were regularly at the Portico of Solomon with one accord.

[RNT] <u>Acts 5:12</u> **Many signs and wonders were done among the people by the hands of the apostles.** They were all with one purpose in Solomon's Colonnade.

[T4T] <u>Acts 5:12</u> **God was enabling the apostles to do many amazing miracles among the people.** All the believers were meeting together regularly in the temple courtyard at the place called Solomon's Porch.

[TCNT] <u>Acts 5:12</u> **Many signs and wonders continued to occur among the people, through the instrumentality of the Apostles**, whose custom it was to meet all together in the Colonnade of Solomon;

[TLB] <u>Acts 5:12</u> Meanwhile, the apostles were meeting regularly at the Temple in the area known as Solomon's Hall, and **they did many remarkable miracles among the people.**

[UDB] <u>Acts 5:12</u> **Yahweh was enabling the apostles to do many amazing miracles that showed the truth of what they were preaching among the people.** All the believers were meeting together regularly in the temple courtyard at the place called Solomon's Porch.

[Wuest-NT] <u>Acts 5:12</u> **And by the hands of the apostles, attesting miracles and miracles which excite wonder and amazement, many of them, were constantly being performed among the people.** And they were in perfect unanimity, all of them, in Solomon's covered colonnade.

<u>Acts 5:15</u> Insomuch that they brought forth the sick into the streets, and laid them on beds and couches, that at the least the shadow of Peter passing by might overshadow some of them.

[CWB] <u>Acts 5:15</u> Peter became so well known in Jerusalem that people brought their sick and placed them on mats along the streets, hoping that as Peter passed, his shadow would fall on them and heal them.

[PNT] <u>Acts 5:15</u> Insomuch that they brought forth their sick into the streets, and laid them on beds and couches, that when Peter came, the shadow passing by, might overshadow some of them: for they were freed from every infirmity which every one had.

[T4T] <u>Acts 5:15</u> The apostles were doing amazing miracles, so people were bringing those who were sick into the streets and laying them on stretchers and mats, in order that when Peter came by he would touch them, or at least his shadow might come upon some of them and heal them.

[TLB] <u>Acts 5:15</u> Sick people were brought out into the streets on beds and mats so that at least Peter's shadow would fall across some of them as he went by!

[TPT] <u>Acts 5:15</u> In fact, when people knew Peter was going to walk by, they carried the sick out to the streets and laid them down on cots and mats, knowing the incredible power emanating from him would overshadow them and heal them.

<u>Acts 5:16</u> There came also a multitude out of the cities round about unto Jerusalem, bringing sick folks, and them which were vexed with unclean spirits: and they were healed every one.

[Authentic-NT] <u>Acts 5:16</u> The concourse of those bringing the ailing and people afflicted by foul spirits even came from towns all round Jerusalem, and every one of them was cured.

[AUV-NT 2005] <u>Acts 5:16</u> Large crowds also came from the towns surrounding Jerusalem, bringing people who were sick and those troubled by evil spirits, and all of them were [miraculously] healed.

[BSB-NT] <u>Acts 5:16</u> Crowds also gathered from the towns around Jerusalem, bringing the sick and those tormented by unclean spirits, and all of them were healed.

[CEB] <u>Acts 5:16</u> Even large numbers of persons from towns around Jerusalem would gather, bringing the sick and those harassed by unclean spirits. Everyone was healed.

[ISV] <u>Acts 5:16</u> Crowds continued coming in—even from the towns around Jerusalem—bringing their sick and those who were troubled by unclean spirits, and all of them were healed.

[NIRV] <u>Acts 5:16</u> Crowds even gathered from the towns around Jerusalem. They brought their sick people. They also brought those who were suffering because of evil spirits. All of them were healed.

[REM-NT] <u>Acts 5:16</u> Masses of people from all over the country came to Jerusalem; they brought those who were sick or afflicted by an evil spirit, and everyone was healed.

[TLB] <u>Acts 5:16</u> And crowds came in from the Jerusalem suburbs, bringing their sick folk and those possessed by demons; and every one of them was healed.

[TPT] <u>Acts 5:16</u> Great numbers of people swarmed into Jerusalem from the nearby villages. They brought with them the sick and those troubled by demons—and everyone was healed!

<u>Acts 6:8</u> And Stephen, full of faith and power, did great wonders and miracles among the people.

[AMPC] <u>Acts 6:8</u> Now Stephen, full of grace (divine blessing and favor) and power (strength and ability) worked great wonders and signs (miracles) among the people.

[Authentic-NT] <u>Acts 6:8</u> Stephen, full of fervor and power, performed great signs and wonders among the people.

[CEB] <u>Acts 6:8</u> Stephen, who stood out among the believers for the way God's grace was at work in his life and for his exceptional endowment with divine power, was doing great wonders and signs among the people.

[CWB] <u>Acts 6:8</u> Stephen not only functioned as a deacon, but was empowered by the Holy Spirit to preach, to work miracles and to heal the sick.

[Fenton] <u>Acts 6:8</u> Stephen, especially, full of active benevolence, produced great and wonderful evidences for the people.

[MSG] <u>Acts 6:8</u> Stephen, brimming with God's grace and energy, was doing wonderful things among the people, unmistakable signs that God was among them.

[Nary-NT] <u>Acts 6:8</u> And Stephen being full of grace and fortitude did wonders, and great miracles among the people.

[NCV] <u>Acts 6:8</u> Stephen was richly blessed by God who gave him the power to do great miracles and signs among the people.

[NLT] <u>Acts 6:8</u> Stephen, a man full of God's grace and power, performed amazing miracles and signs among the people.

[Phillips] <u>Acts 6:8</u> Stephen, full of grace and spiritual power, continued to perform miracles and remarkable signs among the people.

[TTNT] <u>Acts 6:8</u> Stephen, full of God's grace and power, performed extraordinary wonders and miraculous signs among the people.

[TVB] <u>Acts 6:8</u> Stephen continually overflowed with extraordinary grace and power, and he was able to perform a number of miraculous signs and wonders in public view.

[Wuest-NT] <u>Acts 6:8</u> And Stephen, full of grace and of power, was constantly performing great miracles among the people that aroused wonder and amazement, and miracles that had for their purpose the attestation of the message of the one performing the miracle as one that was inspired of God.

<u>Acts 8:6-7</u> And the people with one accord gave heed unto those things which Philip spake, **hearing and seeing the miracles which he did. ⁷For unclean spirits, crying with loud voice, came out of many that were possessed with them: and many taken with palsies, and that were lame, were healed.**

[ACV] <u>Acts 8:6-7</u> And the multitudes unanimously heeded the things that were spoken by Philip during their **listening and seeing the signs that he did. ⁷For of many of those who had unclean spirits, they came out, crying in a great voice. And many who were paralyzed, and who were lame, were healed.**

[AMP] <u>Acts 8:6-7</u> The crowds gathered and were paying close attention to everything Philip said, **as they heard [the message] and saw the [miraculous] signs which he was doing [validating his message]. ⁷For unclean spirits (demons), shouting loudly, were coming out of many who were possessed; and many who had been paralyzed and lame were healed.**

[BOOKS-NT] <u>Acts 8:6-7</u> When the crowds heard Philip and **saw the signs he performed, they all paid close attention to what he said. ⁷For with shrieks, impure spirits came out of many, and many who were paralyzed or lame were healed.**

[BWE-NT] <u>Acts 8:6-7</u> And all the people together listened to what Philip said because **they heard and saw the big works which he did. ⁷Many people who were held by bad spirits were made free from them. The spirits came out of them crying loudly. Many other sick people were healed too. People who could not stand, and others who were lame, were healed.**

[CEB] <u>Acts 8:6-7</u> The crowds were united by what they heard Philip say and **the signs they saw him perform, and they gave him their undivided attention. ⁷With loud shrieks, unclean spirits came out of many people, and many who were paralyzed or crippled were healed.**

[FAA] <u>Acts 8:6-7</u> And the crowds paid unanimous attention to the words spoken by Philip when they heard them and **saw the signs which he performed. ⁷For the unclean spirits of many who were possessed by them came out, shouting with a loud voice, and many who were paralysed or lame were healed.**

[GoodSpeed-NT] <u>Acts 8:6-7</u> When the people heard Philip and **saw the signs that he showed they were all interested in what he had to say, ⁷for with loud cries foul spirits came out of many who had been possessed by them, and many paralytics and lame people were cured.**

[Haweis-NT] <u>Acts 8:6-7</u> And the multitudes with united minds were very attentive to the things spoken by Philip, when they heard him, and **saw the miracles which he did. ⁷For the unclean spirits, roaring**

with great cries, came forth out of many who were possessed: and many who were paralytic and lame were healed.

[NJB] <u>Acts 8:6-7</u> The people unanimously welcomed the message Philip preached, because **they had heard of the miracles he worked and because they saw them for themselves.** [7] **For unclean spirits came shrieking out of many who were possessed, and several paralytics and cripples were cured.**

[NLV] <u>Acts 8:6-7</u> The people all listened to what Philip said. As they listened, **they watched him do powerful works.** [7] **There were many people who had demons in their bodies. The demons cried with loud voices when they went out of the people. Many of the people could not move their bodies or arms and legs. They were all healed.**

[TLB] <u>Acts 8:6-7</u> Crowds listened intently to what he had to say because of the miracles he did. [7] **Many evil spirits were cast out, screaming as they left their victims, and many who were paralyzed or lame were healed,**

[TPT] <u>Acts 8:6-7</u> The crowds were eager to receive Philip's message and **were persuaded by the many miracles and wonders he performed.** [7] **Many demon-possessed people were set free and delivered as evil spirits came out of them with loud screams and shrieks, and many who were lame and paralyzed were also healed.**

[UDB] <u>Acts 8:6-7</u> Many people there heard Philip speak and saw the miraculous things that he was doing. **So they all paid close attention to his words.** [7] **For example, Philip commanded evil spirits to come out of many people, and they came out screaming. Also, many people who were paralyzed and many others who were lame were healed.**

<u>Acts 8:13</u> Then Simon himself believed also: and when he was baptized, he continued with Philip, and wondered, **beholding the miracles and signs which were done**.

[Anderson-NT] <u>Acts 8:13</u> And Simon himself also believed; and after he was immersed, he continued with Philip; and, **seeing the mighty deeds and the signs which were done**, he was astonished.

[AS] <u>Acts 8:13</u> Moreover, Simon himself confides also, and being baptized, he was being steadfast-by Philip, and he himself was set-apart, **beholding-the-experience of powers and great signs occurring**.

[CBC] <u>Acts 8:13</u> Then Simon himself also believed: and when he was baptized, he was continuing with Philip, and was amazed, **beholding the great mighty works which were done**.

[Elkhazen-NT] <u>Acts 8:13</u> Then Simon himself believed also; and being baptized, he adhered to Philip. And being astonished, **wondered to see the signs and exceeding great miracles which were done**.

[Godbey-NT] <u>Acts 8:13</u> But Simon himself also believed: and being baptized, was constantly with Philip, both **seeing the miracles and the great dynamites performed**, was astonished.

[Moffatt-NT 1917] <u>Acts 8:13</u> indeed Simon himself believed, and after his baptism kept close to Philip, utterly astonished to **see the signs and striking miracles which were taking place**.

[SENT] <u>Acts 8:13</u> And Simon became a believer too, and got baptized. He was listening carefully to Philip, and he was astonished, **watching the miracles and the massive displays of power that were happening**.

[WGCIB] <u>Acts 8:13</u> Then Simon himself believed also and, being baptized, he remained devoted to Philip. He was astonished and **wondered at the signs and exceedingly great miracles which were done**.

<u>Acts 9:34</u> And Peter said unto him, Aeneas, **Jesus Christ maketh thee whole**: arise, and make thy bed. And he arose immediately.

[Anderson-Sinaitic NT] <u>Acts 9:34</u> And Peter said to him: Aeneas, **Jesus Christ restores thee to health**: arise, and make thy bed for thyself. And he immediately arose.

[ASV] <u>Acts 9:34</u> And Peter said unto him, Aeneas, **Jesus Christ healeth thee**: arise and make thy bed. And straightway he arose.

[Authentic-NT] <u>Acts 9:34</u> 'Jesus Christ cures you, Aeneas,' Peter said to him. 'Rise, and make your bed.'

[AUV-NT 2003] <u>Acts 9:34</u> Peter said to him, "Aeneas, **Jesus Christ is healing you**, so get up and make your bed." And immediately he got up [out of his bed, completely healed].

[Barclay-NT] <u>Acts 9:34</u> 'Aeneas,' Peter said to him. '**Jesus Christ is curing you**. Get up, and make your own bed.' There and then he got up.

[Dillard-NT] <u>Acts 9:34</u> And Peter said unto him, Eneas, **Anointed Jesus maketh thee whole**: arise, and make thy bed. And he arose immediately.

[Doddridge-NT] <u>Acts 9:34</u> And Peter seeing him, and perceiving in himself a strong intimation that the divine power would be exerted for his recovery, said to him, Aeneas, **Jesus, the true Messiah, in whose name I preach and act, now at this instant healeth thee**, and operates, while I speak, to strengthen and restore thy weakened frame: with a dependence therefore upon his almighty agency, arise and make thy bed. And upon this the palsy left him, and the disabled man was all at once so strengthened, that he arose immediately, and did it.

[ESV] <u>Acts 9:34</u> And Peter said to him, "Aeneas, **Jesus Christ heals you**; rise and make your bed." And immediately he rose.

[Knox] <u>Acts 9:34</u> And Peter said to him, Aeneas, **Jesus Christ sends thee healing**; rise up, and make thy bed; whereupon he rose up at once.

[Mace-NT] <u>Acts 9:34</u> Peter said to him, Eneas, **Jesus, who is the Messiah, gives thee health**: rise, and make your bed your self: upon which he immediately rose.

[T4T] <u>Acts 9:34</u> Peter said to him, "Aeneas, **Jesus Christ heals you right now**! Get up and roll up your mat!" Right away Aeneas stood up.

[TGNT] <u>Acts 9:34</u> So Peter said to him, "Aeneas, **Jesus the Anointed heals you**! Get up and take care of your bed!" Immediately he got up,

[TLV] <u>Acts 9:34</u> Peter said to him, "Aeneas, **Messiah Yeshua heals you**. Get up and pack up your bed." Immediately, he got up!

[TNT] <u>Acts 9:34</u> Peter said to him, 'Aeneas, **Jesus Christ brings you healing**. Get up, and make yourself a meal.' He got up at once.

[Wuest-NT] <u>Acts 9:34</u> And Peter said to him, **Jesus Christ is healing you right now**. Arise at once and immediately spread your bed out evenly for comfort, doing this for yourself. And immediately he arose.

<u>Acts 9:40</u> But Peter put them all forth, and kneeled down, and prayed; and **turning him to the body said, Tabitha, arise. And she opened her eyes**: and when she saw Peter, she sat up.

[AMPC] <u>Acts 9:40</u> But Peter put them all out [of the room] and knelt down and prayed; then **turning to the body he said, Tabitha, get up! And she opened her eyes**; and when she saw Peter, she raised herself and sat upright.

[BOOKS-NT] <u>Acts 9:40</u> Peter sent them all out of the room; then he got down on his knees and prayed. **Turning toward the dead woman, he said, "Tabitha, get up." She opened her eyes**, and seeing Peter she sat up.

[EEBT] <u>Acts 9:40</u> Peter put all these women out of the room. He went down on his knees and he prayed to God. Then **he turned his head towards the dead body. 'Tabitha', he said. 'Stand up!' She opened her eyes**. And when she saw Peter, she sat up.

[REM-NT] <u>Acts 9:40</u> Peter had everyone leave the room, then he knelt down and talked to Jesus. When finished, **he turned toward the dead woman and said, "Tabitha, get up." She opened her eyes**, looked at Peter, and sat up.

[Sindlinger-NT] <u>Acts 9:40</u> After he asked everyone else to leave the room, Peter knelt down and asked God to bring Tabitha back to life. **When he turned toward her and asked her to get up, she opened her eyes and sat up**.

[T4T] <u>Acts 9:40</u> But Peter sent them all out of the room. Then he got down on his knees and prayed. Then, **turning toward Tabitha's body, he said, "Tabitha, stand up!" Immediately she opened her eyes** and, when she saw Peter, she sat up.

[Thomson] <u>Acts 9:40</u> Then Peter, having put them all out, kneeled down and prayed, and **turning to the body, he said, Tabitha, arise. Upon which she opened her eyes**, and seeing Peter, sat up.

<u>Acts 10:38</u> How God anointed Jesus of Nazareth with the Holy Ghost and with power: who went about doing good, and **healing all that were oppressed of the devil**; for God was with him.

[AMPC] <u>Acts 10:38</u> How God anointed and consecrated Jesus of Nazareth with the [Holy] Spirit and with strength and ability and power; how He went about doing good and, in particular, **curing all who were harassed and oppressed by [the power of] the devil**, for God was with Him.

[Anderson-Sinaitic NT] <u>Acts 10:38</u> Jesus of Nazareth, how God anointed him with the Holy Spirit and power, who went about doing good and **giving health to all that were oppressed by the devil**, for God was with him;

[AUV-NT 2005] <u>Acts 10:38</u> This message was about Jesus from Nazareth and how God specially chose Him [and signified it] by giving Him the Holy Spirit and power. He traveled all over doing good [for people] and **healing everyone who was [being] oppressed by the devil**, for God was with Him.

[Barclay-NT] <u>Acts 10:38</u> You know about Jesus of Nazareth, and how God anointed him with the Holy Spirit and with power, and how he went about helping everyone, and **curing all those who were under the tyranny of the devil**, because God was with him.

[Berkeley] <u>Acts 10:38</u> how God anointed Jesus of Nazareth with the Holy Spirit and with power; who traversed the land doing good and **healing all that were overpowered by the devil**; for God was with Him.

[BLE] <u>Acts 10:38</u> Jesus from Nazareth, how God anointed him with Holy Spirit and power; who went along doing good and **healing all who were tyrannized over by the Devil**, because God was with him

[CE] <u>Acts 10:38</u> how God anointed Jesus of Nazareth with the Holy Spirit and with power, and he went about doing good and **healing all who were in the power of the devil**; for God was with him.

[CEV] <u>Acts 10:38</u> God gave the Holy Spirit and power to Jesus from Nazareth. He was with Jesus, as he went around doing good and **healing everyone who was under the power of the devil**.

[Doddridge-NT] <u>Acts 10:38</u> I mean the report [concerning] Jesus of Nazareth, how God anointed him with the Holy Spirit, and with a power of performing the most extraordinary miracles in attestation of his divine mission; who went about, and passed through the whole country, doing good wherever he came, and particularly **healing all those who were oppressed by the tyranny of the devil, dispossessing those malignant spirits of darkness with a most apparent and irresistible superiority to them**; for God himself was with him, and wrought by him to produce those astonishing effects.

[GNC-NT] <u>Acts 10:38</u> You know of Jesus of Nazareth, and how God anointed him with the Holy Spirit and bestowed upon him the power which flows from this; how Jesus went from place to place, doing kindnesses to men and women, and **bringing healing to all those who had fallen into the power of the devil's tyranny**. And he was able to do all this because he had God by his side.

[GNT] <u>Acts 10:38</u> You know about Jesus of Nazareth and how God poured out on him the Holy Spirit and power. He went everywhere, doing good and **healing all who were under the power of the Devil**, for God was with him.

[Hanson-NT] <u>Acts 10:38</u> how God anointed him with holy spirit and power; who went about doing good, and **curing all who were oppressed by the accuser**, for God was with him.

[Jerusalem] <u>Acts 10:38</u> God had anointed him with the Holy Spirit and with power, and because God was with him, Jesus went about doing good and **curing all who had fallen into the power of the devil**.

[Mace-NT] <u>Acts 10:38</u> how Jesus of Nazareth divinely inspired by the holy spirit, and with miraculous power, went about doing good, and **healing all that were under the oppression of the devil**: because God was with him.

[Madsen-NT] <u>Acts 10:38</u> He was anointed by God with the Holy Spirit and with great power. You know how he went through the land, helping and **bringing healing to all who had fallen into the power of the Adversary**. The power of God was with him,

[Moffatt] <u>Acts 10:38</u> how God consecrated Jesus of Nazaret with the holy Spirit and power, and how he went about doing good and **curing all who were harassed by the devil**; for God was with him.

[Morgan-NT] <u>Acts 10:38</u> How God anointed Jesus, the Nazarene, with the holy spirit, and power, who traveled benefiting and **healing all oppressed, by the devil**, for God was with him.

[MSG] <u>Acts 10:38</u> Then Jesus arrived from Nazareth, anointed by God with the Holy Spirit, ready for action. He went through the country helping people and **healing everyone who was beaten down by the Devil**. He was able to do all this because God was with him.

[NCV] <u>Acts 10:38</u> You know about Jesus from Nazareth, that God gave him the Holy Spirit and power. You know how Jesus went everywhere doing good and **healing those who were ruled by the devil**, because God was with him.

[Original-NT] <u>Acts 10:38</u> telling of Jesus of Nazareth, whom God anointed with holy Spirit and power, who went about doing good and **curing all who were in the Devil's clutches**; for God was with him.

[Phillips] <u>Acts 10:38</u> You must have heard how God anointed him with the power of the Holy Spirit, of how he went about doing good and **healing all who suffered under the devil's power**—because God was with him.

[Sawyer-7590] <u>Acts 10:38</u> how God anointed him with the Holy Spirit and power, who went about doing good and **curing all that were subjugated by the devil, for God was with him;**

[Spencer-NT] <u>Acts 10:38</u> how God anointed Him with the Holy Ghost and with power; how He went about doing good and **curing all who were tyrannized over by the devil**, for God was with Him.

[TLB] <u>Acts 10:38</u> And you no doubt know that Jesus of Nazareth was anointed by God with the Holy Spirit and with power, and he went around doing good and **healing all who were possessed by demons**, for God was with him.

[TPT] <u>Acts 10:38</u> "Jesus of Nazareth was anointed by God with the Holy Spirit and with great power. He did wonderful things for others and **divinely healed all who were under the tyranny of the devil**, for God had anointed him.

[UDB] <u>Acts 10:38</u> You know that Yahweh gave his Holy Spirit to Jesus, the man from the town of Nazareth, and gave him the power to do miracles. You also know how Jesus went to many places, always doing good deeds and healing people. **He was healing all the people whom the devil was causing to suffer**. Jesus was able to do those things because Yahweh was always helping him."

[Westminster] <u>Acts 10:38</u> how "God anointed him with the Holy Spirit" and with power, how he went about doing good and **healing all that were mastered by the devil**, because God was with him.

<u>Acts 14:3</u> Long time therefore abode they speaking boldly in the Lord, which gave testimony unto the word of his grace, and **granted signs and wonders to be done by their hands**.

[Barclay-NT] <u>Acts 14:3</u> They spent some considerable time there, speaking fearlessly with complete confidence in the Lord, who confirmed the message of his grace by **enabling them to perform wonderful demonstrations of the divine power in action**.

[Beck] <u>Acts 14:3</u> For a long time Paul and Barnabas continued to speak boldly, trusting in the Lord, who gave His approval to the words of His love **by letting their hands do miracles and wonders**.

[BOOKS-NT] <u>Acts 14:3</u> So Paul and Barnabas spent considerable time there, speaking boldly for the Lord, who confirmed the message of his grace by **enabling them to perform signs and wonders**.

[CEV] <u>Acts 14:3</u> Paul and Barnabas stayed there for a while, having faith in the Lord and bravely speaking his message. **The Lord gave them the power to work miracles and wonders**, and he showed that their message about his gift of undeserved grace was true.

[CLV] <u>Acts 14:3</u> They, indeed, then, tarry a considerable time, speaking boldly in the Lord, Who is testifying to the word of His grace, **granting signs and miracles to occur through their hands**."

[ERV] <u>Acts 14:3</u> So Paul and Barnabas stayed in Iconium a long time, and they spoke bravely for the Lord. They told the people about God's grace. The Lord proved that what they said was true by **causing miraculous signs and wonders to be done through them**.

[FBV-NT] <u>Acts 14:3</u> Paul and Barnabas stayed there a long time, speaking to them boldly in the Lord, who confirmed their message of grace through **the miraculous signs that they were enabled to perform**.

[MLV] <u>Acts 14:3</u> Therefore, they indeed stayed a considerable time there, speaking boldly in the Lord, who was testifying to the word of his favor, **giving signs and wonders to happen through their hands**.

[NLV] <u>Acts 14:3</u> Paul and Barnabas stayed there a long time preaching with the strength the Lord gave. **God helped them to do powerful works when they preached which showed He was with them.**

[Original-NT] <u>Acts 14:3</u> They therefore spent some time there speaking boldly for the Master, who confirmed his gracious Message by **permitting signs and wonders to be performed through their instrumentality**.

[REM-NT] <u>Acts 14:3</u> So Paul and Barnabas spent many hours there speaking fearlessly for the Lord who confirmed them as distributors of the Remedy by **enabling them to do miracles and wonders**.

[TLB] <u>Acts 14:3</u> Nevertheless, they stayed there a long time, preaching boldly, and the Lord proved their message was from him **by giving them power to do great miracles.**

[TTNT] <u>Acts 14:3</u> Even so, they spent some time there and continued to preach boldly for the Lord, who endorsed their message of His grace by **empowering them to perform miraculous signs and wonders**.

<u>Acts 14:8-10</u> And there sat a certain man at Lystra, impotent in his feet, being a cripple from his mother's womb, who never had walked: [9]The same heard Paul speak: who stedfastly beholding him, and perceiving that he had faith to be healed[sozo], [10]Said with a loud voice, Stand upright on thy feet. And he leaped and walked.

[BOOKS-NT] <u>Acts 14:8-10</u> In Lystra there sat a man who was lame. He had been that way from birth and had never walked. [9]He listened to Paul as he was speaking. Paul looked directly at him, saw that he had faith to be healed [10]and called out, "Stand up on your feet!" At that, the man jumped up and began to walk.

[BSB-NT] <u>Acts 14:8-10</u> In Lystra sat a man crippled in his feet, who was lame from birth and had never walked. [9]This man was listening to the words of Paul, who looked intently at him and saw that he had faith to be healed. [10]In a loud voice Paul called out, "Stand up on your feet!" And the man jumped up and began to walk.

[CEB] <u>Acts 14:8-10</u> In Lystra there was a certain man who lacked strength in his legs. He had been crippled since birth and had never walked. Sitting there, he [9]heard Paul speaking. Paul stared at him and saw that he believed he could be healed. [10]Raising his voice, Paul said, "Stand up straight on your feet!" He jumped up and began to walk.

[EEBT] <u>Acts 14:8-10</u> There was a man who lived in Lystra. He could not walk because his feet were not strong. His feet had been weak since he was born. So he had never walked. [9]He was sitting near to Paul and he was listening to Paul's words. Paul could see that the man believed his message. Also the man believed that he could become well. And Paul knew that. [10]So Paul looked at the man and Paul said loudly, 'Stand up on your feet!' So the man jumped up and he began to walk about.

[ESV] <u>Acts 14:8-10</u> Now at Lystra there was a man sitting who could not use his feet. He was crippled from birth and had never walked. [9]He listened to Paul speaking. And Paul, looking intently at him and seeing that he had faith to be made well, [10]said in a loud voice, "Stand upright on your feet." And he sprang up and began walking.

[Green-NT] <u>Acts 14:8-10</u> And a certain man at Lystra was sitting crippled in his feet, lame from him mother's womb, who had never walked. [9]This man heard Paul speaking; who, looking steadily at him and seeing that he had faith to be restored, [10]said with a loud voice, Stand up straight upon thy feet. And he bounded up and walked.

[ICB] <u>Acts 14:8-10</u> In Lystra there sat a man who had been born crippled; he had never walked. [9]This man was listening to Paul speak. Paul looked straight at him and saw that the man believed God could heal him. [10]So he cried out, "Stand up on your feet!" The man jumped up and began walking around.

[Madsen-NT] <u>Acts 14:8-10</u> In Lystra there lived a man who had no strength in his feet and therefore always had to sit. He was lame from birth and had never been able to walk. [9]He was one of the audience when Paul was speaking. Paul looked at him and recognized that he was full of trust in the healing power of the Spirit. [10]And he said to him with a loud voice, 'Get up and stand upright on your feet!' And he sprang up and walked about.

[MSG] <u>Acts 14:8-10</u> There was a man in Lystra who couldn't walk. He sat there, crippled since the day of his birth. [9]He heard Paul talking, and Paul, looking him in the eye, saw that he was ripe for God's work, ready to believe. [10]So he said, loud enough for everyone to hear, "Up on your feet!" The man was up in a flash—jumped up and walked around as if he'd been walking all his life.

[PNT] <u>Acts 14:8-10</u> And there sat a certain man, impotent in his feet, from his mother's womb, who never had walked. ⁹The same heard Paul speak; being in fear: who stedfastly beholding him, and perceiving that he had faith to be healed, ¹⁰Said with a loud voice, I say to thee, in the name of the Lord Jesus Christ, Stand up right on thy feet. And he presently immediately leaped and walked.

[REAL] <u>Acts 14:8-10</u> and some man was sitting in Lystra, paralyzed in his feet—a cripple from his mother's womb who had never walked— ⁹he heard Paul speak. He was focusing on the man, and he was discerning that he had faith to be healed. ¹⁰He said in a loud voice, "Stand upright on your feet," and he leaped up, and he walked,

[REM-NT] <u>Acts 14:8-10</u> There was a crippled man in Lystra, who was paralyzed from birth and had never walked. ⁹He embraced what Paul taught. Paul looked at him and saw that he trusted God and could be healed. ¹⁰Paul called out to him, "Stand up on your feet and walk!" Instantly the man jumped up and began to walk.

[T4T] <u>Acts 14:8-10</u> Once while Paul was preaching to people in Lystra, a man was sitting there who was crippled in his legs. When his mother bore him he had crippled legs, so he was never able to walk. ⁹He listened as Paul was speaking about the Lord Jesus. Paul looked directly at him and could see in the man's face that he believed that the Lord Jesus could make him well. ¹⁰So Paul called out to him, "Stand up!" When the man heard that, he immediately jumped up and began to walk normally.

[Worrell-NT] <u>Acts 14:8-10</u> And at Lystra there was sitting a certain man, impotent in his feet; lame from his mother's womb, who never walked. ⁹The same was hearing Paul speaking, who, looking intently on him, and perceiving that he had faith to be healed, ¹⁰said with a loud voice, "Stand up on your feet, erect!" And he leaped up, and was walking about.

<u>Acts 14:19-20</u> And there came thither certain Jews from Antioch and Iconium, who persuaded the people, and, having stoned Paul, drew him out of the city, **supposing he had been dead. ²⁰Howbeit, as the disciples stood round about him, he rose up**, and came into the city: and the next day he departed with Barnabas to Derbe.

[AUV-NT 2005] <u>Acts 14:19-20</u> But Jews came to [Lystra] from Antioch [in Pisidia] and Iconium. When they persuaded the crowds [to reject Paul's message] they stoned him and dragged him out of town, **assuming he was dead. ²⁰But as the disciples stood around [Paul's apparently lifeless body], he [surprisingly] stood up [fully restored to health]** and entered the town. On the following day he went with Barnabas to Derbe.

[CBC] <u>Acts 14:19-20</u> But there came thither certain Jews from Antioch and Iconium, and having persuaded the crowd, and, having stoned Paul, dragged him outside the city, **reckoning he was dead, as was the fact. ²⁰But, as the disciples encircled him, he having risen up [by Divine power]** and came into the city: and on the morrow he departed with Barnabas unto Derbe.

[Doddridge-NT] <u>Acts 14:19-20</u> But though they were so happy as to make some converts to it, they were soon interrupted in their work; for quickly after this, [some] Jews came thither from the neighboring cities of Antioch and Iconium, and persuaded the multitude to disbelieve what they taught: and representing them to be deceivers, they prejudiced their minds to such a degree against their persons and their doctrine, that the very people who but just before would have adored them as deities, now rose to put them to death as malefactors: and accordingly having stoned Paul in a tumultuous manner in the streets, they dragged him out of the city, **supposing him to be dead. ²⁰But as the disciples were gathered about him with a view of performing the last office of affection to him, in bearing him to his funeral with proper regard, to their unspeakable surprise they found himself so restored by the power of Christ, that he immediately rose up as in perfect health**, and his bruises were so healed that he entered into the city again, and was not only able to walk about it, but the next day found that he was capable of undertaking a journey, and departed with Barnabas to Derby, a city of Lycaonia, on the borders of Cappadocia; as they did not think it convenient to proceed in their progress to Galatia, Phrygia, or any more distant province.

[GNT] <u>Acts 14:19-20</u> Some Jews came from Antioch in Pisidia and from Iconium; they won the crowds over to their side, stoned Paul and dragged him out of the town, **thinking that he was dead. ²⁰But when the believers gathered around him, he got up** and went back into the town. The next day he and Barnabas went to Derbe.

[REM-NT] <u>Acts 14:19-20</u> Then some Jews who rejected the Remedy arrived from Antioch and Iconium, and won the crowd over with lies. The mob stoned Paul and dragged him out of the city, **assuming he was dead. ²⁰But when the members of the Lord's spiritual health-care team gathered around him, he got up** and went back into the city. The next day he set out with Barnabas for Derbe.

[TPT] <u>Acts 14:19-20</u> Some of the Jews who had opposed Paul and Barnabas in Antioch and Iconium arrived and stirred up the crowd against them. They stoned Paul and dragged his body outside the city and **left him for dead. ²⁰When the believers encircled Paul's body, he miraculously stood up!** Paul stood and immediately went back into the city. The next day he left with Barnabas for Derbe.

[TTNT] <u>Acts 14:19-20</u> But when some Jews from Antioch and Iconium arrived, they turned the crowd against them. They stoned Paul and dumped his body outside the city, **thinking he was dead. ²⁰But when the believers gathered around him in prayer, he stood up** and then went back into the city. Both Paul and Barnabas left for Derbe on the following day.

[UDB] <u>Acts 14:19-20</u> However, some Jews came from Antioch and Iconium and persuaded many of the people of Lystra that the message Paul had been telling them was not true. The people who believed what those Jews said became angry with Paul. They let the Jews throw stones at him until he fell down, unconscious. They all thought that he was dead, so they dragged him outside the city and **left him lying there. ²⁰But some of the believers in Lystra came and stood around Paul, where he was lying on the ground. And Paul became conscious! He stood up** and went back into the city with the believers. The next day, Paul and Barnabas left the city of Lystra and traveled to the city of Derbe.

[Wuest-NT] <u>Acts 14:19-20</u> Then there arrived Jews from Antioch and Iconium, and having persuaded the crowds and having stoned Paul, they dragged him by his feet outside of the city, **thinking that he had died. ²⁰However, after the disciples had gathered around him, he arose suddenly** and went into the city. And on the next day he went forth with Barnabas to Derbe.

<u>Acts 16:18</u> And this did she many days. But Paul, being grieved, turned and **said to the spirit, I command thee in the name of Jesus Christ to come out of her. And he came out the same hour**.

[AUV-NT 2003] <u>Acts 16:18</u> And she kept this up for a number of days. But Paul was very disturbed [over what she was doing] and [finally] turned [to her] and **said to the spirit [in the girl], "I command you in the name of Jesus Christ to come out of her." And the evil spirit did come out [of her] immediately.**

[BBE] <u>Acts 16:18</u> And this she did on a number of days. But Paul was greatly troubled and, turning, **said to the spirit, I give you orders in the name of Jesus Christ, to come out of her. And it came out that very hour.**

[BOOKS-NT] <u>Acts 16:18</u> She kept this up for many days. Finally Paul became so annoyed that he turned around and **said to the spirit, "In the name of Jesus Christ I command you to come out of her!" At that moment the spirit left her.**

[EEBT] <u>Acts 16:18</u> The slave girl followed us and she shouted this for many days. But Paul was not happy about it. So he turned round and he spoke to the bad spirit. **'I am using the authority of Jesus to order you. Leave this woman.' The spirit left her immediately.**

[Noyes] <u>Acts 16:18</u> And this she did for many days. But Paul, being much displeased, turned and **said to the spirit, I command thee in the name of Jesus Christ to come out of her. And it came out immediately.**

[Phillips] <u>Acts 16:18</u> She continued this behaviour for many days, and then Paul, in a burst of irritation, turned round and **spoke to the spirit in her. 'I command you in the name of Jesus Christ to come out of her!' And it came out immediately.**

[TLB] <u>Acts 16:18</u> This went on day after day until Paul, in great distress, turned and **spoke to the demon within her. "I command you in the name of Jesus Christ to come out of her," he said. And instantly it left her.**

[TTT-NT] <u>Acts 16:18</u> And Paul was grieved, and turning to her, **said to the spirit, "I command you in the name of Jesus Christ to leave her." And at that hour it left her.**

[VW] <u>Acts 16:18</u> And this she did for many days. But Paul, greatly disturbed, turned and **said to the spirit, I command you in the name of Jesus Christ to come out of her. And he came out that very instant.**

<u>Acts 17:25</u> Neither is worshipped with men's hands, as though he needed any thing, **seeing he giveth to all life**[zoé]**, and breath, and all things;**

[BWE-NT] <u>Acts 17:25</u> Men cannot worship him by things they make with their hands because he does not need anything. **He is the one who gives life and breath and everything else to all people.**

[CJB] <u>Acts 17:25</u> nor is he served by human hands, as if he lacked something; **since it is he himself who gives life and breath and everything to everyone.**

[EEBT] <u>Acts 17:25</u> Men make things for God. But God does not need anything that men have made. God himself causes everything to live. **He gives to living things everything that they need.**

[KNT] <u>Acts 17:25</u> Nor does he need to be looked after by human hands, as though he lacked something, **since he himself gives life and breath and all things to everyone.**

[NEB] <u>Acts 17:25</u> It is not because he lacks anything that he accepts service at men's hands, **for he is himself the universal giver of life and breath and all else.**

[NIRV] <u>Acts 17:25</u> He is not served by human hands. He doesn't need anything. Instead, **he himself gives life and breath to all people. He also gives them everything else they have.**

[Phillips] <u>Acts 17:25</u> nor is he ministered to by human hands, as though he had need of anything—**seeing that he is the one who gives to all men life and breath and everything else.**

[REM-NT] <u>Acts 17:25</u> Human beings do not provide for him—as if there was anything he needed. No! He is the source of all and gives of himself for our good. **From him come life, health, and everything else.**

[T4T] <u>Acts 17:25</u> He does not need to have anything made for him by people {to have people make anything for him}, because everything that exists belongs to him. **He is the one who causes us /all people to live and breathe, and he gives us all the things that we need.**

[TLB] <u>Acts 17:25</u> and human hands can't minister to his needs—for he has no needs! **He himself gives life and breath to everything, and satisfies every need there is.**

<u>**Acts 19:11-12**</u> And God wrought special miracles by the hands of Paul: [12]So that from his body were brought unto the sick handkerchiefs or aprons, and the diseases departed from them, and the evil spirits went out of them.

[Anderson-NT] <u>**Acts 19:11-12**</u> Mighty deeds, also, that were unusual, did God perform by the hands of Paul; [12]so that handkerchiefs or aprons were carried from his body to the sick, and diseases departed from them, and the evil spirits came out of them.

[Beck] <u>**Acts 19:11-12**</u> God did extraordinary miracles by Paul's hands. [12]When handkerchiefs and aprons that had touched his skin were taken to the sick, their sicknesses left them, and the evil spirits went out of them.

[BLE] <u>**Acts 19:11-12**</u> And God did extraordinary miracles by Paul's hands, [12]even to the extent that handkerchiefs or aprons from his body were carried to the sick and they were freed from their diseases and the evil spirits came out.

[BOOKS-NT] <u>**Acts 19:11-12**</u> God did extraordinary miracles through Paul, [12]so that even handkerchiefs and aprons that had touched him were taken to the sick, and their illnesses were cured and the evil spirits left them.

[Boothroyd] <u>**Acts 19:11-12**</u> And God wrought signal miracles by the hands of Paul; [12]So that from his body were brought unto the sick handkerchiefs or aprons, and the diseases departed from them, and the evil spirits went out of them.

[CEB] <u>**Acts 19:11-12**</u> God was doing unusual miracles through Paul. [12]Even the small towels and aprons that had touched his skin were taken to the sick, and their diseases were cured and the evil spirits left them.

[CJB] <u>**Acts 19:11-12**</u> God did extraordinary miracles through Sha'ul. [12]For instance, handkerchiefs and aprons that had touched him were brought to sick people; they would recover from their ailments; and the evil spirits would leave them.

[CLV] <u>**Acts 19:11-12**</u> Besides, powerful deeds, not the casual kind, God did through the hands of Paul, [12]so the handkerchiefs or aprons from his cuticle are carried away to the infirm also, to clear the diseases from them. Besides, wicked spirits go out.

[DLNT] <u>**Acts 19:11-12**</u> And God was doing not the ordinary miracles by the hands of Paul— [12]so that handkerchiefs or aprons were even being carried-forth from his skin to the ones being sick, and the diseases were being released from them, and the evil spirits were going out.

[EEBT] <u>**Acts 19:11-12**</u> God was working by Paul and God was doing many powerful things. These were things that nobody had done before. [12]People took pieces of cloth and clothes that Paul gave to them. Paul had used these things. People took the cloths to those who were ill. After they received them, the sick people became well again. And bad spirits also left them.

[ERV] <u>**Acts 19:11-12**</u> God used Paul to do some very special miracles. [12]Some people carried away handkerchiefs and clothes that Paul had used and put them on those who were sick. The sick people were healed, and evil spirits left them.

[GNT] <u>**Acts 19:11-12**</u> God was performing unusual miracles through Paul. [12]Even handkerchiefs and aprons he had used were taken to the sick, and their diseases were driven away, and the evil spirits would go out of them.

[Knox] <u>**Acts 19:11-12**</u> And God did miracles through Paul's hands that were beyond all wont; [12]so much so, that when handkerchiefs or aprons which had touched his body were taken to the sick, they got rid of their diseases, and evil spirits were driven out.

[KNT] <u>Acts 19:11-12</u> God performed unusual works of power through Paul's hands. [12]People used to take handkerchiefs or towels that had touched his skin and put them on the sick, and then their diseases would leave them and evil spirits would depart.

[Mace-NT] <u>Acts 19:11-12</u> the miracles which God wrought by the ministry of Paul being of such an extraordinary nature, that by applying the handkerchiefs, [12]or aprons that had touched his skin, to the distempered, they were cured, and the evil spirits came out of the possessed.

[MKJV] <u>Acts 19:11-12</u> And God did works of power through the hands of Paul, [12]so that even handkerchiefs or aprons from his skin being brought onto the sick, the diseases were released, and the evil spirits went out of them.

[MSG] <u>Acts 19:11-12</u> God did powerful things through Paul, things quite out of the ordinary. [12]The word got around and people started taking pieces of clothing—handkerchiefs and scarves and the like—that had touched Paul's skin and then touching the sick with them. The touch did it—they were healed and whole.

[NAB] <u>Acts 19:11-12</u> So extraordinary were the mighty deeds God accomplished at the hands of Paul [12]that when face cloths or aprons that touched his skin were applied to the sick, their diseases left them and the evil spirits came out of them.

[Nary-NT] <u>Acts 19:11-12</u> And God wrought extraordinary miracles by the hands of Paul. [12]Insomuch, that the very handkerchiefs or aprons, which were brought from his body, and applied to the sick, cured their diseases, and evil spirits went out of them.

[NEB] <u>Acts 19:11-12</u> And through Paul God worked miracles of an unusual kind: [12]when handkerchiefs and scarves which had been in contact with his skin were carried to the sick, they were rid of their diseases and the evil spirits came out of them.

[NLV] <u>Acts 19:11-12</u> God used Paul to do powerful special works. [12]Pieces of cloth and parts of his clothes that had been next to his body were put on sick people. Then they were healed of their diseases and demons came out of them.

[Original-NT] <u>Acts 19:11-12</u> God effected extraordinary miracles through Paul's instrumentality, [12]so that even handkerchiefs and loincloths were taken away for the sick after physical contact with him, and by this means there were freed from their diseases and the evil spirits left them.

[Pickering-NT] <u>Acts 19:11-12</u> Further, God kept working unusual miracles by the hands of Paul, [12]so that even handkerchiefs or aprons that he touched were applied to the sick, and the diseases left them and the wicked spirits went out from them.

[REM-NT] <u>Acts 19:11-12</u> God's healing love flowed through Paul in amazing ways. [12]Scarves, napkins, or other pieces of cloth that had touched Paul were taken to the sick, and when the fabric touched the sick, their illness was cured, and any evil influences departed.

[SENT] <u>Acts 19:11-12</u> And God was bringing about extraordinary displays of power through Paul's hands. [12]It even got to the point that handkerchiefs and towels that had touched his skin were taken to the sick, and their illnesses left them. Evil spirits would leave too.

[T4T] <u>Acts 19:11-12</u> Also, God gave Paul the power to do amazing miracles. [12]If those who were sick could not come to Paul, handkerchiefs or aprons that Paul had touched would be taken and placed on the sick people {others would take and place on the sick people handkerchiefs or aprons that Paul had touched}. As a result, those sick people would people become well, and evil spirits that troubled people would leave.

[TVB] <u>Acts 19:11-12</u> Meanwhile, God did amazing miracles through Paul. [12]People would take a handkerchief or article of clothing that had touched Paul's skin and bring it to their sick friends or relatives, and the patients would be cured of their diseases or released from the evil spirits that oppressed them.

[Weekes-NT] <u>Acts 19:11-12</u> And God wrought works of power of no common sort by the hands of Paul: [12]so that even napkins or aprons were carried away to the sick from his touch, and the diseases were removed from them, and the wicked spirits went out.

[Weymouth-NT] <u>Acts 19:11-12</u> God also brought about extraordinary miracles through Paul's instrumentality. [12]Towels or aprons, for instance, which Paul had handled used to be carried to the sick, and they recovered from their ailments, or the evil spirits left them.

[Williams-NT] <u>Acts 19:11-12</u> God also continued to do such wonder-works through Paul [12]as an instrument that the people carried off to the sick, towels or aprons used by him, and at their touch they were cured of their diseases, and the evil spirits went out of them.

<u>Acts 20:9-10</u> And there sat in a window a certain young man named Eutychus, being fallen into a deep sleep: and as Paul was long preaching, he sunk down with sleep, and **fell down from the third loft, and was taken up dead.** [10]**And Paul went down, and fell on him, and embracing him said, Trouble not yourselves; for his life is in him.**

[Barclay-NT] <u>Acts 20:9-10</u> A young man, Eutychus, was sitting in the window-seat. As Paul went on taking, he grew sleepier and sleepier. Completely overcome by sleep, **he fell from the third storey to the ground below, and was picked up dead.** [10]**Paul went down and took him in his arms, and lay on top of him. 'Stop this uproar,' he said. 'His life is still in him.'**

[CWB] <u>Acts 20:9-10</u> As Paul talked, a young man named Eutychus sat in the open window to catch the cool night breeze. While listening to Paul, he fell asleep, lost his balance and **fell from the third story to the ground. The believers rushed down, but when they tried to help him up, they found he was dead.** [10]**Paul ran downstairs, knelt beside the body, hugged him and prayed earnestly to the Lord. Then he turned to the believers and said, "Don't worry. He's alive."**

[ERV] <u>Acts 20:9-10</u> There was a young man named Eutychus sitting in the window. Paul continued talking, and Eutychus became very, very sleepy. Finally, he went to sleep and **fell out of the window. He fell to the ground from the third floor. When the people went down and lifted him up, he was dead.** [10]**Paul went down to where Eutychus was, knelt down beside him, and put his arms around him. He said to the other believers, "Don't worry. He is alive now."**

[EXB] <u>Acts 20:9-10</u> A young man named Eutychus was sitting in the window. As Paul continued talking, Eutychus was falling into a deep sleep. Finally, he went sound asleep and **fell to the ground from the third floor. When they picked him up, he was dead.** [10]**Paul went down to Eutychus, ·knelt down [or threw himself on him; like Elisha], and ·put his arms around [embraced] him. He said, "Don't ·worry [fear]. ·He is alive now [For his life/soul is in him]."**

[Rendall-Acts] <u>Acts 20:9-10</u> And there sat in the window a certain young man named Eutychus, who becoming oppressed with deep sleep as Paul discoursed, and being still more overcome with the sleep, **fell down from the third story, and was taken up dead.** [10]**And Paul went down, and fell on him, and embracing him said, Make not this ado; for his life is in him.**

[T4T] <u>Acts 20:9-10</u> A young man whose name was Eutychus was there. He was seated on the sill of an open window on the third story of the house. As Paul continued talking for a long time, Eutychus became sleepier and sleepier. Finally, he was sound/really asleep. **He fell out of the window from the third story down to the ground. Some of the believers went down immediately and picked him up. But he was dead.** [10]**Paul also went down. He lay down and stretched out on top of the young**

man and put his arms around him. Then he said to the people who were standing around, "Do not worry, he is alive again now!"

[Thomson] <u>Acts 20:9-10</u> And a certain young man named Eutychus, who was sitting in an open window, bending backwards in a deep sleep, was, while Paul was continuing his discourse, bent quite back with the sleep, and **fell from the third story, and was taken up dead. ¹⁰But Paul going down, threw himself upon him, and taking him in his arms, said, Be not troubled, for his life is in him.**

[TNIV] <u>Acts 20:9-10</u> Seated in a window was a young man named Eutychus, who was sinking into a deep sleep as Paul talked on and on. When he was sound asleep, **he fell to the ground from the third story and was picked up dead. ¹⁰Paul went down, threw himself on the young man and put his arms around him. "Don't be alarmed," he said. "He's alive!"**

[TPT] <u>Acts 20:9-10</u> Sitting in an open window listening was a young man named Eutychus. As Paul's sermon dragged on, Eutychus became drowsy and fell into a deep slumber. Sound asleep, **he fell three stories to his death below. ¹⁰Paul went downstairs, bent over the boy, and embraced him. Taking him in his arms, he said to all the people gathered, "Stop your worrying. He's come back to life!"**

[TTNT] <u>Acts 20:9-10</u> Seated on the windowsill was a young man called Eutychus, who fell asleep while Paul was speaking at such length. While asleep **he fell to his death from the third story. ¹⁰Paul went down to him, bent down to him and embraced him. "There is nothing to be alarmed about," he said, "he is alive!"**

[TVB] <u>Acts 20:9-10</u> A young fellow named Eutychus, seeking some fresh air, moves to an open window. Paul keeps on talking. Eutychus perches in the open window itself. Paul keeps talking. Eutychus drifts off to sleep. Paul continues talking until Eutychus, now overcome by deep sleep, drops out of the window and **falls three stories to the ground, where he is found dead. ¹⁰Paul joins us downstairs, bends over, and takes Eutychus in his arms. Paul: It's OK. He's alive again.**

[WEBBE] <u>Acts 20:9-10</u> A certain young man named Eutychus sat in the window, weighed down with deep sleep. As Paul spoke still longer, being weighed down by his sleep, **he fell down from the third floor and was taken up dead. ¹⁰Paul went down and fell upon him, and embracing him said, "Don't be troubled, for his life is in him."**

<u>Acts 28:3-5</u> And when Paul had gathered a bundle of sticks, and laid them on the fire, there came a viper out of the heat, and fastened on his hand. ⁴And when the barbarians saw the venomous beast hang on his hand, they said among themselves, No doubt this man is a murderer, whom, though he hath escaped the sea, yet vengeance suffereth not to live. **⁵And he shook off the beast into the fire, and felt no harm.**

[AMP] <u>Acts 28:3-5</u> But when Paul had gathered a bundle of sticks and laid them on the fire, a viper crawled out because of the heat and fastened itself on his hand. ⁴When the natives saw the creature hanging from his hand, they began saying to one another, "Undoubtedly this man is a murderer, and though he has been saved from the sea, Justice [the avenging goddess] has not permitted him to live." ⁵Then **Paul [simply] shook the creature off into the fire and suffered no ill effects.**

[BWE-NT] <u>Acts 28:3-5</u> Paul gathered some sticks of wood. He put them on the fire. A bad snake came out of the heat and hung onto his hand. ⁴The people of Malta saw the snake hanging on his hand. 'Oh,' they said to each other. 'This man has no doubt killed someone. He did not die in the water, but it is not right for him to live.' **⁵Paul shook the snake off into the fire. It did not hurt him.**

[CB] <u>Acts 28:3-5</u> When Paul had gathered a bundle of sticks, and laid them on the fire, a snake came out of the heat and clamped onto his hand. ⁴When the natives saw the venomous snake hanging onto his hand, they said to themselves, "This man must be a murderer, and even though he escaped the sea, vengeance won't allow him to live." **⁵But Paul shook the snake off into the fire, and suffered no injury**.

[CWB] <u>Acts 28:3-5</u> Paul gathered wood with the rest of us. As he threw his bundle of sticks on the fire, a small poisonous snake driven out by the heat, struck his hand and hung on. ⁴When the natives saw this deadly snake, they jumped back and said, "This man must be a murderer, because even though he escaped the sea, the goddess Justice will not let him live." **⁵But Paul shook the snake off into the fire and was unaffected.**

[EHV] <u>Acts 28:3-5</u> As Paul gathered a bundle of sticks and laid it on the fire, a viper came out because of the heat and fastened itself on his hand. ⁴When the natives saw the snake hanging from his hand, they said to one another, "No doubt this man is a murderer. Though he escaped from the sea, Justice has not allowed him to live." ⁵However, **Paul shook the snake off into the fire and was not harmed**.

[Etheridge-NT] <u>Acts 28:3-5</u> And Paulos took many sticks and placed upon the fire; and there came forth a viper from the heat of the fire, and bit (him) in his hand. ⁴And when the Barbaroyee saw it hang upon his hand, they said, Perhaps this man is a murderer, whom, though he is escaped from the sea, justice suffereth not to live. ⁵But **Paulos shook his hand, and cast the viper into the fire, and nothing of evil befell him.**

[FBV-NT] <u>Acts 28:3-5</u> Paul collected a bundle of firewood and threw it on the fire. But a poisonous snake was driven out of the bundle because of the heat and bit him, fastening itself on his hand. ⁴When the people there saw the snake hanging from his hand, they said to each other, "This man must be a murderer. Even though he escaped death from the sea, Justice won't let him live." ⁵However **Paul shook the snake off into the fire, and suffered no ill-effects**.

[NIV] <u>Acts 28:3-5</u> Paul gathered a pile of brushwood and, as he put it on the fire, a viper, driven out by the heat, fastened itself on his hand. ⁴When the islanders saw the snake hanging from his hand, they said to each other, "This man must be a murderer; for though he escaped from the sea, the goddess Justice has not allowed him to live." **⁵But Paul shook the snake off into the fire and suffered no ill effects.**

[REM-NT] <u>Acts 28:3-5</u> Paul gathered some brushwood, and as he was putting it on the fire, a viper, driven out by the heat, bit him, latching on to his hand. ⁴When the islanders saw this, they said, "This man must be a killer; for even though he escaped the sea, justice has found him and will not allow him to live." **⁵But Paul just smiled and shook the snake off into the fire, and suffered no ill effects**.

[TPT] <u>Acts 28:3-5</u> When Paul had gathered an armful of brushwood and was setting it on the fire, a venomous snake was driven out by the heat and latched onto Paul's hand with its fangs. ⁴When the islanders saw the snake dangling from Paul's hand, they said to one another, "No doubt about it, this guy is a murderer. Even though he escaped death at sea, Justice has now caught up with him!" ⁵But **Paul shook the snake off, flung it into the fire, and suffered no harm at all**.

[TTNT] <u>Acts 28:3-5</u> Paul gathered an armful of wood but as he put it on the fire a poisonous viper, driven out by the heat, fastened onto his hand. ⁴When the local people saw the snake hanging from his hand, they said to each other: "This man must be guilty of murder. He may have escaped from the sea but justice has been served on him and he cannot live." **⁵However, Paul merely shook the snake off into the fire, totally unharmed.**

[Williams-NT] <u>Acts 28:3-5</u> Paul, too, gathered a bundle of sticks, and as he put them on the fire, because of the heat, a viper crawled out of them and fastened itself upon his hand. ⁴When the natives saw the reptile hanging from his hand, they said to one another, "Beyond a doubt this man is a murderer, for though he has been rescued from the sea, justice will not let him live." **⁵But he simply shook the reptile off into the fire and suffered no harm.**

Acts 28:8 And it came to pass, that the father of Publius lay sick of a fever and of a bloody flux: to whom **Paul entered in, and prayed, and laid his hands on him, and healed him.**

[AUV-NT 2005] **Acts 28:8** And it happened that Publius' father lay sick with a fever and dysentery. **Paul went [to his house] and, after praying and placing hands on him, healed him.**

[BBE] **Acts 28:8** And the father of Publius was ill, with a disease of the stomach; to whom **Paul went, and put his hands on him, with prayer, and made him well.**

[CEV] **Acts 28:8** His father was in bed, sick with fever and stomach trouble, and **Paul went to visit him. Paul healed the man by praying and placing his hands on him.**

[Haweis-NT] **Acts 28:8** And it so happened that the father of Publius was then confined to his bed with an attack of fever and dysentery: unto whom **Paul went in, and after praying, laid his hands upon him, and healed him.**

[Purver] **Acts 28:8** And the Father of Publius lay oppressed with a Fever, and a Bloody-flux; to whom **Paul went in, and having prayed, put Hands on him, and healed him.**

[TGNT] **Acts 28:8** Now it happened that Publius' father was bedridden with fever and dysentery. But **Paul came to him, and after praying and placing his hand on him, miraculously healed him.**

[TPT] **Acts 28:8** His father lay sick in bed, suffering from fits of high fever and dysentery. So **Paul went into his room, and after praying, placed his hands on him. He was instantly healed.**

[TTT-NT] **Acts 28:8** And it happened that the father of Publius was ill with a fever and dysentery; and **Paul went in to him, and having prayed, placed his hands on him, and he was healed.**

Acts 28:9 So when this was done, others also, which had diseases in the island, came, and were healed:

[Ballentine-NT] **Acts 28:9** After this the rest of those in the island who had diseases kept coming to him and kept being cured.

[BBE] **Acts 28:9** And when this took place, all the others in the island who had diseases came and were made well.

[CEV] **Acts 28:9** After this happened, everyone on the island brought their sick people to Paul, and they were all healed.

[CWB] **Acts 28:9** News of this spread and soon other sick people on the island came to Paul, and he healed them all.

[ERV] **Acts 28:9** After this happened, all the other sick people on the island came to Paul, and he healed them too.

[Lee-NT] **Acts 28:9** And when this happened, the rest also in the island who had sicknesses came to him and were healed.

[MSG] **Acts 28:9** Word of the healing got around fast, and soon everyone on the island who was sick came and got healed.

[NIRV] **Acts 28:9** Then the rest of the sick people on the island came. They too were healed.

[TPT] **Acts 28:9** When the people of the island heard about this miracle, they brought all the sick to Paul, and they were also healed.

ROMANS

Romans 1:16-17 For I am not ashamed of the gospel of Christ: for **it is the power of God unto salvation to every one that believeth**; to the Jew first, and also to the Greek. [17]For therein is the righteousness of God revealed from faith to faith: as it is written, **The just shall live by faith.**

[AUV-NT 2003] **Romans 1:16-17** I am not ashamed of the good news, because **it is God's power for [bringing] salvation to every person who believes [in Jesus]**; first to Jews and then to Greeks. [17]For the Gospel reveals how a person can be made right with God. It is through faith [in Jesus], from beginning to end, just as it is written, "**The righteous person will [obtain] life by [his] faith [in God].**"

[Barclay-NT] **Romans 1:16-17** I am quite sure that the good news will never let me down, **for it is the saving power of God to everyone who accepts it**, first to the Jews, then to the Greeks. [17]In it God's way of setting men right with himself is revealed as beginning and ending in faith, just as it stands written: '**It is the man who is right with God through faith who will find life.**'

[BV-KJV-NT] **Romans 1:16-17** You see, I am not ashamed of the good news of the Anointed King; **for it is God's ability for a rescue to everyone who trusts**, both Jewish first and Greek. [17]You see, God's right way in it is uncovered from trust for trust, just as it has been written in Habakkuk 2:4, "**The person who does what is right will live from trust.**"

[BWE-NT] **Romans 1:16-17** I am not ashamed of the good news of Jesus Christ. **The good news is the power God uses to save every one who believes**. The good news was for the Jews first, but also for those who are not Jews. [17]The good news shows how God puts a person right. God puts a person right when that person believes in his Son and keeps on believing. The holy writings say, '**A person who is put right because he believes, will live for ever.**'

[Conybeare-NT] **Romans 1:16-17** For [even in the chief city of the world] I am not ashamed of the Glad-tidings of Christ, seeing **it is the mighty power whereby God brings salvation to every man** that has faith therein, to the Jew first, and also to the Gentile. [17]For therein God's righteousness is revealed, a righteousness which springs from Faith, and which Faith receives—as it is written: "**By faith shall the righteous live.**"

[ERV] **Romans 1:16-17** I am proud of the Good News, because **it is the power God uses to save everyone who believes**—to save the Jews first, and now to save those who are not Jews. [17]The Good News shows how God makes people right with himself. God's way of making people right begins and ends with faith. As the Scriptures say, "**The one who is right with God by faith will live forever.**"

[FBV-NT] **Romans 1:16-17** I'm certainly not ashamed about the good news, for **it's God's power to save everyone who trusts in him**—to the Jewish people first, and then to everyone else as well. [17]For in the good news God is revealed as good and right, trustworthy from start to finish. As Scripture says, "**Those who are right with God live by trusting him.**"

[GNC-NT] **Romans 1:16-17** And indeed, I am not ashamed of the gospel: **it is the power displayed by God for the salvation of everyone who has faith**, Jew first and then Greek. [17]And in this gospel there is revealed the righteousness which has God for its source, the righteousness that springs from faith and leads to faith. As it is written in scripture, "**The righteous man shall gain life by his faith.**"

[Haweis-NT] **Romans 1:16-17** For I am not ashamed of the Gospel of Christ: for **it is the power of God for salvation to every one who believeth**; to the Jew first, and also to the Greek. [17]For the righteousness of God by faith is therein revealed for belief; as it is written, "**Now the just by faith shall live.**"

[Heberden-NT] Romans 1:16-17 For I am not ashamed of the gospel of Christ; for **it is the gracious manifestation of the power of God unto salvation to every one who believeth Christ to be the son of God, and believing obeyeth his precepts; it is the appointed means of pardon and acceptance**, offered to the Jew first, then also to the Greek, the Gentile. [17]For in it, by the Gospel dispensation, the righteousness of God is revealed, openly declared to all men, from faith to faith, by faith continually increasing; as it is written, "**the righteous shall live by faith.**"

[ICB] Romans 1:16-17 I am not ashamed of the Good News. **It is the power God uses to save everyone who believes**—to save the Jews first, and then to save the non-Jews. [17]The Good News shows how God makes people right with himself. God's way of making people right with him begins and ends with faith. As the Scripture says, "**The person who is made right with God by faith will live forever.**"

[MSG] Romans 1:16-17 It's news I'm most proud to proclaim, **this extraordinary Message of God's powerful plan to rescue everyone who trusts him**, starting with Jews and then right on to everyone else! [17]God's way of putting people right shows up in the acts of faith, confirming what Scripture has said all along: "**The person in right standing before God by trusting him really lives.**"

[NIRV] Romans 1:16-17 I want to preach it because I'm not ashamed of the good news. **It is God's power to save everyone who believes**. It is meant first for the Jews. It is meant also for the Gentiles. [17]The good news shows God's power to make people right with himself. God's power to be made right with him is given to the person who has faith. It happens by faith from beginning to end. It is written, "**The one who is right with God will live by faith.**"

[NJB] Romans 1:16-17 For I see no reason to be ashamed of the gospel; **it is God's power for the salvation of everyone who has faith**—Jews first, but Greeks as well— [17]for in it is revealed the saving justice of God: a justice based on faith and addressed to faith. As it says in scripture: **Anyone who is upright through faith will live.**

[NLT] Romans 1:16-17 For I am not ashamed of this Good News about Christ. **It is the power of God at work, saving everyone who believes**—the Jew first and also the Gentile. [17]This Good News tells us how God makes us right in his sight. This is accomplished from start to finish by faith. As the Scriptures say, "**It is through faith that a righteous person has life.**"

[OEB-NT] Romans 1:16-17 For I am not ashamed of the good news; **it is the power of God which brings salvation to everyone who believes in Christ**, to the Jew first, but also to the Greek. [17]For in it there is a revelation of the divine righteousness resulting from faith and leading on to faith; as scripture says—'**Through faith the righteous will find life.**'

[Original-NT] Romans 1:16-17 For I am not ashamed of the News: **it is God's means of deliverance** for all who believe, whether Jews or Gentiles. For by it God's justice is revealed by faith for faith, as it is stated, "**By faith the just shall live**".

[REM-NT] Romans 1:16-17 I am not ashamed of spreading the good news about God and his character, methods and principles, as **this is God's power which heals everyone who believes and trusts in him**: firstly to the Jews—those initially called to assist in spreading the Remedy, and then to the Gentiles—those most recently called to help spread the Remedy. [17]For the good news is a revelation of God's true righteousness—character, methods and principles—that restores trust in God and results in re-creation of a righteous and Christlike character in humans, just as it is written: "**The Christlike will live by choosing what is right in governance of themselves, and by trusting God with how things turn out.**"

[Rutherford-NT] Romans 1:16-17 In this Gospel I glory. It is the power of God providing salvation for every one who has faith, Jew and Greek alike. [17]There is revealed in it a righteousness that is of God, created by faith, realized in faith, precisely as the scripture expresses it, "But the righteousness as possessed with faith shall live."

[SG] Romans 1:16-17 For I am not ashamed of the good news, for **it is God's power for the salvation** of everyone who has faith, of the Jew first and then of the Greek. [17]In it God's way of uprightness is disclosed through faith and for faith, just as the Scripture says, "**The upright will have life because of his faith**."

[Spencer-NT] Romans 1:16-17 For I am not ashamed of the Gospel, since **it is a divine power for the salvation of every believer**—Jew first, and then Greek. [17]For justification from God is revealed in it by faith to the increase of faith; for it is written, "but **the just man shall live by faith**."

[TLB] Romans 1:16-17 For I am not ashamed of this Good News about Christ. **It is God's powerful method of bringing all who believe it to heaven**. This message was preached first to the Jews alone, but now everyone is invited to come to God in this same way. [17]This Good News tells us that God makes us ready for heaven—makes us right in God's sight—when we put our faith and trust in Christ to save us. This is accomplished from start to finish by faith. As the Scripture says it, "**The man who finds life will find it through trusting God**."

[TPT] Romans 1:16-17 I refuse to be ashamed of sharing the wonderful message of God's liberating power unleashed in us through Christ! **For I am thrilled to preach that everyone who believes is saved**—the Jew first, and then people everywhere! [17]This gospel unveils a continual revelation of God's righteousness—a perfect righteousness given to us when we believe. And it moves us from receiving life through faith, to the power of living by faith. This is what the Scripture means when it says: "**We are right with God through life-giving faith!**"

[TTNT] Romans 1:16-17 I could never be ashamed of believing and proclaiming the gospel. I know that **it is God's powerful way of making salvation available to everyone who believes in Jesus**, first the Jews to whom He came as Man, then also for people of other nations. [17]All who believe the good news of Jesus are saved because they are placed in a right relationship with God, regardless of who they are or of what they have done in the past. This relationship with God can only be received as a gift from Him, and is given to those who place their faith in who Jesus is and what He has done for them. It is a matter of faith from beginning to end. Nothing we could ever do by our own efforts could ever make us pleasing to God or place us in a relationship of righteousness with Him; of being made fully acceptable to Him. This is borne out by the fact that the scriptures declare that **those who are acceptable to God will live by faith**.

[TVB] Romans 1:16-17 For I am not the least bit embarrassed about the gospel. I won't shy away from it, because **it is God's power to save every person who believes**: first the Jew, and then the non-Jew. [17]You see, in the good news, God's restorative justice is revealed. And as we will see, it begins with and ends in faith. As the Scripture declares, "**By faith the just will obtain life**."

[Wand-NT] Romans 1:16-17 I am not ashamed to proclaim the Gospel. **It represents the power of God to save everyone** who believes, the Jew first and then the Greek. [17]In it the justice of God's way is made clear in proportion to our belief. That is why the Scripture says, '**Belief is the good man's very breath of life**.'

[Way-NT] Romans 1:16-17 In the Glad-tidings there is no feature of which I am ashamed. **It is the means through which God exerts faith** in the Message–of the Jew, as having the precedence, but of the Greek also. [17]God's gift of righteousness is revealed in it, lifting men from one step of faith to another. This is the import of that passage of Scripture which says, 'IT IS FROM THE SOIL OF FAITH THAT THE RIGHTEOUS SHALL GROW UP INTO REAL LIFE.'

Romans 4:17 (As it is written, I have made thee a father of many nations,) before him whom he believed, even God, who quickeneth the dead, and **calleth those things which be not as though they were**.

[ACV] Romans 4:17 (as it is written, I have made thee a father of many nations), before him whom he believed, of God who makes the dead alive, and **who calls things not existing, as existing**.

[AMPC] Romans 4:17 As it is written, I have made you the father of many nations. [He was appointed our father] in the sight of God in Whom he believed, Who gives life to the dead and **speaks of the nonexistent things that [He has foretold and promised] as if they [already] existed**.

[AUV-NT 2005] Romans 4:17 just as it is written, "I [i.e., God] have made you [i.e., Abraham] forefather of many nations." He received this promise in the presence of God, in whom he believed, and who gives life [back] to dead people and **who refers to things [promised] as though they were [already] fulfilled**.

[Barclay-NT] Romans 4:17 As scripture says of him: 'I have appointed you as father of many nations.' This promise was made in the presence of God, the God in whom Abraham had put his faith, the God who makes the dead live, the God **whose summons goes out to things which do not yet exist, as if they already did exist**.

[Berkeley] Romans 4:17 as it is written, "I have appointed you a father of many nations." All this in the presence of God in whom he believed, who makes the dead live and **calls into existence what has no being**.

[BSB-NT] Romans 4:17 As it is written: "I have made you a father of many nations." He is our father in the presence of God, in whom he believed, the God who gives life to the dead and **calls into being what does not yet exist**.

[CB] Romans 4:17 (As it is written, I have made you a father of many nations), in the presence of God in whom he believed, who could raise the dead, and **bring things into existence from nothing**.

[CEB] Romans 4:17 As it is written: I have appointed you to be the father of many nations. So Abraham is our father in the eyes of God in whom he had faith, the God who gives life to the dead and **calls things that don't exist into existence**.

[CJB] Romans 4:17 This accords with the Tanakh, where it says, "I have appointed you to be a father to many nations." Avraham is our father in God's sight because he trusted God as the one who gives life to the dead and **calls nonexistent things into existence**.

[CWB] Romans 4:17 The Scriptures confirm that God said to Abraham, "I have made you the spiritual father of many nationalities." This promise was given to Abraham because he had faith that God would raise the dead and **create a whole new world in order to keep His promise**.

[DLNT] Romans 4:17 just as it has been written that "I have made you a father of many nations"— before God Whom he believed, the One giving-life-to the dead and **calling the things not being as being**,

[EEBT] Romans 4:17 The Old Testament says that God spoke to Abraham. 'I have chosen that you will become the father of people from many countries', God said. God himself promised this to Abraham, who believed him. Abraham believed God, who causes dead people to become alive again. God speaks, and he causes things to be. **He causes things to be that were not there before**.

[ERV] Romans 4:17 As the Scriptures say, "I have made you a father of many nations." This is true before God, the one Abraham believed—the God who gives life to the dead and **speaks of things that don't yet exist as if they are real**.

[FBV-NT] Romans 4:17 As Scripture says, "I've made you the father of many nations." For in the presence of God, Abraham trusted in the God who makes the dead alive and **speaks into existence what didn't previously exist**.

[GNT] <u>Romans 4:17</u> as the scripture says, "I have made you father of many nations." So the promise is good in the sight of God, in whom Abraham believed—the God who brings the dead to life and **whose command brings into being what did not exist.**

[Guyse-NT] <u>Romans 4:17</u> This was intimated in what is recorded, concerning God's changing his name from Abram to Abraham; because (said he) I have ordained, constituted, and will actually make thee a father of many nations. This included his being so, in a spiritual sense, to believing Gentiles, as well as Jews, in the account of that God in whom he believed, according to the promise, that in him, meaning in his seed, all the families of the earth should be blessed: He, I say, believed in that God, even the great Jehovah, who quickens the dead in trespasses and sins, and will raise the dead bodies of believers to an immortal life, according to the working of his mighty power, whereby he was able to give life to Gentile sinners, and to invigorate the bodies of Abraham and Sarah, when they were in a manner dead, as to the purpose of having children, in the ordinary course of nature; **and who speaks of the things that at present have no existence, and, by natural causes and appearances, are never likely to be at all, as though they already actually were**; as he did, when he promised, that a son should be born of those aged persons; and that a spiritual seed, should, in due season, be raised to Abraham, from among the idolatrous heathens, who where looked upon with contempt, as things that were not, and who, at that time, were not the people of God.

[Knox] <u>Romans 4:17</u> and so it was written of him, I have made thee the father of many nations. We are his children in the sight of God, in whom he put his faith, who can raise the dead to life, and send **his call to that which has no being, as if it already were.**

[Madsen-NT] <u>Romans 4:17</u> according to the word of scripture: I have chosen you to be the father of many peoples. With faithful trust he turned to that divine power which gives life to what is dead and **calls into being what is not in being.**

[MCC-NT] <u>Romans 4:17</u> Because He believed God, the Enlivener of the Dead; and **the Caller of Non-entities, as if Entities.**

[Moffatt-NT 1917] <u>Romans 4:17</u> (as it is written, I have made you a father of many nations). Such a faith implies the presence of the God in whom he believed, a God who makes the dead live and **calls into being what does not exist.**

[MSG] <u>Romans 4:17</u> We call Abraham "father" not because he got God's attention by living like a saint, but because God made something out of Abraham when he was a nobody. Isn't that what we've always read in Scripture, God saying to Abraham, "I set you up as father of many peoples"? Abraham was first named "father" and then became a father because he dared to trust God to do what only God could do: raise the dead to life, **with a word make something out of nothing.**

[NEB] <u>Romans 4:17</u> For he is the father of us all, as Scripture says: 'I have appointed you to be father of many nations.' This promise, then, was valid before God, the God in whom he put his faith, the God who makes the dead live and **summons things that are not yet in existence as if they already were.**

[NLT] <u>Romans 4:17</u> That is what the Scriptures mean when God told him, "I have made you the father of many nations." This happened because Abraham believed in the God who brings the dead back to life and **who creates new things out of nothing.**

[NLV] <u>Romans 4:17</u> The Holy Writings say, "I have made you a father of many nations." This promise is good because of Who God is. He makes the dead live again. **He speaks, and something is made out of nothing.**

[Original-NT] <u>Romans 4:17</u> as it is stated, "I have made you father of many nations". Anticipating this, he relied on God the "Giver of life from the dead" and **the Namer of things as existing which as yet are non-existent.**

[REM-NT] <u>Romans 4:17</u> As it is written: "I have made you the father of many different ethnic groups." The God in whom Abraham trusted—the Creator God who is the source of all life and **who calls things into existence from nothingness**—considers all of us who trust him to be descendants of Abraham.

[Shuttleworth-NT] <u>Romans 4:17</u> as it is written, "I have made thee a father of many nations:" a promise confirmed to him whilst he stood in the presence of that God who can raise the dead to life, and **who calls the things as yet unborn as though they already existed**.

[Stringfellow-NT] <u>Romans 4:17</u> just as it stands written, A father of many nations I have established you before him whom he believed, (namely) God, who makes alive the dead, and **issues his commands to the things which do not exist as if they did:**

[Thomson] <u>Romans 4:17</u> who; as it is written, "I have made thee a father of many nations" is the father of us all in the sight of him in whom he believed—namely God who reanimateth the dead, and **calleth up things not yet in existence as if actually existing**.

[TLB] <u>Romans 4:17</u> That is what the Scriptures mean when they say that God made Abraham the father of many nations. God will accept all people in every nation who trust God as Abraham did. And this promise is from God himself, who makes the dead live again and **speaks of future events with as much certainty as though they were already past**.

[TNIV] <u>Romans 4:17</u> As it is written: "I have made you a father of many nations." He is our father in the sight of God, in whom he believed—the God who gives life to the dead and **calls into being things that were not**.

[TTNT] <u>Romans 4:17</u> This fulfils God's Word to Abraham: "I have made you a father of many nations." In God's eyes, Abraham is a father to all who believe. He believed that God gives life to those who are spiritually dead and **is able to speak of things that have not happened as if they had already taken place**, so sure is His Word.

[TTT-NT] <u>Romans 4:17</u> as it is written, As a father of many nations I have placed you; before God whom he believed, who livens the dead, and **calls those things which are not the same as those which are;**

[UDB] <u>Romans 4:17</u> This is what Yahweh said to Abraham in the scriptures: "I will make you the ancestor of many ethnic groups." Abraham received this directly from Yahweh who raises dead people to life and **creates things out of nothing**.

[Wand-NT] <u>Romans 4:17</u> as the Scripture itself points out: 'I have made thee a father of many nations.' The reason for this is that he staked everything on the existence of a God who makes the dead live and **calls into being things that had no previous existence**.

[Way-NT] <u>Romans 4:17</u> In this sense he is the father of us all ('AS A FATHER OF MANY NATIONS HAVE I ORDAINED THEE' is the Scripture expression) in the eyes of Him whose promise he believed, that is, of God, who can make the dead live again, and **who is continually anticipating the birth of things that give as yet no token of existence**.

<u>Romans 4:19-21</u> And **being not weak in faith**, he considered not his own body now dead, when he was about an hundred years old, neither yet the deadness of Sara's womb: **20He staggered not at the promise of God through unbelief; but was strong in faith**, giving glory to God; 21And **being fully persuaded** that, what he had promised, he was able also to perform.

[AENT] <u>Romans 4:19-21</u> And **he was not sickly in his faith** while contemplating his aged body (for he was a hundred years old) and (as well) the dormancy of Sarah's womb. **20And he did not hesitate at**

the promise of Elohim as one without faith; but he was strong in faith and gave glory to Elohim; [21]And felt assured, that what Elohim had promised to him, he was able to fulfill.

[AMPC] Romans 4:19-21 He did not weaken in faith when he considered the [utter] impotence of his own body, which was as good as dead because he was about a hundred years old, or [when he considered] the barrenness of Sarah's [deadened] womb. [20]No unbelief or distrust made him waver (doubtingly question) concerning the promise of God, but he grew strong and was empowered by faith as he gave praise and glory to God, [21]Fully satisfied and assured that God was able and mighty to keep His word and to do what He had promised.

[ASV] Romans 4:19-21 And without being weakened in faith he considered his own body now as good as dead (he being about a hundred years old), and the deadness of Sarah's womb; [20]yet, looking unto the promise of God, he wavered not through unbelief, but waxed strong through faith, giving glory to God, [21]and being fully assured that what he had promised, he was able also to perform.

[Barclay-NT] Romans 4:19-21 His faith did not waver, although he was well aware that his body was as good as dead—for he was about a hundred years old—and that the life was gone from Sarah's womb. [20]He never allowed lack of faith to make him question God's promise. So far from that, his faith was so strengthened that he praised God [21]in the unshakable conviction that God is able, not only to make promises, but also to make his promises come true.

[Berkeley] Romans 4:19-21 And there was no weakening of his faith, when he recognized the impotence of his own body at the age of one hundred, as well as Sarah's inability to bear. [20]He did not in unbelief hesitate about God's promise, but, empowered by faith, he rendered praise to God [21]in the complete conviction that He was able to make good His promise.

[BWE-NT] Romans 4:19-21 He did not stop believing when he thought about his own body. It was almost dead. He was about one hundred years old. He did not stop believing when he thought about Sarah, even though she had never given birth to any children. [20]He did not stop believing God's promise. He believed God very much. He did not praise God for his own faith, but for God's promise. [21]He was sure that God was able to do what he had promised to do.

[CAB] Romans 4:19-21 And not weakening in faith, he did not consider his own body, already having been worn out (being about a hundred years old), and the deadness of Sarah's womb, [20]he did not waver at the promise of God in unbelief, but was empowered by faith, giving glory to God, 21 and being fully convinced that what He had promised He was also able to do.

[CEB] Romans 4:19-21 Without losing faith, Abraham, who was nearly 100 years old, took into account his own body, which was as good as dead, and Sarah's womb, which was dead. [20]He didn't hesitate with a lack of faith in God's promise, but he grew strong in faith and gave glory to God. [21]He was fully convinced that God was able to do what he promised.

[Conybeare-NT] Romans 4:19-21 And having no feebleness in his faith, he regarded not his own body which was already dead (being about a hundred years old), nor the deadness of Sarah's womb; [20]at the promise of God (I say) he doubted not faithlessly, but was filled with the strength of Faith, and gave glory to God; [21]being fully persuaded that what He has promised, He is able also to perform.

[Darby] Romans 4:19-21 and not being weak in faith, he considered not his own body already become dead, being about a hundred years old, and the deadening of Sarah's womb, [20]and hesitated not at the promise of God through unbelief; but found strength in faith, giving glory to God; [21]and being fully persuaded that what he has promised he is able also to do;

[Doddridge-NT] Romans 4:19-21 And having received such a promise, not being feeble in faith, how feeble soever he might be in his animal constitution, he considered not his own body, which, with regard to the probability of begetting children, was now dead, being about an hundred years old; nor the deadness of Sarah's womb, of whom the sacred historian tells us, "that it ceased to be with her after the manner of women." [20]Amidst all these difficulties and discouragements, **he objected not to the promise of God through unbelief, but was strengthened by the exercise of the most vigorous and triumphant faith**, thereby giving a due and becoming glory to the great God, the Lord of universal nature; [21]And **was confidently persuaded**, that what he had thus graciously promised, he was, and ever is, able to perform, though that performance should, to sensible view, seen ever so improbable.

[Erasmus-NT] <u>Romans 4:19-21</u> For he did not doubt, although he himself was worn out and had a barren wife, that nevertheless he would be the father of many nations and the originator of a posterity so numerous that it could be equal to the multitude of the stars. For after God had led him into the country and had pointed out to him the heavens filled with a countless density of stars, he said: Just as you are not able to count these fires, so the descendants which will come forth from you will be innumerable. Although this seemed not at all probable or realistic at that time because of the weakness of age, nevertheless, **though he was weak in strength of body, he was not weak in the vigour of his faith**, and he did not begin to search for proofs that this could or could not happen as doubters would do; nor was he concerned that the strength of his body had already been spent and that he was incapable of begetting children, inasmuch as he had now entered his one hundredth year. He did not consider the age of his wife whose reproductive organs also had now withered through age, so that even if he himself had not yet failed in his ability to reproduce, still she was unfit for childbearing. [20]**None of these difficulties, I say, entered into his mind. He did not mistrust; he did not hesitate, but relied on the promises of God with his whole heart, as strong in faith as he was weak in body. Despairing of his own strength, he maintained a most certain hope from the strength of the promises, and claiming nothing for himself in this matter**, he transferred all glory and praise to God alone. [21]**By his own unshaken trust** he attested at once that God was truthful—since he was unwilling to deceive anyone, and omnipotent—since he was able to fulfil whatever he had promised, however much this exceeded human strength.

[ERV] <u>Romans 4:19-21</u> Abraham was almost a hundred years old, so he was past the age for having children. Also, Sarah could not have children. Abraham was well aware of this, but **his faith in God never became weak.** [20]**He never doubted that God would do what he promised. He never stopped believing. In fact, he grew stronger in his faith** and just praised God. [21]**Abraham felt sure** that God was able to do what he promised.

[Godbey-NT] <u>Romans 4:19-21</u> and **being not weak in faith**, he considered not his body already dead, being about a hundred years old, and the deadness of Sarah's womb: [20]but **he staggered not at the promise of God through unbelief**; but was **filled with dynamite through faith**, having given glory to God; [21]and **being fully assured** that whatsoever he has promised, he is able also to perform.

[GT] <u>Romans 4:19-21</u> He understood that his body was practically dead (He was about 100 years old.) and that Sarah couldn't have children either. But **Abraham's faith didn't weaken.** [20]**He did not doubt God's promise. He believed. His faith made him even stronger.** He gave glory to God. [21]**He was convinced** that God was able to do what He had promised.

[GW] <u>Romans 4:19-21</u> Abraham **didn't weaken**. Through faith he regarded the facts: His body was already as good as dead now that he was about a hundred years old, and Sarah was unable to have children. [20]**He didn't doubt God's promise out of a lack of faith. Instead, giving honor to God for the promise, he became strong because of faith** [21]**and was absolutely confident** that God would do what he promised.

[Hanson-NT] <u>Romans 4:19-21</u> and **without being weakened in faith**, he considered his own body as then dead, he being about a hundred years old, and the deadness of Sarah's womb; [20]**but he disputed** not the promise of God, by unbelief, but **grew strong in the faith**, giving glory to God; [21]**having been fully assured** that what he had promised he was able also to perform.

[Jerusalem] <u>Romans 4:19-21</u> Even the thought that his body was past fatherhood—he was about a hundred years old—and Sarah too old to become a mother, **did not shake his belief.** [20]**Since God had promised it, Abraham refused either to deny it or even to doubt it, but drew strength from faith** and gave glory to God, [21]**convinced that God had power** to do what he had promised.

[Macknight-NT] <u>Romans 4:19-21</u> And **not being weak in faith**, he did not consider his own body now dead, being about an hundred years old, neither the deadness of Sarah's womb. [20]**Therefore against the promise of God he did not dispute through unbelief**, but **was strong in faith**, giving glory to God. [21]**And was fully persuaded**, that what was promised, he was able certainly to perform.

[Macknight-NTc] <u>Romans 4:19-21</u> And **not being weak, either in his conceptions or in his belief of the power and veracity of God**, he did not consider his own body now dead, in respect of procreating children, being about an hundred years old, neither the deadness of Sarah's womb, as obstacles to his having a numerous progeny by her, though she was ninety years old. [20]**Therefore against the promise of God he did not dispute through unbelief, by alleging that the thing was impossible**; but **having the firmest persuasion of the veracity of God**, he gave the glory of that perfection to God, by waiting patiently for the performance of his promise. [21]**And was fully persuaded**, that what was promised, God was able even to perform; although the longer he waited, the accomplishment of the promise must have appeared, to an ordinary faith, the more difficult.

[Martin-NT] <u>Romans 4:19-21</u> And **his faithfulness did not weaken**, (though) he recognized that his own body had already died, being a hundred years old, and that Sara's womb was dead. [20]**But he did not desert the promise of God by unfaithfulness, but was strengthened by faithfulness [trust]**, giving glory to God. [21]**(He was) fully convinced that (God) was able to do what he promised.**

[Moffatt-NT 1917] <u>Romans 4:19-21</u> **His faith never quailed**, even when he noted the utter impotence of his own body (for he was about a hundred years old) or the impotence of Sara's womb; [20]**no unbelief made him waver about God's promise; his faith won strength** as he gave glory to God [21]and **felt convinced that He was able to do what He had promised.**

[Murdock-NT] <u>Romans 4:19-21</u> And **he was not sickly in his faith**, while contemplating his inert body, (for he was a hundred years old,) and the inert womb of Sarah. [20]**And he did not hesitate at the promise of God, as one lacking faith; but he was strong in faith**, and gave glory to God; [21]**and felt assured**, that what God had promised to him, he was able to fulfill.

[Original-NT] <u>Romans 4:19-21</u> **His faith never weakened** with consciousness of the impotence of his own body—he was nearly a hundred years old at the time—and of Sarah's incapacity for motherhood. [20]**He did not challenge the promise of God incredulously**, but **fortified by faith** he gave God credence, [21]and **was fully assured** that what he had promised was practicable, and that he would carry it out.

[REM-NT] <u>Romans 4:19-21</u> **Without doubting God for a moment**, he accepted it in the reality that he was one hundred years old and his ability to procreate was severely limited, and Sarah had gone through menopause and was beyond child bearing years. [20]Even though in human understanding the promise seemed hopeless, **Abraham did not waver in his confidence in God**, but praised God as he [21]**realized that God was able to miraculously fulfill the promise.**

[SENT] <u>Romans 4:19-21</u> **His faith did not weaken** as he thought about his own body, which had pretty much already died. (He was a hundred years old or so.) He didn't doubt as he thought about the infertility of Sarah's womb, either. **[20]He went for the promise of God**, and didn't slip into unbelief. Just the opposite: **he was empowered by faith,** and gave glory to God. **[21]He was totally convinced that God was capable of doing what had been promised**.

[TLB] Romans 4:19-21 And because **his faith was strong**, he didn't worry about the fact that he was too old to be a father at the age of one hundred, and that Sarah his wife, at ninety, was also much too old to have a baby. [20]But Abraham never doubted. **He believed God, for his faith and trust grew ever stronger**, and he praised God for this blessing even before it happened. **[21]He was completely sure** that God was well able to do anything he promised.

[TPT] Romans 4:19-21 In spite of being nearly one hundred years old when the promise of having a son was made, **his faith was so strong that it could not be undermined** by the fact that he and Sarah were incapable of conceiving a child. [20]**He never stopped believing God's promise, for he was made strong in his faith** to father a child. And **because he was mighty in faith and convinced** that God had all the power needed to fulfill his promises, Abraham glorified God!

[TVB] Romans 4:19-21 **His faith did not fail**, although he was well aware that his impotent body, after nearly 100 years, was as good as dead and that Sarah's womb, too, was dead. [20]In spite of all this, **his faith in God's promise did not falter. In fact, his faith grew** as he gave glory to God [21]**because he was supremely confident** that God could deliver on His promise.

[TWTY-RCT-NT-V1] Romans 4:19-21 **Also, having not become weak or poor, powerless or lacking in this trust and reliance, obedience and confidence, certainty and guarantee, assurance and dependence in the Trustworthy One**, he perceived and observed, understood and considered attentively, fixed his eyes and mind upon, noticed and envisaged, thought about and contemplated, studied, examined and reflected upon his own flesh and mortal body, as it was already starting to die and become lifeless, deceased and inanimate (as he presently existed at that time at about a hundred years old), and he also thought about the deadness and barrenness of Sarah's womb. [20]**But nevertheless, never did he separate or sunder, distinct or doubt in, hesitate or waver, debate or take issue with, dispute or evaluate his trust and reliance, obedience and confidence, certainty and guarantee, assurance and dependence concerning the promise and gracious pledge, offer and vow of God, but nevertheless, notwithstanding and on the contrary, he was empowered and strengthened, enabled and invigorated in this trust and reliance, obedience and confidence, certainty and guarantee, assurance and dependence**, therefore actively giving and granting, supplying and furnishing, bestowing and delivering, committing and permitting, extending and presenting glory and splendour, magnificence and excellence, pre-eminence and dignity, brightness, favour and majesty to God. [21]Also, having become fully convinced and assured, certain and completely satisfied that concerning this, **whatever He, God, has made and declared, professed and announced with a promise and gracious pledge, offer and vow, He is and exists as powerful and mighty, able and capable, forceful and influenceable, authorised and significant enough to do and perform, accomplish and execute, practise and bring about, undertake, keep and carry out, construct and establish it as well**.

[Wand-NT] Romans 4:19-21 **His faith must have been truly extraordinary**, for he was a hundred years old and he knew that he and his wife were both impotent. [20]**But he did not in the least degree doubt the promise God had made.** Through this trustfulness **he regained his virility**. He acknowledged the supreme power of God [21]and **was convinced that He was strong enough to do what He had promised**.

Romans 8:2 For the law of the Spirit of life[zoé] in Christ Jesus hath made me free from the law of sin and death.

[ACV] <u>Romans 8:2</u> For the law of the Spirit of life in Christ Jesus freed me from the law of sin and of death.

[AUV-NT 2003] <u>Romans 8:2</u> For the Holy Spirit's law which provides [never ending] life for those in [fellowship with] Christ Jesus has freed me from the law that requires [spiritual] death for sinning.

[Barclay-NT] <u>Romans 8:2</u> For, when through union with Christ Jesus I came under the law of the life-giving Spirit, I was emancipated from the law of the death-bringing sin.

[Belsham-NT] <u>Romans 8:2</u> For the law of the spirit of life by Christ Jesus, has set me at liberty from the law of sin and death.

[CWB] <u>Romans 8:2</u> For the Holy Spirit has given me a new life in Christ and has freed me from the controlling power of my sinful nature which always stands ready to put me back on the road to death.

[Erasmus-NT] <u>Romans 8:2</u> We have ceased to live by the will of carnal desires and passions now that the law of Christ—which is spiritual and the bearer of life, more efficacious, and conquering—has liberated us from the law of sin and from death, the companion of sin.

[ERV] <u>Romans 8:2</u> That is because in Christ Jesus the law of the Spirit that brings life made you free. It made you free from the law that brings sin and death.

[Hall] <u>Romans 8:2</u> For the efficacy and power of that Good Spirit, which gives life to all faithful ones, applying unto my soul the blood and all-sufficient merits of Christ my Saviour, have set me free from the tyranny of sin and of death, so as neither of them shall be able to prevail against me.

[Haweis-NT] <u>Romans 8:2</u> For the law of the Spirit of life in Christ Jesus hath liberated me from the law of sin and of death.

[Jordan-NT] <u>Romans 8:2</u> For the Spirit's law of new life in Christ Jesus released you from the claims of the law of sin and destruction.

[Knox] <u>Romans 8:2</u> The spiritual principle of life has set me free, in Christ Jesus, from the principle of sin and of death.

[Moffatt-NT 1917] <u>Romans 8:2</u> the law of the Spirit brings the life which is in Christ Jesus, and that law has set me free from the law of sin and death.

[MSG] <u>Romans 8:2</u> A new power is in operation. The Spirit of life in Christ, like a strong wind, has magnificently cleared the air, freeing you from a fated lifetime of brutal tyranny at the hands of sin and death.

[MSTC] <u>Romans 8:2</u> For the law of the spirit, that bringeth life through Jesus Christ, hath delivered me from the law of sin, and death:

[NIRV] <u>Romans 8:2</u> Because of what Christ Jesus has done, you are free. You are now controlled by the law of the Holy Spirit who gives you life. The law of the Spirit frees you from the law of sin that brings death.

[NLT] <u>Romans 8:2</u> And because you belong to him, the power of the life-giving Spirit has freed you from the power of sin that leads to death.

[NLV] <u>Romans 8:2</u> The power of the Holy Spirit has made me free from the power of sin and death. This power is mine because I belong to Christ Jesus.

[NOG] <u>Romans 8:2</u> The standards of the Spirit, who gives life through Christ Yeshua, have set you free from the standards of sin and death.

[Phillips] <u>Romans 8:2</u> For the new spiritual principle of life 'in' Christ Jesus lifts me out of the old vicious circle of sin and death.

[Rutherford-NT] Romans 8:2 The law of that Spirit that endows thee with life in Christ Jesus has emancipated thee from the law of sin and of death.

[SENT] Romans 8:2 Because the Spirit of Life's own law has set you free in Christ Jesus from the law of sin and death.

[TGNT] Romans 8:2 because the Spirit's law of life from Anointed Jesus freed you from the law of Failure and Death.

[TLB] Romans 8:2 For the power of the life-giving Spirit—and this power is mine through Christ Jesus—has freed me from the vicious circle of sin and death.

[Walker-NT] Romans 8:2 For the law and power of the Spirit of life, in and through Christ Jesus, hath made me free from the law and the dominion of sin and death.

[Wilson-NT] Romans 8:2 for the Law of the Spirit of Life by the Anointed Jesus, liberated me from the Law of Sin and of Death.

[Wuest-NT] Romans 8:2 for the law of the Spirit, that of the life in Christ Jesus, freed you once for all from the law of the sinful nature and of death.

Romans 8:11 But if the Spirit of him that raised up Jesus from the dead dwell in you, he that raised up Christ from the dead **shall also quicken your mortal bodies by his Spirit that dwelleth in you**.

[AMPC] Romans 8:11 And if the Spirit of Him Who raised up Jesus from the dead dwells in you, [then] He Who raised up Christ Jesus from the dead **will also restore to life your mortal (short-lived, perishable) bodies through His Spirit Who dwells in you**.

[Authentic-NT] Romans 8:11 And if the Spirit that raised up Jesus from the dead resides in you, then he that raised Christ Jesus from the dead **will also give life to your mortal bodies by very reason of his Spirit indwelling in you**.

[Ballentine-NT] Romans 8:11 Now if the spirit of him who raised up Jesus from the dead is living in you, he who raised up Christ Jesus from the dead **will endow your mortal bodies with life by means of his Spirit which is living in you**.

[Berkeley] Romans 8:11 If then the Spirit of Him who raised Jesus from the dead, dwells in you, then the Resurrector of Christ Jesus from the dead **will through the Spirit that dwells in you make also your mortal bodies live**.

[BLE] Romans 8:11 And if the Spirit of him who raised Jesus from the dead resides in you, he who raised Christ Jesus from the dead **will bring to life your mortal bodies too through his Spirit your inmate**.

[BV-KJV-NT] Romans 8:11 If the Spirit of the One who got Jesus up from the dead has a house in you, the One who got the Anointed King up from the dead **will also give your dying bodies life through His Spirit that is housed in you**.

[ERV] Romans 8:11 God raised Jesus from death. And if God's Spirit lives in you, he will also give life to your bodies that die. Yes, God is the one who raised Christ from death, and **he will raise you to life through his Spirit living in you**.

[GNC-NT] Romans 8:11 Moreover, if the Spirit of him who raised Jesus from the dead dwells within you, then he who raised Christ Jesus from the dead **will give life to your perishable bodies, doing so on behalf of the Spirit, whom you have dwelling within you**.

[Madsen-NT] <u>Romans 8:11</u> If the Spirit of HIM who awakened Jesus from the dead lives in you, then HE who raised Christ Jesus from the dead **will create life for your death-riddled bodies also. He does that, because HIS Spirit dwells in you**.

[Montgomery-NT] <u>Romans 8:11</u> But if the Spirit of Him who raised up Jesus from dead is dwelling in you, He who raised up Jesus from the dead is dwelling in you, He who raised up Christ Jesus from the dead **will also make your dying bodily self live by his indwelling Spirit in your lives**.

[MSG] <u>Romans 8:11</u> It stands to reason, doesn't it, that if the alive-and-present God who raised Jesus from the dead moves into your life, he'll do the same thing in you that he did in Jesus, bringing you alive to himself? When God lives and breathes in you (and he does, as surely as he did in Jesus), you are delivered from that dead life. **With his Spirit living in you, your body will be as alive as Christ's**!

[Phillips] <u>Romans 8:11</u> Once the Spirit of him who raised Christ Jesus from the dead lives within you he will, by that same Spirit, **bring to your whole being, yes even your mortal bodies, new strength and vitality. For he now lives in you**.

[Rotherham] <u>Romans 8:11</u> If, moreover, the Spirit of him that raised Jesus from among the dead dwelleth in you, he that raised from among the dead Christ Jesus, **shall make alive [even] your death-doomed bodies, through means of his indwelling Spirit within you**.

[Spencer-NT] <u>Romans 8:11</u> But if the Spirit of Him who raised Jesus from the dead resides in you, He who raised Christ Jesus from the dead **will impart life even to your mortal bodies by means of His Spirit dwelling in you**.

[TGNT] <u>Romans 8:11</u> Now if the Spirit that raised Jesus from the dead has taken up residence in you, this same One **will also raise up your mortal bodies by means of his Spirit residing in you**.

[TPT] <u>Romans 8:11</u> Yes, God raised Jesus to life! And since God's Spirit of Resurrection lives in you, **he will also raise your dying body to life by the same Spirit that breathes life into you**!

[TTNT] <u>Romans 8:11</u> This Spirit who lives in you is the same Spirit who raised Jesus from the dead. If He could do that, then **He is certainly able to give God's life to your natural bodies, because His Spirit lives in you**.

[Way-NT] <u>Romans 8:11</u> He who raised the Messiah Jesus from the dead **will thrill with a new life your very bodies—those mortal bodies of your—by the agency of His own Spirit, which now has its home in you**.

[Wuest-NT] <u>Romans 8:11</u> And assuming that the Spirit of the One who raised up Jesus out from among the dead is in residence in you, He who raised from among the dead Christ Jesus, **will also make alive your mortal bodies through the agency of the Spirit who is resident in you**.

<u>Romans 10:17</u> So then faith cometh by hearing, and hearing by the word of God.

[ABP] <u>Romans 10:17</u> So the belief is from report, and the report through the word of God.

[Ballentine-NT] <u>Romans 10:17</u> So faith comes from hearing, and hearing by means of the message of Christ.

[Barclay-NT] <u>Romans 10:17</u> So then, faith must be the consequence of hearing the message, and the message comes through the word which tells of Christ and which was sent by him.

[Barnstone-NT] <u>Romans 10:17</u> Then faith comes from what is heard, and what they hear is through the word.

[BV-KJV-NT] <u>Romans 10:17</u> Clearly trust is from what is heard, and what is heard is through a statement of God.

[Conybeare-NT] <u>Romans 10:17</u> So, then, faith comes by teaching; and our teaching comes by the Word of God.

[Darby] <u>Romans 10:17</u> So faith then [is] by a report, but the report by God's word.

[Heberden-NT] <u>Romans 10:17</u> Truly faith is derived from hearing; and the hearing, which is profitable to salvation, is through the preaching of the word of God.

[Moffatt] <u>Romans 10:17</u> (You see, faith must come from what is heard, and what is heard comes from word of Christ.)

[NEB] <u>Romans 10:17</u> We conclude that faith is awakened by the message, and the message that awakens it comes through the word of Christ.

[NET] <u>Romans 10:17</u> Consequently faith comes from what is heard, and what is heard comes through the preached word of Christ.

[NMB-NT] <u>Romans 10:17</u> So then, faith comes by hearing, and hearing comes by the word of God.

[NWT] <u>Romans 10:17</u> So faith follows the thing heard. In turn, what is heard is through the word about Christ.

[Spencer-NT] <u>Romans 10:17</u> So then, faith comes by hearing, but hearing by the mandate of Christ.

[T4T] <u>Romans 10:17</u> So then, I tell you that people are believing in Christ as a result of hearing the message about him, and people are hearing the message as a result of people preaching about Christ!

[TTNT] <u>Romans 10:17</u> Faith in the truth can only come when you have heard the truth, and that truth is contained in the words of Christ.

[Wauck-NT] <u>Romans 10:17</u> So faith comes from what's heard, and what's heard comes through Christ's word.

FIRST CORINTHIANS

<u>1 Corinthians 3:16</u> Know ye not that ye are the temple of God, and that the Spirit of God dwelleth in you?

[AMPC] <u>1 Corinthians 3:16</u> Do you not discern and understand that you [the whole church at Corinth] are God's temple (His sanctuary), and that God's Spirit has His permanent dwelling in you [to be at home in you, collectively as a church and also individually]?

[BV-KJV-NT] <u>1 Corinthians 3:16</u> Don't you realize that you are God's temple, and God's Spirit has a house in you?

[BWE-NT] <u>1 Corinthians 3:16</u> You know that you are God's house. The spirit of God lives in you.

[CPDV] <u>1 Corinthians 3:16</u> Do you not know that you are the Temple of God, and that the Spirit of God lives within you?

[NLV] <u>1 Corinthians 3:16</u> Do you not know that you are a house of God and that the Holy Spirit lives in you?

[Original-NT] <u>1 Corinthians 3:16</u> Do you not realize that you are God's temple, and that the Divine Spirit resides in you?

[Shuttleworth-NT] <u>1 Corinthians 3:16</u> I have said that you are God's building. So you are; you are God's temple, and the inhabitant within you is God's Holy Spirit.

[TGNT] <u>1 Corinthians 3:16</u> Do you not know that you are the temple of God, and that the Spirit of God has taken up residence in you?

[TTNT] <u>1 Corinthians 3:16</u> Surely you understand that you are God's temple, His dwelling place, because His Spirit lives in you?

[Weymouth-NT] <u>1 Corinthians 3:16</u> Do you not know that you are God's Sanctuary, and that the Spirit of God has His home within you?

[Williams-NT] <u>1 Corinthians 3:16</u> Are you not conscious that you are God's temple, and that the Spirit of God has His permanent home in you?

[Wuest-NT] <u>1 Corinthians 3:16</u> Do you not all know that all of you are God's inner sanctuary and that the Spirit of God is making His home in you?

<u>1 Corinthians 6:19-20</u> What? know ye not that your body is the temple of the Holy Ghost which is in you, which ye have of God, and ye are not your own? **[20]For ye are bought with a price: therefore glorify God in your body, and in your spirit, which are God's.**

If God has purchased us, then He should be responsible for repairing any damage to His property—healing is His (the owner's) responsibility.

[AMP] <u>1 Corinthians 6:19-20</u> Do you not know that your body is a temple of the Holy Spirit who is within you, whom you have [received as a gift] from God, and that you are not your own [property]? **[20]You were bought with a price [you were actually purchased with the precious blood of Jesus and made His own]. So then, honor and glorify God with your body.**

[AMPC] <u>1 Corinthians 6:19-20</u> Do you not know that your body is the temple (the very sanctuary) of the Holy Spirit Who lives within you, Whom you have received [as a Gift] from God? You are not your own, **[20]You were bought with a price [purchased with a preciousness and paid for, made His own]. So then, honor God and bring glory to Him in your body.**

[AUV-NT 2003] <u>1 Corinthians 6:19-20</u> Or, do you not know that your [physical] body is a temple for the Holy Spirit, who lives in you and who was given to you by God? You do not belong to yourselves, **[20]for you were bought [by God] for a price. So, honor God with your [physical] body.**

[Barclay-NT] <u>1 Corinthians 6:19-20</u> Are you not aware that your body is the temple of the Holy Spirit, who dwells within us, and whom we have received from God, and that you therefore do not belong to yourselves? **[20]He bought you for himself—and it did not cost him nothing. Therefore honour God with your body.**

[BWE-NT] <u>1 Corinthians 6:19-20</u> Do you not know that your body is the house of the Holy Spirit who lives in you? God gave the Holy Spirit to you. Remember, you do not belong to yourself. **[20]But you were bought and paid for. So then, bring glory to God with your bodies.**

[CEV] <u>1 Corinthians 6:19-20</u> You surely know that your body is a temple where the Holy Spirit lives. The Spirit is in you and is a gift from God. You are no longer your own. **[20]God paid a great price for you. So use your body to honor God.**

[Cornish-NT] <u>1 Corinthians 6:19-20</u> Your bodies are spiritual structures, the spirit that dwells in you is of God, and your bodies are correspondingly spiritual, as temples, rather than animal organisms; **[20]they owe allegiance not to the physical self, but to Him who redeemed them at a price. God Himself is to be glorified in your bodies.**

[EEBT] <u>1 Corinthians 6:19-20</u> Your body is the home of God's Spirit, who is completely good and separate from everything bad. You should know that. God gave his Spirit to you and he lives in you. You do not belong to yourselves any longer. But you belong to God, **[20]because God bought you. He paid the price for you. So, show how great and how good God is. Use your body to show that.**

[ICB] 1 Corinthians 6:19-20 You should know that your body is a temple for the Holy Spirit. The Holy Spirit is in you. You have received the Holy Spirit from God. You do not own yourselves. **[20]You were bought by God for a price. So honor God with your bodies.**

[Knox] 1 Corinthians 6:19-20 Surely you know that your bodies are the shrines of the Holy Spirit, who dwells in you. And he is God's gift to you, so that you are no longer your own masters. **[20]A great price was paid to ransom you; glorify God by making your bodies the shrines of his presence.**

[KNT] 1 Corinthians 6:19-20 Or don't you know that your body is a temple of the holy spirit within you, the spirit God gave you, so that you don't belong to yourselves? **[20]You were quite an expensive purchase! So glorify God in your body.**

[Madsen-NT] 1 Corinthians 6:19-20 Do you not know that your body is a temple of the indwelling Holy Spirit in you? You have received it from God: you do not belong to yourselves. **[20]Your freedom was bought for you for a high price. So now let your body become a revelation of God.**

[MSG] 1 Corinthians 6:19-20 Or didn't you realize that your body is a sacred place, the place of the Holy Spirit? Don't you see that you can't live however you please, squandering what God paid such a high price for? The physical part of you is not some piece of property belonging to the spiritual part of you. **[20]God owns the whole works. So let people see God in and through your body.**

[Nary-NT] 1 Corinthians 6:19-20 Or do ye not know, that your members are the temple of the Holy Ghost, which is in you, whom ye have from God, and ye are not your own? **[20]For ye are bought at a dear rate. Glorify and carry God in your body.**

[NIRV] 1 Corinthians 6:19-20 Don't you know that your bodies are temples of the Holy Spirit? The Spirit is in you, and you have received the Spirit from God. You do not belong to yourselves. **[20]Christ has paid the price for you. So use your bodies in a way that honors God.**

[Norlie-NT] 1 Corinthians 6:19-20 And don't you know that your body is a temple of the Holy Spirit? He lives within you, a gift from God the Father. So you are not your own. **[20]You have been brought, and at what a price! Honor God, therefore, with your body and with your spirit, both of which belong to God!**

[Original-NT] 1 Corinthians 6:19-20 Or are you ignorant that your body is the temple of the holy Spirit which is in you, which you have received from God, and that you are not your own, **[20]having been acquired at a high price? Then praise God with your body.**

[Phillips] 1 Corinthians 6:19-20 Have you forgotten that your body is the temple of the Holy Spirit, who lives in you and is God's gift to you, and that you are not the owner of your own body? **[20]You have been bought, and at a price! Therefore bring glory to God in your body.**

[REM-NT] 1 Corinthians 6:19-20 Don't you comprehend what is happening? Your brain and body are designed as a complete unit to be a sacred temple for the Holy Spirit who comes from God and lives within you—intimately, in a bond of sacred love. You are not a self-originating or self-sustaining being: you belong in intimate connection with God! **[20]It cost God an infinite price to restore this connection with you, so let God and his love be revealed in the way you treat your body.**

[Shuttleworth-NT] 1 Corinthians 6:19-20 Know you not also that your bodies are the temple of that Holy Spirit which dwells within you, and which God himself gave to you: and that they are not your own property, but God's, **[20]purchased for him by the blood of Christ? Glorify then God both in your bodies, and in your spirits, for both are alike God's property.**

[TLB] <u>1 Corinthians 6:19-20</u> Haven't you yet learned that your body is the home of the Holy Spirit God gave you, and that he lives within you? Your own body does not belong to you. **²⁰For God has bought you with a great price. So use every part of your body to give glory back to God because he owns it.**

[TPT] <u>1 Corinthians 6:19-20</u> Have you forgotten that your body is now the sacred temple of the Spirit of Holiness, who lives in you? You don't belong to yourself any longer, for the gift of God, the Holy Spirit, lives inside your sanctuary. **²⁰You were God's expensive purchase, paid for with tears of blood, so by all means, then, use your body to bring glory to God!**

[TTNT] <u>1 Corinthians 6:19-20</u> Surely you realise that God has made your body a temple of the Holy Spirit, who now lives in you? This is God's doing; and so you do not belong to yourself, to do as you please. **²⁰God has purchased you for Himself; He has paid the price for you with His Son's blood. So honour Him in the way you use your body!**

[Weymouth-NT] <u>1 Corinthians 6:19-20</u> Or do you not know that your bodies are a sanctuary of the Holy Spirit who is within you—the Spirit whom you have from God? **²⁰And you are not your own, for you have been redeemed at infinite cost. Therefore glorify God in your bodies.**

<u>1 Corinthians 11:29-31</u> For he that eateth and drinketh unworthily, eateth and drinketh damnation to himself, not discerning the Lord's body. **³⁰For this cause many are weak and sickly among you, and many sleep. ³¹For if we would judge ourselves, we should not be judged.**

[Authentic-NT] <u>1 Corinthians 11:29-31</u> For he who eats and drinks is eating and drinking a judgment on himself, not discerning the body. **³⁰That is why many of you are infirm and ailing, and a number have gone to their rest. ³¹If we have passed judgment on ourselves we shall not be judged.**

[AUV-NT 2003] <u>1 Corinthians 11:29-31</u> For a person who eats and drinks without determining the significance of the body [of Jesus], eats and drinks judgment upon himself. **³⁰Because of this, many people among you are weak and ill, and a number have fallen asleep. ³¹But if we [had] examined ourselves [properly], we would not be judged.**

[Cornish-NT] <u>1 Corinthians 11:29-31</u> But if you discerned that infinite eternal body, if you understood the meaning of Christ's death in the flesh, and what is signified by the shedding of his blood, and the giving up of his mortal life and material body— **³⁰then, my brethren, there would not be so much sickness and disease and death in your midst as there still is. ³¹but by first judging yourselves, you would then escape the general ruin.**

[Haweis-NT] <u>1 Corinthians 11:29-31</u> For he that eateth and drinketh unworthily, eateth and drinketh condemnation to himself, not distinguishing the Lord's body. **³⁰For this cause many are diseased and infirm among you, and some asleep [in death]. ³¹For if we thoroughly judged ourselves, we should not be judged of the Lord.**

[MSG] <u>1 Corinthians 11:29-31</u> If you give no thought (or worse, don't care) about the broken body of the Master when you eat and drink, you're running the risk of serious consequences. **³⁰That's why so many of you even now are listless and sick, and others have gone to an early grave. ³¹If we get this straight now, we won't have to be straightened out later on.**

[Norlie-NT] <u>1 Corinthians 11:29-31</u> For if one eats and drinks unworthily he eats and drinks judgment on himself, not recognizing the Lord's body. **³⁰Because of this indifference, many of you are feeble and sickly, and some have died. ³¹But, if we examined ourselves carefully, we should escape this misfortune.**

[TTNT] <u>1 Corinthians 11:29-31</u> For anyone who eats and drinks without recognising that he shares in the Lord's body only brings judgment on himself. **³⁰No wonder many among you are weak and sick, and some have even died, if that is how you behave. ³¹But if we judge ourselves and first repent of our sins, then we would not place ourselves under such judgment.**

[Wand-NT] <u>1 Corinthians 11:29-31</u> He who partakes of this food without recognizing it as the Body eats and drinks to his own condemnation. **³⁰For this reason many among you are weak and sickly and some are just spiritual corpses. ³¹But if we judge ourselves we shall not be judged.**

[Williams-NT] <u>1 Corinthians 11:29-31</u> For whoever eats and drinks without recognizing His body, eats and drinks a judgment on himself. **³⁰This is why many of you are sick and feeble, and a considerable number are falling asleep. ³¹But if we properly saw ourselves, we would not bring down upon us this judgment.**

<u>1 Corinthians 12:9</u> To another faith by the same Spirit; to another **the gifts of healing** by the same Spirit;

[AMPC] <u>1 Corinthians 12:9</u> To another [wonder-working] faith by the same [Holy] Spirit, to another the **extraordinary powers of healing** by the one Spirit;

[AS] <u>1 Corinthians 12:9</u> furthermore, to another confidence, by-within the same Breath, but to another the **Grace of healing**, by the same Breath,

[ASV] <u>1 Corinthians 12:9</u> to another faith, in the same Spirit; and to another **gifts of healings**, in the one Spirit;

[AUV-NT 2003] <u>1 Corinthians 12:9</u> Still another person is given [supernatural] faith by the same Holy Spirit; yet another person is given gifts **[providing the ability] to perform [supernatural] healings** by that one Holy Spirit.

[BBE] <u>1 Corinthians 12:9</u> To another faith in the same Spirit; and to another the **power of taking away disease**, by the one Spirit;

[Bowes-NT] <u>1 Corinthians 12:9</u> To another faith in the same Spirit; but to another **gracious gifts of healings** in the one Spirit;

[Erasmus-NT] <u>1 Corinthians 12:9</u> to another by the inspiration of the same Spirit has come the strength of faith that moves even mountains from their place, according to the promise of the Lord; to another through the same Spirit has come **the power to heal disease.**

[Goodspeed-NT] <u>1 Corinthians 12:9</u> another, from his union with the same Spirit receives faith, another, by one and the same Spirit, **the ability to cure the sick,**

[Green-NT] <u>1 Corinthians 12:9</u> and to another faith, in the same Spirit; to another **endowments of healings**, in the one Spirit;

[Guyse-NT] <u>1 Corinthians 12:9</u> To another is given, by the same Holy Spirit, a full assent to the truth of the gospel, and boldness in preaching it, together with a firm trust in Christ for all divine assistance, that shall be needful in every dangerous and difficult service, to which he may be called: **To another is communicated the gift of healing all manner of bodily diseases, in an instant, without the use of ordinary means**, for confirmation of the gospel, by the same good Spirit:

[Knox] <u>1 Corinthians 12:9</u> one, through the same Spirit, is given faith; another, through the same Spirit, **powers of healing**;

[MLV] <u>1 Corinthians 12:9</u> and miraculous faith to different one in the same Spirit; and **gifts of healing** to another in the same Spirit;

[NLV] <u>1 Corinthians 12:9</u> One person receives the gift of faith. Another person receives **the gifts of healing**. These gifts are given by the same Holy Spirit.

[Shuttleworth-NT] <u>1 Corinthians 12:9</u> To another again is given a submiss and firm confidence in the doctrines of revelation; to another, **the gift of healing diseases**; but still again it is the same Spirit which manifests itself under these distinct appearances:

[TCNT] <u>1 Corinthians 12:9</u> To another faith by the same Spirit; to another **power to cure diseases** by the one Spirit; to another supernatural powers;

<u>1 Corinthians 12:28</u> And God **hath set some in the church**, first apostles, secondarily prophets, thirdly teachers, after that **miracles, then gifts of healings**, helps, governments, diversities of tongues.

[Ainslie-NT] <u>1 Corinthians 12:28</u> **And God hath set some in the church**, first apostles, second prophets, third teachers, then **mighty powers, then gifts of healings**, helps, governments, diversities of tongues.

[Bowes-NT] <u>1 Corinthians 12:28</u> And these indeed God has placed in the assembly; first apostles, secondly prophets, thirdly teachers, after that **mighty works, then gracious gifts of healings**; helps, directors, varieties of tongues.

[BWE-NT] <u>1 Corinthians 12:28</u> God **has given each person their right place in the church**. First, there are the apostles. Second, there are prophets who speak words from God. Third, there are those who teach. **Then there are those who do big works. Then there are those who have the gifts to heal people**, those who help in the work of the church people, those who lead and guide others, and those who speak God's words in different kinds of tongues or languages.

[EXB] <u>1 Corinthians 12:28</u> **In the church God has ·given a place** first to [appointed/placed first] apostles, second to prophets, and third to teachers, **then those who do ·miracles [acts of powers], those who have gifts of healing**, those who can help others, those who are able to ·govern [lead], and those who can speak ·in different languages [or with ecstatic utterance; different kinds of tongues].

[KJ3] <u>1 Corinthians 12:28</u> And God placed some in the assembly, firstly, apostles; secondly, prophets; thirdly, teachers; then **works of power; then gifts of healing**, helps, governings, kinds of languages.

[Madsen-NT] <u>1 Corinthians 12:28</u> The divine Ground of the World has placed all in the congregation: the first as apostles, the second as prophets. Thirdly, as teachers; then follow the **bearers of particular powers, those who possess the gift of healing**, the shepherds of souls, those who guide and order, those skilled in speaking in tongues.

[Noyes] <u>1 Corinthians 12:28</u> **God appointed some in the church to be**, in the first place, apostles, in the second place, prophets, in the third place, teachers, then **miracles, then gifts of healing**, those of helping and of governing, divers kinds of tongues. Are all apostles?

[NWT] <u>1 Corinthians 12:28</u> And **God has assigned the respective ones in the congregation**: first, apostles; second, prophets; third, teachers; then **powerful works; then gifts of healings**; helpful services; abilities to direct; different tongues.

[OEB-NT] <u>1 Corinthians 12:28</u> In the church God has appointed, first, apostles, secondly preachers, thirdly teachers; then he has given **supernatural powers, then power to cure diseases**, aptness for helping others, capacity to govern, varieties of the gift of 'tongues.'

[Pickering-NT] <u>1 Corinthians 12:28</u> And those whom God has appointed in the Church are: first apostles, second prophets, third teachers; after that **miracles, then presents of healings**, helps, administrations, kinds of languages.

[SENT] <u>1 Corinthians 12:28</u> And God appoints people in the community: first apostles, second prophets, third teachers. Then **displays of power, gifts of healings**, acts of service, gifts of management, various inspired languages.

[T4T] <u>1 Corinthians 12:28</u> **God has placed** apostles in our congregations. Apostles are first in rank. Next in rank are those who speak messages which come directly from God. Next in rank are those who teach spiritual truth. Then there are **those who have the power to work miracles, those who have the ability to heal sick people**, those who have the ability to help others, those who have the ability to govern the affairs of the congregation, and those who have the ability to speak messages in languages that they have not learned.

[TLB] <u>1 Corinthians 12:28</u> **Here is a list of some of the parts he has placed in his Church**, which is his body: Apostles, Prophets—those who preach God's Word, Teachers, **Those who do miracles, Those who have the gift of healing**; Those who can help others, Those who can get others to work together, Those who speak in languages they have never learned.

SECOND CORINTHIANS

<u>2 Corinthians 1:10</u> Who delivered us from so great a death, and doth deliver: in whom we trust that he will yet deliver us;

[AMP] <u>2 Corinthians 1:10</u> He rescued us from so great a threat of death, and will continue to rescue us. On Him we have set our hope. And He will again rescue us [from danger and draw us near],

[AMPC] <u>2 Corinthians 1:10</u> [For it is He] Who rescued and saved us from such a perilous death, and He will still rescue and save us; in and on Him we have set our hope (our joyful and confident expectation) that He will again deliver us [from danger and destruction and draw us to Himself],

[Authentic-NT] <u>2 Corinthians 1:10</u> It was he who shielded me from imminent death, and shields me now, and whom I trust, with your co-operation in prayer on my behalf, to continue to shield me,

[CEB] <u>2 Corinthians 1:10</u> God rescued us from a terrible death, and he will rescue us. We have set our hope on him that he will rescue us again,

[CEV] <u>2 Corinthians 1:10</u> God saved us from the threat of death, and we are sure that he will do it again and again.

[CWB] <u>2 Corinthians 1:10</u> In the past He has saved us from being killed. This time He saved our bodies from giving way, and we have confidence that in the future He will continue to do for us what He thinks is best.

[GT] <u>2 Corinthians 1:10</u> God has rescued us from such life and death situations and He will rescue us in the future. We have placed all our hopes on Him. He will always rescue us

[ICB] <u>2 Corinthians 1:10</u> God saved us from these great dangers of death. And he will continue to save us. We have put our hope in him, and he will save us again.

[Johnson-NT] <u>2 Corinthians 1:10</u> Having reached our limits and beyond, we could only trust in God. And God freed us to live, he continues to free us, and we believe he will free us in the future.

[Mace-NT] <u>2 Corinthians 1:10</u> and he did deliver me from so terrible a death, and on him I have relied for further deliverance: especially,

[NIRV] <u>2 Corinthians 1:10</u> God has saved us from deadly dangers. And he will continue to do it. We have put our hope in him. He will continue to save us.

[NLV] <u>2 Corinthians 1:10</u> Yes, God kept us from what looked like sure death and He is keeping us. As we trust Him, He will keep us in the future.

[NOG] <u>2 Corinthians 1:10</u> He has rescued us from a terrible death, and he will rescue us in the future. We are confident that he will continue to rescue us,

[REM-NT] <u>2 Corinthians 1:10</u> And sure enough, he has delivered us from many deadly threats, and he will continue to deliver us. We have placed all our hope in him, and he will continue to provide for our needs and deliver us from danger.

[Rotherham] <u>2 Corinthians 1:10</u> Who, out of so great a death, rescued us, and will rescue, —unto whom we have turned our hope, [that], even yet, he will rescue:

[Shuttleworth-NT] <u>2 Corinthians 1:10</u> And who has rescued us from this grievous peril of our lives, and even now holds his guardian arm over us; as we are humbly assured he will still continue to do during the remainder of our course.

[Sindlinger-NT] <u>2 Corinthians 1:10</u> God spared our lives and will do so again.

[T4T] <u>2 Corinthians 1:10</u> And even though we were in terrible danger and were about to die, God rescued us. And he will continue to rescue us whenever we are in trouble. We confidently expect that he will continue to rescue us time after time.

[TTNT] <u>2 Corinthians 1:10</u> And that is what it was like, as if we had been delivered from death itself. Now we can be confident that He will always deliver us, no matter what we have to face in the future.

<u>2 Corinthians 1:20</u> For all the promises of God in him are yea, and in him Amen, unto the glory of God by us.

[Authentic-NT] <u>2 Corinthians 1:20</u> In him there came 'Yes', for every promise of God is fulfilled in him who is the 'Yes'. That is why, through him, we make the affirmation 'Amen' to God in praising him.

[Barclay-NT] <u>2 Corinthians 1:20</u> In him all God's promises find their yes. That is why when to the glory of God we say 'Amen' we say it through him— 'through Jesus Christ our Lord.'

[BBE] <u>2 Corinthians 1:20</u> For he is the Yes to all the undertakings of God: and by him all the words of God are made certain and put into effect, to the glory of God through us.

[Beck] <u>2 Corinthians 1:20</u> For all God's promises He is the Yes that makes them come true. And so He makes it possible for us to give glory to God by saying, "It is true."

[BOOKS-NT] <u>2 Corinthians 1:20</u> For no matter how many promises God has made, they are "Yes" in Christ. And so through him the "Amen" is spoken by us to the glory of God.

[BWE-NT] <u>2 Corinthians 1:20</u> To the many promises God has made Christ can say 'Yes'. He can make them all come true. So then, it is because of Christ that we can say, 'Yes, it is so!' when we praise God.

[CJB] <u>2 Corinthians 1:20</u> For however many promises God has made, they all find their "Yes" in connection with him; that is why it is through him that we say the "Amen" when we give glory to God.

[Conybeare-NT] <u>2 Corinthians 1:20</u> for all the promises of God have in Him the yea [which seals their truth]; wherefore also through Him the Amen [which acknowledges their fulfillment,] is uttered to the praise of God by our voice.

[EEBT] <u>2 Corinthians 1:20</u> Everything that God has promised becomes 'Yes' because of Christ. That is why, by Christ, we can thank God. By him, we can agree that all God's promises are true. And we can say how very great and good God is.

[Erasmus-NT] <u>2 Corinthians 1:20</u> For any promises that have been made are dependable through him, and they are unquestionable because of the very one to whom this glory is due. For the promises that we have set before you are not ours. Their author is God; we are only servants and messengers. It contributes to his glory if what we proclaim in his name is found true and efficacious.

[GNT] <u>2 Corinthians 1:20</u> for it is he who is the "Yes" to all of God's promises. This is why through Jesus Christ our "Amen" is said to the glory of God.

[Johnson-NT] <u>2 Corinthians 1:20</u> Each of us affirmed that Jesus is God's yes to life. Every promise God has made to us finds its fulfillment in Christ. He is God's consummate yes to existence and the key to God's ultimate fulfillment through us.

[KNT] <u>2 Corinthians 1:20</u> All God's promises, you see, find their Yes in him; and that's why we say the Yes, the Amen through him when we pray to God and give him glory.

[Mace-NT] <u>2 Corinthians 1:20</u> for all the promises of God do center in him, and are verified by him to the glory of God by our preaching.

[Macrae] <u>2 Corinthians 1:20</u> For, all the promises of God are in him yea, and amen (immutable truth), to the glory of God by us.

[MSG] <u>2 Corinthians 1:20</u> Whatever God has promised gets stamped with the Yes of Jesus. In him, this is what we preach and pray, the great Amen, God's Yes and our Yes together, gloriously evident.

[MW-NT] <u>2 Corinthians 1:20</u> For whatever the promises of God are, the "Yes" and the "Amen" are in him, to the glory of God through us.

[NEB] <u>2 Corinthians 1:20</u> He is the Yes pronounced upon God's promises, every one of them. That is why, when we give glory to God, it is through Christ Jesus that we say 'Amen'.

[NJB] <u>2 Corinthians 1:20</u> For in him is found the Yes to all God's promises and therefore it is 'through him' that we answer 'Amen' to give praise to God.

[NLT] <u>2 Corinthians 1:20</u> For all of God's promises have been fulfilled in Christ with a resounding "Yes!" And through Christ, our "Amen" (which means "Yes") ascends to God for his glory.

[OEB-NT] <u>2 Corinthians 1:20</u> For, many as were the promises of God, in Christ is the 'Yes' that fulfills them. Therefore, through Christ again, let the 'Amen' rise, through us, to the glory of God.

[PLAWL] <u>2 Corinthians 1:20</u> For all the promises of God in him are yea and in him Amen (i.e. true and certain through him), unto the glory of God (demonstrated in the confirmation of them) by us.

[Purver] <u>2 Corinthians 1:20</u> For all the Promises whatever of God are in him Yes, and in him So let it be, to the Glory of God by us.

[REM-NT] <u>2 Corinthians 1:20</u> All of God's promises are realized through unity with Christ, and through him we are healed and restored in his image to be the final piece of evidence that brings glory to our God of love.

[TLB] <u>2 Corinthians 1:20</u> He carries out and fulfills all of God's promises, no matter how many of them there are; and we have told everyone how faithful he is, giving glory to his name.

[TPT] <u>2 Corinthians 1:20</u> For all of God's promises find their "yes" of fulfillment in him. And as his "yes" and our "amen" ascend to God, we bring him glory!

[TTNT] <u>2 Corinthians 1:20</u> No matter how many promises God gives us, they are all affirmed in Christ with a mighty 'Yes.' We can say 'Amen,' 'It shall be so', to all that is said through Him, and such faithful affirmation gives glory to God.

[Way-NT] <u>2 Corinthians 1:20</u> The same is true of all the promises of God: they are affirmed by His 'I will,' ay, and they are sealed by His 'Amen'; and so God is glorified through our faith in His promises.

<u>2 Corinthians 4:10-11</u> Always bearing about in the body the dying of the Lord Jesus, **that the life**[zoé] **also of Jesus might be made manifest in our body**. [11]For we which live are alway delivered unto death for Jesus' sake, that **the life**[zoé] **also of Jesus might be made manifest in our mortal flesh**.

[AMPC] <u>2 Corinthians 4:10-11</u> Always carrying about in the body the liability and exposure to the same putting to death that the Lord Jesus suffered, **so that the [resurrection] life of Jesus also may be shown forth by and in our bodies**. [11]For we who live are constantly [experiencing] being handed over to death for Jesus' sake, **that the [resurrection] life of Jesus also may be evidenced through our flesh which is liable to death**.

[AUV-NT 2003] <u>2 Corinthians 4:10-11</u> We always carry around in our [physical] bodies the [threat of] dying, as Jesus did, **so that the life of Jesus may be demonstrated in our bodies also**. [11]For while we live, we are always exposed to death for Jesus' sake, so that **the life of Jesus may be demonstrated in our mortal bodies**.

[CEB] <u>2 Corinthians 4:10-11</u> We always carry Jesus' death around in our bodies **so that Jesus' life can also be seen in our bodies**. [11]We who are alive are always being handed over to death for Jesus' sake **so that Jesus' life can also be seen in our bodies that are dying**.

[DLNT] <u>2 Corinthians 4:10-11</u> at-all-times carrying-around in our body the dying of Jesus in order that **the life of Jesus may also be made-evident in our body**. [11]For we the ones living are always being handed-over to death for the sake of Jesus, **in order that the life of Jesus may also be made-evident in our mortal flesh**.

[Madsen-NT] <u>2 Corinthians 4:10-11</u> At all times we are clothed in our bodily existence with the death of Jesus, so **that the power of life of Jesus also may become shiningly revealed in our bodily nature**. [11]Although we live, yet we are constantly exposed to the powers of death through our share in the Being of Jesus, so **that the power of life of Jesus may be revealed in our physical body, although it is subject to death**.

[Montgomery-NT] <u>2 Corinthians 4:10-11</u> Wherever I go, I am always carrying about in my body the dying of Jesus, in order that **the life also of Jesus may be made manifest in this body of mine**. [11]For, alive though I am, I am always given over to death for the sake of Jesus, **that the life also of Jesus may shine forth in my dying flesh**.

[REM-NT] <u>2 Corinthians 4:10-11</u> In this defective body, which tempts to selfishness, we surrender to die to self—as Jesus did—**so that the perfect life of Jesus may be fully revealed in us**. [11]For we who are alive are only alive because we surrender to die to selfishness—for Jesus' cause—**so that his perfect life may be reproduced in our decaying bodies**.

[TLB] <u>2 Corinthians 4:10-11</u> These bodies of ours are constantly facing death just as Jesus did; so it is clear to all that it is only the living Christ within who keeps us safe. [11]Yes, we live under constant danger to our lives because we serve the Lord, but **this gives us constant opportunities to show forth the power of Jesus Christ within our dying bodies**.

[Worsley-NT] <u>2 Corinthians 4:10-11</u> cast down, but not destroyed; always bearing about in the body the dying of the Lord Jesus, that the life also of Jesus might be manifested in our body. [11]For we, who are yet living, are always exposed to death for the sake of Jesus, **that the life also of Jesus may be manifested in our mortal flesh**.

[Wuest-NT] <u>2 Corinthians 4:10-11</u> always bearing about in our body the dying of the Lord Jesus in order **that the life of Jesus might be clearly and openly shown in our body,** [11]for, as for us, we who are living are perpetually being delivered over to death for Jesus' sake in order **that the life of Jesus might be clearly and openly shown in our mortal body.**

GALATIANS

<u>Galatians 3:11</u> But that no man is justified by the law in the sight of God, it is evident: for, **The just shall live by faith.**

[AMP] <u>Galatians 3:11</u> Now it is clear that no one is justified [that is, declared free of the guilt of sin and its penalty, and placed in right standing] before God by the Law, for **"The righteous (the just, the upright) shall live by faith."**

[AUV-NT 2003] <u>Galatians 3:11</u> Now it is evident that no person can be made right with God by [obeying all the requirements of] the law of Moses for, **"The righteous person will obtain life by [his] faith [in God]."**

[Barnstone-NT] <u>Galatians 3:11</u> No one is justified with God, who lives by law, **since clearly the just live by faith.**

[BOOKS-NT] <u>Galatians 3:11</u> Clearly no one who relies on the law is justified before God, because **"the righteous will live by faith."**

[CEB] <u>Galatians 3:11</u> But since no one is made righteous by the Law as far as God is concerned, it is clear that **the righteous one will live on the basis of faith.**

[Green-NT] <u>Galatians 3:11</u> But that by law no one is justified with God, is clear, because, **The just one will live from faith:**

[Hebert-NT] <u>Galatians 3:11</u> But that by law none is justified with God is evident. Because, **"The just out of faith shall live."**

[Macknight-NTc] <u>Galatians 3:11</u> Besides, that by works of law no one can be justified before God, is manifest from Habakkuk, who hath said nothing of men's being just by works, but hath declared, that **the just by faith shall live eternally.**

[Madsen-NT] <u>Galatians 3:11</u> It is quite clear that no human being can be perfect before God in the sense of the Law. **The life of one who has a share in the higher life flows out of faith.**

[Medway-NT] <u>Galatians 3:11</u> The Bible also says that no one becomes righteous by keeping the laws when it says, **"People can only become righteous and live righteously by believing God."**

[MOTB] <u>Galatians 3:11</u> for an absolute perfect performance of all that the law requires is necessary in order to justification by the law, and that man can never render. The law-principle says: Do all that the law requires and thou shalt live; **the faith-principle says: Trust in God and thou shalt live.**

[OEB-NT] <u>Galatians 3:11</u> Again, it is evident that no one is pronounced righteous before God through law, for we read—**'Through faith the righteous will find life.'**

[REM-NT] <u>Galatians 3:11</u> Clearly, no one is healed and set right with God by working to follow a set of rules, because **"Those set right with God live by trust."**

[SG] <u>Galatians 3:11</u> That no one is accepted as upright by God for obeying the Law is evident because **the upright will have life because of his faith.**

[Stevens-NT] <u>Galatians 3:11</u> So far from having hope of being saved by the law, man had fallen under its curse and was helpless, but Christ, by taking the curse upon himself, freed us from it, that **we might be justified and saved simply by trusting in him and his work for us**.

[TLB] <u>Galatians 3:11</u> Consequently, it is clear that no one can ever win God's favor by trying to keep the Jewish laws because God has said that the only way we can be right in his sight is by faith. As the prophet Habakkuk says it, "**The man who finds life will find it through trusting God**."

[TTNT] <u>Galatians 3:11</u> So clearly no one can be made acceptable before God by the religious law for "**those who are right before God shall live by faith**."

[TWTY-RCT-NT-V1] <u>Galatians 3:11</u> Furthermore, it is clearly known and seen, visible and manifest, evident and plain, conspicuous and noticeable that concerning this, no one, nobody and nothing is shown or made, rendered or exhibited, pronounced or declared to be righteous or just, upright or virtuous, faultless or guiltless, fair, approved or accepted in, by or through a law or commandment, custom or rule, tradition or order, statue or ordinance, law-code or moral tradition before and in the immediate proximity and presence of God, for concerning this, "**The righteous and just, upright and virtuous, faultless and guiltless, fair, approved and accepted, those observing the commandments of the Supreme One and those in a right relationship with Him shall live and breathe, be active and powerful, strong and fresh, efficient and endless, vigorous and blessed from out of trust and reliance, obedience and confidence, certainty and guarantee, assurance and dependence in the Supreme One**."

[Wade] <u>Galatians 3:11</u> And that no one stands right with God through obedience to Law is evident from this, that "**the righteous in consequence of having faith shall live**";

[Wand-NT] <u>Galatians 3:11</u> However, it is clear that no one can win acquittal before God by keeping the Law, for it says, '**The just man shall live by his faith**.'

<u>Galatians 3:13-14</u> **Christ hath redeemed us from the curse of the law, being made a curse for us**: for it is written, Cursed is every one that hangeth on a tree: [14]**That the blessing of Abraham might come on the Gentiles through Jesus Christ**; that we might receive the promise of the Spirit through faith.

According to Deut 28, sickness and disease are part of the curse. Jesus paid the price so we don't have to be subject to sickness and disease in this life.

[Berkeley] <u>Galatians 3:13-14</u> **Christ has bought us free from the curse of the Law inasmuch as He became a curse for us**, for it is written, "Cursed is every one who is hanging on a beam," [14]**in order that in Christ Jesus the blessing of Abraham might be realized for the nations** and that we through faith might receive the promise of the Spirit.

[CJB] <u>Galatians 3:13-14</u> **The Messiah redeemed us from the curse pronounced in the Torah by becoming cursed on our behalf**; for the Tanakh says, "Everyone who hangs from a stake comes under a curse. [14]**Yeshua the Messiah did this so that in union with him the Gentiles might receive the blessing announced to Avraham**, so that through trusting and being faithful, we might receive what was promised, namely, the Spirit.

[CLV] <u>Galatians 3:13-14</u> **Christ reclaims us from the curse of the law, becoming a curse for our sakes**, for it is written, Accursed is everyone hanging on a pole, [14]**that the blessing of Abraham may be coming to the nations in Christ Jesus**, that we may be obtaining the promise of the spirit through faith.

[CWB] <u>Galatians 3:13-14</u> Since we are incapable of doing this, **Christ fulfilled the law for us and took upon Himself our disobedience, which the law condemns. He took our curse upon Himself**.

As the Scriptures say, "The Man who is nailed to a tree is cursed by everyone because the curse of sin is upon Him." **[14]Christ died for us so the spiritual blessings that God promised to Abraham might come to Jews and Gentiles alike**, including the promise of the Holy Spirit whom we also receive by faith.

[Doddridge-NT] <u>Galatians 3:13-14</u> But ever adored be the riches of divine grace, **Christ hath redeemed us who believe in his name from the terrible curse of the law, and bought us off from that servitude and misery to which it inexorably doomed us, by being himself made a curse for us, and enduring the penalty which our sins had deserved:** for such was the death which he bore in our stead; not only when considered as a capital punishment, which universally implies something of this, but as thus stigmatized by the express declaration of the law against everyone in such a particular circumstance; for it is written, "Cursed is everyone that hangeth on a tree." Now Christ, as you well know, was hung upon a tree; he expired on the cross, and his dead body hung for some time upon it. [14]And this, in his adorable condescension, he submitted to for us and our salvation; that the curse having been borne by him in our room, **the blessing of Abraham, in all its extent of spiritual benefits, and that adoption which was given in him, might come, not only on believing Jews, but on the Gentiles also, through Christ Jesus** the great anointed Saviour; and particularly that we, even the whole church of christian converts, might, through the exercise of a living and sincere faith in him, receive the promise of the Spirit as the seal of our adoption, both in the effusion of its miraculous gifts, so far as they may conduce to the edification of the church, and in the rich abundance of its saving graces.

[EEBT] <u>Galatians 3:13-14</u> As a result of the Jews' rules, God would have had to punish us. God would have had to make us separate from himself. But **Christ bought us, to make us free, because God punished him on our behalf**. It says in the Old Testament: 'When people hang someone on a tree to kill him, that person must be separate from God.' **[14]Christ did this so that the Gentiles could receive good things from God. They could receive, by Jesus Christ, what God had promised to Abraham**. So then, if we believe Christ, we can receive God's Spirit. We can receive the Spirit that God promised.

[Erasmus-NT] <u>Galatians 3:13-14</u> **Christ alone of all was not subject to the curse, for he was wholly innocent and owed nothing to the law. We were guilty and for this reason accursed. But he freed the guilty from the curse, changing our guilt into innocence and our curse into a blessing. He is very far from wanting you to be led into servitude to the law. How has he liberated you? Though innocent himself, he paid the penalty owed for our crimes, thus taking upon himself the curse which held us firmly in its grasp. He did this though otherwise free from the curse and a partner in the blessing. Did he not take our crimes upon himself when as a criminal among criminals he underwent the ignominious punishment of the cross to redeem us?** For we read in Deuteronomy: 'Cursed is anyone who hangs on a tree.' **[14]Why, however, did God want this to happen? Clearly in order that the curse brought by the law might be removed and that the blessing through faith formerly promised to Abraham might take its place.** And further, that the blessing might replace the curse not only among the Jews but also among the gentiles, not through the benefit of the law which Christ wanted abolished, but through the kindness of Jesus Christ. Thus, reconciled to God and freed from the burden of the burdensome law through his death, we will obtain through faith the evangelical blessing promised to the descendants of Abraham, descendants I say, not according to the flesh, but according to the Spirit. Let us have faith in a trustworthy God, for he will not deceive anyone. He will fulfil what he has promised.

[ERV] <u>Galatians 3:13-14</u> **The law says we are under a curse for not always obeying it. But Christ took away that curse. He changed places with us and put himself under that curse**. The Scriptures say, "Anyone who is hung on a tree is under a curse." **[14]Because of what Jesus Christ did, the blessing**

God promised to Abraham was given to all people. Christ died so that by believing in him we could have the Spirit that God promised.

[EXB] Galatians 3:13-14 Christ ·took away [redeemed us from; bought our freedom from] the curse ·the law put on us [of the law]. ·He changed places with us and put himself under that curse [...by becoming a curse for us]. [For; Because] It is written in the Scriptures, "Anyone ·whose body is displayed [who is hung] on a tree is cursed." [14]**Christ did this so that God's blessing promised to Abraham might come through Jesus Christ to the Gentiles**. ·Jesus died so that by our believing [...so that by faith] we could receive the Spirit that God promised.

[GT] Galatians 3:13-14 The law put us under condemnation, but Christ took that condemnation away. He changed places with us; he put himself under that condemnation. It is written, "When a person's body is hung on a tree, it shows that the person has been condemned." [14]**Christ did this so that God's promised blessing to Abraham could be given to all people.** This blessing comes through Christ Jesus. God wanted us to receive the promise of the Holy Spirit through faith.

[GW] Galatians 3:13-14 Christ paid the price to free us from the curse that the laws in Moses' Teachings bring by becoming cursed instead of us. Scripture says, "Everyone who is hung on a tree is cursed." [14]**Christ paid the price so that the blessing promised to Abraham would come to all the people of the world** through Jesus Christ and we would receive the promised Spirit through faith.

[ICB] Galatians 3:13-14 So the law put a curse on us, but Christ took away that curse. He changed places with us and put himself under that curse. It is written in the Scriptures, "Everyone whose body is displayed on a tree is cursed." [14]**Christ did this so that God's blessing promised to Abraham might come to the non-Jews**. This blessing comes through Jesus Christ. Jesus died so that we could have the Spirit that God promised and receive this promise by believing.

[NCV] Galatians 3:13-14 Christ took away the curse the law put on us. He changed places with us and put himself under that curse. It is written in the Scriptures, "Anyone whose body is displayed on a tree is cursed." [14]**Christ did this so that God's blessing promised to Abraham might come through Jesus Christ to those who are not Jews**. Jesus died so that by our believing we could receive the Spirit that God promised.

[NEB] Galatians 3:13-14 Christ bought us freedom from the curse of the law by becoming for our sake an accursed thing; for Scripture says, 'Cursed is everyone who is hanged on a tree.' [14]**And the purpose of it all was that the blessing of Abraham should in Jesus Christ be extended to the Gentiles**, so that we might receive the promised Spirit through faith.

[NLT] Galatians 3:13-14 But Christ has rescued us from the curse pronounced by the law. When he was hung on the cross, he took upon himself the curse for our wrongdoing. For it is written in the Scriptures, "Cursed is everyone who is hung on a tree." [14]**Through Christ Jesus, God has blessed the Gentiles with the same blessing he promised to Abraham**, so that we who are believers might receive the promised Holy Spirit through faith.

[NLV] Galatians 3:13-14 Christ bought us with His blood and made us free from the Law. In that way, the Law could not punish us. Christ did this by carrying the load and by being punished instead of us. It is written, "Anyone who hangs on a cross is hated and punished." [14]**Because of the price Christ Jesus paid, the good things that came to Abraham might come to the people who are not Jews.** And by putting our trust in Christ, we receive the Holy Spirit He has promised.

[NWT] Galatians 3:13-14 Christ purchased us, releasing us from the curse of the Law by becoming a curse instead of us, because it is written: "Accursed is every man hung upon a stake." [14]**This was so that the blessing of Abraham would come to the nations by means of Christ Jesus**, so that we might receive the promised spirit through our faith.

[Phillips] <u>Galatians 3:13-14</u> **Now Christ has redeemed us from the curse of the Law by himself becoming a curse for us**. For the scripture is plain: Cursed is every one that hangeth on a tree. [14]**God's purpose is therefore plain: that the blessing given to Abraham might reach the gentiles through Christ Jesus,** and the promise of the Spirit might become ours by faith.

[REM-NT] <u>Galatians 3:13-14</u> Christ saved us from where the law leaves us—diagnosed as terminal and abandoned to die—by being himself abandoned on the cross in order to restore us to trust and to purge humanity from the infection of selfishness and death; for it is written: "Abandoned to die is everyone who is hung on a tree." [14]**He saved us from a futile, self-focused works system in order that the blessings of love, life, and freedom—given to Abraham—might come to the Gentiles through Jesus Christ,** so that by trust we might receive the full enlightenment, renewal, and regeneration of heart and mind that comes by the Spirit.

[TCNT] <u>Galatians 3:13-14</u> **Christ ransomed us from the curse pronounced in the Law, by taking the curse on himself for us,** for Scripture says—'Cursed is any one who is hanged on a tree.' [14]**And this he did that the blessing given to Abraham might be extended to the Gentiles through their union with Jesus Christ;** that so, through our faith, we also might receive the promised gift of the Spirit.

[TLB] <u>Galatians 3:13-14</u> **But Christ has bought us out from under the doom of that impossible system by taking the curse for our wrongdoing upon himself.** For it is written in the Scripture, "Anyone who is hanged on a tree is cursed" (as Jesus was hung upon a wooden cross). [14]**Now God can bless the Gentiles, too, with this same blessing he promised to Abraham; and all of us as Christians can have the promised Holy Spirit through this faith.**

[TPT] <u>Galatians 3:13-14</u> **Yet, Christ paid the full price to set us free from the curse of the law. He absorbed it completely as he became a curse in our place.** For it is written: "Everyone who is hung upon a tree is doubly cursed." [14]**Jesus, our Messiah, was cursed in our place and in so doing, dissolved the curse from our lives, so that all the blessings of Abraham can be poured out upon even non-Jewish believers.** And now God gives us the promise of the wonderful Holy Spirit who lives within us when we believe in him.

[TVB] <u>Galatians 3:13-14</u> **the Anointed One, the Liberating King, has redeemed us from the curse of the law by becoming a curse for us.** It was stated in the Scriptures, "Everyone who hangs on a tree is cursed by God." [14]**This is what God had in mind all along: the blessing He gave to Abraham might extend to all nations through the Anointed One, Jesus;** and we are the beneficiaries of this promise of the Spirit that comes only through faith.

[Wade] <u>Galatians 3:13-14</u> **Christ, at His own cost, delivered us from the curse of the Law, having for our sake submitted to its curse** (because it is written, "Cursed is everyone who hangs upon a gibbet") [14]**in order that upon the Gentiles there might come in Jesus Christ the blessing pronounced upon Abraham,** and that we all, through our faith, might receive the promised Spirit.

[Wand-NT] <u>Galatians 3:13-14</u> **Now, Christ bought us off the curse of the Law at the cost of being accursed for our sakes,** 'Cursed is everyone who suffers a criminal's death.' [14]**That is how Abraham's blessing may be extended to non-Jews through Christ Jesus:** we may receive the promised Spirit through faith.

[Weymouth-NT] <u>Galatians 3:13-14</u> **Christ has purchased our freedom from the curse of the Law by becoming accursed for us**—because ["Cursed is every one who is hanged upon a tree."] [14]**Our freedom has been thus purchased in order that in Christ Jesus the blessing belonging to Abraham may come upon the nations,** so that through faith we may receive the promised Spirit.

EPHESIANS

Ephesians 1:21-22,2:6 Far above all principality, and power, and might, and dominion, and every name that is named, not only in this world, but also in that which is to come: [22]And hath put all things under his feet, and gave him to be the head over all things to the church, [2:6]**And hath raised us up together, and made us sit together in heavenly places in Christ Jesus:**

If Jesus is far above all the works of the enemy, then we are far above all the works of the enemy. That would include being above all sickness and disease.

[AMP] Ephesians 1:21-22,2:6 far above all rule and authority and power and dominion [whether angelic or human], and [far above] every name that is named [above every title that can be conferred], not only in this age and world but also in the one to come. [22]And He put all things [in every realm] in subjection under Christ's feet, and appointed Him as [supreme and authoritative] head over all things in the church, [2:6]**And He raised us up together with Him [when we believed], and seated us with Him in the heavenly places, [because we are] in Christ Jesus,**

[Authentic-NT] Ephesians 1:21-22,2:6 high above every angelic Rule and Authority, Power and Dominion, and every entity that has existence not only in this world but in that which is to come. [22]He has indeed 'put everything under his feet', and over and above has given him headship of the Community, [2:6]**and has raised us up together, and seated us together in the heavenly spheres in Christ Jesus.**

[Barclay-NT] Ephesians 1:21-22,2:6 There he gave him a place far above all spiritual powers, above every ruler and authority and power and lord, above every possible title of honour, not only in this world but also in the next. [22]He subjected everything to him, and he gave him as the supreme head to the church; [2:6]**Because our union with Christ Jesus he raised us from spiritual death, and gave us a seat with him in the heavenly places.**

[BWE-NT] Ephesians 1:21-22,2:6 He is greater than any ruler, power, chief, or king. His name is greater than any other name, not only in this world, but in the world that will come. [22]And God has put all things under Christ. He has made him the head of the church people in all matters. [2:6]**God raised us from death with Christ Jesus and gave us a place to sit with him in heaven.**

[Cornish-NT] Ephesians 1:21-22,2:6 untouched, unimpeded by the innumerable authorities, influences, powers, potentates of the world, having power over all other names to which authority is lent not only in this age, but in the next. [22]God has "put all things under his feet", made him the head of all things for the Church, [2:6]**God raised us out of it all with Christ, and He sat us down on the right hand of power with Him and gave us dominion,**

[GNT] Ephesians 1:21-22,2:6 Christ rules there above all heavenly rulers, authorities, powers, and lords; he has a title superior to all titles of authority in this world and in the next. [22]God put all things under Christ's feet and gave him to the church as supreme Lord over all things. [2:6]**In our union with Christ Jesus he raised us up with him to rule with him in the heavenly world.**

[GT] Ephesians 1:21-22,2:6 There Christ is far above any ruler, authority, power, lord or title which can be given, not only in this world but also in the next world. [22]God put everything under Christ's feet. God appointed him to be the Head over all things among the called out people. [2:6]**And God raised us from spiritual death and seated us in the heavenly world with Christ Jesus.**

[Knox] Ephesians 1:21-22,2:6 high above all princedoms and powers and virtues and dominations, and every name that is known, not in this world only, but in the world to come. [22]He has put everything under his dominion, and made him the head to which the whole Church is joined, [2:6]**raised us up too, enthroned us too above the heavens, in Christ Jesus.**

[Mace-NT] <u>Ephesians 1:21-22,2:6</u> far above all the principalities, all the powers, all the potentates, all the dominations, and whatever order can be named, not only in this age, but also in the age to come: ²²for he has subjected all things to him, and constituted him supreme head of the church, ^{2:6}**he hath raised us up together, and made us partakers of his heavenly kingdom.**

[Magiera-NT] <u>Ephesians 1:21-22,2:6</u> higher than all rulers and authorities and powers and lordships and higher than every name that is named, not only in this world, but in the coming [one] also. ²²And HE SUBJECTED EVERYTHING UNDER HIS FEET and he gave him who is higher than all [to be] the head of the church, ^{2:6}**and raised us with him and seated us with him in heaven in Jesus Christ,**

[MOUNCE] <u>Ephesians 1:21-22,2:6</u> infinitely superior to every ruler, authority, power, or dominion—every name that can be named—not only in this age but also in the age to come. ²²And he placed all things under Christ's feet and gave him as head over all things to the church, ^{2:6}**and raised us up with him and seated us with him in the heavenly places in Christ Jesus,**

[MSG] <u>Ephesians 1:21-22,2:6</u> in charge of running the universe, everything from galaxies to governments, no name and no power exempt from his rule. And not just for the time being, but forever. ²²He is in charge of it all, has the final word on everything. At the center of all this, Christ rules the church. ^{2:6}**Then he picked us up and set us down in highest heaven in company with Jesus, our Messiah.**

[NCV] <u>Ephesians 1:21-22,2:6</u> God has put Christ over all rulers, authorities, powers, and kings, not only in this world but also in the next. ²²God put everything under his power and made him the head over everything for the church, ^{2:6}**And he raised us up with Christ and gave us a seat with him in the heavens. He did this for those in Christ Jesus**

[NEB] <u>Ephesians 1:21-22,2:6</u> far above all government and authority, all power and dominion, and any title of sovereignty that can be named, not only in this age but in the age to come. ²²He put everything in subjection beneath his feet, and appointed him as supreme head to the church, ^{2:6}**And in union with Christ Jesus he raised us up and enthroned us with him in the heavenly realms,**

[Phillips] <u>Ephesians 1:21-22,2:6</u> a place that is infinitely superior to any command, authority, power or control, and which carries with it a name far beyond any name that could ever be used in this world or the world to come. ²²God has placed everything under the power of Christ and has set him up as supreme head to the Church. ^{2:6}**and has lifted us to take our place with him in Christ Jesus in the Heavens.**

[REM-NT] <u>Ephesians 1:21-22,2:6</u> above all power, rulers and authority, above all other kingdoms, empires or governments, and above every title that can be given—now and forever. ²²And God placed everything under Christ's governance and appointed him the Supreme Head over all creation, including the church— ^{2:6}**God raised the human race from its degraded and detestable state through Jesus Christ's victorious life, and humanity again occupies its seat in God's heavenly counsel—in the person of Jesus Christ our Lord—**

[Smith] <u>Ephesians 1:21-22,2:6</u> Above every beginning, and authority, and power, and property, and every name named, not only in this life, but in that about to be: ²²And placed all things under his, feet, and gave him head over all things to the church, ^{2:6}**And raised together, and seated together in heavenlies in Christ Jesus:**

[TLB] <u>Ephesians 1:21-22,2:6</u> far, far above any other king or ruler or dictator or leader. Yes, his honor is far more glorious than that of anyone else either in this world or in the world to come. ²²And God has put all things under his feet and made him the supreme Head of the Church— ^{2:6}and **lifted us up from the grave into glory along with Christ, where we sit with him in the heavenly realms—all because of what Christ Jesus did.**

[TNT] <u>Ephesians 1:21-22,2:6</u> There he rules supreme over every ruler, authority, power and lordship, high above every title that can be named not only in this age but also in the age to come. ²²And God has put all things under his feet and has given him to the church as its supreme head. **²⁶Because we belong to Christ Jesus he raised up together with him and caused us to share his place of honour in the supernatural world.**

[TPT] <u>Ephesians 1:21-22,2:6</u> And now he is exalted as first above every ruler, authority, government, and realm of power in existence! He is gloriously enthroned over every name that is ever praised, not only in this age, but in the age that is coming! ²²And he alone is the leader and source of everything needed in the church. God has put everything beneath the authority of Jesus Christ and has given him the highest rank above all others. **²⁶He raised us up with Christ the exalted One, and we ascended with him into the glorious perfection and authority of the heavenly realm, for we are now co-seated as one with Christ!**

[TTNT] <u>Ephesians 1:21-22,2:6</u> As a result of this power, Jesus is now reigning far above every other ruler, authority, power and dominion. He is greater than anyone else could ever be, not only in this present age but also in the future age that He will inaugurate. ²²God has placed everything under Jesus' feet. He has appointed Him to have authority over everything for the sake of the church, **²⁶Now He has actually raised us up with Christ and sees us seated with Him in heavenly places because He has placed us in Christ Jesus.**

[TVB] <u>Ephesians 1:21-22,2:6</u> He's above all rule, authority, power, and dominion; over every name invoked, over every title bestowed in this age and the next. ²²God has placed all things beneath His feet and anointed Him as the head over all things for His church. **²⁶He raised us up with Him and seated us in the heavenly realms with our beloved Jesus the Anointed, the Liberating King.**

[TWTY-RCT-NT-V1] <u>Ephesians 1:21-22,2:6</u> up high and far above every individual and collective leader and ruler, authority and magistrate and official with religious, political and governmental authority and anything with power and energy, right and ability, permission and freedom, force and influence, and all dominions and ruling powers, and all individual and collective name and title, character and person, reputation and authority that is addressed or called by name, recognised and publically known; not only or alone in this current age, season and time, but nevertheless, notwithstanding and on the contrary, also in the ones that are intended and destined to, inevitable to and will exist. ²²And "He arranged, subordinated, governed and placed all individual and collective things under and subject to His feet and under His control," and He gave and granted, supplied and furnished, bestowed and delivered, committed and permitted, extended and presented Him as the head and supreme and most prominent cornerstone over and above every individual and collective thing to the called out Ekklesia, assembly and congregation, **²⁶and He raised us up together and caused us to sit together in the heavenly places in, by and with the Anointed Yahushua,**

[UDB] <u>Ephesians 1:21-22,2:6</u> In that place, Messiah rules as supreme over every powerful spirit on every level of authority and over every name that exists. Jesus is much higher than any other being, not only now, but forever. ²²Yahweh has put all beings under the rule of Messiah, as if they were all under his feet. And Yahweh has appointed Messiah as the ruler over everything among all believers everywhere. **²⁶He raised us up from among those who are like dead people, and he gave us seats of honor to rule with Messiah Jesus in heavenly places.**

<u>Ephesians 4:27</u> Neither give place to the devil.

If Paul instructs us to not give place (license, opportunity) to the devil, it means we have the ability through the Name of Jesus to stand successfully against him. This would include the areas related to healing.

[AENT] <u>Ephesians 4:27</u> And give no place to the Accuser.

OUR HEALING COVENANT

[AMP] <u>Ephesians 4:27</u> And do not give the devil an opportunity [to lead you into sin by holding a grudge, or nurturing anger, or harboring resentment, or cultivating bitterness].

[AMPC] <u>Ephesians 4:27</u> Leave no [such] room or foothold for the devil [give no opportunity to him].

[Authentic-NT] <u>Ephesians 4:27</u> nor give the Devil his opportunity.

[AUV-NT 2003] <u>Ephesians 4:27</u> And do not give the devil an opportunity [to lead you into sin].

[Ballentine-NT] <u>Ephesians 4:27</u> Nor give way to the devil.

[Barclay-NT] <u>Ephesians 4:27</u> Give the devil no place or opportunity in your life.

[Beck] <u>Ephesians 4:27</u> Don't give the Devil a chance to work.

[Belsham-NT] <u>Ephesians 4:27</u> and give no advantage to the accuser.

[BLE] <u>Ephesians 4:27</u> and do not give the Devil a chance;

[BWE-NT] <u>Ephesians 4:27</u> Do not let the devil control you.

[CBC] <u>Ephesians 4:27</u> Neither give opportunity to the devil.

[CWB] <u>Ephesians 4:27</u> Don't give the devil a foothold or an opportunity to cause trouble.

[Erasmus-NT] <u>Ephesians 4:27</u> Let harmony, by itself, make you safe against the scoffing of the devil; if it is torn apart by hatreds and mutual affronts, there will be laid open to the foe a fissure through which he may burst in, to your destruction. Against those who are of one mind he is feeble; against the divided, powerful. To him you will be giving a place if a place is given to hatred.

[ERV] <u>Ephesians 4:27</u> Don't give the devil a way to defeat you.

[FAA] <u>Ephesians 4:27</u> nor give the devil any room.

[FBV-NT] <u>Ephesians 4:27</u> and don't give the devil any opportunity.

[GNC-NT] <u>Ephesians 4:27</u> Do not allow the devil to have any chance of success with you.

[Goodspeed-NT] <u>Ephesians 4:27</u> you must not give the devil a chance.

[Heberden-NT] <u>Ephesians 4:27</u> neither give place to the evil suggestions of the devil;

[Jerusalem] <u>Ephesians 4:27</u> or else you will give the devil a foothold.

[Jordan-NT] <u>Ephesians 4:27</u> and don't give in once inch to the devil.

[Kneeland-NT] <u>Ephesians 4:27</u> and give no advantage to the impostor.

[KNT] <u>Ephesians 4:27</u> and don't leave any loophole for the devil.

[Macknight-NT] <u>Ephesians 4:27</u> Neither give space to the devil.

[Macknight-NTc] <u>Ephesians 4:27</u> Neither, by immoderate anger long continued, give time and opportunity to the devil, to tempt you to commit sin in your anger.

[MOTB] <u>Ephesians 4:27</u> do not allow Satan to obtain power over you,

[MSG] <u>Ephesians 4:27</u> Don't give the Devil that kind of foothold in your life.

[MSTC] <u>Ephesians 4:27</u> neither give place unto the backbiter.

[NLV] <u>Ephesians 4:27</u> Do not let the devil start working in your life.

[Norlie-NT] <u>Ephesians 4:27</u> Do not let the devil get that satisfaction.

[NRSV] <u>Ephesians 4:27</u> and do not make room for the devil.

[NTIV] <u>Ephesians 4:27</u> and give not advantage to the slanderer.

[TLB] <u>Ephesians 4:27</u> for when you are angry, you give a mighty foothold to the devil.

[Wauck-NT] <u>Ephesians 4:27</u> and don't give the Devil an opening.

[Weymouth-NT] <u>Ephesians 4:27</u> and do not leave room for the Devil.

[Williams-NT] <u>Ephesians 4:27</u> stop giving the devil a chance.

[Worsley-NT] <u>Ephesians 4:27</u> and give not the devil room to ensnare you.

[Wuest-NT] <u>Ephesians 4:27</u> And stop giving an occasion for acting [opportunity] to the devil.

<u>Ephesians 5:30</u> For we are members of his body, of his flesh, and of his bones.

[ACV] <u>Ephesians 5:30</u> because we are parts of his body, of his flesh and of his bones.

[DLNT] <u>Ephesians 5:30</u> because we are body-parts of His body.

[Doddridge-NT] <u>Ephesians 5:30</u> For it is a most certain as well as delightful truth, that he regards it in this view, and that we are esteemed by him as members of his body, united to him by one spirit, and therefore considered like Eve, when just taken out of Adam's side, as making a part of his flesh and of his bones; whom therefore he would no more permit to be separated from him, than a man would be willing to lose a vital part of himself.

[EOB-NT] <u>Ephesians 5:30</u> Yes, we are members of his body, his very flesh and bones!

[Macrae] <u>Ephesians 5:30</u> For we are esteemed by him as members of his body, of his flesh and of his bones.

[NLV] <u>Ephesians 5:30</u> We are all a part of His body, the church.

[REB] <u>Ephesians 5:30</u> because it is his body, of which we are living parts.

[TWTY-RCT-NT-V1] <u>Ephesians 5:30</u> for concerning this we are and exists as members and limbs of His body and physical presence.

[Wand-NT] <u>Ephesians 5:30</u> for we are limbs of His Body.

[Worsley-NT] <u>Ephesians 5:30</u> for we are members of his body, as if taken out of his flesh, and of his bones, as Eve was out of Adam's.

<u>Ephesians 6:10-17</u> Finally, my brethren, be strong in the Lord, and in the power of his might. [11]Put on the whole armour of God, that ye may be able to stand against the wiles of the devil. [12]For we wrestle not against flesh and blood, but against principalities, against powers, against the rulers of the darkness of this world, against spiritual wickedness in high places. [13]Wherefore take unto you the whole armour of God, that ye may be able to withstand in the evil day, and having done all, to stand. [14]Stand therefore, having your loins girt about with truth, and having on the breastplate of righteousness; [15]And your feet shod with the preparation of the gospel of peace; [16]Above all, taking the shield of faith, wherewith ye shall be able to quench all the fiery darts of the wicked. [17]And take the helmet of salvation, and the sword of the Spirit, which is the word of God:

[AMP] <u>Ephesians 6:10-17</u> In conclusion, be strong in the Lord [draw your strength from Him and be empowered through your union with Him] and in the power of His [boundless] might. [11]Put on the full armor of God [for His precepts are like the splendid armor of a heavily-armed soldier], so that you may be able to [successfully] stand up against all the schemes and the strategies and the deceits of the devil. [12]For our struggle is not against flesh and blood [contending only with physical opponents], but against the rulers, against the powers, against the world forces of this [present] darkness, against the spiritual forces of wickedness in the heavenly (supernatural) places. [13]Therefore, put on the complete armor of God, so that you will be able to [successfully] resist and stand your ground in the evil day [of danger], and having done everything [that the crisis demands], to stand firm [in your place, fully prepared, immovable, victorious]. ¹⁴So stand firm and hold your ground, having tightened the wide band of truth (personal integrity, moral courage) around your waist and having put on the breastplate of righteousness (an upright heart), ¹⁵and having strapped on your feet the gospel of peace in preparation [to face the enemy with firm-footed stability and the readiness produced by the good news]. ¹⁶Above all, lift up the [protective] shield of faith with which you can extinguish all the flaming arrows of the evil one. ¹⁷And take the helmet of salvation, and the sword of the Spirit, which is the Word of God.

[AMPC] <u>Ephesians 6:10-17</u> In conclusion, be strong in the Lord [be empowered through your union with Him]; draw your strength from Him [that strength which His boundless might provides]. ¹¹Put on God's whole armor [the armor of a heavy-armed soldier which God supplies], that you may be able successfully to stand up against [all] the strategies and the deceits of the devil. ¹²For we are not wrestling with flesh and blood [contending only with physical opponents], but against the despotisms, against the powers, against [the master spirits who are] the world rulers of this present darkness, against the spirit forces of wickedness in the heavenly (supernatural) sphere. ¹³Therefore put on God's complete armor, that you may be able to resist and stand your ground on the evil day [of danger], and, having done all [the crisis demands], to stand [firmly in your place]. ¹⁴Stand therefore [hold your ground], having tightened the belt of truth around your loins and having put on the breastplate of integrity and of moral rectitude and right standing with God, ¹⁵And having shod your feet in preparation [to face the enemy with the firm-footed stability, the promptness, and the readiness produced by the good news] of the Gospel of peace. ¹⁶Lift up over all the [covering] shield of saving faith, upon which you can quench all the flaming missiles of the wicked [one]. ¹⁷And take the helmet of salvation and the sword that the Spirit wields, which is the Word of God.

[Anchor] <u>Ephesians 6:10-17</u> For the remaining time become strong in the Lord, that is, by the strength of his power. ¹¹Put on God's [splendid] armor in order to be able to stand firm against the schemes of the devil. ¹²For we are wrestling not with blood and flesh, but with the governments, with the authorities, with the overlords of this dark world, with the spiritual hosts of evil in the heavens. ¹³Therefore take up God's [splendid] armor so that you are able to put up resistance on the darkest day, to carry out everything, and to stand firm. ¹⁴Stand firm now "Girded with truth around your waist. Clad with righteousness for a cuirass, ¹⁵steadfast because the gospel of peace is strapped under your feet. ¹⁶With all [this equipment] take up faith as the shield with which you will be able to quench the fire-missiles of the evil one. ¹⁷Take salvation as your helmet and the sword provided by the Spirit, that is the word of God.

[BBE] <u>Ephesians 6:10-17</u> Lastly, be strong in the Lord, and in the strength of his power. ¹¹Take up God's instruments of war, so that you may be able to keep your position against all the deceits of the Evil One. ¹²For our fight is not against flesh and blood, but against authorities and powers, against the world-rulers of this dark night, against the spirits of evil in the heavens. ¹³For this reason take up all the arms of God, so that you may be able to be strong in the evil day, and, having done all, to keep your place. ¹⁴Take your place, then, having your body clothed with the true word, and having put on the breastplate of righteousness; ¹⁵Be ready with the good news of peace as shoes on your feet; ¹⁶And most of all, using faith as a cover to keep off all the flaming arrows of the Evil One. ¹⁷And take salvation for your head-dress and the sword of the Spirit, which is the word of God:

[Berkeley] <u>Ephesians 6:10-17</u> In conclusion: acquire power in the Lord and in the strength of His might. ¹¹Put on the complete armor that God supplies, so you will be able to stand against the devil's intrigues. ¹²For our wrestling is not against flesh-and-blood opponents, but against the rulers, the authorities, the cosmic powers of this present darkness; against the spiritual forces of evil in the supernatural sphere. ¹³Take up, therefore, the whole armor of God so that you may be able to stand when you have done all the fighting. ¹⁴So stand your ground, with the belt of truth tightened around your waist, the breastplate of righteousness around the body, ¹⁵the readiness of the Gospel of peace bound under your feet; ¹⁶above all taking up the shield of faith, with which you will be able to extinguish all the fire-dipped darts of the evil one. [17]And take hold of the helmet of salvation and the sword of the Spirit—which is the word of God.

[BV-KJV-NT] <u>Ephesians 6:10-17</u> For the rest of the time, my brothers, be improved in the Master and in the power of His strength. [11]Put on God's full body armor with the intent for you to be able to stand facing the Accuser's schemes [12]because the wrestling match for us is not facing blood and a physical body, but facing the top ranks, facing the authorities, facing the global powers of the darkness of this span of time, facing the spiritual elements of the evilness in the heavenly regions. [13]Because of this, take up God's full body armor so that you might be able to stand in opposition to them in the evil day, even after working on and completing absolutely everything to stand. [14]So stand after putting a sash around your waist in truth, putting on the armored vest of the right way, [15]and tying shoes on the feet in preparation of the good news of the peace, [16]over everything, after taking up the shield of the trust, with which you will be able to extinguish all the flaming arrows of the evil one. [17]And accept the head protection of the rescue process and the knife of the Spirit that is God's statement,

[CCB] <u>Ephesians 6:10-17</u> Finally, be strong in the Lord with his energy and strength. [11]Put on the whole armor of God to be able to resist the cunning of the devil. [12]Our battle is not against human forces but against the rulers and authorities and their dark powers that govern this world. We are struggling against the spirits and supernatural forces of evil. [13]Therefore put on the whole armor of God, that in the evil day, you may resist and stand your ground, making use of all your weapons. [14]Take truth as your belt, justice as your breastplate, [15]and zeal as your shoes to propagate the Gospel of peace. [16]Always hold in your hand the shield of faith to repel the flaming arrows of the devil. [17]Finally, use the helmet of salvation and the sword of the Spirit, that is, the Word of God.

[CEV] <u>Ephesians 6:10-17</u> Finally, let the mighty strength of the Lord make you strong. [11]Put on all the armor that God gives, so you can defend yourself against the devil's tricks. [12]We are not fighting against humans. We are fighting against forces and authorities and against rulers of darkness and powers in the spiritual world. [13]So put on all the armor that God gives. Then when that evil day comes, you will be able to defend yourself. And when the battle is over, you will still be standing firm. [14]Be ready! Let the truth be like a belt around your waist, and let God's justice protect you like armor. [15]Your desire to tell the good news about peace should be like shoes on your feet. [16]Let your faith be like a shield, and you will be able to stop all the flaming arrows of the evil one. [17]Let God's saving power be like a helmet, and for a sword use God's message that comes from the Spirit.

[Conybeare-NT] <u>Ephesians 6:10-17</u> Finally, my brethren, let your hearts be strengthened in the Lord, and in the conquering power of His might. [11]Put on the whole armour of God, that you may be able to stand firm against the wiles of the Devil. [12]For the adversaries with whom we wrestle are not flesh and blood, but they are the Principalities, the Powers, and the Sovereigns of this present darkness, the spirits of evil in the heavens. [13]Wherefore, take up with you to the battle the whole armour of God, that you may be able to withstand them in the evil day, and having overthrown them all, to stand unshaken. [14]Stand, therefore, girt with the belt of truth, and wearing the breastplate of righteousness, [15]and shod as ready messengers of the Glad-tidings of peace: [16]and take up to cover you the shield of faith, wherewith you shall be able to quench all the fiery darts of the Evil One. [17]Take, likewise, the helmet of salvation, and the sword of the Spirit, which is the word of God.

[EEBT] <u>Ephesians 6:10-17</u> The last thing that I want to say to you is this. Be strong by the Lord's great power, because you are united with him. [11]Put on the whole armour that God gives to us. So then you will continue to be strong against all the clever ways by which the Devil attacks us. [12]You need to be strong because we are not fighting against human enemies. No, but instead we are fighting against the rulers and the powerful spirits that have authority over this dark world. We are fighting against powerful bad spirits who live in the heavens. ¹³So, take the whole armour that God gives. Then you will be able to stand against the enemy when he attacks. And he will not be able to move you from your place. Then, after you have done everything, you will still be standing strongly in your place. ¹⁴So stand. Always remember and obey God's true message. That will be like a belt round you. Always be right with God. That will be like a strong metal plate that you put over the front of your body. ¹⁵Remember God's good news that makes you friends with God and with each other. That will be like shoes on your feet, to make you ready to fight. ¹⁶Always continue to believe God. That will be like a shield that you hold in front of you. It will put out all the burning arrows that the Devil throws at you. ¹⁷Remember that God has saved you. That will be like a strong metal hat on your head, to keep you safe. Also, remember what God has said. That will be like a strong knife that you can use, by God's Spirit, to fight.

[GNT] <u>Ephesians 6:10-17</u> Finally, build up your strength in union with the Lord and by means of his mighty power. ¹¹Put on all the armor that God gives you, so that you will be able to stand up against the Devil's evil tricks. ¹²For we are not fighting against human beings but against the wicked spiritual forces in the heavenly world, the rulers, authorities, and cosmic powers of this dark age. ¹³So put on God's armor now! Then when the evil day comes, you will be able to resist the enemy's attacks; and after fighting to the end, you will still hold your ground. ¹⁴So stand ready, with truth as a belt tight around your waist, with righteousness as your breastplate, ¹⁵and as your shoes the readiness to announce the Good News of peace. ¹⁶At all times carry faith as a shield; for with it you will be able to put out all the burning arrows shot by the Evil One. ¹⁷And accept salvation as a helmet, and the word of God as the sword which the Spirit gives you.

[GT] <u>Ephesians 6:10-17</u> Last of all, be clothed with the Lord Jesus and the power of his strength. ¹¹Put on all of God's armor. Then you will be able to stand against the evil tricks of the devil. ¹²Our fight is not against men. No, it is against rulers, against authorities, against world powers of this darkness, and against evil spiritual beings in the heavenly world. ¹³This is why you must take up all of God's armor. Then when the time for battle comes, you will be able to resist; and after you have fought your best, you will stand. ¹⁴So stand firm, using truth as a belt around your waist. Put on the chest plate of being made right. ¹⁵With shoes on your feet, be ready to tell the Good News about peace. ¹⁶And along with everything else, take up faith for a shield. With this, you will be able to put out all the burning arrows of the evil one. ¹⁷Take the helmet of deliverance from sin; and take the sword of the Spirit. (This is the word of God.

[KNT] <u>Ephesians 6:10-17</u> What else is there to say? Just this: be strong in the Lord, and in the strength of his power. ¹¹Put on God's complete armour. Then you'll be able to stand firm against the devil's trickery. ¹²The warfare we're engaged in, you see, isn't against flesh and blood. It's against the leaders, against the authorities, against the powers that rule the world in this dark age, against the wicked spiritual elements in the heavenly places. ¹³For this reason, you must take up God's complete armour. Then, when wickedness grabs its moment, you'll be able to withstand, to do what needs to be done, and still to be on your feet when it's all over. ¹⁴So stand firm! Put the belt of truth round your waist; put on justice as your breastplate; ¹⁵for shoes on your feet, ready for battle, take the good news of peace. ¹⁶With it all, take the shield of faith; if you've got that, you'll be able to quench all the flaming arrows of the evil one. ¹⁷Take the helmet of salvation, and the sword of the spirit, which is God's word.

[LGV-NT] <u>Ephesians 6:10-17</u> Finally, my brothers, be strong in the Master and in the power of His strength! ¹¹Put on the full armor of God so that you may be able to withstand the trickery of the devil, ¹²because we do not struggle with flesh and blood, but with authorities, with powers, with the princes of the darkness of this age, against spiritual conspirators in the celestial dominions. ¹³Therefore take up the full armor of God, so that you may be able to stand firm in that day, the perilous one, and having accomplished everything, to stand firm. ¹⁴Therefore, stand firm having girded your groin with truth, having put on the breastplate of righteousness, ¹⁵and having feet bound with the readiness of the message of peace. [16]Above all, raising the shield of faith with which you will be able to extinguish all the fiery arrows of the wicked one. [17]Also take the helmet of salvation, also the sword of the Breath which is the spoken word of God,

[LTPB] <u>Ephesians 6:10-17</u> Of the rest, brothers, be strengthened in the Lord and in his power's might. [11]Dress yourselves in God's weapons, so you can stand against the devil's plots, [12]because the struggle for us is not against flesh and blood, yet against princes and powers, against the rulers of this world's shadows, against wicked spiritualities in the skies. [13]Therefore, take God's armor, so you can resist on the harmful day and, perfected in all ways, stand. [14]Stand, then, your waists covered in truth, dressed in the breastplate of justice, [15]and feet shoed in the preparation of the gospel's peace; [16]taking up in all circumstances faith's shield, in which you can put out all the wicked one's flaming spears. [17]Take salvation's helmet and Spirit's sword, which is God's word,

[Mace-NT] <u>Ephesians 6:10-17</u> Finally, my brethren, place your strength in the transcendent power of the Lord. [11]put on the set of divine armour, that ye may be able to stand against the wiles of the devil. [12]for our conflict is not barely with men, but with principalities, with potentates, with the princes of darkness, with wicked aereal spirits. [13]wherefore invest yourselves with the set of divine armour, that ye may be able to withstand in the difficult day, and having overcome all to maintain your ground. [14]stand firm, the belt of truth round your waist, let justice invest you like mail: [15]wing your feet with the gospel of peace: [16]cover all with the shield of faith, to repel all the fiery darts of the adversary: [17]let salvation be your helmet, and the divine doctrine your spiritual sword.

[Macrae] <u>Ephesians 6:10-17</u> Finally, my brethren, be strong in the Lord, even in his mighty power. [11]Put on the complete armour of God, to be able to withstand the devil's wiles. [12]For our wrestling is not with flesh and blood alone, but with (diabolical) principalities and powers, who rule in the darkness (i.e. ignorance, error, and wickedness) of this world, with wicked spirits, with respect to heavenly things. [13]Therefore, take the whole armour of God, that ye may be able to resist in the evil day, and by doing all, to stand. [14]Stand, therefore, having your loins girded with the girdle of truth (and sincerity), having on righteousness as a breastplate; [15]And having your feet shod (and fitted for thorny paths) with (the passive virtues of self-denial and patience), the preparation for the practice of the gospel of peace (in bearing the cross, or, suffering for the gospel). [16]Besides all these, having faith as a shield for protection, whereby ye shall be able to quench all the fiery darts (or furious suggestions) of the wicked one, as driving you to infidelity or despair. [17]And have the hope of salvation as a helmet for your head, and the sword of the Spirit, which is the word of God.

[Madsen-NT] <u>Ephesians 6:10-17</u> What it comes to in the end is this: let the intense strength of his might flow through those who want to serve the Lord. [11]Put on the full armour of God that you may resist the well-aimed attacks of the Adversary. [12]For our part is not to fight against powers of flesh and blood, but against spirit-beings, mighty in the stream of time, against spirit-beings, powerful in the moulding of earth's substance, against the cosmic powers whose darkness rules the present time, against beings who, in the spiritual worlds, are themselves the powers of evil. [13]Therefore courageously take up the armour of God, that you can resist the evil on the day when it unfolds its greatest strength. You should stand firm, following everything through to the very end. [14]Stand fast, girded about the loins with truth. Put on the breastplate of the higher life which fulfils our human destiny. [15]Shoe your feet with preparedness to spread the message of peace that comes from the angels. [16]In all your deeds continually hold to your hearts' vision of Christ's presence, with which you can quench all the flaming darts of the evil one. [17]Take into your thoughts the certainty of the coming world-healing, that it protect you as with a helmet, and grasp the sword of the Spirit which is the word of God which you utter.

[Moffatt] <u>Ephesians 6:10-17</u> To conclude. Be strong in the Lord and in the strength of his might; [11]put on God's armour, so as to be able to stand against the stratagems of the devil. [12]For we have to struggle, not with blood and flesh but with the angelic Rulers, the angelic Authorities, the potentates of the dark present, the spirit-forces of evil in the heavenly sphere. [13]So take God's armour, that you may be able to make a stand upon the evil day and hold your ground by overcoming all the foe. [14]Hold your ground, tighten the belt of truth about your loins, wear integrity as your coat of mail, [15]and have your feet shod with the stability of the gospel of peace; [16]above all, take faith as your shield, to enable you to quench all the fire-tipped darts flung by the evil one, [17]put on salvation as your helmet, and take the Spirit as your sword (that is, the word of God),

[NEB] <u>Ephesians 6:10-17</u> Finally then, find your strength in the Lord, in his mighty power. [11]Put on all the armour which God provides, so that you may be able to stand firm against the devices of the devil. [12]For our fight is not against human foes, but against cosmic powers, against the authorities and potentates of this dark world, against the superhuman forces of evil in the heavens. [13]Therefore, take up God's armour; then you will be able to stand your ground when things are at their worst, to complete every task and still to stand. [14]Stand firm, I say. Buckle on the belt of truth; for coat of mail put on integrity; [15]let the shoes on your feet be the gospel of peace, to give you firm footing; [16]and, with all these, take up the great shield of faith, with which you will be able to quench all the flaming arrows of the evil one. [17]Take salvation for helmet; for sword, take that which the Spirit gives you the words that come from God.

[NIRV] <u>Ephesians 6:10-17</u> Finally, let the Lord make you strong. Depend on his mighty power. [11]Put on all of God's armor. Then you can remain strong against the devil's evil plans. [12]Our fight is not against human beings. It is against the rulers, the authorities and the powers of this dark world. It is against the spiritual forces of evil in the heavenly world. [13]So put on all of God's armor. Evil days will come. But you will be able to stand up to anything. And after you have done everything you can, you will still be standing. [14]So remain strong in the faith. Put the belt of truth around your waist. Put the armor of godliness on your chest. [15]Wear on your feet what will prepare you to tell the good news of peace. [16]Also, pick up the shield of faith. With it you can put out all the flaming arrows of the evil one. [17]Put on the helmet of salvation. And take the sword of the Holy Spirit. The sword is God's word.

[NLV] <u>Ephesians 6:10-17</u> This is the last thing I want to say: Be strong with the Lord's strength. [11]Put on the things God gives you to fight with. Then you will not fall into the traps of the devil. [12]Our fight is not with people. It is against the leaders and the powers and the spirits of darkness in this world. It is against the demon world that works in the heavens. [13]Because of this, put on all the things God gives you to fight with. Then you will be able to stand in that sinful day. When it is all over, you will still be standing. [14]So stand up and do not be moved. Wear a belt of truth around your body. Wear a piece of iron over your chest which is being right with God. [15]Wear shoes on your feet which are the Good News of peace. [16]Most important of all, you need a covering of faith in front of you. This is to put out the fire-arrows of the devil. [17]The covering for your head is that you have been saved from the punishment of sin. Take the sword of the Spirit which is the Word of God.

[Norlie-NT] <u>Ephesians 6:10-17</u> Just one thing more: My brethren, get your strength from the almighty power of the Lord. [11]Put on His whole armor, so that you may be able to resist the devil's cunning tactics. [12]For our struggle is not so much against wicked men, but rather against the forces, authorities and master-spirits that rule this world in its present darkness. Yes, our war is against the wicked spiritual forces of the underworld itself. [13]You must, therefore, arm yourself with God's whole armor. In that way you may be able to make a stand when the evil day comes and, when it is all over, you will still be holding your own. [14]Stand up, then, put the belt of truth around your waist, and let righteousness be your breastplate. [15]Let your feet be shod in readiness to proclaim the glad tidings of peace. [16]And by all means, take with you the shield of faith, with which you will be able to quench all the fiery arrows shot by the wicked enemy. [17]Make use also of the helmet of salvation and the sword of the Spirit, which is the Word of God.

[Original-NT] <u>Ephesians 6:10-17</u> Finally, make yourselves strong in the Lord and in the power of his might. [11]Array yourselves in the full armour of God, so that you may stand up to the artfulness of the Adversary. [12]For we are not contending with mortals but with angelic Rulers and Authorities, with the Overlords of the Dark State, the spirit forces of evil in the heavenly spheres. [13]Therefore take to yourselves the full armour of God that you may be able to withstand in the evil day, and having completely overcome, to go on standing. [14]Stand, therefore, with your loins girded with truth, clad in the corselet of rectitude, [15]with your feet shod with the sureness of the News of peace. [16]To complete your equipment, hold before you the shield of faith, with which you will be able to extinguish the flaming darts of the Evil One, [17]and take the helmet of preservation, and the sword of the Spirit—which means God's Word.

[REAL] <u>Ephesians 6:10-17</u> Finally my brothers, be miraculously powered in the Lord and in the Dominion of his force. [11]Put on God's weapons, so you have miracle power to stand against the devil's methods. [12]For this reason, we are not wrestling against blood and flesh, but against governors, against authorities, against the world dominions of the darkness of this age, against spiritual evil in the heavens. [13]So take on God's weapons for yourselves, so you have miracle power to resist on the Day of Evil. Also, having done everything—stand by. [14]So—stand by, having bound your hips with Truth. Also, put on the Breastplate of Justice and Right Standing, [15]and the Shoes of the Preparation of the Good News Message of Peace on your feet. [16]On top of everything, take the Door-Shield of Faith, so you have miracle power to put out fire in all the arrows from the evil. [17]Also, receive the Helmet of Rescue and the Battle Sword of the Spirit—this is God's revealed Word.

[Shuttleworth-NT] <u>Ephesians 6:10-17</u> Finally, my brethren, be strong in holiness, and in the protecting power of the Lord; [11]and put on accordingly that armour which righteousness only can supply, that, so armed, you may be able to stand against the machinations of the devil. [12]For the Christian's warfare is not against flesh and blood, which is able to destroy the body, but against spiritual beings leagued for his eternal destruction, the various orders of evil angels who rule over the dark elements of this world, and who surround the earth, looking down upon us, and seeking whom they may devour. [13]Wherefore, I repeat, put on the whole armour of God, that you may be able to stand in the evil day, and to stand victorious and uninjured. [14]Stand, therefore, having your loins girt about with sincerity and truth; and having put on the breastplate of righteousness; [15]and having your feet shod with holy zeal to go on the blessed mission of preaching the Gospel of peace: [16]but above all, bearing before you the shield of faith, that with it you may be able to extinguish all the fiery darts of the evil one: [17]and take the helmet of salvation, and the sword of the Holy Spirit, which is the inspired word of God:

[TCNT] <u>Ephesians 6:10-17</u> For the future, find strength in your union with the Lord, and in the power which comes from his might. [11]Put on the full armor of God, so that you may be able to stand your ground against the stratagems of the Devil. [12]For ours is no struggle against enemies of flesh and blood, but against all the various Powers of Evil that hold sway in the Darkness around us, against the Spirits of Wickedness on high. [13]Therefore take up the full armor of God, that, when the evil day comes, you may be able to withstand the attack, and, having fought to the end, still to stand your ground. [14]Stand your ground, then, 'with truth for your belt,' and 'with righteousness for your breast-plate,' [15]And with the readiness to serve the Good News of Peace as shoes for your feet. [16]At every onslaught take up faith for your shield; for with it you will be able to extinguish all the flaming darts of the Evil One. [17]And receive 'the helmet of Salvation,' and 'the sword of the Spirit'—which is the Message of God—always with prayer and supplication.

[TLB] <u>Ephesians 6:10-17</u> Last of all I want to remind you that your strength must come from the Lord's mighty power within you. [11]Put on all of God's armor so that you will be able to stand safe against all strategies and tricks of Satan. [12]For we are not fighting against people made of flesh and blood, but against persons without bodies—the evil rulers of the unseen world, those mighty satanic beings and great evil princes of darkness who rule this world; and against huge numbers of wicked spirits in the spirit world. [13]So use every piece of God's armor to resist the enemy whenever he attacks, and when it is all over, you will still be standing up. [14]But to do this, you will need the strong belt of truth and the breastplate of God's approval. [15]Wear shoes that are able to speed you on as you preach the Good News of peace with God. [16]In every battle you will need faith as your shield to stop the fiery arrows aimed at you by Satan. [17]And you will need the helmet of salvation and the sword of the Spirit—which is the Word of God.

[TNT] <u>Ephesians 6:10-17</u> Finally, draw upon the Lord's power and let him supply you with his mighty strength. [11]Put on God's armour, in order that you may be able to make a stand against the devil's stratagems. [12]We are not fighting against human enemies, but against the rulers and the authorities, against the world-rulers of this dark age, against the spirit-forces of evil in the supernatural world. [13]So take up God's armour, in order that you may be able to resist in the evil day, and when you can do no more, still hold your ground. [14]Hold your ground, then. Make truth the belt round your waist, and righteousness your breastplate. [15]Let your readiness to preach the Gospel of peace be as shoes for your feet. [16]Let faith be the constant shield with which you will be able to put out all the fire-tipped darts of the Evil One. [17]Take the gift of salvation as your helmet, and as your sword take what the Spirit gives you, God's word.

[TTNT] <u>Ephesians 6:10-17</u> Above all, be strong in your faith and dependence on the Lord, on His might and power. [11]He has provided His protection for you in several ways. Clothed with His gifts and resources, you will be able to stand against all the devil's disruptive tactics. [12]Your battle is not against people but against the negative spiritual forces that influence and control them; against the spiritual rulers, authorities and powers that are at work in this world that is in bondage to the darkness of sin. They are in league with those evil spiritual forces that exist outside the world. [13]So accept everything God has made available to you, to enable you to stand steadfast when evil attacks. Yes, no matter what happens you are able to stand firm and to remain standing. [14]You stand firm with His truth like a belt you keep around your waist for support. His righteousness is like a breastplate that protects you. [15]You wear the shoes of the gospel so that you are always ready for any eventuality and can walk in peace. [16]Your faith is like a shield that you have to take hold of and that enables you to overcome anything the devil throws at you. [17]The assurance of your salvation is like a protective helmet, enabling you to counter all the devil's lies and efforts to deceive you in your thinking.

[TVB] <u>Ephesians 6:10-17</u> Finally, brothers and sisters, draw your strength and might from God. [11]Put on the full armor of God to protect yourselves from the devil and his evil schemes. [12]We're not waging war against enemies of flesh and blood alone. No, this fight is against tyrants, against authorities, against supernatural powers and demon princes that slither in the darkness of this world, and against wicked spiritual armies that lurk about in heavenly places. [13]And this is why you need to be head-to-toe in the full armor of God: so you can resist during these evil days and be fully prepared to hold your ground. [14]Yes, stand—truth banded around your waist, righteousness as your chest plate, [15]and feet protected in preparation to proclaim the good news of peace. [16]Don't forget to raise the shield of faith above all else, so you will be able to extinguish flaming spears hurled at you from the wicked one. [17]Take also the helmet of salvation and the sword of the Spirit, which is the word of God.

[TWTY-RCT-NT-V1] <u>Ephesians 6:10-17</u> Finally; be strengthened, empowered and enabled by Yahuweh and by the force and power, strength and might of His physical strength and ability, power and superiority, capacity and increased force. [11]Put on, dress and clothe yourselves with the full and complete defensive and offensive armour and weaponry of God for the advantage of having the power and might, ability and capability, force and influence, authority and significance to stand upright and firm, steadfast and established, fixed and unmoveable, upheld and sustained, maintained and authorised against the schemes and artificial devices, stratagems and tricks, deceptions and crafty procedures of the Devil, the false accuser and slanderer, [12]for the fact that concerning this it does not exist for you to fight or wrestle, battle or be in conflict against blood and flesh, the human body, but nevertheless, notwithstanding and on the contrary, to be so against the schemes and artificial devices, stratagems and tricks, deceptions and crafty procedures, against the LORD of this dark and ignorant, ungodly and immoral world and cosmos, against the evil and troublesome, sorrowful and poor, pitiable and unfit, unattractive and useless, worthless and morally reprehensible, morally corrupt and wicked, annoying and unethical, diseased and blind, perilous and criminal, vicious and malignant, harmful and incompetent, bad and wretched, pernicious and noxious spiritual forces. [13]Through the means of and on the grounds of, on account of and for the reason of, on the basis of and because of this, take up and receive, adopt and lift up, raise and obtain the full and complete defensive and offensive armour and weaponry of God so that, in order that and with the result that you might have the power and might, ability and capability, force and influence, authority and significance to stand upright and firm, steadfast and established, fixed and unmoveable, upheld and sustained, maintained and authorised against and to resist and oppose, withstand and refuse to yield in, by and with the evil and troublesome, sorrowful and poor, pitiable and unfit, unattractive and useless, worthless and morally reprehensible, morally corrupt and wicked, annoying and unethical, diseased and blind, perilous and criminal, vicious and malignant, harmful and incompetent, bad and wretched, pernicious and noxious day, and having performed and accomplished, achieved and produced, brought about and done, made and completed all individual things to stand upright and firm, steadfast and established, fixed and unmoveable, upheld and sustained, maintained and authorised. [14]Then and therefore, accordingly, consequently and these things being so, stand upright and firm, steadfast and established, fixed and unmoveable, upheld and sustained, maintained and authorised, having fastened and girdled your waist in, by and with real and disclosed, expressed and certain, upright and dependable, genuine and reliable, sincere and honest truth and facts, and having dressed, clothed and put on the breastplate of righteousness and validation, acceptance, vindication and uprightness, justification and acquittance, [15]and having tied and bound the feet with footwear and sandals in, by and with the preparation and basis, foundation and readiness of the good news, glad tiding and message, proclamation and victorious declaration of peace and tranquillity, harmony and concord, security and safety, prosperity and freedom, felicity and the assurance of salvation. [16]In, by and with all individual and collective things, take up and receive, adopt and lift up, raise and obtain the large shield of trust and reliance, obedience and confidence, certainty and guarantee, assurance and dependence, in, by and with what you are powerful and mighty, able and capable, forceful, influenceable and authorised to quench and stifle, suppress and extinguish, put out and thwart all the individual and collective flaming, ignited and glowing darts and javelins, arrows and missiles of the evil and troublesome, sorrowful and poor, pitiable and unfit, unattractive and useless, worthless and morally reprehensible, morally corrupt and wicked, annoying and unethical, diseased and blind, perilous and criminal, vicious and malignant, harmful and incompetent, bad and wretched, pernicious and noxious one. [17]And take up and receive, deliberately accept and readily grasp, embrace and welcome the helmet of deliverance and preservation, salvation and safety and the sword of the Spirit which is and exists as God's word and saying, statement and message, proclamation and subject matter,

[Wand-NT] <u>Ephesians 6:10-17</u> For the rest let all alike realize the strength they possess in the Lord and in the power of His might. [11]Arm yourselves with the full equipment that God has provided to enable his soldiers to hold their own against the tactics of the Devil. [12]We need it all, for our contest is not against flesh and blood but against demonic rulers, potentates, dictators of this dark age, forces of evil in the spiritual sphere. [13]Therefore take the whole divine equipment, which will enable you to maintain your stand in the evil day and to remain victorious on the field of battle. [14]Let truth be your girdle, your breastplate of righteousness [15]and your sandals the quick gospel of peace. [16]So take your stand, holding before you the long shield of faith with which to smother all the incendiary missiles hurled at you by the enemy. [17]To protect your head you must wear the helmet of salvation; and your right hand must grasp the sword of the Spirit, which is the word of God.

[Way-NT] <u>Ephesians 6:10-17</u> Be ye strengthened in the Lord's presence, And in the power of His might. [11]Array yourselves in the armour-panoply that God supplies, That you may be able to hold your post unflinching Against the Devil's stratagems. [12]For we have to close in grapple not with human flesh and blood alone, But with Principalities, with Powers, With the Lords of Darkness whose present sway is world-wide, With the spirit-host of Wicked Beings that haunt the upper air. [13]Therefore take up the God-given panoply, That you may be able in that grim day to face the foe unflinchingly, To achieve all your duty, and to stand unstaggered still. [14]Stand firm then Your loins girded with the belt of truth, Arrayed in the corslet of righteousness, [15]Your feet shod with that preparedness to face the foe Which is a fruit of the Glad-tidings of peace. [16]To cover them all, take up the shield of faith, Fenced by which you will be able to quench all the fire-darts of that Wicked One. [17]The helmet also of salvation receive ye from His hand, And the sword of the Spirit, Which is the Word of God.

[Weymouth-NT] <u>Ephesians 6:10-17</u> In conclusion, strengthen yourselves in the Lord and in the power which His supreme might imparts. [11]Put on the complete armour of God, so as to be able to stand firm against all the stratagems of the Devil. [12]For ours is not a conflict with mere flesh and blood, but with the despotisms, the empires, the forces that control and govern this dark world—the spiritual hosts of evil arrayed against us in the heavenly warfare. [13]Therefore put on the complete armour of God, so that you may be able to stand your ground on the day of battle, and, having fought to the end, to remain victors on the field. [14]Stand therefore, first fastening round you the girdle of truth and putting on the breastplate of uprightness [15]as well as the shoes of the Good News of peace—a firm foundation for your feet. [16]And besides all these take the great shield of faith, on which you will be able to quench all the flaming darts of the Wicked one; [17]and take the helmet of salvation, and the sword of the Spirit which is the word of God.

PHILIPPIANS

<u>Philippians 1:6</u> Being confident of this very thing, that he which hath begun a good work in you will perform it until the day of Jesus Christ:

[AMP] <u>Philippians 1:6</u> I am convinced and confident of this very thing, that He who has begun a good work in you will [continue to] perfect and complete it until the day of Christ Jesus [the time of His return].

[Anchor] <u>Philippians 1:6</u> since I am confident about this point, that the One who inaugurated a good work among you will bring it to completion by the Day of Christ Jesus.

[Ballentine-NT] <u>Philippians 1:6</u> For I am sure of this, that he who began a generous work in you will perfect it up to the very day of the coming of Jesus Christ.

[CEB] <u>Philippians 1:6</u> I'm sure about this: the one who started a good work in you will stay with you to complete the job by the day of Christ Jesus.

[CENT] <u>Philippians 1:6</u> For I am confident of this, that he who began a good work in you will carry it on to completion until the day of Christ Jesus.

[FBV-NT] <u>Philippians 1:6</u> I'm absolutely sure that God who began this good work in you will continue working and bring it to a successful conclusion when Jesus Christ returns.

[Kneeland-NT] <u>Philippians 1:6</u> being confident of this very thing, that he, who hath begun a good work in you, will continue completing it until the day of Jesus Christ.

[MSG] <u>Philippians 1:6</u> There has never been the slightest doubt in my mind that the God who started this great work in you would keep at it and bring it to a flourishing finish on the very day Christ Jesus appears.

[NIRV] <u>Philippians 1:6</u> God began a good work in you. And I am sure that he will carry it on until it is completed. That will be on the day Christ Jesus returns.

[NJB] <u>Philippians 1:6</u> I am quite confident that the One who began a good work in you will go on completing it until the Day of Jesus Christ comes.

[NLT] <u>Philippians 1:6</u> And I am certain that God, who began the good work within you, will continue his work until it is finally finished on the day when Christ Jesus returns.

[REM-NT] <u>Philippians 1:6</u> I am completely confident of this: God, who began his good work of healing and restoring you to his original ideal, will continue healing you right up to the day Jesus Christ returns to take us home.

[TGNT] <u>Philippians 1:6</u> And I am confident that the One who initiated a good work in you will keep making installments on it to the very Day of Anointed Jesus.

[TLB] <u>Philippians 1:6</u> And I am sure that God who began the good work within you will keep right on helping you grow in his grace until his task within you is finally finished on that day when Jesus Christ returns.

[TPT] <u>Philippians 1:6</u> I pray with great faith for you, because I'm fully convinced that the One who began this glorious work in you will faithfully continue the process of maturing you and will put his finishing touches to it until the unveiling of our Lord Jesus Christ!

[TTNT] <u>Philippians 1:6</u> This causes me to be confident that, because the Lord has begun such a good work in you, He will enable you to complete the purpose He has for you as you await the Lord Jesus Christ's return.

[TVB] <u>Philippians 1:6</u> I am confident that the Creator, who has begun such a great work among you, will not stop in mid-design but will keep perfecting you until the day Jesus the Anointed, our Liberating King, returns to redeem the world.

<u>Philippians 2:8-11</u> And being found in fashion as a man, he humbled himself, and became obedient unto death, even the death of the cross. [9]Wherefore God also hath highly exalted him, and given him a name which is above every name: [10]That at the name of Jesus every knee should bow, of things in heaven, and things in earth, and things under the earth; [11]And that every tongue should confess that Jesus Christ is Lord, to the glory of God the Father.

[Authentic-NT] <u>Philippians 2:8-11</u> and disclosed in physical appearance as a man, he abased himself, and became subject to death, death by the cross. [9]That is why God has so exalted him, [10]that at the name of Jesus every knee, heavenly, earthly and infernal, should bend, [11]and every tongue acclaim Jesus Christ as Master, to the glory of God the Father.

[AUV-NT 2003] <u>Philippians 2:8-11</u> He humbled Himself [by] becoming obedient [to God] to the point of death, even death on a cross. [9]Therefore, God also exalted Him to the highest position and gave Him the name, which is superior to every [other] name. [10][This was] so that, in [honor of] the name of Jesus, everyone's knee in heaven, on earth and under the earth should bow, [11]and that everyone's mouth should confess that Jesus Christ is Lord, to the glory of God the Father.

OUR HEALING COVENANT

[BV-NT] <u>Philippians 2:8-11</u> And after being found in an entity as a person, He put Himself down low when He became obedient up to death, a death from a cross. ⁹For this reason, God also put Him up high and in an act of generosity gave Him the name over every name, ¹⁰so that in the name of Jesus every knee would double over (of heavenly beings, of earthly beings, and of underground beings) ¹¹and every tongue would acknowledge out loud that Jesus is the Master, the Anointed King, for the magnificence of Father God.

[CCB] <u>Philippians 2:8-11</u> He humbled himself by being obedient to death, death on the cross. ⁹That is why God exalted him and gave him the Name which outshines all names, ¹⁰so that at the Name of Jesus all knees should bend in heaven, on earth and among the dead, ¹¹and all tongues proclaim that Christ Jesus is the Lord to the glory of God the Father.

[FBV-NT] <u>Philippians 2:8-11</u> Coming in human form, humbling himself, he submitted himself to death—even death on a cross. ⁹That's why God placed him in the position of greatest honor and power, and gave him the most prestigious name— ¹⁰so that in the name of Jesus everyone should bow in respect, whether in heaven or on earth or under the earth, ¹¹and all will declare that Jesus Christ is Lord, to the glory of God the Father.

[GNT] <u>Philippians 2:8-11</u> He was humble and walked the path of obedience all the way to death—his death on the cross. ⁹For this reason God raised him to the highest place above and gave him the name that is greater than any other name. ¹⁰And so, in honor of the name of Jesus all beings in heaven, on earth, and in the world below will fall on their knees, ¹¹and all will openly proclaim that Jesus Christ is Lord, to the glory of God the Father.

[Haweis-NT] <u>Philippians 2:8-11</u> and found in fashion as man, he humbled himself, becoming obedient to death, even to the death of the cross. ⁹Wherefore God also hath transcendently exalted him, and bestowed on him a name which is above every name: ¹⁰that to the name of Jesus every knee should bow, of beings celestial and terrestrial, and infernal; ¹¹and every tongue should confess that the Lord Jesus [is] Messiah, to the glory of God the Father.

[Mace-NT] <u>Philippians 2:8-11</u> and his whole exterior showing nothing more than a mere man, he abased himself, and carried his submission so far as to die, even the death of the cross. ⁹wherefore God has highly exalted and given him a name, which is above every name; ¹⁰that at the name of Jesus both angels and men, the living and the dead, should pay their adorations, ¹¹and that every nation should confess that Jesus Christ is the Lord, to the glory of God the father.

[Martin-NT] <u>Philippians 2:8-11</u> he rejected any status, becoming obedient to the point of death—even crucifixion. ⁹That's why God lifted him up, and gave him the name [title] that is above every name; ¹⁰so that in Jesus' name, every knee may bow—heavenly, earthly, or of the underworld— ¹¹and every tongue acknowledge the Lord Jesus Christ, for the glory of God the Father.

[MSG] <u>Philippians 2:8-11</u> Having become human, he stayed human. It was an incredibly humbling process. He didn't claim special privileges. Instead, he lived a selfless, obedient life and then died a selfless, obedient death—and the worst kind of death at that: a crucifixion. ⁹Because of that obedience, God lifted him high and honored him far beyond anyone or anything, ever, ¹⁰so that all created beings in heaven and on earth—even those long ago dead and buried—will bow in worship before this Jesus Christ, ¹¹and call out in praise that he is the Master of all, to the glorious honor of God the Father.

[NLV] <u>Philippians 2:8-11</u> After He became a man, He gave up His important place and obeyed by dying on a cross. ⁹Because of this, God lifted Jesus high above everything else. He gave Him a name that is greater than any other name. ¹⁰So when the name of Jesus is spoken, everyone in heaven and on earth and under the earth will bow down before Him. ¹¹And every tongue will say Jesus Christ is Lord. Everyone will give honor to God the Father.

[Phillips] Philippians 2:8-11 he humbled himself by living a life of utter obedience, to the point of death, and the death he died was the death of a common criminal. [9]That is why God has now lifted him to the heights, and has given him the name beyond all names, [10]so that at the name of Jesus 'every knee shall bow', whether in Heaven or earth or under the earth. [11]And that is why 'every tongue shall confess' that Jesus Christ is Lord, to the glory of God the Father.

[REM-NT] Philippians 2:8-11 And after becoming human, he voluntarily humbled himself to perfectly reveal God's character of love, choosing to love at all costs. He wouldn't even use his power to prevent his own death on the cross and thus he overcame selfishness with love! [9]This is why (because his love is without limit) God has exalted him to the highest place in all the universe and has given him a name of recognition and respect above any other, [10]so that at the name of Jesus, every intelligent being—whether in heaven or on earth—will bow in acknowledgement of his true character and worthiness, [11]and every intelligent being will confess that Jesus Christ is truly Lord—the eternal visible expression of God's glory and character.

[Stanhope-NT] Philippians 2:8-11 And stooping so very low, as to die, nay to die the most painful and ignominious Death, in obedience to his Heavenly Father's Will, and for the common benefit of Mankind. [9]This unparalleled Act of Obedience God hath rewarded, by advancing his human Nature to Universal Dominion. [10]That the Man Christ Jesus should now rule over, and be adored by, all Creatures; That all Nations should acknowledge this King, and by submitting to his Laws and Government, promote the Glory of God the Father; [11]Who delights to be honored in the Belief and Obedience, paid to his Blessed Son, and his Gospel.

[TPT] Philippians 2:8-11 He humbled himself and became vulnerable, choosing to be revealed as a man and was obedient. He was a perfect example, even in his death—a criminal's death by crucifixion! [9]Because of that obedience, God exalted him and multiplied his greatness! He has now been given the greatest of all names! [10]The authority of the name of Jesus causes every knee to bow in reverence! Everything and everyone will one day submit to this name—in the heavenly realm, in the earthly realm, and in the demonic realm. [11]And every tongue will proclaim in every language: "Jesus Christ is Lord Yahweh," bringing glory and honor to God, his Father!

[TTNT] Philippians 2:8-11 He was a man in every respect, even though He retained His divinity. Even so, He humbled Himself to such an extent that He obeyed the Father's will, that He should die the death of a criminal on the cross. [9]Because of His obedience, God the Father has now exalted Him to the highest place in heaven, and has given Him the name that is far superior to any other name. [10]Every knee in heaven, on earth and even in the underworld, will bow at the name of Jesus. [11]Every tongue will have to acknowledge that Jesus Christ is Lord, for this is the Father's glorious will.

[TVB] Philippians 2:8-11 He humbled Himself, obedient to death—a merciless death on the cross! [9]So God raised Him up to the highest place and gave Him the name above all. [10]So when His name is called, every knee will bow, in heaven, on earth, and below. [11]And every tongue will confess "Jesus, the Anointed One, is Lord," to the glory of God our Father!

[TWTY-RCT-NT-V1] Philippians 2:8-11 and being found and discovered by inspection and inquiry to be as and like the shape and form, figure and nature of man, He humbled Himself, ranking Himself below others, coming to be, appearing and arising as obedient continually until death and separation, the parting of the soul from the body, even death and separation on an upright stake. [9]So therefore, for this reason and for this purpose, God exalted, lifted and raised Him up to the highest position of honour, superiority and rank and graciously and freely bestowed, favourably granted and kindly gave Him the name and title, character and person, reputation and authority that is above and beyond every individual and collective name and title, character and person, reputation and authority, [10]so that and in order that in, by and with the name and title, character and person, reputation and authority of Yahushua, every individual and collective knee might bend and bow, in heaven, the abode of the Supreme One, and those that exist on and belong to the earth, and those in the underworld, the realm of the dead, ¹¹and every individual and collective tongue and language might confess and profess, acknowledge openly and joyfully praise and glorify concerning that Messiah Yahushua is the Sovereign Master for and on behalf of the glory and magnificence, excellence and pre-eminence, dignity and favour, honour and esteem, majesty and splendour of God the Father.

[UDB] <u>Philippians 2:8-11</u> And he humbled himself by taking on human form, and in his humility he obeyed Yahweh even though obedience to Yahweh meant he had to die, and he died a terrible death, the death of a criminal, death on the cross. ⁹Because of Messiah's obedience to him, Yahweh honored him very much; he honored him more than anyone else who has ever lived, ¹⁰so that when everyone hears the name "Jesus" everyone will bow down to honor him, people who are in heaven, and on earth, and under the earth; ¹¹so that everyone will say the same praises, that Jesus Messiah is Lord, and they will praise Yahweh the Father because of him.

[Wuest-NT] <u>Philippians 2:8-11</u> And being found to be in outward guise as man, He stooped very low, having become obedient [to God the Father] to the extent of death, even such a death as that upon a cross. ⁹Because of which voluntary act of supreme self-renunciation God also supereminently exalted Him to the highest rank and power, and graciously bestowed upon Him the Name, the name which is above every name, ¹⁰in order that in recognition of the Name [all which the Lord Jesus is in His Person and work] which Jesus possesses, every knee should bow, of things in heaven, of things on earth, and of things under the earth, ¹¹and in order that every tongue should plainly and openly agree to the fact that Jesus Christ is Lord, resulting in the glory of God the Father.

<u>Philippians 2:13</u> For it is God which worketh in you both to will and to do of his good pleasure.

[AMP] <u>Philippians 2:13</u> For it is [not your strength, but it is] God who is effectively at work in you, both to will and to work [that is, strengthening, energizing, and creating in you the longing and the ability to fulfill your purpose] for His good pleasure.

[Anchor] <u>Philippians 2:13</u> For the One at work in and among you is God, both to will and to work above and beyond goodwill.

[AUV-NT 2003] <u>Philippians 2:13</u> for it is God who is at work in you, both to motivate the desire and to carry out what pleases Him.

[Ballentine-NT] <u>Philippians 2:13</u> For it is God who is working in you both to will and to act in the interest of his kindly purpose.

[Berkeley] <u>Philippians 2:13</u> for God is the Energizer within you, so as to will and to work for His delight.

[Bowes-NT] <u>Philippians 2:13</u> For it is God who energizes in you both the willing and the energy for his good pleasure.

[BWE-NT] <u>Philippians 2:13</u> For God is at work in you. He helps you want to do it. And he helps you do what he wants you to do.

[CB] <u>Philippians 2:13</u> God is working through you to bring about His plans.

[CWB] <u>Philippians 2:13</u> always recognizing that it is God who is at work in you. He is the One who gives you the will and power to obey Him.

[GoodSpeed-NT] <u>Philippians 2:13</u> For it is God who in his good will is at work in your hearts, inspiring your will and your action.

[ICB] Philippians 2:13 Yes, God is working in you to help you want to do what pleases him. Then he gives you the power to do it.

[ISV] Philippians 2:13 For it is God who is producing in you both the desire and the ability to do what pleases him.

[KNT] Philippians 2:13 After all, God himself is the one who's at work among you, who provides both the will and the energy to enable you to do what pleases him.

[Mace-NT] Philippians 2:13 for it is God that influences your desires and endeavours, out of his benevolence to you.

[Macknight-NT] Philippians 2:13 For it is God who inwardly worketh in you, from benevolence, both to will and to work effectually.

[Madsen-NT] Philippians 2:13 For it is God who awakens the will in you and who brings about the fulfilment so that everything can become good.

[NLT] Philippians 2:13 For God is working in you, giving you the desire and the power to do what pleases him.

[Phillips] Philippians 2:13 For it is God who is at work within you, giving you the will and the power to achieve his purpose.

[REM-NT] Philippians 2:13 because it is God himself working in you to heal, restore and recreate you perfectly in his image, enabling you to understand the truth and empowering you to do what is right—all in perfect harmony with his will.

[Shuttleworth-NT] Philippians 2:13 For you have God's own Spirit to assist your endeavors; which in its mercy can give you both will to attempt, and ability to perform.

[TLB] Philippians 2:13 For God is at work within you, helping you want to obey him, and then helping you do what he wants.

[Tomson-NT] Philippians 2:13 For it is God which worketh in you both the will and the deed, even of his good pleasure.

[TVB] Philippians 2:13 because God is energizing you so that you will desire and do what always pleases Him.

[UDB] Philippians 2:13 For Yahweh is working in your hearts so that you will want to do and then actually do the good things that please him.

[Way-NT] Philippians 2:13 You have not to do it in your unaided strength: it is God who is all the while supplying the impulse, giving you the power to resolve, the strength to perform, the execution of His good-pleasure.

[Whiting-NT] Philippians 2:13 For it is God, who of his own good pleasure, worketh in you both to will and to act.

Philippians 2:27,30 For indeed he [Epaphroditus] was sick nigh unto death: but God had mercy on him; and not on him only, but on me also, lest I should have sorrow upon sorrow. **³⁰Because for the work of Christ he was nigh unto death**, not regarding his life, to supply your lack of service toward me.

Epaphroditus nearly worked himself to death. There was no direct sin involved; yet we can push our bodies beyond their natural ability and die early. The Lord intervened through His kindness, but the fix was a simple natural fix—rest an appropriate amount because even Jesus rested when He was on the earth.

[Besorah] Philippians 2:27,30 For indeed he was sick, near to death, but Elohim had compassion on him and not only on him but on me as well, lest I should have sadness upon sadness. **³⁰because for**

the work of Messiah he was near death, risking his life, to fill up what was lacking in your service toward me.

[BV-KJV-NT] <u>Philippians 2:27,30</u> (you see, he actually was weak, near to death, but God showed forgiving kindness to him, not only to him, but also to me, so that I would not have sadness on sadness). **30because he was near up to the point of death because of the work of the Anointed King when he exposed his soul** so that he might fill up what you lacked, the ministry to me.

[EEBT] <u>Philippians 2:27,30</u> **Certainly, he was very ill, and he almost died. But God was kind to him**. God was also kind to me, so that I was not even more sad. **30Epaphroditus nearly died because he worked for Christ**. He would have died so that he could help me. He helped me because you could not help me yourselves.

[LEB] <u>Philippians 2:27,30</u> **For indeed he was sick, coming near to death, but God had mercy on him** and not on him only, but also on me, so that I would not have grief upon grief. **30because on account of the work of Christ he came near to the point of death**, risking his life in order that he might make up for your inability to serve me.

[MCC-NT] <u>Philippians 2:27,30</u> **For He was indeed sick, next Door to Death; but God commiserated Him**; yet not Him only, but Me also; that I might not have Sorrow upon Sorrow. **30Because, for Christ's Work, He approached quite near to Death**; disregarding Life, that He might supply the Deficiency of your [personal] Service toward Me.

[NET] <u>Philippians 2:27,30</u> **In fact he [Epaphroditus] became so ill that he nearly died. But God showed mercy to him**—and not to him only, but also to me—so that I would not have grief on top of grief. **30since it was because of the work of Christ that he almost died**. He risked his life so that he could make up for your inability to serve me.

[NLV] <u>Philippians 2:27,30</u> **It is true, he [Epaphroditus] was sick. Yes, he almost died, but God showed loving-kindness to him** and to me. If he had died, I would have had even more sorrow. **30He came close to death while working for Christ**. He almost died doing things for me that you could not do.

[REM-NT] <u>Philippians 2:27,30</u> **And he was very sick and almost died, but God graciously intervened** and not only saved his life, but spared me much grief and sadness. **30He almost died promoting the message of Jesus, and most certainly risked his life** in order to provide me the help that distance kept you from providing.

[Sawyer-7590] <u>Philippians 2:27,30</u> **For indeed he was sick nigh to death; but God had mercy on him**, and not on him only but on me also, lest I should have sorrow upon sorrow. **30because on account of the work he was nigh to death**, not having consulted properly for his life, that he might fully supply your lack of service to me.

[TPT] <u>Philippians 2:27,30</u> **It's true he almost died, but God showed him mercy and healed him**. And I'm so thankful to God for his healing, as I was spared from having the sorrow of losing him on top of all my other troubles! **30Because of me, he put his life on the line**, despising the danger, so that he could provide for me with what you couldn't, since you were so far away. And he did it all because of his ministry for Christ.

[TTNT] <u>Philippians 2:27,30</u> **He was very sick and almost died; but God showed His mercy and healed him**. That was God showing mercy to me as well as him, to save me from any further sorrow on top of what I was already experiencing. **30It was because of his faithfulness to the work of Christ that he almost died**. He was prepared to risk his life to help me in ways you are unable to fulfil.

[TVB] Philippians 2:27,30 In fact, he nearly died. But once again, God was exceedingly kind and covered him with His mercy. And I, too, by His mercy, have been spared sorrow on top of sorrow. [30]**because he placed his life in grave danger for the work of the Anointed**; he risked his life to serve me when you couldn't.

[YLT] Philippians 2:27,30 for he [Epaphroditus] also ailed nigh to death, but God did deal kindly with him, and not with him only, but also with me, that sorrow upon sorrow I might not have. [30]**because on account of the work of the Christ he drew near to death,** having hazarded the life that he might fill up your deficiency of service unto me.

Philippians 4:6-8 Be careful for nothing; but in every thing by prayer and supplication with thanksgiving let your requests be made known unto God. [7]And the peace of God, which passeth all understanding, shall keep your hearts and minds through Christ Jesus. [8]Finally, brethren, whatsoever things are true, whatsoever things are honest, whatsoever things are just, whatsoever things are pure, whatsoever things are lovely, whatsoever things are of good report; if there be any virtue, and if there be any praise, think on these things.

[AMP] Philippians 4:6-8 Do not be anxious or worried about anything, but in everything [every circumstance and situation] by prayer and petition with thanksgiving, continue to make your [specific] requests known to God. [7]And the peace of God [that peace which reassures the heart, that peace] which transcends all understanding, [that peace which] stands guard over your hearts and your minds in Christ Jesus [is yours]. [8]Finally, believers, whatever is true, whatever is honorable and worthy of respect, whatever is right and confirmed by God's word, whatever is pure and wholesome, whatever is lovely and brings peace, whatever is admirable and of good repute; if there is any excellence, if there is anything worthy of praise, think continually on these things [center your mind on them, and implant them in your heart].

[AMPC] Philippians 4:6-8 Do not fret or have any anxiety about anything, but in every circumstance and in everything, by prayer and petition (definite requests), with thanksgiving, continue to make your wants known to God. [7]And God's peace [shall be yours, that tranquil state of a soul assured of its salvation through Christ, and so fearing nothing from God and being content with its earthly lot of whatever sort that is, that peace] which transcends all understanding shall garrison and mount guard over your hearts and minds in Christ Jesus. [8]For the rest, brethren, whatever is true, whatever is worthy of reverence and is honorable and seemly, whatever is just, whatever is pure, whatever is lovely and lovable, whatever is kind and winsome and gracious, if there is any virtue and excellence, if there is anything worthy of praise, think on and weigh and take account of these things [fix your minds on them].

[AUV-NT 2005] Philippians 4:6-8 Do not worry about anything, but in everything, by prayer and [special] petition, along with thanksgivings, you should make your requests known to God. [7]And [when you do], the peace from God, which surpasses all comprehension, will guard your hearts and thoughts [from anxiety] in [fellowship with] Christ Jesus. [8]Finally, brothers, give [careful] thought to these things: Whatever is true, whatever is noble, whatever is right, whatever is pure, whatever is lovable, and whatever is commendable. If it is excellent; if it is praiseworthy; [think about it].

[Beck] Philippians 4:6-8 Don't worry about anything, but in everything go to God, and pray to let Him know what you want, and give thanks. [7]Then God's peace, better than all our thinking, will guard your hearts and minds in Christ Jesus. [8]Finally, my fellow Christians, keep your minds on all that is true or noble, right or pure, lovely or appealing, on anything that is excellent or that deserves praise.

[Berkeley] Philippians 4:6-8 Entertain no worry, but under all circumstances let your petitions be made known before God by prayer and pleading along with thanksgiving. [7]So shall the peace of God, that surpasses all understanding, keep guard over your hearts and your thoughts in Christ Jesus.

[8]Furthermore, brothers, whatever is true, whatever is honorable, whatever is just, whatever is lovely, whatever is kindly spoken, whatever is lofty and whatever is praise-worthy, put your mind on these.

[BLE] <u>Philippians 4:6-8</u> Do not worry over anything, but in everything let the things you have to ask for be made known to God by prayer and petition with thanksgiving. [7]And God's peace beyond the highest reach of any mind will guard your hearts and thoughts in Christ Jesus. [8]For the rest, brothers, as many things as are true, as are worthy, as are honest, as are pure, as are lovable, as would sound well to speak of, whatever there is of virtue and whatever there is for praise, take account of these things;

[BV-KJV-NT] <u>Philippians 4:6-8</u> Worry about nothing, but in everything by the prayer and the plea with thankfulness, your requests must be made known to God. [7]And the peace of God, that has a higher position than every way of thinking, will guard your hearts and your thought processes in the Anointed King Jesus. [8]For the rest of the time, brothers, as many things as are true, as many as are respectful, as many as are right, as many as are consecrated, as many as are friendly, as many as are good sounding, if there is any achievement and if there is any praise, consider these things.

[BWE-NT] <u>Philippians 4:6-8</u> Do not worry about anything. Talk to God about everything. Thank him for what you have. Ask him for what you need. [7]Then God will give you peace, a peace which is too wonderful to understand. That peace will keep your hearts and minds safe as you trust in Christ Jesus. [8]Here, my brothers, are some things I want you to think about. Think about things that are true, honest, right, clean and pure, things that are lovely, and things that are good to talk about. If they are good, and if they bring praise to God, think about these things.

[CEB] <u>Philippians 4:6-8</u> Don't be anxious about anything; rather, bring up all of your requests to God in your prayers and petitions, along with giving thanks. [7]Then the peace of God that exceeds all understanding will keep your hearts and minds safe in Christ Jesus. [8]From now on, brothers and sisters, if anything is excellent and if anything is admirable, focus your thoughts on these things: all that is true, all that is holy, all that is just, all that is pure, all that is lovely, and all that is worthy of praise.

[CEV] <u>Philippians 4:6-8</u> Don't worry about anything, but pray about everything. With thankful hearts offer up your prayers and requests to God. [7]Then, because you belong to Christ Jesus, God will bless you with peace that no one can completely understand. And this peace will control the way you think and feel. [8]Finally, my friends, keep your minds on whatever is true, pure, right, holy, friendly, and proper. Don't ever stop thinking about what is truly worthwhile and worthy of praise.

[Doddridge-NT] <u>Philippians 4:6-8</u> In the mean time, whatever necessities or whatever oppressions may arise, be anxious about nothing, so as to disquiet or distress your minds; but in every thing that occurs, in every condition and on every occasion, let your petitions be made known, and breathed out before God, in humble prayer and fervent supplication, to be still mingled with thanksgiving, as there is always room for praise, and always occasion for it, even in circumstances of the greatest affliction and distress. [7]And if you exercise such a temper, the peace which the blessed Spirit of God diffuses over the souls of his people, that peace which far surpasses all understanding, which none can conceive but he who feels it, and which none can feel but by divine communication, shall guard and defend your hearts and your minds in Christ Jesus, so that nothing shall be able to break in upon that sweet and sacred tranquility. [8]As for what remains, my brethren, let me despatch it in a few words. Be always intent on raising your characters to the greatest height you possibly can: whatever things are true and sincere, whatever things [are] grave and venerable, whatever things [are] righteous and equitable, whatever things [are] chaste and pure, whatever things [are] friendly and kind, whatever things [are] reputable and truly ornamental, if [there be] any real virtue in them, and if [there be] any just praise resulting from them, think frequently of these things, consider what they are, how highly you are obliged to regard them, and endeavour more and more to abound in the practice of them.

[FBV-NT] <u>Philippians 4:6-8</u> Don't worry about anything, but take everything to God in prayer, explaining your requests to him and thanking him for all he does. [7]Then the peace that comes from God, which is better than we can ever imagine, will keep your hearts and minds protected in Christ Jesus. [8]Lastly, whatever is true, honorable, right, pure, beautiful, commendable, whatever is truly good and deserves to be praised, think about these kinds of things.

[Harwood-NT] <u>Philippians 4:6-8</u> Suffer not your minds to be corroded with anxious cares about any thing: in every situation of life do you, with fervent prayer and devout gratitude, address your petitions to the Supreme. [7]And that immense goodness of Deity, which he hath displayed to the heathen world, which infinitely transcends all of our most enlarged conceptions, will maintain your hearts and minds in an inviolable attachment to your Christian principles. [8]Finally, my Christian brethren, whatever things are true, whatever venerable, whatever equitable, whatever pure, whatever amiable, whatever commendable, if there is any thing virtuous, any thing laudable, let this engage your attention and culture:

[Haweis-NT] <u>Philippians 4:6-8</u> Be not anxious about any thing, but in every case by prayer and supplication, with thanksgiving, let your petitions be made known unto God. [7]And the peace of God which surpasseth all comprehension, shall guard your hearts and minds in Christ Jesus. [8]Finally, brethren, whatsoever things are true, whatsoever things are serious, whatsoever things are just, whatsoever things are pure, whatsoever things are amiable, whatsoever things are laudable, if there be any virtue, or any thing praise-worthy, pay attention to these things.

[ICB] <u>Philippians 4:6-8</u> Do not worry about anything. But pray and ask God for everything you need. And when you pray, always give thanks. [7]And God's peace will keep your hearts and minds in Christ Jesus. The peace that God gives is so great that we cannot understand it. [8]Brothers, continue to think about the things that are good and worthy of praise. Think about the things that are true and honorable and right and pure and beautiful and respected.

[Jerusalem] <u>Philippians 4:6-8</u> There is no need to worry; but if there is anything you need, pray for it, asking God for it with prayer and thanksgiving, [7]and that peace of God, which is so much greater than we can understand, will guard your hearts and your thoughts, in Christ Jesus. [8]Finally, brothers, fill your minds with everything that is true, everything that is noble, everything that is good and pure, everything that we love and honour, and everything that can be thought virtuous or worthy of praise.

[KNT] <u>Philippians 4:6-8</u> Don't worry about anything. Rather, in every area of life let God know what you want, as you pray and make requests, and give thanks as well. [7]And God's peace, which is greater than we can ever understand, will keep guard over your hearts and minds in King Jesus. [8]For the rest, my dear family, these are the things you should think through: whatever is true, whatever is holy, whatever is upright, whatever is pure, whatever is attractive, whatever has a good reputation; anything virtuous, anything praiseworthy.

[Madsen-NT] <u>Philippians 4:6-8</u> Let no anxiety take root in your hearts, but let your concerns in all things be known to God by sending your thankful thoughts upwards in supplication and prayer. [7]And the peace of God which transcends anything that the intellect can grasp will keep safe your hearts and thoughts in the Being of Christ. [8]And lastly, dear brothers, I say to you: all that is true, all that is worthy of reverence, all that is good and holy, all that is lovely to look at and beautiful to hear, all that has virtue and all that deserves praise: let these be the content of your thinking.

[MSG] <u>Philippians 4:6-8</u> Don't fret or worry. Instead of worrying, pray. Let petitions and praises shape your worries into prayers, letting God know your concerns. [7]Before you know it, a sense of God's wholeness, everything coming together for good, will come and settle you down. It's wonderful what happens when Christ displaces worry at the center of your life. [8]Summing it all up, friends, I'd say you'll do best by filling your minds and meditating on things true, noble, reputable, authentic, compelling, gracious—the best, not the worst; the beautiful, not the ugly; things to praise, not things to curse.

[NEB] <u>Philippians 4:6-8</u> The Lord is near; have no anxiety, but in everything make your requests known to God in prayer and petition with thanksgiving. [7]Then the peace of God, which is beyond our utmost understanding, will keep guard over your hearts and your thoughts, in Christ Jesus. [8]And now, my friends, all that is true, all that is noble, all that is just and pure, all that is lovable and gracious, whatever is excellent and admirable fill all your thoughts with these things.

[NOG] <u>Philippians 4:6-8</u> Never worry about anything. But in every situation let God know what you need in prayers and requests while giving thanks. [7]Then God's peace, which goes beyond anything we can imagine, will guard your thoughts and emotions through Christ Yeshua. [8]Finally, brothers and sisters, keep your thoughts on whatever is right or deserves praise: things that are true, honorable, fair, pure, acceptable, or commendable.

[Phillips] <u>Philippians 4:6-8</u> Don't worry over anything whatever; whenever you pray tell God every detail of your needs in thankful prayer, [7]and the peace of God, which surpasses human understanding, will keep constant guard over your hearts and minds as they rest in Christ Jesus. [8]My brothers I need only add this. If you believe in goodness and if you value the approval of God, fix your minds on whatever is true and honourable and just and pure and lovely and admirable.

[REAL] <u>Philippians 4:6-8</u> Do not be anxious for anything, but make your requests known to God in everything, through worship and petition and giving thanks, [7]and God's peace, that is superior to all understanding, is going to protect your hearts and minds in Anointed Jesus. [8]Finally, brothers, whatever is true, whatever is honest, whatever is right, whatever is pure, whatever is friendly, whatever is of good reputation—if there is any virtue, and if there is any praise, take an inventory of these things.

[Stevens-NT] <u>Philippians 4:6-8</u> Be not distracted by anxious care, but in prayer and praise commit your wants and desires to God. [7]And the peace which God bestows, which, more than all human reasoning or forethought brings rest to the soul, will guard your hearts and thoughts in Christ Jesus. [8]Finally, brethren, whatever is worthy of reverence, true, just, pure, lovely, and fair, —in short, whatever moral excellence there is, and whatever praise it deserves, carefully reflect upon it. Observe my instruction and example, and God shall bless you with his peace.

[T4T] <u>Philippians 4:6-8</u> Do not worry about anything. Instead, in every situation, pray to God, tell him what you need, and ask him to help you. Also thank him for what he does for you. [7]As a result, God will enable you not to worry about anything (OR, God will protect your minds in every way). That is, he will cause you to have inner peace because you have a relationship with Christ Jesus. You will not be able to understand how you can be so peaceful in such difficult circumstances! [8]My fellow believers, there is one more thing I want you to do. Whatever is true, whatever is worthy of respect, whatever is right, whatever is morally pure, whatever is pleasing, whatever is admirable, whatever is good, whatever deserves praise, those are the things that you should continually think about.

[TLB] <u>Philippians 4:6-8</u> Don't worry about anything; instead, pray about everything; tell God your needs, and don't forget to thank him for his answers. [7]If you do this, you will experience God's peace, which is far more wonderful than the human mind can understand. His peace will keep your thoughts and your hearts quiet and at rest as you trust in Christ Jesus. [8]And now, brothers, as I close this letter, let me say this one more thing: Fix your thoughts on what is true and good and right. Think about things that are pure and lovely, and dwell on the fine, good things in others. Think about all you can praise God for and be glad about.

[TPT] <u>Philippians 4:6-8</u> Don't be pulled in different directions or worried about a thing. Be saturated in prayer throughout each day, offering your faith-filled requests before God with overflowing gratitude. Tell him every detail of your life, [7]then God's wonderful peace that transcends human understanding, will make the answers known to you through Jesus Christ. [8]So keep your thoughts continually fixed on all that is authentic and real, honorable and admirable, beautiful and respectful, pure and holy, merciful and kind. And fasten your thoughts on every glorious work of God, praising him always.

[Way-NT] <u>Philippians 4:6-8</u> Let no anxieties fret you: nay, in every matter let the things you would ask be made known by means of prayer—by definite requests—linked with thanksgiving, at God's throne. [7]And so the peace that God gives, the peace that transcends all conception, shall be the fortress-warder of your hearts, of all your thoughts, in this your life in Messiah Jesus. [8]Finally, brothers, what things soever are true, what things soever claim respect, are just, are pure, are winsome, are in fair repute—all that is virtuous, all that wins praise—be these alone the things whereof you take account.

[Williams-NT] <u>Philippians 4:6-8</u> Stop being worried about anything, but always, in prayer and entreaty, and with thanksgiving, keep on making your wants known to God. [7]Then, through your union with Christ Jesus, the peace of God, that surpasses all human thought, will keep guard over your hearts and thoughts. [8]Now, brothers, practice thinking on what is true, what is honorable, what is right, what is pure, what is lovable, what is high-toned, yes, on everything that is excellent or praiseworthy.

[WTNT] <u>Philippians 4:6-8</u> Do not worry about anything, but in everything, by prayer and petition with thanksgiving, let your requests be known to God. [7]And the peace of God that transcends all our dreams will guard your hearts and your thoughts in Christ Jesus. [8]Finally, brothers, whatever is true, whatever is noble, whatever is pure, whatever is lovely, whatever is praiseworthy, yes, on moral excellence and praise—let your thoughts dwell.

[Wuest-NT] <u>Philippians 4:6-8</u> Stop worrying about even one thing, but in everything by prayer whose essence is that of worship and devotion and by supplication which is a cry for your personal needs, with thanksgiving let your requests for the things asked for be made known in the presence of God, [7]and the peace of God which surpasses all power of comprehension shall mount guard over your hearts and minds in Christ Jesus. [8]Finally, brethren, whatever things have the character of truth, whatever things are worthy of reverence, whatever things are righteous, whatever things are pure, whatever things are lovely, whatever things are attractive, whatever excellence there is or fit object of praise, these things make the subject of careful reflection.

COLOSSIANS

<u>Colossians 1:12-13</u> Giving thanks unto the Father, which hath made us meet to be partakers of the inheritance of the saints in light: [13]Who hath delivered us from the power of darkness, and hath translated us into the kingdom of his dear Son:

The power or authority of darkness is where sickness and disease come from. If we have been delivered from its authority, then we have also been delivered or set free from sickness and disease.

[ACV] <u>Colossians 1:12-13</u> Giving thanks to the Father who made us qualified for the share of the portion of the sanctified in light. [13]Who rescued us out of the power of darkness, and transferred us into the kingdom of the Son of his love,

[AMPC] <u>Colossians 1:12-13</u> Giving thanks to the Father, Who has qualified and made us fit to share the portion which is the inheritance of the saints (God's holy people) in the Light. [13][The Father] has delivered and drawn us to Himself out of the control and the dominion of darkness and has transferred us into the kingdom of the Son of His love,

[Authentic-NT] <u>Colossians 1:12-13</u> I give thanks to the Father, who has qualified you to share the lot of the saints in Light, [13]who has rescued us from the dominion of Darkness and transferred us to the Kingdom of his dear Son,

[AUV-NT 2003] <u>Colossians 1:12-13</u> [May you] give thanks to the Father who has enabled you to share in the inheritance of the saints in [the kingdom of] light. [13]He rescued us from the domain of [spiritual] darkness and transferred us into the kingdom of the Son whom He loves,

[BBE] <u>Colossians 1:12-13</u> Giving praise to the Father who has given us a part in the heritage of the saints in light; [13]Who has made us free from the power of evil and given us a place in the kingdom of the Son of his love;

[CLV] <u>Colossians 1:12-13</u> at the same time giving thanks to the Father, Who makes you competent for a part of the allotment of the saints, in light, [13]Who rescues us out of the jurisdiction of Darkness, and transports us into the kingdom of the Son of His love,

[DLNT] <u>Colossians 1:12-13</u> giving-thanks to the Father having qualified you for your part of the share of the saints in the light, [13]Who delivered us out of the authority of darkness and transferred us into the kingdom of the Son of His love,

[FBV-NT] <u>Colossians 1:12-13</u> May you happily praise the Father, who has made it possible for us to share in the inheritance of God's people who live in the light. [13]He rescued us from the tyranny of darkness and brought us into the kingdom of the Son he loves,

[Haweis-NT] <u>Colossians 1:12-13</u> giving thanks to God, even the Father, who hath made us meet for a portion in the inheritance of the saints in light; [13]who hath plucked us out from the dominion of darkness, and transferred us into the kingdom of the Son of his love:

[KJC-NT] <u>Colossians 1:12-13</u> Giving thanks unto the Father, which has made us suitable to be partakers of the inheritance of the saints in light: [13]Who has delivered us from the power of darkness, and has translated us into the kingdom of his dear Son:

[KNT] <u>Colossians 1:12-13</u> And I pray that you will learn to give thanks to the father, who has made you fit to share the inheritance of God's holy ones in the light. [13]He has delivered us from the power of darkness, and transferred us into the kingdom of his beloved son.

[Magiera-NT] <u>Colossians 1:12-13</u> you should give thanks to God the Father, who has made us worthy for a portion of the inheritance of the holy [ones] in light [13]and has delivered us from the authority of darkness and has transferred us to the kingdom of his beloved Son,

[MLV] <u>Colossians 1:12-13</u> giving-thanks to the Father, who made us sufficient for the part of the inheritance of the holy-ones in the light. [13]He rescued us out of the authority of darkness and transplanted us into the kingdom of the Son of his love;

[MSG] <u>Colossians 1:12-13</u> thanking the Father who makes us strong enough to take part in everything bright and beautiful that he has for us. [13]God rescued us from dead-end alleys and dark dungeons. He's set us up in the kingdom of the Son he loves so much,

[NASB] <u>Colossians 1:12-13</u> giving thanks to the Father, who has qualified us to share in the inheritance of the saints in Light. [13]For He rescued us from the domain of darkness, and transferred us to the kingdom of His beloved Son,

[NENT] <u>Colossians 1:12-13</u> and at the same time giving thanks with joy to that Father who equipped us for the inheritance of the holy ones in the light, [13]who rescued us from the authority of the darkness and changed our standing into the kingdom of the son of his love.

[NIRV] <u>Colossians 1:12-13</u> We want you to give thanks with joy to the Father. He has made you fit to have what he will give to all his holy people. You will all receive a share in the kingdom of light. [13]He has saved us from the kingdom of darkness. He has brought us into the kingdom of the Son he loves.

[Phillips] <u>Colossians 1:12-13</u> You will be able to thank the Father because you are privileged to share the lot of the saints who are living in the light. [13]For he rescued us from the power of darkness, and re-established us in the kingdom of his beloved Son.

[SENT] <u>Colossians 1:12-13</u> You'll be thanking the Father in the midst of it for equipping you to have a part in this calling—the calling of the holy ones who live in the light. [13]The Father has saved us from the realm of darkness, and has moved us over into the kingdom of his dear Son.

[TCNT] <u>Colossians 1:12-13</u> And you will give thanks to the Father who made you fit to share the lot which awaits Christ's People in the realms of Light. [13]For God has rescued us from the tyranny of Darkness, and has removed us into the Kingdom of his Son, who is the embodiment of his love,

[TGNT] <u>Colossians 1:12-13</u> with joy. We thank the Father, who qualifies you for your portion of the inheritance of those who are holy and in the light, [13]and who rescued us out of the jurisdiction of darkness and moved us into the kingdom of the Son he loves—

[TTNT] <u>Colossians 1:12-13</u> thanking God the Father for all He has done in you. Yes, it is His work in you that means you are now qualified to share in the inheritance He has prepared for all those He has called and set apart to belong to the Kingdom of light. [13]For He has already rescued us from the devil's dominion of darkness and has brought us into His own Kingdom, the Kingdom that belongs to the Son He loves.

[UDB] <u>Colossians 1:12-13</u> We pray that you will be rejoicing and thanking Yahweh our Father, because he has declared you worthy to be with the others whom he has set apart for himself; this is so he can give you all the things that he is keeping for you when you are with him in the light of his presence. [13]Yahweh our Father has rescued us from the evil that controlled us; he has made his Son, whom he loves, to rule over us now.

[Wand-NT] <u>Colossians 1:12-13</u> giving thanks the while to the Father who has made it possible for you to claim your share of the inheritance with the Saints in the Kingdom of Light. [13]It was He who rescued us out of the power of darkness and established us as citizens in the Kingdom of His beloved Son

[YLT] <u>Colossians 1:12-13</u> Giving thanks to the Father who did make us meet for the participation of the inheritance of the saints in the light, [13]who did rescue us out of the authority of the darkness, and did translate [us] into the reign of the Son of His love,

<u>Colossians 2:10</u> And ye are complete in him, which is the head of all principality and power:

[Barclay-NT] <u>Colossians 2:10</u> It is in your union with him that your life reaches perfected completeness. He is supreme over every demonic power and authority.

[CJB] <u>Colossians 2:10</u> And it is in union with him that you have been made full—he is the head of every rule and authority.

[Douay-Rheims-Peters] <u>Colossians 2:10</u> And you are in him replenished, who is the head in all Principality and Power:

[ERV] <u>Colossians 2:10</u> And because you belong to Christ you are complete, having everything you need. Christ is ruler over every other power and authority.

[EWG-NT] <u>Colossians 2:10</u> and in him ye are made full, who is the head of all principality and power:

[ICB] <u>Colossians 2:10</u> And in him you have a full and true life. He is ruler over all rulers and powers.

[JLDavies-NT] <u>Colossians 2:10</u> and you are in him fulfilled, who is the head of all principality and power,

[Knox] <u>Colossians 2:10</u> and it is in him that you find your completion; he is the fountain head from which all dominion and power proceed.

[Lamsa] <u>Colossians 2:10</u> And it is through him that you also have been made complete, for he is the head of all angelic orders and powers,

[Moffatt-NT 1917] <u>Colossians 2:10</u> it is in him that you reach your full life, and he is the Head of every angelic Ruler and Power;

[NEB] <u>Colossians 2:10</u> and in him you have been brought to completion. Every power and authority in the universe is subject to him as Head.

[Norlie-NT] <u>Colossians 2:10</u> And you have come to fulness of life through union with Him who is the fountainhead of all authority and power.

[Numerical] <u>Colossians 2:10</u> and in him ye are filled up; who is the head of all principality and authority;

[Phillips] <u>Colossians 2:10</u> More-over, your own completeness is realised in him, who is the ruler over all authorities, and the supreme head over all powers.

[Sawyer-7620] <u>Colossians 2:10</u> And you are complete in him, who is the head of every empire and authority,

[TLB] <u>Colossians 2:10</u> so you have everything when you have Christ, and you are filled with God through your union with Christ. He is the highest Ruler, with authority over every other power.

[TPT] <u>Colossians 2:10</u> And our own completeness is now found in him. We are completely filled with God as Christ's fullness overflows within us. He is the Head of every kingdom and authority in the universe!

[TWTY-RCT-NT-V1] <u>Colossians 2:10</u> Also, in, by and with Him all of you are and exist as fully complete and richly supplied, perfectly imbued with power, influence and energy, for He is and exists as the head, the supreme and most prominent cornerstone of all creation, the foundation and chief builder from the origin and beginning of time and the one with unlimited authority and power, right and ability.

[Wade] <u>Colossians 2:10</u> and in Him, Who is the Head of every Angelic Ruler and Authority, you have attained to the fulness of your Spiritual development.

[WMB] <u>Colossians 2:10</u> and in him you are made full, who is the head of all principality and power.

[Wuest-NT] <u>Colossians 2:10</u> And you are in Him, having been completely filled full with the present result that you are in a state of fullness, in Him who is the Head of every principality and authority,

<u>Colossians 2:15</u> And having spoiled principalities and powers, he made a shew of them openly, triumphing over them in it.

[AMP] <u>Colossians 2:15</u> When He had disarmed the rulers and authorities [those supernatural forces of evil operating against us], He made a public example of them [exhibiting them as captives in His triumphal procession], having triumphed over them through the cross.

[AMPC] <u>Colossians 2:15</u> [God] disarmed the principalities and powers that were ranged against us and made a bold display and public example of them, in triumphing over them in Him and in it [the cross].

[Authentic-NT] <u>Colossians 2:15</u> After having despoiled the angelic Rulers and Authorities, he paraded them in public, having led them in triumph by the cross.

[AUV-NT 2003] <u>Colossians 2:15</u> [In doing this] Christ disarmed the rulers and authorities and made a public display of them, triumphing over them through the cross.

[Ballentine-NT] <u>Colossians 2:15</u> He has rid himself of all the powers of evil and has held them up to open contempt by triumphing over them on the cross.

[Beck] <u>Colossians 2:15</u> He stripped rulers and powers of their armor and made a public show of them as He triumphed over them in Christ.

[Berkeley] <u>Colossians 2:15</u> and, disarming the princes and authorities, He publicly exposed them to disgrace as He personally triumphed over them.

[CCB] <u>Colossians 2:15</u> Victorious through the cross, he stripped the rulers and authorities of their power, humbled them before the eyes of the whole world and dragged them behind him as prisoners.

[ClarkePyle] <u>Colossians 2:15</u> And by the same sufferings on the cross, has made Christ the conqueror of sin and Satan, depriving them of their former wicked power and influences over mankind, and leading them, as it were, captives in triumph.

[Erasmus-NT] <u>Colossians 2:15</u> Nor is there any reason for us to fear the tyranny of Satan after Christ on the cross conquered, through his own death, death's source, by recovering us like glorious spoils snatched away from demonic principalities and powers over which he triumphed when he had conquered them. For then did he frankly and openly display them not only to men but also to angels when he had vanquished and indeed despoiled them, carrying them in a triumph, as it were; and displaying his adversaries ruined and shattered, not through the help of angels or men, but by his own power, he hung upon the cross such a magnificent trophy that from high above it was visible to all.

[ERV] <u>Colossians 2:15</u> He defeated the rulers and powers of the spiritual world. With the cross he won the victory over them and led them away, as defeated and powerless prisoners for the whole world to see.

[FBV-NT] <u>Colossians 2:15</u> He stripped away the power of spiritual rulers and authorities, and having publicly revealed what they were truly like, he led them captive behind him in victory.

[JLDavies-NT] <u>Colossians 2:15</u> having stripped off principalities and powers he made a show of them confidently, triumphing over them in him.

[Knox] <u>Colossians 2:15</u> and the dominions and powers he robbed of their prey, put them to an open shame, led them away in triumph, through him.

[Macknight-NTc] <u>Colossians 2:15</u> Further, ye Gentiles are made complete by Christ, in respect of government and protection; for having spoiled evil angels of every denomination of their usurped power, Christ hath shewed them openly as vanquished, triumphing over them by his cross; so that ye need not be afraid of the devil, who formerly seduced and oppressed you.

[Moffatt] <u>Colossians 2:15</u> when he cut away the angelic Rulers and Powers from us, exposing them to all the world and triumphing over them in the cross.

[Montgomery-NT] <u>Colossians 2:15</u> Principalities and powers he disarmed, and openly displayed them as his trophies, when he triumphed over them in the cross.

[MSG] <u>Colossians 2:15</u> He stripped all the spiritual tyrants in the universe of their sham authority at the Cross and marched them naked through the streets.

[NEB] <u>Colossians 2:15</u> On that cross he discarded the cosmic powers and authorities like a garment; he made a public spectacle of them and led them as captives in his triumphal procession.

[Norlie-NT] <u>Colossians 2:15</u> So by the cross He disarmed the principalities and powers of evil; and in triumph He made a public spectacle of them.

[Noyes] <u>Colossians 2:15</u> and having disarmed principalities and powers, he made a public show of them, and led them captive in triumph in him.

[Phillips] <u>Colossians 2:15</u> And then, having drawn the sting of all the powers and authorities ranged against us, he exposed them, shattered, empty and defeated, in his own triumphant victory!

[REV-NT] <u>Colossians 2:15</u> He stripped naked the rulers and the authorities, and He (through him), made a public spectacle of them, leading them as captives in a Triumph procession.

[Sawyer-7590] <u>Colossians 2:15</u> [and] having subjugated principalities and powers, he made a public exhibition of them, leading them in triumph by it.

[Shuttleworth-NT] <u>Colossians 2:15</u> By these wondrous means has our blessed Redeemer stripped all the spiritual powers who were leagued for your destruction of their means of annoyance, and led them away in triumph.

[TPT] <u>Colossians 2:15</u> Then Jesus made a public spectacle of all the powers and principalities of darkness, stripping away from them every weapon and all their spiritual authority and power to accuse us. And by the power of the cross, Jesus led them around as prisoners in a procession of triumph. He was not their prisoner; they were his!

[Wand-NT] <u>Colossians 2:15</u> And at the same time he stripped away like a cast-off garment every demonic Rule and Authority and made a public exhibition of them, openly triumphing over them on the cross.

FIRST THESSALONIANS

<u>1 Thessalonians 5:23</u> And the very God of peace sanctify you wholly; and I pray God **your whole spirit and soul and body be preserved blameless** unto the coming of our Lord Jesus Christ.

The Lord is interested in our entire lives—spirit, soul, and body—not just our spirit.

[AUV-NT 2005] <u>1 Thessalonians 5:23</u> And may God Himself, who gives peace, dedicate you completely, and may **your spirit, soul and body [i.e., your entire person] be kept without just blame** at [i.e., until] the return of our Lord Jesus Christ.

[BLE] <u>1 Thessalonians 5:23</u> And may he, the God of peace, sanctify you to perfection, and **your spirits and souls and bodies be kept faultlessly safe and sound** at the coming of our Lord Jesus Christ.

[BWE-NT] <u>1 Thessalonians 5:23</u> May God himself, who gives peace, make you pure and clean. You are set apart and belong only to him. And **may your spirit and soul and body all together be kept free from fault** until our Lord Jesus Christ comes.

[CEB] <u>1 Thessalonians 5:23</u> Now, may the God of peace himself cause you to be completely dedicated to him; and **may your spirit, soul, and body be kept intact and blameless** at our Lord Jesus Christ's coming.

[Conybeare-NT] <u>1 Thessalonians 5:23</u> Now may the God of peace Himself sanctify you wholly; and **may your whole nature, your spirit and soul and body, be preserved blameless**, when you stand before our Lord Jesus Christ at His appearing.

[GNT] <u>1 Thessalonians 5:23</u> May the God who gives us peace make you holy in every way and **keep your whole being—spirit, soul, and body—free from every fault** at the coming of our Lord Jesus Christ.

[Knox] <u>1 Thessalonians 5:23</u> So may the God of peace sanctify you wholly, **keep spirit and soul and body unimpaired**, to greet the coming of our Lord Jesus Christ without reproach.

[MCC-NT] <u>1 Thessalonians 5:23</u> Then may the God of Peace Himself sanctify you quite perfectly; and may **your whole Frame, Spirit, Soul and Body, be preserved unblameable**, till our Lord Jesus Christ's Advent.

[MSG] <u>1 Thessalonians 5:23</u> May God himself, the God who makes everything holy and whole, make you holy and whole, **put you together—spirit, soul, and body—and keep you fit** for the coming of our Master, Jesus Christ.

[NASB] <u>1 Thessalonians 5:23</u> Now may the God of peace Himself sanctify you entirely; and **may your spirit and soul and body be preserved complete**, without blame at the coming of our Lord Jesus Christ.

[NCV] <u>1 Thessalonians 5:23</u> Now may God himself, the God of peace, make you pure, belonging only to him. **May your whole self—spirit, soul, and body—be kept safe and without fault** when our Lord Jesus Christ comes.

[NEB] <u>1 Thessalonians 5:23</u> May God himself, the God of peace, make you holy in every part, and **keep you sound in spirit, soul, and body, without fault** when our Lord Jesus Christ comes.

[Norlie-NT] <u>1 Thessalonians 5:23</u> May the God of peace himself sanctify you completely! And **may your spirit and soul and body be kept sound and without reproach** till the coming of our Lord Jesus Christ!

[OEB-NT] <u>1 Thessalonians 5:23</u> May God himself, the giver of peace, make you altogether holy; and **may your spirits, souls, and bodies be kept altogether faultless** until the coming of our Lord Jesus Christ.

[Smith] <u>1 Thessalonians 5:23</u> And the same God of peace consecrate you perfectly compete; and **your whole spirit and soul and body be kept faultless** to the arrival of our Lord Jesus Christ.

[TNT] <u>1 Thessalonians 5:23</u> May God himself, the giver of peace, make you entirely holy. **May he keep you undamaged, spirit, soul and body**, so that when our Lord Jesus Christ comes you will be blameless.

[TWTY-RCT-NT-V1] <u>1 Thessalonians 5:23</u> Now, may the God of peace and tranquillity, harmony and concord, security and safety, exemption from chaos, prosperity and freedom, felicity and the assurance of salvation Himself sanctify, cleanse and set you all apart through and through, wholly and completely, altogether and utterly, totally and entirely, perfectly and in every way, and **may the whole and complete, entire, total and every part of your spirit and soul and mortal body and flesh be kept and guarded, held on to and retained, attended to and maintained, kept an eye on and watched over, preserved and protected as faultless and blameless** at, by and with the presence and advent, coming and arrival of our Sovereign Master, Yahushua the Anointed Messiah.

[Wade] <u>1 Thessalonians 5:23</u> And may God Himself, the Source of Peace, make you perfectly holy; and **may each one's spirit, soul, and body be preserved in their integrity, free from all blame**, against the Coming of our Lord Jesus Christ.

SECOND THESSALONIANS

<u>2 Thessalonians 1:11</u> Wherefore also we pray always for you, that our God would count you worthy of this calling, and **fulfil all the good pleasure of his goodness, and the work of faith with power**:

OUR HEALING COVENANT

Surely it is a good desire to be well physically and if so, then healing can be accomplished with faith and with power.

[Anderson-Sinaitic NT] <u>2 Thessalonians 1:11</u> To which end also we pray always for you, that our God may count you worthy of the calling, and **fulfil all the good pleasure of goodness, and the work of faith in power**.

[Barclay-NT] <u>2 Thessalonians 1:11</u> Our constant prayer for you is that God will find you worthy of the invitation he sent to you, and that he may turn all your good intentions into action, and **powerfully help you to live the life that faith demands**.

[BLE] <u>2 Thessalonians 1:11</u> To this same end we are always praying for you that our God may deem you worthy to be called and **may potently bring to full realization every impulse of goodwill and work of faith,**

[BOOKS-NT] <u>2 Thessalonians 1:11</u> With this in mind, we constantly pray for you, that **our God may make you worthy of his calling, and that by his power he may bring to fruition your every desire for goodness** and your every deed prompted by faith.

[CEB] <u>2 Thessalonians 1:11</u> We are constantly praying for you for this: that our God will make you worthy of his calling and **accomplish every good desire and faithful work by his power.**

[CSB] <u>2 Thessalonians 1:11</u> In view of this, we always pray for you that our **God will make you worthy of his calling, and by his power fulfill your every desire to do good** and your work produced by faith,

[EWG-NT] <u>2 Thessalonians 1:11</u> To which end we also pray always for you, that our **God may count you worthy of your calling, and fulfill every desire of goodness and every work of faith, with power;**

[GNT] <u>2 Thessalonians 1:11</u> That is why we always pray for you. We ask our God to make you worthy of the life he has called you to live. **May he fulfill by his power all your desire for goodness and complete your work of faith.**

[Goodspeed-NT] <u>2 Thessalonians 1:11</u> To this end we always pray for you too, asking our God to find you worthy of the call he has given you, and **by his power to fulfil every desire you may have for goodness, and every effort of your faith,**

[Mace-NT] <u>2 Thessalonians 1:11</u> Wherefore we continually pray, that our God would **by his power effect all the gracious designs of his goodness, and accomplish the work of faith in you;**

[Madsen-NT] <u>2 Thessalonians 1:11</u> That is the aim of our unceasing prayer for you: that **the Godhead, who reigns over us, will make you worthy of HIS enduring call upon you, and that HE will fulfil all HIS will for good towards you, as well as making your faith effective and blessed with power;**

[Montgomery-NT] <u>2 Thessalonians 1:11</u> To this end I am making my constant prayer for you, beseeching God to make you worthy of your calling, and **to fulfil mightily every desire of goodness and effort of faith;**

[NEB] <u>2 Thessalonians 1:11</u> With this in mind we pray for you always, that our God may count you worthy of his calling, and **mightily bring to fulfilment every good purpose and every act inspired by faith,**

[NLT] <u>2 Thessalonians 1:11</u> So we keep on praying for you, asking our God to enable you to live a life worthy of his call. **May he give you the power to accomplish all the good things your faith prompts you to do.**

[OEB-NT] <u>2 Thessalonians 1:11</u> With this in view, our constant prayer for you is that our **God may count you worthy of the call that you have received, and by his power make perfect your delight in all goodness and the efforts that have resulted from your faith.**

[REM-NT] <u>2 Thessalonians 1:11</u> Understanding this reality, we keep your case before God: that he will restore you fully—**making you fit to live in his presence—and that he will fill all your ideas and efforts in spreading the Remedy with his power so that his kingdom will be promoted successfully.**

[Shuttleworth-NT] <u>2 Thessalonians 1:11</u> Wherefore we offer up our prayers continually for you that God would count you worthy of that glorious summons, and fulfill in you all the purposes of his grace and love, and **complete within you by his powerful assistance the workings of your faith.**

[TLB] <u>2 Thessalonians 1:11</u> And so we keep on praying for you, that our God will make you the kind of children he wants to have—**will make you as good as you wish you could be!—rewarding your faith with his power.**

[TTNT] <u>2 Thessalonians 1:11</u> We always pray for you along these lines, that our **God will consider you worthy of His calling; that by His power He may fulfil every one of your good intentions and the actions you undertake in faith.**

[Williams-NT] <u>2 Thessalonians 1:11</u> With this in view we are always praying for you too, that our God may make you worthy of His call, and **by His power fully satisfy your every desire for goodness, and complete every activity of your faith,**

[Wuest-NT] <u>2 Thessalonians 1:11</u> To which end also we are praying always for you, namely, that our God may count you worthy of the station in life to which He has called you, and **fulfill every delight [you Thessalonian saints have] in goodness and every work that finds its source in faith with power,**

FIRST TIMOTHY

<u>1 Timothy 5:23</u> Drink no longer water, but use a little wine for thy stomach's sake and thine often infirmities.

Sometimes, the Lord will give us supernatural revelation to change something in the natural realm to obtain our healing. It is still supernatural, and we thank God for the leading of the Holy Spirit.

[AMP] <u>1 Timothy 5:23</u> No longer continue drinking [only] water, but use a little wine for the sake of your stomach and your frequent illnesses.

[Barclay-NT] <u>1 Timothy 5:23</u> Don't go on drinking nothing but water. Use a little wine for the sake of your stomach and your frequent attacks of sickness.

[CCB] <u>1 Timothy 5:23</u> (Do not drink only water but take a little wine to help your digestion, because of your frequent illness.

[ERV] <u>1 Timothy 5:23</u> Timothy, stop drinking only water, and drink a little wine. This will help your stomach, and you will not be sick so often.

[GNT] <u>1 Timothy 5:23</u> Do not drink water only, but take a little wine to help your digestion, since you are sick so often.

[HRB] <u>1 Timothy 5:23</u> Do not drink water in excess, but use a little wine on account of your stomach and your frequent illnesses.

[ICB] <u>1 Timothy 5:23</u> Timothy, you stop drinking only water and drink a little wine. This will help your stomach, and you will not be sick so often.

[Jerusalem] <u>1 Timothy 5:23</u> You should give up drinking only water and have a little wine for the sake of your digestion and the frequent bouts of illness that you have.

[Knox] <u>1 Timothy 5:23</u> (No, do not confine thyself to water any longer; take a little wine to relieve thy stomach, and thy frequent attacks of illness.)

[Mace-NT] <u>1 Timothy 5:23</u> Discontinue the drinking of bare water, take a little wine out of regard to your weak stomach, and your frequent indispositions.

[NIRV] <u>1 Timothy 5:23</u> Stop drinking only water. If your stomach is upset, drink a little wine. It can also help the other sicknesses you often have.

[Phillips] <u>1 Timothy 5:23</u> (By the way, I should advise you to drink wine in moderation, instead of water. It will do your stomach good and help you to get over your frequent spells of illness.)

[REM-NT] <u>1 Timothy 5:23</u> As you travel, don't be so insistent on drinking water only—impure water may be causing many of your digestive problems. Drink a little wine, as it will often kill the contaminants and reduce your risk of sickness.

[Sindlinger-NT] <u>1 Timothy 5:23</u> By the way, I know you usually drink water, but it might be helpful to drink a little wine for your frequent ailments.

[TPT] <u>1 Timothy 5:23</u> (If drinking the water causes you to have stomach ailments, drink some wine instead.)

[TVB] <u>1 Timothy 5:23</u> Concerning your health, Timothy, don't just drink water; drink a little wine. It is good for your stomach and will help with your frequent ailments.

[Williams-NT] <u>1 Timothy 5:23</u> Stop drinking water only, but take a little wine to strengthen your stomach and relieve its frequent attacks.

<u>1 Timothy 6:12</u> **Fight the good fight of faith,** lay hold on eternal life[zoé], whereunto thou art also called, and hast professed a good profession before many witnesses.

[Barclay-NT] <u>1 Timothy 6:12</u> **Strain every nerve, as the noble athlete of faith,** to win the prize of eternal life. It was to this you were called, when you nobly and publicly confessed your faith in the presence of many witnesses.

[BSB-NT] <u>1 Timothy 6:12</u> **Fight the good fight of the faith.** Take hold of the eternal life to which you were called when you made the good confession before many witnesses.

[GoodSpeed-NT] <u>1 Timothy 6:12</u> **Enter the great contest of faith!** Take hold of eternal life, to which God called you, when before many witnesses you made the great profession of faith.

[Haweis-NT] <u>1 Timothy 6:12</u> **Strain every nerve in the noble conflict of faith,** lay fast hold on eternal life, unto which also thou hast been called, and hast confessed the good confession before many witnesses.

[Macknight-NT] <u>1 Timothy 6:12</u> **Combat the good combat of faith:** Lay hold on eternal life, to which also thou wast called; and confess the good confession in the presence of many witnesses.

[MOTB] <u>1 Timothy 6:12</u> **Manfully wage the warfare to which your faith inspires you,** making the life eternal the goal of your striving, for to this were you summoned at your conversion and committed by your public confession of Christ.

[Original-NT] <u>1 Timothy 6:12</u> **Fight the gallant contest of the Faith** to the finish. Put up a real struggle for Eternal Life, to which you were called. Having made the noble confession before many witnesses,

[Phillips] <u>1 Timothy 6:12</u> **Fight the worthwhile battle of the faith**, keep your grip on that life eternal to which you have been called, and to which you boldly professed your loyalty before many witnesses.

[REM-NT] <u>1 Timothy 6:12</u> **Stay focused and purposely apply God's methods to your life every day**. Embrace the full healing and restoration to eternal life that have been freely offered you, and which you wisely accepted in the presence of many witnesses.

[Spencer-NT] <u>1 Timothy 6:12</u> **Strive in the noble contest of the faith**, seize hold of the life eternal to which thou wert called and of which thou madest that noble confession before many witnesses.

[TGNT] <u>1 Timothy 6:12</u> **Fight for the best in the contest of faith**, and seize the eternal life into which you were called, along with the good agreement you made in front of many witnesses.

[TPT] <u>1 Timothy 6:12</u> **So fight with faith for the winner's prize!** Lay your hands upon eternal life, for this is your calling—celebrating in faith before the multitude of witnesses!

[TTNT] <u>1 Timothy 6:12</u> So **fight the good fight of the faith**, living in the good of the eternal life given you when you were called, when you made your public confession of faith in Christ Jesus.

[Weymouth-NT] <u>1 Timothy 6:12</u> **Exert all your strength in the honourable struggle for the faith**; lay hold of the Life of the Ages, to which you were called, when you made your noble profession of faith before many witnesses.

SECOND TIMOTHY

<u>2 Timothy 1:7</u> For God hath not given us the spirit of fear; but of power, and of love, and of a sound mind.

[AMP] <u>2 Timothy 1:7</u> For God did not give us a- spirit of timidity or cowardice or fear, but [He has given us a spirit] of power and of love and of sound judgment and personal discipline [abilities that result in a calm, well-balanced mind and self-control].

[AMPC] <u>2 Timothy 1:7</u> For God did not give us a spirit of timidity (of cowardice, of craven and cringing and fawning fear), but [He has given us a spirit] of power and of love and of calm and well-balanced mind and discipline and self-control.

[BV-KJV-NT] <u>2 Timothy 1:7</u> You see, God did not give us a spirit of cowardice, but of ability, of love, and of proper focus.

[CBC] <u>2 Timothy 1:7</u> For God gave not us a spirit of cowardice; but of power, and of love, and of a sober mind.

[CEB] <u>2 Timothy 1:7</u> God didn't give us a spirit that is timid but one that is powerful, loving, and self-controlled.

[ClarkePyle] <u>2 Timothy 1:7</u> And you have no reason to be discouraged from the most violent oppositions you meet withal; for the spiritual powers and endowments God bestows on the Gospel ministers, are sufficient to set us above all slavish fear and cowardice, and to fix us in an immovable love to him and his true religion, and in a prudent and discreet exercise of our ministry.

[CLV] <u>2 Timothy 1:7</u> for God gives us, not a spirit of timidity, but of power and of love and of sanity."

[FBV-NT] <u>2 Timothy 1:7</u> God didn't give us a spirit that makes us fearful, but a spirit of power and love and good sense.

[GNT] <u>2 Timothy 1:7</u> For the Spirit that God has given us does not make us timid; instead, his Spirit fills us with power, love, and self-control.

[GT] <u>2 Timothy 1:7</u> God did not give us a cowardly attitude. No, God gave us one of power, of giving of self to others, for their good, expecting nothing in return, and good sense.

[Guyse-NT] <u>2 Timothy 1:7</u> You ought by no means to be discouraged in the exercise of those gifts, on account of the opposition of your adversaries: For the temper and disposition, which God by his spirit has formed in us, whom he hath called and fitted for holy ministrations, is not a spirit of cowardice and dread of our enemies, whether men or devils; but is a spirit of holy fortitude and undaunted courage to encounter all difficulties and dangers; and of fervent love to Christ and his cause, and to immortal souls; and of sobriety and good judgment, in a due government of our passions, and in stedfastly adhering to, and patiently suffering for, the true gospel of Christ.

[JMNT] <u>2 Timothy 1:7</u> for you see, God does not give to us (or: did not supply for us) a spirit of cowardice (or: a Breath-effect or attitude of timidity in us), but rather [a spirit and attitude] of ability and of power, as well as of love and of soundness in frame of mind (of wholeness in thinking; of healthiness of attitude; of sanity; of sensibility; of controlled reasonableness; of rational moderation; anatomically: of a saved diaphragm).

[Jordan-NT] <u>2 Timothy 1:7</u> For God has not given us the heart of a coward but of a strong man filled with love and self discipline.

[Kneeland-NT] <u>2 Timothy 1:7</u> For God hath not given us a spirit of fear, but of power, and of love, and of prudence.

[Mace-NT] <u>2 Timothy 1:7</u> for the spirit, which God has given us, is not a spirit of timidity, but of fortitude, of benevolence, and of moderation.

[Macknight-NTc] <u>2 Timothy 1:7</u> For God hath not infused into us a spirit of cowardice which shrinks at danger, but of courage, such as becometh those who possess the gifts of inspiration and miracles, and of benevolence, which disposes us to communicate the gospel to all mankind, and of self-government, to behave with prudence on every occasion.

[MCC-NT] <u>2 Timothy 1:7</u> For God has not given Us an Impulse of Dismay, but of Power, and of Love, and of Discretion.

[NIRV] <u>2 Timothy 1:7</u> God gave us his Spirit. And the Spirit doesn't make us weak and fearful. Instead, the Spirit gives us power and love. He helps us control ourselves.

[NMB-NT] <u>2 Timothy 1:7</u> For God has not given to us the spirit of fear, but of power, and of love, and soberness of mind.

[Numerical] <u>2 Timothy 1:7</u> for God hath not given us a spirit of cowardice, but of power and of love and of wise discretion.

[REAL] <u>2 Timothy 1:7</u> because God has not given us the spirit of fear, but of miracle power, and of unconditional love, and of a sound mind.

[REB] <u>2 Timothy 1:7</u> For the spirit that God gave us is no cowardly spirit, but one to inspire power, love, and self-discipline.

[Shuttleworth-NT] <u>2 Timothy 1:7</u> For the precious gift was not communicated that it might lie dormant through timidity, but that it might operate by miracles, and works of Christian charity, and well-regulated zeal.

[T4T] <u>2 Timothy 1:7</u> Remember that God has put his Spirit within us. His Spirit does not cause us to be afraid. Instead, he causes us to be powerful to work for God, and he helps us to love others and to control what we say and do.

[TLB] <u>2 Timothy 1:7</u> For the Holy Spirit, God's gift, does not want you to be afraid of people, but to be wise and strong, and to love them and enjoy being with them.

[TVB] <u>2 Timothy 1:7</u> You see, God did not give us a cowardly spirit but a powerful, loving, and disciplined spirit.

[Weymouth-NT] <u>2 Timothy 1:7</u> For the Spirit which God has given us is not a spirit of cowardice, but one of power and of love and of sound judgement.

[Wuest-NT] <u>2 Timothy 1:7</u> for God did not give to us a spirit of fearfulness but of power and of a divine and self-sacrificial love and of a sound mind.

<u>2 Timothy 4:18</u> And the Lord shall deliver me from every evil work, and will preserve[sozo] me unto his heavenly kingdom: to whom be glory for ever and ever. Amen.

Every reasonable person would have to agree that sickness and disease is an evil work.

[BBE] <u>2 Timothy 4:18</u> **The Lord will keep me safe from every evil work** and will give me salvation in his kingdom in heaven: to whom be glory for ever and ever. So be it.

[BLE] <u>2 Timothy 4:18</u> **The Lord will rescue me out of the way of every deed of evil** and will save me into his heavenly kingdom; to whom be glory forever and ever. Amen.

[CEB] <u>2 Timothy 4:18</u> **The Lord will rescue me from every evil action** and will save me for his heavenly kingdom. To him be the glory forever and always. Amen.

[CEV] <u>2 Timothy 4:18</u> **The Lord will always keep me from being harmed by evil,** and he will bring me safely into his heavenly kingdom. Praise him forever and ever! Amen.

[CJB] <u>2 Timothy 4:18</u> **The Lord will rescue me from every evil attack** and bring me safely into his heavenly Kingdom. To him be the glory forever and ever. Amen.

[Goodspeed-NT] <u>2 Timothy 4:18</u> **The Lord will rescue me from any harm** and bring me safely to his heavenly kingdom. To him be glory forever and ever. Amen.

[Harwood-NT] <u>2 Timothy 4:18</u> **And the Lord will extricate me from every fatal evil,** and conduct me in safety to his celestial kingdom—to him be glory through all the endless ages of eternity! Amen.

[KNT] <u>2 Timothy 4:18</u> **The Lord will snatch me clear from every wicked deed** and will save me for his heavenly kingdom. Glory to him for the ages of ages, Amen!

[Mace-NT] <u>2 Timothy 4:18</u> **and the Lord will deliver me from every malicious design,** and preserve me for his heavenly kingdom. to him be glory to endless ages. amen.

[Moffatt-NT 1917] <u>2 Timothy 4:18</u> **The Lord will rescue me from every assault of evil,** he will bring me safe to his own realm in heaven. To him be glory for ever and ever! Amen.

[NAB] <u>2 Timothy 4:18</u> **The Lord will rescue me from every evil threat** and will bring me safe to his heavenly kingdom. To him be glory forever and ever. Amen.

[NEB] <u>2 Timothy 4:18</u> **And the Lord will rescue me from every attempt to do me harm,** and keep me safe until his heavenly reign begins. Glory to him for ever and ever! Amen.

[NJB] <u>2 Timothy 4:18</u> **The Lord will rescue me from all evil attempts on me,** and bring me safely to his heavenly kingdom. To him be glory for ever and ever. Amen.

[Original-NT] <u>2 Timothy 4:18</u> **The Lord will continue to rescue me from every evil agency** and preserve me for his heavenly Kingdom. To him be glory for ever and ever. Amen.

[Phillips] <u>2 Timothy 4:18</u> **I am sure the Lord will rescue me from every evil plot**, and will keep me safe until I reach his heavenly kingdom. Glory be to him for ever and ever, amen!

[T4T] <u>2 Timothy 4:18</u> Therefore, **I am sure that the Lord will rescue me from everything that is truly evil** and will bring me safely to heaven, where he rules. Praise him forever! Amen! /May it be so!

[TLB] <u>2 Timothy 4:18</u> **Yes, and the Lord will always deliver me from all evil** and will bring me into his heavenly Kingdom. To God be the glory forever and ever. Amen.

[TWTY-RCT-NT-V1] <u>2 Timothy 4:18</u> **The Sovereign Master shall save and deliver, rescue and guard, set free and shield, maintain and support, protect and liberate, free and redeem, draw and snatch me away from every individual and collective evil and troublesome, sorrowful and poor, pitiable and unfit, unattractive and useless, worthless and morally reprehensible, morally corrupt and wicked, annoying and unethical, diseased and blind, perilous and criminal, vicious and malignant, harmful and incompetent, bad and wretched, pernicious and noxious work and business, employment and undertaking, act and deed, function and occupation, matter and accomplishment, task and labour**, and He shall deliver and preserve, save and rescue me from danger and destruction, ruin and annihilation, being brought into His heavenly and celestial kingdom and royal power, dominion and rule, kingship, reign and authority. To Him be the glory and splendour, magnificence and excellence, pre-eminence and dignity, brightness, favour and majesty to and for eternity and forever, the unbroken age and the perpetuity of time. Yes, truly this is a firm and reliable statement of truth.

[Weekes-NT] <u>2 Timothy 4:18</u> **The Lord will rescue me from every evil-doing**, and will preserve me unto his heavenly kingdom; and to him be the glory unto the ages of the ages; Amen.

[Weymouth-NT] <u>2 Timothy 4:18</u> **The Lord will deliver me from every cruel attack** and will keep me safe in preparation for His heavenly Kingdom. To Him be the glory until the Ages of the Ages! Amen.

[Wuest-NT] <u>2 Timothy 4:18</u> **The Lord will draw me to himself away from every pernicious work actively opposed to that which is good**, and will keep me safe and sound for His kingdom, the heavenly one, to whom be the glory forever and forever. Amen.

[YLT] <u>2 Timothy 4:18</u> **and the Lord shall free me from every evil work**, and shall save [me]—to his heavenly kingdom; to whom [is] the glory to the ages of the ages! Amen.

TITUS

<u>Titus 3:7</u> That being justified by his grace, we should be made heirs according to the hope of eternal life[zoé].

[AUV-NT 2003] <u>Titus 3:7</u> [This was] so that, being made right with God by His unearned favor, we could have the hope of [possessing our] inheritance of never ending life [in heaven].

[BWE-NT] <u>Titus 3:7</u> He did this so that we can be put right with God, by his kindness. He did this so that we can become his children. So now we can look forward to everlasting life.

[FBV-NT] <u>Titus 3:7</u> Now that we are set right by his grace we have become heirs having the hope of eternal life.

[GNT] <u>Titus 3:7</u> so that by his grace we might be put right with God and come into possession of the eternal life we hope for.

[NLV] <u>Titus 3:7</u> Because of this, we are made right with God by His loving-favor. Now we can have life that lasts forever as He has promised.

[Noyes] <u>Titus 3:7</u> that having been accepted as righteous by his grace, we might become heirs according to the hope of everlasting life.

[TGNT] <u>Titus 3:7</u> Being cleared of all charges by that favor, we can become heirs according to the hope of eternal life.

[TLV] <u>Titus 3:7</u> so that being set right by His grace, we might become heirs with the confident hope of eternal life!

[TTNT] <u>Titus 3:7</u> So we are made completely acceptable to God by His grace and have become heirs with the expectation of eternal life. This is the Word of truth on which you can depend.

[TVB] <u>Titus 3:7</u> All of this happened so that through His grace we would be accepted into God's covenant family and appointed to be His heirs, full of the hope that comes from knowing you have eternal life.

[UDB] <u>Titus 3:7</u> By this gift, Yahweh has declared that everything is made right between him and us. And more than that, we will share in everything that the Lord Jesus has to give us, especially everlasting life with him.

[Wakefield-NT] <u>Titus 3:7</u> that, upon our acquittal by this favour of his, we might be heirs, in expectation, of eternal life.

PHILEMON

<u>Philemon 1:6</u> That the communication of thy faith may become effectual by the acknowledging of every good thing which is in you in Christ Jesus.

Receiving our healing by faith is a very effective way of communicating our faith to others.

[AMP] <u>Philemon 1:6</u> I pray that the sharing of your faith may become effective and powerful because of your accurate knowledge of every good thing which is ours in Christ.

[CB] <u>Philemon 1:6</u> That sharing your faith may be effective through acknowledging that every good thing comes from Christ Jesus.

[CEV] <u>Philemon 1:6</u> As you share your faith with others, I pray they may come to know all the blessings Christ has given us.

[CWB] <u>Philemon 1:6</u> I pray that God will enable you to share your faith even more effectively and to help you understand more fully all the good that comes to us through Christ.

[Etheridge-NT] <u>Philemon 1:6</u> (I have prayed) that there may be communication of thy faith (in) yielding fruits, in works and in the (manifestation of the) knowledge of all good which thou hast in Jeshu Meshiha.

[FHV-NT] <u>Philemon 1:6</u> I pray, that as you realize the good things that are ours in Christ, you may be active in sharing your faith.

[GT] <u>Philemon 1:6</u> I pray that you will actively share your faith with a real understanding of every good thing which we have in Christ.

[KNT] <u>Philemon 1:6</u> My prayer is this: that the partnership which goes with your faith may have its powerful effect, in realizing every good thing that is at work in us to lead us into the King.

[MSG] <u>Philemon 1:6</u> And I keep praying that this faith we hold in common keeps showing up in the good things we do, and that people recognize Christ in all of it.

[NIVUK] <u>Philemon 1:6</u> I pray that your partnership with us in the faith may be effective in deepening your understanding of every good thing we share for the sake of Christ.

[Norlie-NT] <u>Philemon 1:6</u> And I, therefore, pray that this faith, which you have in common with them, may bring about a better understanding of all the blessings that you have in Christ Jesus.

[TCNT] <u>Philemon 1:6</u> And I pray that your participation in the Faith may result in action, as you come to a fuller realization of everything that is good and Christlike in us.

[TLB] <u>Philemon 1:6</u> And I pray that as you share your faith with others it will grip their lives too, as they see the wealth of good things in you that come from Christ Jesus.

[TPT] <u>Philemon 1:6</u> I pray for you that the faith we share may effectively deepen your understanding of every good thing that belongs to you in Christ.

[TTNT] <u>Philemon 1:6</u> I pray that, as you share your faith with others, so you may become fully aware of everything good that we have in Christ.

[UASV] <u>Philemon 1:6</u> and I pray that the fellowship of your faith may become effective through the accurate knowledge of every good thing that is in you for the sake of Christ.

[Wand-NT] <u>Philemon 1:6</u> In doing so, I add a prayer for the brothers themselves that they may share in your loyalty to such an extent as to realize all the benefits that flow from our Christian profession.

[YLT] <u>Philemon 1:6</u> that the fellowship of thy faith may become working in the full knowledge of every good thing that [is] in you toward Christ Jesus;

HEBREWS

Hebrews 1:1-4 God, who at sundry times and in divers manners spake in time past unto the fathers by the prophets, ²Hath in these last days spoken unto us by his Son, whom he hath appointed heir of all things, by whom also he made the worlds; ³Who being the brightness of his glory, and the express image of his person, and upholding all things by the word of his power, when he had by himself purged our sins, sat down on the right hand of the Majesty on high; ⁴Being made so much better than the angels, as he hath by inheritance obtained a more excellent name than they.

[AMP] <u>Hebrews 1:1-4</u> God, having spoken to the fathers long ago in [the voices and writings of] the prophets in many separate revelations [each of which set forth a portion of the truth], and in many ways, ²has in these last days spoken [with finality] to us in [the person of One who is by His character and nature] His Son [namely Jesus], whom He appointed heir and lawful owner of all things, through whom also He created the universe [that is, the universe as a space-time-matter continuum]. ³The Son is the radiance and only expression of the glory of [our awesome] God [reflecting God's Shekinah glory, the Light-being, the brilliant light of the divine], and the exact representation and perfect imprint of His [Father's] essence, and upholding and maintaining and propelling all things [the entire physical and spiritual universe] by His powerful word [carrying the universe along to its predetermined goal]. When He [Himself and no other] had [by offering Himself on the cross as a sacrifice for sin] accomplished purification from sins and established our freedom from guilt, He sat down [revealing His completed work] at the right hand of the Majesty on high [revealing His Divine authority], [4]having become as much superior to angels, since He has inherited a more excellent and glorious name than they [that is, Son—the name above all names].

[AMPC] Hebrews 1:1-4 In many separate revelations [each of which set forth a portion of the Truth] and in different ways God spoke of old to [our] forefathers in and by the prophets, [2][But] in the last of these days He has spoken to us in [the person of a] Son, Whom He appointed Heir and lawful Owner of all things, also by and through Whom He created the worlds and the reaches of space and the ages of time [He made, produced, built, operated, and arranged them in order]. [3]He is the sole expression of the glory of God [the Light-being, the out-raying or radiance of the divine], and He is the perfect imprint and very image of [God's] nature, upholding and maintaining and guiding and propelling the universe by His mighty word of power. When He had by offering Himself accomplished our cleansing of sins and riddance of guilt, He sat down at the right hand of the divine Majesty on high, [4][Taking a place and rank by which] He Himself became as much superior to angels as the glorious Name (title) which He has inherited is different from and more excellent than theirs.

[AUV-NT 2005] Hebrews 1:1-4 In times past God spoke to our forefathers through the prophets in many parts and in various ways, [2][but] during these final days He has spoken to us through His Son, whom He appointed to be heir of all things [and] through whom He created the universe. [3]This Son expresses the radiance of God's splendor and represents His very Being, and He sustains everything by His powerful word. After He had provided cleansing for [people's] sins, He sat down at the right side of the Majesty [i.e., God] on high [i.e., in heaven]. [4]He had become as much superior [in rank] to the angels as the name He inherited [i.e., "Son."] was superior to theirs [i.e., the name "angels" means "messengers"].

[Ballentine-NT] Hebrews 1:1-4 In former times it was only partially, And in many different ways, God spoke to our forefathers In those through whom he revealed himself. [2]But in these last days he has once for all spoken to us In his son, Whom he appointed heir of everything, And through whom he made the worlds. [3]He is the reflected perfection of God, And the imprint of the divine nature. And it is he who sustains everything By the expression of his power. So when he had cleared men from the guilt of sin, He sat down on the right of the Majesty on high. [4]And he became as much greater than the angels As the name he inherited is of more dignity than theirs.

[Barclay-NT] Hebrews 1:1-4 Long ago God spoke to our ancestors by means of the prophets, but the revelation which was given through them was fragmentary and varied. [2]But now, as time as we know it is coming to an end, he has spoken in one whose relation to himself is that of Son, that Son into whose possession he gave all things, and by whose agency he created the present world and the world to come. [3]This Son is the radiance of his glory, just as the mark is the exact impression of the seal. It is he who sustains all things by the dynamic power of his word. And, after he had effected the cleaning of men from their sins, he took his place at the right hand of the Majesty in the heights of heaven, [4]for he was as much superior to the angels as the title he had been given as his possession by God was greater than theirs.

[BBE] Hebrews 1:1-4 In times past the word of God came to our fathers through the prophets, in different parts and in different ways; [2]But now, at the end of these days, it has come to us through his Son, to whom he has given all things for a heritage, and through whom he made the order of the generations; [3]Who, being the outshining of his glory, the true image of his substance, supporting all things by the word of his power, having given himself as an offering making clean from sins, took his seat at the right hand of God in heaven; [4]Having become by so much better than the angels, as the name which is his heritage is more noble than theirs.

[EEBT] Hebrews 1:1-4 Many years ago, God spoke to our grandfathers (Israel's people) by the prophets (people who spoke God's messages). He spoke many times and in many different ways. [2]But in these last times, he has spoken to us by his Son. In the beginning, God made the whole world and everything that there is by his Son. And God has chosen that everything should be his Son's. ³The Son shines with the bright light that comes from God. The Son's nature is a copy of God's nature. He shows us completely what God is like. The Son's powerful word causes everything in the world to continue. The Son himself made it possible for us to be clean from everything that we do wrong. After he had done that, he sat down in heaven. He sat at the right side of God, who is the greatest ruler, with all authority. ⁴God has caused his Son to be much greater and much better than the angels. God has given him a much greater and much better name than the angels' names.

[ERV] <u>Hebrews 1:1-4</u> In the past God spoke to our people through the prophets. He spoke to them many times and in many different ways. ²And now in these last days, God has spoken to us again through his Son. He made the whole world through his Son. And he has chosen his Son to have all things. ³The Son shows the glory of God. He is a perfect copy of God's nature, and he holds everything together by his powerful command. The Son made people clean from their sins. Then he sat down at the right side of God, the Great One in heaven. ⁴The Son became much greater than the angels, and God gave him a name that is much greater than any of their names.

[MSG] <u>Hebrews 1:1-4</u> Going through a long line of prophets, God has been addressing our ancestors in different ways for centuries. ²Recently he spoke to us directly through his Son. By his Son, God created the world in the beginning, and it will all belong to the Son at the end. ³This Son perfectly mirrors God, and is stamped with God's nature. He holds everything together by what he says—powerful words! The Son Is Higher than Angels ⁴far higher than any angel in rank and rule.

[Phillips] <u>Hebrews 1:1-4</u> God, who gave to our forefathers many different glimpses of the truth in the words of the prophets, ²has now, at the end of the present age, given us the truth in the Son. Through the Son God made the whole universe, and to the Son he has ordained that all creation shall ultimately belong. ³This Son, radiance of the glory of God, flawless expression of the nature of God, himself the upholding power of all that is, having effected in person the cleansing of men's sin, took his seat at the right hand of the majesty on high— ⁴thus proving himself, by the more glorious name that he had been given, far greater than all the angels of God.

[REM-NT] <u>Hebrews 1:1-4</u> God has been speaking to us throughout all human history. In the past, he worked through his inspired spokespersons (and in other ways) to send his message of truth, love and hope. ²But in these more recent times, God's very thoughts have been made audible and visible to us in the person of his Son, who is the rightful heir of all things, and through whom the entire universe was created. ³Jesus Christ is the radiant glory of God's methods and principles lived out in human flesh. He is the exact manifestation of God's character—the complete revelation of his being—sustaining all things by his powerful word. After he provided the Remedy necessary to heal mankind from the infection of sin and selfishness, he took his seat at the right hand of the Majesty in heaven, ⁴thus his superiority to the angels became known throughout the entire universe, just as the name he inherited is superior to theirs.

[TGNT] <u>Hebrews 1:1-4</u> God spoke to our ancestors through the prophets little by little and in many ways in times past. ²But in these last days he spoke to us through his Son, who has been named heir of everything, and through whom he made the ages. ³He is the radiance of God's majesty and the exact likeness of his core being, besides holding everything up by his powerful pronouncement. After cleaning away failures, he was seated at the right hand of the Highest Majesty, ⁴making him far above the Messengers and inheriting a superior Name.

[TLB] <u>Hebrews 1:1-4</u> Long ago God spoke in many different ways to our fathers through the prophets, in visions, dreams, and even face to face, telling them little by little about his plans. ²But now in these days he has spoken to us through his Son to whom he has given everything and through whom he made the world and everything there is. ³God's Son shines out with God's glory, and all that God's Son is and does marks him as God. He regulates the universe by the mighty power of his command. He is the one who died to cleanse us and clear our record of all sin, and then sat down in highest honor beside the great God of heaven. ⁴Thus he became far greater than the angels, as proved by the fact that his name "Son of God," which was passed on to him from his Father, is far greater than the names and titles of the angels.

[TPT] <u>Hebrews 1:1-4</u> Throughout our history God has spoken to our ancestors by his prophets in many different ways. The revelation he gave them was only a fragment at a time, building one truth upon another. ²But to us living in these last days, God now speaks to us openly in the language of a Son, the appointed Heir of everything, for through him God created the panorama of all things and all time. ³The Son is the dazzling radiance of God's splendor, the exact expression of God's true nature—his mirror image! He holds the universe together and expands it by the mighty power of his spoken word. He accomplished for us the complete cleansing of sins, and then took his seat on the highest throne at the right hand of the majestic One. ⁴He is infinitely greater than angels, for he inherited a rank and a Name far greater than theirs.

[TTNT] <u>Hebrews 1:1-4</u> In the past God spoke to our forefathers through the prophets, on many occasions and in a variety of ways. ²Now, however, He has spoken to us through His Son, whom He has made the heir of everything that has been created. For through Jesus, God created the entire universe, and He is the One who shines with God's own glory. ³When He became man He expressed God's nature perfectly. Not only is He the Word through whom everything was brought into being, but the whole of creation is sustained through Him. The reason He became man was to provide the means by which we can be purified from all our sins. This He accomplished, and so He now sits in triumph at God's right hand, reigning in Majesty in heaven. ⁴When He returned to heaven He took His rightful place, far superior to that of the angels; for the name of Jesus is so much greater than the name of any created being in heaven or on earth.

[TVB] <u>Hebrews 1:1-4</u> Long ago, at different times and in various ways, God's voice came to our ancestors through the Hebrew prophets. ²But in these last days, it has come to us through His Son, the One who has been given dominion over all things and through whom all worlds were made. ³This is the One who—imprinted with God's image, shimmering with His glory—sustains all that exists through the power of His word. He was seated at the right hand of God once He Himself had made the offering that purified us from all our sins. ⁴This Son of God is elevated as far above the heavenly messengers as His holy name is elevated above theirs.

[Wade] <u>Hebrews 1:1-4</u> It was in many fragmentary portions and by many varied methods that God long ago conveyed His communications to our ancestors through the Prophets; ²but at the end of the present period of history He has communicated with us through One Who is a Son—a Son Whom He has constituted heir of all things; for through Him He also made the world, with its successive Ages. ³He, being the Radiance of God's Glory and the Imprint of His Reality (reproducing It was truly as the seal reproduces the signet) and sustaining the Universe by the expression of His mighty Will, after having secured for us purification from our sins, took His seat at the right hand of the Majesty on high, ⁴being thereby shewn to be as much superior to the Angels as the Title which He has inherited is ore exalted than theirs.

[Wand-NT] <u>Hebrews 1:1-4</u> In the old days God spoke to our ancestors in a partial and inconclusive way through the prophets. ²Now, at the end of this era, He has spoken to us through His Son. Him He has made heir of the whole universe, since it was through His agency that He created the World. ³He is the reflection of the Father's Glory and bears impressed upon Him the very character of the Father. By the power of His commanding word, the Son sustains the universe, and now that He has made atonement for sins, He has sat down on the right hand of the Majesty on high. [4]The Son's superiority to the angels is revealed to its full extent in the special Name allotted to him.

[WilliamNorton-NT-G] <u>Hebrews 1:1-4</u> God, who of old, by the many parts [of his word], and in many ways, spoke to [our] fathers by the prophets, [2]has, in these last of the days, spoken to us by [his] Son, whom he has made inheritor of all things, by means of whom he also made the worlds; [3]who, being the forth-shining of [his] glory, and the stamped-image of what he himself is, and upholding all things by the word of his might; when he had by means of himself effected the purging away of our sins, sat down at the right hand of [God's] Greatness in the high [heavens]; [4]having became greater than the angels in such high degree as he has inherited a name which excels theirs.

[WilliamNorton-NT-P] <u>Hebrews 1:1-4</u> God, in all kinds of parts, and in all kinds of ways, spoke with our fathers by the prophets from of old; [2]and in these the last days, he has spoken with us by his Son, whom he has made inheritor of everything, and by whom he made the worlds; [3]who himself is the brightness of his glory, and the image of what he is, and who upholds everything by the might of his word; and who by means of himself effected the purging away of our sins, and sat down at the right hand of [God's] Greatness in the high [heavens]; [4]and he in everything is greater than angels, in proportion as the name which he has inherited excels theirs.

<u>Hebrews 2:9,14-15</u> But we see Jesus, who was made a little lower than the angels for the suffering of death, crowned with glory and honour; that **he by the grace of God should taste death for every man**. [14]Forasmuch then as the children are partakers of flesh and blood, he also himself likewise took part of the same; **that through death he might destroy him that had the power of death, that is, the devil**; [15]And deliver them who through fear of death were all their lifetime subject to bondage.

[AENT] <u>Hebrews 2:9,14-15</u> We see that he is Y'shua, who humbled himself to become a little lower than the Messengers through his suffering and death, but now he is crowned with honor and glory because **he tasted death for the sake of everyone apart from Elohim**. [14]For because the children participated in flesh and blood, he also, in like manner, took part in the same; that, **by his death, he might bring to nothing him who held the kingdom of death, namely Satan**; [15]and might release them who, through fear of death, are all their lives subject to bondage.

[AMP] <u>Hebrews 2:9,14-15</u> But we do see Jesus, who was made lower than the angels for a little while [by taking on the limitations of humanity], crowned with glory and honor because of His suffering of death, **so that by the grace of God [extended to sinners] He might experience death for [the sins of] everyone**. [14]Therefore, since [these His] children share in flesh and blood [the physical nature of mankind], He Himself in a similar manner also shared in the same [physical nature, but without sin], **so that through [experiencing] death He might make powerless (ineffective, impotent) him who had the power of death—that is, the devil—** [15]and [that He] might free all those who through [the haunting] fear of death were held in slavery throughout their lives.

[AMPC] <u>Hebrews 2:9,14-15</u> But we are able to see Jesus, Who was ranked lower than the angels for a little while, crowned with glory and honor because of His having suffered death, in order that by the grace (unmerited favor) of God [to us sinners] **He might experience death for every individual person**. [14]Since, therefore, [these His] children share in flesh and blood [in the physical nature of human beings], He [Himself] in a similar manner partook of the same [nature], **that by [going through] death He might bring to nought and make of no effect him who had the power of death—that is, the devil—** [15]And also that He might deliver and completely set free all those who through the [haunting] fear of death were held in bondage throughout the whole course of their lives.

[Authentic-NT] <u>Hebrews 2:9,14-15</u> But as regards being made 'only slightly inferior to angels', we do see Jesus by experiencing death having been 'crowned with dignity and honour', that thus **in God's**

mercy he should taste death for all mankind. [14]Since, therefore, the children have human nature, so did he share it equally with them; **so that by death he might put out of commission him who wields the power of death, namely the Devil**, [15]and release all those inhibited throughout their lives by fear of death.

[AUV-NT 2005] <u>Hebrews 2:9,14-15</u> But we do see Jesus, who was made a little bit lower than the angels [i.e., by suffering death as a human being], and was crowned with splendor and honor because He suffered death. It was by God's unearned favor that **He would experience death for every person**. [14]Therefore, since the children share in [bodies of] flesh and blood, Christ also, in the same way, took on a human body so that, **through His death, He could destroy [the dominion of] him who had the power to cause death, that is, the devil**. [15]And [also He could] release all of those people who, because of their fear of death, were [kept] in bondage all their lives.

[Beck] <u>Hebrews 2:9,14-15</u> But we do see Jesus, who for a little while was made lower than the angels, now crowned with glory and honor because He suffered death in order **by God's grace to taste death for everyone**. [14]Now since all these children have flesh and blood, He in the same way took on flesh and blood **in order to die and so take away all the powers of him who had the power of death, that is, the devil**. [15]and to free those who, terrified by death, had to be slaves all their lives.

[BLE] <u>Hebrews 2:9,14-15</u> but him who was made a little inferior to the angels, Jesus, we do see garlanded with glory and honor so that **by God's grace he may taste death for everyone**. [14]So, since the children have been sharing flesh and blood, he himself similarly participated in the same, **that through death he might quell him who wields the might of death—that is, the Devil—** [15]and deliver those who for the fear of death were doomed to slavery all their lives.

[BV-KJV-NT] <u>Hebrews 2:9,14-15</u> We see Jesus as the one who has been made some bit less than angels, who because of the hardship of the death has been crowned with an award wreath of magnificence and value, in order that **by God's generosity He might taste death on behalf of everyone**. [14]So since the young children have shared a physical body and blood, He Himself also, correspondingly, took part in the same things, so that **through the death He might make useless the one who has the power of the death (that is, the Accuser)** [15]and He might discharge these people, as many as with fear of death through every bit of the "to be living" part were guilty for the penalty of slavery.

[CJB] <u>Hebrews 2:9,14-15</u> But we do see Yeshua—who indeed was made for a little while lower than the angels—now crowned with glory and honor because he suffered death, so **that by God's grace he might taste death for all humanity**. [14]Therefore, since the children share a common physical nature as human beings, he became like them and shared that same human nature; so **that by his death he might render ineffective the one who had power over death (that is, the Adversary)** [15]and thus set free those who had been in bondage all their lives because of their fear of death.

[Douay-Rheims] <u>Hebrews 2:9,14-15</u> But we see Jesus, who was made a little lower than the angels, for the suffering of death, crowned with glory and honour: that, **through the grace of God, he might taste death for all**. [14]Therefore because the children are partakers of flesh and blood, he also himself in like manner hath been partaker of the same: that, **through death, he might destroy him who had the empire of death, that is to say, the devil**: [15]And might deliver them, who through the fear of death were all their lifetime subject to servitude.

[ECB] <u>Hebrews 2:9,14-15</u> And we see Yah Shua, who was lowered somewhat less than Elohim for the suffering of death, wreathed with glory and honor; that he **by the charism of Elohim tasted death for every man**. [14]So since, as the children partake of flesh and blood, he also himself likewise partook of the same; so **that through death he inactivated him who had the power of death—that is, Diabolos**; [15]and released them, as many as through awe of death who through all their lifetime were subject to servitude.

[ERV] <u>Hebrews 2:9,14-15</u> For a short time Jesus was made lower than the angels, but now we see him wearing a crown of glory and honor because he suffered and died. **Because of God's grace, Jesus died for everyone.** ¹⁴These children are people with physical bodies. So Jesus himself became like them and had the same experiences they have. Jesus did this so that, **by dying, he could destroy the one who has the power of death—the devil.** ¹⁵Jesus became like these people and died so that he could free them. They were like slaves all their lives because of their fear of death.

[EXB] <u>Hebrews 2:9,14-15</u> But we see Jesus, who for a short time was made lower than the angels. This was so **that, by God's grace, he could ·die [taste death] for everyone**. And now, because he suffered and died, he is ·wearing a crown of [crowned with] glory and honor. [Jesus fulfills humanity's destiny: to be crowned with glory and honor;] ¹⁴[Therefore] Since these children ·are people with physical bodies [have in common their flesh and blood], Jesus himself ·became like them [shared their humanity; likewise shared the same things]. He did this so that, **by dying, he could destroy the one who has the power of death—the devil**— ¹⁵and free those who were ·like slaves [held in slavery] all their lives because of their fear of death.

[GoodSpeed-NT] <u>Hebrews 2:9,14-15</u> but we do see Jesus, who was "made for a little while inferior to angels, crowned with glory and honor" because he suffered death, so that **by the favor of God he might taste the bitterness of death on behalf of every human being**. ¹⁴Therefore since these children referred to have the same mortal nature, Jesus also shared it, like them, in order that **by his death he might dethrone the lord of death, the devil,** ¹⁵and free from their slavery men who had always lived in fear of death.

[Hanson-NT] <u>Hebrews 2:9,14-15</u> but we behold Jesus, who was made "for a little while inferior to angels," because of the suffering of death crowned with glory and honor, that **by God's favor he should taste death for every [man]**. ¹⁴Since then the children participate in blood and flesh, he also himself in a similar manner participated in the same, in order that **by means of death he may annihilate him that has the power of death, that is, the accuser;** ¹⁵and liberate all those who, through fear of death, were during their whole lifetime held in slavery.

[ISV] <u>Hebrews 2:9,14-15</u> But we do see someone who was made a little lower than the angels. He is Jesus, who is crowned with glory and honor because he suffered death, so that **by the grace of God he might experience death for everyone.** ¹⁴Therefore, since the children have flesh and blood, he himself also shared the same things, so that **by his death he might destroy the one who has the power of death (that is, the Devil)** ¹⁵and might free those who were slaves all their lives because they were terrified by death.

[Moffatt] <u>Hebrews 2:9,14-15</u> what we do see is Jesus who was put lower than the angels for a little while to suffer death, and who has been crowned with glory and honour, that **by God's grace he might taste death for everyone.** ¹⁴Since the children then share blood and flesh, he himself participated in their nature, so that **by dying he might crush him who wields the power of death (that is to say, the devil)** ¹⁵and release from thraldom those who lay under a life-long fear of death.

[Montgomery-NT] <u>Hebrews 2:9,14-15</u> What we do see is Jesus, who was made for a time a little lower than the angels, now crowned with glory and honor, because of the suffering of death, in order that **through God's grace he might taste death for every man.** ¹⁴Therefore, since the children are sharers in flesh and blood, he also similarly partook of the same, in order that **through death he might render powerless him that had the power of death, that is, the devil;** ¹⁵And might deliver those who through fear of death had been subject to life-long bondage.

[MSG] <u>Hebrews 2:9,14-15</u> What we do see is Jesus, made "not quite as high as angels," and then, through the experience of death, crowned so much higher than any angel, with a glory "bright with

Eden's dawn light." **In that death, by God's grace, he fully experienced death in every person's place**. [14]Since the children are made of flesh and blood, it's logical that the Savior took on flesh and blood in order to rescue them by his death. **By embracing death, taking it into himself, he destroyed the Devil's hold on death** [15]and freed all who cower through life, scared to death of death.

[Nary-NT] <u>Hebrews 2:9,14-15</u> But we see Jesus, who was little less than the angels, crowned with glory and honour because of the sufferings of his death; **God out of his grace and goodness, being willing that he should die for all men**. [14]For as much then as the children were partakers of flesh and blood, he also did partake of the same; that **by death he may destroy him who had the empire of death, that is, the devil**; [15]And that he might deliver those, who for fear of death, were all their life time obnoxious to slavery.

[NEB] <u>Hebrews 2:9,14-15</u> In Jesus, however, we do see one who for a short while was made lower than the angels, crowned now with glory and honour because he suffered death, so that, **by God's gracious will, in tasting death he should stand for us all**. [14]The children of a family share the same flesh and blood; and so he too shared ours, so that **through death he might break the power of him who had death at his command, that is, the devil**; [15]and might liberate those who, through fear of death, had all their lifetime been in servitude.

[NLT] <u>Hebrews 2:9,14-15</u> What we do see is Jesus, who was given a position "a little lower than the angels"; and because he suffered death for us, he is now "crowned with glory and honor." Yes, **by God's grace, Jesus tasted death for everyone**. [14]Because God's children are human beings—made of flesh and blood—the Son also became flesh and blood. For only as a human being could he die, and only **by dying could he break the power of the devil, who had the power of death**. [15]Only in this way could he set free all who have lived their lives as slaves to the fear of dying.

[NLV] <u>Hebrews 2:9,14-15</u> But we do see Jesus. For a little while He took a place that was not as important as the angels. But **God had loving-favor for everyone. He had Jesus suffer death on a cross for all of us**. Then, because of Christ's death on a cross, God gave Him the crown of honor and shining-greatness. [14]It is true that we share the same Father with Jesus. And it is true that we share the same kind of flesh and blood because Jesus became a man like us. He died as we must die. **Through His death He destroyed the power of the devil who has the power of death**. [15]Jesus did this to make us free from the fear of death. We no longer need to be chained to this fear.

[OANT] <u>Hebrews 2:9,14-15</u> But we see that he is Yeshua, who became a little lower than the Angels for the suffering of his death, and glory and honor are placed upon his head, **for God himself, by his grace, tasted death in the place of every person**. [14]For because the children shared together in flesh and blood, he also shared in these things in the same form, so that **by his death he would destroy the one who had held the authority of death, who is Satan**, [15]And he would free those who, by the fear of death, all their lives were subjected to bondage.

[REM-NT] <u>Hebrews 2:9,14-15</u> But we see Jesus—who was positioned a little lower than the angels— now crowned with glory for perfectly revealing God's character, and honored for vindicating God's methods and principles of selfless love, because he voluntarily chose to die rather than use his power to save self **so that by the graciousness of God, he might consume death in order to heal everyone**. [14]And since the children are human (with flesh and blood), he too became human (with flesh and blood) so that **by his death he might reveal the truth about God, consume selfishness with love, destroy him who through his lies about God holds the power of death—that is, the devil—** [15]and free the minds of those who have lived all their lives enslaved by their misunderstanding of God and their fear of death.

[Shuttleworth-NT] <u>Hebrews 2:9,14-15</u> We have seen Jesus Christ made a little inferior to the angels, by taking upon himself the human nature, and we have also seen him, after his passage through the grave, crowned with glory and honor: that **by God's mercy towards us he might taste of death for the redemption of all mankind.** ¹⁴As then those children whom he came to redeem were of human flesh and blood, he himself condescended, for their sake, to assume the same nature with them, in order that **by submitting to death he might destroy the power of the lord of death, namely the devil;** ¹⁵and might release from the apprehensions connected with the thoughts of death all who till that time had been subject to those slavish terrors.

[Smith] <u>Hebrews 2:9,14-15</u> But we see Jesus, made some little while less than angels by the suffering of death, crowned with glory and honour; so that **by the grace of God he should taste of death for all.** ¹⁴Since therefore the young children participated in flesh and blood, he also likewise participated with them; that **by death he might leave unemployed him having the strength of death, that is, the devil;** ¹⁵And deliver them, as many as by fear of death were always to live bound by slavery.

[Thomson] <u>Hebrews 2:9,14-15</u> But we see him who was made a little lower than angels [namely] Jesus, on account of suffering death crowned with glory and honour, **that so he by the favour of God might taste death for every man.** ¹⁴As the children therefore were partakers of flesh and blood, he himself likewise partook of the same in order that he might, **by his death, put a stop to the operation of him who hath the power of death, that is the devil;** ¹⁵and deliver from bondage them who were all their lives liable to the fear of death.

[TLB] <u>Hebrews 2:9,14-15</u> but we do see Jesus—who for a while was a little lower than the angels—crowned now by God with glory and honor because he suffered death for us. **Yes, because of God's great kindness, Jesus tasted death for everyone in all the world.** ¹⁴Since we, God's children, are human beings—made of flesh and blood—he became flesh and blood too by being born in human form; for only as a human being could he die and **in dying break the power of the devil who had the power of death.** ¹⁵Only in that way could he deliver those who through fear of death have been living all their lives as slaves to constant dread.

[TPT] <u>Hebrews 2:9,14-15</u> But we see Jesus, who as a man, lived for a short time lower than the angels and has now been crowned with glorious honor because of what he suffered in his death. For it was **by God's grace that he experienced death's bitterness on behalf of everyone!** ¹⁴Since all his "children" have flesh and blood, so Jesus became human to fully identify with us. He did this, **so that he could experience death and annihilate the effects of the intimidating accuser who holds against us the power of death.** ¹⁵By embracing death Jesus sets free those who live their entire lives in bondage to the tormenting dread of death.

[TTNT] <u>Hebrews 2:9,14-15</u> When He became man He was in a slightly inferior position to the angels; but now He is crowned with glory and honour because **He suffered death on behalf of all humanity.** This is the measure of the grace and favour God has shown us. ¹⁴Jesus shared in our humanity, having flesh and blood like us, so that **through His death on the cross, He could utterly destroy the devil, the one who holds the power of death.** ¹⁵Now all those who have spent their lives in bondage because of their fear of death and what lay beyond, are set free.

<u>**Hebrews 4:14-16**</u> Seeing then that we have a great high priest, that is passed into the heavens, Jesus the Son of God, let us hold fast our profession. ¹⁵For we have not an high priest which cannot be touched with the feeling of our infirmities; but was in all points tempted like as we are, yet without sin. **¹⁶Let us therefore come boldly unto the throne of grace, that we may obtain mercy, and find grace to help in time of need.**

[Alford-NT] <u>Hebrews 4:14-16</u> Seeing then that we have a great high priest, that is passed through the heavens, Jesus the Son of God, let us hold fast our confession. [15]For we have not an high priest unable to sympathize with our infirmities; but rather one in all points tempted in like manner, yet without sin. **[16]Let us therefore come boldly unto the throne of grace, that we may obtain mercy, and find grace to help while yet there is time.**

[AMP] <u>Hebrews 4:14-16</u> Inasmuch then as we [believers] have a great High Priest who has [already ascended and] passed through the heavens, Jesus the Son of God, let us hold fast our confession [of faith and cling tenaciously to our absolute trust in Him as Savior]. [15]For we do not have a High Priest who is unable to sympathize and understand our weaknesses and temptations, but One who has been tempted [knowing exactly how it feels to be human] in every respect as we are, yet without [committing any] sin. **[16]Therefore let us [with privilege] approach the throne of grace [that is, the throne of God's gracious favor] with confidence and without fear, so that we may receive mercy [for our failures] and find [His amazing] grace to help in time of need [an appropriate blessing, coming just at the right moment].**

[Bowes-NT] <u>Hebrews 4:14-16</u> Having therefore a great High-priest, who has passed through the heavens, Jesus the Son of God, let us hold fast the confession. [15]For we have not an High-priest unable to sympathize with our weaknesses; but tried in all things according to our likeness, apart from sin. **[16]Let us therefore approach with freedom of speech the throne of grace, that we may receive mercy and find grace for seasonable support.**

[BV-NT] <u>Hebrews 4:14-16</u> So having a great head priest who has gone through the heavenly regions, Jesus, the Son of God, we should hold tightly to the acknowledgment. [15]You see, we don't have a head priest who is not able to empathize with our weaknesses, but who has experienced trouble in each and everything, in each likeness, without sin. **[16]So we may come with openness to the throne of the generosity so that we might receive forgiving kindness and find generosity for well-timed help.**

[CWB] <u>Hebrews 4:14-16</u> He gave us a wonderful High Priest, Jesus the Son of God, who came to live with us and who has now gone up to heaven into the very presence of God, ministering there on our behalf. So let's hold firmly to the faith we profess. [15]We don't have a High Priest who doesn't understand us or who's incapable of feeling our pain. He was tempted in every way more powerfully than we will ever be tempted, yet He never sinned. **[16]So let's approach our Father's throne with confidence, asking Him for mercy and grace to help us, especially in our time of need.**

[ERV] <u>Hebrews 4:14-16</u> We have a great high priest who has gone to live with God in heaven. He is Jesus the Son of God. So let us continue to express our faith in him. [15]Jesus, our high priest, is able to understand our weaknesses. When Jesus lived on earth, he was tempted in every way. He was tempted in the same ways we are tempted, but he never sinned. **[16]With Jesus as our high priest, we can feel free to come before God's throne where there is grace. There we receive mercy and kindness to help us when we need it.**

[FBV-NT] <u>Hebrews 4:14-16</u> Since we have such a great high priest who has ascended to heaven, Jesus the Son of God, let us make sure we hold on to what we say we believe. [15]For the high priest we have isn't one who doesn't sympathize with our weaknesses, but one who was tempted in all the ways we are, but did not sin. **[16]So we should go confidently to God on his throne of grace so we can receive mercy, and discover the grace to help us when we really need it.**

[Fenton] <u>Hebrews 4:14-16</u> Having, therefore, a great High Priest gone into the heavens, Jesus the Son of God, let us cling to this confession. [15]For we have not a High Priest unable to sympathize with our weaknesses; but equally tried in all things like ourselves, yet sinless. **[16]Let us go, therefore, with freedom to the throne of the Giver, so that we may receive mercy; and we shall find a perfectly supporting gift.**

[Haweis-NT] <u>Hebrews 4:14-16</u> Having then a great high-priest passed through the heavens, Jesus the Son of God, let us hold fast the confession. [15]For we have not an high-priest incapable of a fellow-feeling with our infirmities, but one tempted in all points, in exact resemblance with ourselves, sin excepted. **[16]Let us therefore approach with boldness the throne of grace, that we may receive mercy, and find grace for seasonable help.**

[HBIV] <u>Hebrews 4:14-16</u> Having therefore a great high priest, who has passed through the heavens, Jesus the Son of God, let us hold fast our confession. [15]For we have not a high priest who can not sympathize with our infirmities, but one who has in all points been tried like as we are, apart from sin. **[16]Let us therefore come boldly to the throne of grace, that we may receive mercy, and find grace for well-timed help.**

[ISV] <u>Hebrews 4:14-16</u> Therefore, since we have a great high priest who has gone to heaven, Jesus the Son of God, let us live our lives consistent with our confession of faith. [15]For we do not have a high priest who is unable to sympathize with our weaknesses. Instead, we have one who in every respect has been tempted as we are, yet he never sinned. **[16]So let us keep on coming boldly to the throne of grace, so that we may obtain mercy and find grace to help us in our time of need.**

[Mace-NT] <u>Hebrews 4:14-16</u> who is passed into the heavens, Jesus the son of God, let us hold fast our profession. for we have [15]not an high priest who is incapable of compassionating our miseries; since he was exposed to the same trials as we are, sin only excepted. let [16]us therefore approach with confidence to the throne of grace, that we may obtain the seasonable assistance of divine mercy and favour.

[Madsen-NT] <u>Hebrews 4:14-16</u> Since then we have a great High Priest who has passed through all the heavens, sphere by sphere, Jesus, the Son of God, let us hold to our confession with all our strength. [15]For we do not have a High Priest who cannot suffer our weaknesses with us. He made himself like us and endured the same temptations in everything, only he remained free of sin. **[16]Let us then approach the throne of grace with confident freedom, that we may experience compassionate goodness and find a share in the grace which sends us help in the right hour.**

[Magiera-NT] <u>Hebrews 4:14-16</u> Therefore, because we have a great high priest, Jesus Christ, the Son of God, who went up to heaven, we should persist in confession of him. [15]For we do not have a high priest who is not able to feel our weakness, but one who was tempted in everything like us, [yet] without sin. **[16]Therefore, we should boldly come near the throne of his grace to receive mercies and to find grace for help in time of adversity.**

[MCC-NT] <u>Hebrews 4:14-16</u> Therefore We having a mighty Hierarch, Who has passed into the Heavens, Jesus the Son of God; let us retain our Profession. [15]For We have not an High-priest who is incapable of Sympathising with our Infirmities; but Who has been tempted in all Respects to a Similitude, devoid of Sin. **[16]Therefore let Us proceed with Confidence to the Throne of Grace; that We may obtain Mercy, and may find Favour toward seasonable Assistance.**

[MSG] <u>Hebrews 4:14-16</u> Now that we know what we have—Jesus, this great High Priest with ready access to God—let's not let it slip through our fingers. [15]We don't have a priest who is out of touch with our reality. He's been through weakness and testing, experienced it all—all but the sin. **[16]So let's walk right up to him and get what he is so ready to give. Take the mercy, accept the help.**

[REM-NT] <u>Hebrews 4:14-16</u> Therefore, since we have a great high priest (a great physician) who has gone through the heavens—Jesus, the Son of God—let us hold confidently to the truth about God and his plan to heal and restore us. [15]For we do not have a heavenly physician (a great high priest) who is unable to appreciate our weakness, suffering and struggles, but we have one who in his humanity was tempted in every way—exactly as we are—yet without sin, without ever giving in to selfish temptations. **[16]Therefore, let us approach the throne of God's grace without fear, but confidently, realizing**

that he longs to dispense all the resources of heaven to heal us so that we may receive mercy, grace, and every benefit to give us victory in our time of need.

[SG] <u>Hebrews 4:14-16</u> Since then we have in Jesus, the Son of God, a great high priest who has gone up into heaven, let us keep firm hold of our religion. [15]For our high priest is not one who is incapable of sympathy with our weaknesses, but he has been tempted in every way just as we have, without committing any sin. [16]**So let us come with courage to God's throne of grace to receive his forgiveness and find him responsive when we need his help.**

[Smith] <u>Hebrews 4:14-16</u> Having therefore a great chief priest, passed to the heavens, Jesus the Son of God, we should hold firmly the assent. [15]For we have not a chief priest unable to suffer with our weaknesses; but tried in all things as a resemblance, without sin. [16]**We should therefore go with freedom of speech to the throne of grace, that we receive mercy, and find grace for timely assistance.**

[Stevens-NT] <u>Hebrews 4:14-16</u> Since, then, we have so exalted a Mediator, Jesus, our risen and glorified Lord, let us continue loyal and faithful to him. [15]For though he is so highly exalted, yet he is full of compassionate feeling for our weaknesses; he has passed through a full course of moral trial like our own, without yielding to sin. [16]**We may therefore fearlessly approach his heavenly seat in the assurance that he will receive us with favor and will strengthen us to resist and overcome the power of evil when we are tempted.**

[TGNT] <u>Hebrews 4:14-16</u> So then, since we have a great Ruling Priest who has passed through the heavens, Jesus the God-Man, we must hold tightly to our commitment. [15]For we do not have a Ruling Priest who can't sympathize with our weaknesses, but one who has been tempted in every way yet without failing. [16]**Because of that, we can boldly approach the throne of favor, so we may receive mercy and find favor for help at just the right time.**

[TLB] <u>Hebrews 4:14-16</u> But Jesus the Son of God is our great High Priest who has gone to heaven itself to help us; therefore let us never stop trusting him. [15]This High Priest of ours understands our weaknesses since he had the same temptations we do, though he never once gave way to them and sinned. [16]**So let us come boldly to the very throne of God and stay there to receive his mercy and to find grace to help us in our times of need.**

[Way-NT] <u>Hebrews 4:14-16</u> To resume my argument with my fellow-believers: —since, as I said before, we have a great High-priest, who has already ascended through the skies, Jesus the son of God, let us cling to the faith that we profess. [15]Our weaknesses, our errors, need not discourage us; for we have not such a High-priest as is incapable of sympathizing with our frailties, but one who has been assaulted by temptations in all respects consonant with the likeness of His nature to ours, yet without falling into sin. [16]Let us, then, approach God's throne of grace with a fearlessly-outspoken plea, that we may gain God's mercy, and find His grace bestowed for our help just when it can best avail us.

[WilliamNorton-NT-G] <u>Hebrews 4:14-16</u> Having, therefore, a great High Priest, who has passed through the heavens, Jesus, the Son of God, let us hold fast our profession. [15]For we have not a high priest who is not able to have fellow-feeling with [us] in our weaknesses, but one who has been put to test in all things, like as [we are], without sin. [16]Let us, therefore, go near with confidence to [his] throne of gracious favour, that we may take hold of mercy, and find gracious favour for seasonable help.

<u>Hebrews 9:12</u> Neither by the blood of goats and calves, but by his own blood he entered in once into the holy place, having obtained eternal redemption for us.

[AMP] <u>Hebrews 9:12</u> He went once for all into the Holy Place [the Holy of Holies of heaven, into the presence of God], and not through the blood of goats and calves, but through His own blood, having obtained and secured eternal redemption [that is, the salvation of all who personally believe in Him as Savior].

[AUV-NT 2005] <u>Hebrews 9:12</u> And He did not enter [the heavenly Holy of Holies] by means of the blood of goats and calves but, by means of His own blood He entered the Holy of Holies [i.e., heaven] once for all time, [after] having obtained never ending redemption [i.e., salvation for us on the cross].

[Ballentine-NT] <u>Hebrews 9:12</u> and not through the blood of goats and calves, but through his own blood, entered once for all into the Holy Place, having procured enteral deliverance.

[Barnstone-NT] <u>Hebrews 9:12</u> And not by blood of goats and bulls but through His unique blood. He entered once into the holy place to gain for us eternal redemption.

[Beck] <u>Hebrews 9:12</u> And He didn't use the blood of goats and calves but through His own blood He entered only once into the Holy of Holies and paid a price that frees us forever.

[BWE-NT] <u>Hebrews 9:12</u> He did not take the blood of goats and young cows. He took his own blood. And he went into the Most Holy Place just once. He paid for our sins and made us free for ever.

[CEB] <u>Hebrews 9:12</u> He entered the holy of holies once for all by his own blood, not by the blood of goats or calves, securing our deliverance for all time.

[ERV] <u>Hebrews 9:12</u> Christ entered the Most Holy Place only one time—enough for all time. He entered the Most Holy Place by using his own blood, not the blood of goats or young bulls. He entered there and made us free from sin forever.

[GoodSpeed-NT] <u>Hebrews 9:12</u> taking with him no blood of goats and calves, but his own, and secured our permanent deliverance.

[Knox] <u>Hebrews 9:12</u> It is his own blood, not the blood of goats and calves, that has enabled him to enter, once for all, into the sanctuary; the ransom he has won lasts for ever.

[KNT] <u>Hebrews 9:12</u> and not with the blood of goats and calves but with his own blood. He entered, once and for all, into the holy place, accomplishing a redemption that lasts for ever.

[LITV] <u>Hebrews 9:12</u> nor through the blood of goats and of calves, but through His own blood, He entered once for all into the Holy of Holies, having procured everlasting redemption.

[Madsen-NT] <u>Hebrews 9:12</u> through the power of his own blood he has entered once and for all into the innermost sanctuary and has achieved an eternal redemption.

[NIRV] <u>Hebrews 9:12</u> He did not enter by spilling the blood of goats and calves. He entered the Most Holy Room by spilling his own blood. He did it once and for all time. In this way, he paid the price to set us free from sin forever.

[NLV] <u>Hebrews 9:12</u> Christ went into the Holiest Place of All one time for all people. He did not take the blood of goats and young cows to give to God as a gift in worship. He gave His own blood. By doing this, He bought us with His own blood and made us free from sin forever.

[Original-NT] <u>Hebrews 9:12</u> and not with blood of goats and calves, but with his own blood, procuring permanent redemption.

[Phillips] <u>Hebrews 9:12</u> It was not with goats' or calves' blood but with his own blood that he entered once and for all into the holy place, having won for us men eternal reconciliation with God.

[Shuttleworth-NT] <u>Hebrews 9:12</u> And not carrying with him the blood of goats or of calves, but the precious sacrifice of his own blessed blood, has entered once and for ever into the heavenly holy of holies, having offered for us one great and sufficient expiation which never will require repetition.

[TPT] <u>Hebrews 9:12</u> And he has entered once and forever into the Holiest Sanctuary of All, not with the blood of animal sacrifices, but the sacred blood of his own sacrifice. And he alone has made our salvation secure forever!

[TTNT] <u>Hebrews 9:12</u> And when He entered into the eternal Holy of holies He did not carry with Him an offering of the blood of goats and calves. No, He entered into the Holy of holies only once, with the offering of His own blood. And by that blood He made it possible for us to be one with God eternally. He literally bought us with the price of His own blood!

[Walker-NT] <u>Hebrews 9:12</u> Neither by the blood of goats and calves, but by shedding His own blood He entered in once for all into the holy place, the presence of God, having obtained by the perfection of His offering eternal redemption for us.

<u>Hebrews 10:23</u> Let us hold fast the profession of our faith without wavering; (for he is faithful that promised;)

[AMP] <u>Hebrews 10:23</u> Let us seize and hold tightly the confession of our hope without wavering, for He who promised is reliable and trustworthy and faithful [to His word];

[Barclay-NT] <u>Hebrews 10:23</u> Let us hold inflexibly to the hope which we tell the world we possess, for we can rely on the word of him who promised it to us.

[Berkeley] <u>Hebrews 10:23</u> Let us hold unwaveringly our grip on the hope we confess, for He who promised is faithful.

[BWE-NT] <u>Hebrews 10:23</u> We must hold on to God's promise that we have said we believed. And we must never let go. He has promised and he will do it.

[CB] <u>Hebrews 10:23</u> Let us stay true to the declaration of our faith, unwavering, for He who promises is trustworthy.

[Etheridge-NT] <u>Hebrews 10:23</u> and let us persevere in the confession of our hope, and not swerve; for faithful is He who hath promised us.

[EXB] <u>Hebrews 10:23</u> Let us hold ·firmly [without wavering] to the hope that we have confessed, because ·we can trust God to do what he promised [the one who promised is faithful].

[Fenton] <u>Hebrews 10:23</u> Let us unshrinkingly possess the confession of this hope—for the Promiser is faithful

[GW] <u>Hebrews 10:23</u> We must continue to hold firmly to our declaration of faith. The one who made the promise is faithful.

[Hammond-NT] <u>Hebrews 10:23</u> Let not all the afflictions and dangers that can approach us move us so much as to waver in our Christian profession, which, having the hope of eternal life joined with it, is fortification enough against all the terrors of this world, having God's fidelity engaged to make good the promise to us.

[Knox] <u>Hebrews 10:23</u> Do not let us waver in acknowledging the hope we cherish; we have a promise from one who is true to his word.

[Morgan-NT] <u>Hebrews 10:23</u> We retain the unwavering profession of faith, for he having promised is faithful.

[NEB] <u>Hebrews 10:23</u> Let us be firm and unswerving in the confession of our hope, for the Giver of the promise may be trusted.

[NENT] <u>Hebrews 10:23</u> we should hold fast to the acknowledgment of hope without nodding our heads. For the one who promised is reliable.

[Newcome] <u>Hebrews 10:23</u> let us hold fast the steady profession of our hope; (for he is faithful that hath promised:)

[Original-NT] <u>Hebrews 10:23</u> Let us adhere inflexibly to the confession of our Hope; for he who has promised is faithful.

[Phillips] <u>Hebrews 10:23</u> In this confidence let us hold on to the hope that we profess without the slightest hesitation—for he is utterly dependable—

[Sacred-NT] <u>Hebrews 10:23</u> let us hold fast the confession of the hope, unmoved; for he is faithful, who has promised.

[Sawyer-7590] <u>Hebrews 10:23</u> let us hold firmly the profession of the faith, without declining; for he is faithful that promised;

[Stevens-NT] <u>Hebrews 10:23</u> And let us steadfastly adhere to the assurance of salvation given us in Christ, for this promise of God will not fail of its fulfilment.

[T4T] <u>Hebrews 10:23</u> We must unwaveringly keep professing what we believe. Since God faithfully does all he promised to do, we must confidently expect him to keep doing that.

[TCNT] <u>Hebrews 10:23</u> Let us maintain the confession of our hope unshaken, for he who has given us his promise will not fail us.

[TTNT] <u>Hebrews 10:23</u> So let us not allow anything to distract us from the hope of what lies ahead of us in fulfilment of all He has promised us, for He is faithful in keeping His Word.

[UDB] <u>Hebrews 10:23</u> We must unwaveringly keep stating what we believe. Since Yahweh faithfully does all he promised to do, we must confidently expect him to do these things.

[Wand-NT] <u>Hebrews 10:23</u> Let us cling to the statement of our hope without any weakening, for He who gave us the promise is utterly trustworthy.

[Worsley-NT] <u>Hebrews 10:23</u> Let us inflexibly retain the profession of our hope, (for He is faithful who hath promised)

<u>Hebrews 10:35-36</u> **Cast not away therefore your confidence, which hath great recompence of reward.** [36]For ye have need of patience, that, after ye have done the will of God, ye might receive the promise.

[Ballentine-NT] <u>Hebrews 10:35-36</u> **So do not throw away your boldness. For it has great reward.** [36]For you need endurance so that you may do God's will and receive the promise.

[BLE] <u>Hebrews 10:35-36</u> **So do not throw up your confidence, which has great wages payable.** [36]For staying power is what it takes, that after doing God's will you may receive the fulfillment of the promise:

[BOOKS-NT] <u>Hebrews 10:35-36</u> **So do not throw away your confidence; it will be richly rewarded.** [36]You need to persevere so that when you have done the will of God, you will receive what he has promised.

[BWE-NT] <u>Hebrews 10:35-36</u> **So do not stop believing God now. Your faith will bring you much reward.** [36]You must not give up believing. Then you will do what God wants you to do. Then you will get what he promised you.

[ERV] <u>Hebrews 10:35-36</u> **So don't lose the courage that you had in the past. Your courage will be rewarded richly.** [36]You must be patient. After you have done what God wants, you will get what he promised you.

[Moffatt-NT 1917] <u>Hebrews 10:35-36</u> **Now do not drop that confidence of yours; it carries with it a rich hope of reward**. [36]Steady patience is what you need, so that after doing the will of God you may get what you have been promised.

[MSG] <u>Hebrews 10:35-36</u> **So don't throw it all away now. You were sure of yourselves then. It's still a sure thing!** [36]But you need to stick it out, staying with God's plan so you'll be there for the promised completion.

[NIRV] <u>Hebrews 10:35-36</u> **So don't throw away your bold faith. It will bring you rich rewards.** [36]You need to be faithful. Then you will do what God wants. You will receive what he has promised.

[REM-NT] <u>Hebrews 10:35-36</u> **So don't become discouraged and lose confidence; your trust will be richly rewarded**. [36]Maintain your focus and continue to implement God's methods in your lives, and you will receive all that he has promised;

[Smith] <u>Hebrews 10:35-36</u> **Throw not away therefore your freedom of speech, which has great payment of reward**. [36]For ye have need of patience, that, having done the will of God, ye might receive the promise.

[T4T] <u>Hebrews 10:35-36</u> **So, do not become discouraged when they cause you to suffer {you are persecuted}, because if you continue to trust in God, he will greatly reward you**. [36]You must patiently continue to trust in him in order that, because of your doing what God wants you to do, he will give you what he has promised.

[TCNT] <u>Hebrews 10:35-36</u> **Do not, therefore, abandon the confidence that you have gained, for it has a great reward awaiting it.** [36]You still have need of patient endurance, in order that, when you have done God's will, you may obtain the fulfillment of his promise.

[TLB] <u>Hebrews 10:35-36</u> **Do not let this happy trust in the Lord die away, no matter what happens. Remember your reward!** [36]You need to keep on patiently doing God's will if you want him to do for you all that he has promised.

[TPT] <u>Hebrews 10:35-36</u> **So don't lose your bold, courageous faith, for you are destined for a great reward!** [36]You need the strength of endurance to reveal the poetry of God's will and then you receive the promise in full.

[Way-NT] <u>Hebrews 10:35-36</u> **Do not, then, fling away your fearless trust, for it includes a glorious repayment for all**. [36]Yes, you have need of steadfast endurance, so that you may perform the will of God, and so receive the fulfilment of His promise.

[WilliamNorton-NT-P] <u>Hebrews 10:35-36</u> **Therefore destroy not the confidence which ye have, and for which there will be a great reward**. [36]For patient endurance is needful for you, that ye may do the will of God, and receive what is promised.

[Williams-NT] <u>Hebrews 10:35-36</u> **So you must never give up your confident courage, for it holds a rich reward for you.** [36]Indeed, to carry out the will of God and to receive the blessing He has promised, you need endurance, for:

[Worsley-NT] <u>Hebrews 10:35-36</u> **Cast not away therefore your couragious profession, which hath a great recompence of reward**. [36]For ye have need of patience, that having done the will of God ye may receive the promise.

<u>Hebrews 10:38</u> **Now the just shall live by faith**: but if any man draw back, my soul shall have no pleasure in him.

[Ainslie-NT] <u>Hebrews 10:38</u> **Now my just man shall live by faith**: but if he draw back, my soul shall have no pleasure in him.

[Ballentine-NT] <u>Hebrews 10:38</u> **But my righteous one shall live as a result of his faith**. And if he shall shrink back, My soul hath no pleasure in him.

[CJB] <u>Hebrews 10:38</u> **But the person who is righteous will live his life by trusting**, and if he shrinks back, I will not be pleased with him."

[ERV] <u>Hebrews 10:38</u> **The person who is right with me will live by trusting in me**. But I will not be pleased with the one who turns back in fear."

[Mace-NT] <u>Hebrews 10:38</u> **the just shall have life by trusting in me**, but if he revolt, he will be the object of my displeasure.

[TLB] <u>Hebrews 10:38</u> **And those whose faith has made them good in God's sight must live by faith, trusting him in everything**. Otherwise, if they shrink back, God will have no pleasure in them.

[TPT] <u>Hebrews 10:38</u> And he also says, "**My righteous ones will live from my faith**. But if fear holds them back, my soul is not content with them!"

[TTNT] <u>Hebrews 10:38</u> **But he who is at one with God will live by faith**. If he shrinks away from the truth because of fear, I will not be pleased with him."

[Way-NT] <u>Hebrews 10:38</u> 'A<small>ND MY RIGHTEOUS SERVANT SHALL WIN LIFE FROM HIS FAITH: YET, IF HE SHRINK BACK, MY SOUL HATH NO PLEASURE IN HIM.</small>'

<u>Hebrews 11:1</u> Now faith is the substance of things hoped for, the evidence of things not seen.

[AMP] <u>Hebrews 11:1</u> Now faith is the assurance (title deed, confirmation) of things hoped for (divinely guaranteed), and the evidence of things not seen [the conviction of their reality—faith comprehends as fact what cannot be experienced by the physical senses].

[AMPC] <u>Hebrews 11:1</u> Now faith is the assurance (the confirmation, the title deed) of the things [we] hope for, being the proof of things [we] do not see and the conviction of their reality [faith perceiving as real fact what is not revealed to the senses].

[Anchor] <u>Hebrews 11:1</u> Now faith is [the] groundwork of things hoped for, [the] basis for testing things not seen.

[Anderson-NT] <u>Hebrews 11:1</u> Now, faith is confidence with respect to things hoped for, persuasion with respect to things not seen:

[AUV-NT 2005] <u>Hebrews 11:1</u> Now, [having] faith is being sure of [receiving] what is hoped for, and certain [of the existence] of what is not visible.

[BBE] <u>Hebrews 11:1</u> Now faith is the substance of things hoped for, and the sign that the things not seen are true.

[Belsham-NT] <u>Hebrews 11:1</u> Now faith is the confident expectation of things hoped for, the firm conviction of things not seen.

[Berkeley] <u>Hebrews 11:1</u> But faith forms a solid ground for what is hoped for, a conviction of unseen realities.

[BLE] <u>Hebrews 11:1</u> And faith is assuming the validity of hopes, putting unseen things to the test.

[CEB] <u>Hebrews 11:1</u> Faith is the reality of what we hope for, the proof of what we don't see.

[ERV] <u>Hebrews 11:1</u> Faith is what makes real the things we hope for. It is proof of what we cannot see.

[Etheridge-NT] <u>Hebrews 11:1</u> Now FAITH is the persuasion concerning things which are in hope, as if they were in reality, and a revelation of those which are not seen.

[Green-NT] <u>Hebrews 11:1</u> Now faith is a grounded assurance of things hoped for, a clear warrant of matters not seen.

[GT] <u>Hebrews 11:1</u> Faith is the title-deed to the things we hope for. Faith is being sure of things we cannot see.

[GW] <u>Hebrews 11:1</u> Faith assures us of things we expect and convinces us of the existence of things we cannot see.

[Haak] <u>Hebrews 11:1</u> Now faith is a firm ground of the things which are hoped, (and) an argument of things which are not seen.

[HNT] <u>Hebrews 11:1</u> Now faith is to be confident of what we hope for, to be convinced of what we do not see.

[Jerusalem] <u>Hebrews 11:1</u> Only faith can guarantee the blessings that we hope for, or prove the existence of the realities that at present remain unseen.

[Mace-NT] <u>Hebrews 11:1</u> Now faith is the foundation of our hopes of happiness, and the persuasion we have about things not evident to our senses.

[Madsen-NT] <u>Hebrews 11:1</u> Faith is the intrinsic working-in-advance of that which we hope for, an inner proof of that which still rests, unseen, in the lap of the future.

[Murdock-NT] <u>Hebrews 11:1</u> Now faith is the persuasion of the things that are in hope, as if they were in act; and [it is] the manifestness of the things not seen.

[NAB] <u>Hebrews 11:1</u> Faith is the realization of what is hoped for and evidence of things not seen.

[NCV] <u>Hebrews 11:1</u> Faith means being sure of the things we hope for and knowing that something is real even if we do not see it.

[NET] <u>Hebrews 11:1</u> Now faith is being sure of what we hope for, being convinced of what we do not see.

[Norlie-NT] <u>Hebrews 11:1</u> Now, faith means that we are sure of getting the things we hope for; it means that we are certain as to things we cannot see.

[Original-NT] <u>Hebrews 11:1</u> Now faith is the solid ground of our expectations, the proof of unseen actualities.

[REV-NT] <u>Hebrews 11:1</u> Now trust is firm confidence in things hoped for, a conviction regarding things not seen.

[Shuttleworth-NT] <u>Hebrews 11:1</u> Let me then now remind you what faith is. It is not the visible and tangible fruition of things present, but that which gives a substantial value to things as yet in remote futurity; it is that faculty of the mind by which we lay hold of the objects of the invisible world, as though they were actually subject to the perceptions of the bodily senses.

[Spencer-NT] <u>Hebrews 11:1</u> Now faith is the firm confidence of things hoped for, a sure insight into things unseen.

[TLB] <u>Hebrews 11:1</u> What is faith? It is the confident assurance that something we want is going to happen. It is the certainty that what we hope for is waiting for us, even though we cannot see it up ahead.

[TTNT] <u>Hebrews 11:1</u> True faith is being sure of the hope we have and being certain that we shall see what has been promised, even though we do not see these things at present.

[Wand-NT] <u>Hebrews 11:1</u> Now faith is a conviction of the fulfillment of our hopes, and a continual reliance upon the unseen world.

[Whiting-NT] <u>Hebrews 11:1</u> Now faith is the certain persuasion of things hoped for, the demonstration of things not seen:

<u>Hebrews 11:6</u> **But without faith it is impossible to please him**: for he that cometh to God must believe that he is, and that he is a rewarder of them that diligently seek him.

[ACV] <u>Hebrews 11:6</u> And **apart from faith it is impossible to please him**. For he who comes to God must believe that he is, and becomes a rewarder of those who search for him.

[Anchor] <u>Hebrews 11:6</u> **Now, without faith it is impossible to please him**, for it is necessary for the one who approaches God to believe that he is and [that] he becomes a wage-payer to those who seek him.

[AUV-NT 2005] <u>Hebrews 11:6</u> And **unless one has faith, it is impossible for him to be pleasing to God**, for the person who comes to God must believe that He exists and that He rewards those who seek Him.

[BSB-NT] <u>Hebrews 11:6</u> And **without faith it is impossible to please God**, because anyone who approaches Him must believe that He exists and that He rewards those who earnestly seek Him.

[CEB] <u>Hebrews 11:6</u> **It's impossible to please God without faith** because the one who draws near to God must believe that he exists and that he rewards people who try to find him.

[CWB] <u>Hebrews 11:6</u> **But it's impossible to please God without having faith**. Those who come to God must not only believe that He exists, but that He cares and rewards those who search for Him.

[EEBT] <u>Hebrews 11:6</u> **Unless we believe God, it is impossible for us to make God happy**. Anyone who comes to God must believe him. That person must believe that God is really there. And they must believe that God is good to people. God gives good things to everyone who really wants to find him.

[ERV] <u>Hebrews 11:6</u> **Without faith no one can please God.** Whoever comes to God must believe that he is real and that he rewards those who sincerely try to find him.

[Mace-NT] <u>Hebrews 11:6</u> **now without faith it is impossible to be acceptable to him**: for he that presents himself to God, cannot but believe he exists, and that he is a rewarder of those who make their addresses to him.

[MSG] <u>Hebrews 11:6</u> **It's impossible to please God apart from faith**. And why? Because anyone who wants to approach God must believe both that he exists and that he cares enough to respond to those who seek him.

[Phillips] <u>Hebrews 11:6</u> **And without faith it is impossible to please him**. The man who approaches God must have faith in two things, first that God exists and secondly that God rewards those who search for him.

[REM-NT] <u>Hebrews 11:6</u> **But without trust in God, it is impossible to please him**. Those who come to God must do more than believe that he exists: they must recognize the truth of his absolute trustworthiness of character as revealed in Christ, and understand that he desires to heal and restore all those who trust him. Otherwise, fear will never be removed.

[TLB] <u>Hebrews 11:6</u> **You can never please God without faith**, without depending on him. Anyone who wants to come to God must believe that there is a God and that he rewards those who sincerely look for him.

[TPT] <u>Hebrews 11:6</u> And **without faith living within us it would be impossible to please God**. For we come to God in faith knowing that he is real and that he rewards the faith of those who give all their passion and strength into seeking him.

[TTNT] <u>Hebrews 11:6</u> **By now you can see that it is impossible to please God without faith.** In our relationship with Him, we have to believe that He not only exists, but actually wants to answer us when we pray. He longs to give us what we need when we seek Him with sincere and earnest faith.

<u>Hebrews 11:11</u> **Through faith also Sara herself received strength to conceive seed,** and was delivered of a child when she was past age, because she judged him faithful who had promised.

[AMP] <u>Hebrews 11:11</u> **By faith even Sarah herself received the ability to conceive [a child],** even [when she was long] past the normal age for it, because she considered Him who had given her the promise to be reliable and true [to His word].

[AMPC] <u>Hebrews 11:11</u> **Because of faith also Sarah herself received physical power to conceive a child,** even when she was long past the age for it, because she considered [God] Who had given her the promise to be reliable and trustworthy and true to His word.

[Baxter-NT] <u>Hebrews 11:11</u> **And Sarah past Age, brought forth Isaac,** because she trusted God's Promise, against natural probability.

[Elkhazen-NT] <u>Hebrews 11:11</u> By faith also Sara herself, being barren, received strength to conceive seed, even past the time of age; because she believed that he was faithful who had promised,

[Etheridge-NT] <u>Hebrews 11:11</u> **By faith Saro, who was barren, received strength to conceive seed,** and, which (thing) was not in the time of her years, gave birth (to a son); because she was sure that he who had promised to her was faithful.

[Haweis-NT] <u>Hebrews 11:11</u> **By faith also that very Sarah, who was barren, received ability for the conception of seed,** and past the usual time of life brought forth a child, because she accounted that he who promised it, would be true to his promise.

[Knox] <u>Hebrews 11:11</u> **It was faith that enabled Sara, barren till then, to conceive offspring,** although she was past the age of child-bearing; she believed that God would be faithful to his word.

[Phillips] <u>Hebrews 11:11</u> **It was by faith that even Sarah gained the physical vitality to conceive** despite her great age, and she gave birth to a child when far beyond the normal years of child-bearing. She did this because she believed that the One who had given the promise was utterly trustworthy.

[TLB] <u>Hebrews 11:11</u> **Sarah, too, had faith, and because of this she was able to become a mother** in spite of her old age, for she realized that God, who gave her his promise, would certainly do what he said.

[TPT] <u>Hebrews 11:11</u> **Sarah's faith embraced the miracle power to conceive** even though she was barren and was past the age of childbearing, for the authority of her faith rested in the One who made the promise, and she tapped into his faithfulness.

[TTT-NT] <u>Hebrews 11:11</u> **By faith even barren Sarah herself received strength to conceive seed,** and beyond a reasonable age bore a child; for she determined the one who promised to be faithful.

[TWTY-RCT-NT-V1] <u>Hebrews 11:11</u> **And by trust and reliance, obedience and confidence, certainty and guarantee, assurance and dependence in the Supreme One, Sarah herself, even though she was sterile and barren and past the suitable and right age and proper time, received and seized, grasped and ascertained, took and collected, acquired and obtained authority and power, right and ability, permission and freedom, energy and might, force and influence, capability and significance for and on behalf of laying down the foundation for seed, the power to conceive and therefore bear children,** since and because she thought and considered, seemed and deemed, reckoned and regarded He who made and declared, professed and announced the promise and gracious pledge, offer and vow as trustworthy and certain, firm and reliable, verifiable and stable, dependable and guaranteed, steadfast and enforced, established and validated.

Hebrews 12:12-13 Wherefore lift up the hands which hang down, and the feeble knees; [13]And make straight paths for your feet, lest that which is lame be turned out of the way; **but let it rather be healed**.

[Barclay-NT] **Hebrews 12:12-13** So then, fill the listless hands with energy; strengthen the trembling knees; [13]make straight paths for your feet to walk in, **so that the lame limb may not be dislocated, but cured**.

[BBE] **Hebrews 12:12-13** For this cause let the hands which are hanging down be lifted up, and let the feeble knees be made strong, [13]And make straight roads for your feet, so that the feeble may not be turned out of the way, **but may be made strong**.

[Berkeley] **Hebrews 12:12-13** So, straighten out your listless hands and your shaky knees; [13]step out straight ahead with your feet, so that lame legs may not be dislocated **but rather grow healthy**.

[CEB] **Hebrews 12:12-13** So strengthen your drooping hands and weak knees! [13]Make straight paths for your feet so that if any part is lame, **it will be healed rather than injured more seriously**.

[CLV] **Hebrews 12:12-13** Wherefore stiffen the flaccid hands and the paralyzed knees, [13]and make upright tracks for your feet, that the lame one may not turn aside, **yet rather may be healed**.

[FBV-NT] **Hebrews 12:12-13** So strengthen your feeble hands, and your weak knees! [13]Make straight paths to walk on, so that those who are crippled won't lose their way, **but will be healed**.

[GNT] **Hebrews 12:12-13** Lift up your tired hands, then, and strengthen your trembling knees! [13]Keep walking on straight paths, so that the lame foot may not be disabled, **but instead be healed**.

[Goodspeed-NT] **Hebrews 12:12-13** So tighten your loosening hold! Stiffen your wavering stand! [13]And keep your feet in straight paths, so that limbs that are lame may not be dislocated **but instead be cured**.

[HNT] **Hebrews 12:12-13** Therefore lift up the nerveless hands and the paralysed knees, [13]and make even tracks for your feet, so that what is lame may not be dislocated **but rather cured**.

[ISV] **Hebrews 12:12-13** Therefore, strengthen your tired arms and your weak knees, [13]and straighten the paths of your life, so that your lameness may not become worse, **but instead may be healed**.

[NEB] **Hebrews 12:12-13** Come, then, stiffen your drooping arms and shaking knees, and keep your steps from wavering. [13]Then the disabled limb will not be put out of joint, **but regain its former powers**.

[NLV] **Hebrews 12:12-13** So lift up your hands that have been weak. Stand up on your weak legs. [13]Walk straight ahead so the weak leg will not be turned aside, **but will be healed**.

[Phillips] **Hebrews 12:12-13** So tighten your loosening grip and steady your trembling knees. [13]Keep your feet on a steady path, so that the limping foot does not collapse **but recovers strength**.

[Smith] **Hebrews 12:12-13** Wherefore set upright the relaxed hands, and palsied knees; [13]And make straight wheel-ruts to your feet, lest the lame thing turned aside; and **it should rather be healed**.

Hebrews 13:8 Jesus Christ the same yesterday, and to day, and for ever.

If Jesus never changes, then if He ever healed, He is still healing today. If everyone that came to Him got healed when He was on the earth, then everyone that will forever come to Him has the legal right to be healed—otherwise Jesus has changed.

[AMPC] **Hebrews 13:8** Jesus Christ (the Messiah) is [always] the same, yesterday, today, [yes] and forever (to the ages).

[CLV] **Hebrews 13:8** Jesus Christ, yesterday and today, is the Same One for the eons also.

[EEBT] <u>Hebrews 13:8</u> Jesus Christ is the same today as he was yesterday. And he will be the same always.

[Goodspeed-NT] <u>Hebrews 13:8</u> Jesus Christ is the same today that he was yesterday, and he will be so forever.

[Nary-NT] <u>Hebrews 13:8</u> Jesus Christ was yesterday, is to day, and will be the same for ever.

[Phillips] <u>Hebrews 13:8</u> Jesus Christ is always the same, yesterday, today and for ever.

[Rotherham] <u>Hebrews 13:8</u> Jesus Christ, yesterday, and today, is the same, —and unto the ages.

[T4T] <u>Hebrews 13:8</u> Jesus Christ is the same now as he was previously, and he will be the same forever.

[TCNT] <u>Hebrews 13:8</u> Jesus Christ is the same yesterday and to-day—yes, and for ever!

[TPT] <u>Hebrews 13:8</u> Jesus, the Anointed One, is always the same—yesterday, today, and forever.

[TTNT] <u>Hebrews 13:8</u> Jesus Christ is the same today as He has been in the past, and He will always remain the same for all eternity.

[Wade] <u>Hebrews 13:8</u> Jesus Christ, the object of their faith, is, in the past, in the present, and for all time to come, ever the Same.

[Wand-NT] <u>Hebrews 13:8</u> Jesus Christ is for you just what He was for them, the same yesterday, to-day and for ever.

JAMES

<u>James 4:7</u> Submit yourselves therefore to God. Resist the devil, and he will flee from you.

If the devil will flee, run, fly, scamper away from you just by resisting him, then so will sickness and disease.

[AMP] <u>James 4:7</u> So submit to [the authority of] God. Resist the devil [stand firm against him] and he will flee from you.

[AMPC] <u>James 4:7</u> So be subject to God. Resist the devil [stand firm against him], and he will flee from you.

[Authentic-NT] <u>James 4:7</u> Submit yourselves to God therefore, but oppose the Devil and he will fly from you.

[Barclay-NT] <u>James 4:7</u> So then, accept the authority of God. Take a stand against the devil, and he will run away from you.

[Bassett] <u>James 4:7</u> Submit ye then to God, but withstand the devil, and he shall flee from you.

[BBE] <u>James 4:7</u> For this cause be ruled by God; but make war on the Evil One and he will be put to flight before you.

[BLE] <u>James 4:7</u> So be submissive to God; but stand up against the devil and he will run from you.

[CEV] <u>James 4:7</u> Surrender to God! Resist the devil, and he will run from you.

[Doddridge-NT] <u>James 4:7</u> Subject yourselves therefore to God; and in being listed in his army, keep the rank which he has assigned you; resist the devil steadily and courageously, as the great enemy of your eternal salvation: and though he may for a while combat you with his varied temptations, he will at length flee from you, and your progress in religion, and your victory over your spiritual adversaries, will grow daily more easy.

[Fenton] <u>James 4:7</u> Subject yourselves therefore to God; but repel the Devil, and he will fly from you.

[Haweis-NT] <u>James 4:7</u> Be in subjection then to God. Resist the devil, and he will fly from you.

[Kneeland-NT] <u>James 4:7</u> Submit yourselves therefore to God: resist the impostor, and he will flee from you:

[LDB-NT] <u>James 4:7</u> So surrender your will completely to God. Then take a strong and determined stance like a soldier against the devil, and he will run from you.

[MSG] <u>James 4:7</u> So let God work his will in you. Yell a loud no to the Devil and watch him scamper.

[NCV] <u>James 4:7</u> So give yourselves completely to God. Stand against the devil, and the devil will run from you.

[NEB] <u>James 4:7</u> Be submissive then to God. Stand up to the devil and he will turn and run.

[Shuttleworth-NT] <u>James 4:7</u> Submit yourselves then to God's blessed protection, and under his support resist the devil, and he will flee from you.

[Smith] <u>James 4:7</u> Be subjected therefore to God. Resist the accuser, and he will flee from you.

[T4T] <u>James 4:7</u> So submit yourselves to God. Resist the devil/Refuse to do what the devil wants, and as a result he will run away from you.

[TNT] <u>James 4:7</u> So submit to God. Stand up to the devil and he will run away from you;

[Wilson-NT] <u>James 4:7</u> Be you subject therefore to God. Stand opposed to the Enemy, and he will flee from you.

[Wuest-NT] <u>James 4:7</u> Be subject with implicit obedience to God at once and once for all. Stand immovable against the onset of the devil and he will flee from you.

<u>James 5:14-16</u> Is any sick among you? let him call for the elders of the church; and let them pray over him, anointing him with oil in the name of the Lord: [sozo]**And the prayer of faith shall save**[sozo] **the sick, and the Lord shall raise him up**; and if he have committed sins, they shall be forgiven him. [16]Confess your faults one to another, and **pray one for another, that ye may be healed.** The effectual fervent prayer of a righteous man availeth much.

The Greek word for "save" is often translated as healed or made whole in the King James version. In the context of praying for the sick, it would have been better to use the word "heal" in this verse as many other translations do below.

[AMP] <u>James 5:14-16</u> Is anyone among you sick? He must call for the elders (spiritual leaders) of the church and they are to pray over him, anointing him with oil in the name of the Lord; [15]**and the prayer of faith will restore the one who is sick, and the Lord will raise him up**; and if he has committed sins, he will be forgiven. [16]Therefore, confess your sins to one another [your false steps, your offenses], and **pray for one another, that you may be healed and restored.** The heartfelt and persistent prayer of a righteous man (believer) can accomplish much [when put into action and made effective by God—it is dynamic and can have tremendous power].

[Anderson-Sinaitic NT] <u>James 5:14-16</u> Is any one among you sick? Let him call for the elders of the church, and let them pray over him, anointing him with oil in the name of the Lord. [15]And **the prayer of faith shall save the sick, and the Lord shall raise him up**; and if he have committed sins, it shall be forgiven him. [16]Confess your sins one to another, and **pray for one another, that you may be restored to health:** the prayer of a righteous man, being energetic, avails much.

[BBE] <u>James 5:14-16</u> Is anyone among you ill? let him send for the rulers of the church; and let them say prayers over him, putting oil on him in the name of the Lord. [15]**And by the prayer of faith the man who is ill will be made well, and he will be lifted up by the Lord**, and for any sin which he has done he will have forgiveness. [16]So then, make a statement of your sins to one another, and **say prayers for one another so that you may be made well.** The prayer of a good man is full of power in its working.

[BLE] James 5:14-16 Is anyone among you sick? let him call in the elders of the church, and let them pray over him, putting oil on him in the name of the Lord, [15]**and the prayer of faith shall make the sufferer well, and the Lord shall raise him**; and if he has committed sins he shall be forgiven. [16]So confess your sins to each other and **pray for each other that you may be healed.** Great is the efficacy of a righteous man's strenuous prayer.

[BOOKS-NT] James 5:14-16 Is anyone among you sick? Let them call the elders of the church to pray over them and anoint them with oil in the name of the Lord. [15]**And the prayer offered in faith will make the sick person well; the Lord will raise them up.** If they have sinned, they will be forgiven. [16]Therefore confess your sins to each other and **pray for each other so that you may be healed.** The prayer of a righteous person is powerful and effective.

[BWE-NT] James 5:14-16 Is any one of you sick? He should call for the leaders of the church people. They should talk to God about him and put oil on him in the name of the Lord. [15]**Because they talk to God, and believe, he will hear them. The sick man will be healed. The Lord will make him well again.** If the sick man has done wrong things, the Lord will forgive him. [16]So tell one another the wrong things you have done. **And tell God about each other's needs, so that you will be healed.** When a good man talks to God, big things can be done.

[CEB] James 5:14-16 If any of you are sick, they should call for the elders of the church, and the elders should pray over them, anointing them with oil in the name of the Lord. [15]**Prayer that comes from faith will heal the sick, for the Lord will restore them to health.** And if they have sinned, they will be forgiven. [16]For this reason, confess your sins to each other and **pray for each other so that you may be healed.** The prayer of the righteous person is powerful in what it can achieve.

[CLV] James 5:14-16 Is anyone infirm among you? Let him call to him the elders of the ecclesia, and let them pray over him, rubbing him with olive oil in the name of the Lord. [15]**And the vow of faith will be saving the faltering and the Lord will be rousing him up**, and, if he should have done sins, it will be forgiven him. [16]Then confess sins to one another and **pray for one another, so that you may be healed.** The operative petition of the just is availing much.

[ERV] James 5:14-16 Are you sick? Ask the elders of the church to come and rub oil on you in the name of the Lord and pray for you. [15]**If such a prayer is offered in faith, it will heal anyone who is sick. The Lord will heal them.** And if they have sinned, he will forgive them. [16]So always tell each other the wrong things you have done. **Then pray for each other. Do this so that God can heal you.** Anyone who lives the way God wants can pray, and great things will happen.

[Etheridge-NT] James 5:14-16 and if he be sick, let him call for the presbyters of the church, and they will pray over him and anoint him with oil in the name of our Lord. [15]**And the prayer of faith shall make whole him who was sick, and our Lord shall raise him up**; and if he have committed sins, they shall be forgiven him. [16]But confess your faults one to another, and **pray one for another, that you may be healed.** For great is the power of that prayer which the righteous prayeth.

[EXB] James 5:14-16 Anyone who is sick should call the church's elders. They should pray for and ·pour oil on the person [anoint that person with olive oil; anointing probably indicates dedicating or setting aside the person to God's care] in the name of the Lord. [15]**And the prayer that is said with faith will ·make the sick person well [save the sick; the same Greek word is commonly used for both physical healing and spiritual salvation]; the Lord will ·heal [raise up] that person.** And if the person has sinned, the sins will be forgiven. [16][Therefore,] Confess your sins to each other and **pray for**

each other so God can heal you. ·When a believing person prays, great things happen [The prayer of a righteous person is powerful and effective].

[GT] James 5:14-16 If one of you is sick, he should call for the elders of the called out people. They will pray for him and put oil on him in the name of the Lord. **¹⁵Prayer to God made in faith will make the sick person well. The Lord will raise him up.** If this person has sinned, then God will forgive him. ¹⁶Admit your sins to one another. **Pray for each other. God will make you well.** When a person is right with God, the power of his sincere prayer is tremendous!

[HCSB] James 5:14-16 Is anyone among you sick? He should call for the elders of the church, and they should pray over him after anointing him with olive oil in the name of the Lord. **¹⁵The prayer of faith will save the sick person, and the Lord will restore him to health**; if he has committed sins, he will be forgiven. ¹⁶Therefore, confess your sins to one another and **pray for one another, so that you may be healed**. The urgent request of a righteous person is very powerful in its effect.

[KNT] James 5:14-16 Are any among you sick? They should call for the elders of the church, and they should pray over the sick person, anointing them with oil in the name of the Lord. **¹⁵Faithful prayer will rescue the sick person, and the Lord will raise them up.** If they have committed any sin, it will be forgiven them. ¹⁶So confess your sins to one another, and **pray for one another, that you may be healed.** When a righteous person prays, that prayer carries great power.

[MOUNCE] James 5:14-16 Is anyone among you sick? He should call for the elders of the church and have them pray over him, anointing him with oil in the name of the Lord; ¹⁵and **the prayer offered in faith will restore the one who is sick and the Lord will raise him up.** And if he has committed sins, he will be forgiven. ¹⁶Therefore confess your sins to one another and **pray for one another so that you may be healed.** The active prayer of a righteous person has great power.

[MSG] James 5:14-16 Are you sick? Call the church leaders together to pray and anoint you with oil in the name of the Master. **¹⁵Believing-prayer will heal you, and Jesus will put you on your feet.** And if you've sinned, you'll be forgiven—healed inside and out. ¹⁶Make this your common practice: Confess your sins to each other and **pray for each other so that you can live together whole and healed.** The prayer of a person living right with God is something powerful to be reckoned with.

[MW-NT] James 5:14-16 Is any among you sick? Let him call for the elders of the congregation, and let them pray over him, anointing him with oil in the name of the Lord. ¹⁵Then **the prayer of faith will heal the one who is sick, and the Lord will raise him up.** If he has committed sins, he will be forgiven. ¹⁶Confess your offenses to each other, and **pray for each other, that you may be healed.** The earnest entreaty of a righteous man is very powerful.

[NIRV] James 5:14-16 Is anyone among you sick? Then that person should send for the elders of the church to pray over them. They should ask the elders to anoint them with olive oil in the name of the Lord. **¹⁵The prayer offered by those who have faith will make the sick person well. The Lord will heal them.** If they have sinned, they will be forgiven. ¹⁶So confess your sins to one another. **Pray for one another so that you might be healed.** The prayer of a godly person is powerful. Things happen because of it.

[NJB] James 5:14-16 Any one of you who is ill should send for the elders of the church, and they must anoint the sick person with oil in the name of the Lord and pray over him. **¹⁵The prayer of faith will save the sick person and the Lord will raise him up again**; and if he has committed any sins, he will be forgiven. ¹⁶So confess your sins to one another, and **pray for one another to be cured**; the heartfelt prayer of someone upright works very powerfully.

[NLT] James 5:14-16 Are any of you sick? You should call for the elders of the church to come and pray over you, anointing you with oil in the name of the Lord. **¹⁵Such a prayer offered in faith will heal**

the sick, and the Lord will make you well. And if you have committed any sins, you will be forgiven. [16]Confess your sins to each other and **pray for each other so that you may be healed.** The earnest prayer of a righteous person has great power and produces wonderful results.

[NLV] James 5:14-16 Is anyone among you sick? He should send for the church leaders and they should pray for him. They should pour oil on him in the name of the Lord. [15]**The prayer given in faith will heal the sick man, and the Lord will raise him up.** If he has sinned, he will be forgiven. [16]Tell your sins to each other. And **pray for each other so you may be healed.** The prayer from the heart of a man right with God has much power.

[NWT] James 5:14-16 Is there anyone sick among you? Let him call the elders of the congregation to him, and let them pray over him, applying oil to him in the name of Jehovah. [15]**And the prayer of faith will make the sick one well, and Jehovah will raise him up.** Also, if he has committed sins, he will be forgiven. [16]Therefore, openly confess your sins to one another and **pray for one another, so that you may be healed.** A righteous man's supplication has a powerful effect.

[Phillips] James 5:14-16 If anyone is ill he should send for the church elders. They should pray over him, anointing him with oil in the Lord's name. [15]**Believing prayer will save the sick man; the Lord will restore him** and any sins that he has committed will be forgiven. [16]You should get into the habit of admitting your sins to each other, and **praying for each other, so that you may be healed.** Tremendous power is made available through a good man's earnest prayer.

[Rotherham] James 5:14-16 Sick, is any among you? Let him call unto him the elders of the assembly, and let them pray for him, anointing him with oil in the name [of the Lord]; — [15]**And, the prayer of faith, shall save the exhausted one, and the Lord will raise him up,** and, if he have committed, sins, it shall be forgiven him. [16]Be openly confessing, therefore, one to another, your sins, and **be praying in each other's behalf, —that ye may be healed.** Much availeth, the supplication of a righteous man, when it is energised:

[T4T] James 5:14-16 Whoever among you is sick should call the leaders of the congregation to come to pray for him. They should put olive oil on him and, with the Lord's authority (OR, calling on the Lord to heal him), pray. [15]**And if they truly trust in the Lord when they pray, the sick person will be healed. The Lord will heal him.** And if that person has sinned in a way that caused him to be/and because of that he became sick, if he confesses what he did/says that he did what is wrong, he will be forgiven {the Lord will forgive him}. [16]So, because the Lord is able to heal the sick and to forgive sins, tell each other the sinful things that you have done, and **pray for each other in order that you may be healed {that God may heal you} physically and spiritually.** If righteous people pray and ask fervently for God to do something, God will act powerfully and will certainly do it.

[TLB] James 5:14-16 Is anyone sick? He should call for the elders of the church and they should pray over him and pour a little oil upon him, calling on the Lord to heal him. [15]**And their prayer, if offered in faith, will heal him, for the Lord will make him well;** and if his sickness was caused by some sin, the Lord will forgive him. [16]Admit your faults to one another and **pray for each other so that you may be healed.** The earnest prayer of a righteous man has great power and wonderful results.

[Weymouth-NT] James 5:14-16 Is any one ill? Let him send for the Elders of the Church, and let them pray over him, after anointing him with oil in the name of the Lord. [15]**And the prayer of faith will restore the sick man, and the Lord will raise him up to health;** and if he has committed sins, they shall be forgiven. [16]Therefore confess your sins to one another, and **pray for one another, so that you may be cured.** The heartfelt supplication of a righteous man exerts a mighty influence.

[Williams-NT] James 5:14-16 Is anyone sick among you? He should call in the elders of the church, and they should pray over him, and anoint him with oil in the name of the Lord, [15]and **the prayer that is**

offered in faith will save the sick man; the Lord will raise him to health, and if he has committed sins, he will be forgiven. ¹⁶So practice confessing your sins to one another, and **praying for one another, that you may be cured.** An upright man's prayer, when it keeps at work, is very powerful.

[YLT] <u>James 5:14-16</u> is any infirm among you? let him call for the elders of the assembly, and let them pray over him, having anointed him with oil, in the name of the Lord, ¹⁵and **the prayer of the faith shall save the distressed one, and the Lord shall raise him up**, and if sins he may have committed, they shall be forgiven to him. ¹⁶Be confessing to one another the trespasses, and **be praying for one another, that ye may be healed;** very strong is a working supplication of a righteous man;

FIRST PETER

<u>1 Peter 2:24</u> Who his own self bare our sins in his own body on the tree, that we, being dead to sins, should live unto righteousness: **by whose stripes ye were healed**.

This is the fulfillment of the prophecy started in Isaiah 53:5, seen in the ministry of Jesus in Matthew 8:17, and provided to the whole church here in 1 Peter 2:24.

[AMP] <u>1 Peter 2:24</u> He personally carried our sins in His body on the cross [willingly offering Himself on it, as on an altar of sacrifice], so that we might die to sin [becoming immune from the penalty and power of sin] and live for righteousness; **for by His wounds you [who believe] have been healed**.

[AMPC] <u>1 Peter 2:24</u> He personally bore our sins in His [own] body on the tree [as on an altar and offered Himself on it], that we might die (cease to exist) to sin and live to righteousness. **By His wounds you have been healed**.

[CLV] <u>1 Peter 2:24</u> Who Himself carries up our sins in His body on to the pole, that, coming away from sins, we should be living for righteousness; **by Whose welt you were healed**.

[EXB] <u>1 Peter 2:24</u> Christ [himself] ·carried [bore] our sins in his body on the ·cross [tree] so we would ·stop living for [die to] sin and start living for ·what is right [righteousness]. **And you are healed ·because of [by] his wounds**.

[GNC-NT] <u>1 Peter 2:24</u> In his own body he carried our sins up to the cross, so that, our sins having been done away with, we should spend our lives in pursuit of righteousness. **His wounds were the means through which we received healing**.

[GW] <u>1 Peter 2:24</u> Christ carried our sins in his body on the cross so that freed from our sins, we could live a life that has God's approval. **His wounds have healed you**.

[Hanson-NT] <u>1 Peter 2:24</u> who bore our sins himself, in his body, on the tree, that we, having died to sins, might live to righteousness; **by whose hurt you were healed**.

[HNT] <u>1 Peter 2:24</u> Our sins he bore himself in his body on the gibbet, That we might break with sin and live for uprightness; And **by his bleeding wound you were cured**.

[ICB] <u>1 Peter 2:24</u> Christ carried our sins in his body on the cross. He did this so that we would stop living for sin and start living for what is right. And **we are healed because of his wounds.**

[Mace-NT] <u>1 Peter 2:24</u> he himself canceled our sins by the crucifixion of his body, that we being set free from sin, might live in the service of virtue. **It is by his bruises that you were healed:**

[Moffatt] <u>1 Peter 2:24</u> he bore our sins in his own body on the gibbet, that we might break with sin and live the good life; **it is by his wounds that you have been healed.**

[MSG] 1 Peter 2:24 He used his servant body to carry our sins to the Cross so we could be rid of sin, free to live the right way. **His wounds became your healing**.

[Palmer] 1 Peter 2:24 who himself in his body carried our sins up onto a tree, in order that by dying to sins, we might live to righteousness; **by whose bruise you have been healed**.

[Phillips] 1 Peter 2:24 And he personally bore our sins in his own body on the cross, so that we might be dead to sin and be alive to all that is good. **It was the suffering that he bore which has healed you**.

[TCNT] 1 Peter 2:24 And he 'himself carried our sins' in his own body to the cross, so that we might die to our sins, and live for righteousness. '**His bruising was your healing**.'

[TLB] 1 Peter 2:24 He personally carried the load of our sins in his own body when he died on the cross so that we can be finished with sin and live a good life from now on. **For his wounds have healed ours!**

[TTNT] 1 Peter 2:24 This is He who took all our sins upon Himself when He hung on the cross, so that now we might die to a life of sin and live in ways that are right and pleasing to God. **It is through His wounds that we are healed and set free completely**.

[TTT-NT] 1 Peter 2:24 who himself bore our sins in his own body upon a tree; so that we might live to righteousness, who by our sins were dead—**by his own lash wounds we have been healed.**

[Weekes-NT] 1 Peter 2:24 He himself bore our sins in his own body upon the cross, in order that we, having become separated from our sins, should be alive to righteousness; for **by his bruise ye have been healed**.

[Wuest-NT] 1 Peter 2:24 who himself carried up to the Cross our sins in His body and offered himself there as on an altar, doing this in order that we, having died with respect to our sins, might live with respect to righteousness, **by means of whose bleeding stripe** [the word "stripe is in the singular here; a picture of our Lord's back after the scourging, one mass of raw, quivering flesh with no skin remaining, trickling with blood] **you were healed,**

1 Peter 5:7-9 Casting all your care upon him; for he careth for you. ⁸Be sober, be vigilant; because **your adversary the devil, as a roaring lion, walketh about, seeking whom he may devour: ⁹Whom resist stedfast in the faith,** knowing that the same afflictions are accomplished in your brethren that are in the world.

[AMP] 1 Peter 5:7-9 casting all your cares [all your anxieties, all your worries, and all your concerns, once and for all] on Him, for He cares about you [with deepest affection, and watches over you very carefully]. ⁸Be sober [well balanced and self-disciplined], be alert and cautious at all times. **That enemy of yours, the devil, prowls around like a roaring lion [fiercely hungry], seeking someone to devour. ⁹But resist him, be firm in your faith [against his attack—rooted, established, immovable],** knowing that the same experiences of suffering are being experienced by your brothers and sisters throughout the world. [You do not suffer alone.]

[AMPC] 1 Peter 5:7-9 Casting the whole of your care [all your anxieties, all your worries, all your concerns, once and for all] on Him, for He cares for you affectionately and cares about you watchfully. ⁸Be well balanced (temperate, sober of mind), be vigilant and cautious at all times; **for that enemy of yours, the devil, roams around like a lion roaring [in fierce hunger], seeking someone to seize upon and devour. ⁹Withstand him; be firm in faith [against his onset—rooted, established, strong, immovable, and determined],** knowing that the same (identical) sufferings are appointed to your brotherhood (the whole body of Christians) throughout the world.

[AUV-NT 2003] 1 Peter 5:7-9 Place all your anxious cares upon God [in prayer], because He genuinely cares about you. ⁸Be sensible and alert; **your enemy the devil is prowling around like a roaring lion**

looking for someone to [kill and] eat. ⁹**You should withstand his efforts by maintaining a strong faith [in God]**, remembering that your [Christian] brothers in [the rest of] the world are experiencing [and enduring] suffering similar to yours.

[Ballentine-NT] <u>1 Peter 5:7-9</u> throwing all your anxiety on him. For he cares for you. ⁸Be sober. Be watchful. **Your adversary the devil, like a roaring lion, is walking about, seeking whom he may devour. ⁹Withstand him, steadfast in your faith,** knowing that the same sufferings are being accomplished in your brothers who are in the world.

[CWB] <u>1 Peter 5:7-9</u> Leave all your anxieties and worries with Him because He cares for you. ⁸Stay alert and be careful because **the devil is roaming around like a hungry lion seeking to destroy anyone he can. ⁹Stand firm in the faith and resist the devil,** knowing that believers everywhere are going through the same things you are.

[GW] <u>1 Peter 5:7-9</u> Turn all your anxiety over to God because he cares for you. ⁸Keep your mind clear, and be alert. **Your opponent the devil is prowling around like a roaring lion as he looks for someone to devour. ⁹Be firm in the faith and resist him,** knowing that other believers throughout the world are going through the same kind of suffering.

[Hanson-NT] <u>1 Peter 5:7-9</u> casting all your anxiety on him, because he cares for you. ⁸Be sober, be vigilant; **your opponent, the accuser, walks about like a roaring lion, seeking to devour; ⁹whom withstand steadfast in the faith**, knowing that the same sufferings are being accomplished in your brotherhood in the world.

[HRB] <u>1 Peter 5:7-9</u> "Casting all your anxiety onto Him," because it matters to Him concerning you. ⁸Be sensible, watch, because **your adversary the Devil walks about as a roaring lion seeking someone he may devour; ⁹therefore resist him, being steadfast in the faith**: and know that the same sufferings befall your brethren that are in the world.

[Jordan-NT] <u>1 Peter 5:7-9</u> Let him in on all your problems, because you mean much to him. ⁸Sober up now, and get with it. **That old roaring lion—your adversary, the Devil—is stalking around looking for someone to gobble up. ⁹Put steel in your faith and stand up to him**, realizing that the brotherhood in other parts of the world is enduring the same kind of persecution.

[Moffatt] <u>1 Peter 5:7-9</u> let all your anxieties fall upon him, for his great interest is in you. ⁸Keep cool, keep awake. **Your enemy the devil prowls like a roaring lion, looking out for someone to devour. ⁹Resist him; keep your foothold in the faith**, and learn to pay the same tax of suffering as the rest of your brotherhood throughout the world.

[NEB] <u>1 Peter 5:7-9</u> Cast all your cares on him, for you are his charge. ⁸Awake! be on the alert! **Your enemy the devil, like a roaring lion, prowls round looking for someone to devour. ⁹Stand up to him, firm in faith**, and remember that your brother Christians are going through the same kinds of suffering while they are in the world.

[Phillips] <u>1 Peter 5:7-9</u> You can throw the whole weight of your anxieties upon him, for you are his personal concern. ⁸Be self-controlled and vigilant always, **for your enemy the devil is always about, prowling like a lion roaring for its prey. ⁹Resist him, standing firm in your faith**, remembering that the strain is the same for all your fellow-Christians in other parts of the world.

[REM-NT] <u>1 Peter 5:7-9</u> Pour out all your worries, frustrations and burdens upon him, because he cares for you. ⁸Stay calm and keep a clear head: do not allow your emotions to take charge, because **Satan, your enemy, is stalking around, roaring like a lion, seeking to consume you with fear and doubt. ⁹But resist him and don't be afraid; keep your trust in God strong**, because you know that your fellow believers throughout the world are also being attacked in the same way.

[TGNT] <u>1 Peter 5:7-9</u> Load upon him the entire weight of your worries, because he cares about you. ⁸Be alert and keep watch! **Your prosecutor, the Slanderer, prowls around like a roaring lion looking for someone to gulp down. ⁹Stand against him! Be solid in the faith**, because you know that your brothers and sisters out in the world are fulfilling the same sufferings as you.

[TPT] <u>1 Peter 5:7-9</u> Pour out all your worries and stress upon him and leave them there, for he always tenderly cares for you. ⁸Be well balanced and always alert, because **your enemy, the devil, roams around incessantly, like a roaring lion looking for its prey to devour. ⁹Take a decisive stand against him and resist his every attack with strong, vigorous faith.** For you know that your believing brothers and sisters around the world are experiencing the same kinds of troubles you endure.

[TTNT] <u>1 Peter 5:7-9</u> Because He is so concerned about you, He wants you to lay all your problems, troubles and anxieties on Him. ⁸Keep firm control of yourselves so that you do not live to please your natural, sinful desires. And be constantly aware that **your enemy the devil is always prowling around like a roaring lion, looking for those he can devour. ⁹Resist him firmly because your faith gives you the power to do so.** Your brothers in other parts of the world are experiencing the same kinds of trials that you have to face.

[Wakefield-NT] <u>1 Peter 5:7-9</u> casting all your anxiety upon him, for he careth for you. ⁸Be sober, be watchful; **for your slanderous adversary, like a roaring lion, is going about and seeking whom he may devour. ⁹Him resist by standing firm in the faith**; knowing that the same sufferings are accomplished by your brethren in the world.

[Wand-NT] <u>1 Peter 5:7-9</u> Hand over all your anxieties to Him, for you are His care. ⁸Don't get excited but be continually on the watch, **for the Devil like a roaring lion is continually on the prowl to see of whom he can make a meal. ⁹Against him stand steadfast in your faith**, remembering that the same tribute of suffering is being paid by the rest of the brotherhood throughout the world.

[Wycliffe-Noble] <u>1 Peter 5:7-9</u> and cast ye all your busyness into him, for to him is care of you. [ye casting into him all your busyness, for to him is care of you.] ⁸Be ye sober, and wake ye, **for your adversary, the devil, as a roaring lion goeth about, seeking whom he shall devour. ⁹Whom against stand ye, strong in the faith**, witting that the same passion is made to that brotherhood of you, that is in the world [witting the same passion to be done to that your brotherhood, that is in the world].

SECOND PETER

<u>2 Peter 1:3</u> According as his divine power hath given unto us all things that pertain unto life[zoé] and godliness, through the knowledge of him that hath called us to glory and virtue:

The well-being of our physical bodies would be part of those things that pertain to our lives. If so, divine health and healing has been given to us.

[AMP] <u>2 Peter 1:3</u> For His divine power has bestowed on us [absolutely] everything necessary for [a dynamic spiritual] life and godliness, through true and personal knowledge of Him who called us by His own glory and excellence.

[AMPC] <u>2 Peter 1:3</u> For His divine power has bestowed upon us all things that [are requisite and suited] to life and godliness, through the [full, personal] knowledge of Him Who called us by and to His own glory and excellence (virtue).

[AUV-NT 2005] <u>2 Peter 1:3</u> God's divine power has given us everything [necessary] for [abundant] life and godly living, through the knowledge of Him [i.e., God], who called us by His own splendor and goodness.

[BOOKS-NT] <u>2 Peter 1:3</u> His divine power has given us everything we need for a godly life through our knowledge of him who called us by his own glory and goodness.

[ERV] <u>2 Peter 1:3</u> Jesus has the power of God. And his power has given us everything we need to live a life devoted to God. We have these things because we know him. Jesus chose us by his glory and goodness,

[Haweis-NT] <u>2 Peter 1:3</u> as his divine power hath freely given us all things tending to life and godliness, through the acknowledgment of him who hath called us to glory and fortitude:

[Knox] <u>2 Peter 1:3</u> See how all the gifts that make for life and holiness in us belong to his divine power; come to us through fuller knowledge of him, whose own glory and sovereignty have drawn us to himself!

[Montgomery-NT] <u>2 Peter 1:3</u> For his power divine has granted to us everything needful for life and godliness, through the knowledge of him who called us by his own glory and virtue.

[MSG] <u>2 Peter 1:3</u> Everything that goes into a life of pleasing God has been miraculously given to us by getting to know, personally and intimately, the One who invited us to God. The best invitation we ever received!

[NIRV] <u>2 Peter 1:3</u> God's power has given us everything we need to lead a godly life. All of this has come to us because we know the God who chose us. He chose us because of his own glory and goodness.

[NJB] <u>2 Peter 1:3</u> By his divine power, he has lavished on us all the things we need for life and for true devotion, through the knowledge of him who has called us by his own glory and goodness.

[Norlie-NT] <u>2 Peter 1:3</u> His divine power has given us everything we need for our physical and spiritual life. This has come to us through our getting to know Him who has called us to share His glory and virtue.

[Phillips] <u>2 Peter 1:3</u> He has by his own action given us everything that is necessary for living the truly good life, in allowing us to know the one who has called us to him, through his own glorious goodness.

[Sacred-NT] <u>2 Peter 1:3</u> As his divine power has gifted to us all things which are necessary to life and godliness, through the knowledge of him who has called us to glory and virtue.

[SENT] <u>2 Peter 1:3</u> After all, his divine power has given us everything we need for life and reverence for God. We're given all this through the knowledge of the One who has called us to his own glory and virtue.

[TPT] <u>2 Peter 1:3</u> Everything we could ever need for life and complete devotion to God has already been deposited in us by his divine power. For all this was lavished upon us through the rich experience of knowing him who has called us by name and invited us to come to him through a glorious manifestation of his goodness.

[Wand-NT] <u>2 Peter 1:3</u> Through knowing Him who has invited us to share His own honor and glory we have been made recipients by the Divine Power of everything that promotes life and piety.

[Weekes-NT] <u>2 Peter 1:3</u> since his divine power hath bestowed upon us all things that tend toward life and true piety, through the clear knowledge of him who called us by his own majesty and excellence,

[Wuest-NT] <u>2 Peter 1:3</u> Seeing that all things to us His divine power has generously given, the things which pertain to life and godliness, through the experiential knowledge [which the believer has] of the One who called us [into salvation] by means of His own glory and virtue,

<u>2 Peter 3:9</u> **The Lord is not slack concerning his promise**, as some men count slackness; but is longsuffering to us-ward, not willing that any should perish, but that all should come to repentance.

[AMP] <u>2 Peter 3:9</u> **The Lord does not delay [as though He were unable to act] and is not slow about His promise**, as some count slowness, but is [extraordinarily] patient toward you, not wishing for any to perish but for all to come to repentance.

[AMPC] <u>2 Peter 3:9</u> **The Lord does not delay and is not tardy or slow about what He promises**, according to some people's conception of slowness, but He is long-suffering (extraordinarily patient) toward you, not desiring that any should perish, but that all should turn to repentance.

[BBE] <u>2 Peter 3:9</u> **The Lord is not slow in keeping his word**, as he seems to some, but he is waiting in mercy for you, not desiring the destruction of any, but that all may be turned from their evil ways.

[Boothroyd] <u>2 Peter 3:9</u> **The Lord is not slow concerning his promise**, as some men count slowness; but is long-suffering towards us, not willing that any should perish, but that all should come to repentance.

[CEV] <u>2 Peter 3:9</u> **The Lord isn't slow about keeping his promises**, as some people think he is. In fact, God is patient, because he wants everyone to turn from sin and no one to be lost.

[GT] <u>2 Peter 3:9</u> **The Lord is not slow to keep His promise** (as some people think of 'slow'). No, He is patient with you. He wants everyone to find room for a change in their hearts. He doesn't want anyone to be lost.

[HBIV] <u>2 Peter 3:9</u> **The Lord is not tardy in respect to the promise,** as some account tardiness; but is long-suffering toward you, not wishing that any should perish, but that all should come to repentance.

[Heberden-NT] <u>2 Peter 3:9</u> **therefore the Lord is not neglectful of his promise**, as some esteem negligence; but he is long suffering towards us, not being willing that any should perish, but that all should go on to repentance.

[Kenrick] <u>2 Peter 3:9</u> **The Lord delayeth not His promise**, as some imagine, but for your sake He is slow, not willing that any should perish, but that all should return to penance.

[Mace-NT] <u>2 Peter 3:9</u> **the Lord does not delay the accomplishment of his promise**, as some do imagine. but he waits with patience upon our account, as being unwilling that any should perish, but that all should come to repentance.

[NCV] <u>2 Peter 3:9</u> **The Lord is not slow in doing what he promised**—the way some people understand slowness. But God is being patient with you. He does not want anyone to be lost, but he wants all people to change their hearts and lives.

[NTSR] <u>2 Peter 3:9</u> **The Lord is not slow about his promise** as some count slowness, but is forbearing towards you, not wishing that any should perish, but that all should reach repentance.

[Shuttleworth-NT] <u>2 Peter 3:9</u> **If then the Lord appears at this moment slow to execute his judgments, it is not a slowness which proceeds from want of power, but from want of will**; from his patient long-suffering; from his suspending again and again the day of his visitation, in the still lingering hope that none should finally perish, but that all may come to repentance.

[TLB] <u>2 Peter 3:9</u> **He isn't really being slow about his promised return**, even though it sometimes seems that way. But he is waiting, for the good reason that he is not willing that any should perish, and he is giving more time for sinners to repent.

[TPT] <u>2 Peter 3:9</u> **This means that, contrary to man's perspective, the Lord is not late with his promise to return**, as some measure lateness. But rather, his "delay" simply reveals his loving patience toward you, because he does not want any to perish but all to come to repentance.

[TVB] <u>2 Peter 3:9</u> **Now the Lord is not slow about enacting His promise**—slow is how some people want to characterize it—no, He is not slow but patient and merciful to you, not wanting anyone to be destroyed, but wanting everyone to turn away from following his own path and to turn toward God's.

[ULB] <u>2 Peter 3:9</u> **The Lord does not move slowly concerning his promises**, as some consider slowness to be. Instead, he is patient toward you. He does not desire for any of you to perish, but for everyone to make room for repentance.

[Wakefield-NT] <u>2 Peter 3:9</u> **The Lord is not slow with his promise**, as some men account it slowness; but is patient for your sakes, being desirous that none should be lost, but all come over to repentance.

FIRST JOHN

<u>1 John 3:8</u> He that committeth sin is of the devil; for the devil sinneth from the beginning. **For this purpose the Son of God was manifested, that he might destroy the works of the devil.**

Sickness and disease are works of the devil. This verse tells us one of the main reasons Jesus came to earth was to destroy the works of the devil.

[AMP] <u>1 John 3:8</u> The one who practices sin [separating himself from God, and offending Him by acts of disobedience, indifference, or rebellion] is of the devil [and takes his inner character and moral values from him, not God]; for the devil has sinned and violated God's law from the beginning. **The Son of God appeared for this purpose, to destroy the works of the devil.**

[AMPC] <u>1 John 3:8</u> [But] he who commits sin [who practices evildoing] is of the devil [takes his character from the evil one], for the devil has sinned (violated the divine law) from the beginning. **The reason the Son of God was made manifest (visible) was to undo (destroy, loosen, and dissolve) the works the devil [has done].**

[AUV-NT 2003] <u>1 John 3:8</u> [But] the person who continues to live a sinful life belongs to the devil, because the devil has continued to sin since the beginning. For this is the reason that **the Son of God came [into the world]; it was to destroy the works [i.e., the influence of] the devil [in people's lives].**

[BBE] <u>1 John 3:8</u> The sinner is a child of the Evil One; for the Evil One has been a sinner from the first. **And the Son of God was seen on earth so that he might put an end to the works of the Evil One.**

[CLV] <u>1 John 3:8</u> Yet he who is doing sin is of the Adversary, for from the beginning is the Adversary sinning. **For this was the Son of God manifested, that He should be annulling the acts of the Adversary.**

[Hanson-NT] <u>1 John 3:8</u> he who practices sin is of the accuser; for the accuser sins from [the] beginning. **For this was the son of God manifested, that he might annihilate the works of the accuser.**

[Jerusalem] <u>1 John 3:8</u> to lead a sinful life is to belong to the devil, since the devil was a sinner from the beginning. **It was to undo all that the devil has done that the Son of God appeared.**

[Jordan-NT] <u>1 John 3:8</u> And he who practices evil is devil-inspired, because from the start the Devil practices evil. **For this very reason the Son of God was born that he might break up the Devil's doings.**

[Kneeland-NT] <u>1 John 3:8</u> he who committeth sin, is of the impostor; for the impostor hath sinned from the beginning: **for this purpose the Son of God was manifested, that he might destroy the works of the impostor.**

[Mace-NT] <u>1 John 3:8</u> he that lives in sin, imitates the devil; for the devil was a sinner from the beginning. **For this purpose the son of God appeared, that he might destroy the works of the devil.**

[Martin-NT] <u>1 John 3:8</u> The one who keeps on (with) shortcomings [failures], is from the devil. The devil has been a failure from the beginning. **This is why God's Son was revealed, that he might destroy the devil's activity.**

[NJB] <u>1 John 3:8</u> Whoever lives sinfully belongs to the devil, since the devil has been a sinner from the beginning. **This was the purpose of the appearing of the Son of God, to undo the work of the devil.**

[NOG] <u>1 John 3:8</u> The person who lives a sinful life belongs to the devil, because the devil has been committing sin since the beginning. **The reason that the Son of God appeared was to destroy what the devil does.**

[Phillips] <u>1 John 3:8</u> But the man whose life is habitually sinful is spiritually a son of the devil, for the devil has been a sinner from the beginning. **Now the Son of God came to earth with the express purpose of undoing the devil's work.**

[REM-NT] <u>1 John 3:8</u> He who does what is selfish is practicing the devil's methods and principles, as the devil is the originator of selfishness. **The reason the Son of God came to earth was to destroy the devil's work of selfishness and bring the universe back into unity with God and his law of love!**

[TVB] <u>1 John 3:8</u> The one persisting in sin belongs to the diabolical one, who has been all about sin from the beginning. **That is why the Son of God came into our world: to destroy the plague of destruction inflicted on the world by the diabolical one.**

[Wand-NT] <u>1 John 3:8</u> He who continues in sin is of the Devil, for the Devil has been a sinner from the beginning. **That is the reason why the Son of God appeared, that he might neutralize what the Devil has done.**

[Wuest-NT] <u>1 John 3:8</u> The one who is habitually committing sin is out of the devil as a source, because from the beginning the devil has been sinning. **For this purpose there was manifested the Son of God, in order that He might bring to naught the works of the devil.**

[YLT] <u>1 John 3:8</u> he who is doing the sin, of the devil he is, because from the beginning the devil doth sin; **for this was the Son of God manifested, that he may break up the works of the devil;**

<u>1 John 4:4</u> Ye are of God, little children, and have overcome them: because **greater is he that is in you, than he that is in the world.**

[AMP] <u>1 John 4:4</u> Little children (believers, dear ones), you are of God and you belong to Him and have [already] overcome them [the agents of the antichrist]; because **He who is in you is greater than he (Satan) who is in the world [of sinful mankind].**

[Baxter-NT] <u>1 John 4:4</u> But your Faith in Christ is of the Spirit of God, who dwelleth and worketh in you, and you have overcome the worldly seducing Spirit, its Doctrines, Baits and Temptations; for **God's Spirit which is in you, is more powerful that the Spirit which deludeth the World.**

[Fenton] <u>1 John 4:4</u> You, children, are from God, and have defeated them; because **the One Who is with you is mightier than the one who is in the world.**

[Knox] <u>1 John 4:4</u> You, little children, who take your origin from God, have gained the mastery over it; **there is a stronger power at work in you, than in the world.**

[Mace-NT] <u>1 John 4:4</u> ye are of God, my dear children, and you have overcome them: because **he that is in you, is superior to him that is in the world.**

[Madsen-NT] <u>1 John 4:4</u> Little children, you are of God and have conquered the hostile powers; for he who works in you is greater than he who is at work in the world.

[MSG] <u>1 John 4:4</u> My dear children, you come from God and belong to God. You have already won a big victory over those false teachers, for **the Spirit in you is far stronger than anything in the world.**

[NCV] <u>1 John 4:4</u> My dear children, you belong to God and have defeated them; because **God's Spirit, who is in you, is greater than the devil, who is in the world.**

[Phillips] <u>1 John 4:4</u> You, my children, who belong to God have already defeated them, because **the one who lives in you is stronger than the anti-Christ in the world.**

[TTNT] <u>1 John 4:4</u> However, dear children, because you belong to God you have overcome these false spirits and those influenced by them. **The Spirit of God lives in you and He is far greater than this spirit of antichrist that is at work in the world.**

[Wade] <u>1 John 4:4</u> You, my dear children, belong to God, and have been victorious over these false Preachers, because **greater is He Who is active in you than he who is active in the world.**

[Wand-NT] <u>1 John 4:4</u> But you, children, are of God, and have risen superior to the false prophets, because **He who is in you is greater than he who is in the world.**

<u>1 John 5:4-5</u> For whatsoever is born of God overcometh the world: and **this is the victory that overcometh the world, even our faith.** [5]Who is he that overcometh the world, but he that believeth that Jesus is the Son of God?

[AMP] <u>1 John 5:4-5</u> For everyone born of God is victorious and overcomes the world; and **this is the victory that has conquered and overcome the world—our [continuing, persistent] faith [in Jesus the Son of God].** [5]Who is the one who is victorious and overcomes the world? It is the one who believes and recognizes the fact that Jesus is the Son of God.

[Anderson-NT] <u>1 John 5:4-5</u> For whatever is begotten of God, overcomes the world; and **this is the victorious principle that overcomes the world, even our faith.** [5]Who is he that overcomes the world, but he that believes that Jesus is the Son of God?

[BWE-NT] <u>1 John 5:4-5</u> Everyone who is God's child wins a victory over the world. **We win because we believe God.** [5]Who wins a victory over the world? It is only the person who believes that Jesus is the Son of God.

[ERV] <u>1 John 5:4-5</u> because everyone who is a child of God has the power to win against the world. **It is our faith that has won the victory against the world.** [5]So who wins against the world? Only those who believe that Jesus is the Son of God.

[FBV-NT] <u>1 John 5:4-5</u> Everyone who is born of God defeats the world. **The way we gain victory and defeat the world is by trusting God.** [5]Who can defeat the world? Only those who trust in Jesus, believing he is the Son of God.

[FHV-NT] <u>1 John 5:4-5</u> Everyone who has God for his Father overcomes the world. **This is the victory that overcomes the world, even our faith.** [5]Who is he that overcomes the world, but he who believes that Jesus is the Son of God?

[GT] <u>1 John 5:4-5</u> Everyone who is a child of God conquers the world. **It is our faith which conquers the world.** [5]Who is the person who conquers the world? Only the one who believes that Jesus is God's Son.

[Knox] <u>1 John 5:4-5</u> Whatever takes its origin from God must needs triumph over the world; **our faith, that is the triumphant principle which triumphs over the world**. [5]He alone triumphs over the world, who believes that Jesus is the Son of God.

[Moffatt-NT 1917] <u>1 John 5:4-5</u> for whatever is born of God conquers the world. **Our faith, that is the conquest which conquers the world**. [5]Who is the world's conqueror but he who believes that Jesus is the Son of God?

[Phillips] <u>1 John 5:4-5</u> In fact, **this faith of ours is the only way in which the world can be conquered**. [5]For who could ever be said to conquer the world but the man who really believes that Jesus is God's Son?

[SENT] <u>1 John 5:4-5</u> Because every child born from God wins the battle with the world. And **this faith of ours is the victory that has won the battle with the world**. [5]Who's the winner of this battle? Isn't it the person that believes that Jesus is God's Son?

[Wuest-NT] <u>1 John 5:4-5</u> because everything that has been born of God is constantly coming off victorious over the world. And **this is the victory that has come off victorious over the world, our faith**. [5]Who is he who is constantly coming off victorious over the world but the one who believes that Jesus is the Son of God?

<u>1 John 5:14-15</u> And this is the confidence that we have in him, that, **if we ask any thing according to his will, he heareth us**: [15]And if we know that he hear us, whatsoever we ask, we know that we have the petitions that we desired of him.

[AMP] <u>1 John 5:14-15</u> This is the [remarkable degree of] confidence which we [as believers are entitled to] have before Him: that **if we ask anything according to His will, [that is, consistent with His plan and purpose] He hears us**. [15]And if we know [for a fact, as indeed we do] that He hears and listens to us in whatever we ask, we [also] know [with settled and absolute knowledge] that we have [granted to us] the requests which we have asked from Him.

[Ballentine-NT] <u>1 John 5:14-15</u> And the boldness which we have towards him is this, that **if we keep asking anything according to his will, he keeps listening to us**. [15]And if we know he is listening to us, whatever we are asking, we know we have the petitions which we have asked from him.

[Bowes-NT] <u>1 John 5:14-15</u> And this is the liberty of access we have towards him, **that if we ask any thing, according to his will, he hears us**: [15]And if we know that he hears us, whatever we ask, we know that we have the petitions which we petitioned from him.

[BWE-NT] <u>1 John 5:14-15</u> And we are sure God will do this. **If we ask him for anything that he wants us to have, he will listen to us**. [15]And if we know he listens to us when we ask for anything, then we know that we have what we asked him for.

[Davidson-NT] <u>1 John 5:14-15</u> And this is the openness that we have toward him, **that if we ask any thing according to his will he hears us**. [15]And if we know that he hears us whatsoever we ask, we know that we have the petitions that we have asked from him.

[ERV] <u>1 John 5:14-15</u> We can come to God with no doubts. **This means that when we ask God for things (and those things agree with what God wants for us), God cares about what we say**. [15]He listens to us every time we ask him. So we know that he gives us whatever we ask from him.

[Fenton] <u>1 John 5:14-15</u> And this is the privilege which we possess towards Him, that **if we ask for anything in accordance with His intention, He listens to us;** [15]and if we are assured that He hears us, whatever we may be asking, we know that we shall have the requests that we ask from him.

[HCSB] <u>1 John 5:14-15</u> Now this is the confidence we have before Him: **Whenever we ask anything according to His will, He hears us.** ¹⁵And if we know that He hears whatever we ask, we know that we have what we have asked Him for.

[Mace-NT] <u>1 John 5:14-15</u> Besides, we have this confidence in him, that **if we ask any thing according to his will, he will hear us**. ¹⁵and since we are sure that he hears all our prayers, we are sure that the petitions we presented to him, will be answered.

[MSG] <u>1 John 5:14-15</u> And how bold and free we then become in his presence, **freely asking according to his will, sure that he's listening**. ¹⁵And if we're confident that he's listening, we know that what we've asked for is as good as ours.

[NWT] <u>1 John 5:14-15</u> And this is the confidence that we have toward him, **that no matter what we ask according to his will, he hears us**. ¹⁵And if we know that he hears us concerning whatever we are asking, we know that we are to have the things we ask for, since we have asked them of him.

[Original-NT] <u>1 John 5:14-15</u> The confidence we have, then, where God is concerned, is this, that **if we ask anything which is in accordance with his will he will listen to us**. ¹⁵And if we know that he listens to our requests, we know equally that we shall obtain whatever it may be we have asked him for.

[REM-NT] <u>1 John 5:14-15</u> We can therefore be confident in approaching God, because **we know he is eager to hear whatever we ask in harmony with his will**. ¹⁵And since we know he gladly hears us, we know that we have what we have asked of him.

[Shuttleworth-NT] <u>1 John 5:14-15</u> We are moreover unhesitatingly convinced, that **if we ask any thing of him according to his will, as communicated to us by his blessed Son, he will favourably hear us**: ¹⁵and if he favourably hear us, we are no less confident that we shall receive at his hands the object of our petitions.

[Smith] <u>1 John 5:14-15</u> And this is the freedom of speech which we have toward him, that, **if we ask anything according to his will, he hears us**: ¹⁵And if we know that he hear us, whatever we ask, we know that we have the petitions which we have asked of him.

[TGNT] <u>1 John 5:14-15</u> **We can boldly approach God with any request that is according to his will; he will hear us**. ¹⁵And if we know he hears us, whatever we request is ours.

[TPT] <u>1 John 5:14-15</u> Since we have this confidence, we can also have great boldness before him, for **if we present any request agreeable to his will, he will hear us**. ¹⁵And if we know that he hears us in whatever we ask, we also know that we have obtained the requests we ask of him.

[TTNT] <u>1 John 5:14-15</u> So you can have great confidence when you come before God in prayer. **You can be sure that if you ask anything according to His revealed will, He certainly hears you**. ¹⁵And if you are confident that He hears what you say, no matter what you ask, you can be sure that you have whatever you have asked of Him!

SECOND JOHN

<u>2 John 1:8</u> Look to yourselves, that we lose not those things which we have wrought, but that **we receive a full reward**.

[AMP] <u>2 John 1:8</u> Watch yourselves, so that you do not lose what we have accomplished together, but that **you may receive a full and perfect reward [when He grants rewards to faithful believers]**.

[BLB-NT] <u>2 John 1:8</u> Watch yourselves, so that you should not lose what things we have worked for, but **you may receive a full reward**.

[CB] <u>2 John 1:8</u> Be aware of yourself, so that you do not backpedal and lose all that we has gained for you, but instead, that **we shall gain our reward**.

[Knox] <u>2 John 1:8</u> Be on your guard, or you will lose all you have earned, instead of **receiving your wages in full**.

[Mace-NT] <u>2 John 1:8</u> be upon your guard, that we may not lose the fruit of our labours, but that **we may receive our full reward**.

[MSG] <u>2 John 1:8</u> And be very careful around them so you don't lose out on what we've worked so diligently in together; **I want you to get every reward you have coming to you**.

[NLV] <u>2 John 1:8</u> Watch yourselves! You do not want to lose what we have worked for. **You want to get what has been promised to you**.

[Phillips] <u>2 John 1:8</u> Take care of yourselves; don't throw away all the labour that has been spent on you, **but persevere till you receive your full reward**.

[Sawyer-7590] <u>2 John 1:8</u> Take heed to yourselves, that you lose not the labor which you performed, **but receive a full reward**.

[TTNT] <u>2 John 1:8</u> Therefore be careful, ensuring that you do not lose what we have worked for, so that **you may receive the full reward of your faith**.

THIRD JOHN

<u>3 John 1:2</u> Beloved, I wish above all things that thou mayest prosper and be in health, even as thy soul prospereth.

Sometimes, the condition of our mind can affect the healing of our bodies.

[AMP] <u>3 John 1:2</u> Beloved, I pray that in every way you may succeed and prosper and be in good health [physically], just as [I know] your soul prospers [spiritually].

[AMPC] <u>3 John 1:2</u> Beloved, I pray that you may prosper in every way and [that your body] may keep well, even as [I know] your soul keeps well and prospers.

[BBE] <u>3 John 1:2</u> My loved one, it is my prayer that you may do well in all things, and be healthy in body, even as your soul does well.

[Beck] <u>3 John 1:2</u> Dear friend, I pray that you're doing well in every way and are also healthy, just as your soul is doing well.

[CCB] <u>3 John 1:2</u> Dear friend, may everything go well with you and may you enjoy health of body and soul.

[Douay-Rheims] <u>3 John 1:2</u> Dearly beloved, concerning all things I make it my prayer that thou mayest proceed prosperously, and fare well as thy soul doth prosperously.

[Hall] <u>3 John 1:2</u> As thy soul is in a good and comfortable condition, so I wish that thy body and estate may be also.

[ISV] <u>3 John 1:2</u> Dear friend, I pray that you are doing well in every way and that you are healthy, just as your soul is healthy.

[NLV] <u>3 John 1:2</u> Dear friend, I pray that you are doing well in every way. I pray that your body is strong and well even as your soul is.

[Phillips] <u>3 John 1:2</u> My prayer for you, my very dear friend, is that you may be as healthy and prosperous in every way as you are in soul.

[Spencer-NT] <u>3 John 1:2</u> Dearly beloved, I pray that thou mayest be prosperous in everything, and enjoy good health, just as thy soul prospers.

[T4T] <u>3 John 1:2</u> Dear friend, I ask God that things may go well for you in every way, specifically, that you will be physically healthy just like you are spiritually healthy.

[TLB] <u>3 John 1:2</u> Dear friend, I am praying that all is well with you and that your body is as healthy as I know your soul is.

[TPT] <u>3 John 1:2</u> Beloved friend, I pray that you are prospering in every way and that you continually enjoy good health, just as your soul is prospering.

[TWTY-RCT-NT-V1] <u>3 John 1:2</u> Beloved and esteemed, dearly loved and highly regarded one; I pray and vow, beseech and wish, invocate and ask the Supreme One about and concerning, regarding and on account of, because of and with respect to all individual and collective things, that you may prosper and be successful, lead along the true path and guided well, and that you will be well and sound, kept healthy and firm, reliable and righteous, whole and constant, just as and exactly as your soul prospers and is successful, lead along the true path and is guided well.

[USAV] <u>3 John 1:2</u> Beloved one, I pray that in all things you continue to prosper and enjoy good health, just as your soul is prospering.

[Wade] <u>3 John 1:2</u> Beloved friend, I pray that all may go well with you materially, and especially that you may keep in good health, just as it goes well with your soul spiritually.

[Wuest-NT] <u>3 John 1:2</u> Beloved, in all things I am praying that you will be prospering, and that you will be continually having good health just as your soul is prospering.

JUDE

<u>Jude 1:3</u> Beloved, when I gave all diligence to write unto you of the common salvation, it was needful for me to write unto you, and exhort you that ye should **earnestly contend for the faith** which was once delivered unto the saints.

The word "salvation" is from the same root as "saved" or "sozo" in the Greek and includes healing and health as part of its provision. This same word is translated as "health" in Acts 27:34.

[AMP] <u>Jude 1:3</u> Beloved, while I was making every effort to write you about our common salvation, I was compelled to write to you [urgently] appealing that you **fight strenuously for [the defense of] the faith** which was once for all handed down to the saints [the faith that is the sum of Christian belief that was given verbally to believers].

[CEB] <u>Jude 1:3</u> Dear friends, I wanted very much to write to you concerning the salvation we share. Instead, I must write to **urge you to fight for the faith** delivered once and for all to God's holy people.

[EEBT] <u>Jude 1:3</u> My friends that I love, I was wanting very much to write to you. I was wanting to write about how God has saved all of us. But instead, now I must write to you about something else. **I must ask you very strongly to be like people who fight to keep God's true message safe. You must not**

let anyone stop you believing it. **You must not let anyone stop you obeying it**. God has given this true message to his people, and his message will never change.

[ERV] Jude 1:3 Dear friends, I wanted very much to write to you about the salvation we all share together. But I felt the need to write to you about something else: I want to **encourage you to fight hard for the faith** that God gave his holy people. God gave this faith once, and it is good for all time.

[Etheridge-NT] Jude 1:3 My beloved, while giving all diligence to write to you concerning our common salvation, it is needful for me to write to you, exhorting you (in particular) to **do battle for the faith** which was once delivered to the saints.

[FBV-NT] Jude 1:3 My friends, I was already looking forward to writing to you about the salvation that we share. But now I need to write urgently to you and encourage you to **vigorously defend the truth about God**, given once and for all time to God's holy people.

[IRENT] Jude 1:3 Beloved ones, as one who is ever eager to write to you about the salvation we have in our life in common, I now feel compelled instead to write to you to exhort you to **contend earnestly for the faith delivered once fully for all time**, to those who have consecrated themselves to God.

[Madsen-NT] Jude 1:3 Beloved, always I have wanted to write to you about the salvation in which we all share. Now it has become necessary for me to write to you to urge you to **fight for the substance of the faith**, which has been handed on in the same way to all who strive for salvation.

[MSG] Jude 1:3 Dear friends, I've dropped everything to write you about this life of salvation that we have in common. I have to write **insisting—begging!—that you fight with everything you have in you for this faith** entrusted to us as a gift to guard and cherish.

[REM-NT] Jude 1:3 My dear friends, I have longed to write to you about God's healing plan (his Remedy in which we share), but instead, I must write to warn you to **defend the truth about God as revealed by Jesus**—this precious truth that is the foundation of our faith and the secret with which we have been entrusted.

[T4T] Jude 1:3 You whom I love, I was very eager/very much wanted to write to you about that which we all share/have in common, which is how God/Jesus Christ has saved us. But now I realize that it is necessary for me to write to you in order to exhort you to **defend the truth about Christ that we believe**. Jesus and his apostles gave that truth once for all to us who belong to God, and we must not let it be changed {anyone revise/change it}.

[TPT] Jude 1:3 Dearly loved friend, I was fully intending to write to you about our amazing salvation we all participate in, but felt the need instead to challenge you to **vigorously defend and contend for the beliefs** that we cherish. For God, through the apostles, has once for all entrusted these truths to his holy believers.

[TTNT] Jude 1:3 My dear friends, because I have been so keen to write to you about the salvation we share, it has been necessary for me to urge you to **fight for the faith which has been revealed to the saints**, the revelation received once for all time.

[Tyndale21-NT] Jude 1:3 Dearly loved, when I gave all diligence to write to you about our common salvation, I felt the need to write and urge that you to **continually labor for the faith** that was once given to the saints.

[Wand-NT] Jude 1:3 Beloved, I was busy writing to you on the subject of our common salvation, when the necessity suddenly arose to write and urge you to **throw yourselves into a new contest on behalf of that faith** which was handed over once for all to the keeping of the Christian folk.

[WEBBE] Jude 1:3 Beloved, while I was very eager to write to you about our common salvation, I was constrained to write to you exhorting you to **contend earnestly for the faith** which was once for all delivered to the saints.

[Wuest-NT] Jude 1:3 Divinely loved ones, when giving every diligence to be writing to you concerning the salvation possessed in common by all of us, I had constraint laid upon me to write to you, **beseeching you to contend with intensity and determination for the Faith** once for all entrusted into the safe-keeping of the saints.

Jude 1:20 But ye, beloved, building up yourselves on your most holy faith, praying in the Holy Ghost,

[EHV] Jude 1:20 But you, dear friends, continue to build yourselves up in your most holy faith as you keep praying in the Holy Spirit.

[ERV] Jude 1:20 But you, dear friends, use your most holy faith to build yourselves up even stronger. Pray with the help of the Holy Spirit.

[Etheridge-NT] Jude 1:20 But you, my beloved, in your holy faith be edified anew, praying in the Holy Spirit,

[GT] Jude 1:20 But, you to whom I give myself, build up your lives on your most holy faith, praying with the Holy Spirit.

[GW] Jude 1:20 Dear friends, use your most holy faith to grow. Pray with the Holy Spirit's help.

[Mace-NT] Jude 1:20 but you, my brethren, improve yourselves in your most holy faith, present your addresses by the holy spirit,

[Newcome] Jude 1:20 But, Ye, beloved, building up yourselves in your most holy faith, praying through the Holy Spirit,

[REB] Jude 1:20 But you, my friends, must make your most sacred faith the foundation of your lives. Continue to pray in the power of the Holy Spirit.

[TPT] Jude 1:20 But you, my delightfully loved friends, constantly and progressively build yourselves up on the foundation of your most holy faith by praying every moment in the Spirit.

[Wade] Jude 1:20 But you, Beloved, whilst fortifying your characters with the help of your most holy Faith, and praying with the aid of Holy Spirit,

[Wand-NT] Jude 1:20 But you, beloved, build yourselves up on the foundations of your most holy faith, and pray in the power of the Holy Spirit

[Williams-NT] Jude 1:20 But you, dearly beloved, must continue to build yourselves up on the groundwork of your most holy faith and to pray in the Holy Spirit;

REVELATION

Revelation 11:11 And after three days and an half the Spirit of life[zoē] from God entered into them, and they stood upon their feet; and great fear fell upon them which saw them.

[AMP] Revelation 11:11 But after three and a half days, the breath of life from God came into them, and they stood on their feet; and great fear and panic fell on those who were watching them.

[AUV-NT 2003] <u>Revelation 11:11</u> And after three and a half days, God breathed life into them and they stood up on their feet, and the people who saw them became terrified.

[BSB-NT] <u>Revelation 11:11</u> But after the three and a half days, the breath of life from God entered the two witnesses, and they stood on their feet, and great fear came over those who saw them.

[FBV-NT] <u>Revelation 11:11</u> But three and half days later God's life-giving breath entered them and they stood on their feet. Those who saw this were absolutely terrified.

[GNT] <u>Revelation 11:11</u> After three and a half days a life-giving breath came from God and entered them, and they stood up; and all who saw them were terrified.

[LTPB] <u>Revelation 11:11</u> After three and a half days, life's breath from God entered into them. They stood on their feet, and great fear fell on those who saw them.

[OEB-NT] <u>Revelation 11:11</u> After three days and a half 'the life-giving breath of God entered these men, and they stood up on their feet,' and a great terror took possession of those who were watching them.

[TVB] <u>Revelation 11:11</u> At the end of the three and a half days, the spirit of life that comes from God entered their corpses, raising them, and they stood again on their feet. Those who looked on were terrified by what they saw.

[UDB] <u>Revelation 11:11</u> But after three and a half days, Yahweh will cause them to breathe again and live. They will stand up, and the people who see them will be terrified.

[Waple-Rev] <u>Revelation 11:11</u> And after three days and a half, the Spirit of Life from God entered into them [i.e. they were wonderfully revived] and they stood upon their feet [i.e. were in a posture of Service and Defence, and appeared with Courage and Readiness to perform their Duty] and great fear fell upon all them which saw them [revived so wonderfully, to the Joy of their friends, and the Consternation of their Enemies.]

<u>Revelation 12:11</u> And they overcame him by the blood of the Lamb, and by the word of their testimony; and they loved not their lives unto the death.

[AMP] <u>Revelation 12:11</u> And they overcame and conquered him because of the blood of the Lamb and because of the word of their testimony, for they did not love their life and renounce their faith even when faced with death.

[AUV-NT 2005] <u>Revelation 12:11</u> And they [i.e., the brothers] gained the victory over Satan by the blood of the Lamb, and by [remaining true to] the message of their testimony. And they did not love their lives [so much that they refused] to die [for their faith].

[Ballentine-NT] <u>Revelation 12:11</u> And they overcame him because of the blood of the Lamb, and because of the message of their witness.

[Barclay-NT] <u>Revelation 12:11</u> The blood of the Lamb, and their fearless declaration of their faith, have won for them the victory over him.

[BLE] <u>Revelation 12:11</u> and they won against him because of the Lamb's blood and because of the word of their testimony, and did not love their lives even in the face of death.

[Brichto] <u>Revelation 12:11</u> They overwhelmed him by the blood of the Lamb, And by the word of their testimony to him. They did not love their lives so much as not to die for him.

[Browne-Rev] <u>Revelation 12:11</u> And they themselves did-conquer him on-account-of the blood of the Tender-Lamb, and on-account-of the word of their witnessing, and they loved not their soul until death.

[ECB] <u>Revelation 12:11</u> And they triumph over him through the blood of the Lamb and through the word of their witness; and they love not their souls to the death.

[ERV] <u>Revelation 12:11</u> They defeated him by the blood sacrifice of the Lamb and by the message of God that they told people. They did not love their lives too much. They were not afraid of death.

[Fenton] <u>Revelation 12:11</u> And they have conquered him by the blood of the Lamb, and by the fact of their evidence; and they loved not their life better than death.

[GNT] <u>Revelation 12:11</u> They won the victory over him by the blood of the Lamb and by the truth which they proclaimed; and they were willing to give up their lives and die.

[ICB] <u>Revelation 12:11</u> And our brothers defeated him by the blood of the Lamb's death and by the truth they preached. They did not love their lives so much that they were afraid of death.

[Levi-Rev] <u>Revelation 12:11</u> And they have beaten him through the blood of the Lamb, and through the word of their witnessing; they did not love their own soul but suffered their own death.

[MSG] <u>Revelation 12:11</u> They defeated him through the blood of the Lamb and the bold word of their witness. They weren't in love with themselves; they were willing to die for Christ.

[NIRV] <u>Revelation 12:11</u> They had victory over him by the blood the Lamb spilled for them. They had victory over him by speaking the truth about Jesus to others. They were willing to risk their lives, even if it led to death.

[NJB] <u>Revelation 12:11</u> They have triumphed over him by the blood of the Lamb and by the word to which they bore witness, because even in the face of death they did not cling to life.

[NLV] <u>Revelation 12:11</u> They had power over him and won because of the blood of the Lamb and by telling what He had done for them. They did not love their lives but were willing to die.

[Norlie-NT] <u>Revelation 12:11</u> They defeated him by the blood of the Lamb and by the preaching of the Word, and not by loving their own lives; they were willing to die.

[OEB-NT] <u>Revelation 12:11</u> Their victory was due to the blood of the Lamb, and to the message to which they bore their testimony. In their love of life they shrank not from death.

[Original-NT] <u>Revelation 12:11</u> They overcame him by the blood of the Lamb, and the declaration of their testimony.

[TLB] <u>Revelation 12:11</u> They defeated him by the blood of the Lamb and by their testimony; for they did not love their lives but laid them down for him.

[Waple-Rev] <u>Revelation 12:11</u> And they [i.e. our Brethren] overcame him [in this judiciary Trial before the Throne of God; and all his subtil arts, and powerful instruments, in the times of Persecution;] by the Blood of the Lamb [i.e. by Faith in Christ's Blood; and by his Merits and Passion alone;] and by the word of their Testimony [i.e. by the Gospel which they Preached purely, and Efficaciously, and the Testimonies they had given under the four first Seals;] and [because,] they Loved not their Lives [no not] unto the Death [but despised them, and willingly and cheerfully laid them down for Christ, and his Gospel's sake.

[Weekes-NT] <u>Revelation 12:11</u> And they prevailed over him by means of the blood of the Lamb, and by means of the word of their testimony; and they loved not their life even unto death.

<u>Revelation 22:2</u> In the midst of the street of it, and on either side of the river, was there the tree of life[zoé], which bare twelve manner of fruits, and yielded her fruit every month: and **the leaves of the tree were for the healing of the nations**.

[BLE] <u>Revelation 22:2</u> through the middle of its main avenue; and on this side of the river and on that side were trees of life producing twelve crops of fruit, bringing in their fruit each month; and **the leaves of the trees were for curing the diseases of the nations**.

[BSB-NT] <u>Revelation 22:2</u> down the middle of the main street of the city. On either side of the river stood a tree of life, producing twelve kinds of fruit and yielding a fresh crop for each month. And **the leaves of the tree are for the healing of the nations.**

[CPDV] <u>Revelation 22:2</u> In the midst of its main street, and on both sides of the river, was the Tree of Life, bearing twelve fruits, offering one fruit for each month, and **the leaves of the tree are for the health of the nations.**

[FCConybeare-Rev] <u>Revelation 22:2</u> And along the bank of the river she had the tree of life, which had fruit twelve TIMES; one by one month it gave its fruit, and **leaves of the tree were [for the] healing of all the heathen.** AND FROM ALL TREES OF WHICH THEY ATE THEY WERE BLESSED,

[Goodspeed-NT] <u>Revelation 22:2</u> and ran through the middle of the principal street of the city. On both sides of the river grew the tree of life. It bore twelve kinds of fruit, yielding a different kind each month, and **its leaves were a cure for the heathen.**

[Harwood-NT] <u>Revelation 22:2</u> On each side of the street, and of the river, was planted the tree of life, producing twelve kinds of fruit, which every month attained their full maturity—**the leaves of this tree are a sovereign remedy for every indisposition.**

[ICB] <u>Revelation 22:2</u> down the middle of the street of the city. The tree of life was on each side of the river. It produces fruit 12 times a year, once each month. **The leaves of the tree are for the healing of all people.**

[Knox] <u>Revelation 22:2</u> On either side of the river, mid-way along the city street, grows the tree that gives life, bearing its fruit twelvefold, one yield for each month. And **the leaves of this tree bring health to all the nations.**

[Macrae] <u>Revelation 22:2</u> In the midst of the street of it, and on each side of the river, was the tree of life; (it also was in the middle between its street, and the river being on each side;) it bare twelve kinds of fruits, and yielded one kind every month; and **its leaves were for the healing of the nations, (to prevent diseases).**

[NIRV] <u>Revelation 22:2</u> It flowed down the middle of the city's main street. On each side of the river stood the tree of life, bearing 12 crops of fruit. Its fruit was ripe every month. **The leaves of the tree bring healing to the nations.**

[NLT] <u>Revelation 22:2</u> It flowed down the center of the main street. On each side of the river grew a tree of life, bearing twelve crops of fruit, with a fresh crop each month. **The leaves were used for medicine to heal the nations.**

[Weymouth-NT] <u>Revelation 22:2</u> On either side of the river, midway between it and the main street of the city, was the Tree of Life. It produced twelve kinds of fruit, yielding a fresh crop month by month, and **the leaves of the tree served as medicine for the nations.**

[Williams-NT] <u>Revelation 22:2</u> down the middle of the city's Broadway. On both sides of the river grew the tree of life, which bore twelve kinds of fruit, yielding a different kind each month, and **its leaves contained the remedy to cure the nations.**

<u>Revelation 22:17</u> And the Spirit and the bride say, Come. And let him that heareth say, Come. And let him that is athirst come. And whosoever will, **let him take the water of life**[zoé] **freely.**

[Beck] <u>Revelation 22:17</u> "Come!" say the Spirit and the bride. If you hear this, say, "Come!" If you are thirsty, come. **If you want it, take the water of life—it costs nothing.**

[CEB] <u>Revelation 22:17</u> The Spirit and the bride say, 'Come!' Let the one who hears say, 'Come!' And let the one who is thirsty come! **Let the one who wishes receive life-giving water as a gift.**

[CEV] <u>Revelation 22:17</u> The Spirit and the bride say, "Come!" Everyone who hears this should say, "Come!" If you are thirsty, come! **If you want life-giving water, come and take it. It's free!**

[CPDV] <u>Revelation 22:17</u> And the Spirit and the Bride say: "Draw near." And whoever hears, let him say: "Draw near." And whoever thirsts, let him draw near. And whoever is willing, **let him accept the water of life, freely.**

[ESV] <u>Revelation 22:17</u> The Spirit and the Bride say, "Come." And let the one who hears say, "Come." And let the one who is thirsty come; **let the one who desires take the water of life without price.**

[GT] <u>Revelation 22:17</u> The Spirit and the bride are saying, "Come!" Let the person who is listening say, "Come!" Let the person who is thirsty come. **Let him take as much of the living water as he wants.**

[LDB-NT] <u>Revelation 22:17</u> "You must come!" is the urgent invitation from both the Spirit and the bride. If you have heard and accepted the Great News for yourself, you must now urgently invite others to "Come!" There are so many who are thirsty who must be invited to come. And **let the person who is interested know that in order to live he must accept the Water of Life as a gift from God. It is free!**

[Macrae] <u>Revelation 22:17</u> Now, the Spirit and (church adorned as) the bride say, Come—And let him that hears, say, Come—And let him that is thirsty come. And whoever will, **let him receive the water of life (eternal joy and happiness) freely.**

[Martin-NT] <u>Revelation 22:17</u> The Spirit and the Bride are saying, "Come!" And whoever is listening must say "Come"! The one who is thirsty must come—whoever wishes—**he must take the living water (as a) gift.**

[NAB] <u>Revelation 22:17</u> The Spirit and the bride say, "Come." Let the hearer say, "Come." Let the one who thirsts come forward, and **the one who wants it receive the gift of life-giving water.**

[REM-NT] <u>Revelation 22:17</u> The Spirit and the bride call, "Come home!" So please, let all who hear the truth call, "Come home!" Whoever is thirsty, let them come home; and whoever wishes, **let them drink freely of the water of life.**

[Thomson] <u>Revelation 22:17</u> Now the spirit and the bride say, Come; and let him who heareth say Come. And let every one who thirsteth come; and **let every one who is willing take of the water of life at free cost.**

[TLB] <u>Revelation 22:17</u> The Spirit and the bride say, 'Come.' Let each one who hears them say the same, 'Come.' Let the thirsty one come—**anyone who wants to; let him come and drink the Water of Life without charge.**

[TNIV] <u>Revelation 22:17</u> The Spirit and the bride say, "Come!" And let those who hear say, "Come!" Let those who are thirsty come; and **let all who wish take the free gift of the water of life.**

[TPT] <u>Revelation 22:17</u> "Come," says the Holy Spirit and the Bride in divine duet. Let everyone who hears this duet join them in saying, "Come." Let everyone gripped with spiritual thirst say, "Come." **And let everyone who craves the gift of living water come and drink it freely. "It is my gift to you! Come."**

[Weymouth-NT] <u>Revelation 22:17</u> The Spirit and the Bride say, 'Come;' and whoever hears, let him say, 'Come;' and let those who are thirsty come. Whoever will, **let him take the Water of Life, without payment**.

[Williams-NT] <u>Revelation 22:17</u> The Spirit and the bride say, "Come." Let everyone who hears this say, "Come." Let everyone who is thirsty come. Let everyone who wishes come and **take the living water without any cost**.

[Wuest-NT] <u>Revelation 22:17</u> And the Spirit and the bride are saying, Be coming. And he who hears, let him say, Be coming. And he who is thirsty, let him be coming. He who is desirous, **let him take at once the water of life gratis**.

LONG *Life*

The last enemy that shall be destroyed is death.
— 1 Corinthians 15:26

With long life will I satisfy him, and shew him my salvation.
— Psalms 91:16

Everyone who dies early doesn't necessarily die of sickness and disease. If you are sick, you can use the verses in this chapter to renew your mind that God is not using sickness and disease to kill you early. If you are well, you can use the verses in this chapter to build your faith up against an early death from other causes.

The first verse above tells us that death is an enemy and is scheduled for destruction. The second verse tells us that it is the Lord's desire that we live a long time on the earth. These two verses alone tell us that it is not God's will that we die young. It is not God's will that our physical bodies deteriorate slowly as we get older—how would that be satisfying after all?

I once had a boss who was a Christian. At the end of the day, I would often see him and tell him, "See you tomorrow!" He would always reply the same way, "The Lord willing!" He's not sure if it is the Lord's will for him to live through the night? He's not sure whether it's God's will to stay on the earth with his young child and wife, or die on the way home and leave an orphan and a widow? How can we in the church not know these things? When my boss would answer that way, I made a mental note to not ride home with him since he had no faith to arrive safely.

I attended a funeral for a teen-aged boy many years ago. He died in a camping accident. The minister conducting the service said that God took the young man because he was needed in heaven! What he was saying was that God in heaven took a child from his mother's arms because, apparently, there are not enough angels in heaven doing their job. Amazing.

If someone steals a child from his mother by killing him and thus destroying her life (steals, kills, destroys), who does that sound like?

The thief cometh not, but for to steal, and to kill, and to destroy: I am come that they might have life, and that they might have it more abundantly.
— John 10:10

It sounds just like the devil. We should never attribute terrible acts on the earth to the Lord. His Word reveals His will to us—He wants us to have a long, satisfied life.

Some people say, "Well, you have to die of something." At the end, doctors may put a cause of death on the certificate, but that doesn't mean you have to spend the last many years of your life bed-ridden or on such heavy medication that you are not aware of your surroundings. That is not satisfaction.

Other people say, "You never know when your time is up." According to Psalm 91:16, I know exactly when my time is up—when I am satisfied!

As with all the promises of God, they won't do us any good unless we actively believe them. In the following verses, note which ones say you will prolong your days if you obey the Lord. This means you have a choice in how long you live. Read the following verses and build your faith up that God wants you to live a long, fulfilled life on this earth.

GENESIS

Genesis 6:3 And the LORD said, My spirit shall not always strive with man, for that he also *is* flesh: yet **his days shall be an hundred and twenty years**.

[BBE] Genesis 6:3 And the Lord said, My spirit will not be in man for ever, for he is only flesh; so the days of **his life will be a hundred and twenty years.**

[CAB] Genesis 6:3 And the Lord God said, My Spirit shall certainly not remain among these men forever, because they are flesh, but **their days shall be one hundred and twenty years.**

[CJB] Genesis 6:3 Adonai said, "My Spirit will not live in human beings forever, for they too are flesh; therefore **their life span is to be 120 years."**

[JPS-OT 1985] Genesis 6:3 The LORD said, "My breath shall not abide in man forever, since he too is flesh; **let the days allowed him be one hundred and twenty years."**—

[LTPB] Genesis 6:3 God said, "My breath will not remain in man in eternity, because he is flesh. **His days will be one hundred twenty years."**

[MOTB] Genesis 6:3 To check the evils arising from the union of humanity with beings supernatural, **God limited the life of man to one hundred and twenty years.**

[Thomson] Genesis 6:3 then the Lord God said, "My breath must not continue in these men to this age, because they are flesh; **their days however, shall be an hundred and twenty years."**

[UDB] Genesis 6:3 Then Yahweh said, "My breath will not remain in people forever, to keep them alive. They are made of weak flesh. **They will live not more than 120 years before they die."**

Genesis 15:15 And thou shalt go to thy fathers in peace; thou shalt be buried in a good old age.

[BBE] Genesis 15:15 As for you, you will go to your fathers in peace; at the end of a long life you will be put in your last resting-place.

[CEB] Genesis 15:15 As for you, you will join your ancestors in peace and be buried after a good long life.

[CLV] Genesis 15:15 Yet you shall come to your forefathers in peace, and be entombed at a good grey-haired age.

[HCSB] Genesis 15:15 But you will go to your fathers in peace and be buried at a ripe old age.

LONG LIFE

[Howard-OT] <u>Genesis 15:15</u> But thou shalt depart unto thy fathers in peace, being nourished in a good old age.

[ISV] <u>Genesis 15:15</u> Now as for you, you'll die peacefully, join your ancestors, and be buried at a good old age.

[Knox] <u>Genesis 15:15</u> For thyself, thou shalt be buried with thy fathers, grown old in comfort;

[LXX-1844] <u>Genesis 15:15</u> But thou shalt depart to thy fathers in peace, nourished in a good old age.

[MSG] <u>Genesis 15:15</u> But not you; you'll have a long and full life and die a good and peaceful death.

[Murphy-OT] <u>Genesis 15:15</u> And thou shalt go to thy fathers in peace; thou shalt be buried in a happy old age.

[NAB] <u>Genesis 15:15</u> You, however, shall join your forefathers in peace; you shall be buried at a contented old age.

[T4T] <u>Genesis 15:15</u> But as for you, you will die peacefully when you are very old.

<u>Genesis 24:1</u> And **Abraham was old,** and well stricken in age: and the Lord had blessed Abraham in all things.

[BBE] <u>Genesis 24:1</u> Now **Abraham was old** and far on in years: and the Lord had given him everything in full measure.

[CB] <u>Genesis 24:1</u> **Abraham lived to a ripe old age**, and the Lord blessed Abraham in everything.

[CEV] <u>Genesis 24:1</u> **Abraham was now a very old man**. The Lord had made him rich, and he was successful in everything he did.

[NLV] <u>Genesis 24:1</u> **Now Abraham was old**. He had lived many years. And the Lord had brought good to Abraham in every way.

<u>Genesis 25:8</u> Then Abraham gave up the ghost, and died in a good old age, an old man, and full of years; and was gathered to his people.

[Anchor] <u>Genesis 25:8</u> When Abraham had breathed his last, dying at a happy ripe age, old and full of years, he was gathered to his kin.

[Bate-OT] <u>Genesis 25:8</u> And Abrem expired, and he died in a good old age, old and done, and was gathered to his people.

[CEB] <u>Genesis 25:8</u> Abraham took his last breath and died after a good long life, a content old man, and he was placed with his ancestors.

[JPS-OT 1985] <u>Genesis 25:8</u> And Abraham breathed his last, dying at a good ripe age, old and contented; and he was gathered to his kin.

[MEV] <u>Genesis 25:8</u> Then Abraham breathed his last and died at a good old age, an old man and full of years; and he was gathered to his people.

[Purver] <u>Genesis 25:8</u> Then he expiring, died in a good old Age, a very ancient Man; and was gathered to his People.

[SG] <u>Genesis 25:8</u> So Abraham came to his death, dying at a ripe old age, an old man, satisfied with life; and he was gathered to his fathers.

Genesis 35:29 And Isaac gave up the ghost, and died, and was gathered unto his people, being old and full of days: and his sons Esau and Jacob buried him.

[AMPC] **Genesis 35:29** And Isaac's spirit departed; he died and was gathered to his people, being an old man, satisfied and satiated with days; his sons Esau and Jacob buried him.

[CEB] **Genesis 35:29** Isaac took his last breath and died. He was buried with his ancestors after a long, satisfying life. His sons Esau and Jacob buried him.

[Jerusalem] **Genesis 35:29** when he breathed his last. He died and was gathered to his people, an old man who had enjoyed his full span of life. His sons Esau and Jacob buried him.

[NEB] **Genesis 35:29** He died and was gathered to his father's kin at a very great age, and his sons Esau and Jacob buried him.

[SG] **Genesis 35:29** then Isaac came to his death; he died and was gathered to his fathers, an old man, satisfied with life; and his sons, Esau and Jacob, buried him.

EXODUS

Exodus 20:12 Honour thy father and thy mother: **that thy days may be long upon the land** which the Lord thy God giveth thee.

This promise is repeated in the New Testament in Ephesians 6:3.

[AMP] **Exodus 20:12** "Honor (respect, obey, care for) your father and your mother, so **that your days may be prolonged in the land** the Lord your God gives you.

[AMPC] **Exodus 20:12** Regard (treat with honor, due obedience, and courtesy) your father and mother, **that your days may be long in the land** the Lord your God gives you.

[CT-OT] **Exodus 20:12** Honor your father and your mother, in order **that your days be lengthened on the land** that the Lord, your God, is giving you.

[Hall] **Exodus 20:12** Honour those, which are any way set over thee, and given them due reverence and obedience, for conscience sake; **that God may give thee a long and happy life, in this thy promised land upon earth**, and an eternal life, figured by the other, in that true land of rest, which is above.

[JUB] **Exodus 20:12** Honour thy father and thy mother **that thy days may be lengthened upon the land** which the Lord thy God gives thee.

[Knox] **Exodus 20:12** Honour thy father and thy mother; so **thou shalt live long to enjoy the land** which the Lord thy God means to give thee.

[NCV] **Exodus 20:12** Honor your father and your mother so **that you will live a long time in the land** that the Lord your God is going to give you.

[SAAS-OT] **Exodus 20:12** "Honor your father and mother that it may be well with you, and **your days may be long upon the good land** the Lord your God is giving you.

[TLB] **Exodus 20:12** "Honor your father and mother, that **you may have a long, good life in the land** the Lord your God will give you.

Exodus 23:26 There shall nothing cast their young, nor be barren, in thy land: **the number of thy days I will fulfil.**

[ABP] <u>Exodus 23:26</u> It will not be barren nor sterile upon your land; the **number of your days I will fill up.**

[BBE] <u>Exodus 23:26</u> All your animals will give birth without loss, not one will be without young in all your land; **I will give you a full measure of life.**

[Beck] <u>Exodus 23:26</u> No woman in your country will miscarry or be barren. **I will give you each a full number of years.**

[CE] <u>Exodus 23:26</u> no woman in your land will be barren or miscarry; and **I will give you a full span of life.**

[EEBT] <u>Exodus 23:26</u> Your women will all have babies. None of the babies will be born before it is ready. **I will give a long life to every person.**

[ERV] <u>Exodus 23:26</u> Your women will all be able to have babies. None of their babies will die at birth. And **I will allow you to live long lives.**

[GW] <u>Exodus 23:26</u> No woman in your land will miscarry or be unable to have children. **I will let you live a normal life span.**

[JPS-OT 1963] <u>Exodus 23:26</u> No woman in your land shall miscarry or be barren. **I will let you enjoy the full count of your days.**

[Moffatt] <u>Exodus 23:26</u> no animal shall drop her young or be barren in your country, and **I will give you a full term of life.**

[MSG] <u>Exodus 23:26</u> there won't be any miscarriages nor barren women in your land. **I'll make sure you live full and complete lives.**

[NIRV] <u>Exodus 23:26</u> In your land no woman will give birth to a dead baby. Every woman will be able to have children. **I will give you a long life.**

[NLT] <u>Exodus 23:26</u> There will be no miscarriages or infertility in your land, and **I will give you long, full lives.**

[NLV] <u>Exodus 23:26</u> Women in your land will not lose their babies before they are born, and will be able to give birth. **I will give you a full life.**

[Orton-OT] <u>Exodus 23:26</u> There shall nothing cast their young, nor be barren in thy land: **the number of thy days I will fulfil, thou shalt live to a good old age.**

[Rotherham] <u>Exodus 23:26</u> There shall be nothing casting its young or barren, in thy land, —**the number of thy days, will I make full.**

[Thomson] <u>Exodus 23:26</u> There shall not be a man childless, nor a woman barren in thy land. **The number of your days I will completely fulfil.**

[TLB] <u>Exodus 23:26</u> There will be no miscarriages nor barrenness throughout your land, and **you will live out the full quota of the days of your life.**

[YLT] <u>Exodus 23:26</u> there is not a miscarrying and barren one in thy land; **the number of thy days I fulfil:**

LEVITICUS

<u>Leviticus 18:5</u> Ye shall therefore keep my statutes, and my judgments: which if a man do, **he shall live in them:** I am the Lord.

[BBE] <u>Leviticus 18:5</u> So keep my rules and my decisions, which, **if a man does them, will be life to him**: I am the Lord.

[Beck] <u>Leviticus 18:5</u> Follow My rules and My decisions. **By doing them a man lives**. I am the Lord.

[Berkeley] <u>Leviticus 18:5</u> Therefore keep My law and My ordinances; **whoever practices them enjoys life** through them. I am the Lord.

[EXB] <u>Leviticus 18:5</u> ·Obey [Guard; Keep] my ·laws [statutes; ordinances; requirements] and ·rules [regulations]; **a person who obeys them will live because of them**. I am the Lord.

[GNT] <u>Leviticus 18:5</u> Follow the practices and the laws that I give you; **you will save your life by doing so**. I am the Lord.

[Moffatt] <u>Leviticus 18:5</u> So keep my rules and regulations; if a man obeys them, **it means life for him**. I am the Eternal.

[NAB] <u>Leviticus 18:5</u> Keep, then, my statutes and decrees, for the man who carries them out **will find life through them**. I am the Lord.

[NLT] <u>Leviticus 18:5</u> If you obey my decrees and my regulations, **you will find life through them**. I am the Lord.

[NLV] <u>Leviticus 18:5</u> So keep My Laws and do what I say. If a man obeys them, **My Laws will be life for him**. I am the Lord.

[NRSV] <u>Leviticus 18:5</u> You shall keep my statutes and my ordinances; **by doing so one shall live**: I am the Lord.

DEUTERONOMY

<u>Deuteronomy 4:40</u> Thou shalt keep therefore his statutes, and his commandments, which I command thee this day, **that it may go well with thee, and with thy children after thee, and that thou mayest prolong thy days upon the earth**, which the LORD thy God giveth thee, for ever.

[BBE] <u>Deuteronomy 4:40</u> Then keep his laws and his orders which I give you today, so **that it may be well for you and for your children after you, and that your lives may be long in the land** which the Lord your God is giving you for ever.

[CEB] <u>Deuteronomy 4:40</u> Keep the Lord's regulations and his commandments. I'm commanding them to you today for your well-being and **for the well-being of your children after you, so that you may extend your time on the fertile land** that the Lord your God is giving you forever.

[Douay-Rheims] <u>Deuteronomy 4:40</u> Keep his precepts and commandments, which I command thee: that **it may be well with thee, and thy children after thee, and thou mayst remain a long time upon the land**, which the Lord thy God will give thee.

[HCSB] <u>Deuteronomy 4:40</u> Keep His statutes and commands, which I am giving you today, **so that you and your children after you may prosper and so that you may live long in the land** the Lord your God is giving you for all time."

[MKJV] <u>Deuteronomy 4:40</u> Therefore, you shall keep His statutes and His commandments which I command you this day, so that **it may go well with you and with your sons after you, and so that you may make your days longer upon the earth** which the LORD your God gives you forever.

[MSG] <u>Deuteronomy 4:40</u> Obediently live by his rules and commands which I'm giving you today **so that you'll live well and your children after you—oh, you'll live a long time in the land** that God, your God, is giving you.

[NABRE] <u>Deuteronomy 4:40</u> And you must keep his statutes and commandments which I command you today, **that you and your children after you may prosper, and that you may have long life on the land** which the Lord, your God, is giving you forever.

[NET] <u>Deuteronomy 4:40</u> Keep his statutes and commandments that I am setting forth today so that **it may go well with you and your descendants and that you may enjoy longevity in the land** that the Lord your God is about to give you as a permanent possession.

<u>Deuteronomy 5:16</u> Honour thy father and thy mother, as the LORD thy God hath commanded thee; **that thy days may be prolonged, and that it may go well with thee**, in the land which the LORD thy God giveth thee.

[BBE] <u>Deuteronomy 5:16</u> Give honour to your father and your mother, as you have been ordered by the Lord your God; **so that your life may be long and all may be well for you** in the land which the Lord your God is giving you.

[Beck] <u>Deuteronomy 5:16</u> Honor your father and mother as the LORD you God has ordered you, **so that you will live long and prosper on the earth** the LORD your God is giving you.

[CEV] <u>Deuteronomy 5:16</u> Respect your father and mother, and **you will live a long and successful life** in the land I am giving you.

[CJB] <u>Deuteronomy 5:16</u> Honor your father and mother, as Adonai your God ordered you to do, so **that you will live long and have things go well with you** in the land Adonai your God is giving you.

[CWB] <u>Deuteronomy 5:16</u> "'Honor your parents. Show respect to them, and **I will bless you with long life, and things will go well for you** in the land I have promised to give you.

[Douay-Rheims] <u>Deuteronomy 5:16</u> Honour thy father and mother, as the Lord thy God hath commanded thee, **that thou mayst live a long time, and it may be well with thee** in the land, which the Lord thy God will give thee.

[ERV] <u>Deuteronomy 5:16</u> 'You must honor your father and your mother. The Lord your God has commanded you to do this. If you follow this command, **you will live a long time, and everything will go well for you in the land** that the Lord your God gives you.

[Fenton] <u>Deuteronomy 5:16</u> Honor your father and your mother, as your Ever-Living God commanded you, so **that your days may be lengthened, and that you may prosper upon the land** which your Ever-Living God gives to you.

[NAB] <u>Deuteronomy 5:16</u> 'Honor your father and your mother, as the LORD, your God, has commanded you, that **you may have a long life and prosperity in the land** which the LORD, your God, is giving you.

[NET] <u>Deuteronomy 5:16</u> Honor your father and your mother just as the Lord your God has commanded you to do, **so that your days may be extended and that it may go well with you** in the land that he is about to give you.

[NLT] <u>Deuteronomy 5:16</u> "Honor your father and mother, as the Lord your God commanded you. **Then you will live a long, full life** in the land the Lord your God is giving you.

OUR HEALING COVENANT

Deuteronomy 5:33 Ye shall walk in all the ways which the Lord your God hath commanded you, that ye may live, and that it may be well with you, and **that ye may prolong your days in the land** which ye shall possess.

[BBE] Deuteronomy 5:33 Go on walking in the way ordered for you by the Lord your God, so that life may be yours and it may be well for you, and **your days may be long in the land** of your heritage.

[CCB] Deuteronomy 5:33 Follow all the way which Yahweh has marked out for you, and you will live and be happy and **you will live long in the land** you are going to conquer.

[CEB] Deuteronomy 5:33 You must walk the precise path that the Lord your God indicates for you so that you will live, and so that things will go well for you, and so **you will extend your time on the land** that you will possess.

[CEV] Deuteronomy 5:33 Follow them, because **they make a path that will lead to a long successful life in the land** the Lord your God is giving you.

[CPDV] Deuteronomy 5:33 For you shall walk in the way that the Lord your God has instructed, **so that you may live, and it may be well with you, and your days may be extended in the land** of your possession.'"

[CSB] Deuteronomy 5:33 Follow the whole instruction the Lord your God has commanded you, **so that you may live, prosper, and have a long life in the land** you will possess.

[EEBT] Deuteronomy 5:33 You must live as the Lord your God says. If you do that, **you will live for many years in your own country**. You will enjoy all your good work.

[Fenton] Deuteronomy 5:33 You shall walk in every way as your Ever-Living God commanded you, **so that you may live, and prosper, and lengthen your days in the country** which you shall possess.

[Knox] Deuteronomy 5:33 but still treading the path which the Lord your God has marked out for you; **so that you may enjoy, in long prosperity, the land** which shall be yours.

[Leeser-OT] Deuteronomy 5:33 altogether in the way, which the Lord your God hath commanded you, shall ye walk; in order that ye may live, and that it may be well with you, and that **ye may remain many days in the land** which ye will possess.

[MSG] Deuteronomy 5:33 Walk straight down the road God commands **so that you'll have a good life and live a long time in the land** that you're about to possess.

[NIV] Deuteronomy 5:33 Walk in obedience to all that the Lord your God has commanded you, **so that you may live and prosper and prolong your days in the land** that you will possess.

[NLT] Deuteronomy 5:33 Stay on the path that the Lord your God has commanded you to follow. **Then you will live long and prosperous lives in the land** you are about to enter and occupy.

Deuteronomy 6:2 That thou mightest fear the Lord thy God, to keep all his statutes and his commandments, which I command thee, thou, and thy son, and thy son's son, all the days of thy life; and that **thy days may be prolonged**.

[BBE] Deuteronomy 6:2 So that living in the fear of the Lord your God, you may keep all his laws and his orders, which I give you: you and your son and your son's son, all the days of your life; and so that **your life may be long**.

[CEB] Deuteronomy 6:2 so that you will fear the Lord your God by keeping all his regulations and his commandments that I am commanding you—both you and your sons and daughters—all the days of your life and so that **you will lengthen your life**.

[GNT] <u>Deuteronomy 6:2</u> As long as you live, you and your descendants are to honor the Lord your God and obey all his laws that I am giving you, so that **you may live in that land a long time**.

[MSG] <u>Deuteronomy 6:2</u> This is so that you'll live in deep reverence before God lifelong, observing all his rules and regulations that I'm commanding you, you and your children and your grandchildren, **living good long lives**.

[NIRV] <u>Deuteronomy 6:2</u> Then you, your children and their children after them will honor the Lord your God as long as you live. Obey all his rules and commands I'm giving you. If you do, **you will enjoy long life**.

[Orton-OT] <u>Deuteronomy 6:2</u> That thou mightest fear the LORD thy God, to keep all his statutes, and his commandments which I command thee, thou, and thy son, and thy son's son, all the days of thy life; and that **thy days may be prolonged, that thou mayest procure length of days and all desirable prosperity**.

[T4T] <u>Deuteronomy 6:2</u> He wants you to have an awesome respect for him, and he wants you and your descendants to always obey all these rules and regulations that I am giving to you, in order that **you may live for a long time**.

[TLB] <u>Deuteronomy 6:2</u> The purpose of these laws is to cause you, your sons, and your grandsons to reverence the Lord your God by obeying all of his instructions as long as you live; if you do, **you will have long, prosperous years ahead of you**.

<u>Deuteronomy 11:9,21</u> **And that ye may prolong your days in the land**, which the LORD sware unto your fathers to give unto them and to their seed, a land that floweth with milk and honey. [21]**That your days may be multiplied**, and the days of your children, in the land which the LORD sware unto your fathers to give them, as the days of heaven upon the earth.

[ABP] <u>Deuteronomy 11:9,21</u> **that you should prolong your days upon the land** of which the Lord swore by an oath to your fathers to give to them, and to their seed after them—a land flowing milk and honey. [21]**that you should multiply your days**, and the days of your sons, upon the land which the Lord swore by an oath to your fathers to give to them, as the days of heaven upon the earth.

[AMP] <u>Deuteronomy 11:9,21</u> so **that you may live long on the land** which the Lord swore (solemnly promised) to your fathers to give to them and to their descendants, a land [of great abundance,] flowing with milk and honey. [21]**so that your days and the days of your children may be multiplied** in the land which the Lord swore to your fathers to give them, as long as the heavens are above the earth.

[BLE] <u>Deuteronomy 11:9,21</u> **and in order that you may have a long time on the soil** Jehovah swore to your fathers to give to them and their descendants, a country that runs milk and honey. [21]**in order that you and your children may have as many days on the soil that Jehovah swore to your fathers** to give you as the days of the sky over the earth.

[CLV] <u>Deuteronomy 11:9,21</u> and **that you may prolong your days on the ground** about which Yahweh had sworn to your fathers to give to them and to their seed, a land gushing with milk and honey. [21]**that your days and the days of your sons may be many** on the ground about which Yahweh had sworn to your fathers to give to them, as many as the days of the heavens over the earth.

[EEBT] <u>Deuteronomy 11:9,21</u> **You will live for a long time in this country**. The LORD promised your ancestors that he would give it to you. It is a country where there is enough very good food and drink for everyone. [21]**If you do that, you and your descendants will live in the country for a long time**. You will continue to live there while there is a sky above the earth.

[MKJV] <u>Deuteronomy 11:9,21</u> and **so that you may make your days longer in the land** which the LORD swore to your fathers to give to them and to their seed, a land that flows with milk and honey. ²¹**so that your days and the days of your sons may be multiplied** in the land which the LORD swore to give to your fathers, like the days of the heavens upon the earth.

[MSG] <u>Deuteronomy 11:9,21</u> **Your obedience will give you a long life on the soil** that God promised to give your ancestors and their children, a land flowing with milk and honey. ²¹**so that you'll live a long time**, and your children with you, on the soil that God promised to give your ancestors for as long as there is a sky over the Earth.

[NET] <u>Deuteronomy 11:9,21</u> and **that you may enjoy long life in the land** the Lord promised to give to your ancestors and their descendants, a land flowing with milk and honey. ²¹**so that your days and those of your descendants may be extended** in the land which the Lord promised to give to your ancestors, like the days of heaven itself.

[NIRV] <u>Deuteronomy 11:9,21</u> **You will live there for a long time**. It's the land the Lord promised to give to Abraham, Isaac and Jacob and their children after them. He gave his word when he made that promise. The land has plenty of milk and honey. ²¹**Then you and your children will live for a long time** in the land. The Lord promised to give the land to Abraham, Isaac and Jacob. Your family line will continue as long as the heavens remain above the earth.

[Thomson] <u>Deuteronomy 11:9,21</u> **that you may prolong your days in that land**, which the Lord, with an oath to your fathers, promised to give to them, and to their seed after them—a land flowing with milk and honey. ²¹**that you may prolong your lives**, that the days of your children in the land which the Lord solemnly promised your fathers to give them, may be as the days of heaven over the earth.

[TLB] <u>Deuteronomy 11:9,21</u> If you obey the commandments, **you will have a long and good life in the land** the Lord promised to your ancestors and to you, their descendants—a wonderful land 'flowing with milk and honey'! ²¹**so that as long as there is sky above the earth, you and your children will enjoy the good life** awaiting you in the land the Lord has promised you.

<u>Deuteronomy 22:7</u> But thou shalt in any wise let the dam go, and take the young to thee; **that it may be well with thee, and that thou mayest prolong thy days**.

[AMPC] <u>Deuteronomy 22:7</u> You shall surely let the mother bird go, and take only the young, **that it may be well with you and that you may prolong your days**.

[BBE] <u>Deuteronomy 22:7</u> See that you let the mother bird go, but the young ones you may take; so **it will be well for you and your life will be long**.

[CCB] <u>Deuteronomy 22:7</u> but you shall let the mother go and take only the young. **Then you shall prosper and live long**.

[GNT] <u>Deuteronomy 22:7</u> You may take the young birds, but you must let the mother bird go, so **that you will live a long and prosperous life**.

[MKJV] <u>Deuteronomy 22:7</u> You shall in every case let the dam go and take the young for yourself, so that **it may be well with you, and you may make your days longer**.

[NAB] <u>Deuteronomy 22:7</u> you shall let her go, although you may take her brood away. **It is thus that you shall have prosperity and a long life**.

[NCV] <u>Deuteronomy 22:7</u> You may take the young birds, but you must let the mother bird go free. Then **things will go well for you, and you will live a long time**.

[NJB] <u>Deuteronomy 22:7</u> Let the mother go; the young you may take for yourself. **Thus will you have prosperity and long life**.

[NOG] <u>Deuteronomy 22:7</u> You may take the chicks, but make sure you let the mother go. **Then things will go well for you, and you will live for a long time.**

[TVB] <u>Deuteronomy 22:7</u> You must let the mother go, but you may take the chicks or eggs for yourself. If you do this, God will bless you; **everything will go well with you, and you'll live a long time**.

<u>Deuteronomy 25:15</u> But thou shalt have a perfect and just weight, a perfect and just measure shalt thou have: **that thy days may be lengthened** in the land which the Lord thy God giveth thee.

[CWB] <u>Deuteronomy 25:15</u> You are to use accurate weights and measures, for then the Lord your God can bless you and **you will live a long and happy life** in the land He is to give you.

[EEBT] <u>Deuteronomy 25:15</u> You must have true and honest things with which to measure and to weigh. If you do that **you will live for a long time** in your country. It is the country that the Lord your God is giving to you.

[ERV] <u>Deuteronomy 25:15</u> You must use weights and measures that are correct and accurate. Then **you will live a long time** in the land that the Lord your God is giving you.

[Fenton] <u>Deuteronomy 25:15</u> You shall have a just and right weight; you shall have a just and right measure; so **that your time may be extended** in the land which your Ever-Living God gives to you

[Kenrick] <u>Deuteronomy 25:15</u> Thou shalt have a just and a true weight; and thy bushel shall be equal and true: **that thou mayest live a long time** upon the land which the Lord thy God giveth thee.

[NET] <u>Deuteronomy 25:15</u> You must have an accurate and correct stone weight and an accurate and correct measuring container, so that **your life may be extended** in the land the Lord your God is about to give you.

<u>Deuteronomy 30:19-20</u> I call heaven and earth to record this day against you, that I have set before you life and death, blessing and cursing: **therefore choose life, that both thou and thy seed may live:** [20]That thou mayest love the Lord thy God, and that thou mayest obey his voice, and that thou mayest cleave unto him: **for he is thy life, and the length of thy days:** that thou mayest dwell in the land which the Lord sware unto thy fathers, to Abraham, to Isaac, and to Jacob, to give them.

[CEB] <u>Deuteronomy 30:19-20</u> I call heaven and earth as my witnesses against you right now: I have set life and death, blessing and curse before you. **Now choose life—so that you and your descendants will live—** [20]by loving the Lord your God, by obeying his voice, and by clinging to him. **That's how you will survive and live long on the fertile land** the Lord swore to give to your ancestors: to Abraham, Isaac, and Jacob.

[CWB] <u>Deuteronomy 30:19-20</u> Today I'm calling heaven and earth as my witnesses that I have given you a choice between life and death, blessings and curses. **Choose life, so that you and your families may be blessed and live.** [20]Give yourselves to the Lord your God and to Him alone. Listen to Him. Hold on to Him and don't let go, **because the Lord is your life and He's the only One who can bless you and make you truly happy. He'll give you many prosperous years** in the land He promised your forefathers, Abraham, Isaac and Jacob."

[ERV] <u>Deuteronomy 30:19-20</u> Today I am giving you a choice of two ways. And I ask heaven and earth to be witnesses of your choice. You can choose life or death. The first choice will bring a blessing. The other choice will bring a curse. **So choose life! Then you and your children will live.** [20]You must love the Lord your God and obey him. Never leave him, **because he is your life. And he will give you a long life in the land** that he, the Lord, promised to give to your ancestors—Abraham, Isaac, and Jacob.

[Fenton] <u>Deuteronomy 30:19-20</u> Bear witness to me, now, Heavens and Earth! I place Life and Death before you, —the Blessing and the Curse! Therefore **choose for yourselves the Life, —that you and your posterity may live!** ²⁰Love your Ever-Living God, listen to His voice, and hold to Him, —**or He will give you life, and extend your time, to rest upon the land** that the Ever-Living promised to your fathers, —Abraham, Isaac, and to Jacob to give them.

[ICB] <u>Deuteronomy 30:19-20</u> Today I ask heaven and earth to be witnesses. I am offering you life or death, blessings or curses. **Now, choose life! Then you and your children may live.** ²⁰Love the Lord your God. Obey him. Stay close to him. He is your life. **And he will let you live many years in the land.** This is the land he promised to give your ancestors Abraham, Isaac and Jacob.

[MSG] <u>Deuteronomy 30:19-20</u> I call Heaven and Earth to witness against you today: I place before you Life and Death, Blessing and Curse. **Choose life so that you and your children will live.** ²⁰And love God, your God, listening obediently to him, firmly embracing him. Oh yes, **he is life itself, a long life settled on the soil** that God, your God, promised to give your ancestors, Abraham, Isaac, and Jacob.

[NIRV] <u>Deuteronomy 30:19-20</u> I'm calling for the heavens and the earth to be witnesses against you this very day. I'm offering you the choice of life or death. You can choose either blessings or curses. But I want you to **choose life. Then you and your children will live.** ²⁰And you will love the Lord your God. You will obey him. You will remain true to him. **The Lord is your very life. He will give you many years in the land.** He promised to give that land to your fathers, to Abraham, Isaac and Jacob.

Deuteronomy 32:46-47 And he said unto them, Set your hearts unto all the words which I testify among you this day, which ye shall command your children to observe to do, all the words of this law. ⁴⁷For it is not a vain thing for you; because it is your life: and **through this thing ye shall prolong your days** in the land, whither ye go over Jordan to possess it.

[AMP] <u>Deuteronomy 32:46-47</u> he said to them, "Take to heart all the words of warning which I am speaking to you today; and you shall command your children to observe them carefully—to do all the words of this law. ⁴⁷For it is not an empty or trivial matter for you; indeed it is your [very] life. **By [honoring and obeying] this word you will live long** in the land, which you are crossing the Jordan to possess."

[BBE] <u>Deuteronomy 32:46-47</u> Moses said to them, Let the words which I have said to you today go deep into your hearts, and give orders to your children to do every word of this law. ⁴⁷And this is no small thing for you, but it is your life, and **through this you may make your days long** in the land which you are going over Jordan to take for your heritage.

[Beck] <u>Deuteronomy 32:46-47</u> he told them: "Take to heart everything I'm warning you about today, so that you will order your children to carefully do everything this law tells them. ⁴⁷This isn't empty talk for you; no, it means your life and **will enable you to live long in the land** you're crossing the Jordan to take over."

[CEB] <u>Deuteronomy 32:46-47</u> he told them: Set your mind on all these words I'm testifying against you right now, because you must command your children to perform carefully all the words of this Instruction. ⁴⁷This is no trivial matter for you—this is your very life! It is **by this means alone that you will prolong your life** on the fertile land you are crossing the Jordan River to possess.

[ERV] <u>Deuteronomy 32:46-47</u> he said to them, "You must be sure to pay attention to all the commands I tell you today. And you must tell your children to obey completely the commands in this Law. ⁴⁷Don't think these teachings are not important. They are your life! **Through these teachings you will live a long time** in the land across the Jordan River that you are ready to take.

[ESV] <u>Deuteronomy 32:46-47</u> he said to them, "Take to heart all the words by which I am warning you today, that you may command them to your children, that they may be careful to do all the words of this law. [47]For it is no empty word for you, but your very life, and **by this word you shall live long** in the land that you are going over the Jordan to possess.

[MSG] <u>Deuteronomy 32:46-47</u> he said, "Take to heart all these words to which I give witness today and urgently command your children to put them into practice, every single word of this Revelation. [47]Yes. This is no small matter for you; it's your life. **In keeping this word you'll have a good and long life** in this land that you're crossing the Jordan to possess."

[NAB] <u>Deuteronomy 32:46-47</u> he said, "Take to heart all the warning which I have now given you and which you must impress on your children, that you may carry out carefully every word of this law. [47]For this is no trivial matter for you; rather, it means your very life, since it is **by this means that you are to enjoy a long life** on the land which you will cross the Jordan to occupy."

[NCV] <u>Deuteronomy 32:46-47</u> he said to them: "Pay careful attention to all the words I have said to you today, and command your children to obey carefully everything in these teachings. [47]These should not be unimportant words for you, but rather they mean life for you! **By these words you will live a long time** in the land you are crossing the Jordan River to take as your own.

[RSV] <u>Deuteronomy 32:46-47</u> he said to them, "Lay to heart all the words which I enjoin upon you this day, that you may command them to your children, that they may be careful to do all the words of this law. [47]For it is no trifle for you, but it is your life, and **thereby you shall live long** in the land which you are going over the Jordan to possess.

[RV] <u>Deuteronomy 32:46-47</u> And he said unto them, Set your heart unto all the words which I testify unto you this day; which ye shall command your children, to observe to do all the words of this law. [47]For it is no vain thing for you; because it is your life, and **through this thing ye shall prolong your days** upon the land, whither ye go over Jordan to possess it.

[TLB] <u>Deuteronomy 32:46-47</u> Moses made these comments: "Meditate upon all the laws I have given you today, and pass them on to your children. [47]These laws are not mere words—they are your life! **Through obeying them you will live long**, plentiful lives in the land you are going to possess across the Jordan River."

[TLV] <u>Deuteronomy 32:46-47</u> he said to them, "Put in your hearts all the words that I call as witness against you today—that you may command your children to keep and do all the words of this Torah. [47]For it is not an empty thing for you, because it is your life! **By this word you will prolong your days** on the land, which you are crossing over the Jordan to possess."

[ULB] <u>Deuteronomy 32:46-47</u> He said to them, "Fix your mind on all the words that I have witnessed to you today, so that you may command your children to keep them, all the words of this law. [47]For this is no trivial matter for you, because it is your life, and **through this thing you will prolong your days** in the land that you are going over the Jordan to possess."

<u>Deuteronomy 34:7</u> And Moses was an hundred and twenty years old when he died: **his eye was not dim, nor his natural force abated**.

[Abegg-OT] <u>Deuteronomy 34:7</u> Moses was a hundred and twenty years old when he died, yet **his sight was unimpaired and his strength was not gone**.

[Bate-OT] <u>Deuteronomy 34:7</u> And Moses was an hundred and twenty years old when he died; **his eye was not dim, nor his freshness gone**.

[Beck] <u>Deuteronomy 34:7</u> When he died, Moses was 120 years old. **His eyesight didn't get poor, and he didn't lose his fresh vigor.**

[CCB] <u>Deuteronomy 34:7</u> Moses was a hundred and twenty years old when he died. **He did not lose his vigor and his eyes still saw clearly.**

[CEV] <u>Deuteronomy 34:7</u> Moses was 120 years old when he died, **yet his eyesight was still good, and his body was strong.**

[CLV] <u>Deuteronomy 34:7</u> Moses was a hundred and twenty years old at his death. **Neither had his eye dimmed nor had his vitality fled.**

[ERV] <u>Deuteronomy 34:7</u> Moses was 120 years old when he died. **He was as strong as ever, and his eyes were still good.**

[Haak] <u>Deuteronomy 34:7</u> Now when Moses was an hundred and twenty years old, when he died: **his eye was not grown dim, and his strength was not decayed.**

[Macrae] <u>Deuteronomy 34:7</u> Moses was a hundred and twenty years old when he died; **neither his eye-sight nor his strength were diminished.**

[MSG] <u>Deuteronomy 34:7</u> Moses was 120 years old when he died. **His eyesight was sharp; he still walked with a spring in his step.**

[NIRV] <u>Deuteronomy 34:7</u> Moses was 120 years old when he died. But **his eyesight was still good. He was still very strong.**

[NOG] <u>Deuteronomy 34:7</u> Moses was 120 years old when he died. **His eyesight never became poor, and he never lost his physical strength.**

JOSHUA

<u>Joshua 14:10-11</u> And now, **behold, the Lord hath kept me alive, as he said, these forty and five years,** even since the Lord spake this word unto Moses, while the children of Israel wandered in the wilderness: and now, lo, **I am this day fourscore and five years old.** [11]**As yet I am as strong this day as I was in the day that Moses sent me: as my strength was then, even so is my strength now,** for war, both to go out, and to come in.

[CE] <u>Joshua 14:10-11</u> Now as he promised, **the Lord has preserved me while Israel was journeying through the desert, for the forty-five years** since the Lord spoke thus to Moses; and although **I am now eighty-five years old,** [11]**I am still as strong today as I was the day Moses sent me forth, with no less vigor** whether for war or for ordinary tasks.

[Thomson] <u>Joshua 14:10-11</u> Now **the Lord hath kept me alive as he said. This is the forty fifth year since the Lord spoke this word to Moses,** and Israel commenced their wanderings in the wilderness. And behold I am now eighty five years of age; [11]**yet I am now as strong as when Moses sent me; as able now as then to go out and come in to battle;**

<u>Joshua 24:29</u> And it came to pass after these things, that Joshua the son of Nun, the servant of the Lord, died, being an hundred and ten years old.

[ERV] <u>Joshua 24:29</u> After that the Lord's servant Joshua son of Nun died. He was 110 years old.

[FAA] <u>Joshua 24:29</u> And it came to pass after these things that Joshua the son of Nun, the servant of the Lord, died, being one hundred and ten years old.

JUDGES

Judges 8:32 And **Gideon the son of Joash died in a good old age**, and was buried in the sepulchre of Joash his father, in Ophrah of the Abiezrites.

[CCB] Judges 8:32 **Gideon the son of Joash died at a happy old age**, and he was buried in the tomb of Joash his father, in Ophrah of Abiezer.

[Fenton] Judges 8:32 **The Gideon-ben-Yoash died with good grey hair**, and they buried him in the tomb of Yoash his father, in Afrah of Abiezer.

[HCSB] Judges 8:32 **Then Gideon son of Joash died at a ripe old age** and was buried in the tomb of his father Joash in Ophrah of the Abiezrites.

[Jerusalem] Judges 8:32 **Gideon son of Joash was blessed in his old age; he died**, and was buried in the tomb of Joash his father, at Ophrah of Abiezer.

[NET] Judges 8:32 **Gideon son of Joash died at a very old age** and was buried in the tomb of his father Joash located in Ophrah of the Abiezrites.

[TLB] Judges 8:32 **Gideon finally died, an old, old man**, and was buried in the sepulcher of his father, Joash, in Ophrah, in the land of the Abiezrites.

RUTH

Ruth 4:15 And **he shall be unto thee a restorer of thy life, and a nourisher of thine old age**: for thy daughter in law, which loveth thee, which is better to thee than seven sons, hath born him.

[Knox] Ruth 4:15 **Here is one that shall bring comfort to thy heart, and support to thy old age**; such a mother is his, such a daughter-in-law is thine, whose love is worth more to thee than seven sons of thy own.

[Leeser-OT] Ruth 4:15 **And may he be unto thee one who refresheth thy soul, and who nourisheth thy old age**; for thy daughter-in-law, who loveth thee, hath born him, she who is better to thee than seven sons.

[NLV] Ruth 4:15 **May he bring you new life and strength while you are old**. For your daughter-in-law who loves you, who is better to you than seven sons, has given birth to him."

[WGCIB] Ruth 4:15 **You should have one to comfort your soul, and cherish your old age**. For he is born of your daughter-in-law: who loves you: and is much better to you, than if you had seven sons."

SECOND SAMUEL

2 Samuel 19:32 Now **Barzillai was a very aged man, even fourscore years old**: and he had provided the king of sustenance while he lay at Mahanaim; for he was a very great man.

[CCB] 2 Samuel 19:32 **Barzillai was a very old man of eighty**, who, being a very wealthy man, had provided the king with food when he remained in Mahanaim.

FIRST KINGS

1 Kings 3:14 And if thou wilt walk in my ways, to keep my statutes and my commandments, as thy father David did walk, then **I will lengthen thy days**.

[BBE] **1 Kings 3:14** And if you go on in my ways, keeping my laws and my orders as your father David did, **I will give you a long life**.

[Beck] **1 Kings 3:14** And if you live according to My ways and keep My rules and commandments as your father did, then **I will also give you a long life**.

[BLE] **1 Kings 3:14** And if you walk in my ways, keeping my usages and commandments, as your father David did, **I will make your days long**.

[CEB] **1 Kings 3:14** And if you walk in my ways and obey my laws and commands, just as your father David did, then **I will give you a very long life**."

[CWB] **1 Kings 3:14** If you walk in my ways, keep my commandments and obey my laws as your father David did, **I will also give you a long and healthy life**."

[ISV] **1 Kings 3:14** If you will live life my way, keeping my statutes and my commands, just like your father David did, **I'll also increase the length of your life**."

[JPS-OT 1963] **1 Kings 3:14** "And **I will further grant you long life**, if you will walk in My ways and observe My laws and commandments, as did your father David."

[Knox] **1 Kings 3:14** And if thou wilt follow the paths I have chosen for thee, as thy father did, keeping charge and commandment of mine, **long life thou shalt have too**.

[Moffatt] **1 Kings 3:14** And if you will live my life, keeping my rules and orders, as did your father David, **I will give you a long life**.

[NET] **1 Kings 3:14** If you follow my instructions by obeying my rules and regulations, just as your father David did, then **I will grant you long life**.

[REAL] **1 Kings 3:14** and if you walk on my routes, to guard my laws and my commands, just like your father David walked, then **I shall lengthen your days**,"

[Rotherham] **1 Kings 3:14** And, if thou wilt walk in my ways, by keeping my statutes, and my commandments, as, David thy father, walked, **then will I lengthen out thy days**.

[T4T] **1 Kings 3:14** If you conduct your life as I want you to, and if you obey all my laws and commandments, as your father David did, **I will enable you to live for many years**."

[TVB] **1 Kings 3:14** If you live a life devoted to Me, if you remain loyal to My laws and commands just as your father David did, then **I will add days to your life**.

[YLT] **1 Kings 3:14** and if thou dost walk in My ways to keep My statutes, and My commands, as David thy father walked, then **I have prolonged thy days**.'

FIRST CHRONICLES

1 Chronicles 23:1 So when David was old and full of days, he made Solomon his son king over Israel.

[BLE] **1 Chronicles 23:1 And David grew old, had lived as long as he wanted to**, and he made his son Solomon king over Israel.

[CLV] <u>1 Chronicles 23:1</u> **When David was old and was satisfied with days,** he made Solomon his son king over Israel.

[JPS-OT 1985] <u>1 Chronicles 23:1</u> **When David reached a ripe old age,** he made his son Solomon king over Israel.

<u>1 Chronicles 29:28</u> And **he died in a good old age, full of days,** riches, and honour: and Solomon his son reigned in his stead.

[BBE] <u>1 Chronicles 29:28</u> And **he came to his end after a long life, full of days** and great wealth and honour; and Solomon his son became king in his place.

[CEV] <u>1 Chronicles 29:28</u> **David was rich and respected and lived to be an old man.** Then he died, and his son Solomon became king.

[CWB] <u>1 Chronicles 29:28</u> **He died at a ripe old age,** wealthy and respected, having enjoyed a long life, and his son Solomon succeeded him.

[ICB] <u>1 Chronicles 29:28</u> **David died when he was old. He had lived a good, long life.** He had received many riches and honors. And David's son Solomon became king after him.

[Kent-OT] <u>1 Chronicles 29:28</u> And **he died in a good old age, satisfied with living,** with riches, and with honor; and Solomon his son reigned in his place.

[Moffatt] <u>1 Chronicles 29:28</u> He **died in a ripe old age, having had life and riches and honour to the full,** and Solomon his son reigned instead of him.

[NIV] <u>1 Chronicles 29:28</u> He **died at a good old age, having enjoyed long life,** wealth and honor. His son Solomon succeeded him as king.

[TVB] <u>1 Chronicles 29:28</u> **Then he died peacefully of old age, after a long life,** riches, and honor. And after he joined with his ancestors in death, his son Solomon reigned over Israel in his place.

SECOND CHRONICLES

<u>2 Chronicles 24:15</u> But Jehoiada waxed old, and was full of days when he died; an hundred and thirty years old was he when he died.

[ERV] <u>2 Chronicles 24:15</u> Jehoiada became old. He had a very long life, and he died when he was 130 years old.

[Kent-OT] <u>2 Chronicles 24:15</u> But when Jehoiada was old and satisfied with living he died. A hundred and thirty years old was he when he died.

[MSG] <u>2 Chronicles 24:15</u> He died at a ripe old age—130 years old!

[Rotherham] <u>2 Chronicles 24:15</u> But Jehoiada waxed old and became satisfied with days, and died, — a hundred and thirty years old, when he died.

[TVB] <u>2 Chronicles 24:15</u> Jehoiada was rewarded for his faithfulness to God with a long life. He was 130 years old when he died,

JOB

Job 5:26 **Thou shalt come to thy grave in a full age**, like as a shock of corn cometh in in his season.

[BLE] **Job 5:26** **You shall come to your grave in rugged vigor** as a stack of grain goes up at its due time.

[CJB] **Job 5:26** **You will come to your grave at a ripe old age**, like a pile of grain that arrives in season.

[CT-OT] **Job 5:26** **You shall come to the grave at a ripe old age**, as the grain stack is taken away in its time.

[Douay-Rheims] **Job 5:26** **Thou shalt enter into the grave in abundance**, as a heap of wheat is brought in its season.

[EEBT] **Job 5:26** **You will live for many years**. Plants grow until the right time to pick them. So you will live until it is the right time for you to die. And you will have good health until you die.

[FV] **Job 5:26** **You shall come to your grave in a full age**, like a shock of grain comes in its season.

[Knox] **Job 5:26** and **when go to the grave thou must, it shall be with strength undiminished**, like ripe corn at harvest-home.

[LITV] **Job 5:26** **You shall come to the grave in full vigor**, like a stack of grain comes up in its season.

[NIRV] **Job 5:26** **You will go down to the grave while you are still very strong**. You will be like a crop that is gathered at the right time.

[Orton-OT] **Job 5:26** **Thou shalt come to thy grave in a full age, not by untimely death, but in a good old age**, like a shock of corn cometh in in his season, when it is carried home fully ripe.

[REB] **Job 5:26** **You will come to the grave in sturdy old age** as sheaves come in due season to the threshing-floor.

[Rotherham] **Job 5:26** **Thou shalt come, yet robust, to the grave**, as a stack of sheaves mounteth up in its season.

[T4T] **Job 5:26** **You will become very old before you die**, like sheaves of grain continue to grow until it is time to harvest them.

[TLB] **Job 5:26** **You shall live a long, good life**; like standing grain, you'll not be harvested until it's time!

Job 12:12 With the ancient is wisdom; and in length of days understanding.

[Beck] **Job 12:12** Aged people are wise, and those who live long understand.

[NIRV] **Job 12:12** Old people are wise. Those who live a long time have understanding.

[Schaff-OT] **Job 12:12** So with the old is sage experience; With length of days doth understanding dwell.

[WSP-OT] **Job 12:12** With the aged is wisdom; And length of days is understanding.

Job 21:23 One dieth in his full strength, being wholly at ease and quiet.

[ABU-Job] **Job 21:23** One dies in his full prosperity; he is wholly at ease, and secure.

[AMP] **Job 21:23** "One dies in his full strength, Being wholly at ease and quiet and satisfied;

[Anchor] <u>Job 21:23</u> One dies in full vigor, Wholly at ease and contented.

[BBE] <u>Job 21:23</u> One comes to his end in complete well-being, full of peace and quiet:

[Berkeley] <u>Job 21:23</u> One man dies in fulness of strength, completely at ease and satisfied.

[Bernard-OT] <u>Job 21:23</u> The one dieth in the very perfection of his strength, being wholly at ease and quiet.

[Boothroyd] <u>Job 21:23</u> One dieth in his perfect strength, Being wholly tranquil and at ease.

[CEB] <u>Job 21:23</u> Someone dies in wonderful health, completely comfortable and well,

[Coleman-OT] <u>Job 21:23</u> One man dieth in his entire strength, Being wholly at ease and quiet.

[CWB] <u>Job 21:23</u> Some men remain healthy until the day they die, completely secure and living at ease.

[Haak] <u>Job 21:23</u> This (man) dieth in the strength of his perfection, where he was at full rest and quiet.

[Kenrick] <u>Job 21:23</u> One man dieth strong and hale, rich and happy.

[Orton-OT] <u>Job 21:23</u> One dieth in his full strength, in his very perfection, or, in the strength of his perfection, being wholly at ease and quiet.

[Renan-OT] <u>Job 21:23</u> Man dies in the midst of his prosperity, Perfectly quiet, perfectly happy.

[Sharpe] <u>Job 21:23</u> One man dieth in his full strength, Being wholly at ease and feeling safe.

[T4T] <u>Job 21:23</u> Some people die while they are very healthy, while they are peaceful, when they are not afraid of anything.

<u>Job 32:7</u> I said, Days should speak, and multitude of years should teach wisdom.

[BBE] <u>Job 32:7</u> I said to myself, It is right for the old to say what is in their minds, and for those who are far on in years to give out wisdom.

[CJB] <u>Job 32:7</u> I said, 'Age should speak; an abundance of years should teach wisdom.'

[CPDV] <u>Job 32:7</u> For I had hoped that greater age would speak, and that a multitude of years would teach wisdom.

[Hall] <u>Job 32:7</u> I said, as in good manners I ought; Those, that are ancient and full of days, should speak; and those, that had many years experience, should be most able to teach wisdom to their younger.

[UDB] <u>Job 32:7</u> I said to myself, 'Let those who are much older speak because older people should be able to say things that are wise.'

<u>Job 42:16-17</u> After this lived Job an hundred and forty years, and saw his sons, and his sons' sons, even four generations. [17]So Job died, being old and full of days.

[CBC] <u>Job 42:16-17</u> After this lived Joban hundred and forty years, and saw his sons, and his sons' sons, even four generations. [17]So Job died, being old and satisfied with days.

[CWB] <u>Job 42:16-17</u> Job lived a hundred and forty years after the Lord healed him. He lived to see his grandchildren and their children down to the fourth generation. [17]Then he died, having lived a long and purposeful life.

[JPS-OT 1985] <u>Job 42:16-17</u> Afterward, Job lived one hundred and forty years to see four generations of sons and grandsons. [17]So Job died old and contented.

[NWT] <u>Job 42:16-17</u> After this Job lived for 140 years, and he saw his children and his grandchildren—four generations. [17]Finally Job died, after a long and satisfying life.

[SG] Job 42:16-17 Thereafter Job lived one hundred and forty years, so that he saw his sons and his sons' sons, four generations. ¹⁷So Job died, an old man, satisfied with life.

[Wycliffe-Noble] Job 42:16-17 Forsooth Job lived after these beatings, or scourgings, an hundred and forty years, and saw his sons, and the sons of his sons, till to the fourth generation; (And after these tribulations, Job lived a hundred and forty years, and he saw his sons, and the sons of his sons, unto the fourth generation;) ¹⁷and he was dead old [and he died old], and full of days, that is, he had length and prosperity of life.

PSALMS

Psalms 21:4 He asked life of thee, and thou gavest it him, even length of days for ever and ever.

[Alexander-OT] Psalms 21:4 Life he asked of thee, thou hast given (it) to him, length of days, perpetuity and eternity.

[Anchor] Psalms 21:4 Life eternal he asked on you, you gave it to him; Length of days, eternity, and everlasting.

[Beck] Psalms 21:4 He asked You for life—You gave it to him.

[CEB] Psalms 21:4 He asked you for life, and you gave it to him, all right—long days, forever and always!

[CEV] Psalms 21:4 He asked to live a long time, and you promised him life that never ends.

[Committee-Ps] Psalms 21:4 When he asked of Thee life, Thou hast made him to live, While the ages shall circle around.

[De Witt-Ps] Psalms 21:4 He asked of Thee life, and life didst Thou give him, Even days long extended, forever and aye.

[FAA] Psalms 21:4 He asked you for life; You gave him it—Length of days, age-long and in perpetuity.

[Farr-Ps] Psalms 21:4 He asked of thee life, and, lo! it was given, His days hast thou made as enduring as heaven.

[Fenton] Psalms 21:4 You gave him the lives that he asked, Extended and lengthened his days.

[Haupt] Psalms 21:4 He asked of Thee life—that Thou hast given him, Long life, for ever and ever.

[Hielscher-Ps] Psalms 21:4 He asked but life of Thee; But Thou hast given him length of days, Even unto eternity.

[Jones-Ps] Psalms 21:4 When life was sought, came endless days, Salvation, strength, and grand displays;

[LTPB] Psalms 21:4 He asked life of You, and You gave him length of days in this age and in the age of ages.

[Maxwell-Ps] Psalms 21:4 He ask'd for life, and thou did'st give Not only length of days To him on the frail earth to live, But life that ne'er decays.

[Merrick-Ps] Psalms 21:4 He asked thee Life, and find it given, Life, lasting as the days of heaven.

[Moffatt] Psalms 21:4 he asked for life, and life thou gavest, life long and lasting.

[MOTB] Psalms 21:4 He prayed for life, and thou didst hear his prayer, and grant him year exceeding many.

[MSG] Psalms 21:4 He wanted a good life; you gave it to him, and then made it a long life as a bonus.

[Norlie-NT] <u>Psalms 21:4</u> He asked life of You; You bestowed it on him—long life, for eternity.

[Orton-OT] <u>Psalms 21:4</u> He asked life of thee, that is, present deliverance, and thou gavest it him, even length of days for ever and ever; thou gavest him the promise of long life, and thou wilt continue the crown to his posterity.

[Purver] <u>Psalms 21:4</u> The Life that he asked thee for, hast thou granted him, a very long Space of Time.

[Smyth-Ps] <u>Psalms 21:4</u> Life he petitioned for; and Life Thou freely gavest him: Even Years to outlast the Date of time, Years as the days of Heaven.

[Sullivan-OT] <u>Psalms 21:4</u> You gave him endless days just as he had asked you, days, lasting, lasting days!

[York-Ps] <u>Psalms 21:4</u> He in his trouble asked life of Thee, And Thou has granted immortality.

<u>Psalms 37:25</u> **I have been young, and now am old**; yet have I not seen the righteous forsaken, nor his seed begging bread.

[CJB] <u>Psalms 37:25</u> **I have been young; now I am old**; yet not once have I seen the righteous abandoned or his descendants begging for bread.

[Ewald-OT] <u>Psalms 37:25</u> **Oh, whether young I was, or old I am**: never saw I the godly forsaken and his seed seeking bread;

[MOTB] <u>Psalms 37:25</u> **Never once in my long life** have I seen the righteous forsaken, or his children forced to beg.

[NIRV] <u>Psalms 37:25</u> **I once was young, and now I'm old**. But I've never seen godly people deserted. I've never seen their children begging for bread.

[Rusling-Ps] <u>Psalms 37:25</u> **I have been young, and now am old**, Yet this firm truth I do unfold; I have not seen, in years now fled, The righteous or his seed want bread.

[Spurrell-OT] <u>Psalms 37:25</u> **Once I was young, now have become old**, But I have never witnessed a righteous man forsaken, Nor his seed seeking bread through want.

[T4T] <u>Psalms 37:25</u> **I was young previously, and now I am an old man**, but in all those years, I have never seen that righteous/godly people have been abandoned by Yahweh, nor have I seen that their children needed to beg for food.

[TLB] <u>Psalms 37:25</u> **I have been young and now I am old**. And in all my years I have never seen the Lord forsake a man who loves him; nor have I seen the children of the godly go hungry.

<u>Psalms 91:16</u> **With long life will I satisfy him**, and shew him my salvation.

[Alexander-OT] <u>Psalms 91:16</u> **(With) length of days will I satisfy him**, and will show him my salvation.

[Anchor] <u>Psalms 91:16</u> **With length of days will I content him**, and make him drink deeply of my salvation.

[BBE] <u>Psalms 91:16</u> **With long life will he be rewarded**; and I will let him see my salvation.

[BLE] <u>Psalms 91:16</u> **Of long life I will give him his fill**, and will let him feast his eyes on my salvation.

[CEB] <u>Psalms 91:16</u> **I'll fill you full with old age**. I'll show you my salvation.

[CEV] <u>Psalms 91:16</u> **You will live a long life** and see my saving power."

[Cotton-Ps] <u>Psalms 91:16</u> **I'll fully satisfy him with extended length of days**; when upon my Salvation I shall cause him for to look.

[De Witt-Ps] <u>Psalms 91:16</u> **His measure of life will I fill with long days**, And his eyes shall behold My salvation.

[Delitzsch-Ps] <u>Psalms 91:16</u> **With length of life will I satisfy him**, And cause him to delight himself in My salvation.

[Douay-Rheims] <u>Psalms 91:16</u> **I will fill him with length of days**; and I will shew him my salvation.

[ERV] <u>Psalms 91:16</u> **I will give my followers a long life** and show them my power to save.

[Ewald-OT] <u>Psalms 91:16</u> "**refresh him with long life**, and cause him to behold my salvation."

[Horsley-OT] <u>Psalms 91:16</u> **I will feast him to the full with length of days**, And shew him my complete salvation.

[Jerusalem] <u>Psalms 91:16</u> **I give them life, long and full**, and show them how I can save.'

[JPS-Ps 1972] <u>Psalms 91:16</u> **I will let him live to a ripe old age**, and show him My salvation.

[JUB] <u>Psalms 91:16</u> **With long life I will satisfy him** and show him my saving health.

[Kennedy-Ps] <u>Psalms 91:16</u> **My saving tenderness shall crown his life with long and happy days.**

[Knox] <u>Psalms 91:16</u> **Length of days he shall have to content him**, and find in me deliverance.

[MEMS-Ps] <u>Psalms 91:16</u> **And when, with undisturbed content, his long and happy life is spent, his end I'll crown with saving health.**

[Merrick-Ps] <u>Psalms 91:16</u> **Thy years prolong**, and to thy heart My health-dispensing grace impart.

[Milborne-Ps] <u>Psalms 91:16</u> **Long Life, with ever peaceful Days, I'll on my Friend bestow**; And to him, by a Thousand Ways, My kind Salvation show.

[MSG] <u>Psalms 91:16</u> **I'll give you a long life**, give you a long drink of salvation!

[NLV] <u>Psalms 91:16</u> **I will please him with a long life**. And I will show him My saving power.

[Norlie-NT] <u>Psalms 91:16</u> **He will have the satisfaction of a long life**, and I shall let him participate in My salvation.

[Sandys-OT] <u>Psalms 91:16</u> **He long, long happily shall live**, And flourish in my saving Grace.

[T4T] <u>Psalms 91:16</u> **I will reward them by enabling them to live a long time**, and I will save them."

[Tate-Ps] <u>Psalms 91:16</u> **His long and happy life is spent**, His end I'll crown with saving health.

[TVB] <u>Psalms 91:16</u> **I'll reward him with many good years on this earth** and let him witness My salvation."

<u>Psalms 92:14</u> They shall still bring forth fruit in old age; they shall be fat and flourishing;

[Abegg-OT] <u>Psalms 92:14</u> They will still bear fruit in ripe old age, and they will stay [healthy] and green.

[Allen-Ps-Third] <u>Psalms 92:14</u> In old age still fruit they bear, Nourished in thy courts with care:

[AMP] <u>Psalms 92:14</u> [Growing in grace] they will still thrive and bear fruit and prosper in old age; They will flourish and be vital and fresh [rich in trust and love and contentment];

[Berkeley] <u>Psalms 92:14</u> In old age they shall still be bearing fruit. They shall be full of life and vitality.

[CEV] <u>Psalms 92:14</u> They will be like trees that stay healthy and fruitful, even when they are old.

[COS-Ps-1] <u>Psalms 92:14</u> And in old age, when others fade, they fruit still forth shall bring; They shall be fat, and full of sap, and aye be flourishing;

[CWB] <u>Psalms 92:14</u> Even in our old age we will bear fruit. We will remain productive and continue to be vigorous for our God.

[Kenrick] <u>Psalms 92:14</u> They shall still increase in a fruitful old age: and shall flourish,

[McFadyen-OT] <u>Psalms 92:14</u> They shall still bear fruit in old age, All sappy and fresh shall they be—

[NEB] <u>Psalms 92:14</u> vigorous in old age like trees full of sap, luxuriant, wide-spreading.

[NLV] <u>Psalms 92:14</u> They will still give fruit when they are old. They will be full of life and strength.

[Norlie-NT] <u>Psalms 92:14</u> In old age they will still be producing fruit; they will be running freely with sap, and will be virile,

[Numerical] <u>Psalms 92:14</u> They shall still be vigorous in old age: they shall have sap and be green:

[NWT] <u>Psalms 92:14</u> Even in old age they will still be thriving; They will remain vigorous and fresh,

[T4T] <u>Psalms 92:14</u> Even when righteous people become old, they do many things that please God. They remain strong and full of energy, like trees that remain full of sap.

[Woodd-Ps] <u>Psalms 92:14</u> When nature declines, they still shall bear fruit, their hopes shall revive, their strength shall recruit; firm stands their foundation, their faith fears no shock.

<u>Psalms 118:17</u> **I shall not die, but live**, and declare the works of the Lᴏᴏᴅ.

[AMPC] <u>Psalms 118:17</u> **I shall not die but live**, and shall declare the works and recount the illustrious acts of the Lord.

[BBE] <u>Psalms 118:17</u> **Life and not death will be my part**, and I will give out the story of the works of the Lord.

[CJB] <u>Psalms 118:17</u> **I will not die; no**, I will live and proclaim the great deeds of Yah!

[MOTB] <u>Psalms 118:17</u> **No! we shall not die, but live**, to tell all that he has done for us.

[Norlie-NT] <u>Psalms 118:17</u> **I shall not die, but will survive** to tell of the Lord's doings.

[WSP-OT] <u>Psalms 118:17</u> **I shall not die, but I shall live**, That I may declare the deeds of Jehovah.

[YLT] <u>Psalms 118:17</u> **I do not die, but live**, And recount the works of Jah,

PROVERBS

<u>Proverbs 3:1-2</u> My son, forget not my law; but let thine heart keep my commandments: **²For length of days, and long life, and peace, shall they add to thee.**

[AMPC] <u>Proverbs 3:1-2</u> My son, forget not my law or teaching, but let your heart keep my commandments; **²For length of days and years of a life [worth living] and tranquility [inward and outward and continuing through old age till death], these shall they add to you.**

[BBE] <u>Proverbs 3:1-2</u> My son, keep my teaching in your memory, and my rules in your heart: **²For they will give you increase of days, years of life, and peace.**

[BLE] <u>Proverbs 3:1-2</u> My son, do not forget my instructions, but let your heart keep my commands, **²Because they will add to your length of life, your years of health, and your welfare.**

[CEB] <u>Proverbs 3:1-2</u> My son, don't forget my instruction. Let your heart guard my commands, **²because they will help you live a long time and provide you with well-being.**

[CEV] <u>Proverbs 3:1-2</u> My child, remember my teachings and instructions and obey them completely. ²**They will help you live a long and prosperous life.**

[CJB] <u>Proverbs 3:1-2</u> My son, don't forget my teaching, keep my commands in your heart; ²**for they will add to you many days, years of life and peace.**

[ERV] <u>Proverbs 3:1-2</u> My son, don't forget my teaching. Remember what I tell you to do. ²**What I teach will give you a good, long life, and all will go well for you.**

[EXB] <u>Proverbs 3:1-2</u> My ·child [son], do not forget my ·teaching [instruction; law], but ·keep my commands in mind [let your heart/mind protect my commands]. ²**Then ·you will live a long time, and your life will be successful [length of days and years of life and peace will be added to you].**

[FrenchSkinner-OT] <u>Proverbs 3:1-2</u> O my son, forget not my teaching, But let thy heart observe my commandments. ²**For length of days, and years of happiness, And prosperity, shall they give in abundance unto thee;**

[GNT] <u>Proverbs 3:1-2</u> My child, don't forget what I teach you. Always remember what I tell you to do. ²**My teaching will give you a long and prosperous life.**

[GW] <u>Proverbs 3:1-2</u> My son, do not forget my teachings, and keep my commands in mind, ²**because they will bring you long life, good years, and peace.**

[HCSB] <u>Proverbs 3:1-2</u> My son, don't forget my teaching, but let your heart keep my commands; ²**for they will bring you many days, a full life, and well-being.**

[Jerusalem] <u>Proverbs 3:1-2</u> My son, do not forget my teaching, let your heart keep my principles, ²**for these will give you lengthier days, longer years of life, and greater happiness.**

[Knox] <u>Proverbs 3:1-2</u> Forget not then, my son, the teaching I give thee; lock these words of mine close in thy bosom; ²**long years they shall bring thee of life well spent, and therewith prosperity.**

[LXX-1844] <u>Proverbs 3:1-2</u> My son, forget not my laws; but let thine heart keep my words: ²**for length of existence, and years of life, and peace, shall they add to thee.**

[MSG] <u>Proverbs 3:1-2</u> Good friend, don't forget all I've taught you; take to heart my commands. ²**They'll help you live a long, long time, a long life lived full and well.**

[NIRV] <u>Proverbs 3:1-2</u> My son, do not forget my teaching. Keep my commands in your heart. ²**They will help you live for many years. They will bring you peace and success.**

[NIV] <u>Proverbs 3:1-2</u> My son, do not forget my teaching, but keep my commands in your heart, ²**for they will prolong your life many years and bring you peace and prosperity.**

[NLT] <u>Proverbs 3:1-2</u> My child, never forget the things I have taught you. Store my commands in your heart. ²**If you do this, you will live many years, and your life will be satisfying.**

[NLV] <u>Proverbs 3:1-2</u> My son, do not forget my teaching. Let your heart keep my words. ²**For they will add to you many days and years of life and peace.**

[NRSV] <u>Proverbs 3:1-2</u> My child, do not forget my teaching, but let your heart keep my commandments; ²**for length of days and years of life and abundant welfare they will give you.**

[NWT] <u>Proverbs 3:1-2</u> My son, do not forget my teaching, And may your heart observe my commandments, ²**Because they will add many days And years of life and peace to you.**

[REB] <u>Proverbs 3:1-2</u> My son, do not forget my teaching, but treasure my commandments in your heart; ²**for long life and years in plenty and abundant prosperity will they bring you.**

[Rotherham] <u>Proverbs 3:1-2</u> My son, mine instruction, do not thou forget, and, my commandment, let thy heart observe; ²**For, length of days and years of life, and blessedness, shall they add to thee.**

LONG LIFE

[SG] <u>Proverbs 3:1-2</u> My son, forget not my teaching, But keep my commands in mind; **²For a long and happy life, With abundant prosperity, will they bring to you.**

[YLT] <u>Proverbs 3:1-2</u> My son! my law forget not, And my commands let thy heart keep, **²For length of days and years, Life and peace they do add to thee.**

<u>Proverbs 3:16</u> **Length of days is in her [wisdom's] right hand**; and in her [wisdom's] left hand riches and honour.

[AMP] <u>Proverbs 3:16</u> **Long life is in her right hand**; In her left hand are riches and honor.

[BBE] <u>Proverbs 3:16</u> **Long life is in her right hand**, and in her left are wealth and honour.

[CEV] <u>Proverbs 3:16</u> **In her right hand Wisdom holds a long life**, and in her left hand are wealth and honor.

[CWB] <u>Proverbs 3:16</u> **Wisdom holds out her right hand and offers a long and happy life**, and in her left hand she offers riches and honor.

[ERV] <u>Proverbs 3:16</u> **With her right hand, Wisdom offers long life**—with the other hand, riches and honor.

[GNT] <u>Proverbs 3:16</u> **Wisdom offers you long life**, as well as wealth and honor.

[LXX-1844] <u>Proverbs 3:16</u> **For length of existence and years of life are in her right hand**; and in her left hand are wealth and glory: out of her mouth proceeds righteousness, and she carries law and mercy upon her tongue.

[MSG] <u>Proverbs 3:16</u> **With one hand she gives long life**, with the other she confers recognition.

[NETS-OT] <u>Proverbs 3:16</u> **for longevity and years of life are in her right hand**, and in her left hand are riches and repute; out of her mouth righteousness comes forth, and she carries law and mercy upon her tongue.

[T4T] <u>Proverbs 3:16</u> **With one hand wisdom enables you to live a long life**, and with the other hand wisdom enables you to become rich and to be honored.

[TLB] <u>Proverbs 3:16</u> **Wisdom gives: a long, good life**, riches, honor,

[TPT] <u>Proverbs 3:16</u> **Wisdom extends to you long life in one hand** and wealth and promotion in the other. Out of her mouth flows righteousness, and her words release both law and mercy.

[TVB] <u>Proverbs 3:16</u> **She holds the secret of a long life in one hand** and riches and fame in her other hand.

<u>Proverbs 4:4</u> He taught me also, and said unto me, Let thine heart retain my words: **keep my commandments, and live.**

[BBE] <u>Proverbs 4:4</u> And he gave me teaching, saying to me, Keep my words in your heart; **keep my rules so that you may have life**:

[ERV] <u>Proverbs 4:4</u> my father taught me this: "Pay attention to what I say. **Obey my commands and you will have a good life.**

[EXB] <u>Proverbs 4:4</u> my father taught me and said, "Hold on to my words with all your heart. ·**Keep [Guard] my commands and you will live.**

[MSG] <u>Proverbs 4:4</u> He would sit me down and drill me: "Take this to heart. **Do what I tell you—live!**

[NLV] <u>Proverbs 4:4</u> he taught me, saying, "Hold my words close to your heart. **Keep my teachings and live.**

[NWT] <u>Proverbs 4:4</u> He taught me and said: "May your heart hold fast to my words. **Keep my commandments and continue living.**

<u>Proverbs 4:10</u> Hear, O my son, and receive my sayings; and **the years of thy life shall be many.**

[BBE] <u>Proverbs 4:10</u> Give ear, O my son, and let your heart be open to my sayings; and **long life will be yours.**

[CEV] <u>Proverbs 4:10</u> My child, if you listen and obey my teachings, **you will live a long time.**

[ICB] <u>Proverbs 4:10</u> My child, listen and accept what I say. Then **you will have a long life.**

[JUB] <u>Proverbs 4:10</u> Hear, O my son, and receive my words, and **the years of thy life shall be multiplied.**

[Knox] <u>Proverbs 4:10</u> Listen, then, my son, and master the charge I give thee, as **thou wouldst have long life.**

[LXX-1844] <u>Proverbs 4:10</u> Hear, my son, and receive my words; and **the years of thy life shall be increased, that the resources of thy life may be many.**

[MSG] <u>Proverbs 4:10</u> Dear friend, take my advice; **it will add years to your life.**

[NEB] <u>Proverbs 4:10</u> Listen, my son, take me words to heart, and **the years of your life shall be multiplied.**

[TPT] <u>Proverbs 4:10</u> My son, if you will take the time to stop and listen to me and embrace what I say, **you will live a long and happy life full of understanding in every way.**

[YLT] <u>Proverbs 4:10</u> Hear, my son, and receive my sayings, **And years of life [are] multiplied to thee.**

<u>Proverbs 9:11</u> For by me thy days shall be multiplied, and the years of thy life shall be increased.

[BSV] <u>Proverbs 9:11</u> For by me your days will be multiplied, and the years of your life will be increased.

[CLV] <u>Proverbs 9:11</u> For by me your days shall increase, And years of life shall be added to you.

[CWB] <u>Proverbs 9:11</u> If you eat from my table, your days will be many, and years will be added to your life.

[Elzas-OT] <u>Proverbs 9:11</u> For by me, thy days shall be multiplied, And years of happiness shall be added to thee.

[ERV] <u>Proverbs 9:11</u> Wisdom will help you live longer; she will add years to your life.

[EXB] <u>Proverbs 9:11</u> ·If you live wisely [Through/By me], you will live a long time; wisdom will add years to your life.

[Knox] <u>Proverbs 9:11</u> Long life I bring thee, and a full tale of years;

[MSG] <u>Proverbs 9:11</u> It's through me, Lady Wisdom, that your life deepens, and the years of your life ripen.

[NCV] <u>Proverbs 9:11</u> If you live wisely, you will live a long time; wisdom will add years to your life.

[NLV] <u>Proverbs 9:11</u> For by me your days will grow in number, and years will be added to your life.

[NOG] <u>Proverbs 9:11</u> You will live longer because of me, and years will be added to your life.

[TPT] <u>Proverbs 9:11</u> Wisdom will extend your life, making every year more fruitful than the one before.

<u>Proverbs 10:27</u> **The fear of the L<small>ORD</small> prolongeth days:** but the years of the wicked shall be shortened.

[AMP] <u>Proverbs 10:27</u> **The [reverent] fear of the Lord [worshiping, obeying, serving, and trusting Him with awe-filled respect] prolongs one's life**, But the years of the wicked will be shortened.

[BBE] <u>Proverbs 10:27</u> **The fear of the Lord gives long life**, but the years of the evil-doer will be cut short.

[BLE] <u>Proverbs 10:27</u> **The fear of Jehovah adds days**; but wrong-doers' years will be shortened.

[CEB] <u>Proverbs 10:27</u> **The fear of the Lord increases one's life**, but the years of the wicked will be cut short.

[CJB] <u>Proverbs 10:27</u> **The fear of Adonai adds length to life**, but the years of the wicked are cut short.

[ERV] <u>Proverbs 10:27</u> **Respect for the Lord will add years to your life**, but the wicked will have their lives cut short.

[GW] <u>Proverbs 10:27</u> **The fear of the Lord lengthens the number of days**, but the years of wicked people are shortened.

[Jerusalem] <u>Proverbs 10:27</u> **The fear of Yahweh adds length to life**, the years of the wicked will be cut short.

[Leeser-OT] <u>Proverbs 10:27</u> **The fear of the Lord increaseth man's days**; but the years of the wicked will be shortened.

[LXX-1844] <u>Proverbs 10:27</u> **The fear of the Lord adds length of days**: but the years of the ungodly shall be shortened.

[MSG] <u>Proverbs 10:27</u> **The Fear-of-God expands your life**; a wicked life is a puny life.

[NAB] <u>Proverbs 10:27</u> **The fear of the Lord prolongs life**, but the years of the wicked are brief.

[NCV] <u>Proverbs 10:27</u> **Whoever respects the Lord will have a long life**, but the life of an evil person will be cut short.

[NIRV] <u>Proverbs 10:27</u> **Having respect for the Lord leads to a longer life**. But the years of evil people are cut short.

[NLV] <u>Proverbs 10:27</u> **The fear of the Lord makes life longer**, but the years of the sinful will be cut off.

[Rotherham] <u>Proverbs 10:27</u> **The reverence of Yahweh, addeth days**, but, the years of the lawless, shall be shortened.

[Schaff-OT] <u>Proverbs 10:27</u> **The fear of Jehovah multiplieth days**, but the years of the wicked are shortened.

[T4T] <u>Proverbs 10:27</u> **If you revere Yahweh, you will live for a long time**; but wicked people die before they become old.

[YLT] <u>Proverbs 10:27</u> **The fear of Jehovah addeth days**, And the years of the wicked are shortened.

<u>Proverbs 11:19</u> **As righteousness tendeth to life**: so he that pursueth evil pursueth it to his own death.

[BLE] <u>Proverbs 11:19</u> **Firmness in the right makes for life**; but one who chases after evil does this for his own death.

[CCB] <u>Proverbs 11:19</u> **Upright living leads to life** but the way of evil leads to death.

[CEV] <u>Proverbs 11:19</u> **Always do the right thing, and you will live**; keep on doing wrong, and you will die.

[ERV] <u>Proverbs 11:19</u> **People who do what is right are on their way to life**, but those who always want to do wrong are on their way to death.

[Fenton] <u>Proverbs 11:19</u> **The Child of Virtue is Life**; The Offspring of Wickedness Death!

[GNT] <u>Proverbs 11:19</u> **Anyone who is determined to do right will live**, but anyone who insists on doing wrong will die.

[JPS-OT 1985] <u>Proverbs 11:19</u> **Righteousness is a prop of life**, But to pursue evil leads to death.

[Koren-OT] <u>Proverbs 11:19</u> **He that is firm in righteousness achieves life**; but he that pursues evil comes to his own death.

[MSG] <u>Proverbs 11:19</u> **Take your stand with God's loyal community and live**, or chase after phantoms of evil and die.

[NIRV] <u>Proverbs 11:19</u> **Surely right living leads to life**. But whoever runs after evil finds death.

[NLT] <u>Proverbs 11:19</u> **Godly people find life**; evil people find death.

[NLV] <u>Proverbs 11:19</u> **He who will not be moved from being right with God will live**, but he who goes

for what is bad will bring about his own death.

[NWT] <u>Proverbs 11:19</u> **The one standing firmly for righteousness is in line for life**, But the one chasing after evil is in line for death.

[WEB] <u>Proverbs 11:19</u> **He who is truly righteous gets life**. He who pursues evil gets death.

<u>Proverbs 17:6</u> **Children's children are the crown of old men**; and the glory of children are their fathers.

[MSG] <u>Proverbs 17:6</u> **Old people are distinguished by grandchildren**; children take pride in their parents.

[Orton-OT] <u>Proverbs 17:6</u> **Children's children are the crown of old men; it is an honor to live to be old** and see many descendants: and the glory of children are their fathers; it is an honour for children to be descended from worthy parents.

[Purver] <u>Proverbs 17:6</u> **The Crown of the Ancient are Children's Children**; and the Ornament of Children are their Fathers.

[SAAS-OT] <u>Proverbs 17:6</u> **The crown of old men is children of children,** And the boasting of children is their fathers. The entire world of goods belongs to the faithful, But to the faithless, not even a penny.

[TLB] <u>Proverbs 17:6</u> **An old man's grandchildren are his crowning glory**. A child's glory is his father.

[TVB] <u>Proverbs 17:6</u> **Grandchildren are the crowning glory and ultimate delight of old age**, and parents are the pride of their children.

<u>Proverbs 18:21</u> **Death and life are in the power of the tongue**: and they that love it shall eat the fruit thereof.

[CE] <u>Proverbs 18:21</u> **Death and life are in the power of the tongue**; those who make it their friend shall eat its fruit.

[CEV] <u>Proverbs 18:21</u> **Words can bring death or life**! Talk too much, and you will eat everything you say.

[EEBT] <u>Proverbs 18:21</u> **Words are able to save life and to cause death**. So you must accept the result of what you say.

[GNT] <u>Proverbs 18:21</u> **What you say can preserve life or destroy it**; so you must accept the consequences of your words.

[Hall] <u>Proverbs 18:21</u> **It is a great power, which the tongue hath, whether for life or death: good words tend to life; evil, unto death,** whether to ourselves or others; and according as a man would rather to improve it, so it shall speed with him either way.

[Jerusalem] <u>Proverbs 18:21</u> **Death and life are in the gift of the tongue**, those who indulge it must eat the fruit it yields.

[Knox] <u>Proverbs 18:21</u> **Of life and death, tongue holds the keys**; use it lovingly, and it will requite thee.

[LXX-1844] <u>Proverbs 18:21</u> **Life and death are in the power of the tongue**; and they that rule it shall eat the fruits thereof.

[NCV] <u>Proverbs 18:21</u> **What you say can mean life or death**. Those who speak with care will be rewarded.

[NEB] <u>Proverbs 18:21</u> **The tongue has power of life and death**; make friends with it and enjoy its fruits.

[TPT] <u>Proverbs 18:21</u> **Your words are so powerful that they will kill or give life**, and the talkative person will reap the consequences.

[TVB] <u>Proverbs 18:21</u> **Words have power in matters of life and death**, and those who love them will savor their fruit.

<u>Proverbs 20:29</u> The glory of young men is their strength: and **the beauty of old men is the gray head.**

[AMP] <u>Proverbs 20:29</u> The glory of young men is their [physical] strength, And **the honor of aged men is their gray head [representing wisdom and experience].**

[CEV] <u>Proverbs 20:29</u> Young people take pride in their strength, but **the gray hairs of wisdom are even more beautiful.**

[T4T] <u>Proverbs 20:29</u> We honor/admire young people because they are strong, but **we respect old people more because they are wise.**

[TPT] <u>Proverbs 20:29</u> We admire the young for their strength and beauty, but **the dignity of the old is their wisdom.**

<u>Proverbs 23:22</u> Hearken unto thy father that begat thee, and **despise not thy mother when she is old.**

[EEBT] <u>Proverbs 23:22</u> Listen to your father. You would not be alive without him. **Your mother will get old. But do not think that she is not important then.**

[T4T] <u>Proverbs 23:22</u> Pay attention to what your father tells you, and **do not neglect/take care of your mother when she is old.**

[TLB] <u>Proverbs 23:22</u> Listen to your father's advice and **don't despise an old mother's experience.**

[TPT] <u>Proverbs 23:22</u> Give respect to your father and mother, for without them you wouldn't even be here. And **don't neglect them when they grow old.**

<u>Proverbs 28:16</u> The prince that wanteth understanding is also a great oppressor: but **he that hateth covetousness shall prolong his days.**

[AMP] <u>Proverbs 28:16</u> A leader who is a great oppressor lacks understanding and common sense [and his wickedness shortens his days], But **he who hates unjust gain will [be blessed and] prolong his days.**

[BBE] <u>Proverbs 28:16</u> The prince who has no sense is a cruel ruler; but **he who has no desire to get profit for himself will have long life.**

[CEB] <u>Proverbs 28:16</u> A prince without understanding is a cruel oppressor, **but one who hates unjust gain will live long.**

[ERV] <u>Proverbs 28:16</u> A foolish ruler hurts the people under him, **but a ruler who hates wrong will rule for a long time.**

[EXB] <u>Proverbs 28:16</u> A ·ruler [prince] without ·wisdom [understanding] will be cruel, **but the one who ·refuses to take [hates] ·dishonest money [unjust gain/profit] will ·rule [or live] a long time.**

[GW] <u>Proverbs 28:16</u> A leader without understanding taxes his people heavily, **but those who hate unjust gain will live longer.**

[ICB] <u>Proverbs 28:16</u> A ruler who is cruel does not have wisdom. But **the one who hates money taken dishonestly will live a long time.**

[Jerusalem] <u>Proverbs 28:16</u> A prince lacking sense is rich in rapacity, **he who hates avarice will lengthen his days.**

[Lamsa] <u>Proverbs 28:16</u> A ruler who lacks understanding is also a great oppressor; but **he who hates deceit shall prolong his life.**

[MSG] <u>Proverbs 28:16</u> Among leaders who lack insight, abuse abounds, **but for one who hates corruption, the future is bright.**

[NIRV] <u>Proverbs 28:16</u> A ruler who is mean to his people takes money from them by force. But **one who hates money gained in the wrong way will rule a long time.**

[NLV] <u>Proverbs 28:16</u> A ruler who takes much from the people who have little does not have understanding. But **he who hates wanting something that belongs to someone else will live a long time.**

[Rotherham] <u>Proverbs 28:16</u> A leader, may lack intelligence, yet abound in oppressions, **The hater of greed, shall lengthen out days.**

[TPT] <u>Proverbs 28:16</u> Abusive leaders fail to employ wisdom, but **leaders who despise corruption will enjoy a long and full life.**

[YLT] <u>Proverbs 28:16</u> A leader lacking understanding multiplieth oppressions, **Whoso is hating dishonest gain prolongeth days.**

ISAIAH

<u>Isaiah 46:4</u> **And even to your old age I am he; and even to hoar hairs will I carry you**: I have made, and I will bear; even I will carry, and will deliver you.

[BBE] <u>Isaiah 46:4</u> **Even when you are old I will be the same, and when you are grey-haired I will take care of you**: I will still be responsible for what I made; yes, I will take you and keep you safe.

[CEVUK2012] <u>Isaiah 46:4</u> **I will still be the same when you are old and grey, and I will take care of you.** I created you. I will carry you and always keep you safe.

[CJB] <u>Isaiah 46:4</u> **Till your old age I will be the same—I will carry you until your hair is white.** I have made you, and I will bear you; yes, I will carry and save you.

[EEBT] <u>Isaiah 46:4</u> **I will do that even until you are old. I will do it until you have grey hairs. I am he who will supply everything. I will supply everything that you need.** I have made you and I will carry you. I will supply everything that you need. And I will save you.

[FAA] <u>Isaiah 46:4</u> **Up to your old age, I am he. And I will support you up to advanced years.** I act and I nurture And I support and deliver.

[Henderson-OT] <u>Isaiah 46:4</u> **Even to old age I will be the same; Even to gray hairs will I carry you:** I have made, and I will bear, Yea, I will carry, and deliver you.

[JPS-OT 1963] <u>Isaiah 46:4</u> **Till you grow old, I will still be the same; When you turn gray, it is I who will carry**; I was the Maker, and I will be the Bearer; And I will carry and rescue [you].

[Knox] <u>Isaiah 46:4</u> **You grow old, but I am still the same; the grey hairs come**, but I ever uphold you; I must carry you, I that created you, I must bear you away to safety.

[LXX-1844] <u>Isaiah 46:4</u> **I am he; and until ye shall have grown old, I am he**: I bear you, I have made, and I will relieve, I will take up and save you.

[McFadyen-OT] <u>Isaiah 46:4</u> **Till old age I am ever the same; Till your hair is grey, I will carry you.** It is I that have borne the burden, It is I that will carry it still; It is I that will carry and save you.

[Moffatt] <u>Isaiah 46:4</u> **even to your old age I will be the same, when you are grey-haired, still I will sustain you**; I have borne the burden, I will carry it, yes, I will carry you and save you.

[MSG] <u>Isaiah 46:4</u> **And I'll keep on carrying you when you're old. I'll be there, bearing you when you're old and gray.** I've done it and will keep on doing it, carrying you on my back, saving you.

[NIRV] <u>Isaiah 46:4</u> **I will continue to carry you even when you are old. I will take good care of you even when your hair is gray.** I have made you, and I will carry you. I will take care of you, and I will save you. I am the Lord.

[NLT] <u>Isaiah 46:4</u> **I will be your God throughout your lifetime—until your hair is white with age.** I made you, and I will care for you. I will carry you along and save you.

[REB] <u>Isaiah 46:4</u> **Till you grow old I am the Lord, and when white hairs come, I shall carry you still;** I have made you and I shall uphold you. I shall carry you away to safety.

<u>Isaiah 53:10</u> Yet it pleased the Lord to bruise him; he hath put him to grief: when thou shalt make his soul an offering for sin, **he shall see his seed, he shall prolong his days**, and the pleasure of the Lord shall prosper in his hand.

[HBIV] <u>Isaiah 53:10</u> But it has pleased Jehovah to crush him with grievous sickness [With the purpose that] if he were to make himself an offering for guilt, **He would see [his] seed, he would prolong his days**, And the pleasure of Jehovah would prosper in his hand.

[JPS-OT 1963] <u>Isaiah 53:10</u> But the Lord chose to crush him by disease, That, if he made himself an offering for guilt, **He might see offspring and have long life**, And that through him the Lord's purpose might prosper.

[Kenrick] <u>Isaiah 53:10</u> And the Lord was pleased to bruise Him in infirmity: if he lay down His life for sin, **He shall see a long-lived seed**, and the will of the Lord shall be prosperous in His hand.

[REB] <u>Isaiah 53:10</u> Yet the Lord took thought for his oppressed servant and healed him who had given himself as a sacrifice for sin. **He will enjoy long life and see his children's children**, and in his hand the Lord's purpose will prosper.

<u>Isaiah 65:22</u> They shall not build, and another inhabit; they shall not plant, and another eat: for as the days of a tree are the days of my people, and mine elect shall long enjoy the work of their hands.

[BBE] <u>Isaiah 65:22</u> They will no longer be building for the use of others, or planting for others to have the fruit: for the days of my people will be like the days of a tree, and my loved ones will have joy in full measure in the work of their hands.

[Besorah] <u>Isaiah 65:22</u> "They shall not build and another inhabit; they shall not plant and another eat. For the days of My people are going to be as the days of a tree and My chosen ones outlive the work of their hands.

[BLE] <u>Isaiah 65:22</u> They shall not build and another live there, they shall not plant and another eat, for my people's lifetime shall be like that of a tree, and my chosen shall wear out the work of their hands.

[Douay-Rheims] <u>Isaiah 65:22</u> They shall not build, and another inhabit; they shall not plant, and another eat: for as the days of a tree, so shall be the days of my people, and the works of their hands shall be of long continuance.

[ERV] <u>Isaiah 65:22</u> Never again will one person build a house and another person live there. Never again will one person plant a garden and another eat the fruit from it. My people will live as long as the trees. My chosen people will get full use of whatever they make.

[FV] <u>Isaiah 65:22</u> They will not build, and another live in them; they will not plant, and another eat; for like the days of a tree are so will be the days of My people, and My elect will long enjoy the work of their hands.

[GNV] <u>Isaiah 65:22</u> They shall not build, and another inhabit: they shall not plant, and another eat: for as the days of the tree are the days of my people, and mine elect shall enjoy in old age the work of their hands.

[HCSB] <u>Isaiah 65:22</u> They will not build and others live in them; they will not plant and others eat. For My people's lives will be like the lifetime of a tree. My chosen ones will fully enjoy the work of their hands.

[ICB] <u>Isaiah 65:22</u> No more will one person build a house and someone else live there. One person will not plant a garden and someone else eat its fruit. My people will live a long time as trees live long. My chosen people will live there and enjoy the things they make.

[KJV-Miller] <u>Isaiah 65:22</u> They shall not build and another inhabit, they shall not plant and another eat for as the days of a tree so will be the days of my people and my chosen will grow old enjoying the work of their hands.

[Knox] <u>Isaiah 65:22</u> that once built houses for others to occupy, planted what others should enjoy; my people shall live to the age of trees and see the work of their own hands wear out before them.

[NCV] <u>Isaiah 65:22</u> No more will one person build a house and someone else live there. One person will not plant a garden and someone else eat its fruit. My people will live a long time, as trees live long. My chosen people will live there and enjoy the things they make.

[NIRV] <u>Isaiah 65:22</u> They will no longer build houses only to have others live in them. They will no longer plant crops only to have others eat them. My people will live to be as old as trees. My chosen ones will enjoy for a long time the things they have worked for.

[Rotherham] <u>Isaiah 65:22</u> They shall not build, and, another, dwell, They shall not plant, and, another, eat, —For, as the days of a tree, shall be the days of my people, And, the work of their own hands, shall my chosen ones, use to the full:

[T4T] Isaiah 65:22 The houses that they build, no one will take those houses away from them and live in them. No one will take a vineyard away from its owner. My chosen people will live a long time, like trees do, and they will enjoy the things that they have done—the houses that they have built and the crops that they have planted.

JOEL

Joel 2:28 And it shall come to pass afterward, that I will pour out my spirit upon all flesh; and your sons and your daughters shall prophesy, **your old men shall dream dreams**, your young men shall see visions:

[AMP] Joel 2:28 "It shall come about after this That I shall pour out My Spirit on all mankind; And your sons and your daughters will prophesy, **Your old men will dream dreams**, Your young men will see visions.

[Douay-Rheims-Peters] Joel 2:28 And it shall be after this: I will power out my spirit upon all flesh: and your sons, and your daughters shall prophecy: **your ancients shall dream dreams**, and your young men shall see visions.

[NET] Joel 2:28 After all of this I will pour out my Spirit on all kinds of people. Your sons and daughters will prophesy. **Your elderly will have revelatory dreams**; your young men will see prophetic visions.

[T4T] Joel 2:28 "Some time later, I will give my Spirit to many people. You sons and daughters will proclaim messages that come directly from me. **Your old men will have dreams** that come from me, and your young men will have visions that come from me.

ZECHARIAH

Zechariah 8:4 Thus saith the LORD of hosts; There shall yet old men and old women dwell in the streets of Jerusalem, and every man with his staff in his hand for very age.

[CPDV] Zechariah 8:4 Thus says the Lord of hosts: Then elderly men and elderly women will dwell in the streets of Jerusalem, and every man will be with his walking stick in his hand, because of the multitude of days.

[EEBT] Zechariah 8:4 The Lord Almighty says, 'Old men and old women will sit in the streets of Jerusalem again. Each will have a stick in his hands because he is so old.

[ERV] Zechariah 8:4 The Lord All-Powerful says, "Old men and women will again be seen in the public places in Jerusalem. People will live so long that they will need their walking sticks.

[NET] Zechariah 8:4 Moreover, the Lord who rules over all says, 'Old men and women will once more live in the plazas of Jerusalem, each one leaning on a cane because of advanced age.

[NIV] Zechariah 8:4 This is what the Lord Almighty says: "Once again men and women of ripe old age will sit in the streets of Jerusalem, each of them with cane in hand because of their age.

[NLT] Zechariah 8:4 "This is what the Lord of Heaven's Armies says: Once again old men and women will walk Jerusalem's streets with their canes and will sit together in the city squares.

[TLB] Zechariah 8:4 The Lord Almighty declares that Jerusalem will have peace and prosperity so long that there will once again be aged men and women hobbling through her streets on canes,

LUKE

Luke 1:36 And, behold, thy cousin Elisabeth, she hath also conceived a son in her old age: and this is the sixth month with her, who was called barren.

[Barclay-NT] **Luke 1:36** Elisabeth, your kinswoman, has also conceived a son in her old age. They said that she could never have a child. But now she is in her sixth month.

[CB] **Luke 1:36** Your cousin Elisabeth, who was called barren, is also pregnant in her old age, and has been for six months.

[Madsen-NT] **Luke 1:36** And see, Elizabeth who is related to you, in spite of her age she also has conceived a son. She is carrying him now in the sixth month, although she is regarded as barren.

[T4T] **Luke 1:36** I also need to tell you something else. Your cousin Elizabeth is very old, and it was thought {people said} that she could not bear any children. But she has been pregnant for almost six months, and will bear a son!

Luke 2:37 And she was a widow of about fourscore and four years, which departed not from the temple, but served God with fastings and prayers night and day.

[Berkeley] **Luke 2:37** and **was a widow of about eighty-four**. She never left the temple, but worshiped night and day in fastings and intercessions.

[CB] **Luke 2:37 She was an 84 year old widow**, who had not strayed from her faith, and served God with fastings and prayers night and day.

[CWB] **Luke 2:37 She had remained a widow and was eighty-four years old**. She spent all her time in the Temple and could be found there any time, day or night, fasting, praying and worshiping God.

[NWT] **Luke 2:37** and **she was a widow now 84 years old**. She was never missing from the temple, rendering sacred service night and day with fasting and supplications.

[Phillips] **Luke 2:37 and was now a widow of eighty-four**. She spent her whole life in the Temple and worshipped God night and day with fastings and prayers.

ACTS

Acts 2:17 And it shall come to pass in the last days, saith God, I will pour out of my Spirit upon all flesh: and your sons and your daughters shall prophesy, and your young men shall see visions, and **your old men shall dream dreams**:

[AUV-NT 2003] **Acts 2:17** God said that 'in the last days [of the Jewish nation?] I will pour out My Holy Spirit upon all people, and your sons and daughters will speak out [in prophecies] and your young men will see [supernatural] visions, and **your old men will have [supernatural] dreams**.

[CWB] **Acts 2:17** 'This is what I will do in the days to come. I will pour out my Spirit on people. Your sons and daughters will proclaim my message. **I will speak to your young men in visions and to your old men in dreams**.

[EEBT] **Acts 2:17** "'This is what I will do in the last days", God says. "I will give my Spirit to all people. Your sons and daughters will speak my message to people. Your young men will see pictures from me in their minds. And **your old men will see things in their dreams**.

[ERV] <u>Acts 2:17</u> 'God says: In the last days I will pour out my Spirit on all people. Your sons and daughters will prophesy. Your young men will see visions. **Your old men will have special dreams.**

[Madsen-NT] <u>Acts 2:17</u> In the last days, so speaks God, I will pour out my Spirit upon all earthly life. Then your sons and your daughters shall begin to speak words of the spirit, your young men shall awaken to seeing in the spirit and **your elders shall dream enlightened dreams.**

[TPT] <u>Acts 2:17</u> 'This is what I will do in the last days—I will pour out my Spirit on everybody and cause your sons and daughters to prophesy, and your young men will see visions, and **your old men will experience dreams from God.**

[Wuest-NT] <u>Acts 2:17</u> And it shall be in the last days, says God, that I will abundantly bestow my Spirit upon all flesh. And your sons shall speak forth by divine inspiration, also your daughters. And your young men shall see visions. And **your old men shall dream with dreams.**

FIRST CORINTHIANS

<u>1 Corinthians 15:26</u> The last enemy that shall be destroyed is death.

[AENT] <u>1 Corinthians 15:26</u> And the last enemy, death, will be abolished.

[Authentic-NT] <u>1 Corinthians 15:26</u> The final enemy to be abolished is death.

[BV-KJV-NT] <u>1 Corinthians 15:26</u> The last enemy is rendered useless: the death.

[CB] <u>1 Corinthians 15:26</u> The last enemy to be destroyed is death itself.

[Cornish-NT] <u>1 Corinthians 15:26</u> and until death itself has been completely obliterated. That will be the end, when death is ended,

[Darby] <u>1 Corinthians 15:26</u> [The] last enemy [that] is annulled [is] death.

[ECB] <u>1 Corinthians 15:26</u> The final enemy to inactivate is death.

[EEBT] <u>1 Corinthians 15:26</u> God will destroy the last enemy. And that enemy is death.

[Erasmus-NT] <u>1 Corinthians 15:26</u> It is through sin that death reigns, and through death that Satan reigns. Once sin has been wiped out, death will cease to reign. Although in the meantime we struggle with all our strength to accomplish this, it will nevertheless not happen fully until the final resurrection has vanquished all the power of mortality—the very last enemy, so to speak, destroyed, the one who was most stubbornly rebelling.

[GNT] <u>1 Corinthians 15:26</u> The last enemy to be defeated will be death.

[Harwood-NT] <u>1 Corinthians 15:26</u> The last foe he shall dethrone and annihilate, is death.

[JMNT] <u>1 Corinthians 15:26</u> [The] last holder of ruin (or: enemy; quality having ill-will) being progressively brought down to idleness (made unemployed and ineffective; rendered useless and unproductive) [is] the Death (or: Death, a last enemy, is being presently nullified and abolished).

[Moffatt] <u>1 Corinthians 15:26</u> (Death is the last for to be put down.)

[NENT] <u>1 Corinthians 15:26</u> Death, the last enemy, has been stripped of power,

[NWT] <u>1 Corinthians 15:26</u> And the last enemy, death, is to be brought to nothing.

[Phillips] <u>1 Corinthians 15:26</u> The last enemy of all to be destroyed is death itself.

[REB] <u>1 Corinthians 15:26</u> and the last enemy to be deposed is death.

[Sharpe] <u>1 Corinthians 15:26</u> Death the last enemy is being destroyed;

[TPT] <u>1 Corinthians 15:26</u> And the last enemy to be subdued and eliminated is death itself.

[TTT-NT] <u>1 Corinthians 15:26</u> The last of all enemies which shall be done away with is death, for all things shall be thrown under his feet.

[Williams-NT] <u>1 Corinthians 15:26</u> Death is the last enemy to be stopped,

EPHESIANS

<u>Ephesians 6:1-3</u> Children, obey your parents in the Lord: for this is right. ²Honour thy father and mother; (which is the first commandment with promise;) ³**That it may be well with thee, and thou mayest live long on the earth.**

[ACV] <u>Ephesians 6:1-3</u> Children, obey your parents in Lord, for this is right. ²Honor thy father and mother, which is the first commandment with promise, ³**so that it may become well with thee, and thou will be long lasting on the earth.**

[AMPC] <u>Ephesians 6:1-3</u> Children, obey your parents in the Lord [as His representatives], for this is just and right. ²Honor (esteem and value as precious) your father and your mother—this is the first commandment with a promise— ³**That all may be well with you and that you may live long on the earth.**

[CEV] <u>Ephesians 6:1-3</u> Children, you belong to the Lord, and you do the right thing when you obey your parents. The first commandment with a promise says, ²"Obey your father and your mother, ³**and you will have a long and happy life."**

[CLV] <u>Ephesians 6:1-3</u> Children, be obeying your parents, in the Lord, for this is just. ²Honor your father and mother' (which is the first precept with a promise), ³**that it may be becoming well with you, and you should be a long time on the earth.**

[CWB] <u>Ephesians 6:1-3</u> Children, obey your parents unless it goes against God's commands, because that's the right thing to do. ²Respect your parents, whether they love the Lord or not, because that's the commandment to which God has attached a special promise: ³**"That things may go well with you and that you may live a longer life."**

[EEBT] <u>Ephesians 6:1-3</u> Children, obey your parents. This is what the Lord wants. It is the right thing to do. ²The first rule that God gave with a promise says: 'Always remember how important your father and your mother are. ³**Then, as a result, you will be happy and you will live for a long time on the earth.'**

[Goodspeed-NT] <u>Ephesians 6:1-3</u> Children, as Christians obey your parents, for that is right. ²"You must honor your father and mother"—that is the first commandment accompanied with a promise— ³**"so that you may prosper and have a long life on earth."**

[Jerusalem] <u>Ephesians 6:1-3</u> Children, be obedient to your parents in the Lord—that is your duty. ²The commandment that has a promise attached to it is: Honour your father and mother, ³**and the promise is: and you will prosper and have a long life in the land.**

[NCV] <u>Ephesians 6:1-3</u> Children, obey your parents as the Lord wants, because this is the right thing to do. ²The command says, "Honor your father and mother." This is the first command that has a promise with it— ³**"Then everything will be well with you, and you will have a long life on the earth."**

[NLV] <u>Ephesians 6:1-3</u> Children, as Christians, obey your parents. This is the right thing to do. ²Respect your father and mother. This is the first Law given that had a promise. ³The promise is this: If you respect your father and mother, **you will live a long time and your life will be full of many good things.**

[TLB] <u>Ephesians 6:1-3</u> Children, obey your parents; this is the right thing to do because God has placed them in authority over you. ²Honor your father and mother. This is the first of God's Ten Commandments that ends with a promise. ³**And this is the promise: that if you honor your father and mother, yours will be a long life, full of blessing.**

[TPT] <u>Ephesians 6:1-3</u> Children, if you want to be wise, listen to your parents and do what they tell you, and the Lord will help you. ²For the commandment, "Honor your father and your mother," was the first of the Ten Commandments with a promise attached: ³**"You will prosper and live a long, full life if you honor your parents."**

PHILEMON

<u>Philemon 1:9</u> Yet for love's sake I rather beseech thee, being such an one as **Paul the aged**, and now also a prisoner of Jesus Christ.

[CB] <u>Philemon 1:9</u> Instead, for the sake of love I, Paul, urge you, **in my old age** and from prison for Jesus Christ.

[CSB] <u>Philemon 1:9</u> I appeal to you, instead, on the basis of love. I, **Paul, as an elderly man** and now also as a prisoner of Christ Jesus,

[EEBT] <u>Philemon 1:9</u> But I am not telling you that you must do it. Instead, I am asking you to do it because you love people. **I am Paul, and I am an old man**. Also, I am in prison now because I am Christ Jesus's servant.

[Macknight-NTc] <u>Philemon 1:9</u> Yet, instead of using my authority, by that love which thou bearest to the saints and to me I rather beseech thee, who am such an one as Paul, thy friend, **grown old in the service of the gospel**; and now also confined with a chain for preaching Jesus Christ:

[MCC-NT] <u>Philemon 1:9</u> I rather through Love exhort [Thee; I] being Such-one as **Paul the Aged**, but now indeed a Chained Man of Jesus Christ.

[Original-NT] <u>Philemon 1:9</u> yet out of affection I prefer to appeal to you, being such as I am, **that old man Paul**, and also at present a prisoner of Christ Jesus.

[TTNT] <u>Philemon 1:9</u> yet I want to appeal to your love. **I, Paul, who am now advancing in years** as a prisoner of Jesus Christ,

HEBREWS

<u>Hebrews 11:13</u> **These all died in faith**, not having received the promises, but having seen them afar off, and were persuaded of them, and embraced them, and confessed that they were strangers and pilgrims on the earth.

[AMPC] <u>Hebrews 11:13</u> **These people all died controlled and sustained by their faith**, but not having received the tangible fulfillment of [God's] promises, only having seen it and greeted it from a great distance by faith, and all the while acknowledging and confessing that they were strangers and temporary residents and exiles upon the earth.

[AUV-NT 2003] <u>Hebrews 11:13</u> **These people [all] continued to have faith until they died**, [even though] they had not obtained [all] the things God had promised, but had [only] seen them and welcomed them from a distance. And they had confessed to being strangers and aliens on earth.

[Barnstone-NT] <u>Hebrews 11:13</u> **All these died in faith** without winning the promises. But seeing them far off they were persuaded to embrace them, and confessed that they were strangers and exiles on the earth.

[BBE] <u>Hebrews 11:13</u> **All these came to their end in faith**, not having had the heritage; but having seen it with delight far away, they gave witness that they were wanderers and not of the earth.

[Berkeley] <u>Hebrews 11:13</u> **Controlled by faith all these went to their death** without realizing the promises, but scanning and hailing them from a distance, all the while confessing that they were guests and visitors on the earth.

[BOOKS-NT] <u>Hebrews 11:13</u> **All these people were still living by faith when they died**. They did not receive the things promised; they only saw them and welcomed them from a distance, admitting that they were foreigners and strangers on earth.

[CCB] <u>Hebrews 11:13</u> **Death found all these people strong in their faith**. They had not received what was promised, but they had looked ahead and had rejoiced in it from afar, saying that they were foreigners and travelers on earth.

[GNT] <u>Hebrews 11:13</u> **It was in faith that all these persons died**. They did not receive the things God had promised, but from a long way off they saw them and welcomed them, and admitted openly that they were foreigners and refugees on earth.

[Greaves-NT] <u>Hebrews 11:13</u> **All these died according to faith**, not having received the promises, but having beheld them from afar and hailed them, and having confessed also that they were strangers and sojourners upon the earth.

[GT] <u>Hebrews 11:13</u> **All of the people died having faith**. They had not yet received the things which God had promised. They saw that those things were far in the future but they welcomed them. They admitted that they were strangers on earth. It was not their home.

[Knox] <u>Hebrews 11:13</u> **It was faith they lived by, all of them, and in faith they died**; for them, the promises were not fulfilled, but they looked forward to them and welcomed them at a distance, owning themselves no better than strangers and exiles on earth.

[Madsen-NT] <u>Hebrews 11:13</u> **These all died in the power of the faith**, without themselves having experienced the fulfilment of the promises. They only saw and greeted it from afar, acknowledging that they were only strangers and guests on the earth.

[MSG] <u>Hebrews 11:13</u> **Each one of these people of faith died** not yet having in hand what was promised, but still believing. How did they do it? They saw it way off in the distance, waved their greeting, and accepted the fact that they were transients in this world.

[TCNT] <u>Hebrews 11:13</u> **All these died sustained by faith**. They did not obtain the promised blessings, but they saw them from a distance and welcomed the sight, and they acknowledged themselves to be only aliens and strangers on the earth.

[TTNT] <u>Hebrews 11:13</u> **All these heroes of faith continued to trust God right up to the time of their deaths**. This does not mean that they saw in their own lifetime the fulfilment of everything promised them. Some things would only be accomplished fully a long time in the future; yet by faith they saw them as fulfilled. They were certain that what God had said would surely happen, even though they may not live to see it all, for they regarded themselves as only temporary residents here on earth.

[VW] <u>Hebrews 11:13</u> **These all died in faith, not having received the promises**, but having seen them afar off were assured of them, embraced them and confessed that they were foreigners and pilgrims on the earth.

[Wuest-NT] <u>Hebrews 11:13</u> **These all died dominated by faith**, not having received the promises, but having seen them afar off and greeted them, also confessed that they were strangers, even those who had settled down alongside of a pagan population upon the earth.

DAYS CAN BE SHORTENED

<u>Deuteronomy 4:26</u> I call heaven and earth to witness against you this day, that ye shall soon utterly perish from off the land whereunto ye go over Jordan to possess it; **ye shall not prolong your days** upon it, but shall utterly be destroyed.

[AMP] <u>Deuteronomy 4:26</u> I call heaven and earth as witnesses against you today, that you will soon utterly perish from the land which you are crossing the Jordan to possess. You shall not live long on it, but will be utterly destroyed.

[Plaisted] <u>Deuteronomy 4:26</u> I call heaven and earth to witness against you this day, that you shall soon completely perish off of the land to which you go over Jordan to possess it; you shall not prolong your days upon it, but shall completely be destroyed.

[T4T] <u>Deuteronomy 4:26</u> Today I am requesting everyone who is in heaven and everyone who is on the earth to watch what you are doing. If you disobey what I am telling you, you will soon all die in the land that you will be crossing the Jordan River to occupy. You will not live very long there; Yahweh will completely get rid of many of you.

<u>Psalms 55:23</u> But thou, O God, shalt bring them down into the pit of destruction: **bloody and deceitful men shall not live out half their days**; but I will trust in thee.

[NET] <u>Psalms 55:23</u> But you, O God, will bring them down to the deep Pit. **Violent and deceitful people will not live even half a normal lifespan**. But as for me, I trust in you.

<u>Psalms 89:45</u> **The days of his youth hast thou shortened**: thou hast covered him with shame. Selah.

[NLV] <u>Psalms 89:45</u> **You have made him old before his time**, and have covered him with shame.

<u>Proverbs 10:27</u> The fear of the LORD prolongeth days: but **the years of the wicked shall be shortened**.

<u>Ecclesiastes 7:17</u> Be not over much wicked, neither be thou foolish: **why shouldest thou die before thy time?**

YOUR FAITH CAN IMPACT YOUR DAYS

<u>Philippians 1:23-24</u> For I am in a strait betwixt two, having a desire to depart, and to be with Christ; which is far better: [24]Nevertheless to abide in the flesh is more needful for you.

[Phillips] <u>Philippians 1:23-24</u> I am torn in two directions—on the one hand I long to leave this world and live with Christ, and that is obviously the best thing for me. [24]Yet, on the other hand, it is probably more necessary for you that I should stay here on earth.

Paul had a choice to go or to stay.

2 Peter 1:14 Knowing that shortly I must put off this my tabernacle, even as our Lord Jesus Christ hath shewed me.

> **[NLV] 2 Peter 1:14** I know that I will soon be leaving this body. Our Lord Jesus Christ has told me this.
>
> *Peter also knew when his time was near.*

2 Kings 20:1-7 In those days was Hezekiah sick unto death. And the prophet Isaiah the son of Amoz came to him, and said unto him, Thus saith the LORD, Set thine house in order; for thou shalt die, and not live. ²Then he turned his face to the wall, and prayed unto the LORD, saying, ³I beseech thee, O LORD, remember now how I have walked before thee in truth and with a perfect heart, and have done that which is good in thy sight. And Hezekiah wept sore. ⁴And it came to pass, afore Isaiah was gone out into the middle court, that the word of the LORD came to him, saying, ⁵Turn again, and tell Hezekiah the captain of my people, **Thus saith the LORD, the God of David thy father, I have heard thy prayer, I have seen thy tears: behold, I will heal**[raphah] **thee**: on the third day thou shalt go up unto the house of the LORD. ⁶**And I will add unto thy days fifteen years**; and I will deliver thee and this city out of the hand of the king of Assyria; and I will defend this city for mine own sake, and for my servant David's sake. ⁷And Isaiah said, **Take a lump of figs. And they took and laid it on the boil, and he recovered**.

2 Chronicles 32:24-25 In those days Hezekiah was sick to the death, and prayed unto the LORD: and **he spake unto him, and he gave him a sign**. ²⁵But **Hezekiah rendered not again according to the benefit done unto him**; for his heart was lifted up: therefore there was wrath upon him, and upon Judah and Jerusalem.

Note in 2 Kings 20:2 Isaiah told the King he was going to die. It doesn't say that it was the will and desire of the Lord—only that it was going to happen.

Note in 2 Kings 20:7 Hezekiah was healed with a natural remedy applied by supernatural revelation.

Note in 2 Chronicles 32 Hezekiah showed no thankfulness to the Lord for being healed and instead got into pride.

John 10:17-18 Therefore doth my Father love me, because I lay down my life, that I might take it again. ¹⁸No man taketh it from me, but I lay it down of myself. **I have power to lay it down, and I have power to take it again**. This commandment have I received of my Father.

> **[BLE] John 10:17-18** That is why the Father loves me, because I lay down my life, to take it again. ¹⁸Nobody has deprived me of it, but I lay it down of my own accord. **I am authorized to lay it down and I am authorized to take it again**; I was given this commission by my Father.
>
> **[CLV] John 10:17-18** Therefore the Father is loving Me, seeing that I am laying down My soul that I may be getting it again. ¹⁸No one is taking it away from Me, but I am laying it down of Myself. **I have the right to lay it down, and I have the right to get it again**. This precept I got from My Father.
>
> **[Darby] John 10:17-18** On this account the Father loves me, because I lay down my life that I may take it again. ¹⁸No one takes it from me, but I lay it down of myself. **I have authority to lay it down and I have authority to take it again**. I have received this commandment of my Father.
>
> **[NCV] John 10:17-18** The Father loves me because I give my life so that I can take it back again. ¹⁸No one takes it away from me; I give my own life freely. **I have the right to give my life, and I have the right to take it back**. This is what my Father commanded me to do.

[NLV] John 10:17-18 For this reason My Father loves Me. It is because I give My life that I might take it back again. ¹⁸No one takes my life from Me. I give it by Myself. **I have the right and the power to take it back again**. My Father has given Me this right and power.

[NWT] John 10:17-18 This is why the Father loves me, because I surrender my life, so that I may receive it again. ¹⁸No man takes it away from me, but I surrender it of my own initiative. **I have authority to surrender it, and I have authority to receive it again**. This commandment I received from my Father.

The words of Jesus do not sound too different from the words of Paul or Peter.

ABOUT THE

Dr. Chip Beaulieu is the founder of Word of Truth Church in Dayton, Tennessee. He was in the ministry of helps for many years before becoming a full-time pastor. Dr. Beaulieu has traveled to many countries preaching the gospel. His strong teaching anointing has touched many lives, and many have been healed in his services. In 2015, he started Healing School at his church and has taught it each week since then.

Connect with the author online:

Homepage: www.daytonwot.org

Facebook: www.facebook.com/chip.beaulieu1

BIBLIOGRAPHY

References

Hagin, Kenneth E. *Healing Scriptures*. Rhema Bible Church, ©1993

Longenecker, David E. *God's Medicine—The Meditation Manual for Divine Healing*.

Sumrall, Dr. Lester *Healing in Every Book of the Bible* LeSEA Publishing ©2002

Bible Translations

[Abegg-OT] – Jr., Martin G. Abegg; Flint, Peter W.; Ulrich, Eugene C. *The Dead Sea Scrolls Bible - The Oldest Known Bible Translated for the First Time into English*. Copyright © 1999 by Martin G. Abegg, Jr., Peter W. Flint and Eugene C. Ulrich. All rights reserved. First edition. San Francisco: Harper

[ABP] – Pool, Charles Van der. *Apostolic Bible Polyglot*. Copyright © 1992. 1st edition.

[ABU-Job] – *The Book of Job* New York: American Bible Society © 1857

[ABU-Proverbs] – Conant, Thomas Jefferson. *The Book of Proverbs*. Copyright © 1872. New York: Sheldon & Company

[ACV] – Porter, Walter L. *A Conservative Version*. Copyright © 2005. Still Voices Publishing

[AENT] – Roth, Andrew Gabriel. *Aramaic English New Testament*. Scripture taken from the Aramaic English New Testament © 2008. Used by permission of Netzari Press. 5th edition. Netzari Press LLC.

[Ainslie-NT] – Ainslie, Robert. *The New Testament Translated from the Greek Text of Tischendorf, (8vo., Lipsiae, 1865: F. A. Brockhaus)*. Copyright © 1869. London: Longmans, Green, Reader, and Dyer; Brighton: H. and C. Treacher.

[Alexander-OT] – Alexander, Joseph Addison. *The Prophecies of Isaiah. Translated and Explained*. Copyright © 1870. New York vol 2. New York: Charles Scribner & Co.

[Alexander-OT] – Alexander, Joseph Addison. *The Psalms Translated and Explained*. Copyright © 1853. New York vol 1-2. New York: Charles Scribner

[Alford-NT] – Alford, Henry. *The New Testament for English Readers*. Copyright © 1872. London, Oxford, and Cambridge: Deighton, Bell, and Co.

[Allen-Ps] – Allen, William. *Psalms and Hymns for Public Worship, Containing All the Psalms and Hymns of Dr. Watts, Which are Deemed Valuable, Together with a New Version of All the Psalms, and Many Original Hymns, Besides a Large Collection from Other Writers*. Copyright © 1835. Boston: WM. Peirce, New York: Leavity, Lord, and Co., Hartford: D. Burgess & Co. Note: different renditions of the same Psalm will be followed with version, e.g. -First

[AMP] – *The Amplified Bible*. Copyright © 2015 by the Lockman Foundation. All rights reserved. The Lockman Foundation

[AMPC] – taken from *The Amplified Bible – Classic Edition*, Old Testament copyright © 1965, 1987 by the Zondervan Corporation, Grand Rapids, Michigan. The Amplified New Testament copyright © 1958, 1987 by The Lockman Foundation, La Habra, California. Used by permission.

[Anchor] – Speiser, Ephraim Avigdor. *The Anchor Bible – Genesis*. Copyright © 1964 by Doubleday & Company, Inc. All Rights Reserved. 2nd edition volume 1. Garden City New York: Doubleday & Company, Inc.

[Anchor] – Levine, Baruch A. *The Anchor Bible – Numbers 21-36*. Copyright © 2000 by Doubleday, a division of Random House, Inc.. 1st edition volume 4a. Doubleday & Company, Inc.

[Anchor] – Boling, Robert G. *The Anchor Bible – Joshua*. Copyright © 1982 by Doubleday & Company, Inc. All Rights Reserved. 1st edition volume 6. Garden City New York: Doubleday & Company, Inc.

OUR HEALING COVENANT

[Anchor] – Pope, Marvin H. *The Anchor Bible – Job*. Copyright © 1965 by Doubleday & Company, Inc. All Rights Reserved. 2nd edition volume 15. Garden City New York: Doubleday & Company, Inc.

[Anchor] – Dahood, Mitchell. *The Anchor Bible – Psalms 1-50*. Copyright © 1965, 1966 by Doubleday & Company, Inc. All Rights Reserved. 1st edition volume 16. Garden City New York: Doubleday & Company, Inc.

[Anchor] – Dahood, Mitchell. *The Anchor Bible – Psalms 51-100*. Copyright © 1968 by Doubleday & Company, Inc. All Rights Reserved. 1st edition volume 17. Garden City New York: Doubleday & Company, Inc.

[Anchor] – Dahood, Mitchell. *The Anchor Bible – Psalms 101-150*. Copyright © 1970 by Doubleday & Company, Inc. All Rights Reserved. 1st edition volume 17a. Garden City New York: Doubleday & Company, Inc.

[Anchor] – McKenzie, John L. *The Anchor Bible – Second Isaiah*. Copyright © 1969 by Doubleday & Company, Inc. All Rights Reserved. 1st edition volume 20. Garden City New York: Doubleday & Company, Inc.

[Anchor] – Mann, C. S. *The Anchor Bible – Mark*. Copyright © 1986 by Doubleday. All Rights Reserved. 1st edition volume 27. Garden City New York: Doubleday & Company, Inc.

[Anchor] – Brown, Raymond Edward. *The Anchor Bible – John 13-21*. Copyright © 1970 by Doubleday & Company, Inc. All Rights Reserved. 1st edition volume 29a. Garden City New York: Doubleday & Company, Inc.

[Anchor] – Reumann, John. *The Anchor Yale Bible - Philippians - A New Translation with Introduction and Commentary*. Copyright © 2008. vol 33b. New Haven: Yale University Press

[Anchor] – Barth, Markus. *The Anchor Bible – Ephesians 4-6*. Copyright © 1974 by Doubleday & Company, Inc. All Rights Reserved. 1st edition volume 34a. Garden City New York: Doubleday & Company, Inc.

[Anchor] – Buchanan, George Wesley. *The Anchor Bible – Hebrews*. Copyright © 1972 by Doubleday & Company, Inc. All Rights Reserved. 1st edition volume 36. Garden City New York: Doubleday & Company, Inc.

[Anderson-NT] – Anderson, Henry Tomkins *The New Testament Translated from the Original Greek,* Cincinnati © 1866

[Anderson-Sinaitic NT] – Anderson, Henry Tomkins. *The New Testament Translated from the Sinaitic Manuscript Discovered by Constantine Tischendorf at Mt. Sinai*. Copyright © 1918. Cincinnati: The Standard Publishing Company

[AS] – Szasz, Emery. *Awful Scrolls, Straight Old and New Testaments*. Copyright © 2018.

[Aston-Ps] – Aston, Walter Hutchinson; Lowth, Robert. *Select Psalms In Verse with Critical Remarks, By Bishop Lowth, and Others, Illustrative of the Beauties of Sacred Poetry*. Copyright © 1811. London: Printed for J. Hatchard

[ASV] – *The Holy Bible Containing the Old and New Testaments Translated Out of the Original Tongues Being the Version Set Forth A.D. 1611 Compared with the Most Ancient Authorities and Revised A.D. 1881-1885. Newly Edited by The American Revision Committee A.D. 1901. American Standard Version*. Copyright © 1929. Grand Rapids, MI: Christian Reformed Publishing House

[ASV-2014] – Huddleston, Jeff D. *American Standard Version - 2014 Edition*. Copyright © 2014 by Jeff D. Huddleston. All rights reserved.

[Authentic-NT] – Schonfield, Hugh J. *The Authentic New Testament*. Copyright © 1956 by Hugh J. Schonfield. London: Dennis Dobson Ltd.

[AUV-NT 2003] – Paul, William Edward. *Understandable Version*. Copyright © 2003. 2nd edition. Franktown CO: Impact Publications

[AUV-NT 2005] – Paul, William Edward. *The New Testament: An Understandable Version*. Copyright © 2005. 3rd edition. Bloomington IN: AuthorHouse

[Ballentine-NT] – Ballentine, Frank Schell *The American Bible* Scranton, PA: Good News Publishing Co. © 1902

[Barclay-NT] – Barclay, Williams. *The New Testament, A New Translation*. London, New York: Collins, © 1968.

[Barnstone-NT] – Barnstone, Willis R. *Restored New Testament*. Copyright © 2009, 2002 by Willis Barnstone. All rights reserved. New York: W. W. Norton & Company, Inc.

[Bartholomew-Ps] – Batholomew, Alfred. *Sacred Lyrics: Being an Attempt to Render the Psalms of David - More Applicable to Parochial Psalmody*. Copyright © 1831. London: Printed for the Author

[Barton-Ps] – Barton, William. *The Book of Psalms in Metre Close and Proper to the Hebrew: Smooth and Pleasant for the Metre: To be sung in usual and known Tunes. Newly Translated with Amendments, and Addition of many fresh Metres. Fitted for the ready use, and understanding of all good Christians*. Copyright © 1682. London: Printed for the Company of Stationers

BIBLIOGRAPHY

[Bassett] – Bassett, Francis Tilney. *The Book of the Prophet Hosea.* London: W. Macintosh, © 1869

[Bassett] – Bassett, Francis Tilney. *The Catholic Epistle of St. James.* London: Samuel Bagster and Sons, © 1876

[Bate-OT] – Bate, Julius. *A New and Literal Translation, from the Original Hebrew of the Pentateuch of Moses, and of the Historical Books of the Old Testament, to the End of the Second Book of Kings: with Notes Critical and Explanatory.* Copyright © 1773. London: W. Faden

[Baxter-NT] – Baxter, Richard. *A Paraphrase of the New Testament.* Copyright © 1695. 2nd edition. London: C. Parkhurst

[Bay-Ps] – Daye, Stephen. *The Bay Psalm Book* New York: Dodd, Mead & Company. Copyright ©1903

[BBE] – *The Bible in Basic English*, Cambridge, MA: University Press, Copyright © 1965, Public Domain

[Beaumont-Ps] – Beaumont, John. *Original Sacred Psalms, or Sacred Songs, Taken from the Psalms of David, and Imitated in the Language of the New Testament, In Twenty Different Metres, Fitted to the Tunes Now in General Use in the British Churches with a New Set of The Christian's Doxologies, Suited to the Various Measures.* Copyright © 1834. Shrewbury: Printed for the Author

[Beck] – Beck, William Fred *The Holy Bible – An American Translation* Copyright © 1976 by Mrs. William F. Beck. Used by permission.

[Belknap-Ps] – Belknap, Jeremy. *Sacred Poetry: Consisting of Psalms and Hymns, Adapted to Christian Devotion, In public and private. Selected from the Best Authors, with Variations and Additions.* Copyright © 1820. New edition. Boston: Thomas Wells

[Belsham-NT] – Belsham, Thomas. *The Epistles of Paul the Apostle.* London: R. Hunter. Copyright ©1822

[Benisch-OT] – Benisch, Abraham. *Jewish School and Family Bible.* Copyright © 1864. London: Longman, Brown, Green, and Longmans

[Berkeley] – Verkuyl, Gerrit. *The Modern Language New Testament - The New Berkeley Version.* The Berkeley Version of the New Testament, copyright 1945, by Gerrit Verkuyl. Assigned 1958 to Zondervan Publishing House. Revised edition copyright © 1969 by the Zondervan Publishing House. Preface copyright © 1970. All rights reserved, including that of translation. Grand Rapids: Zondervan Publishing House

[Bernard-OT] – Bernard, Hermann Hedwig. *The Book of Job, as Expounded to His Cambridge Pupils.* Copyright © 1864. vol 1. London: Hamilton, Adams, and Co.

[Besorah] – *Besorah of Yahusha.* Copyright © 2010. PS: Chosen by Lot

[Birks-OT] – Birks, Thomas Rawson. *The Companion Psalter: Or Four Hundred and Fifty Versions of the Psalms, Selected and Original, for Public or Private Worship.* Copyright © 1874. London: Seeleys and Co.

[BLB-NT] – *The Holy Bible, Berean Literal Bible, BLB.* Copyright ©2016 by Bible Hub. Used by Permission. All Rights Reserved Worldwide. Bible Hub

[BLE] – Byington, Stephen T. *The Bible in Living English*, Watchtower Bible and Tract Society, Copyright ©1972

[BOOKS-NT] – *The Books of the Bible NT.* Copyright © 1973, 1978, 1984, 2011 by Biblica, Inc. ® Used by permission. All rights reserved worldwide. Biblica Inc.

[Boothroyd] – Boothroyd, Benjamin. *The Holy Bible, Containing the Old and New Testaments; Now Translated from the Corrected Texts of the Original Tongue, and with Former Translations Diligently Compared; Together with a General Introduction and Short Explanatory Notes.* Copyright © 1853. London: Partridge and Oakey

[Boswell-Ps] – Boswell, Robert. *The Book of Psalms, in Metre; from the Original, Compared with Many Versions, in Different Languages.* Copyright © 1784. London: Printed for the Editor

[Bowes-NT] – Bowes, John. *The New Testament Translated from the Purest Greek.* Copyright © 1870. Dundee

[Box-OT] – Box, George Herbert. *The Book of Isaiah.* Copyright © 1909. New York: The MacMillan Company

[Brichto] – Brichto, Sidney. *The People's Bible - Apocalypse.* Copyright © 2004. All rights reserved. 1st edition. Great Britain: Sinclair-Stevenson

[Browne-Rev] – Browne, H. *John's Apocalypse, Literally Translated, and Spiritually Interpreted.* Copyright © 1881. Manchester: Tubbs, Brook, and Chrystal, London: Simpkin, Marshall & Co.

[BrownKrueger] – Brown, David L.; Krueger, James. *Geneva Bible - The Pilgrim's Bible.* Copyright © 2001 & 2005.

OUR HEALING COVENANT

[BSB-NT] – *The Holy Bible, Berean Study Bible, BSB*. Copyright ©2016 by Bible Hub Used by Permission. All Rights Reserved Worldwide. Bible Hub

[BSV] – Bond Slave Version. Copyright © 2006.

[Buchanan-Ps] – Buchanan, George; Eadie, John. *Translation of Buchanan's Latin Psalms into English Verse*. Copyright © 1836. Glasgow: Printed by Muir, Gowans, & Co.

[Burgess-Ps] – Burgess, George. *The Book of Psalms; Translated into English Verse*. Copyright © 1840. New York: F. J. Huntington and Co.

[Buttenwieser-OT] – Buttenwieser, Moses *The Psalms Chronologically Treated with a New Translation*. Copyright © 1938 Chicago: The University of Chicago Press

[BV-KJV-NT] – Geide, Ray. *Breakthrough Version*. BREAKTHROUGH VERSION™, BV™ Copyright© 2018 by Ray Geide. Used by permission. All rights reserved worldwide. breakthroughversion.com. version 3.3.3. Breakthrough Version Publishing

[BV-NT] – Geide, Ray. *Breakthrough Version*. BREAKTHROUGH VERSION™, BV™ Copyright© 2018 by Ray Geide. Used by permission. All rights reserved worldwide. breakthroughversion.com. version 3.3.3. Breakthrough Version Publishing

[BWE-NT] – Cressman, Annie. *Bible in Worldwide English*. Copyright © 1998 Taken from THE JESUS BOOK - The Bible in Worldwide English. Copyright SOON Educational Publications, Derby DE65 6BN, UK. Used by permission. Willington Derby: SOON Educational Publications

[BWilliams-Ps] – Williams, Benjamin. *The Book of Psalm as Translated, Paraphrased, or Imitated By Some of the Most Eminent English Poets*. Copyright © 1781. Salisbury: Collins and Johnson

[CAB] – Esposito, Paul W. *Complete Apostle's Bible*. Copyright © 2005 Used by permission. 1st Books

[Campbell-Gs] – Campbell, George. *The Four Gospels, Translated from the Greek, with Preliminary Dissertations, and Notes Critical and Explanatory*. Copyright © 1837. vol 1-2. Andover: Printed and Published by Gould and Newman. New York: Corner of Fulton and Nassau St.

[Cayley-Ps] – Cayley, Charles Bagot. *The Psalms in Metre*. Copyright © 1860. London: Longman, Green, Longman, and Roberts

[CB] – Schlafly, Andrew. *Conservative Bible*. Copyright © 2018.

[CBC] – Bullinger, Ethelbert William. *The Companion Bible (Condensed)*. Copyright © 2008.

[CCB] – *Christian Community Bible*. Copyright © 1995 All Rights Reserved. 17th edition. Quezon City, Philippines: Claretian Publications

[CE] – *Confraternity Version*. Copyright © 1962 New Catholic Edition, Catholic Book Publishing Company, New York.

[CEB] – *Common English Bible* All rights reserved. No part of these materials may be reproduced or transmitted in any form or by any means, electronic or mechanical, including photocopying and recording, or by any information storage or retrieval system, except as may be expressly permitted by the 1976 Copyright Act, the 1998 Digital Millennium Copyright Act, or in writing from the publisher.

[CENT] – Clontz, Timothy Eric. *Common Edition, New Testament*. Common, Copyright © Timothy E. Clontz 1999. All rights reserved.

[CEV] – *Holy Bible - Contemporary English Bible* Scripture quotations marked (CEV) are from the Contemporary English Version Copyright © 1991, 1992, 1995 by American Bible Society, Used by Permission.

[CEV] – *Holy Bible - Contemporary English Version*. Copyright © 1995 American Bible Society. New York: American Bible Society

[CEVUK2012] – *The Contemporary English Version - UK Edition*. Copyright © 2012 American Bible Society. All rights reserved.

[Cheyne-OT] – Cheyne, Thomas Kelly. *The Book of Psalms or the Praises of Israel - A New Translation, with Commentary*. Copyright © 1895. New York. New York: Thomas Whittaker

[Cheyne-OT] – Cheyne, Thomas Kelly. *Introduction to the Book of Isaiah with an Appendix Containing the Undoubted Portions of the Two Chief Prophetic Writers in a Translation*. Copyright © 1895. London: Adam and Charles Black

[Churton-Ps] – Churton, Edward. *The Book of Psalms in English Verse and In Measures Suited for Sacred Music*. Copyright © 1854. Oxford and London: John Henry Parker

BIBLIOGRAPHY

[CJB] –Stern, David H. Taken from the *Complete Jewish Bible*. Copyright © 1998. All rights reserved. Used by permission of Messianic Jewish Publishers, 6120 Day Long Lane, Clarksville, MD 21029. www.messianicjewish.net.

[ClarkePyle] – Clarke, Samuel. *A Paraphrase on the Four Evangelists*. Copyright © 1736. 7th edition vol 1. London: Printed by W. B. for James, John and Paul Knapton. (Matthew and Mark)

[ClarkePyle] – Clarke, Samuel. *A Paraphrase on the Four Evangelists*. Copyright © 1751. 9th edition vol 2. London: Printed for John and Paul Knapton. (Luke and John)

[ClarkePyle] – Pyle, Thomas. *A Paraphrase on the Acts of the Holy Apostles, Upon All the Epistles of the New Testament, and Upon the Revelations*. Copyright © 1817. Oxford - A New Edition vol 1-3. Oxford: Printed by W. Baxter, for Law and Whitaker (Acts/Epistles/Revelation)

[CLV] – *The Sacred Scriptures THE CONCORDANT LITERAL VERSION*, Copyright © Concordant Publishing Concern P.O. Box 449, Almont, MI 48003, U.S.A. 810-798-3563

[Cohn-OT] – Cohn, Adam. *Modernized Tanakh*. © Adam Cohn 2013 - This work is licensed under the Creative Commons Attribution 3.0 Unported License. To view a copy of this license, visit http://creativecommons.org/licenses/by/3.0/

[Coleman-OT] – Coleman, John Noble. *The Book of Job*. Copyright © 1869. London: James Nisbet & Co.

[Coleman-OT] – Coleman, John Noble. *The Book of Ecclesiastes*. Copyright © 1867. 2nd edition. Edinburg: Andrew Elliot

[Coles-Ps] – Coles, Abraham. *A New Rendering of the Hebrew Psalms into English Verse*. Copyright © 1888 D. Appleton & Company: New York.

[Collier-Ps] – Collier, Edward Augustus. *Lyrics from the Psalter - A Metrical Rendering of Selections from the Psalms*. Copyright © 1907. Pittsburgh: The United Presbyterian Board of Publication

[Committee-Ps] – *The Psalter; or Book of Psalms*. The Committee of the Reformed Presbyterian Synod. Copyright © 1893 New York.

[Condon-Mk] – Schmid, Josef; Condon, Kevin. *The Gospel According to Mark*. Copyright © 1968. Cork: The Mercier Press

[Conybeare-NT] – *The Life and Epistles of St. Paul*. By Rev. William John Conybeare & Rev. John Saul Howson. volumes 1&2. New York: Charles Scribner Copyright © 1864

[Cornish-NT] – Cornish, Gerald Warre. *St. Paul from the Trenches - A Rendering of the Epistles to the Corinthians and Ephesians done in France during the Great War*. Copyright © 1948. Boston: Houghton Mifflin Company

[COS-Ps-1] – Church of Scotland; Brown, John. The Psalms of David in Metre. Copyright © 1991. Philadelphia. Philadelphia: Hogan & Thompson

[Cottle-Ps] – Cottle, Joseph. *A Version of the Psalms of David, Attempted in Metre*. Copyright © 1805. 2nd edition. London: Printed for Longman and Co.

[Cotton-Ps] – Matther, Cotton. *The Book of Psalms, In a Translation Exactly conformed unto the Original; But all in Blank Verses, Fitted unto the Tunes commonly used in our Churches. Which pure offering is accompanied with Illustrations, digging for Hidden Treasures in it; And Rules to Employ it upon the Glorious and Various Intentions of it. Whereto are added, Some other Portions of the Sacred Scripture, to Enrich the Cantional*. Copyright © 1718. Boston: Printed by S. Kneeland, for B. Eliot, S. Gerrish, D. Henchman, and J. Edwards

[CPDV] – Jr., Ronald L. Conte. *Catholic Public Domain Version*. Public Domain.

[Cradock-Ps] – Cradock, Thomas. *A New Version of the Psalms of David*. Copyright © 1756. New Version. Annapolis: Printed by Jonas Green

[CSB] – *Christian Standard Bible*. Scripture quotations marked CSB have been taken from the Christian Standard Bible®, Copyright © 2017 by Holman Bible Publishers. Used by permission. Christian Standard Bible® and CSB® are federally registered trademarks of Holman Bible Publishers.

[CT-OT] – Rosenberg, A. J. *Judaica Press Prophets and Writings*. English Translation Copyright © Judaica Press. All rights reserved. Chabad.org. Judaica Press

[CWB] – Blanco, Jack John. *The Clear Word*. Copyright © 2003 by Review and Herald® Publishing Association. Final revision.

[D'Onston-Gs] – D'Onston, Roslyn. *The Patristic Gospels - An English Version of the Holy Gospels as They Existed in the Second Century*. Copyright © 1904. London: Grant Richards

OUR HEALING COVENANT

[Darby] – Darby, John Nelson. *The Darby Bible*, Copyright © 1890, Public Domain

[Davidson-NT] – Davidson, Samuel. *The New Testament Translated from the Critical Text of Von Tischendorf*. Copyright © 1876. 2nd edition. London: Henry S. King & Co.

[Davis-Ps] – Davis, Abijah. *An American Version of the Psalms of David. Suited to the State of the Church in the Present Age of the World*. Copyright © 1813. Philadelphia: Printed by the author by D. Heartt

[De Witt-Ps] De Witt, John. *The Psalms A New Translation*. Copyright © 1891 New York: Anson D. F. Randolph and Co.

[Delitzsch-Ps] – Delitzsch, Franz. *Biblical Commentary on The Psalms*. Copyright © 1881. Edinburgh 2nd edition vol 1-3. Edinburgh: T. & T. Clark

[Didham-Ps] – Didham, Richard Cunningham. *A New Translation of the Psalms*. Copyright © 1869. London: Williams and Norgate

[Dillard-NT] – Dillard, W. D. *Teaching and Acts of Jesus of Nazareth and His Apostles, Literally Translated Out of the Greek*. Copyright © 1885. Chicago

[DLNT] – Magill, Michael J. *Disciples' Literal New Testament* Scripture quotations are from the Disciples' Literal New Testament, Copyright © 2011. Used by permission. All rights reserved.

[Doddridge-NT] – Doddridge, Philip. *Family Expositor*. Copyright © 1831. London: Frederick Westley and A. H. Davis

[Douay-Rheims] – *Douay Rheims Version of the Holy Bible*, Douay Bible House, New York, New York, 1942

[Douay-Rheims-Peters] – *The Original and True Rheims New Testament of Anno Domini 1582; The Original and True Douay Old Testament of Anno Domini 1610*. Copyright © 2005 Dr. William G. von Peters Ph.D. 2005 copyright assigned to VSC Corp. All rights reserved for all media formats domestic and international.

[Driver-OT] – Driver, Samuel Rolles. *The Parallel Psalter Being The Prayer-Book Version of the Psalms and a New Version Arranged on Opposite Pages with an Introduction and Glossaries*. Copyright © 1904. 2nd edition. Oxford: At the Clarendon Press

[Driver-OT] – Driver, Samuel Rolles. *The Book of the Prophet Jeremiah - A Revised Translation with Introductions and Short Explanations*. Copyright © 1908. 2nd edition. London: Hodder and Stoughton

[Eakin-Hab] – Eakin, Thomas. *The Text of Habakkuk Chap. 1:1-2:4 - A Dissertation Submitted to the University of Toronto for the Degree of Doctor of Philosophy*. Copyright © 1905. University of Toronto

[EB] – Nicoll, William Robertson; Cox, Samuel. *The Book of Ecclesiastes*. Copyright © 1907. NYL. New York: A. C. Armstrong and Son, London: Hodder and Stoughton

[ECB] – Jahn, Herb. *exeGeses Companion Bible*. Copyright © 1994.

[EEBT] – *EasyEnglish Bible*. Copyright © MissionAssist 2018 – Charitable Incorporated Organisation 1162807 easyenglish.bible. Wycliffe Associates

[EHV] – *Evangelical Heritage Version*. The Evangelical Heritage Version (EHV), New Testament & Psalms Copyright ©2017. The Wartburg Project

[Elkhazen-NT] – Elkhazen, Pierre. *NewTestamentEng*. Copyright © 2015 Computer Club 2000+ medjugorjenet.com, medjugorjenet.webs03.com. V2015.

[Elzas-OT] – Elzas, Abraham. *The Proverbs of Solomon, Translated from the Hebrew Text, with Notes, Critical and Explanatory*. Copyright © 1871. Leeds: Charles Goodall, J. W. Bean & Son, and the Translator, London: Trübner & Co.

[EOB-NT] – Brugaletta, John; et. al. *The Eastern / Greek Orthodox Bible - New Testament*. Copyright © 2008.

[Erasmus-NT] – Erasmus. *Collected Works of Erasmus volume 42. Paraphrases on Romans and Galatians*. Copyright © 1984. University of Toronto Press

[ERV] – *The HOLY BIBLE: EASY-TO-READ VERSION* © 2014 by Bible League International and used by permission.

[ESB-NT] – Killian, Trennis E. *The Easy Study Bible*. Copyright © 2011 by Trennis E. Killian.

[ESV] – The ESV® Bible (*The Holy Bible, English Standard Version*®), copyright © 2001 by Crossway, a publishing ministry of Good News Publishers. Used by permission. All rights reserved

[Etheridge-NT] – Etheridge, John Wesley. *New Testament - Acts, Epistles, and Revelation*. Copyright © 1849. London: Longman, Green, Brown, and Longmans

BIBLIOGRAPHY

[Ewald-OT] – Ewald, Georg Heinrich August Von; Johnson, E. *Commentary on the Psalms.* Copyright © 1880. vol 1. London, Edinburgh: Williams and Norgate

[Ewald-OT] – Ewald, Georg Heinrich August Von; Johnson, E. *Commentary on the Psalms.* Copyright © 1881. vol 2. London, Edinburgh: Williams and Norgate

[EWG-NT] – Huddleston, Jeff D. *Every Word of God.* Copyright © 2018 by Jeff D. Huddleston. All rights reserved.

[EXB] – *The Expanded Bible* Scripture taken from The Expanded Bible. Copyright ©2011 by Thomas Nelson. Used by permission. All rights reserved.

[FAA] – Thomason, Graham G. Far Above All Translation. Copyright © 2009-2017. Anyone is permitted to copy and distribute this text or any portion of this text. www.FarAboveAll.com.

[Farr-Ps] – Farr, Edward. *A New Version of the Psalms of David, In All the Various Metres Suited to Psalmody, Divided into Subjects, and Designated According to Bishop Horne, &c.* Copyright © 1836. London: B. Fellowes

[FBV-NT] – Gallagher, Dr. Jonathan. Free Bible Version. Copyright © 2018 Dr. Jonathan Gallagher. This work is licensed under a Creative Commons Attribution-NoDerivs License. freebibleversion.org.

[FCConybeare-Rev] – Conybeare, Frederick Cornwalls. *The Armenian Version of Revelation and Cyril of Alexandria's Scholia on the Incarnation and Epistle of Easter.* Copyright © 1907. London: The Text and Translation Society

[Fenton] – Fenton, Ferrar, *The Holy Bible in Modern English*, Destiny Publisher, Massachusetts © 1903

[FHV-NT] – McCord, Carl Hugo. *The Everlasting Gospel - New Testament with Psalms, Proverbs and More.* Copyright © 2007 Freed-Hardeman University. All rights reserved. 5th edition. Freed-Hardeman University

[Folsom-Gs] – Folsom, Nathaniel S. *The Four Gospels.* Copyright © 1869. Boston: A. Williams and Company

[Fox-OT] – Fox, Everett. *The Five Books of Moses.* Copyright © 1983, 1986, 1990, 1995 by Schocken Books Inc. All rights reserved under International and Pan-American Copyright Conventions. New York: Schocken Books, Inc.

[FrenchSkinner-OT] – French, William; Skinner, George. *A New Translation of the Proverbs of Solomon from the Original Hebrew with Explanatory Notes.* Copyright © 1831. Cambridge: Printed by J. Smith; London: John Murray

[FV] – Coulter, Fred. *The Holy Bible in Its Original Order: A New English Translation: A Faithful Version with Commentary.* Copyright © 2007-2010 York Publishing Company - www.restoringtheoriginalbible.com. ALL RIGHTS RESERVED. Second edition. York Publishing Company

[Fysh-Ps] – Fysh, Frederic. *A Lyrical Literal Version of the Psalms.* Copyright © 1850. vol 1. London: Seeleys

[GAC-Ps] – General Association of Connecticut. *Psalms and Hymns, for Christian Use and Worship;.* Copyright © 1855. New Haven: Durrie and Peck. Boston: Tappan & Whittemore; New-York: Clark, Austin & Smith; Philadelphia: Peck & Bliss; Albany: E. H. Pease & Co.; Rochester: Erastus Darrow; Buffalo: Danforth, Hawley & Co.; Detroit: A. McFarren; Chicago: D. B. Cooke & Co. Note: the selected version follows the heading, e.g. -First.

[Garstang-OT] – Garstang, Walter. *A Translation, Out of the Ancient Biblical Hebrew, of The Book of Kohéleth else "Ecclesiastes, or The Preacher."* Copyright © 1886. London: Simkin, Marshall & Co., Liverpool: Edward Howell

[Geddes-Ps] – Geddes, Alexander. *A New Translation of the Book of Psalms, from the Original Hebrew; with Various Readings and Notes.* Copyright © 1807. London: Printed for J. Johnson

[GHBWright-OT] – Wright, George Henry Bateson. *The Book of Job. A New Critically Revised Translation, with Essays on Scansion, Date Etc.* Copyright © 1883. London: Williams and Norgate

[Gilpin-NT] – Gilpin, William. *An Exposition of the New Testament; Intended as an Introduction to the Study of the Scriptures, by Pointing out the Leading Senses, and Connection of the Sacred Writers.* Copyright © 1790. London: Printed for R. Blamire, in the Strand.

[Ginsburg-OT] – Ginsburg, Christian David. *Coheleth, Commonly Called The Book of Ecclesiastes: Translated from the Original Hebrew, with a Commentary, Historical and Critical.* Copyright © 1868. Halle Sax: Julius Fricke

[Glickman-Sos] – Glickman, S. Craig. *A Song for Lovers.* Copyright © 1976 by InterVarsity Press. All rights reserved. Downers Grove: InterVarsity Press

[GNC-NT] – Cassirer, Heinz Walter. *God's New Covenant - A New Testament Translation.* Copyright © 1989 by Olive Cassirer. All rights reserved. Grand Rapids: William B. Eerdmans Publishing Company

OUR HEALING COVENANT

BIBLIOGRAPHY

[Haupt-Ecc] – Haupt, Paul. *The Book of Ecclesiastes - A New Metrical Translation With an Introduction and Explanatory Notes.* Copyright © 1905. London. London: Kegan Paul, Trench, Trübner & Co.

[Haweis-NT] – Haweis, Thomas. *A Translation of the New Testament from the Original Greek.* Copyright © 1795. London: T. Chapman

[Hawkins-Ps] – Hawkins, Ernest. *The Book of Psalms, As Used in the Daily Service, with Short Headings and Explanatory Notes.* Copyright © 1859. 2nd edition. London: Bell & Daldy

[Hawley-Ps] – Hawley, M. L. *The Psalms in Meter.* Copyright © 1868. New York: Published for the Author. Carlton & Lanahan

[HBIV] – *The Holy Bible Containing the Old and New Testament - An Improved Version.* Copyright © 1913. Philadelphia: American Baptist Publication Society

[HCSB] – *The Holman Christian Standard Bible®,* Copyright © 1999, 2000, 2002, 2003, 2009 by Holman Bible Publishers. Used by permission. Holman Christian Standard Bible®, Holman CSB®, and HCSB® are federally registered trademarks of Holman Bible Publishers.

[Heberden-NT] – Heberden, William. *A Literal Translation of the Apostolic Epistles and Revelation with a Concurrent Commentary.* Copyright © 1839. London: Printed for J. G. & F. Rivington

[Hebert-NT] – Hebert, Charles. *The New Testament Scriptures in the Order in Which They Were Written: A Very Close Translation from the Greek Text of 1611, with Brief Explanations. The First Portion: The Six Primary Epistles, to Thessalonica, Corinth, Galatia, and Rome, A.D. 52-58.* Copyright © 1882. First portion. London: Henry Frowde

[Henderson-OT] – Henderson, Ebenezer. *The Book of the Prophet Ezekiel, Translated from the Original Hebrew, with a Commentary, Critical, Philological, and Exegetical.* Copyright © 1868. Andover. Andover: Warren F. Draper, Boston: W. H. Halliday and Company, Philadelphia: Smith, English, and Co.

[Henderson-OT] – Henderson, Ebenezer. *The Book of the Prophet Isaiah, Translated from the Original Hebrew, with a Commentary, Critical, Philological, and Exegetical.* Copyright © 1857. London 2nd edition. London: Hamilton, Adams, and Co.

[Heylyn-Gs] – Heylyn, John. *Theological Lectures at Westminster-Abbey. With an Interpretation of the New Testament. Part the First. Containing. The Four Gospels. To Which Are Added, Select Discourses upon the Principal Pointed of Revealed Religion.* Copyright © 1749. London: Printed for J. and R. Tonson and S. Draper in the Strand

[Hielscher-Ps] – Hielscher, Helen Hughes. *Songs of the Son of Isai - A Metrical Arrangement of the Psalms of David.* Copyright © 1916. Boston: Sherman, French & Company

[HNT] – Moffatt, James. *The Historical New Testament.* Copyright © 1901. 2nd and revised edition. Edinburgh: T. & T. Clarke.

[HOB-OT] – Publishing, Papoutsis. *Holy Orthodox Bible.* Copyright © 2009. Papoutsis Publishing. All Rights Reserved. Peter Papoutsis

[Holdens-Pr] – Holden, George. *An Attempt Towards an Improved Translation of the Proverbs of Solomon, from The Original Hebrew, with Notes Critical and Explanatory, and a Preliminary Dissertation.* Copyright © 1819. Liverpool: Printed for the author

[Horsley-OT] – Horsley, Samuel. *The Book of Psalms; Translated from the Hebrew: with Notes, Explanatory and Critical.* Copyright © 1815. vol 1. London: Sold by F. C. & J. Rivington

[Horsley-OT] – Horsley, Samuel. *Hosea. Translated from the Hebrew: with Notes Explanatory and Critical: Second Edition, Corrected, with Additional Notes. And A Sermon, Now First Published, on Christ's Descent into Hell.* Copyright © 1804. 2nd edition. London: Printed for J. Hatchard

[Howard-OT] – Howard, Henry Edward John. *The Book of Genesis, According to the Version of the LXX. Translated into English, with Notes of Its Omissions and Insertions, and with Notes on the Passages in which It Differs from Out Authorized Translation.* Copyright © 1855. Cambridge: Macmillan & Co.

[HPAJ] – *The Holy Peshitta of the Assembly of Jerusalem.* Copyright © 1987–2018 The Holy Peshitta of the Assembly of Jerusalem.

[HRB] – Esposito, Don. *Hebraic Roots Bible - A Literal Translation.* © Copyright Word of Truth Publications, 2009, 2012, 2015. 3rd edition.

[HRV] – Trimm, James Scott. *Hebraic Roots Bible: A Literal Translation.* © 2009 James Scott Trimm. All rights reserved.

[ICB] – *The International Children's Bible®.* Copyright © 1986, 1988, 1999 by Thomas Nelson. Used by permission. All rights reserved.

OUR HEALING COVENANT

[IRENT] – Kwon, Oun J. *Invitation to Reading in English New Testament*. Public Domain.

[ISV] – *The Holy Bible: International Standard Version*®. Copyright © 1996-forever by The ISV Foundation. ALL RIGHTS RESERVED INTERNATIONALLY. Used by permission.

[Jenour-Isa] – Jenour, Alred. *The Book of the Prophet Isaiah Translated from the Hebrew; with Critical and Explanatory Notes, and Practical Remarks; to which is Prefixed a Preliminary Dissertation on the Nature and Use of Prophecy*. Copyright © 1830. vol 1-2. London: Printed for R. B. Seeley and W. Burnside

[Jerusalem] – *The Jerusalem Bible* © 1966 by Darton Longman & Todd Ltd and Doubleday and Company Ltd.

[JGC-Ps] – Campbell, John George. *The Book of Psalms. Literally Rendered into Verse*. Copyright © 1877. London: Macmillan and Co. Note: source of the Psalm follows the heading, e.g. -Zain.

[JLDavies-NT] – Davies, John Llewelyn. *The Epistles of St. Paul to the Ephesians, the Colossians, and Philemon: with Introductions and Notes, and an Essay on the Traces of Foreign Elements in the Theology of These Epistles*. Copyright © 1866. London: Macmillan and Co.

[JMNT] – Mitchell, Jonathan. *Jonathan Mitchell New Testament*. Copyright © 2014 Used by permission. Harper Brown Publishing

[JMontgomery-Ps] – Montgomery, James. *Songs of Zion; Being Imitations of Psalms*. Copyright © 1824. 2nd edition-London. London: Printed for Longman, Hurst, Rees, Orme, Brown, and Green

[Johnson-NT] – Johnson, Ben Campbell *Matthew and Mark: A Relational Paraphrase* Copyright © 1978 by Ben Campbell Johnson. All rights reserved.

[Johnson-NT] – Johnson, Ben Campbell *Luke and John: An Interpretive Paraphrase* Copyright © 1976 by Ben Campbell Johnson. All Rights Reserved. Published by A Great Love.

[Johnson-NT] – Johnson, Ben Campbell *The Heart of Paul: A Relational Paraphrase of the New Testament* Copyright © 1976 by Ben Campbell Johnson. All Rights Reserved. Published by Word Books, Waco, Texas.

[Jones-Ps] – Jones, Abner. *The Psalms of David Rendered into English Verse of Various Measures, Divided According to Their Musical Cadence, and Comprised in their own Limits: In Which Their Responsive Lines Are Kept Unbroken, the Devout and Exalted Sentiments with Which They Everywhere Abound, Expressed in Their Own Familiar and Appropriate Language, and the Graphic Imagery, by Which They Are Rendered Vivid, Preserved Entire*. Copyright © 1860. New York: Mason Brothers

[Jordan-NT] – Jordan, Clarence. *Clarence Jordan's Cotton Patch Gospel – Paul's Epistles*. Copyright © 1968. New York: Association Press

[Jordan-NT] – Jordan, Clarence. *Clarence Jordan's Cotton Patch Gospel - Luke and Acts*. Copyright © 1969. New York: Association Press

[Jordan-NT] – Jordan, Clarence. *Clarence Jordan's Cotton Patch Gospel - Hebrews and the General Epistles*. Copyright © 1973. New Century Publishers, Inc.

[Jordan-NT] – Jordan, Clarence. *Clarence Jordan's Cotton Patch Gospel - Matthew and John*. Copyright © 1970. New York: Association Press

[JosephStock-Isa] – Stock, Joseph. *The Book of the Prophet Isaiah: In Hebrew and English. The Hebrew Text metrically arranged: the Translation Altered from that of Bishop Lowth. With Notes Critical and Explanatory*. Copyright © 1803. Bath: Printed by R. Cruttwell

[JPS-OT 1917] – JPS. *The Holy Scriptures According to the Masoretic Text - A New Translation with the Aid of Previous Versions and with Constant Consultation of Jewish Authorities*. Copyright © 1917 by The Jewish Publication Society of America. 1st edition. Philadelphia: Jewish Publication Society of America

[JPS-OT 1963] – JPS. *The Torah - The Five Books of Moses - The New JPS Translation of The Holy Scriptures According to the Traditional Hebrew Text*. Copyright © 1992 by The Jewish Publication Society of America. 3rd edition. Philadelphia, Jerusalem: Jewish Publication Society of America

[JPS-OT 1963] – JPS. *The Prophets Nev'im - The New JPS Translation of The Holy Scriptures According to the Traditional Hebrew Text*. Copyright © 1978 by The Jewish Publication Society of America. All rights reserved. Philadelphia, Jerusalem: Jewish Publication Society of America

[JPS-OT 1985] – JPS. *The Old Testament - JPS 1985*. Copyright © 1985 Jewish Publication Society. All rights reserved. Jps.org. Philadelphia: Jewish Publication Society of America

BIBLIOGRAPHY

[JPS-Ps 1972] – JPS. *The Book of Psalms - A New Translation According to the Traditional Hebrew Text*. Copyright © 1992. Revised edition with updated translation 1997. All rights reserved. Revised edition. Philadelphia: Jewish Publication Society of America

[JSharpe-Mic] – Sharpe, John. Micah, *A New Translation with Notes for English Readers and Hebrew Students*. Copyright © 1876. Cambridge: J. Hall & Son, London: Whitaker & Co.; Simpkin, Marshall & Co.; and Bell & Sons, Oxford: Jas. Parker & Co.

[JUB] – *The Jubilee Bible* (from the Scriptures of the Reformation) edited by Russell M. Stendal Copyright © 2000, 2001, 2010

[Keble-Ps] – Keble, John. *The Psalter or Psalms of David: In English Verse*. Copyright © 1869. 4th edition. Oxford and London: James Parker and Co.

[Kennedy-Ps] – Kennedy, Benjamin Hall. *The Psalter or Psalms of David, in English Verse*. Copyright © 1876. Cambridge: Deighton, Bell and Co., London: G. Bell and Sons

[Kenrick] – Kenrick, Francis Patrick. *The Pentateuch : Translated from the Vulgate*. Copyright © 1860. Baltimore: Kelly, Hedian & Piet Publishers. *The Book of Job and the Prophets*. Copyright © 1859. Baltimore: Kelly, Hedian & Piet Publishers. *The Psalms, Books of Wisdom, and Canticle of Canticles*. Copyright © 1857. Baltimore: Lucas Brothers. *The New Testament*. Copyright © 1862. 2nd edition. Baltimore: Kelly, Hedian & Piet Publishers

[Kent-OT] – Kent, Charles Foster. The Student's Old Testament. Copyright © 1904. Volumes 1-6. New York: Charles Scribner's Sons

[KIT-NT] – *The Kingdom Interlinear Translation of the Greek Scriptures*. Copyright © 2018 Watch Tower Bible and Tract Society of Pennsylvania. Revised edition. Watchtower Bible and Tract Society of Pennsylvania

[KJ21] – Scripture taken from The Holy Bible, 21st Century King James Version (KJ21®), Copyright © 1994, Deuel Enterprises, Inc., Gary, SD 57237, and used by permission.

[KJ3] – Green, Jay Patrick. *KJ3 - Literal Translation of the Bible*. Copyright © 2005 – By Jay P. Green, Sr.–All Rights Reserved. Sovereign Grace Publishing

[KJC-NT] – McGinnis, Bill. *King James Clarified*. Public Domain. Version 1.1.

[KJV-Miller] – Miller, Fred P. *Fred Miller's Revised King James Version*. Copyright © 2003 Fred Miller.

[Kneeland-NT] – Kneeland, Abner. *The New Testament Being the English Only of the Greek and English Testament; Translated from the Original Greek according to Griesbach; upon the basis of the fourth London edition of the Improved Version, with an attempt to further improvements from the translations of Campbell, Wakefield, Scarlett, Macknight, and Thomson*. Copyright © 1823. Philadelphia: Published by the Editor

[Knox] – Knox, Monsignor Ronald. *The Holy Bible: A Translation from the Latin Vulgate in the Light of the Hebrew and Greek Originals*. Copyright © 1944, 1948, 1950 by Sheed & Ward, Inc., New York. Used by permission.

[KNT] – Wright, Nicholas Thomas. *Kingdom New Testament*. Scripture is taken from The Kingdom New Testament. Copyright © 2011 by Rt. Rev. Nicholas Thomas Wright. Published by Society for Promoting Christian Knowledge. All rights reserved. Used by permission. Society for Promoting Christian Knowledge

[Koren-OT] – *The Koren Jerusalem Bible*. Copyright © 2008 Creative Commons Attribution-ShareAlike (CC BY-NC) 4.0 International copyleft license. www.KorenPub.com. Jerusalem: Koren Publishers

[Lamsa] – Lamsa, George M. *Holy Bible From The Ancient Eastern Text*. Copyright © 1957. Philadelphia: A. J. Holman Co.

[Lang-Ps] – Lang, John Dunmore. *Specimens of an Improved Metrical Translation of the Psalms of David, Intended for the use of the Presbyterian Church in Australia and New Zealand. With a Preliminary Dissertation, and Notes, Critical and Explanatory*. Copyright © 1840. Philadelphia: Printed by Adam Waldie

[LDB-NT] – Johnson, Raymond Walter. *The New Testament - God's New Agreement With Mankind Through His Son Jesus the Messiah - A captivating, accurate new translation, with special, authoritative notes, for the last generation*. Copyright © 1999 by Life Messengers. All rights reserved. Seattle: Life Messengers

[LEB] – Harris, W. Hall. *Lexham English Bible*. Scripture quotations marked (LEB) are from the Lexham English Bible. Copyright © 2012 Logos Bible Software. Lexham is a registered trademark of Logos Bible Software. 4th edition. Logos

[Lee-NT] – Lee, Witness et. al. *The New Testament: Recovery Version*. COPYRIGHT © 1997- 2018 LIVING STREAM MINISTRY. All rights reserved. Reproduction in whole or in part without permission is prohibited. Revised edition. Anaheim, California: Living Streams Ministries

[Leeser-OT] – Leeser, Isaac. *Twenty-Four Books of the Holy Scriptures*. Hebrew Publishing Company, New York, New York

[Levi-Rev] – Levi, Peter. *The Revelation of John - Translated and Introduced*. Copyright © 1992 by Peter Levi. All rights reserved. Great Britain: Kyle Cathie Limited

[Lewis-Gs] – Lewis, Agnes Smith. *Some Pages of the Four Gospels Retranscribed from the Sinaitic Palimpsest with a Translation of the Whole Text*. Copyright © 1896. London: C. J. Clay and Sons.

[LGV-NT] – *Last Generation Version of the New Testament*. Copyright © 4Winds Fellowships. Free to distribute in any form. Tim Warner

[Lingard-Gs] – Lindgard, John. *A New Version of the Four Gospels; with Notes Critical and Explanatory by a Catholic*. Copyright © 1836. London: Joseph Booker

[LitProph-OT] – Lowth, Robert. *Isaiah: A New Translation; with a Preliminary Dissertation, and Notes. Critical, Philological, and Explanatory*. Copyright © 1836. 11th edition vol 1. London: Printed for Thomas Tegg and Son

[LitProph-OT] – Blayney, Benjamin. Jeremiah, and Lamentations. *A New Translation: with Notes Critical, Philological, and Explanatory*. Copyright © 1836. 3rd edition vol 2. London: Printed for Thomas Tegg and Son

[LitProph-OT] – Newcome, William. *An Attempt Towards an Improved Version, Metrical Arrangement, and an Explanation of The Prophet Ezekiel*. Copyright © 1836. vol 3. London: Printed for Thomas Tegg and Son

[LitProph-OT] – Wintle, Thomas. *Daniel, an Improved Version Attempted; with a Preliminary Dissertation, and Notes Critical, Historical, and Explanatory*. Copyright © 1836. vol 4. London: Printed for Thomas Tegg and Son

[LitProph-OT] – Newcome, William; Horsley, Samuel. *An Attempt Towards an Improved Version, Metrical Arrangement, and an Explanation, of The Twelve Minor Prophets*. Copyright © 1836. Now greatly enlarged and Improved. vol 5. London: Printed for Thomas Tegg and Son

[LITV] – Green Sr., Jay Patrick. Scripture taken from the *Literal Translation of the Holy Bible* © 1976-2000 Used by permission of the copyright holder.

[LTN-OT] – Kaplan, Aryeh. *The Living Torah: The Five Books of Moses: A New Translation Based on Traditional Jewish Sources*. Copyright © 2000 World ORT. New York: Moznaim Publishing Corp.

[LTPB] – Cunyus, John G. *The Latin Testament Project Bible*. © Copyright 2008-2016, John G. Cunyus. All Rights to the English Translation and Commentary Reserved. Searchlight Press

[LXX-1844] – *Septuagint*, The morphologically analyzed text of CATSS LXX prepared by CATSS under the direction of R. Kraft (Philadelphia team). ed. A. Rahlfs (Stuttgart: Württembergische Bibelanstalt, 1935; repr. in 9th ed., 1971)

[Lyte-Ps] – Lyte, Henry Francis; Appleyard, John. *The Poetic Works of the Rev. H. F. Lyte, M.A.* Copyright © 1907. London: Elliot Stock

[Mace-NT] – Mace, Daniel. *New Testament in Greek and English*. Copyright © 1739. London: J. Roberts

[Macknight-NT] – Macknight, James. *A New Literal Translation, from the Original Greek, of All the Apostolical Epistles*. Copyright © 1835. New Edition. Philadelphia: Desilver, Thomas, and Co. Note: [Macknight-NT] denotes a verse from the translation column while [Macknight-NTc] is from the commentary / paraphrase column.

[Macrae] – Macrae, David. *A Revised Translation and Interpretation of the Sacred Scriptures*. Copyright © 1815. Glasgow: R. Hutchinson & Co.

[Madsen-NT] – Madsen, Jon. *The New Testament: A Rendering*. Copyright © 1994 Floris Books. Floris Books

[Magiera-NT] – Magiera, Janet M. *Aramaic Peshitta New Testament Translation*. Copyright © 2009. Messianic Edition.

[Marson-Ps] – Marson, Charles Latimer. *The Psalms at Work - Being the English Church Psalter with Notes on the Use of the Psalms*. Copyright © 1909. 4th edition. London: Elliot Stock

[Martin-NT] – Martin, Ruth P. *The Pioneer's New Testament*. Copyright © 2014 by Ruth P. Martin. 4th edition.

[Maxwell-Ps] – Maxwell, James. *A New Version of the Whole Book of Psalms in Metre*. Copyright © 1773. Glasgow: Printed by William Smith

[MCC-NT] – Williams, William. *A Modern, Correct, and Close, Translation of the New Testament; with Occasional Observations, and Arranged in Order of Time. With a Special Explanation of the Apocalypse*. Copyright © 1812. London: Printed for John Stockdale, Piccadilly

BIBLIOGRAPHY

[McFadyen-OT] – McFadyen, John Edgar. *The Psalms in Modern Speech and Rhythmical Form*. Copyright © 1916. 2nd edition. London: James Clarke. *The Wisdom Books in Modern Speech and Rhythmical Form*. Copyright © 1917. London: James Clarke. *Isaiah in Modern Speech*. Copyright © 1918. London: James Clarke. *Jeremiah in Modern Speech*. Copyright © 1919. London: James Clarke

[McSwiney-Ps] – McSwiney, James. *Translation of the Psalms and Canticles*. Copyright © 1901. St. Louis MO: B.Herder. [-H] is from Hebrew translation in column one. [-V] is from the Vulgate translation in column two.

[Medway-NT] – Medway, Brian. *No Copyright Version*. Public Domain.

[MEMS-Ps] – MEMS. *The Whole Book of Psalms, In Metre; with Hymns, Suited to the Feasts and Fasts of the Church, and Other Occasions of Public Worship*. Copyright © 1829. Boston: Massachusetts Episcopal Missionary Society

[Merrick-Ps] – Merrick, James. *A Version or Paraphrase of the Psalms*. Copyright © 1789. London: Thomas Payne

[MEV] – *Holy Bible - Modern English Version*. Scripture taken from the Modern English Version. Copyright © 2014 by Military Bible Association. Used by permission. All rights reserved. Lake Mary FL: Passio

[Milborne-Ps] – Milbourne, Luke. *The Psalms of David, in English Metre; Translated from the Original, and Suited to all the Tunes now Sung in CHURCHES: With the Additions of Several New*. Copyright © 1698. London: Printed for W. Rogers at the Sun, R. Clavill at the Peacock, and B. Tooke at the Middle Temple Gates, all in Fleetstreet

[Miller-Pr] – Miller, John. *A Commentary on the Proverbs with a New Translation*. Copyright © 1872. New York: Anson D. F. Randolph & Company

[Ming-Ps] – Protestant Episcopal Church. *The Whole Book of Psalms in Metre; with Hymns, Suited to the Feasts and Fasts of the Church and Other Occasions of Public Worship*. Copyright © 1806. New York: Printed by Alexander Ming

[Mitchell] – Mitchell, Stephen. *A Book of Psalms - Selected and Adapted from the Hebrew*. Copyright © 1996 by Stephen Mitchell. All rights reserved. 1st edition. HarperCollins Publishers

[MKJV] – Green, Sr. Jay Patrick. *Modern King James Version* Scripture taken from the Holy Bible, Modern King James Version Copyright © 1962 – 1998 Used by permission of the copyright holder.

[MLV] – Walker, G. Allen. *Holy Bible Modern Literal Version*. Copyright © 2015, G. Allen Walker, co-editor of the MLV. mlvbible.com. CreateSpace Independent Publishing Platform

[Moffatt] – Moffatt, James A. R. *The Bible, A New Translation*. Copyright © 1922, 1924,1925,1926, 1935 by Harper Collins, San Francisco; copyright © 1950, 1952, 1953, 1954; and copyright © 1994 by Kregel Publications, Grand Rapids, Michigan. Used by permission.

[Moffatt-NT 1917] – Moffatt, James. *The New Testament - A New Translation in Modern Speech*. Copyright © 1917. New Edition Revised. New York: Hodder & Stoughton, George H. Doran Company

[Montefiore-Gs] – Montefiore, C. G. *The Synoptic Gospels*. Copyright © 1909. volume 1. London: Macmillan and Co.

[Montefiore-Gs] – Montefiore, C. G. *The Synoptic Gospels*. Copyright © 1927. volume 2, 2nd edition. London: Macmillan and Co.

[Montgomery-NT] – Montgomery, Helen Maria Barrett. *Centenary Translation of the New Testament Published to Signalize the Completion of the First Hundred Years of Work of the American Baptist Publication Society*. Copyright © 1924. 2nd edition. Philadelphia: The American Baptist Publication Society

[Morgan-NT] – Morgan, Jonathan. *The New Testament of Our Lord and Saviour Jesus Christ. Translated from the Greek, into Pure English; with Explanatory Notes, on Certain Passages, wherein the Author differs from other translators*. Copyright © 1848. Portland: S. H. Colesworthy; Boston: B. B. Mussey, New-York: P. Price; Philadelphia: J. Gibon, Cincinnati: A. T. Ames; Louisville: Noble and Dean.

[MOTB] – Sanders, Frank Knight; Kent, Charles Foster. *The Messages of the Bible - Volume 1 - The Messages of the Earlier Prophets*. Copyright © 1899. 3rd edition vol 1. New York: Charles Scribner's Sons

[MOTB] – Sanders, Frank Knight; Kent, Charles Foster; Edgar, John; McFadyen. *The Messages of the Bible - Volume 4 - The Messages of the Prophetic and Priestly Historians*. Copyright © 1901. 1st edition vol 4. New York: Charles Scribner's Sons

[MOTB] – Sanders, Frank Knight; Kent, Charles Foster; Edgar, John; McFadyen. *The Messages of the Bible - Volume 5 - The Messages of the Psalmists*. Copyright © 1904. 1st edition vol 5. New York: Charles Scribner's Sons

OUR HEALING COVENANT

[MOTB] – Sanders, Frank Knight; Kent, Charles Foster; Riggs, James Steven. *The Messages of the Bible - Volume 10 - The Messages of Jesus According to the Gospel of John.* Copyright © 1918. vol 10. New York: Charles Scribner's Sons

[MOTB] – Sanders, Frank Knight; Kent, Charles Foster; Stevens, Barker. *The Messages of the Bible - Volume 11 - The Messages of Paul.* Copyright © 1900. vol 11. New York: Charles Scribner's Sons

[MOUNCE] – Mounce, Robert H; Mounce, William D. *Mounce Reverse-Interlinear New Testament.* Copyright © 2011 by Robert H Mounce and William D Mounce. Used by permission. All rights reserved worldwide.

[MP1650] – *Metrical Psalms 1650.* Copyright © 1650. British and Foreign Bible Society

[MSG] – Peterson, Eugene H. *The Message.* Scripture taken from *The Message.* Copyright © 1993, 1994, 1995, 1996, 2000, 2001, 2002. Used by permission of NavPress Publishing Group.

[MSTC] – McDonnell, Shawn. *Modern Spelling Tyndale Coverdale.* Scriptures quoted from the MODERN SPELLING TYNDALE/COVERDALE BIBLE® copyright © 2008 by Shawn McDonnell, and free for all non-commercial use. Used By Permission. Lulu.com

[Muhlenberg-Ps] – Muhlenberg, William Augustus. *Church Poetry: Being Portions of the Psalms in Verse, and Hymns Suited to the Festivals and Fasts, and Various Occasions of the Church. Selected and Altered from Various Authors.* Copyright © 1823. Philadelphia: S. Potter & Co.

[Murdock-NT] – Murdock, James. *The New Testament, or the Book of the Holy Gospel.* Copyright © 1851. New York: Standford and Swords

[Murphy-OT] – Murphy, James Gracey. *A Critical and Exegetical Commentary on the Book of Genesis. With a New Translation.* Copyright © 1873. Boston: Estes and Lauriat

[MW-NT] – Gruber, Daniel. *The Messianic Writings.* Copyright © 2011. Daniel Gruber. All Rights reserved under International and Pan-American Copyright Conventions. Elijah Publishing

[NAB] – *The New American Bible* © 2010, 1991, 1986, 1970 Confraternity of Christian Doctrine, Washington, D.C. and are used by permission of the copyright owner. All Rights Reserved. No part of the New American Bible may be reproduced in any form without permission in writing from the copyright owner.

[NABRE] – *The New American Bible.* Revised edition. The New American Bible, revised edition © 2010, 1991, 1986, 1970 Confraternity of Christian Doctrine, Washington, D.C. and are used by permission of the copyright owner. All Rights Reserved. No part of the New American Bible may be reproduced in any form without permission in writing from the copyright owner. wwwmigrate.usccb.org/bible/permissions/index.cfm. Confraternity of Christian Doctrine, Inc., Washington, DC

[Nary-NT] – Nary, Cornelius. *The New Testament of Our Lord and Saviour Jesus Christ.* Copyright © 1719. Revised edition.

[NASB] – *The New American Standard Bible®,* Copyright © 1960, 1962, 1963, 1968, 1971, 1972, 1973, 1975, 1977, 1995 by The Lockman Foundation. Used by permission

[NCV] – *The Scriptures - New Century Version.* Scriptures quoted from *The Holy Bible, New Century Version®,* copyright © 2005 by Thomas Nelson, Inc. Used by permission. Thomas Nelson

[NEB] – *The New English Bible,* copyright © 1961, 1970 by The Delegates of the Oxford University Press and The Syndics of the Cambridge University Press. Used by permission.

[NENT] – Daniels, Frank. *Non Ecclesiastical New Testament.* Copyright © 1995, 2007, 2018 Frank Daniels.

[NET] – *The NET Bible®,* New English Translation®, copyright ©1996-2006 by Biblical Studies Press, L.L.C. http://netbible.com. All rights reserved

[NETS-OT] – *A New English Translation of the Septuagint.* Quotations marked NETS-OT are taken from A New English Translation of the Septuagint, ©2007 by the International Organization for Septuagint and Cognate Studies, Inc. Used by permission of Oxford University Press. All rights reserved. Oxford University Press

[Newcome] – Newcome, William. *An Attempt at an Improved Version - New Testament.* Copyright © 1796. Dublin: John Exshaw

[NHEB] – Mitchell, Wayne Alan; Harness, Mark D. *New Heart English Bible.* You may publish, copy, memorize, translate, quote, and use the New Heart English Bible freely without additional permission. 2nd edition.

[NIRV] – *The Holy Bible, NEW INTERNATIONAL READER'S VERSION®.* © 1995, 1996, 1998 Biblica. All rights reserved throughout the world. Used by permission of Biblica.

BIBLIOGRAPHY

[NIV] – *The Holy Bible, New International Version*® Copyright © 1973, 1978, 1984 by International Bible Society. Used by permission of Zondervan Publishing House. All rights reserved. Used by permission.

[NIVUK] – *New International Version - Anglicized Edition*. Holy Bible, New International Version® Anglicized, NIV® Copyright © 1979, 1984, 2011 by Biblica, Inc.® Used by permission. All rights reserved worldwide. Zondervan Publishing House

[NJB] – *The New Jerusalem Bible*. Copyright © 1985 All Rights Reserved. Doubleday & Company

[NKJV] – *The Holy Bible Containing the Old and New Testaments - New King James Version*®. Scripture taken from the New King James Version. Copyright © 1979, 1980, 1982 by Thomas Nelson, Inc. Used by permission. All rights reserved. Nashville: Thomas Nelson

[NLT] – *New Living Translation* Scripture quotations are taken from the *Holy Bible*, New Living Translation, copyright ©1996, 2004, 2007, 2013 by Tyndale House Foundation. Used by permission of Tyndale House Publishers, Inc., Carol Stream, Illinois 60188. All rights reserved.

[NLT] – *Holy Bible - New Living Translation*. Scripture quotations marked (NLT) are taken from the *Holy Bible*, New Living Translation, copyright © 1996. Used by permission of Tyndale House Publishers, Inc., Wheaton, Illinois 60189. All rights reserved. 1st edition. Wheaton, Illinois: Tyndale House Publishers, Inc.

[NLV] – *New Life Version*. © 1969 Christian Literature International. Christian Literature Foundation

[NMB-NT] – Davis, Ruth Magnusson. *New Matthew Bible*. Scripture is taken from The New Matthew Bible. Copyright © 2016 by Ruth Magnusson Davis. Published by Baruch House Publishing. All rights reserved. Used by permission.

[NOG] – *The Names of God Bible*. Scripture is taken from The Names of God Bible, Copyright © 2011. Used by permission of Baker Publishing Group.

[Norlie-NT] – Norlie, Olaf Morgan; Harrison, R. K. *Norlie's Simplified New Testament In Plain English - for Today's Reader. A New Translation from the Greek* with *The Psalms for Today A New Translation in Current English*, Toronto: Wycliffe College, University of Toronto. Copyright © 1961. Grand Rapids: Zondervan Publishing House

[Norton-Gs] – Norton, Andrews. *A Translation of the Gospels*. Copyright © 1856. 2nd edition. Boston: Little, Brown, and Company

[Noyes] – Noyes, George Rapall. *The New Testament: Translated from the Greek Text of Tischendorf*. Copyright © 1891. Eight Thousand. Boston: American Unitarian Association

[NRSV] – *The Holy Bible containing the Old and New Testaments with the Apocryphal / Deuterocanonical Books - New Revised Standard Version*. New Revised Standard Version Bible, copyright © 1989, Division of Christian Education of the National Council of the Churches of Christ in the United States of America. 1st edition. Garden City: Doubleday Book and Music Clubs, Inc.; New York, Oxford: Oxford University Press

[NTIV] – Belsham, Thomas. *The New Testament in an Improved Version*. Copyright © 1809. Boston: Thomas B. Wait and Company

[NTSR] – Schwank, Benesikt; Stöger, Alois. *The New Testament for Spiritual Reading – The Two Epistles of St. Peter*. Copyright © 1963, 1966, 1969. volume 22. New York: Herder and Herder

[Numerical] – Grant, Frederick William. *The Numerical Bible*. Copyright © 1897. 4th edition vol 3. New York: Loizeaux Brothers

[NWT] – *New World Translation*. © 2015 Watch Tower Bible and Tract Society of Pennsylvania. All rights reserved.

[OANT] – Bauscher, Glenn David; Mitchell, Tim. *The Peshitta Aramaic-English New Testament - An Interlinear Translation*. Copyright © 2016 Original Aramaic NT. 8th edition. Lulu.com

[OEB-NT] – Allen, Russell. *Open English Bible*. Copyright © 2010 Russell Allen. Second release.

[Oliver-Ps] – Oliver, Andrew. *A Translation of the Syriac Peshito Version of the Psalms of David; with Notes Critical and Explanatory*. Copyright © 1861. Boston: E. P. Dutton and Company

[Original-NT] – Schonfield, Hugh J. *The Original New Testament*. Copyright © 1985 by Hugh J. Schonfield. All rights reserved. 1st US edition. San Francisco: Harper & Row

[Orton-OT] – Orton, Job. *An Exposition of the Old Testament, with Devotional and Practical Reflections for the Use of Families*. Copyright © 1822. A New Edition vol 1-6. London: Printed for Baldwin, Cradock and Joy; Ogle, Duncan and Co; G. and W. B. Whittaker; and Simkin and Marshall.

[Ottley-Isa] – Ottley, Richard Rusden. *The Book of Isaiah According to the Septuagint (Codex Alexandrinus).* Copyright © 1909. Cambridge: at the University Press. -Heb is translation from Hebrew. -LXX is translation from Septuagint.

[Palmer] – Palmer, David Robert. *The Holy Bible Containing the Old and New Testaments.* Public Domain.

[PalmerBz-NT] – Palmer, David Robert. *The Holy Bible Containing the Old and New Testaments Byzantine Edition.* Public Domain. Edition 10-11-2016.

[Parkhurst-Ps] – Parkhurst, John. *Literal Translation of the Psalms of David.* Copyright © 1830. London: Samuel Bagster and Sons

[Pauli-Isa] – Uzziel, Jonathan Ben; Pauli, Christian William Henry. *The Chaldee Paraphrase on the Prophet Isaiah.* Copyright © 1871. London: London Society's House

[PCB-Ps] – The Parish Church at Bromsgrove. *A Selection of Psalms and Hymns, for the Use of the Congregation of the Parish Church, Bromsgrove.* Copyright © 1859. 2nd edition. Bromsgrove: Printed by Alfred Palmer

[Perowne-Ps] – Perowne, John James Stewart. *The Book of Psalms. A New Translation, with Explanatory Notes for English Readers.* Copyright © 1884. 5th edition. London: George Bell and Sons

[Phillips] – Phillips, John Bertram. *The New Testament in Modern English* by J. B. Phillips. Copyright © 1958. Used by permission.

[Pickering-NT] – Pickering, Wilbur N. *The Sovereign Creator Has Spoken - Objective Authority for Living - The New Testament with Commentary.* Copyright © 2016 Wilbur N. Pickering, Creative Commons Attribution-ShareAlike 3.0, Original work available at http://thechristiancommons.com.

[Plaisted] – Plaisted, David A. *Lighthouse Bible.* Copyright © 2011 David A. Plaisted. 3rd edition. Lulu.com

[PLAWL] – Patrick, Symon; Lowth, William; Arnold, Richard; Whitby, Daniel; Lowman, Moses. *A Critical Commentary and Paraphrase on the Old and New Testament and the Apocrypha.* Copyright © 1845. New Edition vol 4. Philadelphia: Carey and Hart, New York: Wiley and Putnam

[PNT] – Whiston, William. *Mr. Whiston's Primitive New Testament.* Copyright © 1745. Stamford and London

[Priest-Ps] – An English Priest. *The Book of Psalms, Pointed for Chanting, and Adapted to Appropriate Chants.* Copyright © 1858. London: Joseph Masters

[Purver] – Purver, Anthony. *A New and Literal Translation of All the Books of the Old and New Testament; with Notes, Critical and Explanatory.* Copyright © 1764. vol 1-2. London: W. Richardson and S. Clark

[REAL] – *The Real Word of God.* Copyright © 2010 the Trinity Word Trust. Hadarel Corporation

[REB] – *The Revised English Bible with the Apocrypha.* Copyright © Oxford University Press and Cambridge University Press 1989. Oxford University Press, Cambridge University Press

[REM-NT] – Jennings, Timothy R. *The Remedy - A New Testament Expanded Paraphrase.* Copyright © 2018 Come And Reason Ministries, all rights reserved. Permission granted to copy/paste and/or share verses in/to other media.

[REM-NT] – Jennings, Timothy R. *The Remedy - New Testament Expanded Paraphrase in Everyday English.* Copyright © 2018 Come and Reason Ministries, all rights reserved. Permission granted to copy/paste and/or share verses in/to other media. 2nd edition. Chattanooga: Lennox® Publishing

[Renan-OT] – Renan, Ernest. *The Book of Job Translated from the Hebrew. With a Study upon the Age and Character of the Poem.* Copyright © 1889. London: W. M. Thomson

[Rendall-Acts] – Rendall, Frederic. *The Acts of the Apostles. In Greek and English.* Copyright © 1897. London: Macmillan and Co., Limited; New York: The Macmillan Company

[REV-NT] – Schoenheit, John W. *The Revised English Version.* Copyright © 2013 John W. Schoenheit. All rights reserved.

[Rieu-Gs] – Rieu, Emile Victor. *The Four Gospels.* Copyright © 1953 by Penguin Books. Baltimore: Penguin Books

[RJ Miller-Gs] – Miller, Robert J. *The Complete Gospels - Annotated Scholars Version.* Copyright © 1992, 1994 The Complete Gospels: Annotated Scholars Version by Polebridge Press. All rights reserved. Printed in the United States of America. No part of this book may be used or reproduced in any manner whatsoever without written permission except in the case of brief quotations embodied in critical articles and reviews. For information address Polebridge Press, P.O. Box 1526, Sonoma, California, 95476. 3rd edition. Polebridge Press

BIBLIOGRAPHY

[RNT] – Ballantine, William Gay. *Riverside New Testament*. Copyright © 1923. Boston: Hougton Mifflin Company

[RNV] – Castleberry, C. F. *The Sacred Scripture of Yahuwuah, Restored Names Version*. Public Domain. 7-3-2018.

[Rodwell-Isa] – Rodwell, John Medows. *The Prophecies of Isaiah. Translated from the Hebrew*. Copyright © 1886. 2nd edition. London: Frederic Norgate

[Rosenburg-Ps] – Rosenburg, David. *Blues of the Sky Interpreted from the Original Hebrew Book of Psalms*. Copyright © 1976 by David Rosenburg. All rights reserved. 1st edition. New York, Hagerstown, San Francisco, London: Harper & Row, Publishers

[Rotherham] – Rotherham, Joseph Bryant. *Rotherham's Emphasized Bible* (EBR), 1902 – Public Domain.

[RSV] – *The Revised Standard Version of the Bible*. Copyright © 1946, 1952 by the Division of Christian Education of the National Council of the Churches of Christ in the United States of America. Used by permission.

[Rusling-Ps] – Rusling, Joseph. *Portions of the Psalms of David, and Other Parts of Scriptures, in Verse. Designed as a Companion for the Christian*. Copyright © 1838. 2nd edition. Philadelphia: Sold by the Publisher

[Rutherford-NT] – Rutherford, William Gunison. *St. Paul's Epistle to the Romans - A New Translation with a Brief Analysis*. Copyright © 1900. London: Macmillan and Co.

[RV] – *Holy Bible Containing the Old and New Testament Translated Out of the Original Tongues*. Copyright © 1903. Oxford: At the University Press

[RVIC] – Parkinson, James B. *The Revised Version (American Edition) Improved and Corrected*. Copyright © 2012 All rights reserved.

[SAAS-OT] – *The Orthodox Study Bible*. Scripture taken from the St. Athanasius Academy Septuagint™. Copyright © 2008 by St. Athanasius Academy of Orthodox Theology. Used by permission. All rights reserved. Thomas Nelson, Inc.

[Sacred-NT] – Campbell, George; Macknight, James; Doddridge, Philip. *The Sacred Writings of the Apostles and Evangelists of Jesus Christ. Commonly Styled the New Testament. Translated from the Original Greek*. Copyright © 1914. St. Louis 16th edition. St. Louis MO: Christian Board of Publication

[Sandys-OT] – Sandys, George. *A Paraphrase upon the Divine Poems*. Copyright © 1638. London: At the Bells St. Pauls Church-yard

[Sawyer-7590] – Sawyer, Leicester Ambrose. *The New Testament, Translated from the Original Greek, with Chronological Arrangement of the Sacred Books, and Improved Divisions of Chapters and Verses*. Copyright © 1861. Revised and Improved, 12th thousand. Boston: Walker, Wise and Company

[Sawyer-7590] – Sawyer, Leicester Ambrose. *The Holy Bible, Containing the Old and New Testaments. Translated and Arranged, with Notes;* Copyright © 1861. vol 2. Boston: Walker, Wise and Company

[Sawyer-7620] – Sawyer, Leicester Ambrose. *The Bible; Analyzed, Translated and Accompanied with Critical Studies*. Copyright © 1891. Whitesboro: L. A. Sawyer

[Schaff-OT] – Lange, John Peter; Schaff, Philip; Lewis, Taylor; Zöckler, Otto; Evans, L. J. *A Commentary on the Holy Scriptures: Critical, Doctrinal, and Homiletical, with Special Reference to Ministers and Students - Job*. Copyright © 1902. vol 8. New York: Scribner, Armstrong & Co.

[Schaff-OT] – Lange, John Peter; Schaff, Philip; Zöckler, Otto; Aiken, Charles Augustus. *A Commentary on the Holy Scriptures: Critical, Doctrinal, and Homiletical, with Special Reference to Ministers and Students - Proverbs, Ecclesiastes, Song of Solomon*. Copyright © 1898. vol 10. New York: Scribner, Armstrong & Co.

[SECT] – Sharpe, Samuel; Ellicott, Charles John; Craik, Henry; Tregelles, Samuel Prideaux. *Scripture Translations. Proverbs, 1&2 Timothy, Hebrews, Revelation*. Copyright © 1871. Boston: Scriptural Tract Repository

[SENT] – Mealy, J. Webb. *Spoken English New Testament*. Copyright © 2012 James Webb Mealy. All rights reserved.

[SG] – Smith, J. M. Powis; Goodspeed, Edgar J. *The Complete Bible - An American Translation. The Old Testament translated by J. M. Powis Smith and a Group of Scholars. The Apocrypha and the New Testament translated by Edgar J. Goodspeed* © 1945 University of Chicago Press

[Shadwell-Gs] – Shadwell, Lancelot. *The Gospels of Matthew, and of Mark, Newly Rendered into English; with Notes on the Greek Text:*. Copyright © 1861. London: Walker and Co.

[Sharpe] – Sharpe, Samuel. *The Holy Bible*. Copyright © 1883. OT 5th ed. NT 8th ed. Edinburg: Williams and Norgate

BIBLIOGRAPHY

[Shuttleworth-NT] – Shuttleworth, Philip Nicholas. *A Paraphrasic Translation of the Apostolic Epistles, with Notes*. Copyright© 1854. 5th edition. London: Rivingtons

[Sidney-Ps] – Sidney, Philip; Sidney, Mary. *The Psalms of Sir Philip Sidney and the Countess of Pembroke*. Copyright © 1963 by John C. A. Rathmell. All rights reserved. New York University Press

[Sindlinger-NT] – Sindlinger, Daniel Thomas. *The Better Life Bible - New Testament*. All rights reserved. Copyright © 2006 by Dan Sindlinger. Lulu.com

[Slavitt-Ps] – Slavitt, David R. *Sixty-One Psalms of David*. Copyright © 1996. New York: Oxford University Press

[Smith] – Smith, Julia E. *Holy Bible Containing the Old and New Testament*. Copyright © 1876. Hartford, Conn: American Publishing Company

[Smyth-Ps] – Smyth, Miles. *The Psalms of King David Paraphrased And turned into English Verse according to the common Metre As they are usually sung in Parish Churches*. Copyright © 1668. London: Printed for T. Garthwait

[Spencer-NT] – Spencer, Francis Aloysius. *The New Testament of Our Lord and Saviour Jesus Christ Translated into English from the Original Greek*. Copyright © 1951. New York: The Macmillan Company

[Spitsbergen] – Spitsbergen, Mark. *Spitsbergen's Translation*. Copyright © 2018. All rights reserved. Mark Spitsbergen

[Spurrell-OT] – Spurrell, Helen. *A Translation of the Old Testament Scriptures from the Original Hebrew*. Copyright © 1885. London: James Nisbet & Co.

[SPV] – Ho, Jeffrey. *Spirit of Prophecy Version Bible*. Copyright © 2018.

[Stanhope-NT] – Stanhope, George. *A Paraphrase and Comment upon the Epistles and Gospels Appointed to be Used in the Church of England on all Sundays and Holy-Days Throughout the Year*. Copyright © 1732. 5th edition vol 1-2. London: J. and J. Knapton

[Stanhope-NT] – Stanhope, George. *A Paraphrase and Comment upon the Epistles and Gospels Appointed to be Used in the Church of England on all Sundays and Holy-Days Throughout the Year*. Copyright © 1817. 10th edition vol 3-4. London: Printed for James Nun

[Sternhold-Ps] – Sternhold, Thomas; Hopkins, John. *The Whole Book of Psalms, Collected into English Metre*. Copyright © 1836. Stereotype Edition. Oxford: Printed at the University Press by Samuel Collingwood and Co.

[Stevens-NT] – Stevens, George Barker. *The Epistles of Paul in Modern English*. Copyright © 1898. New York: Charles Scribner's Sons

[Stow-Ps] – Stow, John. *A Version of the Psalms of David*. Copyright © 1844. 3rd edition. London: Printed at the Free-School, Gower's Walk, Whitechapel

[Street-Ps] – Street, Stephen. *A New Literal Version of the Book of Psalms: with a Preface and Notes*. Copyright © 1790. vol 1. London: J. Davis

[Stringfellow-NT] – Stringfellow, Ervin Edward. *Acts and Epistles – A Translation and Annotations*. Copyright © 1945. Des Moines, Iowa: William C. Brown Co.

[Sullivan-OT] – Sullivan, Francis. *Tragic Psalms*. Copyright © 1987 by the Pastoral Press. Washington: The Pastoral Press

[Swendenborg-Gs] – Swendenborg, Emanuel; Clowes, John. *The Gospel According to Matthew, Translated from the Original Greek, and Illustrated by Extracts from the Theological Writings of Emanuel Swedenbord, Together with Notes and Observations of the Translator, Annexed to Each Chapter*. Copyright © 1868. 4th edition. London: F. Pitman, 20, Paternoster Row, E.C., C. P. Alvey, 36, Bloombury Street, W.C.; Manchester: J. B. Ledsham, 31, Corporation Street, J. Larkin, 26, Hewitt Street, Hightown.

[Swendenborg-Gs] – Swendenborg, Emanuel; Clowes, John. *The Gospel According to Mark, Translated from the Original Greek, and Illustrated by Extracts from the Theological Writings of Emanuel Swedenbord, Together with Notes and Observations of the Translator, Annexed to Each Chapter*. Copyright © 1858. 2nd edition. London: W. White, 36, Bloombury Street; J. S. Hodson, Portugal Street, Lincoln's Inn.

[T4T] – Deibler, Ellis W.; Jr. *A Translation for Translators*. Copyright © 2008-2017 Ellis W. Deibler, Jr. This translation is made available to you under the terms of the Creative Commons Attribution Share-Alike license 4.0.

[Tackwall-NT] – Taylor, Kenneth Ray. *Tackwells New Testament*. Copyright © 2019.

[Tate-Ps] – Tate, Nahum; Brady, Nicholas. *A New Version of the Psalms of David, Fitted to the Tunes Used in Churches*. Copyright © 1848. London. London: Printed by G. E. Eyre and W. Spottiswoode

OUR HEALING COVENANT

BIBLIOGRAPHY

[Wade] – Wade, George Woosung. *Documents of the New Testament*. Copyright © 1934. London: Thomas Murby & Co.

[Wakefield-NT] – Wakefield, Gilbert. *A Translation of the New Testament*. Copyright © 1820. London: George Kearsley

[Walker-NT] – Walker, Obadiah. A Paraphrase and Annotations Upon All the Epistles of St. Paul. Copyright © 1852. Oxford: University Press

[Wand-NT] – Wand, J. W. C. *The New Testament Letters Prefaced and Paraphrased*. Copyright © 1950 Oxford University Press. 3rd impression. London, New York, Toronto: Oxford University Press (The Epistles)

[Waple-Rev] – Waple, Edward. *The Book of the Revelation Paraphrased; with Annotations on Each Chapter Whereby it is made plain by the meanest Capacity*. Copyright © 1693. London

[Watts-Ps] – Watts, Isaac. *The Psalms of David, Imitated in New Testament Language: Together with Hymns and Spiritual Song. In Three Books*. Copyright © 1857. London. London: T. Nelson and Sons

[Wauck-NT] – Wauck, Mark A. *Letters of Saint Paul*. Copyright © 2008 Society of Saint Paul. All rights reserved. Boston: Pauline Books & Media

[Way-NT] – Way, Author Sanders. *The Letters of St. Paul to the Seven Churches and Three Friends with the Letter to the Hebrews*. Copyright © 1906. 2nd edition, revised. London: Macmillan and Co., Limited; New York: The Macmillan Co.

[WBall-Ps] – Ball, William. *Nugae Sacrae. Or Psalms and Hymns, and Spiritual Songs*. Copyright © 1825. London: J. Hatchard and Son

[WEB] – *World English Bible* Public Domain published by ebible.org

[WEBBE] – *The World English Bible British Edition*. Public Domain.

[Webster] – Webster, Noah *The Webster Bible* © 1833 Public Domain

[Weekes-NT] – Weekes, Robert Dodd. *The New Dispensation - The New Testament Translated from the Greek*. Copyright © 1897. New York and London: Funk and Wagnalls

[Wells-NT] – Wells, Edward. *A Treatise Concerning the Harmony of the Four Gospels: Together, with a Table, representing in One Easy and Clear View the Harmony of the Four Gospels; so far forth as relates to the Order of Time, wherein the several Passages of the Gospel History did succeed One Another*. Copyright © 1718. London: Printed for James Knapton

[Wesley-NT] – Wesley, John. *Explanatory Notes Upon the New Testament*. Copyright © 1856. New York 12th edition. New York: Published by Carlton & Porter

[Westminster] – Lattey, Cuthbert Charles; Murray, John. *The New Testament in the Westminster Version of the Sacred Scriptures*. Copyright © 1948. Small Edition. New York, Toronto: Longmans, Green and Co.

[Weymouth-NT] – Weymouth, Richard Francis. *The New Testament in Modern Speech*. Copyright © 1978 by Kregel Publications. Used by permission.

[WGCIB] – *The Work of God's Children Illustrated Bible*. Public Domain.

[Wheatland-Ps] – Wheatland, Stephen; Silvester, Tipping. *The Psalms of David, Translated into Heroic Verse, in as Literal a Manner, As Rhyme and Metre will allow. With Arguments to each Psalm, and Explanatory Notes*. Copyright © 1754. London: Printed for S. Birt, in Ave-Mary-Lane, and J. Buckland, in Pater-noster Row.

[Whiting-NT] – Whiting, Nathan N. *The Good News of Our Lord Jesus Christ, the Anointed; from the Critical Greek Text of Tittmann*. Copyright © 1849. Boston: Joshua V. Himes

[WilliamNorton-NT] – Norton, William. *A Translation, in English Daily Used, of the Peshito-Syriac Text, and of the Received Greek Text. Of Hebrews, James, 1 Peter, and 1 John. With an Introduction, on the Peshito-Syriac Text, and the Revised Greek Text of 1881*. Copyright © 1889. London: W. K. Bloom. -P from the Peshito column. -G is from the Greek column.

[Williams-NT] – Williams, Charles Bray. *The New Testament - A Translation in the Language of the People*. Copyright © 1960. Boston: Bruce Humphries, Inc.

[Wilson-NT] – Wilson, Benjamin. *The Emphatic Diaglott*. Copyright © 1864. New York: Samuel R. Wells

[Witham-NT] – Witham, Robert. *Annotations on the New Testament of Jesus Christ*. Copyright © 1730.

[Wither-Ps] – Wither, George. *The Psalms of David Translated into Lyrick-Verse*. Copyright © 1881. Manchester: Printed for the Spencer Society

OUR HEALING COVENANT

[WMB] – The World Messianic Bible. Public Domain.

[Woodd-Ps] – Woodd, Basil. *A New Metrical Version of the Psalms of David; with An Appendix of Select Psalms and Hymns, Adapted to the Service of the United Church of England and Ireland; For every Sunday in the Year, Festival Days, Saints' Days, &c.* Copyright © 1821. London: Printed and sold by E. Bridgewater

[Worrell-NT] – Worrell, Adolphus Spalding. *The New Testament Revised and Translated.* Copyright © 1904. Philadelphia: The American Baptist Publication Society

[Worsley-NT] – Worsley, John. *New Testament or New Covenant.* Copyright © 1770. London: R. Hett

[Wrangham-Ps] – Wrangham, Digby Strangeways. *Lyra Regis - The Book of Psalms and Other Lyrical Poetry of the Old Testament Rendered Literally into English Metres.* Copyright © 1885. Leeds: J. S. Fletcher & Co.

[WSP-OT] – Porter, John Scott; Smith, George Vance; Wellbeloved, Charles. *The Holy Scriptures of the Old Covenant in a Revised Translation.* Copyright © 1859. vol 1, © 1861 vol 2, © 1862 vol 3, London: Longman, Brown, Longmans, and Roberts

[WTNT] – Wilton, Clyde C. *The Wilton Translation of the New Testament.* Copyright © 2012 All rights reserved.

[Wuest-NT] – Wuest, Kenneth Samuel. *The New Testament: An Expanded Translation.* Copyright © 1961 by William B. Eerdmans Publishing Co., Grand Rapids, Michigan. Used by permission.

[Wycliffe-Noble] – Noble, Terence P., *Wycliff's NT - Modern Spelling Edition.* Copyright © 2001 All rights reserved. For permission to reproduce significant portions of this book, please contact the publisher.

[Ycard-Ecc] – Ycard, F. *A New Paraphrase upon Ecclesiastes, with an Analysis and Notes Proving, That the Preacher introduces a Refin'd Sensualist, to Oppugn and Invalidate his Penitential Animadversions and Exhortations.* Copyright © 1901. London: Printed for Tho. Bennett, at the Half Moon in St. Paul's Church-yard, R. Parker at the Unicorn, under the Piazza of the Royal Exchange, Peter Buck, at the Temple, near the Inner Temple-gate, Fleetstreet; and E. Castle, next Scotland yard-gate, Charing Cross

[YLT] – Young, Robert. *Young's Literal Translation of the Holy Bible,* © 1862. Public Domain.

[York-Ps] – *A New Metrical Translation of the Book of Psalms. Accentuated for Chanting. An Attempt to Preserve, As Far As Possible, the Leading Characteristics of the Original, in the Language of the English Bible.* Copyright © 1857. London: Samuel Bagster and Sons